Data Analysis and Related Applications 4

Big Data, Artificial Intelligence and Data Analysis Set

coordinated by
Jacques Janssen

Volume 12

Data Analysis and Related Applications 4

New Approaches

Edited by

Yiannis Dimotikalis
Christos H. Skiadas

ISTE

WILEY

First published 2024 in Great Britain and the United States by ISTE Ltd and John Wiley & Sons, Inc.

ISTE Ltd
27-37 St George's Road
London SW19 4EU
UK

www.iste.co.uk

John Wiley & Sons, Inc.
111 River Street
Hoboken, NJ 07030
USA

www.wiley.com

Library of Congress Control Number: 2024937862

British Library Cataloguing-in-Publication Data
A CIP record for this book is available from the British Library
ISBN 978-1-78630-992-1

Contents

1

On the First-Passage Area of a One-Dimensional Diffusion Process with Stochastic Resetting

For a one-dimensional diffusion process with stochastic resetting $\mathcal{X}(t)$, obtained from an underlying diffusion $X(t)$, we study the statistical properties of its first-passage time through zero, when starting from $x > 0$, and its first-passage area, i.e. the random area swept out by $\mathcal{X}(t)$ until its first-passage time through zero. By making use of solutions of certain associated ODEs, we find explicit expressions for the Laplace transforms of the first-passage time and the first-passage area, and their single and joint moments.

1.1. Formulation of the problem and general results

This note deals with the first-passage area (FPA) of a diffusion process with stochastic resetting. It is a continuation of Abundo (2013, 2023b), Abundo and Del Vescovo (2017) and Abundo and Furia (2019), regarding the FPA of jump-diffusions, drifted Brownian motion, Lèvy process and Ornstein–Uhlenbeck process. In fact, here we considered a one-dimensional diffusion process in the presence of stochastic resetting $\mathcal{X}(t)$, obtained from an underlying diffusion $X(t)$; this kind of process is treated, for example, in den Hollander et al. (2019) and Evans et al. (2020) (see also the references in Abundo 2023a). We studied the statistical properties of the first-passage time (FPT) through zero of $\mathcal{X}(t)$, starting from $x > 0$, and its FPA, namely the random area swept out by $\mathcal{X}(t)$ until its FPT through zero. In some cases, we explicitly obtained the Laplace transform of the FPT and FPA, and their single and joint moments. Moreover, we provided the distribution of the maximum displacement of $\mathcal{X}(t)$.

Chapter written by Mario ABUNDO.

In the case that the underlying diffusion $X(t)$ is Brownian motion without drift, the FPA was already studied in Singh and Pal (2022), although the results found therein were obtained using special functions. In contrast, here we used nothing but elementary functions: our arguments were based on classical results for one-dimensional diffusions. In fact, the study of the distributions of the FPT and FPA was carried out via solutions of certain associated ODEs. We focused on the case when the underlying diffusion $X(t)$ is a Wiener process, i.e. a Brownian motion with or without drift, but the results can be extended to other processes.

The FPT and FPA of a diffusion process with stochastic resetting have important applications in many areas, for example, in biology, in the ambit of stochastic models for the activity of a neuron subject to resetting (see, for example, Nobile et al. 1985 and the references contained therein). Other important applications are found in queuing theory, where the first hitting time to zero can be identified with the busy period, i.e. the first instant at which the queue is empty, and the FPA is the total waiting time of the "customers" during a busy period (see, for example, Kearney 2004).

Now, we precisely describe the process $\mathcal{X}(t)$ with stochastic resetting.

We consider a one-dimensional temporally homogeneous diffusion process $X(t)$ driven by the SDE:

$$dX(t) = \mu(X(t))dt + \sigma(X(t))dB_t, \qquad [1.1]$$

and starting from the position $X(0) = x > 0$, where the drift $\mu(\cdot)$ and diffusion coefficient $\sigma(\cdot)$ are regular enough functions, such that there exists a unique strong solution of the SDE [1.1] for a given starting point, and B_t is the standard Brownian motion. We also assume that the FPT of the diffusion $X(t)$ below zero is finite with probability one.

We assume that resetting events can occur according to a homogeneous Poisson process with rate $r > 0$. Until the first resetting event $\mathcal{R}$, the process $\mathcal{X}(t)$ coincides with $X(t)$, and it evolves according to [1.1] with $\mathcal{X}(0) = X(0) = x > 0$. When the reset occurs, $\mathcal{X}(t)$ is set instantly to a position $x_R > 0$. After that, $\mathcal{X}(t)$ evolves again according to [1.1], starting afresh (independently of the past history) from x_R, until the next resetting event occurs, etc. The inter-resetting times turn out to be independent and exponentially distributed random variables with parameter r. In other words, in any time interval $(t, t + \Delta t)$, with $\Delta t \to 0^+$, the process can pass from $\mathcal{X}(t)$ to the position x_R with probability $r\Delta t + o(\Delta t)$, or it can continue its evolution according to [1.1] with probability $1 - r\Delta t + o(\Delta t)$. The process $\mathcal{X}(t)$ so obtained is called diffusion with stochastic resetting. For any C^2 function $f(x)$, its infinitesimal generator is given by (see, for example, Abundo 2013):

$$\begin{aligned}\mathcal{L}f(x) &= \frac{1}{2}\sigma^2(x)f''(x) + \mu(x)f'(x) + r(f(x_R) - f(x)) \\ &\equiv Lf(x) + r(f(x_R) - f(x)),\end{aligned} \qquad [1.2]$$

where $Lf(x) = \frac{1}{2}\sigma^2(x)f''(x) + \mu(x)f'(x)$ is the "diffusion part" of the generator, i.e. regarding the diffusion process $X(t)$.

For an initial position $x > 0$, we are concerned with the FPT of $\mathcal{X}(t)$ through zero, namely:

$$\tau(x) = \inf\{t > 0 : \mathcal{X}(t) = 0 \mid \mathcal{X}(0) = X(0) = x\}, \tag{1.3}$$

and the corresponding FPA

$$A(x) = \int_0^{\tau(x)} \mathcal{X}(t)dt, \tag{1.4}$$

which is the area enclosed between the time axis and the path of the process $\mathcal{X}(t)$ up to the FPT through zero. We assume that both $\tau(x)$ and $A(x)$ are finite with probability one, for any $x > 0$. Note that

$$\tau(x) = \tau_X(x), \text{ if } \tau_X(x) < \sigma; \ \tau(x) = \sigma + \tau(x_R), \text{ if } \tau_X(x) \geq \sigma, \tag{1.5}$$

where $\tau_X(x)$ is the first-hitting time to zero of $X(t)$ starting from $x > 0$ and σ is an exponentially distributed random variable with parameter $r > 0$.

In fact, we limit ourselves to study the case when the underlying process $X(t)$ is a Wiener process, i.e. Brownian motion with or without drift.

The main qualitative difference between the FPT of the process $\mathcal{X}(t)$ and the FPT of the underlying diffusion $X(t)$ is that, for the process $\mathcal{X}(t)$, the moments of the FPT are finite, while for the second one, they may be infinite. This is, for example, the case of Brownian motion starting from $x > 0$, where, as is well known, the first-hitting time to zero is finite with probability 1, but it has infinite expectation.

For $\lambda > 0$, let us consider the Laplace transform (LT) of $\int_0^{\tau(x)} U(\mathcal{X}(s))ds$, $U(x) = ax + b$ $(a, b \geq 0)$ being a polynomial of degree one, i.e.

$$M_\lambda(x) = E\left[e^{-\lambda \int_0^{\tau(x)} U(\mathcal{X}(s))ds}\right]. \tag{1.6}$$

Taking $U(x) = 1$, we obtain the LT of the FPT $\tau(x)$, while for $U(x) = x$, we get the LT of the FPA $A(x)$. The following holds (see Abundo 2023a):

PROPOSITION 1.1.– *The LT $M_\lambda(x)$ of $\int_0^{\tau(x)} U(\mathcal{X}(s))ds$ satisfies the differential problem:*

$$\begin{cases} LM_\lambda(x) - \lambda U(x)M_\lambda(x) - rM_\lambda(x) + rM_\lambda(x_R) = 0, \\ M_\lambda(0) = 1, \\ \lim_{x\to+\infty} M_\lambda(x) = M_\lambda(+\infty) < \infty, \end{cases} \tag{1.7}$$

where L denotes the infinitesimal generator of the underlying diffusion $X(t)$, which is given, for any C^2 function f, by

$$Lf(x) = \frac{1}{2}\sigma^2(x)f''(x) + \mu(x)f'(x), \qquad [1.8]$$

and f' and f'' denote the first and second derivatives of f. □

REMARK 1.1.– *Proposition 1.1 was already proved in Singh and Pal (2022) in the case when $X(t)$ is Brownian motion. Note that, for $r = 0$ (i.e. when no resetting is allowed), we obtain equation (2.12) of Abundo (2013), provided that the jump part in the infinitesimal generator is set to zero, while the second boundary condition is $M_\lambda(+\infty) = 0$.*

If the $n-$th order moment of $\int_0^{\tau(x)} U(\mathfrak{X}(s))ds$ exists finite, it is provided by:

$$T_n(x) := E\left[\left(\int_0^{\tau(x)} U(X(s))ds\right)^n\right] = (-1)^n \left[\frac{\partial^n}{\partial \lambda^n} M_\lambda(x)\right]_{\lambda=0}, n = 1, 2, \ldots. \qquad [1.9]$$

By calculating the $n-$th derivative with respect to λ, at $\lambda = 0$, of both members of [1.7], we obtain that, setting $T_0(x) = 1$, the $n-$th order moments $T_n(x)$ satisfy the ODEs:

$$LT_n(x) - rT_n(x) = -nU(x)T_{n-1}(x) - rT_n(x_R),\ x > 0, \qquad [1.10]$$

with the constraint $T_n(0) = 0$ and the addition of an appropriate further condition (indeed, we need two conditions to obtain the unique solution of [1.10]). Note that for $r = 0$, [1.10] becomes equation (2.19) of Abundo (2013). In particular, for $U(x) \equiv 1$, [1.10] is nothing but the celebrated Darling and Siegert's equation (1953) for the moments of the FPT of a diffusion without resetting.

As regards the joint moments of $\tau(x)$ and $A(x)$, we consider the joint LT of $\tau(x)$ and $A(x)$, i.e. $E[e^{-\lambda_1\tau(x)-\lambda_2 A(x)}]$ ($\lambda_i > 0$):

$$M_{\lambda_1,\lambda_2}(x) = E\left[\exp\left(-\int_0^{\tau(x)} (\lambda_1 + \lambda_2\mathfrak{X}(t))dt\right)\right]. \qquad [1.11]$$

As easily seen, we get:

$$\frac{\partial M_{\lambda_1,\lambda_2}(x)}{\partial \lambda_1}|_{\lambda_1=\lambda_2=0} = -E[\tau(x)],\ \frac{\partial M_{\lambda_1,\lambda_2}(x)}{\partial \lambda_2}|_{\lambda_1=\lambda_2=0} = -E[A(x)], \qquad [1.12]$$

and

$$\frac{\partial^2 M_{\lambda_1,\lambda_2}(x)}{\partial\lambda_1\partial\lambda_2}|_{\lambda_1=\lambda_2=0} = E[\tau(x)A(x)]. \quad [1.13]$$

Applying the same reasoning as before and taking $U(x) = \lambda_1 + \lambda_2 x$, we obtain that $M_{\lambda_1,\lambda_2}(x)$ solves the problem

$$\begin{cases} LM_{\lambda_1,\lambda_2}(x) - rM_{\lambda_1,\lambda_2}(x) = (\lambda_1 + \lambda_2 x)M_{\lambda_1,\lambda_2}(x) - rM_{\lambda_1,\lambda_2}(x_R) \\ M_{\lambda_1,\lambda_2}(0) = 1 \\ \lim_{x\to+\infty} M_{\lambda_1,\lambda_2}(x) = M_{\lambda_1,\lambda_2}(+\infty) < \infty. \end{cases} \quad [1.14]$$

Then, by applying $\frac{\partial^2}{\partial\lambda_1\partial\lambda_2}$ and calculating it for $\lambda_1 = \lambda_2 = 0$, we obtain that $V(x) := E[\tau(x)A(x)]$ is the solution of the problem:

$$\begin{cases} LV(x) - rV(x) = -xE[\tau(x)] - E[A(x)] - rV(x_R) \\ V(0) = 0, \end{cases} \quad [1.15]$$

with a suitable additional condition.

Note that for $r = 0$, [1.15] becomes the analogous equation, respectively, obtained in Abundo and Del Vescovo (2017) and Abundo (2023b), in the case of drifted Brownian motion and Ornstein–Uhlenbeck process without resetting. Of course, now the boundary conditions are different.

1.2. Brownian motion with resetting

In this section, we consider Brownian motion with resetting $\mathcal{X}(t)$, and we find explicit expressions of the LT and single and joint moments of the FPT and FPA, as solutions of certain differential problems. Note that for $r = 0$ the moments of the FPT and FPA are infinite. This follows by the fact that the FPT density of Brownian motion decays as $t^{-3/2}$ at large time t. In contrast, both the FPT density and the FPA density of Brownian motion with resetting decay exponentially fast at large values (see, for example, Abundo 2023a and the references therein); and so, the moments of the FPT and FPA are finite, for $r > 0$.

Since the underlying process of Brownian motion with resetting is $X(t) = B_t$, for any C^2 function $f(x)$, the infinitesimal generator L of $X(t)$ is given by $Lf(x) = \frac{1}{2}f''(x)$ and from [1.7], we get that the LT of $\int_0^{\tau(x)} U(\mathcal{X}(s))ds$ solves the problem:

$$\begin{cases} \frac{1}{2}\frac{\partial^2 M_\lambda}{\partial x^2}(x) - \lambda U(x)M_\lambda(x) - rM_\lambda(x) + rM_\lambda(x_R) = 0, \\ M_\lambda(0) = 1, \\ \lim_{x\to+\infty} M_\lambda(x) = M_\lambda(+\infty) < \infty, \end{cases} \quad [1.16]$$

Taking $U(x) = 1$, we obtain that the LT of the FPT $\tau(x)$ is the solution of:

$$\begin{cases} \frac{1}{2}\frac{\partial^2 M_\lambda}{\partial x^2}(x) - (\lambda + r)M_\lambda(x) + rM_\lambda(x_R) = 0, \\ M_\lambda(0) = 1, \\ \lim_{x\to+\infty} M_\lambda(x) = M_\lambda(+\infty) < \infty, \end{cases} \quad [1.17]$$

By solving, we explicitly obtain (see Abundo 2023a for details) the LT of $\tau(x)$:

$$M_\lambda(x) = E\left[e^{-\lambda\tau(x)}\right] =$$

$$= e^{-x\sqrt{2(\lambda+r)}} + \frac{r}{\lambda + re^{-x_R\sqrt{2(\lambda+r)}}}\left(e^{-x_R\sqrt{2(\lambda+r)}} - e^{-(x+x_R)\sqrt{2(\lambda+r)}}\right). \quad [1.18]$$

REMARK 1.2.– *Formula* [1.18] *extends to all* $x > 0$ *equation (44) of Singh and Pal (2022) that holds for* $x = x_R$. *For* $r = 0$, *namely when no resetting occurs,* [1.18] *provides* $E[e^{-\lambda\tau(x)}] = e^{-x\sqrt{2\lambda}}$, *i.e. the well-known formula of the LT of the FPT through zero of Brownian motion starting from* $x > 0$; *this LT corresponds to the inverse Gaussian density for the FPT.*

As regards the LT of $A(x)$, by taking $U(x) = x$ in [1.16], we obtain that the LT of $A(x)$ is the solution of:

$$\begin{cases} \frac{1}{2}\frac{\partial^2 M_\lambda}{\partial x^2}(x) - rM_\lambda(x) = \lambda x M_\lambda(x) - rM_\lambda(x_R), \\ M_\lambda(0) = 1, \\ \lim_{x\to+\infty} M_\lambda(x) = M_\lambda(+\infty) < \infty, \end{cases} \quad [1.19]$$

Unfortunately, equation [1.19] cannot be solved in terms of elementary functions. For $x = x_R$, its solution, $M_\lambda(x_R) = E[e^{-\lambda A(x_R)}]$, can be written in terms of special functions, precisely Scorer's and Airy functions (see Singh and Pal 2022). For $r = 0$, i.e. for Brownian motion without resetting, equation [1.19] is the Schrodinger equation for a quantum particle moving in a uniform field and it can be solved in terms of the Airy function.

1.2.1. *Moments of the FPT*

Now we calculate the first two moments of $\tau(x)$ by solving the ODE [1.10] with $U(x) = 1$, and $T_n(x) = E[\tau^n(x)], n = 1, 2$.

As for the mean of $\tau(x)$, taking $n = 1$, we have that $T_1(x) = E[\tau(x)]$ is the solution of the problem:

$$\begin{cases} \frac{1}{2}T_1''(x) - rT_1(x) = -1 - rT_1(x_R) \\ T_1(0) = 0, \; T_1(+\infty) < +\infty, \end{cases} \quad [1.20]$$

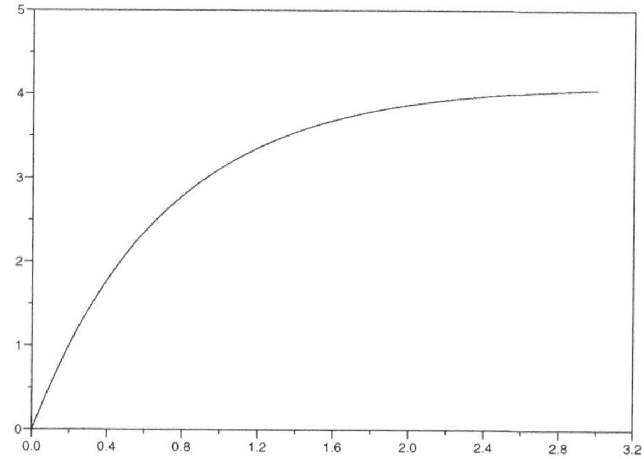

Figure 1.1. *Graph of $E[\tau(x)]$, given by [1.21], as a function of $x > 0$ for $r = x_R = 1$ (on the horizontal axes x)*

The appropriate additional condition is $T_1(\infty) < \infty$. By solving, we get (see Abundo (2023a) for details):

$$T_1(x) = E[\tau(x)] = \frac{1}{r} e^{x_R\sqrt{2r}} \left(1 - e^{-x\sqrt{2r}}\right), \qquad [1.21]$$

and for $x = x_R$:

$$T_1(x_R) = \frac{1}{r}(e^{x_R\sqrt{2r}} - 1), \qquad [1.22]$$

Note that $E[\tau(+\infty)] = \frac{1}{r} e^{x_R\sqrt{2r}} < +\infty$.

REMARK 1.3.– *Formula* [1.21] *extends to all $x > 0$ equation (45) of Singh and Pal (2022) that provides $E[\tau(x_R)]$ (see* [1.22]*). Note that, letting r go to zero in equation* [1.21]*, it follows $E[\tau(x)] = +\infty$, which matches the well-known result for Brownian motion (see, for example, Abundo and Del Vescovo 2017).*

Figure 1.1 shows an example of the shape of $E[\tau(x)]$, given by [1.21], as a function of $x > 0$ for $r = x_R = 1$.

As regards the second-order moment of $\tau(x)$, by taking $n = 2$ and $U(x) = 1$ in [1.10], we get that $T_2(x) = E[\tau^2(x)]$ is the solution of the problem:

$$\begin{cases} \frac{1}{2}T_2''(x) - rT_2(x) = -\frac{2}{r} e^{x_R\sqrt{2r}}(1 - e^{-x\sqrt{2r}}) - rT_2(x_R) \\ T_2(0) = 0, \ T_2(+\infty) < +\infty. \end{cases} \qquad [1.23]$$

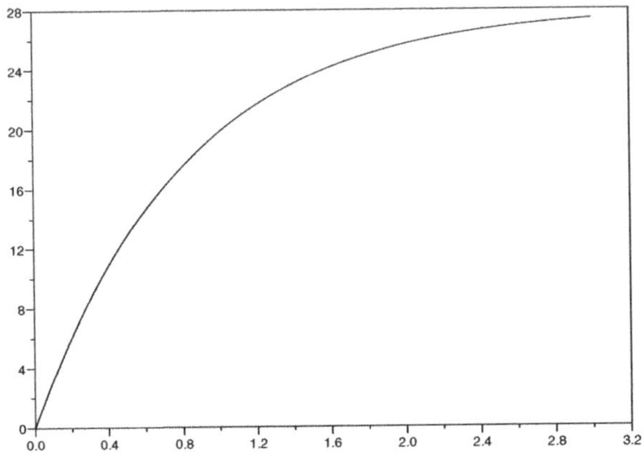

Figure 1.2. *Graph of $E[\tau^2(x)]$ as a function of $x > 0$ for $r = x_R = 1$ (on the horizontal axes x)*

By solving (see Abundo 2023a for details), we get:

$$T_2(x) = E[\tau^2(x)] = e^{x_R\sqrt{2r}}\left(\frac{2}{r^2}e^{x_R\sqrt{2r}} - \frac{2}{r^2} - \frac{2x_R}{r\sqrt{2r}}\right)\left(1 - e^{-x\sqrt{2r}}\right)$$

$$-\frac{2}{r}e^{(x_R - x)\sqrt{2r}}\left(\frac{1}{r} + \frac{x}{\sqrt{2r}}\right) + \frac{2}{r^2}e^{x_R\sqrt{2r}}, \qquad [1.24]$$

and for $x = x_R$:

$$E[\tau^2(x_R)] = e^{x_R\sqrt{2r}}\left(\frac{2}{r^2}e^{x_R\sqrt{2r}} - \frac{2}{r^2} - \frac{2x_R}{r\sqrt{2r}}\right). \qquad [1.25]$$

Figure 1.2 shows an example of the shape of $E[\tau^2(x)]$, given by [1.24], as a function of $x > 0$ for $r = x_R = 1$.

As regards the behaviors of the first two moments of the FPT $\tau(x)$ for $x \to 0^+$ and $x \to +\infty$, from [1.21] we get $E[\tau(x)] = a_1 x + o(x)$, as $x \to 0^+$, where the constant $a_1 = \frac{\sqrt{2r}}{r}e^{x_R\sqrt{2r}}$ depends on r and x_R, and $\lim_{x\to+\infty} E[\tau(x)] = a_1/\sqrt{2r}$.

From [1.24], we get that $E[\tau^2(x)] = a_2 x + o(x)$, as $x \to 0^+$, where $a_2 = \sqrt{2r}E[\tau^2(x_R)] + \frac{\sqrt{2}}{r\sqrt{r}}e^{x_R\sqrt{2r}}$ and $E[\tau^2(x_R)]$ is given by [1.25]. Moreover, $\lim_{x\to+\infty} E[\tau^2(x)] = E[\tau^2(x_R)] + \frac{2}{r^2}e^{x_R\sqrt{2r}}$. Therefore, $Var[\tau(x)] = a_2 x + o(x)$, as $x \to 0^+$, and $\lim_{x\to+\infty} Var[\tau(x)] = E[\tau^2(x_R)] + \frac{2}{r^2}e^{x_R\sqrt{2r}} - \frac{1}{r^2}e^{2x_R\sqrt{2r}}$.

1.2.2. *Moments of the FPA*

We recall that the FPA density of Brownian motion with resetting (i.e. for $r > 0$) decays exponentially fast at large values, so the moments of the FPA are finite (see, for example, Abundo 2023a and the references therein). The LT of the FPA, $E[\exp(-\lambda A(x)]$, was obtained in Singh and Pal (2022) for $x = x_R$ in terms of special functions, and the first two moments of the FPA at $x = x_R$ were there obtained, by calculating the first and second derivatives of $E[\exp(-\lambda A(x_R)]$ with respect to λ at $\lambda = 0$ (see equations (58) and (59) therein). Precisely, it results:

$$E[A(x_R)] = \frac{x_R}{r} e^{x_R\sqrt{2r}} := \alpha_1, \qquad [1.26]$$

$$E[A^2(x_R)] = \frac{2e^{x_R\sqrt{2r}}}{r}\left[\frac{x_R^2}{r}\left(\frac{3}{4} + e^{x_R\sqrt{2r}}\right) + \frac{1}{r^2} - \frac{x_R^3}{2\sqrt{2r}}\right] - \frac{2}{r^3} := \alpha_2. \qquad [1.27]$$

Now, we calculate the first two moments of the FPA $A(x)$ for every $x > 0$ by solving the ODE [1.10] with $U(x) = x$, and $T_n(x) = E[A^n(x)], n = 1, 2$.

As regards the mean of $A(x)$, taking $n = 1$, we have that $T_1(x) = E[A(x)]$ is the solution of the problem:

$$\begin{cases} \frac{1}{2}T_1''(x) - rT_1(x) = -x - rT_1(x_R) \\ T_1(0) = 0, \; T_1(x_R) = \alpha_1; \end{cases} \qquad [1.28]$$

note that $A(+\infty) = +\infty$, so in contrast with the case of the mean FPT, the appropriate additional condition is $T_1(x_R) = \alpha_1$.

By solving (see Abundo 2023a), we get:

$$T_1(x) = E[A(x)] = \frac{x_R}{r} e^{x_R\sqrt{2r}}\left(1 - e^{-x\sqrt{2r}}\right) + \frac{x}{r}. \qquad [1.29]$$

REMARK 1.4.– *Formula* [1.29] *extends to all $x > 0$ equation (58) of Singh and Pal (2022) which provides $E[A(x_R)]$ (see* [1.26]*). Note that, for $r = 0$, it follows $E[A(x)] = +\infty$, which matches the well-known result for Brownian motion (see, for example, Abundo and Del Vescovo 2017).*

For $x \to 0^+$, we have $E[A(x)] = \left(\frac{x_R\sqrt{2r}}{r} e^{x_R\sqrt{2r}} + \frac{1}{r}\right) x + o(x)$, while for large positive x, it holds $E[A(x)] \sim \frac{x}{r}$.

Figure 1.3, shows an example of the shape of $E[A(x)]$, given by [1.29], as a function of $x > 0$, for $r = x_R = 1$.

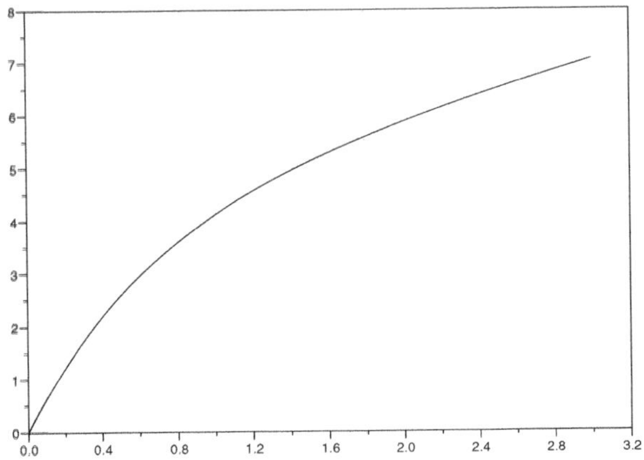

Figure 1.3. *Graph of $E[A(x)]$ as a function of $x > 0$ for $r = x_R = 1$ (on the horizontal axes x)*

As regards the second-order moment of $A(x)$, by taking $n = 2$ in [1.10] with $U(x) = x$, we get that $T_2(x) = E[A^2(x)]$ is the solution of the problem:

$$\begin{cases} \frac{1}{2}T_2''(x) - rT_2(x) = -2xE[A(x)] - rT_2(x_R) \\ T_2(0) = 0, \; T_2(x_R) = \alpha_2, \end{cases} \quad [1.30]$$

where $E[A(x)]$ is given by [1.29].

By solving, we obtain (see Abundo (2023a) for details):

$$T_2(x) = E[A^2(x)] = \left(1 - e^{-x\sqrt{2r}}\right)\left(\alpha_2 + \frac{2}{r^3}\right) +$$

$$+\frac{2x}{r^2}\left(x + x_R e^{x_R\sqrt{2r}}\right) - \frac{x_R x}{r}\left(\frac{x}{\sqrt{2r}} + \frac{1}{2r}\right)e^{-(x-x_R)\sqrt{2r}}. \quad [1.31]$$

Equation [1.31] extends to all values of $x > 0$, the formula found in Singh and Pal (2022) for the expectation of $A^2(x_R)$ (see equation (59) therein).

Figure 1.4 shows the shape of $E[A^2(x)]$, given by [1.31], as a function of $x > 0$, for $r = x_R = 1$. Note that the graph of $E[A^2(x)]$ is not globally concave or convex, but it presents an inflection point. From [1.31], it follows that, for $x \to 0^+$, $E[A^2(x)] = \left[\sqrt{2r}\left(\alpha_2 + \frac{2}{r^3}\right) + \frac{3x_R}{2r^2}e^{x_R\sqrt{2r}}\right]x + o(x)$, and $Var[A(x)]$ has the same behavior, at the first order in x. Moreover, for large $x > 0$, $E[A^2(x)] \sim \frac{2}{r^2}x^2$, and $Var[A(x)] \sim \frac{x^2}{r^2}$.

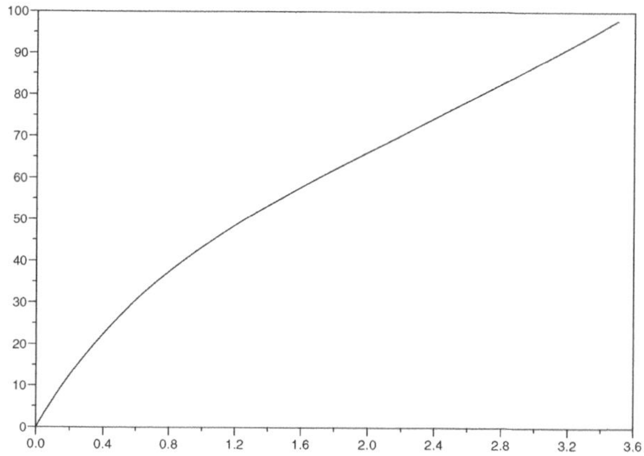

Figure 1.4. *Graph of $E[A^2(x)]$ as a function of $x > 0$ for $r = x_R = 1$ (on the horizontal axes x)*

REMARK 1.5.– *From the previous calculations, we conclude that the following growth conditions (upper bounds) hold:*

$$E[A(x)] \leq const \cdot x, \; E[A^2(x)] \leq const' \cdot x^2, \text{ for large } x > 0. \qquad [1.32]$$

Similar bounds hold for Brownian motion with a negative drift μ (without resetting, i.e. $r = 0$), because in that case, the moments of $A(x)$ grow at most polynomially in x (see Abundo and Del Vescovo 2017).

1.2.3. *Joint moment of* $A(x)$ *and* $\tau(x)$

In this section, we find an explicit expression for $E[A(x)\tau(x)]$, i.e. the joint moment of $A(x)$ and $\tau(x)$. The joint LT of $\tau(x), A(x)$ is $M_{\lambda_1,\lambda_2}(x) = E\left[e^{-\lambda_1\tau(x)}e^{-\lambda_2 A(x)}\right], \lambda_1, \lambda_2 > 0$. By reasoning as before, we find that it satisfies the differential equation:

$$(L - r)M_{\lambda_1,\lambda_2}(x) = (\lambda_1 + \lambda_2 x)M_{\lambda_1,\lambda_2}(x) - rM_{\lambda_1,\lambda_2}(x_R). \qquad [1.33]$$

Then, by taking $\frac{\partial^2}{\partial\lambda_1\partial\lambda_2}$ in both members of equation [1.33] and calculating it at $\lambda_1 = \lambda_2 = 0$, we obtain that $V(x) := E[\tau(x)A(x)]$ satisfies the differential problem:

$$(L - r)V(x) = -xE[\tau(x)] - E[A(x)] - rV(x_R), \; V(0) = 0, \qquad [1.34]$$

with a suitable additional condition.

In fact, since $E[A(x)\tau(x)] \leq \sqrt{E[A^2(x)]}\sqrt{E[\tau^2(x)]}$, by taking into account the behaviors of the moments of the FPA at large x (see [1.32]), we obtain that the additional condition for the ODE [1.34] must be:

$$V(x) = E[\tau(x)A(x)] \le const \cdot x, \text{ for large } x > 0. \quad [1.35]$$

By solving, we obtain (see Abundo 2023a for details):

$$V(x) = -\left[\frac{x_R e^{x_R\sqrt{2r}}}{r^2} + V(x_R)\right] e^{-x\sqrt{2r}} + \bar{V}(x), \quad [1.36]$$

where $V(x_R) = e^{x_R\sqrt{2r}}\left[\left(8e^{x_R\sqrt{2r}} - 1\right)\frac{x_R}{4r^2} - \frac{3x_R^2}{2r\sqrt{2r}}\right]$,
$\bar{V}(x) = V(x_R) + \frac{(e^{x_R\sqrt{2r}}+1)x}{r^2} + \frac{x_R e^{x_R\sqrt{2r}}}{r^2} - e^{-(x-x_R)\sqrt{2r}}\left(\frac{x^2}{2r\sqrt{2r}} + \frac{(1+2x_R\sqrt{2r})x}{4r^2}\right)$.
Therefore, the expressions of $Cov[A(x), \tau(x)] := V(x) - E[\tau(x)]E[A(x)]$ and of the correlation coefficient

$$\rho_{\tau(x),A(x)} := \frac{Cov[\tau(x), A(x)]}{\sqrt{Var[\tau(x)]Var[A(x)]}}, \quad [1.37]$$

follow soon. As easily seen, $\rho_{\tau(x),A(x)}$ turns out to be positive for every $x > 0$, i.e. $\tau(x)$ and $A(x)$ are positively correlated. Moreover, $\lim_{x\to 0^+} \rho_{\tau(x),A(x)} = \rho_0 > 0$, and $\lim_{x\to+\infty} \rho_{\tau(x),A(x)} = \rho_\infty < \rho_0$. The graph of $\rho_{\tau(x),A(x)}$ increases from ρ_0 to a maximum value; after that, it decreases to $\rho_\infty < \rho_0$, as $x \to +\infty$. This kind of behavior for $\rho_{\tau(x),A(x)}$ was also observed for the drifted Brownian motion without reset (see Abundo and Del Vescovo 2017) and Ornstein–Uhlenbeck process without reset (see Abundo 2023b).

Figure 1.5 (top panel) shows the graph of $\rho_{\tau(x),A(x)}$, as a function of $x > 0$ for $r = x_R = 1$ (on the horizontal axes x); the existence of the maximum is revealed by an enlargement around $x = 0.1$ (bottom panel). Figure 1.6 shows another example of the graph of $\rho_{\tau(x),A(x)}$, obtained for $r = 1$ and $x_R = 2$.

1.2.4. *Maximum displacement*

We define the maximum displacement of Brownian motion with resetting $\mathcal{X}(t)$, starting from $x > 0$, as the random variables $\mathcal{M}_x = \max_{t\in[0,\tau(x)]} \mathcal{X}(t)$ (obviously, we have $\mathcal{M}_x \ge x$). Note that the event $\{\mathcal{M}_x \le z\}$ occurs if and only if $\mathcal{X}(t)$ first exits the interval $(0, z)$ through the left end 0. Therefore, for $z \ge x$, we get that the distribution function $F_{\mathcal{M}_x}(z) = P(\mathcal{M}_x \le z)$ is the solution of the differential equation (see, for example, Abundo 2013, 2023b):

$$\begin{cases} \mathcal{L}w(x) = \frac{1}{2}w''(x) + rw(x_R) - rw(x) = 0, \; x \in (0, z) \\ w(0) = 1, \; w(z) = 0, \end{cases} \quad [1.38]$$

where $\mathcal{L}$ is the infinitesimal generator of $\mathcal{X}(t)$ (see [1.2]).

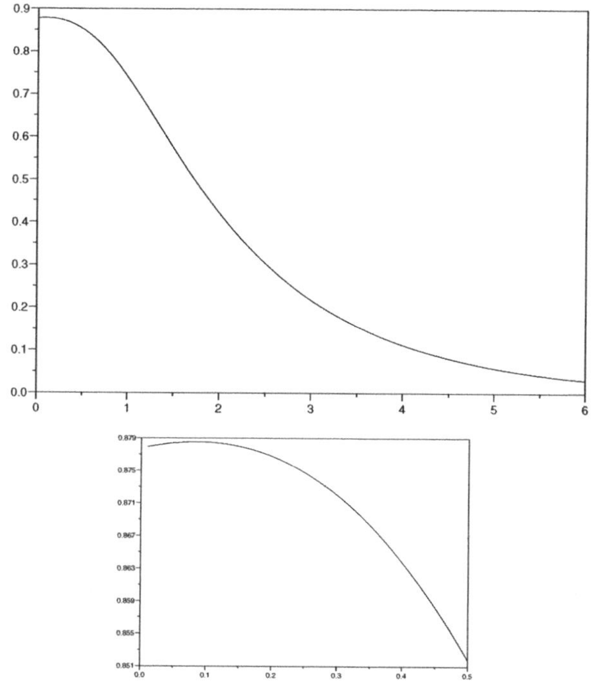

Figure 1.5. *Graph of $\rho_{\tau(x),A(x)}$ as a function of $x > 0$ for $r = x_R = 1$ (on the horizontal axes x); the second panel shows an enlargement around $x = 0.1$*

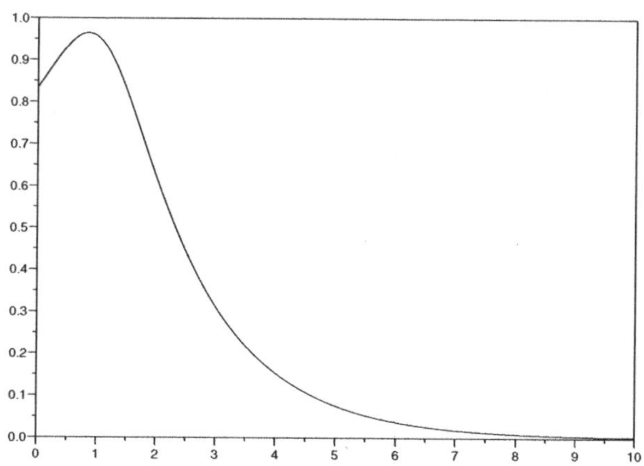

Figure 1.6. *Graph of $\rho_{\tau(x),A(x)}$ as a function of $x > 0$ for $r = 1$ and $x_R = 2$ (on the horizontal axes x)*

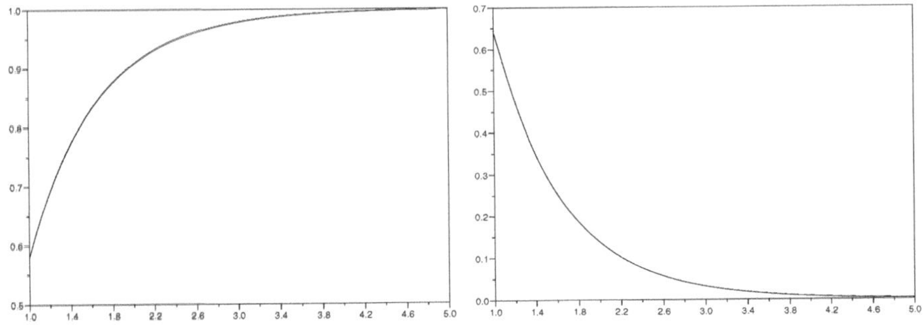

Figure 1.7. *Left panel: distribution function of the maximum displacement* $\mathcal{M}_x$ *of Brownian motion with resetting, for* $x = 1, x_R = 0.5$ *and* $r = 1$; *right panel: the corresponding density (on the horizontal axes* $z \geq x = 1$)

By solving, we get (see Abundo 2023a for details):

$$F_{\mathcal{M}_x}(z) = P(\mathcal{M}_x \leq z) = \begin{cases} 0, & z < x \\ c_1(z)e^{-x\sqrt{2r}} + c_2(z)e^{x\sqrt{2r}} + a(z), & z \geq x, \end{cases} \qquad [1.39]$$

where

$$\begin{cases} c_1(z) = (e^{z\sqrt{2r}} - 1)^{-1}(e^{-z\sqrt{2r}} + e^{-2x_R\sqrt{2r}})^{-1} \\ c_2(z) = -e^{-2x_R\sqrt{2r}}c_1(z) \\ a(z) = 1 - c_1(z) - c_2(z). \end{cases} \qquad [1.40]$$

As seen, the distribution function of $\mathcal{M}_x - x$ appears to have a tail that decays exponentially fast, and so the expectation $E[\mathcal{M}_x]$ results to be finite. By calculating the solution of [1.38] for $r = 0$, we obtain that, for Brownian motion without resetting, the distribution of the maximum displacement is:

$$F_{\mathcal{M}_x}(z) = 1 - \frac{x}{z}, \; z \geq x, \qquad [1.41]$$

and it is zero for $z < x$. This implies that the expectation of the maximum displacement of Brownian motion without resetting is infinite. Figure 1.7 shows an example of the distribution function of the maximum displacement $\mathcal{M}_x$ of Brownian motion with resetting, and the corresponding probability density, obtained by taking the derivative in [1.39], for $x = 1, x_R = 0.5$ and $r = 1$.

1.3. Drifted Brownian motion with resetting

In this section, we consider drifted Brownian motion with resetting $\mathcal{X}(t)$, namely $X(t) = x + B_t + \mu t$, and we find explicit expressions of the LT, the moments of the FPT and FPA, and the maximum displacement of $\mathcal{X}(t)$, as solutions of differential problems. We omit the details, and we limit ourselves to report only the results which can be obtained without using special functions (for more details, see Abundo 2023a).

Note that the FPT through zero of Brownian motion with non-zero drift μ (without resetting), starting from $x > 0$ is finite with probability one, only if the drift is negative. Instead, the FPT through zero of drifted Brownian motion with resetting $\mathcal{X}(t)$ is finite, irrespective of the sign of the drift μ and the moments of the FPT are also finite, for any $0 < r < +\infty$ (see, for example, Pal et al. 2019). The infinitesimal generator of $X(t)$ is now given by $Lf(x) = \frac{1}{2}\frac{df^2}{dx^2} + \mu\frac{df}{dx}$; by proceeding as in the case of undrifted Brownian motion with resetting, the solutions of the various equations can be obtained by taking $\mu + \sqrt{\mu^2 + 2(\lambda + r)}$ in place of $\sqrt{2(\lambda + r)}$ in the corresponding formulae.

1.3.1. *The Laplace transform of* $\tau(x)$

The LT of $\tau(x)$ turns out to be

$$M_\lambda(x) = E\left[e^{-\lambda\tau(x)}\right] = e^{-x\left(\mu+\sqrt{\mu^2+2(\lambda+r)}\,\right)} +$$

$$+M_\lambda(x_R)\tfrac{r}{\lambda+r}\left(1 - e^{-x\left(\mu+\sqrt{\mu^2+2(\lambda+r)}\,\right)}\right), \text{ where}$$

$$M_\lambda(x_R) = \frac{(\lambda+r)e^{-x_R\left(\mu+\sqrt{\mu^2+2(\lambda+r)}\,\right)}}{\lambda+re^{-x_R\left(\mu+\sqrt{\mu^2+2(\lambda+r)}\,\right)}}.$$

REMARK 1.6.– *The above formula is new, because only the undrifted Brownian motion with resetting was studied in Singh and Pal (2022).*

1.3.2. *Moments of the FPT*

The mean of the FPT is:

$$E[\tau(x)] = \frac{1}{r}e^{x_R(\mu+\sqrt{\mu^2+2r})}\left(1 - e^{-x(\mu+\sqrt{\mu^2+2r})}\right). \qquad [1.42]$$

For $\mu = 0$, we again obtain [1.21].

As for the second-order moment of $\tau(x)$, we have:

$$E[\tau^2(x)] =$$

$$= e^{x_R(\mu+\sqrt{\mu^2+2r})}\left(\frac{2}{r^2}e^{x_R(\mu+\sqrt{\mu^2+2r})}-\frac{2}{r^2}-\frac{2x_R}{r\sqrt{\mu^2+2r}}\right)\left(1-e^{-x(\mu+\sqrt{\mu^2+2r})}\right)$$

$$-\frac{2}{r}e^{(x_R-x)(\mu+\sqrt{\mu^2+2r})}\left(\frac{1}{r}+\frac{x}{\sqrt{\mu^2+2r}}\right)+\frac{2}{r^2}e^{x_R(\mu+\sqrt{\mu^2+2r})}. \qquad [1.43]$$

For $\mu = 0$, we again obtain [1.24].

1.3.3. *Mean of the FPA*

The mean of the FPA turns out to be:

$$E[A(x)] = E[A(x_R)]\left(1-e^{-x\left(\mu+\sqrt{\mu^2+2r}\right)}\right)+\frac{x}{r}+\frac{\mu}{r^2}\left(1-e^{-x\left(\mu+\sqrt{\mu^2+2r}\right)}\right), \qquad [1.44]$$

where

$$E[A(x_R)] = e^{x_R\left(\mu+\sqrt{\mu^2+2r}\right)}\left[\frac{x_R}{r}+\frac{\mu}{r^2}\left(1-e^{-x_R\left(\mu+\sqrt{\mu^2+2r}\right)}\right)\right]. \qquad [1.45]$$

For $\mu = 0$, we again obtain $E[A(x_R)] = \frac{x_R}{r}e^{\sqrt{2r}x_R}$ and $E[A(x)] = \frac{x_R}{r}e^{\sqrt{2r}x_R}(1-e^{-x\sqrt{2r}})+\frac{x}{r}$ (see [1.26] and [1.29].

1.3.4. *Maximum displacement*

The distribution function of the maximum displacement $\mathcal{M}_x$ turns out to be:

$$F_{\mathcal{M}_x}(z) = P(\mathcal{M}_x \le z) = \begin{cases} 0, & z < x \\ c_1(z)e^{d_1 x}+c_2(z)e^{d_2 x}+a(z), & z \ge x. \end{cases} \qquad [1.46]$$

where $d_1 = -\mu-\sqrt{\mu^2+2r} < 0$, $d_2 = -\mu+\sqrt{\mu^2+2r} > 0$, and the functions $c_i(z)$ and $a(z)$ are given by:

$$\begin{cases} c_1(z) = -\left[e^{-\left(\mu+\sqrt{\mu^2+2r}\right)z}-1+e^{-2x_R\sqrt{\mu^2+2r}}\left(1-e^{-\left(\mu-\sqrt{\mu^2+2r}\right)z}\right)\right]^{-1} \\ c_2(z) = -c_1e^{-2x_R\sqrt{\mu^2+2r}} \\ a(z) = 1-c_1(z)-c_2(z). \end{cases} \qquad [1.47]$$

For $\mu = 0$ [1.46] becomes [1.39]. Once again, the distribution function of $\mathcal{M}_x - x$ has a tail that decays exponentially fast, and so the expectation $E[\mathcal{M}_x]$ results to be finite. Note that for Brownian motion with drift $\mu < 0$ (without resetting), the distribution of the maximum displacement is:

$$F_{\mathcal{M}_x}(z) = \begin{cases} 0, & z < x \\ \frac{e^{-2\mu x} - e^{-2\mu z}}{1 - e^{-2\mu z}}, & z \geq x, \end{cases} \quad [1.48]$$

and its density is

$$f_{\mathcal{M}_x}(z) = \begin{cases} 0, & z < x \\ \frac{\mu e^{-\mu x} \sinh(\mu x)}{\sinh^2(\mu z)}, & z \geq x, \end{cases} \quad [1.49]$$

from which it follows that, unlike the case $\mu = 0$, the expectation of the maximum displacement of Brownian motion with drift $\mu < 0$ without resetting is

$$E[\mathcal{M}_x] = x - \frac{1 - e^{-2\mu x}}{2\mu} \ln\left(1 - e^{2\mu x}\right) < +\infty.$$

Note that, for $\mu \to 0^-$, the last expression tends to $+\infty$ (see the comment after [1.41]).

1.4. References

Abundo, M. (2013). On the first-passage area of a one-dimensional jump-diffusion process. *Methodol. Comput. Appl. Probab.*, 15, 85–103. doi: 10.1007/s11009-011-9223-1.

Abundo, M. (2023a). The first-passage area of Wiener process with stochastic resetting. arXiv:2306.12154. doi: 10.48550/arXiv.2306.12154.

Abundo, M. (2023b). The first-passage area of Ornstein–Uhlenbeck process revisited. *Stoch. Anal. Appl.*, 41(2), 358–376. doi: 10.1080/07362994.2021.2018335.

Abundo, M. and Del Vescovo, D. (2017). On the joint distribution of first-passage time and first-passage area of drifted Brownian motion. *Methodol. Comput. Appl. Probab.*, 19, 985–996. doi: 10.1007/s11009-017-9546-7.

Abundo, M. and Furia, S. (2019). Joint distribution of first-passage time and first-passage area of certain Lèvy processes. *Methodol. Comput. Appl. Probab.*, 21, 1283–1302. doi: 10.1007/s11009-018-9677-5.

Darling, D.A. and Siegert, A.J.F. (1953). The first passage problem for a continuous Markov process. *Ann. Math. Stat.*, 24, 624–639.

Evans, M.R., Majumdar, S.N., Schehr, G. (2020). Stochastic resetting and applications. *J. Phys. A: Math. Theor.*, 53, 193001.

den Hollander, F., Majumdar, S.N., Meylahn, J.M., Touchette, H. (2019). Properties of additive functionals of Brownian motion with resetting. *J. Phys. A: Math. Theor.*, 52, 175001. doi: 10.1088/1751-8121/ab0efd.

Kearney, M.J. (2004). On a random area variable arising in discrete-time queues and compact directed percolation. *J. Phys. A Math. Gen.*, 37(35), 8421.

Nobile, A.G., Ricciardi, L.M., Sacerdote, L. (1985). Exponential trends of Ornstein–Uhlenbeck first-passage-time densities. *J. Appl. Prob.*, 22, 360–369.

Pal, A., Chatterjee, R., Reuveni, S., Kundu, A. (2019). Local time of diffusion with stochastic resetting. *J. Phys. A Math. Theor.*, 52(26), 264002.

Singh, P. and Pal, A. (2022). First-passage Brownian functionals with stochastic resetting. *J. Phys. A: Math. Theor.*, 55, 234001. doi: 10.1088/1751-8121/ac677c.

2

Statistical Analysis of Groundwater Level in Slovakia

In our analysis, we deal with the statistical evaluation of the groundwater level in the Great Corn Island. Groundwater is one of the most important sources of drinking water. The Great Corn Island is the largest river island in Europe and also the largest reservoir of drinking water in Central Europe. Naturally, it is very important to monitor and measure the state of groundwater here. In this chapter, we used statistical methods to determine sudden and extreme changes in the groundwater level, but we also monitored the gradual development of the groundwater level on selected probes. Another aim was to compare the development of the groundwater level in these probes to each other by means of correlation analysis. All results were obtained by analyses in statistical software R.

2.1. Introduction

Groundwater is an important (and currently one of the most economical) source of drinking water due to its capture, exploitation, quality and protection requirements. It is the main source of drinking water in Slovakia – one of the countries with a strong orientation of water management on groundwater. The usable quantities of these waters are directly dependent on the fluctuation of groundwater levels, while their evaluation is inextricably linked to the data obtained on the long-term observation of groundwater.

A great amount of groundwater analysis has performed made worldwide. Trend analysis of the groundwater level in India is discussed by Halder et al. (2020) and also by Thakur and Thomas (2011). Lu et al. (2014) determined a slight increasing trend in the groundwater level in western Jilin Province, China. Zuansi and Ofterdinger (2016)

Chapter written by Dominika SÓNAK BALLOVÁ, Jana KALICKÁ and Michaela ČERVEŇANSKÁ.

analyzed the groundwater level response to rainfall in Ireland. Our work is extended by change-point detection, which is a useful tool before conducting trend analysis, since undetected sudden change can lead to a misleading trend detection in the observed process.

2.2. Data and methods

The investigated area is a part of the lower Rye Island in Slovakia. Its boundary consists of the rivers Váh and the Small Danube River and several drainage channels. It is a lowland alluvial area, which is protected by dykes against river flooding. Due to the periodic excess of moisture, a network of drainage channels and pumping stations was built in the area to adjust the regime of internal waters and groundwater. It is also a very favorable locality for highly productive agricultural production.

The state hydrological network for groundwater quantity monitoring (or the groundwater observation network) of the Slovak Hydrometeorological Institute belongs to the most extensive monitoring networks of the natural environment within the institute, in terms of the number of observation objects. Figure 2.1 shows the spatial distribution of groundwater level observation objects.

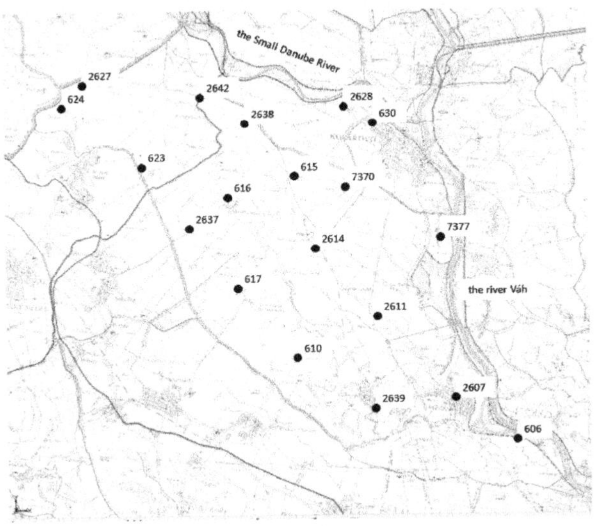

Figure 2.1. *Location of observation objects. For a color version of this figure, see www.iste.co.uk/dimotikalis/data4.zip*

The main goal of the groundwater observation network is to monitor changes in the groundwater level regime and its temperature (continuously or with a weekly step) for the purposes of processing assessments, expertise and studies. Groundwater levels are monitored in observation objects, also called probes (see Figure 2.2).

Figure 2.2. *Probe SHMU. For a color version of this figure, see www.iste.co.uk/dimotikalis/data4.zip*

In order to describe the development of the groundwater level, time series y_t, $t = 1, 2, ..., n$, of the average monthly groundwater level from November 2005 to October 2014 of 19 probes was used. The development of the groundwater level during this period of time is shown graphically for each probe in Figure 2.3.

The monitored period includes the floods that occurred in Slovakia in May and June 2010. These floods were exceptional from a hydrological point of view due to their temporal and spatial distributions. Due to the meteorological situation and its development in April and May, which resulted in the re-occurrence of flood waves in individual river basins in a short period of time, the whole of Slovakia was gradually affected and flood situations occurred simultaneously in almost all river basins. Due to the saturation of the river basins from previous precipitation and their repetition, the retention capacity of river basins was very limited. The groundwater rose, causing major problems. These devastating, almost widespread floods caused the ruptures of dykes, roadwashing, landslides, the destruction of bridges, the demolition of houses or their partial destruction, flooded cellars and underground spaces (garages), contaminated drinking water in wells, flooded railways and farmland. Five people lost their lives, and more than 60 were injured. Thousands lost their homes.

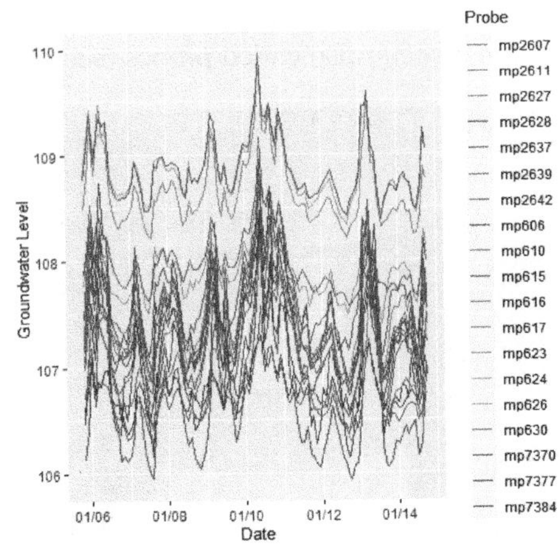

Figure 2.3. *Groundwater level of probes. For a color version of this figure, see www.iste.co.uk/dimotikalis/data4.zip*

2.2.1. Change-point detection methods

First, we focus on the sudden change in the mean value of the hydrological processes. A change-point is a specific time τ in the series, for which y_t follows a common distribution F_1 for $t = 1, 2, ..., \tau$ and for $t = \tau + 1, \tau + 2, ..., n$ it follows distribution F_2, where $F_1 \neq F_2$. The null and alternative hypothesis are:

H_0: The time series is homogeneous.

H_1: There exists at least one statistically significant change in the mean value of the process.

Pettitt's test

Pettitt's test is a rank-based non-parametric method used to test the presence of a sudden single change (switch) in time series. The result of this test is the most probable time of the occurrence of the change. The test statistics is defined as follows:

$$U_{t,n} = \sum_{i=1}^{t} \sum_{j=t+1}^{n} sgn(y_j - y_i) \qquad 1 \leq t \leq n, \qquad [2.1]$$

where

$$sgn(x) = \begin{cases} 1; & x > 0 \\ 0; & x = 0 \\ \text{-}1; & x < 0. \end{cases}$$

For a time series with continuous distribution, the test statistic is given as

$$U_{t,n} = U_{t-1,n} + V_{t,n}, \qquad t = 2, 3, ..., n,$$

where

$$V_{t,n} = \sum_{j=1}^{n} sgn(y_j - y_t), \qquad U_{1,n} = V_{1,n}.$$

The most probable time of the change is given as

$$K_\tau = \mid U_{\tau,n} \mid = \max \mid U_{t,n} \mid .$$

The corresponding p-value is defined as

$$p = 2\exp\left(\frac{-6K_\tau^2}{n^2 + n^3}\right).$$

If $p < \alpha$, we reject the null hypothesis and y_τ is a statistically significant change-point (Pettitt 1979).

Buishand test

The Buishand test is another frequently used test for detecting the abrupt change in the mean value of the process. The test statistic is given as the adjusted partial sum

$$S_0 = 0 \qquad S_k = \sum_{i=1}^{k} (y_i - \bar{y}), k = 1, 2, ..., n.$$

For homogeneous series $S_k \approx 0$. The i-th time period is a change-point, if S_k reaches its maximum or minimum value and it corresponds to negative, respectively, positive shift. The value of $R/\sqrt{n}$ is compared with the critical value of the Buishand test, where R is the rescaled adjusted range

$$R = \frac{\max_{0<k<n} S_k - \min_{0<k<n} S_k}{s},$$

and s is the sample standard deviation (Buishand 1984).

2.2.2. *Trend analysis*

Another, more common approach to a change in time series is the analysis of the long-term development of processes using trend analysis. In hydrometeorology, for the first insight, the presence of a monotonic trend is usually investigated. The null hypothesis and the alternative hypothesis are stated:

H_0: There is no trend in the series.

H_1: There is a statistically significant monotonic (decreasing/increasing) trend in the series.

Mann–Kendall test

The Mann–Kendall test is commonly used for detecting a monotonic trend. The test statistic is given by the formula

$$S = \sum_{i=1}^{n-1} \sum_{j=i+1}^{n} sgn(y_j - y_i)$$

For $n > 40$, S can be approximate by the normal distribution. Thus, the standardized test statistic is given as

$$Z = \begin{cases} \frac{S-1}{\sqrt{D(S)}}; & S > 0 \\ 0\,; & S = 0 \\ \frac{S+1}{\sqrt{D(S)}}; & S < 0. \end{cases}$$

The null hypothesis is rejected if $|Z| > u_{1-\alpha/2}$, where $u_{1-\alpha/2}$ is the $1 - \alpha/2$ quantile of the standard normal distribution (Mann 1945).

2.2.3. *Spearman's rho test*

The test statistic of Spearman's rho test is based on Spearman's correlation, which is defined as:

$$D = 1 - \frac{6\sum_{i=1}^{n}(R_i - i)^2}{n(n^2 - 1)},$$

where R_i is the rank of the i-th observation in time series. The standardized statistic is given as

$$Z_{SR} = D\sqrt{\frac{n-2}{1-D^2}}.$$

If $|\ Z_{SR}\ | > t_{n-2,1-\alpha/2}$, the trend exists. $t_{n-2,1-\alpha/2}$ is the critical value of Student's t distribution (Kendall 1975).

Sen's regression

The magnitude of the trend in the non-parametric case can be computed by Sen's method. The slope of Sen's regression is defined as the median of linear slopes:

$$b = med\Big(\frac{y_j - y_i}{j - i}\Big), \qquad 1 \le i < j \le n.$$

Similar to linear regression, the trend is increasing if $b > 0$ and decreasing if $b < 0$. The intercept is computed for each time step and then the median of all intercepts is the corresponding intercept

$$a = med(y_t - bt).$$

The fitted model is then given by Sen (1968)

$$y = a + bt.$$

2.3. Results

Our analysis was conducted using several packages of the statistical software R (R Core Team 2018). All of the tests were evaluated at the level of significance α=0.05. Firstly, we detected sudden changes in the series. We used Buishand's and Pettitt's test and compared the results of these tests. After detecting a change-point, we used these tests iteratively to look for another change-point in the period before and after the detected change-point. Next, the trend analysis was conducted and lastly the correlation analysis of the groundwater level in the observed probes was evaluated.

Using Pettitt's and Buishand's test, we detected a sudden switch in the mean value of the groundwater level for most of the observed probes. Only, for three of the probes, there was no sudden change detected. For the probes where change-points were detected, the time of the changes were very similar, with no more than two months of time lag. The most common time of change is given in Table 2.1. It is interesting that the sudden change in the groundwater level did not reflect the floods in May and June 2010. The consequence came immediately, almost a year later, in April and May 2011.

Time	Frequency
November 2009	12
December 2009	3
April 2011	7
May 2011	6
January 2013	2

Table 2.1. *Frequency of time of change-point occurrence*

In 2009, a positive shift in the mean value of groundwater level was detected for most of the probes' observations; we can see this for probe 2639 in Figure 2.4, which was followed by a negative switch in 2012 or 2013 for most of the probes. This reflects the longer consequence of floods on the groundwater level. Also, when compared to the long-term average, the groundwater level in the period between 2009 and 2013 is significantly higher.

Next, we focused on the gradual change in the series using the Mann–Kendall test and Spearman's rho test. A monotonic trend was detected only for the groundwater level in three probes. Using the Theil–Sen regression, the magnitude and the nature of these trends was determined. All three probes showed a decreasing tendency of groundwater level. Other probes showed a constant trend.

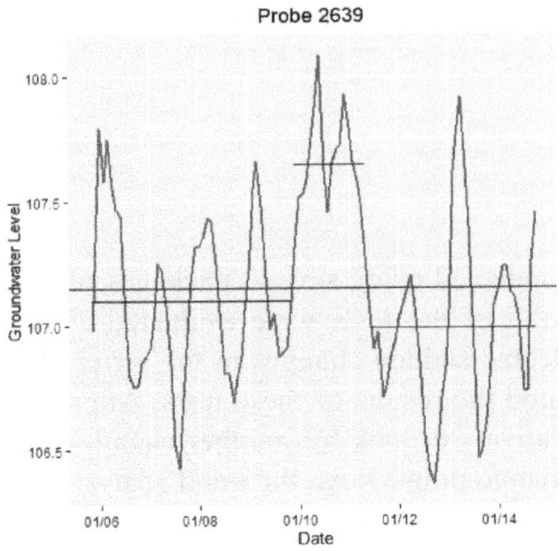

Figure 2.4. *Change-points and long-term mean of probe 2639. For a color version of this figure, see www.iste.co.uk/dimotikalis/data4.zip*

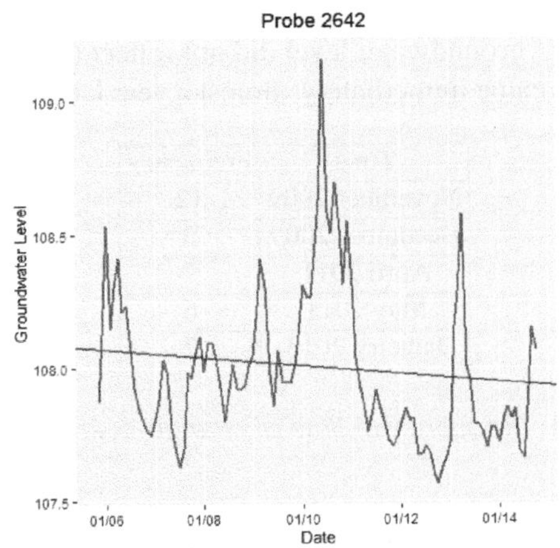

Figure 2.5. *Decreasing trend in probe 2642. For a color version of this figure, see www.iste.co.uk/dimotikalis/data4.zip*

The last part of our analysis was to examine the strength of similarity between the development of groundwater level of the observed probes. For this purpose, the correlation matrix of Spearman's correlation was constructed. In Figure 2.6, we can see that there is a very strong positive correlation in the groundwater level of these probes. We can see that the area's groundwater level is strongly interconnected.

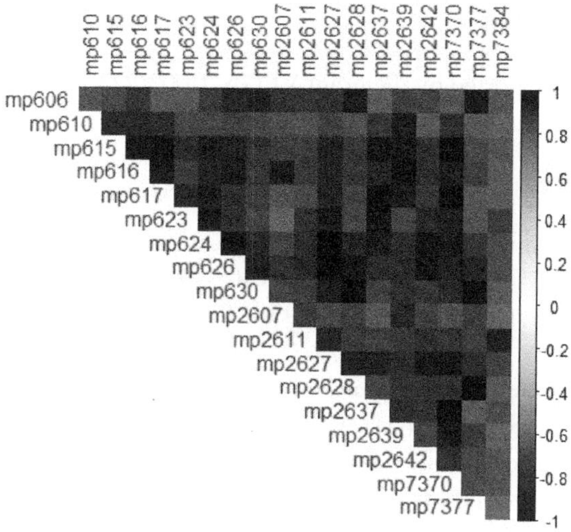

Figure 2.6. *Correlation matrix for the probes. For a color version of this figure, see www.iste.co.uk/dimotikalis/data4.zip*

2.4. Conclusion

The most important parameter for assessing groundwater floods is the minimum depth of the groundwater level below the ground. For this reason, it is necessary to observe groundwater levels for a sufficiently long period of time, even after a flood. However, the depth of the groundwater level is only a static property. It does not contain the dynamic aspects of the groundwater flow. Therefore, it is necessary to include the duration of the increased groundwater level as a presentation of the dynamics of groundwater.

In the area of the lower Rye Island, a sudden rise in the groundwater level has been recorded since the beginning of the hydrological year 2010 (November 2009), with a maximum level at the beginning of June. The level was declining since the end of June, with fluctuating increases in August and September. The reason may be the exceptionally high precipitation totals recorded in May and June, as well as the high supply from the Nitra River (which is a tributary of the river Váh) and the Small Danube River, and the high water levels on the Danube River. The analysis showed us that the increased groundwater levels, compared to the long-term average, lasted in some places until the following hydrological year – until the second half of June 2011, which is in some places a whole year.

This finding is essential in terms of defining the potential danger resulting from the high groundwater level, for example, when creating the potential hazard matrix.

2.5. Acknowledgment

This work was supported by the grant VEGA-1/0036/23.

2.6. References

Bayazit, M. (2015). Nonstationarity of hydrological records and recent trends in trend analysis: A state-of-art review. *Environmental Processes*, 2(3), 527–542.

Buishand, T.A. (1984). Tests for detecting a shift in the mean of hydrological time series. *J. Hydrol.*, 73, 51–69.

Conover, W.J. (1971). *Practical Nonparametric Statistics*. John Wiley & Sons, New York.

Halder, S., Roy, M.B., Roy, P.K. (2020). Analysis of groundwater level trend and groundwater drought using Standard Groundwater Level Index: A case study of an eastern river basin of West Bengal, India. *SM Appl. Sci.*, 2, 507.

Kendall, M.G. (1975). *Rank Correlation Methods*. Griffin, London.

Lehtinen, E., Pulkkinen, U., Pörn, K. (1997). Statistical trend analysis methods for temporal phenomena. SKi Report.

Lu, W.X., Zhao, Y., Chu, H.B., Yang, L.L. (2014). The analysis of groundwater levels influenced by dual factors in western Jilin Province by using time series analysis method. *Appl. Water Sci.*, 4, 251–260.

Mann, H.B. (1945). Nonparametric tests against trend. *Econometrica*, 13, 245–259.

Pettitt, A.N. (1979). A non-parametric approach to the change-point problem. *Appl. Statist.*, 28, 126–135.

Pohlert, T. (2018). Trend: Non-parametric trend tests and change-point detection, R package version 1.1.1 [Online]. Available at: https://CRAN.R-project.org/package=trend.

R Core Team (2018). R: A language and environment for statistical computing. R Foundation for Statistical Computing, Vienna [Online]. Available at: https://www.R-project.org/.

Sen, P.K. (1968). Estimates of the regression coefficient based on Kendall's tau. *J. Amer. Statist. Assoc.*, 63, 1379–1389.

Slovak Hydrometeorological Institute (SHMU) (n.d.). Monitoring kvantity podzemných vôd [Online]. Available at: http://www.shmu.sk/sk/?page=24.

Thakur, G. and Thomas, T. (2011). Analysis of groundwater levels for detection of trend in Sagar district, Madhya Pradesh. *J. Geol. Soc. India*, 77, 303–308.

Wilcoxon, F. (1945). Individual comparisons by ranking methods. *Biomet. Bull.*, 1, 80–83.

Zuansi, C. and Ofterdinger, U. (2016). Analysis of groundwater-level response to rainfall and estimation of annual recharge in fractured hard rock aquifers, NW Ireland. *J. Hydrol.*, 535, 71–84.

3

Stochastic Processes Associated with Fully Nonlinear Parabolic Equations Arising in Financial Mathematics

We consider a triple of stochastic models that allow us to construct probabilistic representation of a solution to the Cauchy problem for a fully nonlinear parabolic equation. One of them is based on forward SDEs only, while two others are based on forward–backward SDEs. We use these probabilistic representations to obtain numerical algorithms to find approximate solutions of the stochastic system applying the Euler scheme and deep learning procedures.

3.1. Semilinear and fully nonlinear PDEs

The aims of this chapter are:

1) To construct probabilistic representations of the Cauchy problem for a fully nonlinear parabolic equation of the type arising in financial mathematics, in particular, in portfolio optimization problem and option pricing theory on markets with friction (under transaction costs, illiquidity and others).

2) To develop, on the basis of these representations, the effective numerical technique to construct approximate solutions of the original problem.

Chapter written by Yana BELOPOLSKAYA and Andrey CHUBATOV.

To give an example of a typical equation arising in financial mathematics, we refer to Liu and Yong (2005), where the authors consider a market with a presence of price impact and derive a generalized Black–Scholes pricing PDE of the form

$$f_t + \frac{\sigma^2(t,x)x^2 f_{xx}}{2[1-\lambda(t,x)xf_{xx}]^2} + (r(t,x) - \delta(t,x))xf_x - r(t,x)f = 0,$$
$$f(T,x) = \phi(x), \quad (t,x) \in [0,T) \times (0,\infty) \qquad [3.1]$$

to compute the replicating cost. Here, functions r, σ are the interest rate of a risk-free asset and a volatility of a stock, while λ and δ are the price impact function of the trader and the dividend yield of the stock.

Similar equations arise when we look for fair option prices on a market, where transaction costs should be taken into account (Kabanov and Safarian 2010) or to solve a problem of portfolio optimization (Touzi 2013).

In this chapter, we consider three probabilistic representations of a solution to the Cauchy problem for a fully nonlinear parabolic equation of the form

$$u_t + \Phi\left(x, u, \nabla u, \nabla^2 u\right) = 0, \quad u(T,x) = h(x), (t,x) \in [0,T) \times R^d. \qquad [3.2]$$

Here and below, we use notations $\nabla u \in R^d$ for a gradient of u and $\nabla^2 u \in R^d \otimes R^d$ for the Hessian of u, in coordinates $\nabla_i u = \frac{\partial u}{\partial x_i}$, $\nabla^2_{ij} u = \frac{\partial^2 u}{\partial x_i \partial x_j}$, $i,j = 1,\dots,d$.

A probabilistic approach to systems of nonlinear parabolic equations was developed by Belopolskaya and Dalecky (1990). To apply this approach to [3.2], we have to consider a differential prolongation of this equation and include [3.2] into a system of semilinear parabolic equations consisting of the equation [3.2] for $u(t,x)$ and equations for $\nabla u(t,x), \dots, \nabla^3 u(t,x)$. As a result, we obtain a semilinear parabolic equation with respect to a vector valued function

$$v(t,x) = \left(u(t,x), \nabla u(t,x), \nabla^2 u(t,x), \nabla^3 u(t,x)\right)$$

which is nonlinear only with respect to the unknown function v itself.

To simplify the exposition, we first consider the case $d = 1$ and a more simple version of the Cauchy problem [3.2], namely,

$$u_t + \Phi\left(x, u_{xx}\right) = 0, \quad u(T,x) = h(x), \quad (t,x) \in [0,T) \times (0,\infty). \qquad [3.3]$$

and introduce notations

$$u^1 = u, \quad u^2 = u_x = \frac{\partial u}{\partial x}, \quad u^3 = u_{xx} = \frac{\partial^2 u}{\partial x^2}, \quad u^4 = u_{xxx} = \frac{\partial^3 u}{\partial x^3}.$$

We consider $u^k, k = 1, \ldots 4$, as components of a vector function $v = (u^1, \ldots, u^4)$ and derive equations to be satisfied by u^k. By formal differentiation of [3.3] with respect to x, we derive an equation for u^2

$$u_t^2 + \Phi_{u^3}(x, u^3)u_{xx}^2 + \Phi_x(x, u^3) = 0 \qquad [3.4]$$

and rewrite the equation [3.3] in the form

$$u^1(T, x) = f(x), \quad (t, x) \in [0, T] \times (0, \infty). \qquad [3.5]$$

Next, we continue the differentiation of [3.2] with respect to x we derive a system of equations with respect to u^m

$$u_t^m + \frac{1}{2}A^2(x, u^3)u_{xx}^m + \sum_{q=1}^{4} B^{mq}(x, v)u_x^q + \sum_{q=1}^{4} c^{mq}(x, v)u^q +$$

$$+G^m(x, v) = 0, \quad m = 1, \ldots, 4, \quad v(T, x) = g(x). \qquad [3.6]$$

Here, $g = (f, f_x, f_{xx}, f_{xxx})^*$, $\frac{1}{2}A^2(x, u^3) = \Phi_{u^3}(x, u^3)$, $G^1 = \Phi - \Phi_{u^3}u^3$, $G^2 = \Phi_x$, $G^3 = \Phi_{xx}$, $G^4 = \Phi_{xxx}$, all $c^{mq}(x, v) = 0$, $B^{mq}(x, v) = 0$, but $c^{34}(x, v) = 2\Phi_{xu^3} + \Phi_{u^3u^3}u^4$, $c^{44}(x, v) = 3\Phi_{xu^3u^3}u^4 + 3\Phi_{xxu^3} + \Phi_{u^3u^3u^3}(u^4)^2$ and $B^{44}(x, v) = 3\Phi_{xu^3} + 3\Phi_{u^3u^3}u^4$.

We say that condition **C 1** holds if the functions $\Phi(x, y), x, y \in R$ and $h(x)$ are bounded and have bounded derivatives up to order 3 and $\Phi_y(x, y) > 0$.

REMARK 3.1.– *If the condition $\Phi_y(x, y) > 0$ is violated, we can still apply the above approach to rewrite [3.3] in the form*

$$u_t + \frac{1}{2}K^2 u_{xx} + \tilde{\Phi}(x, u_{xx}) = 0, \quad u(T, x) = h(x), \quad (t, x) \in [0, T] \times R,$$

where $\tilde{\Phi}(x, y) = \Phi(x, y) - \frac{1}{2}K^2 y$ and $K^2 > 0$.

To construct a stochastic counterpart of the Cauchy problem [3.9], we fix a probability space $(\Omega, \mathcal{F}, P)$ and the Wiener process $w(t)$ defined on this space. Let $\mathcal{F}_t$ denote a flow generated by $w(t)$.

Consider a system of SDEs with respect to $v = (u^1, \ldots, u^4)$,

$$d\xi(\tau) = A(\xi(\tau), v(\tau, \xi(\tau)))dw(\tau), \quad \xi(t) = x, \quad 0 \le t \le \tau \le T, \qquad [3.7]$$

$$d\eta(\tau) = \Big(c(\xi(\tau), v(\tau, \xi(\tau)))\,d\tau + C(\xi(\tau), v(\tau, \xi(\tau)))\,dw(\tau)\Big)\,\eta(\tau), \qquad [3.8]$$

and a closing relation of the form

$$\langle h, v(t,x)\rangle = E\left[\langle \eta(T), g(\xi(T))\rangle + \int_t^T \langle \eta(\tau), G(\xi(\tau), v(\tau,\xi(\tau)))\rangle d\tau\right]. \quad [3.9]$$

Here, $C(x,v) = [A(x,v)]^{-1}B(x,v), \quad \langle h, v\rangle = \sum_{m=1}^4 h_m v_m$.

Systems of the form [3.7]–[3.9] and their links to [3.6] were studied in Belopolskaya and Dalecky (1990). To be more precise, the following assertions were proved.

THEOREM 3.1.– *Assume that condition **C 1** holds and there exists a classical solution $u(t,x)$ of the Cauchy problem [3.6]. Then, the function*

$$v(t,x) = \big(u(t,x), u_x(t,x), u_{xx}(t,x), u_{xxx}(t,x)\big)$$

admits a probabilistic representation of the form [3.9], where the processes $\xi(t)$, $\eta(t)$ satisfy [3.7], [3.8].

THEOREM 3.2.– *Let condition **C 1** hold. Then, there exists an interval $[T_1, T]$ depending on Φ and h such that for all t, τ such that $0 \le T_1 \le t \le \tau \le T$ there exists a solution $\big(\xi_{t,x}(\tau), \eta_{t,h}(\tau), v(t,x)\big)$ of the system [3.7]–[3.9]. In addition, the first component $u_1 = u$ of the function $v(t,x)$ is a unique classical solution of the Cauchy problem [3.6].*

Given the probabilistic representation of a solution to [3.3] extracted from [3.9], we can develop a numerical algorithm via a multiplicative scheme similar to the one constructed in Milstein and Tretjakov (2013) and Belopolskaya and Nemchenko (2020).

Let $\pi : s = t_0 < t_1 < \cdots < t_N = T$, $\Delta_t = \frac{T-s}{N}$ define an equidistant discretization. The relation

$$\langle h, v(t,x)\rangle = E\left[\langle \eta(T), v_0(\xi_{t,x}(T))\rangle\right] = \langle h, U(t,T)v_0(x)\rangle$$

defines an evolution family, acting in the space of bounded continuous functions. As a result, we get $U(t,T)v_0(x) = \lim_{n\to\infty}\prod_{k=1}^n U(t_k, t_{k+1})v_0(x)$. On the contrary, we have

$$\langle h, U(t_k, t_{k+1})v(t_{k+1}, x)\rangle = E\left[\langle \eta_{t_k,h}(t_{k+1}), v(t_{k+1}, \xi_{t_k,x}(t_{k+1}))\rangle\right].$$

To get an approximation of $v(t,x)$, which satisfies [3.12], we construct an approximation to $U(t,T)$. To this end, we consider the explicit Euler scheme

$$\xi_{t_k,x}(t_{k+1}) \sim \bar{\xi}_{t_k,x}(t_{k+1}) = x + A(x, \bar{v}(t_k,x))\Delta_t^{\frac{1}{2}}\epsilon_k, \quad [3.10]$$

$$\eta^m_{t_k,h}(t_{k+1}) \sim \bar{\eta}^m_{t_k,x,h}(t_{k+1}) = h^m + \sum_{l=1}^{d} c^{ml}(x, \bar{v}(t_{k+1}, x))h^l \Delta_t + \\ + \sum_{l=1}^{d} C^{ml}(x, \bar{v}(t_k, x))h^l \Delta_t^{\frac{1}{2}} \epsilon_k, \quad [3.11]$$

where ϵ_k are i.i.d random variables with $P(\epsilon_k = \pm 1) = \frac{1}{2}$. We denote by $S(t_k, t_{k+1})$ a map defined by $S(t_k, t_{k+1})h = \eta(t_{k+1})$ and by $\bar{S}(t_k, t_{k+1})$ its approximation $\bar{S}(t_k, t_{k+1})h = \bar{\eta}(t_{k+1})$. To make the above approximation to be a working numerical algorithm, we have to discretize the space variable as well. Set $x_j = x + j\lambda\Delta_x$, $j = 0, \pm 1, \pm 2, \ldots$, where $\lambda > 0$.

Then, an approximation $\bar{v}^m(t_k, x_j)$ of $v^m(t_k, x_j)$ can be constructed as follows:

$$v^m(t_k, x_j) = E_{t_k,x}\left[\sum_{l=1}^{d} S^{ml}(t_k, t_{k+1})v^l(t_{k+1}, \xi(t_{k+1}))\right] =$$

$$= [U(t_k, t_{k+1})v(t_{k+1}, x)]^m \sim \bar{v}^m(t_k, x) = [\bar{U}(t_k, t_{k+1})v(t_{k+1}, x_j)]^m =$$

$$= \frac{1}{2}\sum_{l=1}^{d} \bar{v}^l\left(t_{k+1}, x_j + a(x, \bar{v}(t_{k+1}, x))\Delta + A(x, \bar{v}(t_{k+1}, x))\Delta^{\frac{1}{2}}\right)\cdot$$

$$\cdot\left(\delta^{ml} + c^{ml}(x, \bar{v}(t_{k+1}, x_j))\Delta + C^{ml}(x, \bar{v}(t_{k+1}, x_j))\Delta^{\frac{1}{2}}\right) +$$

$$\frac{1}{2}\sum_{l=1}^{d} \bar{v}^l\left(t_{k+1}, x_j + a(x, \bar{v}(t_{k+1}, x))\Delta - A(x_j, \bar{v}(t_{k+1}, x_j))\Delta^{\frac{1}{2}}\right)\cdot$$

$$\cdot\left(\delta^{ml} + c^{ml}(x, \bar{v}(t_{k+1}, x_j))\Delta - C^{ml}(x_j, \bar{v}(t_{k+1}, x_j))\Delta^{\frac{1}{2}}\right). \quad [3.12]$$

To obtain $\bar{v}(t_k, x)$ when $x_j < x < x_{j+1},\ k = N-1, \ldots, 1, 0,\ \Delta_t = O(\Delta_x^2)$, we apply a linear interpolation

$$\bar{u}(t_k, x) = \frac{x_{j+1} - x}{\lambda\Delta_x}\bar{u}(t_k, x_j) + \frac{x - x_j}{\lambda\Delta_x}\bar{u}(t_k, x_{j+1}). \quad [3.13]$$

Figures 3.1(a) and (b) present numerical results obtained via the above algorithm for a solution of the Cauchy problem for the equation

$$f_t + \frac{\sigma^2 x^2 f_{xx}}{2[1 - \lambda x f_{xx}]^2} = 0, \quad \text{with} \quad \sigma^2 = 0.08, \lambda = 0.1$$

and initial data $h(x) = \sin^2(x)$ and $h(x) = \sin x$, respectively.

REMARK 3.2.– *In condition **C 1**, if we allow the function $\Phi(x, y)$ to be sublinear in x and have a polynomial growth in y, the above results are true on a certain interval $[T_2, T] \subset [T_1, T]$ Belopolskaya and Dalecky (1990).*

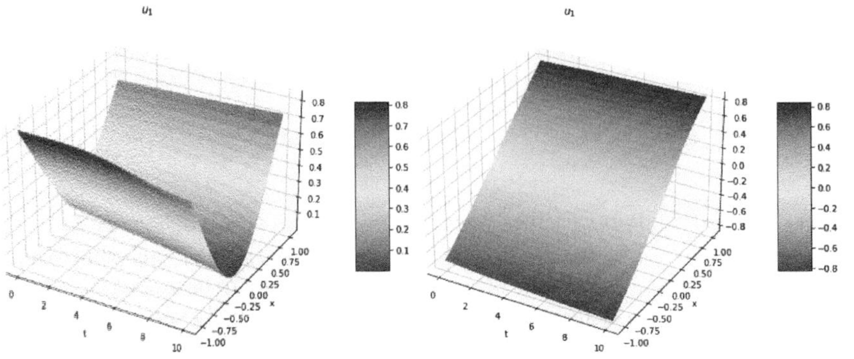

(a) (b)

Figure 3.1. *(a)* $u(T,x) = \sin^2(x)$*, (b)* $u(T,x) = \sin(x)$ *T=10. For a color version of this figure, see www.iste.co.uk/dimotikalis/data4.zip*

REMARK 3.3.– *The above theoretical results can be easily extended to a multidimensional case and to the general Cauchy problem [3.2] Belopolskaya and Woyczynski (2013).*

3.2. BSDE, FBSDE and deep learning algorithms

Connections between quasilinear PDEs and the theory of backward stochastic differential equations (BSDEs) have been well known since pioneer papers by Pardoux and Peng (1990). An extension of this theory to fully nonlinear parabolic equations of the form [3.2] was constructed in Cheridito et al. (2007) and to systems of such equations in Belopolskaya (2014) and Belopolskaya and Woyczynski (2013). Recently, Weinan et al. (2017)–Pham et al. (2021) showed that we can develop an effective algorithm to obtain a numerical solution of the Cauchy problem [3.2] combining the approach from Cheridito et al. (2007) and the neural network technique. Here, we suggest an alternative model based on the forward–backward stochastic differential equation (FBSDE) theory for [3.2] and also apply the neural network technique to construct its numerical solution.

Firstly, we recall the approach suggested in Cheridito et al. (2007). Let us reduce the Cauchy problem [3.2] to the Cauchy problem

$$u_t + \frac{1}{2}\Delta u + \Psi\left(x, u, \nabla u, \nabla^2 u\right) = 0, \quad u(T,x) = h(x), (t,x) \in [0,T] \times R^d, \qquad [3.14]$$

where $\Psi(x,u,q,r) = \Phi(x,u,q,r) - \frac{1}{2}Tr\, r$ and $\Delta = Tr\nabla^2$ is the Laplace operator.

Assume that there is a classical solution $u(t,x)$ of [3.14] and introduce a stochastic process $\zeta(t) = x + w(t) \in R^d$. Then, by the Ito formula applied to a function $V = (u, \nabla u)$ and the process $\zeta(t) = x + w(t)$, we can verify that processes $y(t), z(t), \alpha(t)$ and $\Gamma(t)$ determined by relations

$$y(t) = u(t, \zeta(t)), \quad z(t) = \nabla u(t, \zeta(t)), \tag{3.15}$$

$$\alpha(t) = \nabla\left(u_t(t,\zeta(t)) + \frac{1}{2}\Delta u(t,\zeta(t))\right), \quad \Gamma(t) = \nabla^2 u(t,\zeta(t)), \tag{3.16}$$

satisfy

$$y(t) = h(\zeta(T)) + \int_t^T \Psi\big(\zeta(s), y(s), z(s), \Gamma(s)\big)ds - \int_t^T \langle z(s), dw(s)\rangle, \tag{3.17}$$

$$z(t) = z(0) + \int_0^t \alpha(s)ds + \int_0^t \Gamma(s)dw(s). \tag{3.18}$$

To construct an approximate solution to [3.17], [3.18], we can consider a partition $0 = t_0 < t_1 < \cdots < t_N = T$ and discretize the process $\zeta(t)$ setting

$$\zeta(t_{k+1}) = \zeta(t_k) + w(t_{k+1}) - w(t_k).$$

Next, we rewrite [3.17] as a forward equation to get

$$y(t_{k+1}) = G\big(\zeta(t_k), y(t_k), z(t_k), \Gamma(t_k), \Delta_t, \Delta w\big), \tag{3.19}$$

where

$$G\big(\zeta(t_k), y(t_k), z(t_k), \Gamma(t_k), \Delta_t, \Delta w\big) =$$
$$= y(t_k) - \Psi\big(\zeta(t_k), y(t_k), z(t_k), \Gamma(t_k)\big)\Delta_t + z(t_k)\Delta w$$

and set

$$z(t_{k+1}) = z(t_k) + \alpha(t_k)\Delta_t + \Gamma(t_k)\Delta w. \tag{3.20}$$

Provided we know $\Gamma(t)$ and $\alpha(t)$, we construct an approximate solution of [3.17] in a standard way (Peng and Xu 2011).

Hence, we need to construct approximations

$$\Gamma_k^\theta(x) \text{ of } \nabla^2 u(t_k, x) \text{ and } \alpha_k^\theta(x) \text{ of } \nabla[u_t(t_k,x) + \frac{1}{2}\Delta u(t_k,x)].$$

Assuming that Γ and α are continuous functions, we can construct the required approximations via deep neural networks and consider a system describing the processes y^β and z^β as stochastic processes such that $y_0^\beta = U^\beta(\xi)$, $z_0^\beta = Z^\beta(\xi)$ and for any $k \in \{0, 1, \dots, N-1\}$

$$y^\beta(t_{k+1}) = y^\beta(t_k) - \Psi\big(\zeta(t_k), y(t_k), z(t_k), \Gamma^\beta(t_k)\big)\Delta_t + z^\beta(t_k)\Delta w, \quad [3.21]$$

and

$$z^\beta(t_{k+1}) = z^\theta(t_k) + \alpha_k^\beta(\zeta(t_k))\Delta_t + \Gamma_k^\beta(\zeta(t_k))\Delta w. \quad [3.22]$$

For all suitable β and all $k = 1, \dots, K$, we consider $y^\beta(t_{k+1})$, $z^\beta(t_{k+1})$ given by [3.21] and [3.22], respectively, as approximations of $y(t_{k+1})$ and $z(t_{k+1})$. Besides for all suitable β, we consider $\Gamma_k^\beta(x)$ as an approximation of $\Delta u(t_k, x)$ and $\alpha_k^\beta(x)$ as an approximation of $\nabla[u_t(t_k, x) + \frac{1}{2}\Delta u(t_k, x)]$.

To construct approximations $\Gamma_k^\beta(x)$ and $\alpha_k^\beta(x)$, we can apply the neural network technique (Beck et al. 2019; Pham et al. 2021).

We modify the approach of Cheridito et al. (2007) to an equation of the form

$$u_t + \Phi(x, u, \nabla u, \nabla^2 u) = 0, \quad u(T, x) = h(x), (t, x) \in [0, T) \times R^d \quad [3.23]$$

and assume first that $\Phi(x, u, q, r)$ is C^2-smooth in all arguments $x \in R^d$, $u \in R$, $q \in R^d$, $r \in R^d \otimes R^d$. Set $u^1 = u$, $u^2 = \nabla u$ and by formal differentiation derive an equation for the function $u^2 = \nabla u$

$$\frac{\partial u^2}{\partial t} + \nabla_x \Phi + \nabla_u \Phi u^2 + \nabla_q \Phi \nabla u^2 + \nabla_r \Phi \nabla^2 u^2 = 0,$$
$$u^2(T, x) = \nabla h(x), \quad (t, x) \in [0, T] \times R^d. \quad [3.24]$$

We can rewrite the system [3.23], [3.24] as an equation for a vector function $g = (u^1, u^2) \in R^{d+1}$ or as a system

$$u_t^j + \frac{1}{2} Tr \tilde{A} \nabla^2 u^j \tilde{A} + \langle \tilde{a}, \nabla u^2 \rangle + \tilde{\gamma}^j(x, u, \nabla u, \nabla u^2) = 0, \quad [3.25]$$

where $j = 1, 2$ and

$$\frac{1}{2}[\tilde{A}\tilde{A}^*](x, u, q, r) = \nabla_r \Phi(x, u, q, r), \quad \tilde{a}(x, u, q, r) = \nabla_q \Phi(x, u, q, r),$$
$$\tilde{\gamma}^1(x, u, q, r) = \Phi(x, u, q, r) - \nabla_q \Phi(x, u, q, r) r - \nabla_r \Phi(x, u, q, r) \nabla u^2,$$
$$\tilde{\gamma}^2(x, u, q, r) = \nabla_x \Phi(x, u, q, r) + \nabla_u \Phi(x, u, q, r) q.$$

In the same way as in section 3.1, we can associate with [3.25] a stochastic process that satisfies the SDE

$$d\xi(\theta) = \tilde{a}\big(\xi(\theta), u^1(\theta,\xi(\theta)), u^2(\theta,\xi(\theta)), \nabla u^2(\theta,\xi(\theta))\big)d\theta +$$
$$+ \tilde{A}\big(\xi(\theta), u^1(\theta,\xi(\theta)), u^2(\theta,\xi(\theta)), \nabla u^2(\theta,\xi(\theta))\big)dw(\theta). \quad [3.26]$$

Applying the Ito formula to the processes $u^1(\theta,\xi(\theta))$, $u^2(\theta,\xi(\theta))$ and assuming that $\xi(\theta)$ satisfies [3.26], we get

$$du^1(\theta,\xi(\theta)) = \left[u^1_\theta + \frac{1}{2}Tr\tilde{A}\nabla^2 u^1 \tilde{A}^*\right](\theta,\xi(\theta))d\theta +$$
$$+ \big\langle \nabla u^1(\theta,\xi(\theta)), \tilde{A}dw(\theta)\big\rangle, \quad [3.27]$$

$$du^2(\theta,\xi(\theta)) = \left[u^2_\theta + \frac{1}{2}Tr\tilde{A}\nabla^2 u^2 \tilde{A}^*\right](\theta,\xi(\theta))d\theta + \nabla u^2(\theta,\xi(\theta))\tilde{A}dw(\theta), \quad [3.28]$$

Set

$$y^1(\theta) = u^1(\theta,\xi(\theta)), \quad y^2(\theta) = u^2(\theta,\xi(\theta))$$

and

$$z^1(\theta) = \tilde{A}^*\left(\xi(\theta), u^1(\theta,\xi(\theta)), u^2(\theta,\xi(\theta)), \nabla u^2(\theta,\xi(\theta))\right)\nabla u^1(\theta,\xi(\theta)),$$

$$z^2(\theta) = \tilde{A}^*\left(\xi(\theta), u^1(\theta,\xi(\theta)), u^2(\theta,\xi(\theta)), \nabla u^2(\theta,\xi(\theta))\right)\nabla u^2(\theta,\xi(\theta)).$$

In addition, let

$$A(x,u^1,u^2,z^2) = \tilde{A}^{-1}(x,u^1,u^2,z^2)z^2,$$

$$\gamma^j(x,u^1,u^2,z^2) = \tilde{\gamma}^j(x,\tilde{A}^{-1}(x,u^1,u^2,z^2)z^2).$$

Therefore, we can rewrite the system [3.26]–[3.28] setting $y(t) = (y^1(t), y^2(t))$, $z(t) = (z^1(t), z^2(t))$ in the form

$$d\xi(\theta) = a(\xi(\theta), y(\theta), z^2(\theta))d\theta + A(\xi(\theta), y(\theta), z^2(\theta))dw(\theta), \quad \xi(t) = x, \quad [3.29]$$

$$dy(\theta) = -\gamma(\xi(\theta), y(\theta), z^2(\theta))d\theta + z(\theta)d\hat{w}(\theta),$$
$$y(T) = \kappa = (h(\xi(T)), \nabla h(\xi(T))), \quad \hat{w}(t) = (w(t), w(t)) \in R^d \times R^d. \quad [3.30]$$

As a result, we obtained a strongly coupled forward–backward system of SDEs. As usual, to obtain a closed system, we have to apply the Ito martingale theorem. There are a number of papers devoted to fully coupled FBSDEs with vector valued $y(t) \in R^d$) (Ma and Yong 2007; Ji et al. 2020). In what follows, we assume that conditions A 2.1–A 2.3 from Ji et al. (2020) are held. We roughly state them as condition **C 3**.

We say that condition **C 3** holds if coefficients $A(x, u, q, r)$ and $\gamma^j(x, u, q, r)$, $j = 1, 2$, in [3.29], [3.30] are bounded and Lipschitz continuous as well as functions $u_0(x)$ and $\nabla u_0(x)$ and some conditions of coefficient monotonicity are fulfilled.

THEOREM 3.3.– *Assume that condition* **C 3** *holds. Then, there exists a unique solution of the FBSDE system [3.29], [3.30].*

The proof of this statement we can find, for example, in Belopolskaya (2014) and Abraham and Riviére (2006).

Let us rewrite [3.29], [3.30] as

$$d\xi(\theta) = a(\xi(\theta), y(\theta), z^2(\theta))d\theta + A(\xi(\theta), y(\theta), z^2(\theta))dw(\theta), \quad \xi(t) = x, \tag{3.31}$$

$$dy^j(\theta) = -\gamma^j(\xi(\theta), y(\theta), z^2(\theta))d\theta + z^j(\theta)dw(\theta), \quad j = 1, 2,$$
$$y^1(T) = \kappa_1 = u_0(\xi(T)), \quad y^2(T) = \kappa_2 = \nabla u_0(\xi(T)). \tag{3.32}$$

To solve [3.31], [3.32], we can reduce it to the following variational problem:

$$\inf_{y_0, z(t), 0 \le t \le T} E\left[\|\kappa(\xi_{y_0,z}(T)) - y_{y_0,z}(T)\|^2\right], \tag{3.33}$$

where stochastic processes $\xi_{y_0,x}(t)$ and $y^j_{y_0,x}(t)$ satisfy SDEs

$$\xi_{y_0,z}(\tau) = x + \int_t^\tau a(\xi_{y_0,z}(\theta), y(\theta), z^2(\theta))d\theta +$$
$$+ \int_t^\tau A(\xi_{y_0,z}(\theta), y(\theta), z^2(\theta))dw(\theta), \tag{3.34}$$

$$y^j_{y_0,z}(T) = y^j_0 - \int_t^T \gamma^j(\xi_{y_0,z}(\theta), y(\theta), z^2(\theta))d\theta + \int_t^T z^j(\theta)dw(\theta), \; j = 1, 2, \tag{3.35}$$

where $y_0 = (y_0^1, y_0^2) \in R^{d+1}$- $\mathcal{F}_0$ is a measurable random variable and $z = (z^1, z^2) \in R^d \times (R^d \otimes R^d)$ is an $\mathcal{F}_t$ measurable square integrable process.

We consider $(y_0, z(t), \, 0 \le s \le t \le T)$ as a control in variational problem [3.33].

Note (Ji et al. 2020) that under **C 3**, we have

$$\inf_{y_0, z(t), 0 \le t \le T} E\left[\|\kappa(\xi_{y_0,z}(T)) - y_{y_0,z}(T)\|^2 \right] = 0, \tag{3.36}$$

and $(\xi_{y_0,z}(t), y_{y_0,z}(t), z(t))$ is the unique solution of [3.29], [3.30].

For numerical computations, we follow the methodology suggested by Raissi (2018) and change the loss function [3.33].

The Euler scheme applied to solve the system [3.31], [3.32] with [3.32] rewritten in a forward way on the time interval $[t_k, t_{k+1}]$ of the given partition $\pi : s = t_0 < t_1 < \cdots < t_K = T$ leads to

$$\begin{cases} \bar{\xi}(s) = \xi, \quad \bar{y}(s) = y_0, \\ \xi(t_{k+1}) \sim \bar{\xi}(t_k) + a(\bar{\xi}(t_k), \bar{y}(t_k), \bar{z}^2(t_k))\Delta_t + A(\bar{\xi}(t_k), \bar{y}(t_k), z^2(t_k))\Delta w, \\ y^j(t_{k+1}) \sim \bar{y}^j(t_k) - \gamma^j(\bar{\xi}(t_k), \bar{y}(t_k)), \bar{z}^2(t_k))\Delta_t + \bar{z}^j(t_k)\Delta w. \end{cases} \tag{3.37}$$

REMARK 3.4.– *To justify that [3.37] can be made a closed system, we recall that*

$$M(t) = E\left[\kappa(\xi(T)) + \int_t^T \gamma(\xi(\tau), y(\tau), z(\tau))d\tau \middle| F_t \right]$$

is a square integrable martingale. By the Ito martingale representation theorem, there exists a process $z(t)$ such that

$$M(T) = E[M(T)] + \int_0^T \langle z(\tau), d\hat{w}(\tau)\rangle$$

and the process $z(\tau)$ is unique in the mean square sense. Therefore, we can use the last equality as a required closing relation.

Next, we approximate $z(t_k)$ by $2(K-1)$ neural networks to obtain $z_\beta(t_k)$ and then compute $y_\beta(t_k)$ by the Euler–Maruyama scheme [3.37].

Compared with [3.33], we choose a more detailed loss function of the form

$$\sum_{m=1}^{M} \sum_{k=0}^{K-1} \sum_{j=1}^{2} \left\| \bar{y}^j_m(t_{k+1}) - y^j_{\beta,m}(t_k) - \gamma^{j,k}_{\beta,m}\Delta_t - z^j_{\beta,m}(t_k)A^k_{\beta,m}\Delta w_m \right\|^2 + \\ + \sum_{m=1}^{M} \sum_{j=1}^{2} \left\| y^j_{\beta,m}(t_K) - \kappa^j(\xi_{\beta,m}(t_K)) \right\|^2 \tag{3.38}$$

which corresponds to M different realizations of the Wiener process. The choice of [3.38] allows us to guarantee that $\bar{y}(t_k)$ and $y^\beta(t_k)$ converge to the same limit as $K \to \infty$. Here, we use notations of the form $\xi_{\beta,m}(t_k) = \xi_\beta(t_k, \omega_m)$, $\gamma^{j,k}_{\beta,m} = \gamma^j(\xi_{\beta,m}(t_k), y_{\beta,m}(t_k), z_{\beta,m}(t_k))$, $A^k_{\beta,m} = A(\xi_{\beta,m}(t_k), y_{\beta,m}(t_k), z_{\beta,m}(t_k))$.

Let us describe the required, fully connected neural networks at each time point to approximate the control $z = (z^1, z^2)$ and denote by β_k its parameters at time t_k. The total set of parameters are $\beta = (\beta_{y_s}, \beta_{z(s)}, \beta_1, \dots, \beta_{K-1})$.

To approximate continuous functions $z^1(t_k) : R^d \to R^d$, $z^2(t_k) : R^d \to R^{d\times d}$, we use the neural network technique. We chose two neural networks with $L = 4$ layers, namely each network has one input layer with dimensions d, two hidden layers with dimensions d and one output layer with dimensions d^2 and d, respectively.

For $x \in R^d$ given an activation function

$$\psi_d(x) = \big(\max(x_1, 0), \dots, \max(x_d, 0)\big)$$

and affine transformations $M^{\beta,\alpha}_{q,l} : R^l \to R^q$ of the form

$$M^{\beta,\alpha}_{q,l}(x) = \begin{pmatrix} \beta_{\alpha+1} & \beta_{\alpha+2} & \dots & \beta_{\alpha+l} \\ \beta_{\alpha+l+1} & \beta_{\alpha+l+2} & \dots & \beta_{\alpha+2l} \\ \beta_{\alpha+2l+1} & \beta_{\alpha+2l+2} & \dots & \beta_{\alpha+3l} \\ \vdots & \vdots & \vdots & \vdots \\ \beta_{\alpha+(q-1)l+1} & \beta_{\alpha+(q-1)l+2} & \dots & \beta_{\alpha+ql} \end{pmatrix} \begin{pmatrix} x_1 \\ x_2 \\ x_3 \\ \vdots \\ x_l \end{pmatrix} + \begin{pmatrix} \beta_{\alpha+ql+1} \\ \beta_{\alpha+ql+m} \\ \beta_{\alpha+ql+3} \\ \vdots \\ \beta_{\alpha+ql+q} \end{pmatrix}, \quad [3.39]$$

where $\alpha = d + 1$ we construct two neural networks of the form

$$\mathcal{S}^{1,\beta}_k = M^{\beta,[(2K+k)d+1)](d+1)}_{d,d} \circ \psi_d \circ M^{\beta,[(K+k)d+1](d+1)}_{d,d} \circ \psi_d \circ M^{\beta,(kd+1)(d+1)}_{d,d} \quad [3.40]$$

and

$$\mathcal{S}^{2,\beta}_k = M^{\beta,[(5Kd+kd^2+1)](d+1)}_{d^2,d} \circ \psi_d \circ M^{\beta,[(4K+k)d+1](d+1)}_{d,d} \circ \psi_d \circ M^{\beta,[(3K+k)d+1](d+1)}_{d,d}. \quad [3.41]$$

The functions in [3.40] define the neural network with four layers (one input layer with d neurons, two hidden layers with d neurons each and one output layer with d neurons) and a rectifier function as activation functions. The functions in [3.41] also define the neural network with four layers (one input layer with d neurons, two hidden layers with d neurons each and one output layer with d^2 neurons) and a rectifier function as activation functions. Note that condition $\rho \geq (5Kd + Nd^2 + 1)(d + 1)$ ensures that $M^{\beta,\alpha}_{q,l} : R^l \to R^q$ acts correctly.

Construct approximations $z^j_\beta(t_k)$ of $z^j(t_k), j = 1,2$ using the above neural networks and define the processes $y^1_\beta(t)$, $y^2_\beta(t)$ as stochastic processes such that $y^1_\beta(s) = U_\beta(x)$, $y^2_\beta(s) = z^1_\beta(x)$ and for every $k \in \{0,1\ldots,K-1\}$

$$y^j_\beta(t_{k+1}) = y^j_\beta(t_k) - \gamma^j(\xi_\beta(t_k), y_\beta(t_k), z_\beta(t_k))\Delta_t + z^j_\beta(t_k)\Delta w. \qquad [3.42]$$

For a suitable $\beta \in R^\rho$ and all $k \in \{0,1,\ldots,K\}$, we consider $y_\beta(t_k) : \Omega \to R^{d+1}$ as an approximation of $y(t_k)$ and $z_\beta(t_k) : \Omega \to R^q$, $q = d + d^2$ as an approximation of $z(t_k)$. In addition, we consider $u_\beta(x)$ as approximation of $u(s,x) = y^1(s)$ and $y^2_\beta(s)$ as approximation of $\nabla u(s,x) = y^2(s)$. In addition, we get $z^1_\beta(t_K)$ as approximation of $\nabla u(t_K, x)$ and $z^2_\beta(t_K)$ as approximation of $\nabla^2 u(t_K, x)$.

To find suitable parameters β, we compute the minimizer of the loss function using stochastic gradient descent (SGD)

$$R^\rho \ni \beta \mapsto \hat{L}_K(\beta) = E\left[\|y_\beta(t_K) - \kappa(\xi_\beta(t_K))\|^2\right] \in R. \qquad [3.43]$$

Applying an SGD-based minimization algorithm yields, under suitable assumptions, random approximations of a local minimum point of the function in [3.42]. To this end, we denote by $\psi^n(\beta,\omega)$, $\beta \in R^\rho$, $\omega \in \Omega$ a function of the form

$$\psi^n(\beta,\omega) = \left\|y^n_\beta(t_K,\omega) - \kappa(\xi^n(T,\omega))\right\|^2$$

and the function

$$\Psi^n(\beta,\omega) = \nabla_\beta \psi^n(\beta,\omega),$$

Let

$$\beta^n = \beta^{n-1} - \lambda \Psi^n(\beta^{n-1}),$$

where $\lambda \in (0,\infty)$ is a constant learning rate.

Hence, minimizing over β applying the SGD technique based on simulations of $\xi(t_k)$, $\xi(t_{k+1})$ and Δw, we obtain an approximation of $u(t_k,\cdot)$ and $D_x u(t_k,\cdot)$.

Finally, we get the following scheme of training $u_\beta(t,x)$ to approximate the solution $u(t,x)$ of [3.23]:

1) Given $\xi(t_0)$, we set $y^1_\beta(t_0) = u_\beta(t_0,\xi(t_0))$, $y^2_\beta(t_0) = \nabla u_\beta(t_0,\xi(t_0))$ and $z^1_\beta(t_0) = \nabla u_\beta(t_0,\xi(t_0))$, $z^2_\beta(t_0) = \nabla^2 u_\beta(t_0,\xi(t_0))$.

2) On each time interval $[t_k, t_{k+1}]$, we find $\xi_\beta(t_{k+1})$ and $\bar{y}^j_\beta(t_{k+1})$ using the Euler–Maruyama scheme [3.37] and the networks for $y^j_\beta(t_{k+1})$ and $z^j_\beta(t_{k+1})$

$$y^1_\beta(t_{k+1}) = u_\beta(t_{k+1},\xi(t_{k+1})), \quad y^2_\beta(t_{k+1}) = \nabla u_\beta(t_{k+1},\xi(t_{k+1})),$$
$$z^1_\beta(t_{k+1}) = \nabla u_\beta(t_{k+1},\xi(t_{k+1})), \quad z^2_\beta(t_{k+1}) = \nabla^2 u_\beta(t_{k+1},\xi(t_{k+1})).$$

The loss function is taken as a Monte Carlo approximation of

$$E\left[\sum_{k=1}^{K}\|y_\beta(t_k)-\bar{y}(t_k)\|^2+\left|y_\beta^1(t_K)-h(\xi_\beta(t_K))\right|^2\right]+$$
$$+E\left[\left\|y_\beta^2(t_K)-\nabla h(\xi_\beta(t_K))\right\|^2\right].$$

Then, train a fully connected feedforward networks $\mathcal{S}_\beta^j(t_k)$ given by [3.40], [3.41] to obtain β^* which allow us to minimize the loss function using the SGD method.

3) Connect all subnetworks $\mathcal{S}_\beta^j(t_k)$, $j=1,2$, to obtain a network with outputs $y_\beta^j(t_K)$, where $y_\beta^1(t_K)$ is expected to be an approximation of $u(t_K,\xi(t_K))$.

3.3. Acknowledgments

This work was supported by Grant RSF 22-21-00016.

3.4. References

Abraham, R. and Riviére, O. (2006). Forward-backward stochastic differential equations and PDE with gradient dependent second order coefficients. *ESAIM: Probability and Statistics*, 10, 184–205.

Beck, C., Weinan, E., Jentzen, A. (2019). Machine learning approximation algorithms for high-dimensional fully nonlinear partial differential equations and second-order backward stochastic differential equations. *Journal of Nonlinear Science*, 29, 1563–1619.

Belopolskaya, Y. (2014). Probabilistic counterparts of nonlinear parabolic PDE systems. In *Modern Stochastics and Applications*, Korolyuk, V., Limnios, N., Mishura, Y. et al. (eds). Springer, Cham, 71–94.

Belopolskaya, Y. and Dalecky, Y. (1990). *Stochastic Equations and Differential Geometry*. Kluver, Boston.

Belopolskaya, Y. and Nemchenko, E. (2020). Probabilistic models and numerical algorithms for quasilinear parabolic equations and systems. *Communications on Stochastic Analysis*, 14(1–2), 1–12.

Belopolskaya, Y. and Woyczynski, W.A. (2013). SDEs, BSDEs and fully non-linear parabolic systems. *Rendiconti del Seminario Matematico Università e Politecnico di Torino*, 71(2), 209–218.

Cheridito, P., Soner, H.M., Touzi, N., Victoir, N. (2007). Second order backward stochastic differential equations and fully non-linear parabolic PDEs. *Communications on Pure and Applied Mathematics*, 60(7), 1081–1110.

Hornik, K., Stinchcombe, M., White, H. (1990). Universal approximation of an unknown mapping and its derivatives using multilayer feedforward networks. *Neural Networks*, 3(5), 551–560.

Ji, S., Peng, S., Peng, Y., Zhang, X. (2020). Three algorithms for solving high-dimensional fully-coupled FBSDEs through deep learning. *IEEE Intelligent Systems*, 35(3), 71–84.

Kabanov, Y. and Safarian, M. (2010). *Markets with Transaction Costs: Mathematical Theory*. Springer Finance, Berlin.

Liu, H. and Yong, J. (2005). Option pricing with an illiquid underlying asset market. *Journal of Economic Dynamics & Control*, 29, 2125–2156.

Ma, J. and Yong, J. (2007). *Forward-Backward Stochastic Differential Equations and their Applications*. Springer, Berlin.

Milstein, G. and Tretjakov, M. (2013). *Stochastic Numerics for Mathematical Physics*. Springer, Berlin, Heidelberg.

Pardoux, E. and Peng, S. (1990). Adapted solution of a backward stochastic differential equation. *Systems and Control Letters*, 14(1), 55–61.

Peng, S. and Xu, M. (2011). Numerical algorithms for backward stochastic differential equations with 1-d Brownian motion: Convergence and simulations. *ESAIM: Mathematical Modelling and Numerical Analysis*, 45(2), 335–360.

Pham, H., Warin, X., Germain, M. (2021). Neural networks-based backward scheme for fully nonlinear PDEs. *SN Partial Differential Equations and Applications*, 2(16), 1–27.

Raissi, M. (2018). Forward-backward stochastic neural networks: Deep learning of high-dimensional partial differential equation. *arXiv preprint*, arXiv:1804.07010.

Touzi, N. (2013). *Optimal Stochastic Control, Stochastic Target Problems, and Backward SDE*. Springer, New York.

Weinan, E., Han, J., Jentzen, A. (2017). Deep learning-based numerical methods for high-dimensional parabolic partial differential equations and backward stochastic differential equations. *Communications in Mathematics and Statistics*, 5(4), 349–380.

4

An Improved Shape Parameter Estimation Method for the Pareto Model

The Pareto type I distribution, also referred to as the power-law distribution, holds significant importance as a prevalent continuous probability distribution known for its heavy-tailed nature. Its utility lies in effectively modeling heavy-tailed data and conducting extreme value analysis. Acquiring a profound comprehension of its mathematical properties, statistical characteristics and estimation techniques becomes imperative in order to make well-informed decisions. In this research, we consider a recent class of estimators for the shape parameter of a Pareto distribution. This class of estimators depends on a control parameter that must be properly chosen. We introduce an adaptive procedure for choosing such a parameter. Experimental results indicate that the proposed adaptive estimation method performs favorably when compared to other well-known methods from the literature.

4.1. Introduction

The Pareto type I distribution, also known as the Pareto distribution of the first kind or the power-law distribution, is a widely used continuous probability distribution characterized by heavy tails. This model has the following distribution function:

$$F(x|a,c) = 1 - \left(\frac{x}{c}\right)^{-a}, \quad x > c, \quad a > 0, \quad c > 0, \qquad [4.1]$$

where a and c are the shape and scale parameters, respectively. The parameter a quantifies the heaviness or steepness of the right tail of the distribution. It is also known as the tail or Pareto index (Kleiber and Kotz 2003). As a decreases, the tail becomes heavier. The corresponding probability density function is

$$f(x|a,c) = \frac{ac^a}{x^{a+1}}, \quad x > c, \quad a > 0, \quad c > 0. \qquad [4.2]$$

Chapter written by Frederico CAEIRO and Ayana MATEUS.
These authors contributed equally to this work.

The non-central moments of order k of the Pareto distribution are given by

$$E(X^k) = \frac{ac^k}{a-k}, \quad \text{if } a > k. \qquad [4.3]$$

Therefore, the mean,

$$E(X) = \frac{ac}{a-1},$$

and the variance

$$V(X) = \frac{ac^2}{(a-1)^2(a-2)}$$

exist if $a > 1$ and $a > 2$, respectively. Therefore, the coefficient of variation is $(a(a-2))^{-1/2}$, if $a > 2$. The Pareto distribution has demonstrated its versatility and value as a tool with successful applications in a wide range of fields. Bibliometrics is one field where the Pareto distribution has found extensive use (Glänzel 2008). In the study of scientific publications and citation patterns, researchers often employ the Pareto distribution to understand the concentration of citations among a small number of highly influential papers or authors. In demography, the Pareto distribution is applied to examine population dynamics and the distribution of various demographic factors (Rosen and Resnick 1980). It helps in understanding phenomena such as the concentration of wealth or the size distribution of cities, allowing demographers to study the socio-economic structures and inequalities within societies. Geologists employ the Pareto distribution to study the distribution of natural resources, such as mineral deposits or the magnitude of earthquakes (Crovelli and Barton 1995). In the field of finance, the Pareto distribution is employed to model the behavior of financial assets and returns (Wang 1995). Under a semi-parametric framework, the Pareto type I distribution is often used in the analysis of extreme events (Caeiro et al. 2021; Caeiro and Gomes 2022).

Due to the wide array of applications associated with the Pareto distribution, accurate estimation of the distribution's parameters is vital for understanding data characteristics, making predictions, conducting statistical inference and advancing statistical methodologies. While maximum likelihood estimators are widely used due to their simplicity and closed-form solutions, it is crucial to recognize their limitations in terms of optimal efficiency for small or moderate sample sizes. Alternative estimation methods offer improved efficiency, reduced bias and lower mean squared error, providing more accurate parameter estimates in such scenarios. Quandt (1966) compared the performance of the maximum likelihood estimator with the moments estimator, a least squares estimator, and four quantile estimators. Different least squares estimators were examined by Lu and Tao (2007), Caeiro et al. (2015) and Kim et al. (2017). Robust estimators of the shape parameter were introduced by Brazauskas and Serfling (2000) and Vandewalle et al. (2007). Bayesian estimators can be found in Arnold and Press (1989), Rasheed and Al-Gazi (2014) and Han (2020). Singh and Guo (1995) and Caeiro and Gomes (2011) considered probability weighted moment (PWM) estimators. Haider Bhatti et al. (2019) proposed modified maximum likelihood estimators and (Chen et al. 2019) deal with the estimation of the Pareto parameters with a modification of ranked set sampling. Despite significant advances in the past few decades, this topic remains an active area of research. Recently, Mateus and Caeiro (2021) introduced a class of consistent estimators for the shape parameter of a Pareto type I distribution. These estimators were derived with the method of PWMs and are parameterized by a tuning or control parameter. The inclusion of this control parameter allows adjusting of the bias and variance of the estimator, potentially leading to higher efficiency when compared to the maximum likelihood estimator. The focus of our work is to address the selection of an appropriate control parameter for the aforementioned class of estimators.

This chapter is structured as follows. In section 4.2, we briefly describe the most used estimation methods for the parameters of a Pareto distribution, namely the moment, the maximum likelihood, the least squares, the PWMs and the extended class of the PWMs. In section 4.3, we introduce a data-driven methodology for selecting the control parameter to optimize the performance of the estimators under study. A Monte Carlo simulation study is performed in section 4.4 to compare the finite sample behavior of the new class of estimators with the most used estimators. To illustrate the applicability of our results, a real data application is provided at the end of section 4.4. Section 4.5 concludes this chapter with some conclusions about the performance of the different estimation methods.

4.2. Estimators under study

In this section, we review the most common estimation methods and a class of estimators recently introduced in the literature. In the following, we will assume that $X_1, X_2, \cdots, X_n$ is a sample of size n of independent and identically distributed random variables, with a common Pareto distribution, given in [4.1]. The corresponding sample of non-decreasing order statistics is denoted by $X_{1:n}, X_{2:n}, \cdots, X_{n:n}$.

4.2.1. *Common methods of estimation*

– *Maximum likelihood estimators*: The maximum likelihood (ML) estimators of the parameters a and c, in [4.1], are obtained by maximization of the log-likelihood function, and are given by

$$\hat{a}^{ML} = \left(\frac{1}{n}\sum_{i=1}^{n} \ln X_i - \ln X_{1:n}\right)^{-1}, \qquad \text{and} \qquad \hat{c}^{ML} = X_{1:n}. \qquad [4.4]$$

It is essential to note that, for small sample sizes, alternative estimators can outperform the ML estimators in terms of bias or root mean squared error (RMSE).

– *Moment estimators*: the most commonly used moment estimators are the ones proposed by Quandt (1966):

$$\hat{a}^M = \frac{n\overline{X} - X_{1:n}}{n(\overline{X} - X_{1:n})}, \qquad \text{and} \qquad \hat{c}^M = \left(1 - \frac{1}{n\hat{a}^M}\right) X_{1:n}. \tag{4.5}$$

Since the first non-central moment only exists for values of a greater than 1, the moment estimators presented in equation [4.5] are only consistent under the same condition.

– *Probability weighted moment estimators*: the method of PWMs, proposed by Greenwood et al. (1979), is a valuable technique for estimating distribution parameters in models that possess an explicit quantile function. The PWMs of a continuous random variable X with the distribution function F are defined as

$$M_{k,r,s} = E(X^k(F(X))^r(1 - F(X))^s), \tag{4.6}$$

where k, r and s are real numbers. For the Pareto distribution, the PWMs in [4.6] have the following analytical expression:

$$M_{k,r,s} = c^k \,\mathrm{B}\left(s + 1 - \frac{k}{a}, r + 1\right), \quad s - \frac{k}{a} > -1, \quad r > -1, \tag{4.7}$$

where B stands for the complete beta function. The PWM estimators are obtained by equating $M_{k,r,s}$ with their corresponding sample moments, and then by solving those equations for the unknown parameters. It is usual to work with one of the following PWMs

$$\alpha_r = M_{1,0,r} = E(X(1 - F(X))^r) \quad \text{or} \quad \beta_r = M_{1,r,0} = E(X(F(X))^r), \tag{4.8}$$

with $r = 0, 1, \cdots$. PWM estimators can be built by replacing F in [4.8] by its empirical estimator. Singh and Guo (1995) and Caeiro and Gomes (2011) considered two specific PWMs, namely

$$\alpha_0 = \frac{c}{1 - 1/a} \quad \text{and} \quad \alpha_1 = \frac{c}{2 - 1/a}.$$

They equated these PWMs with their corresponding sample moments and obtained the following PWM estimators for the parameters of the Pareto distribution:

$$\hat{a}^{PWM} = \frac{\hat{\alpha}_0 - \hat{\alpha}_1}{\hat{\alpha}_0 - 2\hat{\alpha}_1} \qquad \text{and} \qquad \hat{c}^{PWM} = \frac{\hat{\alpha}_0\hat{\alpha}_1}{\hat{\alpha}_0 - \hat{\alpha}_1}. \tag{4.9}$$

Note that the PWM estimators in [4.9] are consistent only if $a > 1$.

4.2.2. *Log-generalized probability weighted moment estimator*

Recently, Chen et al. (2017) proposed an extended version or generalized PWM by considering the moments,

$$M^*_{g,r,s} = E(g(X)(F(X))^r(1 - F(X))^s) \tag{4.10}$$

where g is a suitable function, and r and s are real values. Building upon this work, Mateus and Caeiro (2021) investigated PWMs with $g(x) = \ln(x)$ (see also Caeiro and Prata Gomes 2015; Caeiro and Mateus 2023). Such a choice of g ensures the existence of the PWMs in the complete parameter space. Specifically, for the Pareto distribution and with $r = 0$, the expression is given by:

$$M^*_{\ln,0,s} = \frac{\ln(c)}{(1+s)} + \frac{1}{a(1+s)^2}, \quad s > -1. \tag{4.11}$$

Mateus and Caeiro (2021) considered the log-generalized probability weighted moments (LGPWM) of the scale independent variable $X^* = \dfrac{X}{X_{1:n}}$:

$$L_s = E((\ln X^*)(1 - F(X^*))^s), \quad s > -1. \tag{4.12}$$

Note that for the Pareto model, L_s serves as a pivotal quantity for the shape parameter a. Consequently, if $s > -1$, the corresponding empirical estimator of [4.12] is,

$$\tilde{l}_s = \frac{1}{n}\sum_{i=1}^{n}(1 - p_{i:n})^s \ln X_{i:n}. \tag{4.13}$$

where $p_{i:n}$ is an empirical estimate of $F(X_{i:n})$. The most common choices for the empirical estimates are $p_{i:n} = (i - b_1)/n$, with $0 \le b_1 \le 1$ or $p_{i:n} = (i - b_2)/(n + 1 - 2b_2)$, with $-0.5 \le b_2 \le 0.5$, where b_j, $j = 1, 2$ is a continuity correction factor. In this work, we consider the empirical values $p_{i:n} = (i - 0.35)/n$, with $1 \le i \le n$.

By solving the equation $L_s = \tilde{l}_s$ with respect to the parameter a, Mateus and Caeiro (2021) obtained the class of LGPWM for the shape parameter of the Pareto distribution as follows:

$$\hat{a}^{LGPWM} = \left(\frac{(1+s)^2}{n-1}\sum_{i=2}^{n}\left(1 - \frac{i-1}{n-1}\right)^s \ln X^*_{i-1:n-1}\right)^{-1}, \quad s > -1. \tag{4.14}$$

This class of estimators depends on a control parameter $s > -1$. When $s = 0$, the estimator becomes asymptotically equivalent to the ML estimator for the shape parameter. Regarding the estimation of the scale parameter, and since $X_{1:n} \xrightarrow{p} c$, the aforementioned authors suggested that the parameter c could be estimated by the sample minimum,

$$\hat{c}^{LGPWM} = X_{1:n}, \qquad [4.15]$$

which corresponds to the ML estimator of the scale parameter in [4.4].

4.3. An algorithm for selection of the control parameter of the LGPWM shape parameter estimator

In this section, we introduce a data-driven methodology for selecting the control parameter s of the LGPWM shape parameter estimator. The methodology is outlined as follows:

– Consider the LGPWM estimators $\hat{a}^{LGPWM}$ in [4.14], with a control parameter s and $\hat{c}^{LGPWM}$ in [4.15]. The control parameter s takes values in the range $(-0.5, 4)$, discretized in small steps of length 0.02. This allows us to explore a wide range of potential values for s.

– Consider a sample of size n. For each value of s, estimate the shape and scale parameters using the previously mentioned estimators.

– Analyze the fit of the Pareto model by comparing the empirical cumulative distribution function, denoted as $F_n(x)$, with the fitted cumulative distribution function, denoted as $\hat{F}(x) = F(x|\hat{a}, \hat{c})$, with F in [4.1], using an appropriate goodness-of-fit statistic.

– To quantitatively measure the agreement between the observed data and the fitted model, consider one of three commonly used goodness-of-fit test statistics:

- Kolmogorov–Smirnov (KS) statistic

$$D_n = \sup_x |F_n(x) - \hat{F}(x)| = \max\left\{D_n^+, D_n^-\right\} \qquad [4.16]$$

with

$$D_n^+ = \max_{1\leq i\leq n}\left(\left|\frac{i}{n} - \hat{F}(X_{i:n})\right|\right), \quad \text{and} \quad D_n^- = \max_{1\leq i\leq n}\left(\left|\frac{i-1}{n} - \hat{F}(X_{i:n})\right|\right).$$

- Cramér–von Mises (CvM) test statistic

$$W_n^2 = \sum_{i=1}^{n}\left(\frac{2i-1}{2n} - \hat{F}(X_{i:n})\right)^2 + \frac{1}{12n}. \qquad [4.17]$$

- Modified Anderson–Darling (MAD) test statistic (Ahmad et al. 1988)

$$AU_n^2 = \frac{n}{2} - \sum_{i=1}^{n}\left(2 - \frac{2i-1}{n}\right)\log(1 - \hat{F}(X_{i:n})) - 2\sum_{i=1}^{n}\hat{F}(X_{i:n}). \qquad [4.18]$$

Smaller values of the statistics in [4.16], [4.17] and [4.18] correspond to a better fit of the Pareto model.

– Finally, based on the goodness-of-fit statistics, we select the control parameter value that provides the best fit to the sample values. This step involves choosing the combination of shape parameter $\hat{a}$ and scale parameter $\hat{c}$ that minimizes the discrepancy between the observed data and the Pareto model predictions.

4.4. Numerical results

In this section, we analyze simulated and real datasets to assess the performance of the estimation procedures presented in section 4.2. The control parameter s of the LGPWM estimator of the shape parameter is selected using the data-driven method described in section 4.3. This selection relies on the statistics presented in equations [4.16], [4.17] and [4.18], respectively. The LGPWM estimators are denoted as LGPWM-KS, LGPWM-CvM and LGPWM-MAD, where the suffixes KS, CvM and MAD correspond to the statistic test used to select the control parameter. All computations were performed using the R software.

4.4.1. *Simulation study*

In the subsequent section, a Monte Carlo simulation experiment is conducted to illustrate the performance of the aforementioned estimation methods for estimating the shape parameters of the Pareto model. We generated a total of $r = 250$ samples, with sizes of $n = 15, 20, 30, 40, 50, 75$ and 100, from the Pareto distribution. Four combinations of shape and scale parameters were considered, namely (a, c)=$(0.25, 0.5)$, (a, c)=$(0.75, 0.5)$, (a, c)=$(1, 1)$ and (a, c)=$(2, 1.5)$. To assess the accuracy and efficiency of the different estimators, we computed the simulated mean value (E) and the RMSE for each sample size, parameter set and estimator under investigation. The results obtained from the Monte Carlo simulation are summarized in Tables 4.1, 4.2, 4.3 and 4.4.

Upon examination of these tables, it is evident that the estimated mean value and RMSE tend to approach the shape parameter a and zero, respectively, for most estimation methods as the sample size increases. However, this trend does not hold for the moment (M) and PWM estimators. This discrepancy can be attributed to the lack of consistency of the estimators for $a \leq 1$. Furthermore, it is noteworthy that the majority of estimators exhibit a tendency to overestimate the target parameter. With regard to the LGPWM estimator, the findings show that the LGPWM-MAD estimator has the smallest absolute bias and RMSE for small sample sizes.

$\hat{a}$	ML		MOM		PWM		LGPWM-KS		LGPWM-CvM		LGPWM-MAD	
	E	RMSE	E	RMSE	E	RMSE	E	RMSE	E	RMSE	E	RMSE
15	0.289	0.090	1.002	0.752	1.027	0.778	0.310	0.120	0.303	0.115	0.283	0.087
20	0.280	0.076	1.001	0.751	1.020	0.771	0.293	0.093	0.287	0.091	0.275	0.075
30	0.267	0.050	1.000	0.750	1.013	0.763	0.277	0.063	0.272	0.058	0.264	0.049
40	0.264	0.046	1.000	0.750	1.009	0.759	0.272	0.056	0.270	0.055	0.264	0.046
50	0.259	0.035	1.000	0.750	1.007	0.757	0.266	0.044	0.263	0.041	0.259	0.035
75	0.257	0.028	1.000	0.750	1.004	0.754	0.263	0.035	0.261	0.034	0.257	0.029
100	0.255	0.026	1.000	0.750	1.004	0.754	0.260	0.032	0.258	0.030	0.255	0.027

Table 4.1. *Simulated mean value and RMSE of the estimators of the shape parameter a for the Pareto distribution with $(a, c) = (0.25, 0.5)$*

$\hat{a}$	ML		MOM		PWM		LGPWM-KS		LGPWM-CvM		LGPWM-MAD	
	E	RMSE	E	RMSE	E	RMSE	E	RMSE	E	RMSE	E	RMSE
15	0.867	0.270	1.176	0.462	1.273	0.576	0.930	0.360	0.910	0.345	0.848	0.261
20	0.839	0.228	1.145	0.421	1.228	0.524	0.879	0.280	0.861	0.274	0.826	0.225
30	0.801	0.150	1.110	0.372	1.178	0.456	0.830	0.189	0.816	0.175	0.793	0.148
40	0.793	0.138	1.092	0.354	1.145	0.417	0.817	0.169	0.811	0.164	0.791	0.139
50	0.778	0.105	1.080	0.337	1.129	0.396	0.797	0.131	0.790	0.124	0.776	0.106
75	0.772	0.085	1.067	0.322	1.108	0.368	0.788	0.106	0.783	0.101	0.771	0.087
100	0.766	0.078	1.060	0.314	1.097	0.355	0.780	0.096	0.774	0.091	0.766	0.080

Table 4.2. *Simulated mean value and RMSE of the estimators of the shape parameter a for the Pareto distribution with $(a, c) = (0.75, 0.5)$*

$\hat{a}$	ML		MOM		PWM		LGPWM-KS		LGPWM-CvM		LGPWM-MAD	
	E	RMSE	E	RMSE	E	RMSE	E	RMSE	E	RMSE	E	RMSE
15	1.157	0.360	1.359	0.453	1.473	0.590	1.241	0.480	1.213	0.459	1.131	0.348
20	1.118	0.304	1.316	0.392	1.413	0.520	1.172	0.373	1.148	0.365	1.101	0.301
30	1.068	0.200	1.263	0.312	1.345	0.420	1.107	0.252	1.087	0.233	1.058	0.197
40	1.057	0.184	1.236	0.285	1.299	0.364	1.089	0.225	1.081	0.219	1.055	0.186
50	1.037	0.140	1.217	0.253	1.277	0.331	1.062	0.175	1.053	0.165	1.034	0.141
75	1.030	0.113	1.200	0.227	1.251	0.289	1.050	0.142	1.043	0.135	1.028	0.117
100	1.022	0.104	1.189	0.213	1.236	0.270	1.040	0.128	1.032	0.121	1.021	0.107

Table 4.3. *Simulated mean value and RMSE of the estimators of the shape parameter a for the Pareto distribution with $(a, c) = (1, 1)$*

4.4.2. *Real data analysis*

We now analyze the fit of a Pareto model to one real dataset: the population of the 150 largest metropolitan areas in the world. This data is available in Caeiro and

Mateus (2023). In this study, values were converted to millions ($\times 10^{-6}$). In Table 4.5, we provide the descriptive statistics obtained with the function summary in R software.

$\hat{a}$	ML		MOM		PWM		LGPWM-KS		LGPWM-CvM		LGPWM-MAD	
	E	RMSE	E	RMSE	E	RMSE	E	RMSE	E	RMSE	E	RMSE
15	2.313	0.721	2.305	0.695	2.447	0.877	2.481	0.960	2.426	0.919	2.262	0.696
20	2.236	0.608	2.242	0.590	2.356	0.757	2.345	0.747	2.296	0.730	2.202	0.601
30	2.135	0.400	2.152	0.422	2.240	0.570	2.215	0.505	2.175	0.465	2.116	0.394
40	2.114	0.367	2.116	0.393	2.171	0.489	2.178	0.450	2.161	0.438	2.110	0.372
50	2.074	0.280	2.084	0.316	2.137	0.419	2.125	0.350	2.107	0.331	2.068	0.283
75	2.059	0.226	2.071	0.260	2.111	0.336	2.100	0.284	2.087	0.270	2.056	0.233
100	2.044	0.208	2.058	0.239	2.093	0.309	2.079	0.257	2.064	0.242	2.042	0.214

Table 4.4. *Simulated mean value and RMSE of the estimators of the shape parameter a for the Pareto distribution with $(a, c) = (2, 1.5)$*

Min.	1st quart.	Median	Mean	3rd quart.	Max.
2.916	3.571	4.907	7.082	8.744	38.001

Table 4.5. *Summary statistics for the population data*

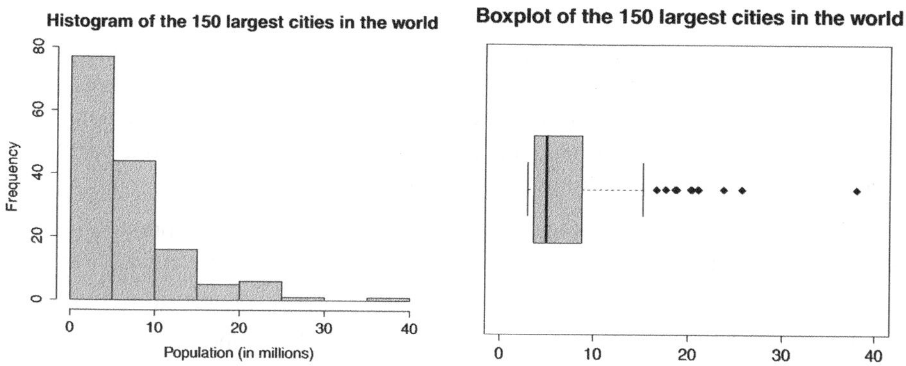

Figure 4.1. *Histogram and boxplot for the population data*

The histogram and boxplot of these observations, in Figure 4.1, confirm the positive skewness of the data and are compatible with the Pareto distribution behavior.

The parameter estimates for the fitted Pareto distribution, provided by the ML, M, PWM and LGPWM estimators, and the values of D_n, W_n^2 and AU_n^2 test statistics in [4.16], [4.17] and [4.18], respectively, are shown in Table 4.6. The smallest value of each test statistic is presented in **bold**. The values of the test statistics show that the new LGPWM estimators are relatively better than any other considered estimators. There are no major differences regarding the LGPWM-KS, LGPWM-CvM and LGPWM-MAD estimators, as all provide similar estimates. Note that not all methods perform well: the $\hat{c}^{PWM}$ estimator produced an inadequate estimate of the scale parameter ($\hat{c}^{PWM} > x_{1:150}$).

	$\hat{a}$	$\hat{c}$	KS	CvM	MAD
ML	1.4599	2.9162	0.0595	0.0979	0.4462
M	1.6953	2.9047	0.1167	0.5929	2.1937
PWM	1.8835	3.3222	0.1800	0.9749	2.1406
LGPWM-KS ($s = 0.5$)	1.3939	2.9162	**0.0435**	0.0536	0.3404
LGPWM-CvM ($s = 1$)	1.3830	2.9162	0.0449	**0.0507**	0.3397
LGPWM-MAD ($s = 1.4$)	1.3875	2.9162	0.0443	0.0517	**0.3394**

Table 4.6. *Parameter estimates and goodness-of-fit statistics for the population data*

4.5. Conclusion

In this chapter, we conducted an investigation on a specific class of estimators for the shape parameter of a Pareto type I distribution, which were derived by extending the PWM technique. Referred to as LGPWM estimators, these estimators require the appropriate selection of a control parameter. A procedure for selecting this parameter has been proposed, and our findings can be summarized as follows:

– The LGPWM class of estimators encompasses the ML estimators as a special case when the control parameter, s, is set to 0. Moreover, these estimators exhibit consistency across the entire parameter space.

– The LGPWM class of estimators demonstrates highly competitive performance, characterized by low absolute bias and RMSE, particularly for small sample sizes.

– The most favorable outcomes in terms of absolute bias and RMSE are achieved when the parameter s is chosen using the MAD statistic.

– These conclusions highlight the effectiveness and robustness of the LGPWM estimators in accurately estimating the shape parameter of the Pareto type I distribution, while also emphasizing the significance of selecting an appropriate control parameter through the proposed procedure.

4.6. Acknowledgments

This work was partially funded by national funds through the FCT – Fundação para a Ciência e a Tecnologia, I.P., under the scope of the projects UIDB/00297/2020 and UIDP/00297/2020 (Center for Mathematics and Applications).

4.7. References

Ahmad, M.I. and Sinclair, C.D., Spurr, B.D. (1988). Assessment of flood frequency models using empirical distribution function statistics. *Water Resources Research*, 24(8), 1323–1328. doi: 10.1029/wr024i008p01323.

Arnold, B.C. and Press, S.J. (1989). Bayesian estimation and prediction for pareto data. *Journal of the American Statistical Association*, 84(408), 1079–1084.

Brazauskas, V. and Serfling, R. (2000). Robust and efficient estimation of the tail index of a single-parameter pareto distribution. *North American Actuarial Journal*, 4(4), 12–27. doi: 10.1080/10920277.2000.10595935.

Caeiro, F. and Gomes, M.I. (2011). Semi-parametric tail inference through probability-weighted moments. *Journal of Statistical Planning and Inference*, 141(2), 937–950.

Caeiro, F. and Gomes, M.I. (2022). Computational study of the adaptive estimation of the extreme value index with probability weighted moments. In *Recent Developments in Statistics and Data Science*, Bispo, R., Henriques-Rodrigues, L., Alpizar-Jara, R., de Carvalho, M. (eds). Springer International Publishing, Cham, 29–39.

Caeiro, F. and Mateus, A. (2023). A new class of generalized probability-weighted moment estimators for the pareto distribution, *Mathematics*, 11(5) [Online]. Available at: https://www.mdpi.com/2227-7390/11/5/1076.

Caeiro, F. and Prata Gomes, D. (2015). A log probability weighted moment estimator of extreme quantiles. In *Theory and Practice of Risk Assessment*, Kitsos, C.P., Oliveira, T.A., Rigas, A., Gulati, S. (eds). Springer International Publishing, Cham, 293–303.

Caeiro, F., Martins, A.P., Sequeira, I.J. (2015). Finite sample behaviour of classical and quantile regression estimators for the pareto distribution. *AIP Conference Proceedings*, 1648(1), 540007. doi: 10.1063/1.4912753.

Caeiro, F., Mateus, A., Soltane, L. (2021). A class of weighted hill estimators. *Computational and Mathematical Methods*. doi: 10.1002/cmm4.1167.

Chen, H., Cheng, W., Zhao, J., Zhao, X. (2017). Parameter estimation for generalized pareto distribution by generalized probability weighted moment-equations. *Communications in Statistics – Simulation and Computation*, 46(10), 7761–7776.

Chen, W., Yang, R., Yao, D., Long, C. (2019). Pareto parameters estimation using moving extremes ranked set sampling. *Statistical Papers*, 62(3), 1195–1211. doi: 10.1007/s00362-019-01132-9.

Crovelli, R.A. and Barton, C.C. (1995). *Fractals and the Pareto Distribution Applied to Petroleum Accumulation-Size Distributions*. Springer, Boston. doi: 10.1007/978-1-4615-1815-0_4.

Glänzel, W. (2008). On some new bibliometric applications of statistics related to the h-index. *Scientometrics*, 77(1), 187–196.

Greenwood, J.A., Landwehr, J.M., Matalas, N.C., Wallis, J.R. (1979). Probability weighted moments: Definition and relation to parameters of several distributions expressable in inverse form. *Water Resources Research*, 15(5), 1049–1054.

Haider Bhatti, S., Hussain, S., Ahmad, T., Aftab, M., Raza, M.A., Tahir, M. (2019). Efficient estimation of pareto model using modified maximum likelihood estimators. *Scientia Iranica*, 26(1), 605–614.

Han, M. (2020). The e-Bayesian estimation and its e-MSE of pareto distribution parameter under different loss functions. *Journal of Statistical Computation and Simulation*, 90(10), 1834–1848.

Kim, J.H., Ahn, S., Ahn, S. (2017). Parameter estimation of the pareto distribution using a pivotal quantity. *Journal of the Korean Statistical Society*, 46(3), 438–450.

Kleiber, C. and Kotz, S. (2003). *Statistical Size Distributions in Economics and Actuarial Sciences*. John Wiley & Sons, Hoboken.

Lu, H.-L. and Tao, S.-H. (2007). The estimation of pareto distribution by a weighted least square method. *Quality & Quantity*, 41(6), 913–926.

Mateus, A. and Caeiro, F. (2021). A new class of estimators for the shape parameter of a pareto model. *Computational and Mathematical Methods*, 3(2), e1133.

Quandt, R.E. (1966). Old and new methods of estimation and the pareto distribution. *Metrika*, 10(1), 55–82.

Rasheed, H.A. and Al-Gazi, N.A.A. (2014). Bayes estimators for the shape parameter of pareto type I distribution under generalized square error loss function. *Mathematical Theory and Modeling*, 4(11), 20–32.

Rosen, K.T. and Resnick, M. (1980). The size distribution of cities: An examination of the pareto law and primacy. *Journal of Urban Economics*, 8(2), 165–186 [Online]. Available at: https://www.sciencedirect.com/science/article/pii/0094119080900431

Singh, V.P. and Guo, H. (1995). Parameter estimations for 2-parameter pareto distribution by pome. *Water Resources Management*, 9(2), 81–93. doi: 10.1007/bf00872461.

Vandewalle, B., Beirlant, J., Christmann, A., Hubert, M. (2007). A robust estimator for the tail index of pareto-type distributions. *Computational Statistics & Data Analysis*, 51(12), 6252–6268.

Wang, S. (1995). Insurance pricing and increased limits ratemaking by proportional hazards transforms. *Insurance: Mathematics and Economics*, 17(1), 43–54.

5

BSDE-θ Scheme for the Heston Model: Valuation of American Options

In this chapter, a numerical forward–backward stochastic differential equations (FBSDEs) approach is used for pricing American options under the Heston model. The motivation behind this approach lies in the Heston model's ability to capture significant market features, including stochastic volatility and the correlation between the underlying asset and the volatility. However, to the best of our knowledge, there is a lack of dedicated investigation on American option pricing using the FBSDE approach under this model. In the present study, the FBSDE representation is obtained and used to develop a numerical scheme, which enables the approximation of option prices and hedge ratios. The primary focus lies in approximating American option price as the solution to the backward stochastic differential equation (BSDE) within the FBSDE representation using a θ *discretization*, which we name as the BSDE-θ scheme. This BSDE-θ scheme offers computational advantages and flexibility for handling both lower and higher dimensions. Finally, numerical experimental studies are conducted to assess the accuracy and stability of the scheme across various choices of θ. Additionally, the impact of the choice of basis functions in the form of global polynomials on the estimation of conditional expectation functions is investigated. The findings indicate that the choice of θ influences the accuracy of the numerical scheme in particular cases. Moreover, the choice of basis functions under consideration does not exhibit any observable impact on the results.

5.1. Background

It is well known that the classical Black–Scholes model for option pricing has limitations, such as the assumption of constant volatility, which does not reflect the observed behavior of financial markets. Due to those limitations, Heston (1993) proposed a model with stochastic volatility that captures changes using a mean-reverting Cox–Ingersoll–Ross process.

Chapter written by Marko DIMITROV, Abigail BERTA, Achref BACHOUCH, Christian EWALD and Ying NI.

Another advantage of the Heston model is the ability to consider the correlation between the underlying asset and its volatility. The volatility generally increases during significant drops in asset prices, implying a negative correlation. The incorporation of the correlation allows the proposed model to be more realistic.

Since the characteristic function of the Heston model is known in a closed form, it is not hard to obtain semi-analytic valuation formulas for European options under this model. For example, Fang and Oosterlee (2009) have developed a so-called COS method for pricing European options, based on Fourier-cosine series expansions.

However, many problems within the area of financial mathematics do not have an analytical pricing formula. Most problems, such as pricing and hedging financial derivatives, can be explained naturally using backward stochastic differential equations (BSDEs) (see El Karoui et al. (1997c)). That is, according to Pardoux and Peng (1990), there exists a unique solution to the BSDE given by

$$\begin{aligned} -dY_t &= f(t, Y_t, Z_t)dt - Z_t dW_t, \\ Y_T &= \xi \end{aligned}$$

i.e. there exists a unique pair of adapter processes (Y, Z) that satisfies the given BSDE under certain assumptions, including the Lipschitz condition. Here, function f is called the generator, and random variable ξ is the terminal condition. In this setting, Y can be considered to be a unique price, and Z is the unique hedging strategy.

Due to their importance, different numerical schemes were proposed to solve BSDEs. The algorithms based on regression, namely least-squares Monte Carlo methods, were presented in Bouchard and Touzi (2004), Gobet et al. (2005) and Lemor et al. (2006). This method was used throughout the chapter.

As the BSDEs are connected to partial differential equations (PDEs) through the nonlinear Feynman–Kac formula, see El Karoui et al. (1997c), in combination with the recently developing deep learning methods, Weinan et al. (2017) introduced a deep learning-based numerical method to solve parabolic PDEs and BSDEs. Later, the same authors in Han et al. (2018) developed a so-called deep BSDE method to solve high-dimensional PDEs. The Deep BSDE method can be used instead of the regression-based Monte Carlo method to improve accuracy and extend the financial derivative valuation to higher dimensions.

One of the schemes to solve BSDEs was proposed by Zhao et al. (2012). The authors there proposed a generalized θ scheme to solve BSDEs with four different parameters $\theta_i, i = 1, 2, 3, 4$, and proved error estimates.

Teng (2018) proposed a regression tree-based method to solve forward–backward stochastic differential equations (FBSDEs) and provided numerical experiments on financial problems, including European option pricing under the Heston model. The author used the generalized θ *scheme* on the BSDE associated with the FBSDE.

In the present study, we consider American option pricing using the FBSDE under the Heston model. We adapt the generalized θ *scheme* by Zhao et al. (2012) to our problem. More specifically, we present a BSDE-θ scheme with five parameters $\theta_i, i = 1, 2, \ldots, 5$ for solving the (F)BSDE under the Heston model. The advantage of this suggested Heston BSDE-θ scheme is that it requires only one of the parameters to price American options. The other four parameters are used in obtaining the Delta and Vega hedging strategies. This BSDE-θ scheme is straightforward and easy to implement, and it can be used for both pricing options under the Heston model and computing the hedge ratios.

We conduct numerical experimental studies to show the scheme's accuracy for evaluating American put option prices under different choices of parameter θ_1. Additionally, a small investigation into the choice of basis functions as global polynomials is presented.

5.2. BSDE numerical schemes

This section introduces the FBSDEs, briefly mentions one well-known numerical scheme to solve BSDEs and shows a derivation of the BSDE-θ numerical schemes for the Heston model. The scheme provides a way to approximate the solution and the hedge ratios.

Consider a filtered probability space $(\Omega, \mathcal{F}, \mathbb{F}, \mathbb{P})$, where $\mathbb{F} = \{\mathcal{F}_t\}_{t\in[0,T]}$ is the augmented natural filtration of the Wiener process $\{W_t\}_{t\in[0,T]}$. In general, the decoupled FBSDEs with the initial condition $X_0 = x_0$, and $X_t \in \mathbb{R}^n$, are given by

$$\begin{aligned}
dX_t &= a(t, X_t)dt + b(t, X_t)dW_t, \\
-dY_t &= f(t, X_t, Y_t, Z_t)dt - Z_t dW_t, \\
Y_T &= \xi = g(X_T),
\end{aligned}$$

where the generator function f is $f : [0, T] \times \mathbb{R}^n \times \mathbb{R}^m \times \mathbb{R}^{m\times d} \longrightarrow \mathbb{R}^m$, ξ is the square-integrable terminal condition, the drift coefficient $a \in \mathbb{R}^n$ and the diffusion coefficient $b \in \mathbb{R}^{n\times d}$.

One of the aims of the numerical schemes to be presented is to find the numerical solutions to the Heston model given by a two-dimensional decoupled FBSDE, i.e. $\{(X_t^2, X_t^2)'\}_{t\in[0,T]}$ is a two-dimensional forward process ($n = 2$), and $\{Y_t\}_{t\in[0,T]}$ is the one-dimensional backward process ($m = 1$).

A popular numerical scheme was proposed by Gobet et al. (2005), where the authors proposed a method based on regression to solve BSDEs. Furthermore, they discussed the choice of function bases – hypercubes, Voronoi partition and global polynomials. The authors extended their research in Lemor et al. (2006), where they considered generalized BSDEs and presented convergence results.

The aforementioned method serves as a basis for our derivation and analysis. That is, the focus will be on the FBSDE representation of the Heston model, the derivation of the BSDE-θ scheme for this model and a numerical experimental study on the scheme.

Before moving onto the Heston model, consider a simpler example of the BSDE representation of the Black–Scholes model under the real-world measure. Assume that $V(t, S_t)$ is a price of a European call option, where the underlying asset follows the geometric Brownian motion

$$dS_t = \mu S_t dt + \sigma S_t dW_t$$

for which the analytical solution is given in Black and Scholes (1973). The derivation of the FBSDE representation is given in El Karoui et al. (1997c) using self-financing portfolio Y_t made of π_t assets and $Y_t - \pi_t$ bonds with the risk-free return rate r. The FBSDE is then

$$\begin{aligned} dS_t &= \mu S_t dt + \sigma S_t dW_t, \\ -dY_t &= \left(-rY_t - \frac{\mu - r}{\sigma} Z_t\right) dt - Z_t dW_t, \\ Y_T &= \xi = \max(S_T - K, 0), \end{aligned}$$

where Z_t is the hedging strategy, i.e. $Z_t = \sigma S_t \pi_t = \sigma S_t \frac{\partial V}{\partial S}$.

5.2.1. *The Heston model*

As mentioned, the Heston model provides more realistic settings for pricing financial derivatives. That is, the Heston model under the real-world measure $\mathbb{P}$ is given by a system of two stochastic differential equations

$$\begin{aligned} dS_t &= \mu^{\mathbb{P}} S_t dt + \sqrt{\nu_t} S_t dW_t^{\mathbb{P},S}, \\ d\nu_t &= \kappa^{\mathbb{P}} \left(\bar{\nu}^{\mathbb{P}} - \nu_t\right) dt + \gamma \sqrt{\nu_t} dW_t^{\mathbb{P},\nu} \end{aligned} \qquad [5.1]$$

where S_t represents the price of the underlying asset at time t, and v_t denotes the instantaneous variance or volatility of the underlying asset. Additionally, parameters are given under the real-world measure $\mathbb{P}$ where $\mu^{\mathbb{P}}$ is the drift rate of the underlying asset, and $\kappa^{\mathbb{P}} > 0$ is called the speed of the mean reversion rate for the variance. The parameter $\bar{\nu}^{\mathbb{P}} > 0$ is the long-term mean of the variance process, and $\gamma > 0$ is the volatility of the variance. The initial level of the variance is given by $\nu_0 > 0$. Wiener processes $W_t^{\mathbb{P},S}$ and $W_t^{\mathbb{P},\nu}$ are correlated with the correlation coefficient $\rho \in [-1, 1]$.

In addition to the previous constraints, the Feller condition (see Feller 1951) given by

$$\frac{2\kappa^{\mathbb{P}}\bar{\nu}^{\mathbb{P}}}{\gamma^2} \geq 1 \qquad [5.2]$$

guarantees that the variance is strictly positive.

Let the function $\lambda(S_t, \nu_t, t)$ be the *market price of volatility risk*. Following Heston (1993), assume that this function is proportional to the variance, i.e. $\lambda(S_t, \nu_t, t) = \lambda\nu_t$ where λ is a constant. According to the Girsanov theorem, the Heston model under the risk-neutral measure $\mathbb{Q}$ is given by

$$\begin{aligned} dS_t &= rS_t dt + \sqrt{\nu_t} S_t dW_t^{\mathbb{Q},S}, \\ d\nu_t &= \kappa^{\mathbb{Q}}\left(\bar{\nu}^{\mathbb{Q}} - \nu_t\right) dt + \gamma\sqrt{\nu_t} dW_t^{\mathbb{Q},\nu} \end{aligned} \qquad [5.3]$$

where r is a constant risk-free interest rate, $\kappa^{\mathbb{Q}} = \kappa^{\mathbb{P}} + \lambda$ and $\bar{\nu}^{\mathbb{Q}} = \frac{\kappa^{\mathbb{P}}\bar{\nu}^{\mathbb{P}}}{\kappa^{\mathbb{P}}+\lambda}$. Here, the Wiener processes under $\mathbb{Q}$ are given by

$$\begin{aligned} dW_t^{\mathbb{Q},S} &= \frac{\mu - r}{\sqrt{\nu_t}} dt + dW_t^{\mathbb{P},S}, \\ dW_t^{\mathbb{Q},\nu} &= \frac{\lambda(S_t, \nu_t, t)}{\gamma\sqrt{\nu_t}} dt + dW_t^{\mathbb{P},\nu} = \frac{\lambda\sqrt{\nu_t}}{\gamma} dt + dW_t^{\mathbb{P},\nu}, \end{aligned} \qquad [5.4]$$

where the last equality used the assumption $\lambda(S_t, \mu_t, t) = \lambda\nu_t$. Note that $W_t^{\mathbb{Q},S}$ and $W_t^{\mathbb{Q},\nu}$ processes are correlated with the same correlation coefficient ρ as under the real-world measure $\mathbb{P}$.

5.2.2. *BSDE representation of the Heston model*

The derivation of the BSDE representation under the risk-neutral measure $\mathbb{Q}$ follows. According to the Feynman–Kac theorem, the solution of the system of SDEs is related to the solution of the PDE for the Heston model

$$\mathcal{L}V + rS\frac{\partial V}{\partial S} + \kappa^{\mathbb{Q}}(\bar{\nu}^{\mathbb{Q}} - \nu)\frac{\partial V}{\partial \nu} - rV = 0,$$

where $V(S, \nu, t) = e^{-r(T-t)}\mathbb{E}^{\mathbb{Q}}\left[g(S_T) \mid S_t = S, \nu_t = \nu\right]$ is the European option price and

$$\mathcal{L} = \frac{\partial}{\partial t} + \frac{1}{2}\nu S^2 \frac{\partial^2}{\partial S^2} + \frac{1}{2}\gamma^2\nu\frac{\partial^2}{\partial \nu^2} + \rho\gamma\nu S\frac{\partial^2}{\partial S \partial \nu}.$$

The BSDE representation of the Heston model under a risk-neutral measure $\mathbb{Q}$ is obtained directly by applying Itô's lemma on $V(t, S_t, \nu_t)$ and Heston's PDE, which yields

$$\begin{aligned} -dY_t &= -rY_t dt - Z_t^1 dW_t^{\mathbb{Q},\nu} - Z_t^2 dW_t^{\mathbb{Q},S} \\ Y_T &= g(X_T), \end{aligned} \quad [5.5]$$

where Y_t refers to the European option price at time t and Z_t^1, Z_t^2 are associated with the hedging strategies as follows:

$$\begin{aligned} Z_t^1 &= \frac{\partial V}{\partial \nu}\gamma\sqrt{\nu_t}, \\ Z_t^2 &= \frac{\partial V}{\partial S}\sqrt{\nu_t}S_t. \end{aligned}$$

Equations [5.3] and [5.5] give the FBSDE formulation of the European option pricing under the Heston model using the risk-neutral measure.

Using equation [5.4], the BSDE given by equation [5.5] can be transformed into its counterpart under the real-world measure as follows:

$$\begin{aligned} -dY_t &= -rY_t dt - Z_t^1 dW_t^{\mathbb{Q},\nu} - Z_t^2 dW_t^{\mathbb{Q},S} \\ &= -rY_t dt - Z_t^1\left(\frac{\lambda\sqrt{\nu_t}}{\gamma}dt + dW_t^{\mathbb{P},\nu}\right) - Z_t^2\left(\frac{\mu - r}{\sqrt{\nu_t}}dt + dW_t^{\mathbb{P},S}\right) \end{aligned}$$

Furthermore, by applying the Cholesky decomposition on the correlated Wiener processes, it follows that

$$\begin{aligned} dW_t^{\mathbb{P},\nu} &= d\widetilde{W}_t^{\mathbb{P},\nu} \\ dW_t^{\mathbb{P},S} &= \rho d\widetilde{W}_t^{\mathbb{P},\nu} + \sqrt{1-\rho^2}d\widetilde{W}_t^{\mathbb{P},S} \end{aligned}$$

where $\widetilde{W}_t^{\mathbb{P},\nu}$ and $\widetilde{W}_t^{\mathbb{P},S}$ are two independent Wiener processes. Next, the transformation becomes

$$\begin{aligned} -dY_t = -rY_t dt &- Z_t^1\left(\frac{\lambda\sqrt{\nu_t}}{\gamma}dt + d\widetilde{W}_t^{\mathbb{P},\nu}\right) \\ &- Z_t^2\left(\frac{\mu - r}{\sqrt{\nu_t}}dt + \rho d\widetilde{W}_t^{\mathbb{P},\nu} + \sqrt{1-\rho^2}d\widetilde{W}_t^{\mathbb{P},S}\right), \end{aligned}$$

or equally,

$$\begin{aligned} -dY_t &= f(Y_t, Z_t^1, Z_t^2)dt - (Z_t^1 + \rho Z_t^2)d\widetilde{W}_t^{\mathbb{P},\nu} - \sqrt{1-\rho^2}Z_t^2 d\widetilde{W}_t^{\mathbb{P},S} \\ Y_T &= g(X_T), \end{aligned} \quad [5.6]$$

where

$$f(Y_t, Z_t^1, Z_t^2) = -rY_t - \frac{\lambda\sqrt{\nu_t}}{\gamma}Z_t^1 - \frac{\mu - r}{\sqrt{\nu_t}}Z_t^2.$$

Finally, equations [5.1] and [5.6] give the FBSDE formulation of the European option pricing under the Heston model using the real-world measure.

REMARK 5.1.– *The FBSDE formulation given by equations* [5.1] *and* [5.6] *is equivalent to the corresponding formulation derived by Teng (2018). Indeed, equation (64) in Teng (2018) simplifies to equation* [5.6] *by recognizing that "*Z_t^1*" and "*Z_t^2*" in Teng (2018) are* $Z_t^1 + \rho Z_t^2$ *and* $\sqrt{1-\rho^2}Z_t^2$*, respectively, using the notation in this chapter.*

REMARK 5.2.– *The FBSDE representations for the European option pricing under the Heston model have been obtained for both the real-world probability measure and the risk-neutral probability measure. Either of these two representations can be used for the pricing problem. However, the representation under the risk-neutral measure is chosen hereafter for two reasons. Firstly, estimating the real-world parameters for real-world dynamics given by equation* [5.1] *is challenging, particularly regarding the market risk of the volatility constant* λ *which requires dedicated research. Conversely, the risk-neutral parameters in equation* [5.1]*, with embedded parameter* λ*, can be conveniently obtained by calibrating the model to market option prices. Secondly, the generator function in the BSDE from equation* [5.5] *is simpler than its counterpart in equation* [5.6] *and satisfies the standard conditions of BSDE, providing an advantage in numerical implementations.*

As mentioned, the values and hedge ratios of an option can be simultaneously calculated as solutions to BSDEs. This is particularly important because option sensitivities cannot be directly observed in the market. A closed form of the Delta hedging strategy $\frac{\partial V}{\partial S}$ is available, which implies that the accuracy of the BSDE methods can be compared by using it as a reference. However, there does not exist an analytical formula for the Vega hedging strategy $\frac{\partial V}{\partial \nu}$, so it has to be estimated using another method, such as the Finite Difference method, to compare with the BSDE methods.

5.2.3. *BSDE-θ scheme under the Heston model*

This section focuses on deriving the BSDE numerical scheme for the Heston BSDE under the risk-neutral measure $\mathbb{Q}$. The notations $\mathbb{P}$ and $\mathbb{Q}$ will be omitted from the superscript in the upcoming derivations. We begin with discussing the European option pricing.

For the derivation, consider partition $0 = t_0 < t_1 < \cdots < t_N = T, N \geq 1$ and natural filtration $\{\mathcal{F}_{t_m}\}_{m=1,2,\ldots,N}$ generated by $\{X_{t_m}\}_{m=1,2,\ldots,N}$.

From equation [5.5], the Heston BSDE can be written as

$$Y_m = Y_{m+1} - \int_{t_m}^{t_{m+1}} rY_s ds - \int_{t_m}^{t_{m+1}} Z_s^1 dW_s^{\nu} - \int_{t_m}^{t_{m+1}} Z_s^2 dW_s^S.$$

Another requirement for the derivation of the BSDE-θ numerical scheme is the θ discretization given by

$$\int_{t_m}^{t_{m+1}} h(s)\mathrm{d}s \approx \theta h(t_m)\Delta t + (1-\theta)h(t_{m+1})\Delta t$$

where $\theta \in [0,1]$ and $\Delta t = t_{m+1} - t_m$.

Next, start deriving the numerical BSDE scheme by taking conditional expectation as suggested in Lemor et al. (2006), where $\mathbb{E}_m[\,\cdot\,] = \mathbb{E}[\,\cdot \mid \mathcal{F}_{t_m}]$, the following holds:

$$\begin{aligned}
Y_m &= \mathbb{E}_m\left[Y_{m+1}\right] - \int_{t_m}^{t_{m+1}} \mathbb{E}_m\left[rY_s\right] ds - \mathbb{E}_m\left[\int_{t_m}^{t_{m+1}} Z_s^1 dW_s^{\nu}\right] \\
&\quad - \mathbb{E}_m\left[\int_{t_m}^{t_{m+1}} Z_s^2 dW_s^S\right] \\
&= \mathbb{E}_m\left[Y_{m+1}\right] - \int_{t_m}^{t_{m+1}} \mathbb{E}_m\left[rY_s\right] ds \\
&\approx \mathbb{E}_m\left[Y_{m+1}\right] - \theta_1 \mathbb{E}_m\left[rY_m\right]\Delta t - (1-\theta_1)\mathbb{E}_m\left[rY_{m+1}\right]\Delta t \\
&\approx \mathbb{E}_m\left[Y_{m+1}\right] - \theta_1 rY_m \Delta t - (1-\theta_1) r\mathbb{E}_m\left[Y_{m+1}\right]\Delta t
\end{aligned}$$

where $\theta_1 \in [0,1]$.

The scheme does not depend on Z_m^1 and Z_m^2, and the generator function is linear, implying that the Lipschitz conditions are satisfied. However, the interest may lie in the numerical scheme for the hedging strategies. Using the Cholesky decomposition

$$\begin{aligned}
dW_t^{\nu} &:= \rho d\widetilde{W}_t^S + \sqrt{1-\rho^2} d\widetilde{W}_t^{\nu}, \\
dW_t^S &:= d\widetilde{W}_t^S.
\end{aligned}$$

where the two Wiener processes are independent, allowing the Heston BSDE to be written as

$$\begin{aligned} dY_t &= rY_t dt - Z_t^1 \left(\rho d\widetilde{W}_t^S + \sqrt{1-\rho^2} d\widetilde{W}_t^\nu \right) - Z_t^2 d\widetilde{W}_t^S \\ &= rY_t dt - Z_t^1 \sqrt{1-\rho^2} d\widetilde{W}_t^\nu - (\rho Z_t^1 + Z_t^2) d\widetilde{W}_t^S \\ Y_T &= g(S_T), \end{aligned}$$

from which it follows that

$$\begin{aligned} Y_m = Y_{m+1} &- \int_{t_m}^{t_{m+1}} rY_s ds - \int_{t_m}^{t_{m+1}} \sqrt{1-\rho^2} Z_s^1 d\widetilde{W}_s^\nu \\ &- \int_{t_m}^{t_{m+1}} (\rho Z_s^1 + Z_s^2) d\widetilde{W}_s^S, \end{aligned} \qquad [5.7]$$

where the two Brownian motions are independent.

Start by determining Z_m^1. Multiplying equation [5.7] by $\Delta\widetilde{W}_{m+1}^\nu$ and taking the conditional expectation yields

$$\begin{aligned} \mathbb{E}_m \left[Y_m \Delta\widetilde{W}_{m+1}^\nu \right] = \mathbb{E}_m \left[Y_{m+1} \Delta\widetilde{W}_{m+1}^\nu \right] &- \int_{t_m}^{t_{m+1}} \mathbb{E}_m \left[rY_s \Delta\widetilde{W}_{m+1}^\nu \right] ds \\ &- \mathbb{E}_m \left[\int_{t_m}^{t_{m+1}} \sqrt{1-\rho^2} Z_s^1 d\widetilde{W}_s^\nu \Delta\widetilde{W}_{m+1}^\nu \right] \\ &- \mathbb{E}_m \left[\int_{t_m}^{t_{m+1}} (\rho Z_s^1 + Z_s^2) d\widetilde{W}_s^S \Delta\widetilde{W}_{m+1}^\nu \right] \end{aligned}$$

which, from independence and properties of stochastic integrals, implies that

$$\begin{aligned} 0 = \mathbb{E}_m \left[Y_{m+1} \Delta\widetilde{W}_{m+1}^\nu \right] &- \int_{t_m}^{t_{m+1}} \mathbb{E}_m \left[rY_s \Delta\widetilde{W}_{m+1}^\nu \right] ds \\ - \int_{t_m}^{t_{m+1}} \mathbb{E}_m \left[\sqrt{1-\rho^2} Z_s^1 \right] ds. \end{aligned}$$

From this, using θ discretization, we have

$$\begin{aligned} 0 \approx \; & \mathbb{E}_m \left[Y_{m+1} \Delta\widetilde{W}_{m+1}^\nu \right] \\ & - \theta_2 \mathbb{E}_m \left[rY_m \Delta\widetilde{W}_{m+1}^\nu \right] \Delta t - (1-\theta_2) \mathbb{E}_m \left[rY_{m+1} \Delta\widetilde{W}_{m+1}^\nu \right] \Delta t \\ & - \theta_3 \mathbb{E}_m \left[\sqrt{1-\rho^2} Z_m^1 \right] \Delta t - (1-\theta_3) \mathbb{E}_m \left[\sqrt{1-\rho^2} Z_{m+1}^1 \right] \Delta t. \end{aligned}$$

or equally

$$Z_m^1 \approx \frac{1 - r(1-\theta_2)\Delta t}{\theta_3\sqrt{1-\rho^2}\Delta t}\mathbb{E}_m\left[Y_{m+1}\Delta\widetilde{W}_{m+1}^{\nu}\right] - \frac{(1-\theta_3)}{\theta_3}\mathbb{E}_m\left[Z_{m+1}^1\right]$$

where $\theta_2 \in [0,1], \theta_3 \in (0,1]$.

Now that the scheme for Z_m^1 is available, the hedging strategy for Z_m^2 can be obtained by multiplying equation [5.7] by $\Delta\widetilde{W}_{m+1}^S$ and taking the conditional expectation as follows:

$$\begin{aligned}\mathbb{E}_m\left[Y_m\Delta\widetilde{W}_{m+1}^S\right] &= \mathbb{E}_m\left[Y_{m+1}\Delta\widetilde{W}_{m+1}^S\right] - \int_{t_m}^{t_{m+1}}\mathbb{E}_m\left[rY_s\Delta\widetilde{W}_{m+1}^S\right]ds \\ &\quad - \mathbb{E}_m\left[\int_{t_m}^{t_{m+1}}\sqrt{1-\rho^2}Z_s^1 d\widetilde{W}_s^{\nu}\Delta\widetilde{W}_{m+1}^S\right] \\ &\quad - \mathbb{E}_m\left[\int_{t_m}^{t_{m+1}}(\rho Z_s^1 + Z_s^2)d\widetilde{W}_s^S\Delta\widetilde{W}_{m+1}^S\right]\end{aligned}$$

which yields

$$\begin{aligned}0 &= \mathbb{E}_m\left[Y_{m+1}\Delta\widetilde{W}_{m+1}^S\right] - \int_{t_m}^{t_{m+1}}\mathbb{E}_m\left[rY_s\Delta\widetilde{W}_{m+1}^S\right]ds \\ &\quad - \int_{t_m}^{t_{m+1}}\mathbb{E}_m\left[(\rho Z_s^1 + Z_s^2)\right]ds.\end{aligned}$$

Finally, it leads to

$$\begin{aligned}0 &\approx \mathbb{E}_m\left[Y_{m+1}\Delta\widetilde{W}_{m+1}^S\right] \\ &\quad - \theta_4\mathbb{E}_m\left[rY_m\Delta\widetilde{W}_{m+1}^S\right]\Delta t - (1-\theta_4)\mathbb{E}_m\left[rY_{m+1}\Delta\widetilde{W}_{m+1}^S\right]\Delta t \\ &\quad - \theta_5\mathbb{E}_m\left[(\rho Z_m^1 + Z_m^2)\right]\Delta t - (1-\theta_5)\mathbb{E}_m\left[(\rho Z_{m+1}^1 + Z_{m+1}^2)\right]\Delta t\end{aligned}$$

or equally

$$\begin{aligned}Z_m^2 &\approx \frac{1 - r(1-\theta_4)\Delta t}{\theta_5\Delta t}\mathbb{E}_m\left[Y_{m+1}\Delta\widetilde{W}_{m+1}^S\right] \\ &\quad - \frac{1-\theta_5}{\theta_5}\mathbb{E}_m\left[(\rho Z_{m+1}^1 + Z_{m+1}^2)\right] - \rho Z_m^1\end{aligned}$$

where $\theta_4 \in [0,1], \theta_5 \in (0,1]$.

To summarize, the BSDE-θ scheme for the European option pricing is given by

$$\begin{aligned}
Y_m &\approx \mathbb{E}_m\left[Y_{m+1}\right] - \theta_1 r Y_m \Delta t - (1-\theta_1) r \mathbb{E}_m\left[Y_{m+1}\right]\Delta t \\
Z_m^1 &\approx \frac{1 - r(1-\theta_2)\Delta t}{\theta_3\sqrt{1-\rho^2}\Delta t}\mathbb{E}_m\left[Y_{m+1}\Delta\widetilde{W}_{m+1}^{\nu}\right] - \frac{(1-\theta_3)}{\theta_3}\mathbb{E}_m\left[Z_{m+1}^1\right] \\
Z_m^2 &\approx \frac{1 - r(1-\theta_4)\Delta t}{\theta_5\Delta t}\mathbb{E}_m\left[Y_{m+1}\Delta\widetilde{W}_{m+1}^{S}\right] \\
&\quad - \frac{1-\theta_5}{\theta_5}\mathbb{E}_m\left[(\rho Z_{m+1}^1 + Z_{m+1}^2)\right] - \rho Z_m^1.
\end{aligned} \quad [5.8]$$

where $\theta_1, \theta_2, \theta_4 \in [0,1]$ and $\theta_3, \theta_5 \in (0,1]$. Here, regression one of the options to estimate the conditional expectation functions.

In particular, we might be interested in the BSDE-θ scheme when $\theta_1 = \theta_2 = \ldots = \theta_5 = 1$ and $\theta_1 = \theta_2 = \ldots = \theta_5 = 0.5$. Note that θ_3 and θ_5 cannot be zero, so the case when $\theta_1 = \theta_2 = \ldots = \theta_5 = 0$ is not of interest when the hedging ratios are required.

The simplified version of the scheme when $\theta_1 = \theta_2 = \ldots = \theta_5 = 1$ is given by

$$\begin{aligned}
Y_m &\approx \mathbb{E}_m\left[Y_{m+1}\right] - rY_m\Delta t \\
Z_m^1 &\approx \frac{1}{\sqrt{1-\rho^2}\Delta t}\mathbb{E}_m\left[Y_{m+1}\Delta\widetilde{W}_{m+1}^{\nu}\right] \\
Z_m^2 &\approx \frac{1}{\Delta t}\mathbb{E}_m\left[Y_{m+1}\Delta\widetilde{W}_{m+1}^{S}\right] - \rho Z_m^1.
\end{aligned}$$

Next, we consider the American option pricing. It is well known that American options can be exercised at any time before maturity. To incorporate the early exercise feature of an American option, an increasing reflection process is introduced into the BSDE formulation, as described in El Karoui et al. (1997b). This process is triggered whenever the solution Y_t of the BSDE falls below the lower bound given by the option's intrinsic value, represented by the payoff at time t denoted as $g(X_t, t)$.

The reflection process, denoted as C, satisfies the following minimal condition:

$$-dY_t = f(s, Y_s, Z_s)ds + C_T - C_t - Z_s dW_s,$$

$$Y_t \geq g(X_t, t), \quad \text{and} \quad \int_0^T (Y_t - g(X_t, t))dC_t = 0, \quad C_0 = 0.$$

To price American options under the Heston model, in our numerical scheme for Y_t in equation [5.8], we introduce an additional step to ensure the exercise value, denoted as $\widetilde{Y}_\tau$, at the optimal stopping time $\tau \in [t, T]$

$$\widetilde{Y}_\tau = \max(Y_\tau, g(X_\tau, \tau)).$$

The proposed numerical scheme, with this additional step, has been proved to approximate Reflected BSDEs (Bouchard and Chassagneux 2008). The uniqueness and existence of the solution for BSDEs with reflection are proven in El Karoui et al. (1997a), while the financial application to American options is demonstrated in El Karoui et al. (1997b). For more detailed discussions on numerical schemes on reflected BSDEs, refer to Bouchard and Chassagneux (2008).

5.3. Numerical experimental studies: valuation of American options

The numerical experimental studies presented in this section focus on pricing American put options under the Heston model using the proposed BSDE-θ scheme.

In addition to checking the scheme's accuracy, the investigation aims to check for what choice of θ_1 the scheme yields the best result for the parameters of interest. Furthermore, as suggested in the literature (e.g. Lemor et al. 2006), the choice of basis functions is essential when applying the regression-based Monte Carlo method for estimating the conditional expectation functions. Due to this, another aim of the numerical study is to check whether there is a significant difference in the valuation when choosing the standard polynomial basis or Laguerre polynomials (see Dattoli 2000) as basis functions in the form of global polynomials. The standard polynomial basis functions of up to order two and Laguerre polynomials of up to order three were used throughout the chapter.

The Euler–Maruyama scheme was used to simulate asset price and volatility processes in [5.4]. The number of simulated paths for the simulation of the Heston model was $M = 600,000$, and the number of time steps was set to $N = 600$. Prices shown in this section are average values of 10 simulations. In addition, variance reduction techniques suggested in Kleijnen et al. (2010) were used to generate processes.

Case 1: Feller condition is satisfied

Firstly, let us consider a set of parameters that satisfy the Feller condition. Such a set is given in Table 5.1.

K	v_0	T	r	γ	$\bar{v}$	κ	ρ
10	0.0625	0.25	0.1	0.9	0.16	5	0.1

Table 5.1. *Parameters for the Heston model to price American put options*

The pricing of American options under the Heston model with these parameters has been previously studied by Clarke and Parrott (1996), Zvan et al. (1998), Oosterlee (2003), Ikonen and Toivanen (2009), Vellekoop and Nieuwenhuis (2009), Persson and von Sydow (2010) and Haentjens and In't Hout (2015). The authors of each of these papers have proposed their unique methods for pricing American options, which do not rely on the BSDE framework. The reference prices, which were employed to calculate the relative errors in the following numerical analysis, were obtained by taking the average of the American put option prices reported by the authors in the above-mentioned studies. The average prices are listed in Table 5.2.

Using the parameters that satisfy the Feller condition, American option prices using the BSDE-θ scheme and Laguerre polynomials are given in Table 5.2 for different choices of θ_1.

	$\theta_1 = 0$	$\theta_1 = 0.5$	$\theta_1 = 1$	Reference price
$S_0 = 8$	2.0000	2.0000	2.0000	1.9999
$S_0 = 9$	1.0486	1.0494	1.0489	1.1077
$S_0 = 10$	0.5006	0.5007	0.5014	0.5205
$S_0 = 11$	0.2081	0.2081	0.2080	0.2141
$S_0 = 12$	0.0803	0.0807	0.0804	0.0820

Table 5.2. *Prices of American put options using the Euler scheme, Laguerre polynomials and BSDE-θ scheme for different choices of θ_1*

In this context, it appears that the performance of the BSDE-θ scheme is not influenced by the selection of θ_1. To further explore the behavior of the scheme in this example, consider a denser set of parameters for θ_1, alongside both standard polynomial and Laguerre polynomial bases.

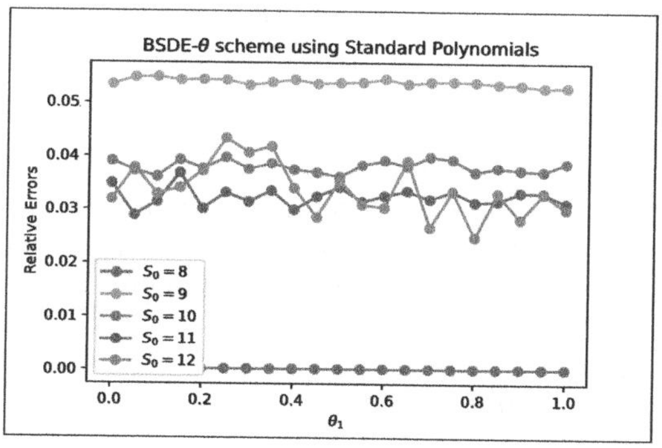

Figure 5.1. *BSDE-θ scheme for pricing American put options using parameters in Table 5.2 and standard polynomials as basis functions under different choices of parameter θ_1. For a color version of this figure, see www.iste.co.uk/dimotikalis/data4.zip*

The accuracy, as shown in Figures 5.1 and 5.2, does in fact depend on the value of θ_1. For instance, in the case of in-the-money options, the pricing for American put options remains relatively consistent, showing little dependence on θ_1. However, for at-the-money and out-of-the-money options, the variability in pricing increases, particularly for those deeply out-of-the-money. It is crucial to note that the accuracy reported here is reliant not only on the reference prices but also on the pricing method employed, both of which can be further improved.

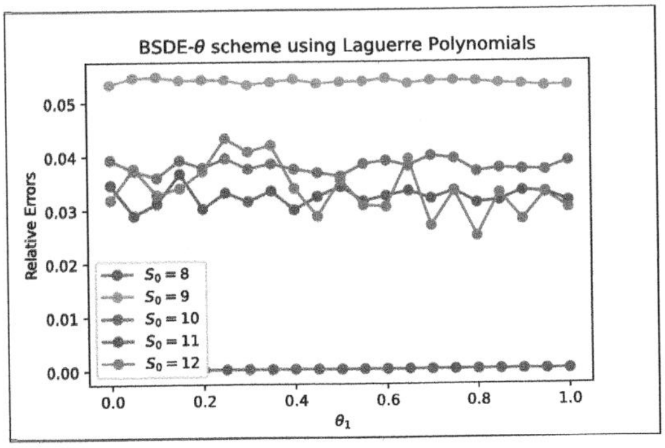

Figure 5.2. *BSDE-θ scheme for pricing American put options using parameters in Table 5.2 and Laguerre polynomials as basis functions under different choices of parameter θ_1. For a color version of this figure, see www.iste.co.uk/dimotikalis/data4.zip*

The scheme's accuracy for in-the-money options, when the initial asset price $S_0 = 8$, remains consistent across different values of θ_1 and represents the greatest accuracy among the five tested initial asset prices. Conversely, with $S_0 = 9$, the scheme exhibits the largest relative error. This discrepancy may be attributed to the chosen reference price.

Finally, the selection of basis functions employed in estimating the conditional expectation functions appears to have a negligible impact on the results. However, according to Gobet et al. (2005), implementing local regression techniques (e.g. hypercubes) or using Voronoi partitions could potentially enhance the accuracy of the scheme.

Case 2: Feller condition is not satisfied

As mentioned, the parameter choice in Table 5.1 satisfies the Feller condition from equation [5.2]. However, the correlation coefficient ρ is positive, which is not reflected in practice. Therefore, it is important to check the BSDE-θ scheme for different choices of parameters where the correlation coefficient is negative. One set of parameters where this holds is given in Table 5.3, but the Feller condition does not hold.

This specific set of parameters was investigated in the context of Bermudan options pricing, using a Fourier-based valuation method by Fang and Oosterlee (2011).

Similarly, Haentjens and In't Hout (2015) explored these parameters in relation to American put option pricing using Alternating Direction Implicit (ADI) schemes. The reference price used in our analysis was derived from the prices established in these prior studies.

K	v_0	T	r	γ	$\bar{v}$	κ	ρ
100	0.0348	0.25	0.04	0.39	0.0348	1.15	−0.64

Table 5.3. *Parameters for the Heston model to price American put options where the Feller condition does not hold*

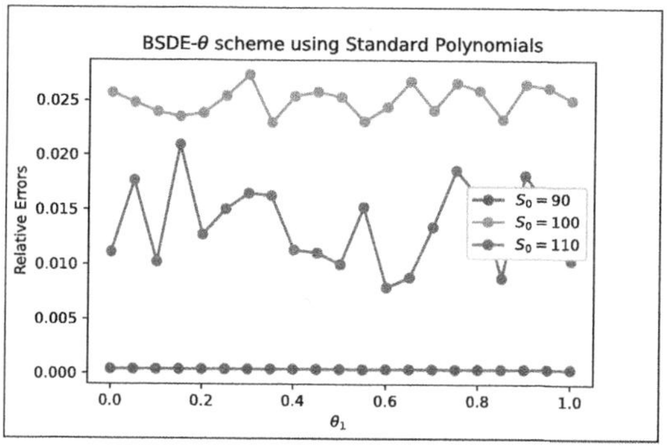

Figure 5.3. *BSDE-θ scheme for pricing American put options using parameters in Table 5.3 and standard polynomials as basis functions under different choices of parameter θ_1. For a color version of this figure, see www.iste.co.uk/dimotikalis/data4.zip*

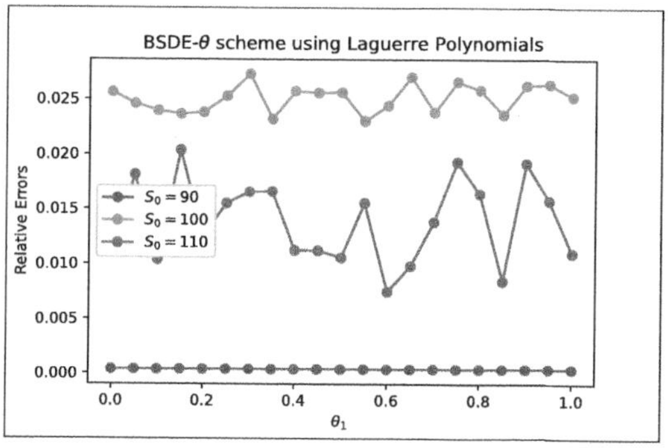

Figure 5.4. *BSDE-θ scheme for pricing American put options using parameters in Table 5.3 and Laguerre polynomials as basis functions under different choices of parameter θ_1. For a color version of this figure, see www.iste.co.uk/dimotikalis/data4.zip*

As observed in the previous example, the accuracy remains consistent for in-the-money options. The pricing for out-of-the-money options exhibits a higher dependency on the choice of θ_1. In terms of accuracy, the results are optimal when the initial asset price, S_0, is set to 90.

5.4. Conclusion and future work

Firstly, a BSDE-θ scheme under the Heston model was derived under the risk-neutral measure. Then, numerical experimental studies for pricing American put options under the Heston model using the proposed BSDE-θ scheme were conducted. The scheme's accuracy was explored for American put options, and the effect of different choices of θ_1 and basis functions on the valuation results were examined.

For the case where the Feller condition is satisfied, the observation was that the BSDE-θ scheme performs well, particularly for in-the-money options. The accuracy of the scheme was evaluated using a reference price obtained from previous studies. The results showed that the scheme depends on θ_1 when pricing at-the-money and out-of-the-money American put options. Furthermore, the comparison of the performance of standard polynomial basis functions and Laguerre polynomials as basis functions was performed, and the choice did not significantly impact the valuation results.

Despite violating the Feller condition, the BSDE-θ scheme still demonstrated high accuracy. Similar to the previous case, the pricing of American options depends on θ_1 when pricing at-the-money and out-of-the-money options, and the choice of basis functions did not substantially affect the valuation results.

Overall, the numerical experimental studies suggest that the BSDE-θ scheme is effective for pricing American put options under the Heston model. The scheme exhibits good accuracy, particularly for in-the-money options, and is robust to parameter choices and basis functions. These findings provide valuable insights for practitioners and researchers interested in pricing American options using the BSDE-θ approach.

Further investigations could focus on hedge ratios, alternative basis functions and a comparison between the Euler–Maruyama scheme and the almost exact scheme (AES), as well as using different methods to estimate conditional expectation functions.

5.5. References

Bender, C. and Denk, R. (2007). A forward scheme for backward SDEs. *Stochastic Processes and their Applications*, 117(12), 1793–1812.

Bergman, Y.Z. (1995). Option pricing with differential interest rates. *The Review of Financial Studies*, 8(2), 475–500.

Black, F. and Scholes, M. (1973). The pricing of options and corporate liabilities. *Journal of Political Economy*, 81(3), 637–654.

Bouchard, B. and Chassagneux, J. (2008). Discrete-time approximation for continuously and discretely reflected BSDEs. *Stochastic Processes and their Applications*, 118(12), 2269–2293.

Bouchard, B. and Touzi, N. (2004). Discrete-time approximation and Monte-Carlo simulation of backward stochastic differential equations. *Stochastic Processes and their Applications*, 111(2), 175–206.

Clarke, N. and Parrott, K. (1996). The multigrid solution of two-factor American put options. Research Report 96-16, Oxford Computing Laboratory, Oxford.

Dattoli, G. (2000). Generalized polynomials, operational identities and their applications. *Journal of Computational and Applied Mathematics*, 118(1–2), 111–123.

El Karoui, N., Kapoudjian, C., Pardoux, E., Peng, S., Quenez, M.C. (1997a). Reflected solutions of backward SDE's, and related obstacle problems for PDE's. *The Annals of Probability*, 25(2), 702–737.

El Karoui, N., Pardoux, E., Quenez, M.C. (1997b). Reflected backward SDEs and American options. In *Numerical Methods in Finance*, Rogers, L.C.G. and Talay, D. (eds). Cambridge University Press, Cambridge.

El Karoui, N., Peng, S., Quenez, M.C. (1997c). Backward stochastic differential equations in finance. *Mathematical Finance*, 7(1), 1–71.

Fang, F. and Oosterlee, C.W. (2009). A novel pricing method for European options based on Fourier-cosine series expansions. *SIAM Journal on Scientific Computing*, 31(2), 826–848.

Fang, F. and Oosterlee, C.W. (2011). A Fourier-based valuation method for Bermudan and barrier options under Heston's model. *SIAM Journal on Financial Mathematics*, 2(1), 439–463.

Feller, W. (1951). Two singular diffusion problems. *Annals of Mathematics*, 51(1), 173–182.

Gobet, E., Lemor, J.-P., Warin, X. (2005). A regression-based Monte Carlo method to solve backward stochastic differential equations. *The Annals of Applied Probability*, 15(3), 2172–2202.

Haentjens, T. and In't Hout, K.J. (2015). ADI schemes for pricing American options under the Heston model. *Applied Mathematical Finance*, 22(3), 207–237.

Han, J., Jentzen, A., Weinan, E. (2018). Solving high-dimensional partial differential equations using deep learning. *Proceedings of the National Academy of Sciences*, 115(34), 8505–8510.

Heston, S.L. (1993). A closed-form solution for options with stochastic volatility with applications to bond and currency options. *The Review of Financial Studies*, 6(2), 327–343.

Hutzenthaler, M., Jentzen, A., Kruse, T. (2019). On multilevel Picard numerical approximations for high-dimensional nonlinear parabolic partial differential equations and high-dimensional nonlinear backward stochastic differential equations. *Journal of Scientific Computing*, 79(3), 1534–1571.

Ikonen, S. and Toivanen, J. (2009). Operator splitting methods for pricing American options under stochastic volatility. *Numerische Mathematik*, 113, 299–324.

Kleijnen, J.P., Ridder, A., Rubinstein, R. (2010). Variance reduction techniques in Monte Carlo methods. CentER Discussion Paper Series No. 2010-117. doi: 10.2139/ssrn.1715474.

Lemor, J.-P., Gobet, E., Warin, X. (2006). Rate of convergence of an empirical regression method for solving generalized backward stochastic differential equations. *Bernoulli*, 12(5), 889–916.

Oosterlee, C.W. (2003). On multigrid for linear complementarity problems with application to American-style options. *Electronic Transactions on Numerical Analysis*, 15(1), 165–185.

Pardoux, E. and Peng, S. (1990). Adapted solution of a backward stochastic differential equation. *Systems & Control Letters*, 14(1), 55–61.

Persson, J. and von Sydow, L. (2010). Pricing American options using a space-time adaptive finite difference method. *Mathematics and Computers in Simulation*, 80(9), 1922–1935.

Teng, L. (2018). A review of tree-based approaches to solve forward-backward stochastic differential equations. *arXiv preprint*, arXiv:1809.00325.

Vellekoop, M. and Nieuwenhuis, H. (2009). A tree-based method to price American options in the Heston model. *The Journal of Computational Finance*, 13(1), 1.

Weinan, E., Jiequn, H., Jentzen, A. (2017). Deep learning-based numerical methods for high-dimensional parabolic partial differential equations and backward stochastic differential equations. *Communications in Mathematics and Statistics*, 5(4), 349–380.

Zhao, W., Li, Y., Zhang, G. (2012). A generalized θ-scheme for solving backward stochastic differential equations. *Discrete & Continuous Dynamical Systems-Series B*, 17(5), 1585–1603.

Zvan, R., Forsyth, P.A., Vetzal, K.R. (1998). Penalty methods for American options with stochastic volatility. *Journal of Computational and Applied Mathematics*, 91(2), 199–218.

6

Age-replacement Policy for Series Systems Under Parameter Uncertainty in Lifetime Distribution

An age-replacement policy provides an optimal preventive replacement interval to minimize the maintenance costs. Most of the previous research proposed an age-replacement policy based on lifetime distribution with certain parameters. However, the parameters of the lifetime distributions may be subject to uncertainties. In addition, the time required to maintain a system is likely to vary from the expected time due to various factors (e.g. location, weather, availability of replacement parts and maintenance personnel).

This research considers series systems consisting of multiple types of units and proposes a model that optimally manages the uncertainty in the parameters of both the lifetime and the maintenance time distributions for an age-replacement policy. The proposed policy makes it possible to obtain the optimal replacement interval according to the priorities of the company providing maintenance for the series systems. The priority, for example, can be minimizing the risk of failure with a limited maintenance budget or minimizing maintenance costs with an upper limit of acceptable failure risk.

6.1. Introduction

Our lives are supported by various systems. Failure of such infrastructural systems must be avoided as it causes financial and temporal damage to society. Therefore, maintenance, which ensures system reliability and recovery from failure conditions, plays an important role in ensuring the longer-term use of systems.

In general, there are two types of maintenance: preventive maintenance, which is performed before a system failure, and corrective maintenance, which is performed

---

Chapter written by Kentaro FUJIOKA, Ying NI and Lu JIN.

after a failure. The former is scheduled in advance and performed to ensure system reliability, and has the characteristics of reducing maintenance time, maintenance cost, system failure rate and failure frequency. The latter is known as "run-to-failure" or "reactive maintenance" and is characterized by long maintenance times and high maintenance costs caused by sudden failures; this has the objective of recovering the system.

Therefore, proper preventive maintenance to avoid breakdowns effectively reduces corrective maintenance costs. On the contrary, it should be noted that frequent preventive maintenance to avoid corrective maintenance may increase preventive maintenance costs.

"Age-replacement policy" and "condition-based maintenance policy" are well known as maintenance policies combining preventive and corrective maintenance. This study addresses the former age-replacement policy.

In an age-replacement policy, a system is replaced at failure or when it reaches a defined preventive replacement interval, whichever occurs first. The replacement interval that minimizes the maintenance cost per unit of time is considered optimal. Aven and Castro (2008) investigated an age-replacement policy based on minor repairs for systems with two causes of failure. They obtained conditions for the existence of an optimal replacement interval and proposed an optimal age-replacement policy under certain safety constraints. Peng et al. (2010) proposed a strategy to minimize the maintenance cost of a system that can fail, subject to degradation and random shocks. The models of Aven and Castro (2008) and Peng et al. (2010) are applicable to two-unit systems, while a more generalized model is needed for multi-unit systems. Shafiee and Finkelstein (2015) represented degradation as a stochastic process and proposed an optimal age-replacement policy for multi-unit systems with economic dependence among units.

In most previous studies (e.g. Aven and Castro (2008)–Shafiee and Finkelstein (2015)), the maintenance time was assumed to be negligibly small compared to the operating time. However, maintenance, especially corrective maintenance, may sometimes take a non-negligible amount of time due to various factors. For example, the maintenance of offshore wind farms may require the transportation of equipment and materials and dispatch of repair personnel. The maintenance time in such cases is non-negligible.

Many studies have examined maintenance times for single-unit systems. The age-replacement policy developed by Barlow and Hunter (1960) is an early example. Cui and Xie (2005) and Li et al. (2019) studied methods to evaluate system availability, considering repair or replacement times. Sanoubar et al. (2021) numerically evaluated age-replacement policies based on minimal repairs, considering the deviation between actual and scheduled maintenance times and the cost impact of not maintaining the system as scheduled. Scarf et al. (2019) proposed an inspection maintenance policy in which periodic inspections are randomly discontinued, and compared the cost and reliability of random and periodic inspections, and discussed the implications for practice. Wang et al. (2020) evaluated the impact of customer time non-compliance on optimizing preventive maintenance policy and estimated the resulting warranty costs. Our previous work (Fujioka and Jin 2022) derived sufficient conditions for the existence and uniqueness of the corresponding optimal solution in series systems considering maintenance time. In these studies, the parameters of the maintenance model are known, and the optimal maintenance policies are sought, based on the parameters of the system lifetime distribution and maintenance time distribution. However, in real-life systems, maintenance is rarely performed as scheduled in all cases due to the weather and other environmental factors at the site or the absence of maintenance personnel.

Therefore, this study focuses on the uncertainty of the parameters of the maintenance model. The risk then refers to the financial risk due to model uncertainty. Specifically, risk or uncertainty is formulated as the variance of the cost rate (expected cost per unit time) when the parameters of the used model are subject to uncertainties. Wu et al. (2017) proposed a method to collectively optimize time-based maintenance policies for a set of single-unit systems, taking into account the risk inherent in the parameters of the lifetime distribution of the system. We extend Wu et al. (2017) to a series system of multiple units.

There are studies in the literature that take into account various types of uncertainty in the maintenance model. For example, Alotaibi et al. (2020) presented a model for the age-replacement policy when maintenance is not performed as planned. They reported implications of practice in age-replacement where the execution of preventive replacement is uncertain. Also, de Jonge et al. (2015) investigated the impact of parameter uncertainty on an optimal age-replacement policy. They evaluated the impact of uncertainty by considering both a simple uniform lifetime distribution and a more realistic Weibull lifetime distribution.

Therefore, as an extension of our previous work (Fujioka and Jin 2022; Wu et al. 2017), we consider series systems consisting of multiple types of units and propose a model that optimally manages the uncertainty in the parameters of both the lifetime and the maintenance time distributions for an age-replacement policy. The proposed policy makes obtaining the optimal replacement interval possible according to the attitude toward risk-providing maintenance for the series systems.

This chapter is constructed as follows. Section 6.2 describes the series system model considered in this study. Section 6.3 provides three optimization problems for this model and describes the conditions for the existence of an optimal replacement interval. Section 6.4 describes the numerical examples of the proposed model and the effect of risk on the optimal replacement interval. Section 6.5 summarizes the main points of this study and points out its limitations.

6.2. The model

Wu et al. (2017) expressed the parameters of the lifetime distribution as $\boldsymbol{\theta}(=\boldsymbol{\theta}_1,\ldots,\boldsymbol{\theta}_n)$. This study also follows the same notation, so the parameter vector for the lifetime distribution for unit i, $i = 1,\ldots,n$, is $\boldsymbol{\theta}_i$. The parameter of the maintenance time distribution is then denoted as $\boldsymbol{\phi}(=\boldsymbol{\phi}_P,\boldsymbol{\phi}_1,\ldots,\boldsymbol{\phi}_n)$, where $\boldsymbol{\phi}_P$ and $\boldsymbol{\phi}_i, i = 1,\ldots,n$ refer to the parameter vectors for the preventive maintenance time and the corrective maintenance time for unit i, respectively.

6.2.1. *Lifetime of units*

We consider a series system consisting of n units of different types. Unit failures are attributed to system failures. We assume that system failures are detected immediately. Let $X_i, i = 1,\ldots,n$ be the lifetime of unit i. The failure rate function is

$$\lambda_i(x \mid \boldsymbol{\theta}_i) = f_i(x \mid \boldsymbol{\theta}_i)/\left(1 - F_i(x \mid \boldsymbol{\theta}_i)\right),$$

where $f_i(x \mid \boldsymbol{\theta}_i)$ and $F_i(x \mid \boldsymbol{\theta}_i)$ are the probability density function and the cumulative distribution function of X_i. Also, assume that both X_i and $X_j, j \neq i$ are independent of each other. Since the system lifetime X_S is the minimum of X_i, the cumulative distribution function of X_S can be expressed as

$$F_S(t \mid \boldsymbol{\theta}) = 1 - \Pr\left[X_S > t\right] = 1 - \prod_{i=1}^{n}\left(1 - F_i(t \mid \boldsymbol{\theta}_i)\right).$$

This cumulative distribution function can be transformed as a sum of subdistribution functions as

$$\Pr\left[X_S \leq t\right] = \sum_{i=1}^{n} \Pr\left[X_S = X_i, X_S \leq t\right].$$

Since X_i are all continuous, we omit the equivalence case. The subdistribution function can be formulated by differentiating with respect to t

$$\begin{aligned}
&\frac{\partial}{\partial t}\Pr\left[X_S = X_i, X_S \leq t\right]\\
&= \lim_{h\to 0}\frac{1}{h}\Pr\left[t - h \leq X_i \leq t, X_j > t \text{ for all } j \neq i\right]\\
&= f_i(t \mid \boldsymbol{\theta}_i)\prod_{j\neq i}\left(1 - F_j(t \mid \boldsymbol{\theta}_i)\right) = \lambda_i(t \mid \boldsymbol{\theta}_i)\left(1 - F_S(t \mid \boldsymbol{\theta})\right).
\end{aligned}$$

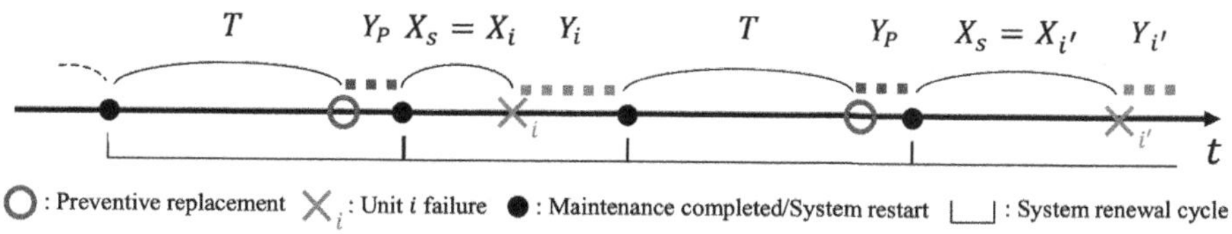

Figure 6.1. *Age-replacement policy for series systems*

Therefore, the subdistribution function becomes

$$\tilde{F}_i(t \mid \boldsymbol{\theta}) = \int_0^t \lambda_i(u \mid \boldsymbol{\theta}_i)\,(1 - F_S(u \mid \boldsymbol{\theta}))\,du,$$

The cumulative distribution function of the system can be expressed using the subdistribution function as

$$F_S(t \mid \boldsymbol{\theta}) = \sum_{i=1}^{n} \tilde{F}_i(t \mid \boldsymbol{\theta}).$$

6.2.2. *Maintenance action and time*

We consider two maintenance actions: preventive maintenance scheduled for the replacement interval T, and corrective maintenance in case of a system failure that occurs until T. Preventive maintenance takes a replacement time Y_P and has a cumulative distribution function $G_P(y \mid \phi_P)$. Corrective maintenance takes a maintenance time Y_i that depends on the failed unit i and has a cumulative distribution function $G_i(y \mid \phi_i)$. It is assumed that both preventive replacement and corrective maintenance fully recover the system to normal operation. This assumption is the same as in a previous study by Shafiee and Finkelstein (2015).

6.2.3. *Maintenance policy*

In this study, the maintenance policy is represented as Figure 6.1, and the system experiences a maintenance action at either the replacement interval T or at the lifetime X_i. In Figure 6.1, one cycle denoted the period from the start of the system to the maintenance completed.

6.2.4. *Cost model and cost rate*

As shown in Figure 6.1, the renewal cycle of a system consists of the operating time until preventive replacement or unit failure, and the corresponding maintenance time. The optimal preventive replacement interval T^* is determined by minimizing the cost rate, which is the ratio of the total expected cost per cycle to the expected cycle time.

Preventive replacement cost c_P is incurred each time a system receives a preventive replacement. The corrective maintenance cost $c_i\ (> c_P)$ is incurred each time the system fails in unit i. Downtime loss per unit of time c_L is incurred when the system is shut down for maintenance. The downtime loss is c_L multiplied by the actual maintenance time.

Under the model of section 6.2, the cost rate $\mathrm{C}(T \mid \boldsymbol{\theta}, \boldsymbol{\phi})$ can be expressed as

$$\mathrm{C}(T \mid \boldsymbol{\theta}, \boldsymbol{\phi}) = \frac{c_P\,(1 - F_S(T \mid \boldsymbol{\theta})) + \sum_{i=1}^{n} c_i \tilde{F}_i(T \mid \boldsymbol{\theta}) + c_L D(T \mid \boldsymbol{\theta}, \boldsymbol{\phi})}{\int_0^T (1 - F_S(t \mid \boldsymbol{\theta}))\, dt + D(T \mid \boldsymbol{\theta}, \boldsymbol{\phi})}, \qquad [6.1]$$

where $D(T \mid \boldsymbol{\theta}, \boldsymbol{\phi})$ is the expected maintenance time within one cycle,

$$D(T \mid \boldsymbol{\theta}, \boldsymbol{\phi}) = \int_0^\infty (1 - G_P(t \mid \boldsymbol{\phi}_P))\, dt\ (1 - F_S(T \mid \boldsymbol{\theta})) + \sum_{i=1}^{n} \int_0^\infty (1 - G_i(t \mid \boldsymbol{\phi}_i))\, dt\, \tilde{F}_i(T \mid \boldsymbol{\theta}). \qquad [6.2]$$

The optimal preventive replacement interval T^* can be derived by differentiating equation [6.1] with respect to T and placing it at 0.

For simplicity, let a_i express the difference between the corrective maintenance and preventive replacement costs.

$$a_i = c_i - c_P$$

Also, let b_i denote the difference between the expected time for corrective maintenance and the expected time for preventive replacement

$$b_i = \int_0^\infty (1 - G_i(t \mid \boldsymbol{\phi}_i))\, dt - \int_0^\infty (1 - G_P(t \mid \boldsymbol{\phi}_P))\, dt.$$

Under a_i and b_i, equations [6.1] and [6.2] can be transformed as follows:

$$\mathrm{C}(T \mid \boldsymbol{\theta}, \boldsymbol{\phi}) = \frac{c_P + c_L \int_0^\infty (1 - G_P(t \mid \boldsymbol{\phi}_P))\, dt + \sum_{i=1}^{n} a_i \tilde{F}_i(T \mid \boldsymbol{\theta}) + c_L \sum_{i=1}^{n} b_i \tilde{F}_i(T \mid \boldsymbol{\theta})}{\int_0^T (1 - F_S(t \mid \boldsymbol{\theta}))\, dt + \int_0^\infty (1 - G_P(t \mid \boldsymbol{\phi}_P))\, dt + \sum_{i=1}^{n} b_i \tilde{F}_i(T \mid \boldsymbol{\theta})}. \qquad [6.3]$$

6.3. Optimization

Regarding the ideas of Wu et al. (2017), the following three optimization problems are applied to the maintenance of series systems.

Option 1

The following objective function allows for explicitly weighted treatment of expected cost and risk:

$$\min_{T\in\mathbb{R}} \mathrm{C}(T \mid \boldsymbol{\theta}, \boldsymbol{\phi}) + \rho \mathrm{V}_{\boldsymbol{\theta},\boldsymbol{\phi}}(\mathrm{C}(T \mid \boldsymbol{\theta}, \boldsymbol{\phi})). \quad [6.4]$$

Here, $\mathrm{C}(T \mid \boldsymbol{\theta}, \boldsymbol{\phi})$ is understood as the expected cost using estimates for the parameters and $\mathrm{V}_{\boldsymbol{\theta},\boldsymbol{\phi}}(\mathrm{C}(T \mid \boldsymbol{\theta}, \boldsymbol{\phi}))$ refer to the variance of the expected cost viewed as a function of the (random variable) estimators for the parameters $\boldsymbol{\theta}, \boldsymbol{\phi}$. We assume that $\rho \in [0, 1]$. The value of ρ reflects the decision-maker's attitude toward risk. For example, if the decision-maker wants to avoid risk, ρ will be set to a large value.

The existence of an optimal replacement interval for option 1 is indicated by satisfying the conditions (i)–(iii) of our previous work (Fujioka and Jin 2022) and (iv).

(i) The failure rate function $\lambda_i(t \mid \boldsymbol{\theta})$ is differentiable and monotonically increasing for any $i \in \{1, 2, \ldots, n\}$.

(ii) The distribution of the corrective maintenance time for any $i \in \{1, 2, \ldots, n\}$ satisfies the following:

$$\int_0^\infty (1 - G_i(t \mid \boldsymbol{\phi}_i))\, dt > \int_0^\infty (1 - G_P(t \mid \boldsymbol{\phi}_P))\, dt.$$

(iii) c_L and c_P satisfy the following:

$$c_L \int_0^T (1 - F_S(t \mid \boldsymbol{\theta}))\, dt > c_P.$$

(iv) The parameters of the preventive replacement time $\boldsymbol{\phi}_P$ are assumed to be known with certainty.

Condition (i) means that the system we considered in this research needs to be an increasing failure rate type. Condition (ii) indicates that preventive maintenance takes less expected time than corrective maintenance. In condition (iii), c_L can be considered as the loss of operating profit per unit time. In other words, condition (iii) means that the expected profit due to operation in one cycle is greater than the sum of minimal repair and preventive maintenance costs c_P. Condition (iv) is reasonable because preventive replacement is scheduled in advance, and its time is unlikely to vary.

Differentiating the objective function with respect to T and setting it to 0, we obtain

$$\frac{\partial \mathrm{C}(T \mid \boldsymbol{\theta}, \boldsymbol{\phi})}{\partial T} + \rho \frac{\partial \mathrm{V}_{\boldsymbol{\theta},\boldsymbol{\phi}}(\mathrm{C}(T \mid \boldsymbol{\theta}, \boldsymbol{\phi}))}{\partial T} = 0. \qquad [6.5]$$

Let T^* denote T satisfying equation [6.5]. Equation [6.5] can be expressed using equation [6.3] as

$$\begin{aligned}
&\sum_{i=1}^{n} (a_i + c_L b_i) \left(\lambda_i (T^* \mid \boldsymbol{\theta}) \int_0^{T^*} (1 - F_S(t \mid \boldsymbol{\theta}))\, dt - \tilde{F}_i (T^* \mid \boldsymbol{\theta}) \right) \\
&+ \sum_{i=1}^{n} \lambda_i (T^* \mid \boldsymbol{\theta}) \left(a_i \int_0^{\infty} (1 - G_P(t \mid \boldsymbol{\phi}_P))\, dt - b_i c_P \right) \\
&= c_P + c_L \int_0^{\infty} (1 - G_P(t \mid \boldsymbol{\phi}_P))\, dt \qquad [6.6] \\
&- \rho \frac{\partial \mathrm{V}_{\boldsymbol{\theta},\boldsymbol{\phi}}(\mathrm{C}(T^* \mid \boldsymbol{\theta}, \boldsymbol{\phi}))}{\partial T^*} \frac{\left\{ \int_0^{T^*} (1 - F_S(t \mid \boldsymbol{\theta}))\, dt + D(T^* \mid \boldsymbol{\theta}, \boldsymbol{\phi}) \right\}^2}{1 - F_S(T^* \mid \boldsymbol{\theta})}.
\end{aligned}$$

Furthermore, differentiating the left-hand side of equation [6.6] by T^*, we obtain

$$\begin{aligned}
&\frac{\partial}{\partial T^*} \left\{ \sum_{i=1}^{n} (a_i + c_L b_i) \left(\lambda_i (T^* \mid \boldsymbol{\theta}) \int_0^{T^*} (1 - F_S(t \mid \boldsymbol{\theta}))\, dt - \tilde{F}_i (T^* \mid \boldsymbol{\theta}) \right) \right. \\
&\left. + \sum_{i=1}^{n} \lambda_i (T^* \mid \boldsymbol{\theta}) \left(a_i \int_0^{\infty} (1 - G_P(t \mid \boldsymbol{\phi}_P))\, dt - b_i c_P \right) \right\} \\
&= \sum_{i=1}^{n} \left\{ (a_i + c_L b_i) \int_0^{T^*} (1 - F_S(t \mid \boldsymbol{\theta}))\, dt \right. \qquad [6.7] \\
&\left. + \left(a_i \int_0^{\infty} (1 - G_P(t \mid \boldsymbol{\phi}_P))\, dt - b_i c_P \right) \right\} \frac{\partial \lambda_i (T^* \mid \boldsymbol{\theta})}{\partial T^*}.
\end{aligned}$$

If conditions (i)–(iii) are satisfied, equation [6.7] leads to the following relationship:

$$\begin{aligned}
&\sum_{i=1}^{n} \left\{ a_i \left(\int_0^{T^*} (1 - F_S(t \mid \boldsymbol{\theta}))\, dt + \int_0^{\infty} (1 - G_P(t \mid \boldsymbol{\phi}_P))\, dt \right) \right. \\
&\left. + b_i \left(c_L \int_0^{T^*} (1 - F_S(t \mid \boldsymbol{\theta}))\, dt - c_P \right) \right\} \frac{\partial \lambda_i (T^* \mid \boldsymbol{\theta})}{\partial T^*} > 0.
\end{aligned}$$

Therefore, the left-hand side of equation [6.6] is a monotonically increasing function.

As T^* increases, the variance of $\boldsymbol{\theta}$ increases, and thus $\mathrm{V}_{\boldsymbol{\theta},\boldsymbol{\phi}}(\mathrm{C}(T^* \mid \boldsymbol{\theta},\boldsymbol{\phi}))$ increases. Hence, in equation [6.6], $\rho\frac{\partial \mathrm{V}_{\boldsymbol{\theta},\boldsymbol{\phi}}(\mathrm{C}(T^*|\boldsymbol{\theta},\boldsymbol{\phi}))}{\partial T^*} \geq 0$. Since $\frac{\{\int_0^{T^*}(1-F_S(t|\boldsymbol{\theta}))dt+D(T^*|\boldsymbol{\theta},\boldsymbol{\phi})\}^2}{1-F_S(T^*|\boldsymbol{\theta})}$ is monotonically increasing with respect to T^*, if $\rho \neq 0$, the right-hand side of equation [6.6] is monotonically decreasing with respect to T^*. Also, if $\rho = 0$, the right-hand side of equation [6.6] is $c_P + c_L \int_0^\infty (1 - G_P(t \mid \phi_P))\, dt$.

Therefore, if condition (iv) is satisfied, the minimum value of the left side of equation [6.6] is 0 (when $T^* = 0$) and the maximum value of the right side is $c_P + c_L \int_0^\infty (1 - G_P(t \mid \phi_P))\, dt$ (when $T^* = 0$), clearly indicating that there exists an optimal solution T^* that satisfies equation [6.5].

Option 2

As shown in the following equation, we can choose T that minimizes the expected cost $C(T \mid \boldsymbol{\theta},\boldsymbol{\phi})$, while imposing the maximum risk ν_0:

$$\begin{aligned} &\min_{T\in\mathbb{R}} \mathrm{C}(T \mid \boldsymbol{\theta},\boldsymbol{\phi}), \\ &\text{subject to: } \mathrm{V}_{\boldsymbol{\theta},\boldsymbol{\phi}}(\mathrm{C}(T \mid \boldsymbol{\theta},\boldsymbol{\phi})) \leq \nu_0, \end{aligned} \qquad [6.8]$$

where ν_0 reflects the decision-maker's attitude toward risk. For example, if the decision-maker wants to avoid risk, ν_0 would be set to a small value.

The Lagrangian function for the optimization problem in option 2 can be written as

$$L(T) = \mathrm{C}(T \mid \boldsymbol{\theta},\boldsymbol{\phi}) + \mu(\mathrm{V}_{\boldsymbol{\theta},\boldsymbol{\phi}}(\mathrm{C}(T \mid \boldsymbol{\theta},\boldsymbol{\phi})) - \nu_0).$$

The Karush–Kuhn–Tucker (KKT) conditions for the solution to be optimal in this nonlinear programming are as follows, where μ is the Lagrange multiplier:

$$\mathrm{V}_{\boldsymbol{\theta},\boldsymbol{\phi}}(\mathrm{C}(T \mid \boldsymbol{\theta},\boldsymbol{\phi})) \leq \nu_0, \qquad [6.9]$$

$$\mu \geq 0,$$

$$\frac{\partial \mathrm{C}(T \mid \boldsymbol{\theta},\boldsymbol{\phi})}{\partial T} + \mu\frac{\partial \mathrm{V}_{\boldsymbol{\theta},\boldsymbol{\phi}}(\mathrm{C}(T \mid \boldsymbol{\theta},\boldsymbol{\phi}))}{\partial T} = 0, \qquad [6.10]$$

$$\mu(\mathrm{V}_{\boldsymbol{\theta},\boldsymbol{\phi}}(\mathrm{C}(T \mid \boldsymbol{\theta},\boldsymbol{\phi})) - \nu_0) = 0. \qquad [6.11]$$

Therefore, in option 2, the following algorithm can be used to obtain the optimal replacement interval.

Step 1

To check whether the constraint in equation [6.9] is satisfied at the replacement interval T that minimizes $C(T \mid \boldsymbol{\theta}, \boldsymbol{\phi})$. If the constraint holds, stop; if not, go to step 2.

Step 2

To solve equations [6.10] and [6.11] and obtain the optimal solution.

Option 3

As shown in the following equation, we can choose T that minimizes the risk $V(.)$ while imposing the maximum cost C_0:

$$\begin{aligned} &\min_{T \in \mathbb{R}} \mathrm{V}_{\boldsymbol{\theta},\boldsymbol{\phi}}(\mathrm{C}(T \mid \boldsymbol{\theta}, \boldsymbol{\phi})), \\ &\text{subject to : } \mathrm{C}(T \mid \boldsymbol{\theta}, \boldsymbol{\phi}) \leq C_0. \end{aligned} \quad [6.12]$$

In this case, C_0 reflects the budget constraint. Option 3 is used primarily for portfolio management in the financial industry. In practice, it is common to plan maintenance under tight budget constraints, and maintenance managers often try to reduce the risk of large budget overruns.

The Lagrangian function for the optimization problem of option 3 can be written as

$$L(T) = \mathrm{V}_{\boldsymbol{\theta},\boldsymbol{\phi}}(\mathrm{C}(T \mid \boldsymbol{\theta}, \boldsymbol{\phi})) + \mu(\mathrm{C}(T \mid \boldsymbol{\theta}, \boldsymbol{\phi}) - C_0)$$

The KKT condition for the solution to be optimal in this nonlinear programming is as follows, where μ is the Lagrange multiplier:

$$\mathrm{C}(T \mid \boldsymbol{\theta}, \boldsymbol{\phi}) \leq C_0, \quad [6.13]$$

$$\mu \geq 0,$$

$$\frac{\partial \mathrm{V}_{\boldsymbol{\theta},\boldsymbol{\phi}}(\mathrm{C}(T \mid \boldsymbol{\theta}, \boldsymbol{\phi}))}{\partial T} + \mu \frac{\partial \mathrm{C}(T \mid \boldsymbol{\theta}, \boldsymbol{\phi})}{\partial T} = 0, \quad [6.14]$$

$$\mu(\mathrm{C}(T \mid \boldsymbol{\theta}, \boldsymbol{\phi}) - C_0) = 0. \quad [6.15]$$

Therefore, in option 3, the following algorithm can be used to obtain the optimal replacement interval.

Step 1

To check whether the constraint in equation [6.13] is satisfied at the replacement interval T that minimizes $\mathrm{V}_{\boldsymbol{\theta},\boldsymbol{\phi}}(\mathrm{C}(T \mid \boldsymbol{\theta}, \boldsymbol{\phi}))$. If the constraint holds, stop; if not, go to step 2.

Step 2

To solve equations [6.14] and [6.15] and obtain the optimal solution.

6.3.1. *A special case*

As a special case, this chapter derives the variance of the cost rate when the lifetime and the maintenance time follow a Weibull distribution. Firstly, the estimators' expectation, variance and covariance for the parameters $\boldsymbol{\theta}_i$ and $\boldsymbol{\phi}_i$ are obtained. Specifically, when $\boldsymbol{\theta}_i = (\theta_{i,0}, \theta_{i,1}), \theta_{i,0}$ refers to shape parameters and $\theta_{i,1}$ to scale parameters in the case of the Weibull distribution. For simplicity, the vector variable $\boldsymbol{\pi}$ of the parameters is defined as follows (e.g. $\boldsymbol{\pi}_1 = (\pi_{1,0}, \pi_{1,1}) = (\theta_{1,0}, \theta_{1,1})$)):

$$\boldsymbol{\pi}\left(=\boldsymbol{\pi}_1,\ldots,\boldsymbol{\pi}_{2n}\right) = \left\{\boldsymbol{\theta}\left(=\boldsymbol{\theta}_1,\ldots,\boldsymbol{\theta}_n\right), \boldsymbol{\phi}\left(=\boldsymbol{\phi}_1,\ldots,\boldsymbol{\phi}_n\right)\right\},$$

$$\boldsymbol{\pi}_k = \begin{cases} \boldsymbol{\theta}_i, i = 1,\ldots,n & (k = 1,\ldots,n) \\ \boldsymbol{\phi}_i, i = 1,\ldots,n & (k = n+1,\ldots,2n) \end{cases}$$

With the above notation, the Weibull distribution function is given by

$$F_k\left(t \mid \boldsymbol{\pi}_k\right) = 1 - \exp\left(-\frac{t^{\pi_{k,0}^{-1}}}{\pi_{k,1}}\right).$$

Assume that there are in total m units under a type I censoring scheme: τ denoted the threshold time and the jth unit i may survive over the time interval $(0, \tau)$ or fail $X_j < \tau$. From Sirvanci and Yang (1984) and Wu et al. (2017), the estimator of $\boldsymbol{\pi}_k$, its expectation, variance and covariance are given by

$$\hat{\pi}_{k,0} = \sum_{j=1}^{m} \frac{(\log\tau - \log X_j) I_j}{M h(p)},$$

$$\hat{\pi}_{k,1} = \sum_{j=1}^{m} \frac{V_j^{\pi_{k,0}^{-1}}}{M},$$

$$\mathrm{E}\left[\hat{\pi}_{k,0}\right] = \pi_{k,0} h(p) [1/(1 - (1-p)^m - p^m)] \times \sum_{k=1}^{m-1} \binom{m}{k} p^k (1-p)^{m-k} / h(k/m).,$$

$$\mathrm{E}\left[\hat{\pi}_{k,1}\right] = \sum_{j=1}^{m} \frac{V_j^{\mathrm{E}[\hat{\pi}_{k,0}]^{-1}}}{M},$$

$$\mathrm{Var}\left[\hat{\pi}_{k,0}\right] = \frac{\pi_{k,0}^2 I_{2p} - \pi_{k,0}^2 p I_{1p}^2 + \pi_{k,0}^2 p^3 (1-p) \left\{\left[(1-p)\log\frac{1}{1-p}\right]^{-1} - \frac{h(p)}{p}\right\}^2}{(p h(p))^2},$$

$$\mathrm{Var}\left[\hat{\pi}_{k,1}\right] = \frac{\pi_{k,1}^2}{p} + \frac{\pi_{k,1}^2}{\pi_{k,0}^2} \left(1 + I_{1p} + \log\pi_{k,1}\right)^2 \mathrm{Var}\left(\pi_{k,0}\right),$$

$$\mathrm{Cov}\left[\hat{\pi}_{k,0}, \hat{\pi}_{k,1}\right] = \frac{1}{\pi_{k,0}^2} \left[-\pi_{k,1}\pi_{k,0}\left(1 + I_{1p} + \log\pi_{k,1}\right) \mathrm{Var}\left(\pi_{k,0}\right)\right],$$

where M is the number of failed units i in $[0, \tau]$, $p = \frac{M}{m}$, $V_j = \min\{X_j, \tau\}$, $I_{1p} = \frac{1}{p}\int_0^p \log\log\frac{1}{1-t}dt$, $I_{2p} = \int_0^p \left(\log\log\frac{1}{1-t}\right)^2 dt$, $h(p) = \log\log\frac{1}{1-p} - I_{1p}$ and I_j is the indicator, $I_j = 1$ if item jth unit i fails in $[0, \tau]$ and $I_j = 0$ otherwise.

Next, we obtain the variance of the cost rate $\mathrm{V}_{\boldsymbol{\theta},\boldsymbol{\phi}}(\mathrm{C}(T \mid \boldsymbol{\theta}, \boldsymbol{\phi}))$ by extending the delta method. From Wu et al. (2017), the parameters estimated based on observations depend on the sample size, so the parameters of lifetime and maintenance time distributions can be treated as random variables. Calculate the variance of $\mathrm{E}[\boldsymbol{\pi}] = \mathrm{E}[\boldsymbol{\pi}_1], \ldots, \mathrm{E}[\boldsymbol{\pi}_{2n}]$ around $C(T \mid \boldsymbol{\theta}, \phi)$ can be written as follows. ($(2n) \times 2$ variables Taylor expansion.)

$$\begin{aligned}\mathrm{C}(T \mid \boldsymbol{\theta}, \boldsymbol{\phi}) &= \mathrm{C}(T \mid \boldsymbol{\pi})\\ &\approx \mathrm{C}(T \mid \mathrm{E}[\boldsymbol{\pi}]) + \sum_{k=1}^{2n}\sum_{j=0}^{1}\left\{(\pi_{k,j} - \mathrm{E}[\pi_{k,j}])\frac{\partial}{\partial \pi_{k,j}}\mathrm{C}(T \mid \mathrm{E}[\boldsymbol{\pi}])\right\}\end{aligned}$$

Assuming that the distributions of lifetime and maintenance time followed by the units are independent of each other, the variance of the cost rate can be obtained as

$$\begin{aligned}&\mathrm{V}_{\boldsymbol{\theta},\boldsymbol{\phi}}(\mathrm{C}(T \mid \boldsymbol{\theta}, \boldsymbol{\phi}))\\ &\approx \sum_{k=1}^{2n}\left\{\mathrm{Var}[\pi_{k,0}]\left(\frac{\partial}{\partial \pi_{k,0}}\mathrm{C}(T \mid \mathrm{E}[\boldsymbol{\pi}])\right)^2 + \mathrm{Var}[\pi_{k,1}]\left(\frac{\partial}{\partial \pi_{k,1}}\mathrm{C}(T \mid \mathrm{E}[\boldsymbol{\pi}])\right)^2\right.\\ &\left.+2\left(\frac{\partial}{\partial \pi_{k,0}}\mathrm{C}(T \mid \mathrm{E}[\boldsymbol{\pi}])\right)\left(\frac{\partial}{\partial \pi_{k,1}}\mathrm{C}(T \mid \mathrm{E}[\boldsymbol{\pi}])\right)\mathrm{Cov}[\pi_{k,0}, \pi_{k,1}]\right\}\end{aligned}$$

6.4. Numerical example

This section illustrates a numerical example of a three-unit series system. As in the special case discussed in the previous section, the lifetime and the maintenance time are assumed to follow Weibull distributions with shape parameter $\pi_{k,0}$ and scale parameter $\pi_{k,1}$, respectively. Numerical examples were created in the following order:

1) For each unit, create a dummy dataset by simulating a sample of size 100 from the Weibull distribution using true values of the set parameters.

2) Using the dummy data ($m = 100$), estimate the parameters according to the method of Sirvanci and Yang (1984) and calculate the expected value, variance and covariance of the estimated values.

3) Using the delta method, compute $\mathrm{V}_{\boldsymbol{\theta},\boldsymbol{\phi}}(\mathrm{C}(T \mid \boldsymbol{\theta}, \boldsymbol{\phi}))$.

4) Solve the optimization problem.

Referring to the availability of 90% for offshore wind power (NEDO 2018), the expected preventive replacement times are set 1/9 times the expected operating time. In addition, corrective maintenance may take more time and cost more than scheduled preventive replacement due to various factors such as ordering replacement parts, preparing maintenance teams and transporting maintenance equipment. Therefore, the true values and estimated values of parameters are listed in Table 6.1, and the maintenance costs were set as follows: $c_P = 10, c_1 = 20, c_2 = 24, c_3 = 22, c_L = 2$.

	$\boldsymbol{\pi}_1 = \boldsymbol{\theta}_1$	$\boldsymbol{\pi}_2 = \boldsymbol{\theta}_2$	$\boldsymbol{\pi}_3 = \boldsymbol{\theta}_3$	$\boldsymbol{\pi}_4 = \boldsymbol{\phi}_1$	$\boldsymbol{\pi}_5 = \boldsymbol{\phi}_2$	$\boldsymbol{\pi}_6 = \boldsymbol{\phi}_3$
$\pi_{i,0}$	0.280	0.290	0.310	0.240	0.230	0.250
$\pi_{i,1}$	3.500	3.500	3.500	0.001	0.001	0.001
	$\hat{\boldsymbol{\pi}}_1 = \hat{\boldsymbol{\theta}}_1$	$\hat{\boldsymbol{\pi}}_2 = \hat{\boldsymbol{\theta}}_2$	$\hat{\boldsymbol{\pi}}_3 = \hat{\boldsymbol{\theta}}_3$	$\hat{\boldsymbol{\pi}}_4 = \hat{\boldsymbol{\phi}}_1$	$\hat{\boldsymbol{\pi}}_5 = \hat{\boldsymbol{\phi}}_2$	$\hat{\boldsymbol{\pi}}_6 = \hat{\boldsymbol{\phi}}_3$
$\hat{\pi}_{i,0}$	0.315	0.321	0.307	0.228	0.264	0.239
$\hat{\pi}_{i,1}$	3.301	3.353	3.784	0.0007	0.0024	0.0007

Table 6.1. *True value and estimated value of parameters (when censoring times are set as follows: $\tau_1 \sim \tau_3 = 1.6, \tau_4 \sim \tau_6 = 0.18$)*

Option 1

For this case, we consider a numerical example of option 1 of equation [6.4]. Figure 6.2 contains plots of the objective function under option 1 for various choices of the constant ρ, $\rho = 0, 0.5, 1.0$. Table 6.2 shows the optimal solution of option 1 at $\rho = 0, 0.5, 1.0$. Figure 6.3 plots the optimal solution with respect to risk parameter ρ for $\rho \in [0, 1]$. Figure 6.4 presents the graph of the optimal replacement interval T^* as a function of $\rho \in [0, 1]$. As shown in Figures 6.2 and 6.4, the optimal replacement interval tends to be shorter when ρ is set to a large value to avoid financial risk. It should be noted here that the monetary units of the cost rate and its variance are different. In addition to variance, standard deviation can also be used. Furthermore, numerical results depend on the method used to derive financial risk, the estimation method and the parameters' precision level. Therefore, as an example, we used the delta method and the estimation method from Sirvanci and Yang (1984). However, it is also possible to capture the risk more accurately, depending on the method chosen.

	T^*	$\mathrm{C}(T^* \mid \boldsymbol{\theta}, \boldsymbol{\phi}) + \rho \mathrm{V}_{\boldsymbol{\theta},\boldsymbol{\phi}}(\mathrm{C}(T^* \mid \boldsymbol{\theta}, \boldsymbol{\phi}))$
$\rho = 0$	0.751	17.2
$\rho = 0.5$	0.384	26.0
$\rho = 1.0$	0.325	28.9

Table 6.2. *Optimal solution of option 1*

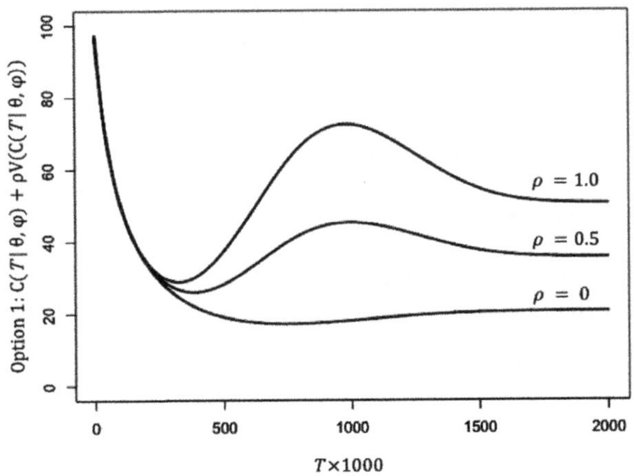

Figure 6.2. *Objective function for option 1 at* $\rho = 0, 0.5, 1.0$

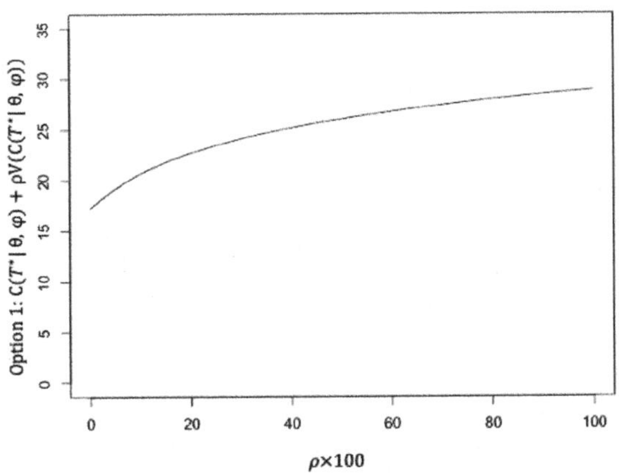

Figure 6.3. *Optimal solution for option 1 when* $\rho \in [0, 1]$

Option 2

If ν_0 is greater than or equal to 45.3, the optimal replacement interval for the objective function is $T^* = 0.751$, unaffected by the constraint in equation [6.9]. For example, let $\nu_0 = 50$. When $T \in [0, 0.814] \cup [1.141, \infty]$, $T^* = 0.751$, the optimal solution is given by $\mathrm{C}(T^* \mid \boldsymbol{\theta}, \boldsymbol{\phi}) = 17.2$. Let $\nu_0 = 60$. When $T \in [0, \infty]$, $T^* = 0.751$, the optimal solution is given by $\mathrm{C}(T^* \mid \boldsymbol{\theta}, \boldsymbol{\phi}) = 17.2$.

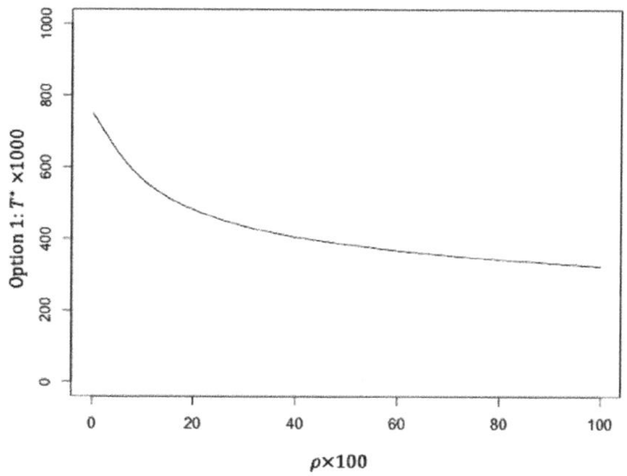

Figure 6.4. *Optimal replacement interval T^* for option 1 when $\rho \in [0, 1]$*

If ν_0 is smaller than 45.3, the optimal replacement interval for the objective function is affected by the constraint in equation [6.9]. For example, let $\nu_0 = 36$. When $T \in [0, 0.657] \cup [1.447, \infty]$, $T^* = 0.657$, the optimal solution is given by $\mathrm{C}(T^* \mid \boldsymbol{\theta}, \boldsymbol{\phi}) = 17.4$. Let $\nu_0 = 26$. When $T \in [0, 0.569]$, $T^* = 0.569$, the optimal solution is given by $\mathrm{C}(T^* \mid \boldsymbol{\theta}, \boldsymbol{\phi}) = 18.1$.

Option 3

In the case of a strict budget limit setting, the range of the replacement interval T is narrower, and T can be taken near the minimum of the cost rate. Therefore, for example, let $C_0 = 20$. When $T \in [0.456, 1.376]$, $T^* = 0.456$, the optimal solution is $\mathrm{V}_{\boldsymbol{\theta},\boldsymbol{\phi}}(\mathrm{C}(T^* \mid \boldsymbol{\theta}, \boldsymbol{\phi})) = 13.86$.

Conversely, in the case of a loose budget limit setting, the range of the replacement interval T is wider. Therefore, for example, let $C_0 = 40$. When $T \in [0.152, \infty]$, $T^* = 0.152$, the optimal solution is $\mathrm{V}_{\boldsymbol{\theta},\boldsymbol{\phi}}(\mathrm{C}(T^* \mid \boldsymbol{\theta}, \boldsymbol{\phi})) = 0.17$.

6.5. Conclusion

We considered series systems consisting of multiple types of units and proposed a model that optimally manages the uncertainty in the parameters of both the lifetime and the maintenance time distributions for an age-replacement policy as an extension of our previous work (Wu et al. 2017; Fujioka and Jin 2022). The proposed policy makes it possible to obtain the optimal replacement interval according to the priorities of the company providing maintenance for the series systems. The priority, for example, can be minimizing the risk of failure with a limited maintenance budget or minimizing maintenance costs with an upper limit of acceptable failure risk.

Under the proposed model, we presented optimization problems for three options; and for each option, we indicated the existence of an optimal replacement interval. Furthermore, we gave numerical examples for the proposed model and considered the effect of risk on the optimal replacement interval.

The system subject to maintenance in this study is a series system, and we considered the uncertainties in the parameters of the lifetime and maintenance time distributions. Therefore, the parameters of each unit are assumed to be independent of each other. As future work, we would like to extend the model from a series system to a parallel system and consider the case where each unit's parameters depend on each other. In addition, although this study used a regeneration process to construct the model, in an existing multi-unit system, it is more economical to replace only the failed unit and use the other units as they are, rather than replacing the entire system after the first unit failure. Therefore, a model other than the regeneration process (e.g. geometric process) may be considered.

6.6. References

Alotaibi, N.M., Cavalcante, C.A.V., Lopes, R.S., Scarf, P.A. (2020). Preventive replacement with defaulting. *IMA Journal of Management Mathematics*, 31, 491–504.

Aven, T. and Castro, I.T. (2008). A minimal repair replacement model with two types of failure and a safety constraint. *European Journal of Operational Research*, 188, 506–515.

Barlow, R. and Hunter, L. (1960). Optimum preventive maintenance policies. *Operations Research*, 8, 90–100.

Cui, L. and Xie, M. (2005). Availability of a periodically inspected system with random repair or replacement times. *Journal of Statistical Planning and Inference*, 131, 89–100.

Fujioka, K. and Jin, L. (2022). Optimal age-replacement policy for series systems considering maintenance time. *Total Quality Science*, 8, 51–60.

de Jonge, B., Klingenberg, W., Teunter, R., Tinga, T. (2015). Optimum maintenance strategy under uncertainty in the lifetime distribution. *Reliability Engineering & System Safety*, 133, 59–67.

Li, J., Chen, Y., Zhang, Y., Huang, H. (2019). Availability modeling for periodically inspection system with different lifetime and repair-time distribution. *Chinese Journal of Aeronautics*, 32, 1667–1672.

NEDO (New Energy and Industrial Technology Development Organization) (2018). Guidebook for landing type offshore wind power generation (final version) [Online]. Available at: https://www.nedo.go.jp/content/100889993.pdf [Accessed 25 April 2022].

Peng, H., Feng, Q., Coit, D.W. (2010). Reliability and maintenance modeling for systems subject to multiple dependent competing failure processes. *IIE Transactions*, 43, 12–22.

Sanoubar, S., He, K., Maillart, L.M., Prokopyev, O.A. (2021). Optimal age replacement in anticipation of timedependent, unpunctual policy implementation. *IEEE Transactions on Reliability*, 70, 1177–1192.

Scarf, P.A., Cavalcante, C.A.V., Lopes, R.S. (2019). Delay-time modelling of a critical system subject to random inspections. *European Journal of Operational Research*, 278, 772–782.

Shafiee, M. and Finkelstein, M. (2015). An optimal age-based group maintenance policy for multi-unit degrading systems. *Reliability Engineering and System Safety*, 134, 230–238.

Sirvanci, M. and Yang, G. (1984). Estimation of the Weibull parameters under type 1 censoring. *Journal of the American Statistical Association*, 79, 183–187.

Wang, X., Li, L., Xie, M. (2020). An unpunctual preventive maintenance policy under two-dimensional warranty. *European Journal of Operational Research*, 282, 304–318.

Wu, S., Coolen, F.P.A., Liu, B. (2017). Optimization of maintenance policy under parameter uncertainty using portfolio theory. *IISE Transactions*, 49, 711–721.

7

New Bicluster Algorithm for Trading

The choice of the rules to follow for a profitable investment in stocks is essentially guided by the trend in their price on the global market. Understanding the trend of stocks in advance determines a significant advantage for the success of investors. Therefore, establishing rules to formulate buying and selling decisions is really essential. Indeed, in recent years, many scholars have thought of combining financial technical indicators with biclusters to determine their rules. By combining the two methodologies, more technical indicators can be considered in order to improve the trading rules. They are usually based on historical stock values, but there are many other factors which can cause changes to a stock price. For example, investor feelings about changes in political scenarios due to telematics or ethical choices, new business projects or even natural disasters greatly influence the stock market. In the most recent studies, sentimental analysis was introduced in price forecasting to consider the psychological factors of investors. Following this new perspective, a modified version of the bicluster method was proposed introducing sentimental analysis so as to improve the possibility of buying or selling a stock with a significant economic gain for investors.

7.1. Introduction

Achieving success in stock trading is contingent upon effectively timing the purchase or sale of stocks (Huang et al. 2019b). This involves analyzing statistical trends, which can be facilitated by using technical indicators. These indicators offer valuable predictions for making trading decisions in the market (Huang et al. 2014). Different combinations of technical indicators yield distinct trading rules (Xue et al. 2015). These trading rules serve the purpose of identifying trading signals, namely, whether to buy, sell, or take no action (Sun et al. 2019).

Chapter written by Gloria GHENO.

In their study, Huang et al. (2019b) considered a range of technical indicators that are crucial in analyzing stock market behavior. These indicators provide valuable insights into various aspects of price movements and market trends. The following is a breakdown of the specific technical indicators explored:

– Simple moving average (SMA): this indicator calculates the average price of a stock over a specified number of days. By smoothing out price fluctuations, it offers a clearer view of the underlying trend.

– Relative strength index (RSI): the RSI measures the velocity and magnitude of price changes. It helps determine whether a stock is overbought or oversold, indicating potential turning points in the market.

– Williams %R: this indicator compares a stock's closing price to its high–low range over a designated period. It assists in identifying potential reversal points by highlighting overbought and oversold conditions.

– Rate of change (ROC): the ROC quantifies the percentage change in price from one period to the next. It aids in assessing the momentum and speed of price movements, providing insights into market dynamics.

– Commodity channel index (CCI): the CCI is a valuable tool for identifying new trends and extreme market conditions. It measures a stock's price deviation from its average over a specific time frame.

– Ease of movement (EMV): the EMV measures the volume required to move prices. By analyzing the relationship between volume and price movements, it helps identify significant buying or selling pressure.

– Ultimate oscillator (UOS): the UOS captures price momentum across three different time frames. It combines short, medium and long-term price movements to provide a comprehensive understanding of market trends.

– BR and AR: these indicators reflect the popularity of a stock among investors. They assess the accumulation and distribution of shares, shedding light on market sentiment.

– K, D and J: these indicators are commonly used in short-term trend analysis. They help traders identify potential entry or exit points, based on price and momentum signals.

– Momentum (MTM): the MTM reflects short-term price volatility. By measuring the rate of price change over a specific period, it highlights the speed and intensity of price movements.

By considering and analyzing these diverse technical indicators, a comprehensive perspective on market trends, price movements and potential trading opportunities can be achieved.

In order to effectively use the combination of multiple technical indicators, several authors (Huang et al. 2014; Xue et al. 2015; Huang et al. 2019b) have proposed the adoption of the bicluster method. Originally introduced for analyzing gene expression (Cheng and Church 2000), the bicluster method has found applications in various economic domains such as marketing (Dolnicar et al. 2012) and new product analysis (Garbuio and Gheno 2021), among others. Unlike traditional clustering methods that group either rows or columns of a matrix, the bicluster method simultaneously groups both columns and rows. This unique characteristic makes it particularly suitable for selecting trading rules.

By using the bicluster algorithm, local coherent patterns are extracted, each consisting of a subset of technical indicators and a subset of time periods (Huang et al. 2019b). This enables the identification of specific combinations of indicators and rules that exhibit consistent and meaningful patterns in the dataset. By focusing on these biclusters, traders and analysts can gain insights into the relationships between technical indicators and trading rules, facilitating the development of effective trading strategies.

Two measures can be used to establish the connection between trading indicators and trading rules:

– Return measure ($return_t$): this measure calculates the return on investment over a specific period. It is determined by the formula:

$$return_t = \frac{cpw_t - cp_t}{cp_t}$$

where cpw_t is the closing price after one week and cp_t denotes the closing price of the t-th trading day.

– Financial rate of return (FRR_t): this measure assesses the relative change in the closing price over a designated period. It is computed as:

$$FRR_t = \frac{acp_t - cp_t}{cp_t} 100\%$$

where cp_t refers to the closing price of the t-th trading day and acp_t represents the average price of the closing prices of N subsequent days, which is given by

$$acp_t = \frac{1}{N} \sum_{j=1}^{t+N-1} cp_j$$

	(Huang et al. 2014)	(Huang et al. 2019b)	(Xue et al. 2015)	(Sun et al. 2019)
Input matrix for bicluster	Financial rate of return (FRR) and technical indicators	Financial rate of return (FRR) and technical indicators	Volume, return and technical indicators	Future return rate (three FRRs: short-, middle-, long-term) and technical indicators
Data normalization	Min–max standard method	– Min–max standard method (technical indicators) – Return replaced by -3, -2, 1, 0, 1, 2, 3 respectively if (-∞, -3α), [-3α, -2α), [-2α, -α), [-α, α), [α, 2α), [2α ,3α), [3α, +∞)	– Min–max standard method (technical indicators) – Return replaced by -1, 1, 0 respectively if (-∞, -α), (α, +∞), otherwise	– Min–max standard method (technical indicators) – Return replaced by -1, 1, 0 respectively if (-∞, -α), (α, +∞), otherwise
Bicluster contains	m days and n technical indicators	m days and n technical indicators	m days, n technical indicators, returns	m days and n technical indicators
Average 1) of the columns 2) of return/FRR associated	1) Yes 2) No	1) Yes 2) Yes	1) No 2) No	1) Yes 2) No
Trading rules	Support-based metric $support(buy) = \frac{\# rows\ with\ FRR_t \geq T_t}{all\ rows}$ $support(sell) = \frac{\# rows\ with\ FRR_t < T_t}{all\ rows}$ $support(no\ action) = \frac{\# of\ remaining\ rows}{all\ rows}$ The decision (buy, sell or no action) relative to the bicluster is that with the greatest support	Fuzzy rule to find x_{df} Particle swarm optimization algorithm to find β $x_{df} \geq \beta => buy$ $x_{df} < \beta => sell$	Return=1=> buy Return=0=> no action Return=-1=> sell	Majority of 1=> buy Majority of 0=> no action Majority of -1=> sell For each period (short, middle, long)
Testing	No	No	Yes	Yes

Table 7.1.

By using these measures, traders and analysts can effectively evaluate the performance and potential of trading indicators in relation to the trading rules. The return measure provides insights into the profitability of an investment over time, while the FRR compares the closing price with the average price over a defined period, aiding in the assessment of market trends and price movements.

The subsequent table elucidates the distinct approaches used by various authors to derive trading rules (buy, sell, no action) from trading indicators. The initial step is shared by all authors, involving the creation of an input matrix that incorporates the trading indicators and returns. The subsequent step entails data normalization. The third step entails the use of a bicluster algorithm. In most cases, authors calculate the average of the columns (trading indicators and associated return) for each bicluster acquired. In the final step, the trading rules are derived.

Another important aspect is the relation between trading rules and sentiment analysis, which lies in the potential influence of sentiment on market behavior and decision-making. Sentiment analysis involves the analysis of textual data, such as news articles, social media posts and financial reports, to determine the overall sentiment or opinion expressed. Sentiment analysis algorithms use various methods to assess sentiment, including machine learning, statistical analysis and lexicon-based approaches. These algorithms may consider various features such as word choice, sentence structure, context and linguistic patterns to determine the sentiment expressed in the text. The applications of sentiment analysis are diverse and can be found in social media monitoring, customer feedback analysis, brand reputation management, market research and political analysis. By automatically classifying sentiments in large volumes of text, sentiment analysis enables organizations to gain valuable insights and make informed decisions based on public opinion and sentiment trends.

Sentiment analysis can be integrated into trading strategies by incorporating sentiment-related data as an additional input or factor in the decision-making process. For example, positive sentiment toward a particular stock or market sector may indicate potential upward price movement, which could trigger a buy signal according to a trading rule. Conversely, negative sentiment may prompt a sell signal or a decision to refrain from trading.

By considering sentiment analysis alongside other relevant data, traders and investors gain insights into market psychology, crowd sentiment and the impact of news events on market dynamics. This integration aims to capture and respond to market sentiment, thereby improving trading decisions and potentially enhancing returns. Many research papers use investor sentiment to forecast stock prices, exemplified by studies conducted by Li et al. (2014); Pagolu et al. (2016) and

Jing et al. (2021). In addition, Christodoulaki et al. (2002) and Yang et al. (2017) combine trading analysis with sentiment analysis, using genetic programming.

This work proposes the combination of trading indicators with sentiment analysis using biclusters and various sentiment analysis algorithms.

7.2. Fuzzy logic and trading rules

The approach presented in this paper builds upon the work of (Huang et al. 2019b), who used fuzzy logic to identify the value x_{df} that determines whether to buy, sell or take no action. Fuzzy logic is a mathematical approach for reasoning and decision-making in uncertain, imprecise and vague situations. It enables the representation and manipulation of degrees of truth between 0 and 1 accommodating the inherent fuzziness of real-world phenomena. By using linguistic variables (e.g. small, medium, big and large, or NL, NS, PS and PL) and fuzzy sets, it deals with ambiguous information. Fuzzy rules, based on conditional statements using operators like "and", "or" and "not", allow for flexible and approximate reasoning. Fuzzy logic finds applications in control systems, AI, decision-making, pattern recognition and expert systems, providing a valuable tool for modeling and handling complex systems with uncertainty and imprecision.

To classify the technical indicators in small, medium, big and large (Huang et al. 2019b), use fuzzy theory. The membership functions of four fuzzy sets (small, medium, big and large) are Gaussian:

$$\mu_p(X_i) = e^{-\frac{(x_i - \bar{x}_p)^2}{2\sigma_p^2}} \quad with\, p = small, medium, big, large$$

where X_i is the average of the column of the bicluster relative to the technical indicator i. Their parameters, which are not estimated in contrast to Huang et al. (2019a), who estimate them, are:

$$\bar{x}_{small} = 0\ \bar{x}_{medium} = \frac{1}{3}\ \bar{x}_{big} = \frac{2}{3}\ \bar{x}_{large} = 1$$

$$\sigma_{small}^2 = \sigma_{medium}^2 = \sigma_{big}^2 = \sigma_{large}^2 = \frac{1}{36}$$

To classify the FRR in negative large (NL), negative small (NS), positive small (PS) and positive large (PL), Huang et al. (2019b) used four Gaussian membership functions:

$$\mu_w(Y) = e^{-\frac{(y-\bar{y}_w)^2}{2\sigma_w^2}} \quad with\ w = NL, NS, PS, PL$$

where Y is the average of the FRRs linked to the time periods of the bicluster. The parameters of the membership functions are:

$$\bar{y}_{NL} = -3\ \bar{y}_{NS} = -1\ \bar{y}_{PS} = 1\ \bar{y}_{PL} = 3$$

$$\sigma_{NL}^2 = \sigma_{NS}^2 = \sigma_{PS}^2 = \sigma_{PL}^2 = 1$$

They consider the union of the four fuzzy sets (small, medium, big and large), and so the membership function of the union is:

$$\mu_{A_i} = max[\mu_{small}(X_i), \mu_{medium}(X_i), \mu_{big}(X_i), \mu_{large}(X_i)]$$

They also consider the union of the four fuzzy sets (NL, NS, PS, PL), and so the membership function of the union is:

$$\mu_{FRR} = max[\mu_{NL}(Y), \mu_{NS}(Y), \mu_{PS}(Y), \mu_{PL}(Y)]$$

The rule-based system consists of R rules, where in the antecedents, there are the conditions for the n trading indicators X_i, and consequently, there is the FRR:

$$Rule^r: \underbrace{X_1\ is\ A_1^{(r)}\ and\ X_2\ is\ A_2^{(r)}\ and \ldots X_n\ is\ A_n^{(r)}}_{multiple\ conjunctive\ antecedents}\ then\ \underbrace{FRR^{(r)}\ is\ A_{FRR}^{(r)}}_{consequent}$$

The membership function of the multiple conjunction antecedents (which can be seen as the intersection of the n conditions) is:

$$\mu_{A^{(r)}} = \min[\mu_{A_1^{(r)}}(X_1), \mu_{A_2^{(r)}}(X_2), \ldots, \mu_{A_n^{(r)}}(X_n)]$$

Because in the model proposed by Huang et al. (2019b) only four types of A_{FRR} exist (NS, NL, PS, PL), they group the R rules into four clusters and the relative membership function becomes (it is necessary to remember that the rules in the same cluster are linked by "or" operator):

$$\mu_{A_w} = max\ of\ all\ membership\ functions\ \mu_{A^{(r)}}\ with\ consequent\ w$$

with w = NS, NL, PS, PL.

In order to enhance understanding, an example is provided. The starting point is a bicluster, with respective average values for the columns: $I_A = 0.3, I_B = 0.6$ and $FRR = -1.1$. Now, it is necessary to calculate to which subset the values observed of I_A, I_B and FRR belong.

$$\mu_{I_A} = \mu_{A_1} = \max[\mu_{small}(I_A = 0.3), \mu_{medium}(I_A = 0.3), \mu_{big}(I_A = 0.3), \mu_{large}(I_A = 0.3)]$$

$$\mu_{I_B} = \mu_{A_2} = \max[\mu_{small}(I_B = 0.6), \mu_{medium}(I_B = 0.6), \mu_{big}(I_B = 0.6), \mu_{large}(I_B = 0.6)]$$

$$\mu_{FRR} = \max[\mu_{NL}(FRR = -1.1), \mu_{NS}(FRR = -1.1), \mu_{PS}(FRR = -1.1), \mu_{PL}(FRR = -1.1)]$$

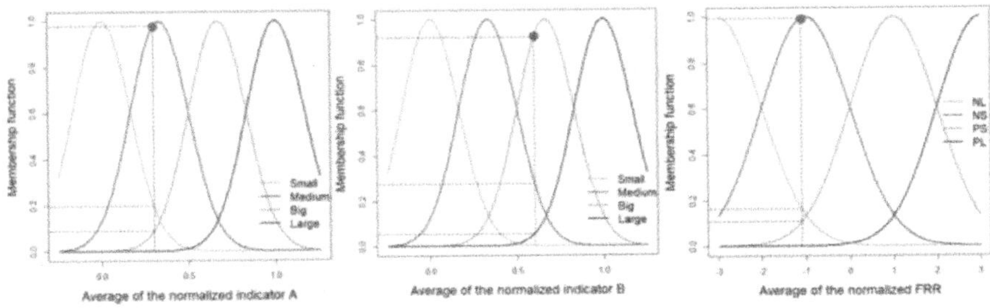

Figure 7.1. *Membership functions for calculating the fuzzy rule. For a color version of this figure, see www.iste.co.uk/dimotikalis/data4.zip*

Based on Figure 7.1, it can be determined that "I_A *is medium*", "I_B *is big*" and "*FRR is NS*". Consequently, the following rule can be formulated:

$$Fuzzy\ rule: If\ I_A\ is\ medium\ and\ I_B\ is\ big\ then\ FRR\ is\ NS$$

Since the conjunction between "I_A *is medium*" and "I_B *is big*" is represented by the logical operator "and", it is necessary to determine the minimum values between the membership functions of these two antecedents:

$$\mu_{Rule} = \mu_{A^{(1)}} = min[\mu_{I_A}(I_A = 0.3), \mu_{I_B}(I_B = 0.6)]$$

Based on Figure 7.2, it can be observed that the minimum value is $\mu_{I_B}(0.6)$, which is used for truncating the membership function of FRR. When there is only one rule, taking in account μ_{Rule}, the truncated membership function of FRR is obtained.

Now this example is expanded to incorporate two rules, including the previous one and an addition rule. The first rule is expressed as follows:

$$Fuzzy\ rule\ 1: If\ I_A\ is\ medium\ and\ I_B\ is\ big\ then\ FRR\ is\ NS$$

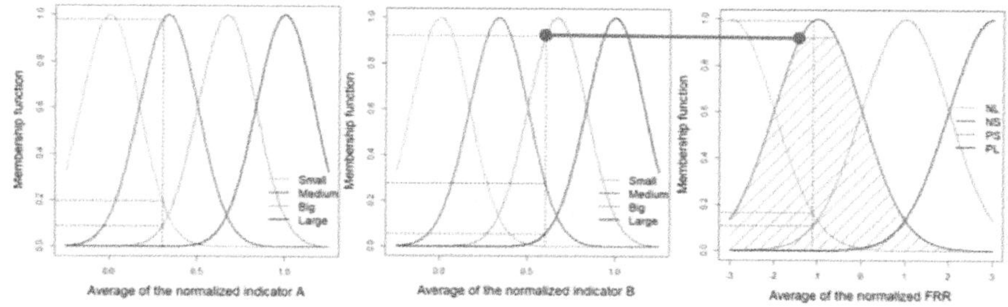

Figure 7.2. *From membership function to truncated function. For a color version of this figure, see www.iste.co.uk/dimotikalis/data4.zip*

To obtain the second rule, the following graph is considered, which displays the membership functions of I_A, I_B and FRR.

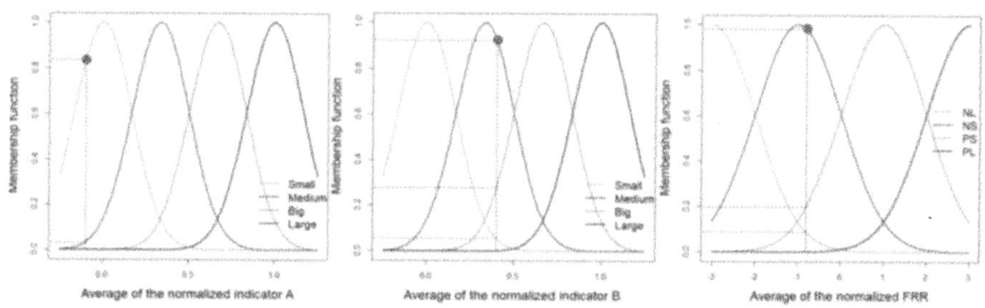

Figure 7.3. *Membership functions for calculating fuzzy rule 2. For a color version of this figure, see www.iste.co.uk/dimotikalis/data4.zip*

Based on the graphs of the membership functions, shown in Figure 7.3, the following rule is derived:

$$Fuzzy\ rule\ 2\text{:}\ If\ I_A\ \ is\ small\ and\ I_B\ is\ medium\ then\ FRR\ is\ NS$$

The aggregation of these two rules is performed due to both having FRR equal to NS. The combined fuzzy rule is as follows:

$$Fuzzy\ rule\text{:}$$

$$If\ I_A\ is\ medium\ and\ I_B\ is\ big\ or\ I_A is\ small\ and\ I_B\ is\ medium$$

$$then\ FRR\ is\ NS$$

Since the two rules are connected by the logical operator "or", the following calculations are made:

$$\mu_{Rule\ 1} = \mu_{A(1)} = min[\mu_{I_A}(I_A = 0.3), \mu_{I_B}(I_B = 0.6)] = 0.9231163$$

$$\mu_{Rule\ 2} = \mu_{A(2)} = min[\mu_{I_A}(I_A = -0.1), \mu_{I_B}(I_B = 0.4)] = 0.8352702$$

$$\mu_{A_{NS}} = \max[\mu_{Rule\ 1}, \mu_{Rule\ 2}] = 0.9231163$$

By using this example, it was demonstrated how it is possible to obtain a truncated result. After finding the truncated result, the defuzzification process is carried out. The purpose of defuzzification is to find a representative crisp value that best represents the fuzzy set or fuzzy membership function. A crisp value refers to a single, specific and definite numerical value without any uncertainty or ambiguity. It is a precise and well-defined number, typically used in contrast to fuzzy values that represent degrees of membership or uncertainty. Crisp values are commonly used in traditional mathematics and computations, where precise values are required. To defuzzify these results, Huang et al. (2019b) use the weighted average method:

$$x_{df} = \frac{\sum_{i=1}^{4} \mu_i \bar{y}_i}{\sum_{i=1}^{4} \mu_i}$$

where, according to the method, $\bar{y}_i = \bar{y}_w$ is the center value of each membership function $\mu_i = \mu_w(Y)$. The weighted average method in fuzzy logic can be seen as a form of statistical mean. In this method, each fuzzy set or membership function is assigned a weight, and the crisp output is obtained by calculating the weighted average of the fuzzy sets. Returning to the previous example, the steps performed for the NS subset are repeated for the other subsets of FRR, namely NL, PL and PS. As a result, four truncated values are obtained, as shown in Figure 7.4.

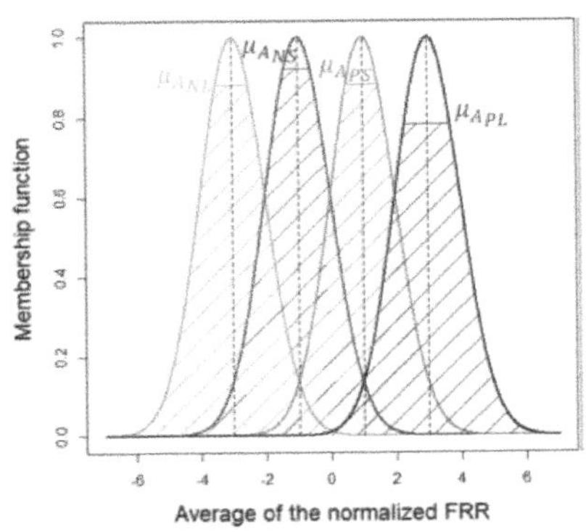

Figure 7.4. *Truncated membership function. For a color version of this figure, see www.iste.co.uk/dimotikalis/data4.zip*

The defuzzification can now be performed using the weighted average method:

$$x_{df} = \frac{\sum_{i=1}^{4} \mu_i \bar{y_i}}{\sum_{i=1}^{4} \mu_i} = \frac{-3\,\mu_{NL} - 1\mu_{NS} + \mu_{PS} + 3\mu_{PL}}{\mu_{NL} + \mu_{NS} + \mu_{PS} + \mu_{PL}}$$

Therefore, an example was provided to explain how the fuzzy method obtains the value x_{df}. To decide if x_{df} is a buy signal or a sell signal, Huang et al. (2019b) use the parameter β:

– if $x_{df} \geq \beta$, then a buy signal;

– if $x_{df} < \beta$, then a sell signal.

The parameter β is calculated using the particle swarm optimization (PSO) algorithm, which is a computational optimization algorithm inspired by the social behavior of bird flocking or fish schooling. PSO is a population-based stochastic search algorithm that aims to find the optimal solution by iteratively improving a candidate solution. In PSO, a population of potential solutions, called particles, move through the search space to find the best solution. Each particle represents a potential solution and has a position and velocity in the search space. The position of a particle represents a candidate solution, and the velocity determines the direction and speed of its movement. The algorithm begins by initializing a population of particles randomly distributed throughout the search space. Each particle is associated with two vectors: the personal best (pbest), which is the best position the particle has encountered so far, and the global best (gbest), which represents the best position found by any particle in the entire population. In each iteration, the particles adjust their velocity based on their current position, personal best and global best. The velocity update equation is influenced by two main factors: cognitive component and social component. The cognitive component enables a particle to remember its own best position, while the social component allows a particle to learn from the best position discovered by other particles in the population. By updating the velocity, the particles move toward promising regions of the search space. Then, their positions are updated based on the new velocity. This process continues iteratively until a termination condition is met, such as reaching a maximum number of iterations or achieving a satisfactory solution. The performance of PSO is evaluated by a fitness function that measures the quality of a candidate solution. The fitness function is problem-specific and reflects the objective of the optimization problem being solved. The objective function in the model proposed by Huang et al. (2019b) is given by:

$$\frac{n_{buy}\,(\beta) + n_{sell}\,(\beta)}{n_{total}\,(\beta)}$$

where n_{buy} and n_{sell} respectively represent the number of correct predicted buy points or sell points. To control the correct prediction, they compare the closing price to time t (cp_t) with the mean of the closing price of the following trading days acp_t. If $cp_t < acp_t$ there is a buy point; if otherwise, a sell point.

7.3. Sentiment analysis, trading indicators and fuzzy rules

In order to enhance the method proposed by Huang et al. (2019b), the integration of the sentiment analysis into the approach is suggested. To accomplish this, two columns, which consider tweets, are included in the input matrix for biclustering.

	Indicator 1	Indicator 2	...	Indicator n	Indicator tweets 1	Indicator tweets 2	FRR
Day 1							
Day 2							
⋮							
Day D							

Table 7.2. *New input matrix*

To generate an indicator for tweets, a modified version of the methodology introduced by Yang et al. (2017) is used. Unlike the approach used by Yang et al. (2017), the calculation of message scores involves the use of the VADER algorithm (Hutto and Gilbert 2014) and LIWC. These methods have been commonly used in financial research papers (e.g. Kirange and Deshmukh (2016); Cristescu et al. (2022).

The first step is the computation of the daily user sentiment, representing the average score of all messages authored by user i within a given day. The calculation is performed as follows:

$$S_{user,m}(i\,,t,m) = \frac{\sum_{j=1}^{J} Score_{j,m}}{J}$$

where $Score_{j,m}$ is calculated by two different methods (m=VADER, LIWC) and J is the number of tweets written by user i on day t.

VADER is a highly effective tool specifically designed for sentiment analysis in social media texts. It uses a combination of lexical and grammatical heuristics along with a pre-constructed sentiment lexicon. This tool is proficient in handling sentiment intensity and context, providing a sentiment polarity score that ranges from -1 to 1, with 0 indicating neutrality. In contrast, LIWC, developed by Pennebaker et al. (2001, 2015), is a text analysis software that focuses on analyzing and categorizing the linguistic and psychological aspects of text using a predefined dictionary of words. LIWC offers valuable insights into various dimensions, including psychological and emotional states, cognitive processes, and the linguistic style used by the author. While VADER primarily emphasizes sentiment analysis, LIWC goes beyond that by identifying and categorizing a wide range of linguistic and psychological features within the text. These include pronouns, verb tense, cognitive processes, social and personal concerns and linguistic styles used by the author.

In summary, VADER and LIWC are both valuable tools in the realm of text analysis, but with different emphases. VADER specializes in sentiment analysis, providing polarity scores, while LIWC offers comprehensive insights into linguistic and psychological aspects. In addition, the determination of the influence of a user within the financial community involves the use of a centrality score. This score helps assess the significance and impact of an individual in the financial domain, considering various factors such as network connections, interactions and contributions within the community (Yang et al. 2017). The centrality score is used to gauge the influence of a user within the financial community, taking into account their network connections and contributions, such that only the relevant users are considered. The daily tweets sentiment score on day t is:

$$S_{tweets}(t,m) = \frac{\sum_{i=1}^{U} \omega_i S_{user,m}(i,t,m)}{U}$$

where U is the number of users, ω_i is the centrality score and $m = VADER, LIWC$. To build the technical indicator of tweets, the smoothing moving average is used:

$$SMA_{tweets}(t,e,m) = \frac{\sum_{s=t-e}^{t-1} S_{tweets}(i,m)}{e}$$

Upon obtaining the new input matrix, it serves as the input for the algorithm, as shown in Figure 7.5.

The dataset used is divided into two parts: input matrix, used to build the algorithm, and testing set, used for testing its performance. The input matrix is segmented into two parts: training set (technical indicators, tweets indicators and FRR), serving as the precise input matrix for biclustering and deriving fuzzy rules and validation set (technical indicators and tweets indicators), used for calculating x_{df}. Each day, a different x_{df} is computed using the rules obtained by training set. The validation set (technical indicators, tweets indicators, cp, and acp) is also used in the calculation of β. The values cp and acp are used to determine $n_{buy}(\beta)$ and $n_{sell}(\beta)$ of the objective function of the PSO algorithm.

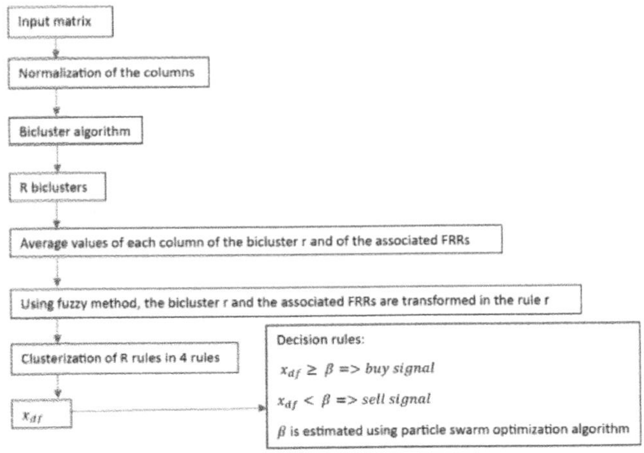

Figure 7.5. *New algorithm*

7.4. Conclusion

Bicluster and trading rules offer numerous benefits in financial markets, including market segmentation, pattern recognition, adaptive trading strategies, risk management and portfolio diversification. By using bicluster analysis, traders and investors can identify distinct market segments, identify recurring patterns, develop adaptive trading strategies, assess and mitigate risks, allocate resources strategically and optimize risk-adjusted returns. In addition, bicluster analysis helps identify low-correlation trading rules, constructing well-diversified portfolios and reducing risk and enhancing returns. By harnessing the power of bicluster analysis, traders and investors can improve their decision-making processes, improve risk management, and achieve consistent and favorable outcomes in the dynamic world of financial markets.

For this reason, many authors have proposed different methods to consider bicluster and trading rules together. However, they do not consider investors' sentiment, which is another important factor to understand the pattern of the market. To enhance the existing model proposed by Huang et al. (2019b), this study proposes the incorporation of sentiment analysis to measure investors' sentiment. By integrating sentiment analysis into the model, it offers a more comprehensive and precise analysis of the market. This addition contributes to a deeper understanding of market dynamics and investor behavior. The use is very easy after the algorithm has calculated the fuzzy rules and the parameter β.

To find out whether to sell or buy a stock on a given day, the investors consider the technical indicators and the tweets indicators of that given day and by the fuzzy rules they determine x_{df}. If $x_{df} < \beta$ they sell; otherwise, they buy.

7.5. References

Cheng, Y. and Church, G.M. (2000). Biclustering of expression data. In *ISMB*, 8(2000), 93–103.

Christodoulaki, E., Kampouridis, M., Kanellopoulos, P. (2002). Technical and sentiment analysis in financial forecasting with genetic programming. *2022 IEEE Symposium on Computational Intelligence for Financial Engineering and Economics (CIFEr)*, 1–8.

Cristescu, M.P., Nerisanu, R.A., Mara, D.A., Oprea, S.V. (2022). Using market news sentiment analysis for stock market prediction. *Mathematics*, 10(22), 4255.

Dolnicar, S., Kaiser, S., Lazarevski, K., Leisch, F. (2012). Biclustering: Overcoming data dimensionality problems in market segmentation. *Journal of Travel Research*, 51(1), 41–49.

Garbuio, M. and Gheno, G. (2021). An algorithm for designing value propositions in the IoT space: Addressing the challenges of selecting the initial class in reference class forecasting. *IEEE Transactions on Engineering Management*, 99, 1–12.

Huang, Q., Wang, T., Tao, D., Li, X. (2014). Biclustering learning of trading rules. *IEEE Transactions on Cybernetics*, 45(10), 2287–2298.

Huang, Q., Hu, B., Zhang, F. (2019a). Evolutionary optimized fuzzy reasoning with mined diagnostic patterns for classification of breast tumors in ultrasound. *Information Sciences*, 502, 525–536.

Huang, Q., Yang, J., Feng, X., Liew, A.W.C., Li, X. (2019b). Automated trading point forecasting based on bicluster mining and fuzzy inference. *IEEE Transactions on Fuzzy Systems*, 28(2), 259–272.

Hutto, C. and Gilbert, E. (2014). Vader: A parsimonious rule-based model for sentiment analysis of social media text. *Proceedings of the International AAAI Conference on Web and Social Media*, 8(1), 216–225.

Jing, N., Wu, Z., Wang, H. (2021). A hybrid model integrating deep learning with investor sentiment analysis for stock price prediction. *Expert Systems with Applications*, 178, 115019.

Kirange, D.K. and Deshmukh, R.R. (2016). Sentiment analysis of news headlines for stock price prediction. Composoft. *An International Journal of Advanced Computer Technology*, 5(3), 2080–2084.

Li, X., Xie, H., Chen, L., Wang, J., Deng, X. (2014). News impact on stock price return via sentiment analysis. *Knowledge-Based Systems*, 69, 14–23.

Pagolu, V.S., Reddy, K.N., Panda, G., Majhi, B. (2016). Sentiment analysis of Twitter data for predicting stock market movements. *2016 International Conference on Signal Processing, Communication, Power and Embedded System (SCOPES)*, 1345–1350. IEEE.

Pennebaker, J.W., Francis, M.E., Booth, R.J. (2001). *Linguistic Inquiry and Word Count: LIWC 2001*. Lawrence Erlbaum Associates, Mahwah.

Pennebaker, J.W., Boyd, R.L., Jordan, K., Blackburn, K. (2015). The development and psychometric properties of LIWC2015. LIWC2015 Development Manual, The University of Texas at Austin.

Sun, J., Huang, Q., Li, X. (2009). Determination of temporal stock investment styles via biclustering trading patterns. *Cognitive Computation*, 11, 799–808.

Xue, Y., Liu, Z., Luo, J., Ma, Z., Zhang, M., Hu, X., Kuang, Q. (2015). Stock market trading rules discovery based on biclustering method. *Mathematical Problems in Engineering*. doi: 10.1155/2015/849286.

Yang, S.Y., Mo, S.Y.K., Liu, A., Kirilenko, A.A. (2017). Genetic programming optimization for a sentiment feedback strength based trading strategy. *Neurocomputing*, 264, 29–41.

8

A Flexible Generalization of the Latent Dirichlet Allocation

Text modeling techniques have been used in a variety of applications in the past, among which is the analysis of documents for latent topics detection. One of the most commonly used tools for topic modeling is the latent Dirichlet allocation (LDA). The LDA allows us to obtain a representation of a document in terms of latent topic structure. The stiffness of the topic prior to distribution, i.e. the Dirichlet, is one of the main limitations of this approach. To overcome this restriction, we take advantage of a generalization of the Dirichlet distribution, the so-called flexible Dirichlet (FD). The FD distribution still maintains some appealing properties of the Dirichlet distribution, for example, interpretability, as well as conjugacy to the multinomial model, while the flexibility is guaranteed by the enriched parameterization. This work proposes a collapsed Gibbs sampling estimation procedure for obtaining estimates of the relevant quantities. The performances of the new model are illustrated through extensive simulation studies.

8.1. Introduction

In the last few decades, topic modeling techniques have grown in interest due to their increasing variety of applications in several fields, such as genomics, spam filters, semantic analysis and social media. In all of these applications, the main goal is to provide representations of text documents in terms of latent topic distributions. Therefore, text modeling approaches can help to identify the main subjects of a text in terms of latent semantic topics and their relevance within a document. One of the most frequently implemented techniques for textual data is the latent Dirichlet allocation Latent Dirichlet Allocation (LDA) (Blei et al. 2003). The LDA is a generative probabilistic model composed of a three-level hierarchical Bayesian structure, where documents are represented as random mixtures over latent topics. In addition, each topic has its own distribution over a set of words $\mathcal{V}$, i.e. the vocabulary.

Chapter written by Alice GIAMPINO, Roberto ASCARI and Sonia MIGLIORATI.

The aforementioned approach further assumes that both topics and words are randomly drawn from multinomial distributions, whose probability vectors are Dirichlet-distributed. However, even though the Dirichlet distribution has many attractive mathematical properties, such as easy tractability, conjugacy to the multinomial model, and simple interpretation of its parameters, it is also known to have some limitations. The main issue is related to the stiffness of its covariance matrix, whose elements are strictly proportional to elements of the barycenter, and the off-diagonal entries can only take negative values. Blei and Lafferty (2007) introduced the correlated topic model (CTM) to enable the presence of a positive correlation between topics. Nonetheless, the logistic normal distribution, used as distribution for the multinomial probability parameters once they have been mapped from the Euclidean space to the simplex, poses a significant challenge to parameter interpretation due to the log-ratio transformation, which allows the model to be specified on the real number space.

Notwithstanding the previously mentioned issues concerning both LDA and CTM, a solution is provided by a generalization of the Dirichlet distribution, the so-called flexible Dirichlet flexible Dirichlet (FD) distribution (Ongaro and Migliorati 2013; Migliorati et al. 2017). The FD is specified directly on the simplex, and it exhibits many appealing properties inherited from the Dirichlet one, such as interpretability, as well as conjugacy to the multinomial model. The benefit of using the FD distribution is due to its enriched parameterization, which guarantees more flexibility in the covariance matrix. As a special case of the FD, it is possible to recover the classic Dirichlet distribution by a suitable choice of its parameters.

In this work, we propose a new model called flexible LDA (FLDA) to find the latent structure of topics over a set of D documents. The focal point of this chapter is to resort to the FD distribution instead of the Dirichlet within the LDA approach. This allows us to model positive correlations as in the CTM, although preserving the interpretability of the LDA. To this end, we propose a collapsed Gibbs sampling (CGS) algorithm for the estimation of the relevant FLDA parameters and find relevant insights into topic distributions over documents.

In the next section, we describe the main models. In particular, we start by presenting the considered distributions on the simplex, such as the Dirichlet and the FD. Then, in section 8.3, we introduce latent topic models with a focus on the LDA and the FLDA. In section 8.4, we describe the main sampling schemes and estimation procedures used for both of the latent topic models presented in the previous section. The performances of the new FLDA model are shown in section 8.5 through some extensive simulation studies.

8.2. Distributions on the simplex

In this section, we define some distributions defined on the T-part simplex, i.e.

$$\mathcal{S}^T = \left\{ \mathbf{x} = (x_1, \ldots, x_T)^\intercal : x_t > 0, \sum_{t=1}^{T} x_t = 1 \right\}.$$

The most popular distribution on $\mathcal{S}^T$ is the Dirichlet, which is characterized by the following probability density function (p.d.f.):

$$\text{Dir}(\mathbf{x}; \boldsymbol{\alpha}) = \frac{\Gamma(\alpha^+)}{\prod_{t=1}^{T} \Gamma(\alpha_t)} \prod_{t=1}^{T} x_t^{\alpha_t - 1}, \qquad [8.1]$$

where $\boldsymbol{\alpha} = (\alpha_1, \ldots, \alpha_T)^\intercal \in \mathbb{R}_+^T$ and $\alpha^+ = \sum_{t=1}^{T} \alpha_t$. The Dirichlet distribution has many relevant statistical properties, including the conjugacy to the multinomial/categorical scheme, which makes it a key prior distribution in a Bayesian framework. Nonetheless, it is commonly known that it deserves a rigid parameterization to its covariance matrix. Indeed, if a random vector $\mathbf{X} \in \mathcal{S}^T$ is Dirichlet distributed (i.e. $\mathbf{X} \sim \text{Dir}(\boldsymbol{\alpha})$), then its mean vector and the elements of its covariance matrix are equal to

$$\mathbb{E}[X_t] = \mu_t = \frac{\alpha_t}{\alpha^+},$$

$$\text{Var}(X_t) = \frac{\mu_t(1 - \mu_t)}{\alpha^+ + 1},$$

$$\text{Cov}(X_t, X_l) = -\frac{\mu_t \mu_l}{\alpha^+ + 1}$$

$(t, l = 1, \ldots, T; t \neq l)$. Inspecting the above equations, it is easy to note that if two elements of $\mathbf{X}$, let us say X_t and X_l, have the same expected value, then they are forced to have the same variance. Furthermore, covariances are strictly proportional to the product of the corresponding expectations and they can take only negative values. The stiffness of this covariance matrix is related to the fact that, once the mean vector $\boldsymbol{\alpha}/\alpha^+$ has been fixed, there is just a single parameter (i.e. α^+) to model the entire covariance matrix. Some alternatives and generalizations of the Dirichlet distribution have been included in the statistical literature, among which is the FD (Ongaro and Migliorati 2013; Migliorati et al. 2017).

The FD is a distribution defined on $\mathcal{S}^T$ and it is characterized by the following p.d.f.:

$$\text{FD}(\mathbf{x}; \boldsymbol{\alpha}, \tau, \mathbf{p}) = \frac{\Gamma(\alpha^+ + \tau)}{\prod_{t=1}^{T} \Gamma(\alpha_t)} \left(\prod_{t=1}^{T} x_t^{\alpha_t - 1} \right) \sum_{i=1}^{T} p_i \frac{\Gamma(\alpha_i)}{\Gamma(\alpha_i + \tau)} x_i^{\tau}, \qquad [8.2]$$

where $\mathbf{p} \in \mathcal{S}^T$ is the vector of mixing weights, $\boldsymbol{\alpha} \in \mathbb{R}_+^T$, $\alpha^+ = \sum_{t=1}^T \alpha_t$ and $\tau > 0$. The FD also allows for a representation as a (structured) finite mixture of Dirichlet distributions, i.e:

$$\mathrm{FD}(\mathbf{x}; \boldsymbol{\alpha}, \tau, \mathbf{p}) = \sum_{t=1}^{T} p_t \mathrm{Dir}(\mathbf{x}; \boldsymbol{\alpha} + \tau \mathbf{e}_t), \quad [8.3]$$

where $\mathbf{e}_t$ is the null vector except for the t-th element which is equal to 1 (i.e. $\mathbf{e}_t$ is one of the vertices of the simplex). It is also noteworthy to mention that the FD includes the Dirichlet distribution as a special case: equation [8.2] coincides with equation [8.1] if $\tau = 1$ and $p_t = \alpha_t/\alpha^+$ for $t = 1, \dots, T$.

The FD distribution is characterized by D additional parameters with respect to the Dirichlet (i.e. $D - 1$ unique elements in $\mathbf{p}$ and τ). As a result, the FD allows for a more flexible modelization of the covariance matrix. Indeed, if $\mathbf{X} \sim \mathrm{FD}(\boldsymbol{\alpha}, \tau, \mathbf{p})$, then the following expressions hold for its first two-order moments:

$$\mathbb{E}\left[X_t\right] = \mu_t = \frac{\alpha_t + \tau p_t}{\alpha^+ + \tau},$$

$$\mathrm{Var}\left(X_t\right) = \frac{\mu_t(1 - \mu_t)}{\alpha^+ + \tau + 1} + \frac{\tau^2 p_t(1 - p_t)}{(\alpha^+ + \tau)(\alpha^+ + \tau + 1)},$$

$$\mathrm{Cov}\left(X_t, X_l\right) = -\frac{\mu_t \mu_l}{\alpha^+ + \tau + 1} - \frac{\tau^2 p_t p_l}{(\alpha^+ + \tau)(\alpha^+ + \tau + 1)}$$

$(t, l = 1, \dots, T; t \neq l)$.

To better grasp the mixture structure of the FD, we can inspect the form of its component-specific barycenters $\boldsymbol{\lambda}_1, \dots, \boldsymbol{\lambda}_T$:

$$\boldsymbol{\lambda}_t = (1 - \delta)\boldsymbol{\alpha}/\alpha^+ + \delta \mathbf{e}_t, \quad \text{where } \delta = \frac{\tau}{\alpha^+ + \tau}. \quad [8.4]$$

From equation [8.4], $\boldsymbol{\lambda}_t$ can be expressed as a weighted average of the vector $\bar{\boldsymbol{\alpha}} = \boldsymbol{\alpha}/\alpha^+$ and the simplex vertex $\mathbf{e}_t$ with a weight depending on τ. Therefore, the vector $\bar{\boldsymbol{\alpha}}$ can be thought of as a "common" barycenter. Figure 8.1 shows the component-specific barycenters' behavior by means of ternary diagrams, which are equilateral triangles that allow for a convenient and common representation of three-part simplex elements (see Aitchison 2003). Specifically, by joining the $\boldsymbol{\lambda}_t$'s (red triangles) with a segment, an equilateral triangle with edges parallel to the simplex's edges is obtained.

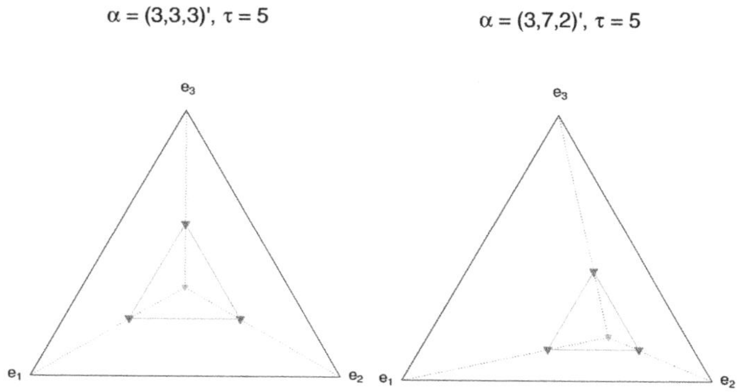

Figure 8.1. *Ternary diagrams showing the FD's mixture structure. Green triangles represent the common barycenter $\bar{\alpha}$, while red triangles represent component-specific mean vectors $\boldsymbol{\lambda}_t$. Left: equal α_t values. Right: different α_t values. For a color version of this figure, see www.iste.co.uk/dimotikalis/data4.zip*

8.3. Latent topic models

In the following, we consider a collection $\mathcal{C}$ of D text documents, commonly referred to as a "corpus". The d-th document can be thought of as a sequence of N_d words, i.e. $\boldsymbol{w}_d = (w_{d,1}, \dots, w_{d,N_d})^\intercal$, where $w_{d,n}$ represents the n-th word in the d-th document, $d = 1, \dots, D$ and $n = 1, \dots, N_d$. Words in the corpus can be indexed by the set $\mathcal{V} = \{1, \dots, V\}$, which represents a "vocabulary" formed by V unique terms.

The topic modeling techniques we will consider assume that each word forming a document is generated according to one among T possible topics. As a result, the d-th document can be expressed as a probability distribution $\boldsymbol{\theta}_d$ over topics $\{1, \dots, T\}$. For example, $\boldsymbol{\theta}_1 = (0.2, 0.3, 0.5)^\intercal$ means that each word forming the first document is generated from topic 1 with a probability of 0.2, from topic 2 with a probability of 0.3 and from topic 3 with a probability of 0.5.

Similarly, the t-th topic is represented as a probability distribution $\boldsymbol{\phi}_t$ over the vocabulary $\mathcal{V}$, $t = 1, \dots, T$. Each topic assigns a (generally different) probability to each word in the vocabulary, leading to topics characterized by different subsets of most-probable words. For example, given $\boldsymbol{\phi}_1 = (0.2, 0.1, 0.06, 0.5, 0.14)^\intercal$ and $\boldsymbol{\phi}_2 = (0.05, 0.1, 0.2, 0.4, 0.25)^\intercal$, topics 1 and 2 assign probability equal to 0.2 and 0.05 to the first word of the vocabulary, respectively.

Therefore, documents and topics can be depicted as points in the T-part ($\mathcal{S}^T$) and V-part simplices ($\mathcal{S}^V$), respectively. This is an easy and compact way to summarize a corpus of text data. In the following, we will refer to the sets of documents and topics as $\Theta = \{\boldsymbol{\theta}_1, \dots, \boldsymbol{\theta}_D\}$ and $\Phi = \{\boldsymbol{\phi}_1, \dots, \boldsymbol{\phi}_T\}$, respectively.

In this work, we restrict our attention to two different topic modeling techniques: the LDA and the FLDA. Under the LDA model (Blei et al. 2003), once the topics $\boldsymbol{\phi}_1, \ldots, \boldsymbol{\phi}_T$ have been drawn (i.i.d. from a Dir($\boldsymbol{\beta}$), with $\boldsymbol{\beta}$ representing a V-dimensional vector with positive elements), the generative process of the d-th document in a corpus is composed of the following steps:

(i) generate the topic distribution $\boldsymbol{\theta}_d \sim \text{Dir}(\boldsymbol{\alpha})$;

(ii) for each word $w_{d,n}$, $n = 1, \ldots, N_d$:
1) generate a topic $z_{d,n}$ from a $Z_{d,n} \sim \text{Categorical}(\boldsymbol{\theta}_d)$;

2) generate a word $w_{d,n}$ from $W_{d,n}|Z_{d,n} = z_{d,n} \sim \text{Categorical}(\boldsymbol{\phi}_{z_{d,n}})$.

In the above generating scheme, the random variable $Z_{d,n}$ defines a latent (i.e. unobservable) topic label for the n-th word. Since the LDA assumes that the $\boldsymbol{\theta}_d$'s and the $\boldsymbol{\phi}_t$'s are Dirichlet-distributed, this technique shares the same limitations discussed in section 8.2. In particular, the distribution for the topic proportions may suffer from the stiffness of Dirichlet's covariance matrix.

We propose an alternative specification for latent topic models, which is given by using the FD as distribution for each element $\boldsymbol{\theta}_d \in \Theta$, while maintaining the Dirichlet prior for topics $\boldsymbol{\phi}_t \in \Phi$. This framework allows us to define the FLDA as a generalization of the classical LDA model, by assuming that

$$\boldsymbol{\phi}_t \sim \text{Dir}(\boldsymbol{\beta}) \quad \text{and} \quad \boldsymbol{\theta}_d \sim \text{FD}(\boldsymbol{\alpha}, \tau, \mathbf{p}).$$

It is possible to prove that the FD is conjugate to the multinomial/categorical scheme, thus

$$\boldsymbol{\theta}_d|\mathbf{z}, \mathcal{C}, \boldsymbol{\alpha}, \tau, \mathbf{p} \sim FD\left(\boldsymbol{\alpha} + \mathbf{c}_d, \tau, \mathbf{p}_d^*/p_d^{*+}\right), \quad \mathbf{c}_d = (c_{1,d,\cdot}, \ldots, c_{T,d,\cdot})^\intercal, \qquad [8.5]$$

where $c_{t,d,\cdot}$ represents the number of words generated by topic t in document d, $p_d^{*+} = \sum_{t=1}^{T} p_{d,t}^*$, and the generic element of $\mathbf{p}_d^* = \left(p_{d,1}^*, \ldots, p_{d,T}^*\right)^\intercal$ is given by

$$p_{d,t}^* = p_t \frac{(\alpha_t + \tau)^{[c_{t,d,\cdot}]}}{(\alpha_t)^{[c_{t,d,\cdot}]}}, \qquad t = 1, \ldots, T, \qquad [8.6]$$

with $x^{[n]} = x(x+1) \cdot \cdots \cdot (x+n-1)$ denoting the rising factorial function.

8.4. Collapsed Gibbs sampling

The estimation procedure for the parameters involved in the LDA and FLDA models (i.e. the elements in Θ and Φ) cannot be fulfilled by using standard techniques such as the maximum likelihood, due to the presence of the topic labels, which are latent variables complicating the complete-data likelihood function. Blei et al. (2003) provided an alternative variational inference approach for estimating the quantities of interest. However, this approach requires some challenging equations to be computed, especially for the FLDA model; and above all, it gives only approximate solutions.

Therefore, we prefer an approach based on Markov Chain Monte Carlo (MCMC) techniques, such as the CGS. Here, the basic idea is to generate one parameter at a time, by drawing it from its full conditional distribution. The main difference with respect to a standard Gibbs sampler is that full conditionals are computed by marginalizing some parameters out. The estimates of the dropped parameters are computed by means of closed-form expressions (e.g. by taking advantage of some conjugacy properties). Griffiths and Steyvers (2004) proposed a CGS approach to estimate the parameters of the LDA model by computing the full conditionals of the topic labels $Z_{d,n}$ and by deriving a closed-form expression for estimates of the elements in Θ and Φ. To sketch the CGS, it is useful to define some quantities:

– $c_{t,d,w} = \sum_{n=1}^{N_d} \mathbb{I}(z_{d,n} = t,\ w_{d,n} = w)$: number of times that word w is assigned to topic t in document d;

– $c_{t,d,\cdot} = \sum_{v=1}^{V} c_{t,d,v}$: number of words assigned to topic t in document d;

– $c_{t,\cdot,w} = \sum_{d=1}^{D} c_{t,d,w}$: number of times word w is assigned to topic t across documents;

– $c_{t,\cdot,\cdot} = \sum_{v=1}^{V} c_{t,\cdot,v}$: the total number of words assigned to topic t.

In the LDA model, the full conditional distribution for $Z_{d,n}$, namely the probability that $w_{d,n}$ is assigned to topic t ($t = 1, \ldots, T$) given all the other topic assignments $\mathbf{z}_{-(d,n)}$, takes the following form:

$$p(t) = p\left(Z_{d,n} = t|\mathbf{z}_{-(d,n)}, C, \boldsymbol{\alpha}, \boldsymbol{\beta}\right) \propto \frac{\left(\alpha_t + c^{-}_{t,d,\cdot}\right)\left(\beta_{w_{d,n}} + c^{-}_{t,\cdot,w_{d,n}}\right)}{\left(\beta^{+} + c^{-}_{t,\cdot,\cdot}\right)} \qquad [8.7]$$

($t = 1, \ldots, T$), where the notation c^{-} refers to the previously defined counts excluding the n-th word of document d, and $w_{d,n}$ indicates which term of the vocabulary is associated with the n-th word in document d. We can sample from these full conditionals by simply generating values from a discrete random variable with support $\{1, 2, \ldots, T\}$ and probability mass function (p.m.f.) given by [8.7].

Thanks to the conjugacy property of the Dirichlet to the multinomial/categorical sampling, we can derive the following posterior expressions:

$$\boldsymbol{\theta}_d|\mathbf{z}, \mathcal{C}, \boldsymbol{\alpha} \sim Dir(\boldsymbol{\alpha} + \mathbf{c}_d), \quad \mathbf{c}_d = (c_{1,d,\cdot}, \ldots, c_{T,d,\cdot})^{\intercal}; \tag{8.8}$$

$$\boldsymbol{\phi}_t|\mathbf{z}, \mathcal{C}, \boldsymbol{\beta} \sim Dir(\boldsymbol{\beta} + \mathbf{c}_t), \quad \mathbf{c}_t = (c_{t,\cdot,1}, \ldots, c_{t,\cdot,V})^{\intercal}. \tag{8.9}$$

These posteriors allow estimating the elements in Θ and Φ. Indeed, by having a sample of size B for the topic labels, namely $\mathbf{z}^{(b)}$, $b = 1, \ldots, B$, we can estimate $\boldsymbol{\theta}_d$ and $\boldsymbol{\phi}_t$ as the posterior mean of [8.8] and [8.9], respectively:

$$\hat{\boldsymbol{\theta}}_d^{(b)} = \frac{\boldsymbol{\alpha} + \mathbf{c}_d^{(b)}}{\alpha^+ + N_d}, \qquad \hat{\boldsymbol{\phi}}_t^{(b)} = \frac{\boldsymbol{\beta} + \mathbf{c}_t^{(b)}}{\beta^+ + c_{t,\cdot,\cdot}^{(b)}}.$$

The CGS scheme for the FLDA is similar to the previous LDA scheme. Indeed, the main difference is related to the expression of the full conditionals, which varies according to the FD distribution imposed on $\boldsymbol{\theta}_d$. It is possible to prove that

$$p(t) = p(Z_{d,n} = t|\mathbf{z}_{-(d,n)}, \mathcal{C}, \boldsymbol{\alpha}, \tau, \mathbf{p}, \boldsymbol{\beta}) \propto$$

$$\propto \frac{\left(\alpha_t + c^-_{t,d,\cdot}\right)\left(\beta_{v_{d,n}} + c^-_{t,\cdot,w_{d,n}}\right)}{\left(\beta^+ + c^-_{t,\cdot,\cdot}\right)} \cdot \left\{\sum_{h=1}^{T} p^*_{d,h} + p^*_{d,t}\left(\frac{\tau_t}{\alpha_t + c^-_{t,d,\cdot}}\right)\right\}, \tag{8.10}$$

$t = 1, \ldots, T$, where $p^*_{d,t}$ is defined as in equation [8.6]. According to the posterior distribution of $\boldsymbol{\theta}_d$ reported in [8.5], an estimate is obtained by computing its posterior mean according to the FD distribution, i.e.

$$\hat{\boldsymbol{\theta}}_d^{(b)} = \frac{\boldsymbol{\alpha} + \mathbf{c}_d^{(b)} + \tau \mathbf{p}_d^{*(b)} / p_+^{(b)}}{\alpha^+ + \tau + N_d}.$$

Finally, the CGS for both the LDA and the FLDA models can be summarized by the following algorithm:

1. Initialize the vector **z** (randomly) and compute the counts $c_{t,d,v}$.
2. For $b = 1, \ldots, B$:

   – For each word in the corpus:
     - sample a new topic $z_{d,n}^{(b)}$ for $w_{d,n}$ from $p(z)$;
     - update the counts $c_{t,d,v}$.

   – Use $\mathbf{z}^{(b)}$ to compute the estimates $\hat{\boldsymbol{\theta}}_d^{(b)}$ and $\hat{\boldsymbol{\phi}}_t^{(b)}$.

where the full conditionals $p(t)$ are given by [8.7] for the LDA and by [8.10) for the FLDA, respectively.

8.5. Simulation study

In this section, we compare the LDA and the FLDA models through a simulation study involving three distinct corpus-generating schemes. All the considered scenarios share the number of topics and the dimension of the corpus. Indeed, we consider corpora containing $D = 250$ documents with an average length of $\varepsilon = 600$ words. Documents have been populated by considering an artificial vocabulary of $V = 300$ unique words, which can be generated according to $T = 3$ latent topics.

The three simulating scenarios differ in the corpus-generating mechanism. In the first scenario, we generate each element $\boldsymbol{\theta}_d \in \Theta$ from a Dirichlet distribution with parameter $\boldsymbol{\alpha} = (10, 25, 15)^\intercal$. In the second scenario, each $\boldsymbol{\theta}_d$ is generated from an FD with parameters $\boldsymbol{\alpha} = (10, 25, 15)^\intercal, \mathbf{p} = (0.5, 0.3, 0.2)^\intercal$ and $\tau = 30$. Finally, we consider a logistic-normal with parameters $\boldsymbol{\mu} = (-2, 3)^\intercal$ and $\boldsymbol{\Sigma} = \begin{bmatrix} 2 & 1 \\ 1 & 6 \end{bmatrix}$ as distribution for generating each $\boldsymbol{\theta}_d$ in the third scenario. Therefore, the underlying true data-generating mechanisms are the LDA (first scenario), the FLDA (second scenario) and the CTM (third scenario) models.

Figure 8.2 shows the generated vectors $\boldsymbol{\theta}_1^*, \dots, \boldsymbol{\theta}_D^*$ in the three scenarios by means of a ternary diagram. It is worth noting that three very different patterns are recovered, characterized by one main group of $\boldsymbol{\theta}_d^*$ values (first scenario), three distinct groups (second scenario) and most $\boldsymbol{\theta}_d^*$ values with one null component (third scenario). These $\boldsymbol{\theta}_d^*$ vectors are going to be considered as the *true* vectors of topic proportions generating the corpora.

Finally, to define the $T = 3$ topics, we generated vectors $\boldsymbol{\phi}_1^*, \boldsymbol{\phi}_2^*$ and $\boldsymbol{\phi}_3^*$ by sampling from a Dirichlet distribution with V-dimensional parameter $\boldsymbol{\beta} = (1, \dots, 1)^\intercal$.

We replicate each scenario $B = 100$ times, by generating B different corpora and fitting both the LDA and the FLDA models. The aim of the simulation study is to compare the reliability of the estimates provided by the two models.

We fit the models by considering the CGS illustrated in the previous section. More specifically, we run a single chain composed of 2,000 iterations and discard 1,000 iterations as a warm-up.

To estimate both the LDA and the FLDA parameters, we need to specify the model hyper-parameters. In the LDA, the only quantity to specify is the T-dimensional vector $\boldsymbol{\alpha}$, which is typically chosen with equal elements $\alpha_1 = \dots = \alpha_T = \alpha$ so as to adopt a symmetric Dirichlet distribution in a weakly informative fashion. Many authors proposed some default values for the common α, such as $\alpha = 0.1$ (Teh et al. 2006) or $\alpha = 50/T$ (Steyvers and Griffiths 2007; Xiao and Stibor 2010; Qiu et al. 2014). In this simulation study, we prefer a value of $\alpha = 1$ so as to select a uniform distribution on the simplex $\mathcal{S}^T$. For the FLDA, the implementation of some default choices is more tricky. Indeed, we have to specify the value of $\boldsymbol{\alpha}$, $\mathbf{p}$ and τ, and these parameters have a direct impact on the cluster structure of the FD distribution, which cannot (and should not) be treated by a default choice. In a scenario with no prior information available, we decide to implement a preliminary step aimed at obtaining values for the $\boldsymbol{\alpha}, \mathbf{p}$ and τ. More precisely, having the estimates $\hat{\boldsymbol{\theta}}_1, \ldots, \hat{\boldsymbol{\theta}}_D$ from the LDA model, we use them as data points to estimate the parameters of an FD distribution. This inferential problem can be handled both via an EM-based procedure (Migliorati et al. 2017) or by a Bayesian approach implemented through the Stan language (Carpenter et al. 2017). Both these approaches provide initial estimates $\hat{\boldsymbol{\alpha}}, \hat{\mathbf{p}}$ and $\hat{\tau}$ that can be used to run the CGS described in section 8.4.

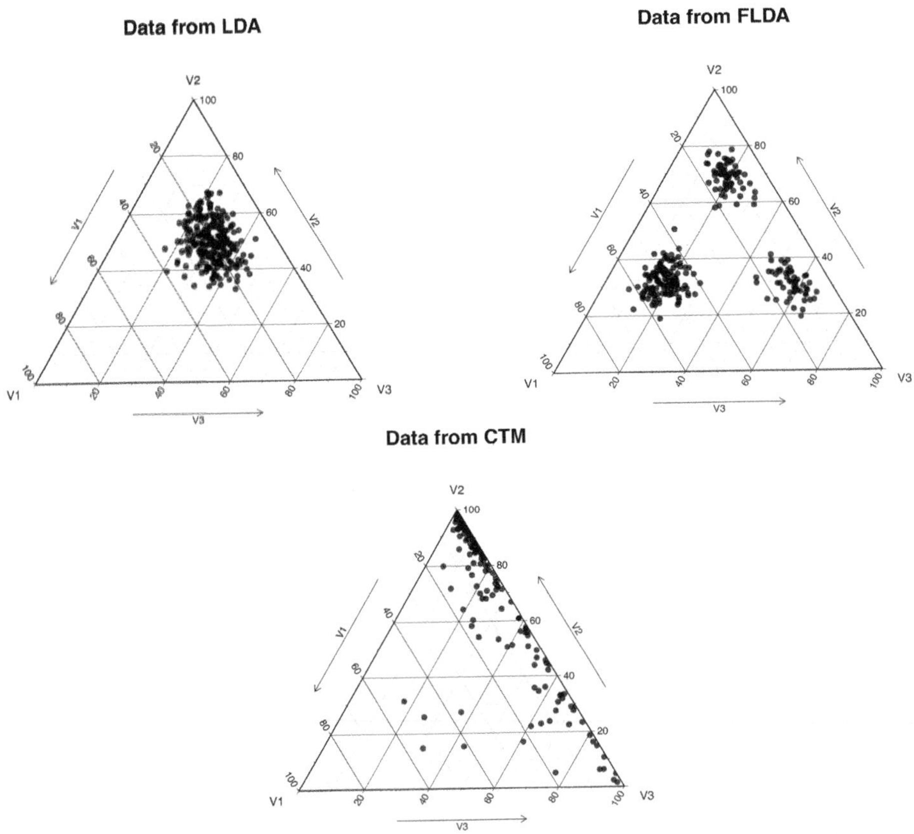

Figure 8.2. *Ternary diagrams representing the vectors of topic proportions generated from the LDA (top left), FLDA (top right) and CTM (bottom) models. For a color version of this figure, see www.iste.co.uk/dimotikalis/data4.zip*

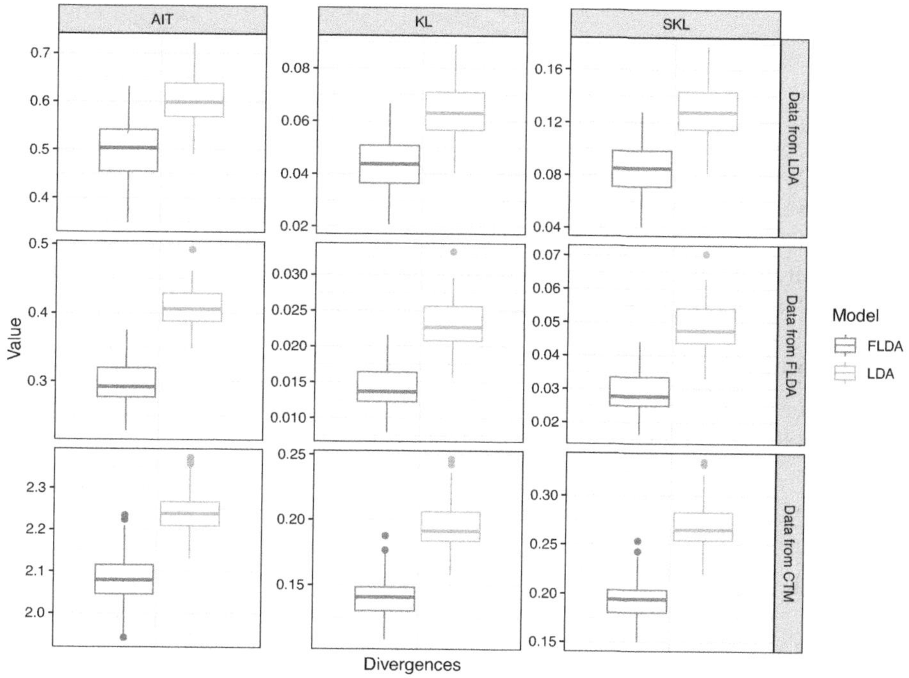

Figure 8.3. *Boxplot representing the mean distance between the estimated θ_d's and the true θ_d^*'s. For a color version of this figure, see www.iste.co.uk/dimotikalis/data4.zip*

To compare the estimates provided by the LDA and the FLDA models, we take advantage of three measures, namely the Kullback–Leibler (KL) divergence (Kullback and Leibler 1951), its symmetrized version (SKL, Kullback and Leibler 1951) and the Aitchison (AIT) distance (Aitchison 1990). These metrics measure the discrepancy existing between two compositional vectors. Thus, larger values are associated with "farther" vectors. In particular, let **x** and **y** be two compositional vectors defined on the same simplex space $\mathcal{S}^T$. Then, the above metrics are defined as:

$$d_{KL}(\mathbf{x}, \mathbf{y}) = \sum_{t=1}^{T} x_t \log\left(\frac{x_t}{y_t}\right),$$

$$d_{SKL}(\mathbf{x}, \mathbf{y}) = d_{KL}(\mathbf{x}, \mathbf{y}) + d_{KL}(\mathbf{y}, \mathbf{x}),$$

and

$$d_{AIT}(\mathbf{x},\mathbf{y}) = \sqrt{\sum_{t=1}^{T}\left(\log\left(\frac{x_t}{\mu_0(\mathbf{x})}\right) - \log\left(\frac{y_t}{\mu_0(\mathbf{y})}\right)\right)^2},$$

where $\mu_0(\mathbf{x}) = \left(\prod_{t=1}^{T} x_t\right)^{1/T}$ denotes the geometric mean of the elements of $\mathbf{x}$.

In this framework, we can use these measures to compare an estimated vector of parameters (i.e. $\hat{\boldsymbol{\theta}}_d$ or $\hat{\boldsymbol{\phi}}_t$) with the true vector ($\boldsymbol{\theta}_d^*$ or $\boldsymbol{\phi}_t^*$).

In particular, Figure 8.3 shows the mean of the distances computed between $\boldsymbol{\theta}_d^*$ and its estimate $\hat{\boldsymbol{\theta}}_d^{(b)}$ in the b-th simulating replicate. For example, each point in the boxplots in the first column of Figure 8.3 represents the value

$$d_{AIT}^{(b)} = \frac{1}{D}\sum_{d=1}^{D} d_{AIT}\left(\hat{\boldsymbol{\theta}}_d^{(b)}, \boldsymbol{\theta}_d^*\right), \quad b = 1, \ldots, B.$$

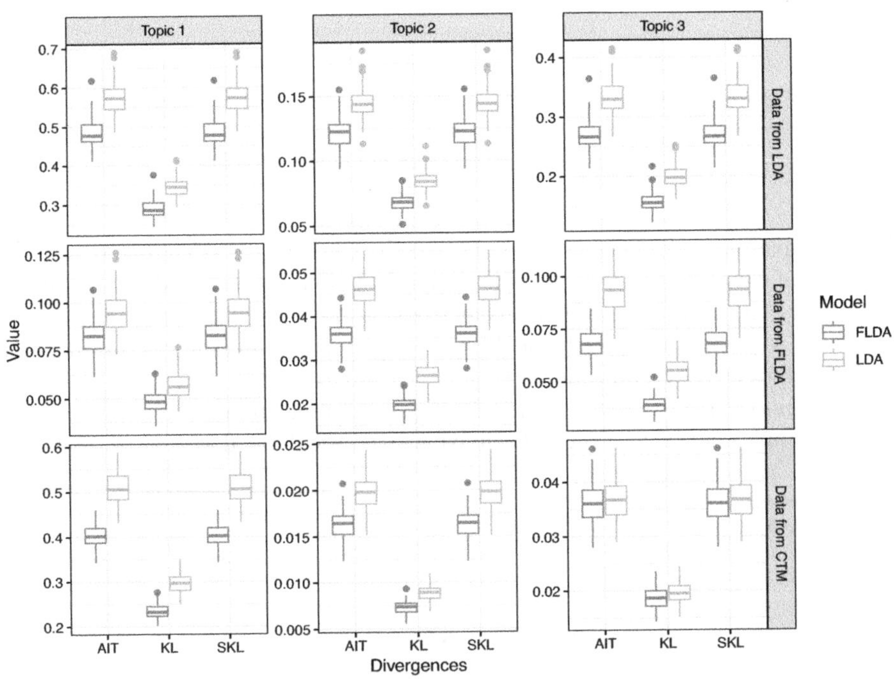

Figure 8.4. *Boxplot of distances between the estimated ϕ_t's and the true ϕ_t^*'s. For a color version of this figure, see www.iste.co.uk/dimotikalis/data4.zip*

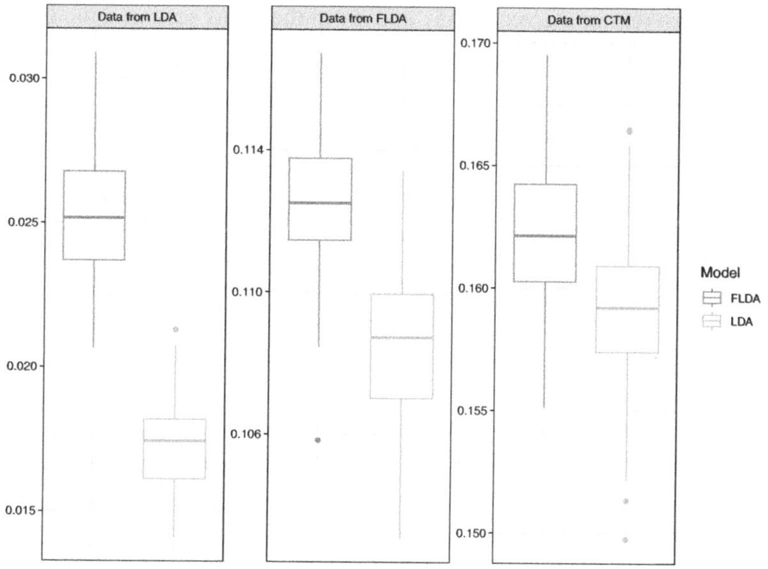

Figure 8.5. *Normalized Pearson's χ^2 statistic evaluating the association between real and predicted words' topic. For a color version of this figure, see www.iste.co.uk/dimotikalis/data4.zip*

It is easy to see that the FLDA model provides estimates for the topic proportions that are closer to the corresponding true values than the LDA's estimates in all the three considered scenarios and according to all the considered metrics. Therefore, the FLDA, contrarily to the LDA, shows robustness with respect to the data generating mechanism.

Interestingly, by focusing on the upper and middle panels, it seems that the better estimates provided by the FLDA model are even more remarkable when the corpus-generating mechanism is the LDA instead of the FLDA mechanism. This is probably due to the additional step of estimating the FD's parameters using the results provided by the LDA model and, consequently, improving it.

Similar considerations hold for the estimation of the topics, namely the parameters ϕ_1, ϕ_2 and ϕ_3. Figure 8.4 shows the boxplots of the distances between the b-th estimate $\hat{\phi}_t^{(b)}$ and the true ϕ_t^*, for example, $d_{AIT,t}^{(b)} = d_{AIT}\left(\hat{\phi}_t^{(b)}, \phi_t^*\right)$. In all the plots, we can note a general superiority of the FLDA model with respect to the classical LDA. The only partial exception is the estimation of the third topic (i.e. ϕ_3) when the corpus is generated according to a correlated topic model (CTM), i.e. a scenario where we expect both the LDA and the FLDA models to perform badly. In that case, the two approaches seem to provide similar results. Please note that in estimating the two remaining vectors ϕ_1 and ϕ_2 in the CTM scenario, the FLDA still provides better estimates.

Finally, since the CGS estimation procedure for both the LDA and FLDA models provides Monte Carlo samples of **z**, we can compare them with the set of true topics associated with each word in the corpus. Such a comparison is performed by considering the normalized Pearson's χ^2 statistic (Agresti 2013). Figure 8.5 summarizes these normalized statistics for the two models in the three simulative scenarios. The FLDA still shows better performance (i.e. predicted topics more associated with real topics) than the LDA.

8.6. References

Agresti, A. (2013). *Categorical Data Analysis*, 3rd edition. John Wiley & Sons Inc., Hoboken.

Aitchison, J. (1990). On coherence in parametric density estimation. *Biometrika*, 77(4), 905–908.

Aitchison, J. (2003). *The Statistical Analysis of Compositional Data.* Blackburn Press, Caldwell.

Blei, D.M. and Lafferty, J.D. (2007). Correlated topic models. *Advances in Neural Information Processing Systems*, 18.

Blei, D.M., Ng, A.Y., Jordan, M.I. (2003). Latent Dirichlet allocation. *Journal of Machine Learning Research*, 3(4–5), 993–1022. doi: 10.1016/b978-0-12-411519-4.00006-9.

Carpenter, B., Gelman, A., Hoffman, M.D., Lee, D., Goodrich, B., Betancourt, M., Brubaker, M., Guo, J., Li, P., Riddell, A. (2017). Stan: A probabilistic programming language. *Journal of Statistical Software*, 76(1). doi: 10.18637/jss.v076.i01.

Griffiths, T.L. and Steyvers, M. (2004). Finding scientific topics. *Proceedings of the National Academy of Sciences*, 101(suppl. 1), 5228–5235.

Kullback, S., and Leibler, R.A. (1951). On information and sufficiency. *The Annals of Mathematical Statistics*, 22(1), 79–86.

Migliorati, S., Ongaro, A., Monti, G.S. (2017). A structured Dirichlet mixture model for compositional data: Inferential and applicative issues. *Statistics & Computing*, 27, 963–983.

Ongaro, A. and Migliorati, S. (2013). A generalization of the Dirichlet distribution, *Journal of Multivariate Analysis*, 114, 412–426.

Qiu, Z., Wu, B., Wang, B., Shi, C., Yu, L. (2014). Collapsed Gibbs sampling for latent Dirichlet allocation on spark. *JMLR: Workshop and Conference Proceedings*, 36, 17–28.

Steyvers, M. and Griffiths, T. (2007). Probabilistic topic models. In *Handbook of Latent Semantic Analysis*, Landauer, T.K., McNamara, D.S., Dennis, S., Kintsch, W. (eds). Psychology Press, London, 439-460.

Teh, Y.W., Newman, D., Welling, M. (2006). A collapsed variational Bayesian inference algorithm for latent Dirichlet allocation. *Advances in Neural Information Processing Systems*, 19.

Xiao, H. and Stibor, T. (2010). Efficient collapsed Gibbs sampling for latent Dirichlet allocation. *JMLR: Workshop and Conference Proceedings*, 13, 63–78.

9

Extreme Value Parameters Estimation: An Overview

The main objective of statistics of extremes is the estimation of parameters of rare events. The extreme value index, ξ, and the extremal index, θ, are parameters that play a central role in extreme value theory (EVT), not only by themselves but also because of their influence in the estimation of other parameters, such as extreme quantiles. Several estimators of ξ and θ have appeared in the literature. However, those estimators depend on tuning parameters that need to be adequately chosen. Computational procedures have been considered and present nice results. Different existing procedures will be reviewed and applied to a case study.

9.1. Introduction and overview of extreme value theory

An important topic in managing risk is the analysis, modeling and prediction of rare but dangerous extreme events. The core problem in risk management is how to model the tails and estimate extreme quantiles of the distribution of the process at risk.

Society, ecosystems, etc. tend to adapt to routine, near-normal conditions; these conditions tend to produce fairly minimal impacts. In contrast, unusual and extreme conditions tend to have much more substantial net impacts, despite, by definition, occurring a much smaller proportion of the time.

EVT is a statistical theory concerning extreme values, i.e. values occurring at the tails of a probability distribution. It is the branch of probability and statistics dedicated to characterizing the very low or quite high values of a variable. When we are dealing with an application and the interest is focused in data away from the central part, the analysis of extreme values requires special attention and special models.

Chapter written by Dora Prata GOMES and M. Manuela NEVES.

There is a large variety of fields of application: Hidrology, Material Science, Ocean Engineering, Structural Engineering, Material Strength, Environment, Finance, Insurance and Statistical Quality Control.

The aim of this chapter is to review the importance of EVT, to present some procedures of estimating the main parameters, to discuss challenges for those procedures and to present an application study.

After a brief review of the background in EVT, in section 9.2, we present the definition and characterization of the parameters under study. Estimation procedures are discussed in sections 9.3 and 9.4, and the application is discussed in section 9.5. This chapter ends with section 9.6, which is dedicated to the conclusions and some ideas on the work in progress.

Let us consider the sample $(X_1, X_2, \ldots, X_n)$ of independent and identically (iid) random variables, with unknown cumulative distribution function (cdf) F and let $M_n \equiv X_{n:n} := \max(X_1, X_2, \ldots, X_n)$. The distribution function of the maximum is given by

$$P(M_n \leq x) = P(X_1 \leq x, \ldots, X_n \leq x) = P(X_1 \leq x) \ldots P(X_n \leq x) = F^n(x).$$

The limit of this function is a degenerate distribution. The asymptotic theory of sample extremes has been developed in "parallel" with the central limit theory. Let $X_1, X_2, X_3, \ldots$ be the iid random variables. The central limit theory is concerned with the limiting behavior of the partial sums $X_1 + X_2 + \cdots + X_n$, or the sample mean, $\overline{X}_n$ when the variance σ^2 is finite,

$$\frac{\sum_{i=1}^{n} X_i - n\mu}{\sigma\sqrt{n}} \equiv \frac{\overline{X}_n - \mu}{\sigma/\sqrt{n}} \underset{n\to\infty}{\longrightarrow} N(0,1).$$

The theory of sample extremes is concerned with the limit behavior of the sample extremes, the maximum M_n or the minimum m_n, as $n \to \infty$. We usually deal with the maxima. Although slightly more complicated, the same theory applies to the minimum because of the relation

$$m_n = \min\left(X_1, \cdots, X_n\right) = -\max\left(-X_1, \cdots, -X_n\right).$$

As an illustration of the behavior of $\overline{X}_n$ and M_n, Figure 9.1 shows that normal distribution fits reasonably well to the sample mean but hardly to the sample maximum. A simulation scheme of 5,000 samples of size $n = 1,000$ from standard uniform random variables was performed.

First results are due to Fréchet (1927), Fisher and Tippett (1928), Gumbel (1935) and Von Mises (1936); however, Gnedenko (1943) and Haan (1970) gave conditions for the existence of sequences $\{a_n > 0\}$ e $\{b_n\}$ such that,

$$\lim_{n\to\infty} \mathbb{P}\left(\frac{M_n - b_n}{a_n} \leq x\right) = \lim_{n\to\infty} F^n(a_n x + b_n) = G_\xi(x),\ \forall x \in \mathbb{R}. \qquad [9.1]$$

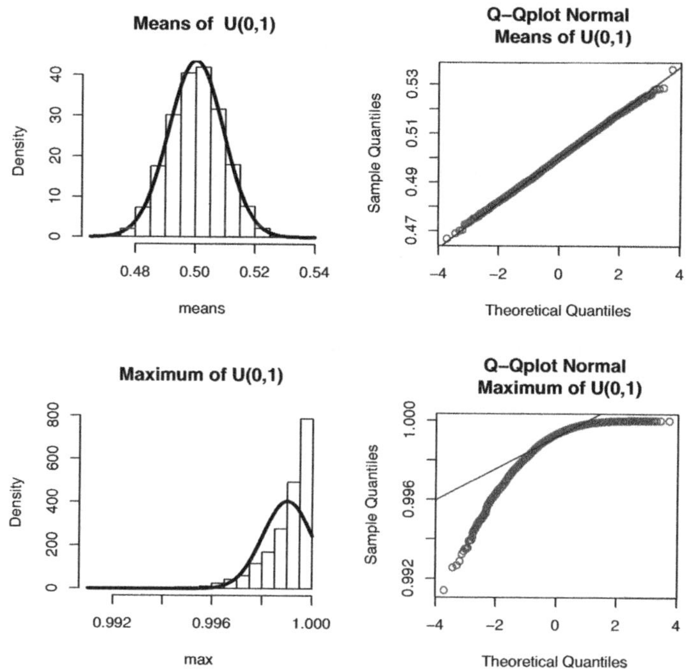

Figure 9.1. *Normal fit and probability plots to the sample average and maximum of random samples ($n = 1,000$) from an uniform distribution. For a color version of this figure, see www.iste.co.uk/dimotikalis/data4.zip*

G_ξ is the Generalized Extreme Value (GEV) distribution function (df), which is given by

$$G_\xi(x) \equiv \text{GEV}_\xi = \begin{cases} \exp[-(1+\xi x)^{-1/\xi}], & 1+\xi x > 0 \ \text{if } \xi \neq 0 \\ \exp[-\exp(-x)], & x \in \mathbb{R} \qquad\quad \text{if } \xi = 0. \end{cases} \qquad [9.2]$$

These models can also incorporate location (λ) and scale ($\delta > 0$) parameters, and we generally represent them as

$$G_\xi(x; \lambda, \delta) \equiv G_\xi((x-\lambda)/\delta).$$

When the limit [9.1] holds, we say that F is in the domain of attraction (for maxima) of G_ξ and write $F \in \mathcal{D}_\mathcal{M}(G_\xi)$. When the sample size $n \longrightarrow \infty$, we can consider the approximation

$$P(M_n \leq x) = F^n(x) \approx G_\xi((x-b_n)/a_n).$$

The shape parameter ξ governs the tail behavior, giving the thickness of the tail. G_ξ incorporates the three (Fisher–Tippett) types, depending upon the value of ξ:

– Gumbel: $\xi = 0$, the right tail is of an exponential type, and F has an infinite or a finite right endpoint.

– Fréchet: $\xi > 0$, the right tail is heavy, of a negative polynomial type, and F has an infinite right endpoint.

– Weibull: $\xi < 0$, the right tail is light, and F has a finite right endpoint ($x^* < +\infty$).

Figure 9.2 shows the plots of density functions for the normal, Gumbel, Weibull and Fréchet (left) and the corresponding cdf (right).

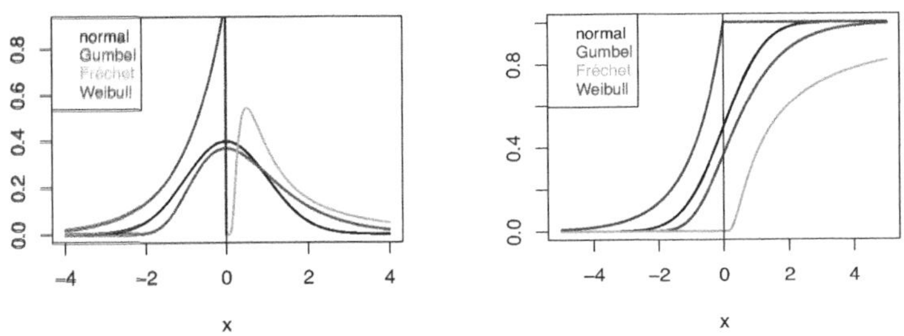

Figure 9.2. *Shapes of GEV distribution compared with the normal. For a color version of this figure, see www.iste.co.uk/dimotikalis/data4.zip*

The maxima of almost all common continuous distributions, after suitable normalization, converge to the GEV, for some value of ξ. Some examples are:

– normal, lognormal, hyperbolic, gamma, chi-squared $\longrightarrow$ Gumbel;

– Pareto, Cauchy, inverse gamma, Student's-t, loggamma $\longrightarrow$ Fréchet;

– uniform, beta $\longrightarrow$ Weibull.

9.2. Some parameters of interest in EVT

The shape parameter ξ is called the extreme value index (EVI); it is the primary parameter of interest in EVT analysis, and is also the basis of other important parameters of extreme events.

Some of the most frequent questions concerning risk management involve extreme quantile estimation. This corresponds to the determination of the value that a variable exceeds with a given (low) probability. A typical example of such measures is the Value-at-Risk (VaR) in the finance area.

A *high quantile* of probability $1-q$ (q small) can be defined as

$$\chi_{1-q} := \inf\{x : F(x) \geq 1-q\} = F^{<-}(1-q),$$

$$\chi_{1-q} := \lambda - \frac{\delta}{\xi}\left[1 - \{-\log(1-q)\}^{-\xi}\right], \quad \xi \neq 0.$$

In practice, it is often observed that extremes cluster in time. For example, it is often observed that the extremes of temperatures, water levels, wind speeds or financial time series cluster in time.

Such short-range clustering is also accommodated by extreme value theory through a new parameter; the so-called extremal index (EI). The extremal index, usually denoted by θ, essentially quantifies the inverse of the mean cluster size, in the above situations, and thus has an appealing physical meaning.

In real problems, when it is not possible to assume independence, the stationarity is the first realistic situation to be considered.

Let $\{X_n\}_{n\geq 1}$ be a stationary sequence. Under adequate conditions, the cdf of the maximum $X_{n:n}$ of a stationary sequence can be directly related to the maximum $Y_{n:n}$ of the associated iid sequence, through the extremal index. The extremal index θ, $0 < \theta \leq 1$, can be informally defined by

$$\mathbb{P}(X_{n:n} \leq x) \approx F^{n\theta}(x) \approx \mathrm{GEV}_\xi\left(\frac{x - b'_n}{a'_n}\right) \quad \begin{cases} a'_n = a_n\theta^\xi \\ b'_n = b_n + a_n\frac{\theta^\xi - 1}{\xi}. \end{cases}$$

Those conditions (see Leadbetter et al. 1983) establish that the stationary sequence has the same Extreme Value distribution limit as the associated iid sequence, but different scale and location parameters:

$$\lambda_\theta = \lambda + \delta\frac{\theta^\xi - 1}{\xi}, \qquad \delta_\theta = \delta\theta^\xi \qquad \xi_\theta = \xi,$$

where (λ, δ, ξ) are the location, scale and shape parameters of GEV_ξ. An adequate estimation of the EI is then needed.

9.3. EVI and EI estimation

In this chapter, we are going to review some EVI and EI estimators derived in a semi-parametric approach, i.e. the only assumption made is that the limit in [9.1] holds, i.e. that the underlying distribution verifies the extreme value condition. In this framework, we do not need to fit a specific parametric model based on scale, shape and location parameters. Estimates are now usually based on the largest k order statistics in the sample, assuming only that the model F underlying the data is in $\mathcal{D}_\mathcal{M}(\mathrm{G}_\xi)$.

The tail shape parameter and the extremal index are the fundamental parameters governing the extreme behavior of the distribution. This section provides a comprehensive analysis of the performance of estimators of both key parameters in extreme value theory. We present three prominent estimators for the tail shape parameter, and we also review three estimators for the extremal index.

9.3.1. *EVI estimators*

The EVI is estimated, on the basis of the k top statistics, with k intermediate, i.e. such that $k = k_n \to \infty$ and $k/n \to 0$, as $n \to \infty$. However, most estimators show a strong dependence on that value k. They usually present a small bias and a high variance for small values of k. Bias increases and variance decreases when k increases.

Currently, there are several different EVI-estimators, and we will now present and compare a few. We will illustrate the application of the following estimators: the classical Hill (H) estimator (Hill 1975), the Corrected Hill (CH) estimator (Caeiro et al. 2005) and a recent class of estimators, the *Lehmer mean-of-order-p* (L_p) estimators (Penalva 2017; Penalva et al. 2020), all defined for $\xi > 0$.

Let $X_{1:n} \le X_{2:n} \le \cdots \le X_{n:n}$ be the order statistics associated with the sample $(X_1, X_2, \ldots, X_n)$ and define the log-excesses as $V_{ik} := \ln X_{n-i+1:n} - \ln X_{n-k:n}$. The Hill estimator, for $\xi > 0$, is defined as:

$$\widehat{\xi}^{\mathrm{H}}(k) \equiv \mathrm{H}(k) := \frac{1}{k}\sum_{i=1}^{k} V_{ik}, \quad k = 1, 2, \ldots, n-1. \qquad [9.3]$$

There are several alternatives to the Hill estimator that are less sensitive to the choice of the level k. Caeiro et al. (2005) introduced a class of *reduced bias* EVI-estimators. The simplest class of reduced-bias EVI-estimators, the Corrected Hill (CH) estimator, is defined as:

$$\hat{\xi}_n^{CH}(k) \equiv \hat{\xi}_{\hat{\beta},\hat{\rho}}^{CH}(k) \equiv \mathrm{CH}(k) := \mathrm{H}(k)\left(1 - \frac{\hat{\beta}(n/k)^{\hat{\rho}}}{1-\hat{\rho}}\right), \quad 1 \le k < n, \qquad [9.4]$$

with $(\hat{\beta}, \hat{\rho})$ being an adequate estimator of the vector of second-order parameters (β, ρ). These are the scale and the shape second-order parameters, controlling the rate of first-order convergence, and they are necessary for establishing distributional properties of the estimators. Details on second-order conditions can be found in Beirlant et al. (2004), Haan and Ferreira (2006) and Fraga Alves et al. (2007), among others (for the estimation of that vector of parameters, see Gomes and Martins 2002 and Fraga Alves et al. 2003).

The estimator CH, in [9.4], cannot only reduce the bias of the classical estimators but also does not increase the asymptotic variance of the estimators, for adequate levels of k and adequate estimation of parameters of second-order $(\beta, \rho) \in (\mathbb{R}, \mathbb{R}^-)$.

The class of *Lehmer mean-of-order-p* (L_p) estimators is defined for $\xi > 0$, as

$$\widehat{\xi}^{\mathrm{L}}(k) \equiv \mathrm{L}_p(k) := \frac{1}{p}\, \frac{\sum_{i=1}^{k} V_{ik}^{p}}{\sum_{i=1}^{k} V_{ik}^{p-1}}, \quad k = 1, 2, \ldots, n-1, \quad \left[\mathrm{L}_1(k) \equiv \mathrm{H}(k)\right]. \qquad [9.5]$$

Properties of this estimator are deeply studied in Penalva (2017) and Penalva et al. (2020).

9.3.2. *EI estimators*

Classical estimators of EI have been developed based on characterizations of θ given by Leadbetter (1983) and O'Brien (1987). For example, $\theta = \lim_{n\to\infty} \theta_n^B(u_n)$, where

$$\frac{1}{\theta_n^B(u_n)} = \frac{r_n \overline{F}(u_n)}{\mathbb{P}(M_{r_n} > u_n)} = E\left[\sum_{i=1}^{r_n} I(X_i > u_n) \Big| M_{r_n} > u_n\right],$$

is the expected number of exceedances over u_n in a block containing at least one such exceedance. Therefore, the EI can be interpreted as the reciprocal of the limiting mean number of exceedances in blocks with at least one exceedance.

If we choose a threshold u and a block length r, then natural estimators for the quantities $\mathbb{P}(M_r > u)$ and $\overline{F}(u)$ lead to the EI blocks estimator of Hsing (1991):

$$\widehat{\Theta}_n^B(u\,;\,r) := \frac{k^{-1}\sum_{i=1}^{k} I\left(\max\left(X_{(i-1)r+1}, \cdots, X_{ir}\right) > u\right)}{r^{-1} n \sum_{i=1}^{n} I\left(X_i > u\right)}, \qquad [9.6]$$

where $k = \lfloor n/r \rfloor$ and $I(\cdot)$ is an indicator function, taking the value 1 if the argument is true; otherwise, 0.

Another interpretation of the extremal index is due to O'Brien (1987). Writing $\theta_n^R(u_n) = \mathbb{P}\left(\max\left(X_2, \cdots, X_{r_n}\right) \le u_n | X_1 > u_n\right)$, under additional conditions, we see that

$$\theta_n^R(u_n) = \theta_n^B(u_n) + o(1).$$

Therefore, $\theta = \lim_{n\to\infty} \theta_n^R(u_n)$ represents the limiting probability that an exceedance is followed by a run of observations below the threshold.

If we choose a threshold u and a run length r, the estimation of the quantities $\mathbb{P}\left(X_1 > u, \max\left(X_2, \cdots, X_{r+1}\right) \leq u\right)$ and $\overline{F}(u)$ lead to obtaining the runs estimator for the EI (Hsing 1993; Weissman and Novak 1998):

$$\widehat{\Theta}_n^R(u\,;\,r) := \frac{(n-r)^{-1}\sum_{i=1}^{n-r} I\left(X_i > u, \max\left(X_{i+1}, \cdots, X_{i+r}\right) \leq u\right)}{n^{-1}\sum_{i=1}^{n} I\left(X_i > u\right)}. \tag{9.7}$$

The previous interpretations identify $\theta = 1$ with exceedances occurring singly in the limit, while $\theta < 1$ implies that exceedances tend to occur in clusters.

The EI is also related to the times between threshold exceedances. For this purpose, introduce the random variable $T(u)$ to be the time between successive exceedances of u, i.e. $\mathbb{P}(T(u) > n) = \mathbb{P}\left(\max(X_2, \cdots, X_{n+1}) \leq u | X_1 > u\right)$, for $n \geq 1$. Ferro and Segers (2003) showed, under some conditions, that

$$\overline{F}(u)T(u) \xrightarrow{d} T_\theta,$$

where T_θ is a random variable distributed according to the mixture distribution $(1-\theta)\delta_0 + \theta\exp(\theta)$, δ_θ and $\exp(\theta)$ represent a delta function with unit mass at 0 and the exponential distribution with mean $1/\theta$. For T_θ, we obtain

$$\frac{E[T_\theta^2]}{(E[T_\theta])^2} = \frac{2}{\theta}. \tag{9.8}$$

Assume that we observe $N = \sum_{i=1}^{n} I\left(X_i > u\right)$ exceedances of u at times $1 \leq S_1 < \cdots < S_N \leq n$. The interexceedance times are $T_i = S_{i+1} - S_i$ for $1 \leq i \leq N-1$. Replacing the theoretical moments of T_θ in the ratio [9.8] with their empirical counterparts yields another estimator for the EI. The intervals estimator suggested by Ferro and Segers (2003) is:

$$\widehat{\Theta}^I(u) := \begin{cases} \dfrac{2\left(\sum_{i=1}^{N-1} T_i\right)^2}{(N-1)\sum_{i=1}^{N-1} T_i^2}, & \text{if } \max T_i \leq 2, \\ \dfrac{2\left(\sum_{i=1}^{N-1} (T_i - 1)\right)^2}{(N-1)\sum_{i=1}^{N-1} (T_i - 1)(T_i - 2)}, & \text{if } \max T_i > 2. \end{cases} \tag{9.9}$$

In runs and blocks estimators (Smith et al. 1994; Weissman and Novak 1998), we have to choice two tuning parameters: the threshold u and the block/run length r, while for intervals estimator, we only need to choice the threshold u.

9.4. Extreme quantile estimation

In many engineering fields, we need to carefully estimate extreme quantiles in order to measure the probability of rare events of the observed phenomena. For example, this is the case in reliability, flood prevention and insurance and finance.

In this section, we review some classical methods to construct estimators for high quantiles, χ_{1-q} with $q \in [0,1]$ close to 0.

Let us again consider the sample $(X_1, X_2, \ldots, X_n)$ of independent and identically random variables with a regularly varying right tail. For these heavy tailed models and for small values of q, we want to extrapolate beyond the sample, estimating not only the EVI and EI but also an extreme quantile χ_{1-q}, i.e. a value such that $F(\chi_{1-q}) = 1 - q$, or equivalently,

$$\chi_{1-q} := F^{\leftarrow}(1-q) = U(1/q), \quad q = q_n \to 0, \quad \text{as } n \to \infty,$$

with the notation $F^{\leftarrow}(y) := \inf\{x : F(x) \geq y\}$ for the generalized inverse function of F and $U(t) := F^{\leftarrow}(1 - 1/t), t \geq 1$, for the reciprocal quantile function.

When extreme quantiles have to be estimated from a given data set, the classical parametric approach can be applied by inverting the GEV distribution,

$$G_{\xi_\theta}(x; \lambda_\theta; \delta_\theta) = \exp\left[-\left(1 + \xi_\theta\left(\frac{x - \lambda_\theta}{\delta_\theta}\right)\right)^{-1/\xi_\theta}\right],$$

where $G_{\xi_\theta}(\chi_{1-q}) = 1 - q$. This approach leads to the following parametric estimator for extreme quantiles in terms of the parameters and the cumulative probability q,

$$\widehat{\chi}_{1-q} := \widehat{\lambda}_\theta - \frac{\widehat{\delta}_\theta}{\widehat{\xi}_\theta}\left[1 - \{-\log(1-q)\}^{-\widehat{\xi}_\theta}\right],$$

with

$$\widehat{\lambda}_\theta = \widehat{\lambda} - \widehat{\delta}\frac{1 - \theta^{\widehat{\xi}}}{\widehat{\xi}}, \quad \widehat{\delta}_\theta = \widehat{\delta}\theta^{\widehat{\xi}} \text{ and } \widehat{\xi}_\theta = \widehat{\xi}. \qquad [9.10]$$

In a semi-parametric spirit, Weissman (1978) proposed the following semi-parametric estimator of an extreme quantile:

$$\widehat{\chi}_{q,\hat{\xi}_n^\bullet}(k) \equiv X_{n-k:n}\, r_n^{\hat{\xi}_n^\bullet(k)}, \; 0 < q < 1, \; 1 \leq k < n, \; r_n \equiv r_n(k;q) = \frac{k}{nq}, \qquad [9.11]$$

where $X_{n-k:n}$ is the $(k+1)$th top-order statistics and $\hat{\xi}_n^\bullet$ can be any consistent estimator for ξ. In this chapter, we will consider H(k), CH(k) and $L_p(k)$ estimators. This quantile estimator is an asymptotic estimator, in the sense that it provides useful estimates when the sample size n is high.

9.5. Application to the daily mean flow discharge in river Tejo

The extreme quantile estimation of heavy tailed distributions has many important applications. Studying and modeling river flow discharge rates are required for river management, including water resources planning, pollution prevention and flood control.

The data under study refers to the daily mean flow discharge rate values (m^3/s) from 1 January, 1974 to 30 June, 2022 of a Portuguese river, Tejo, collected from the "SNIRH: Sistema Nacional de Informação dos Recursos Hídricos". Given that the interest is in extremes, the maximum of each month is taken.

Figure 9.3 displays the data, which shows episodes of increased volatility and relatively extreme flow discharge values.

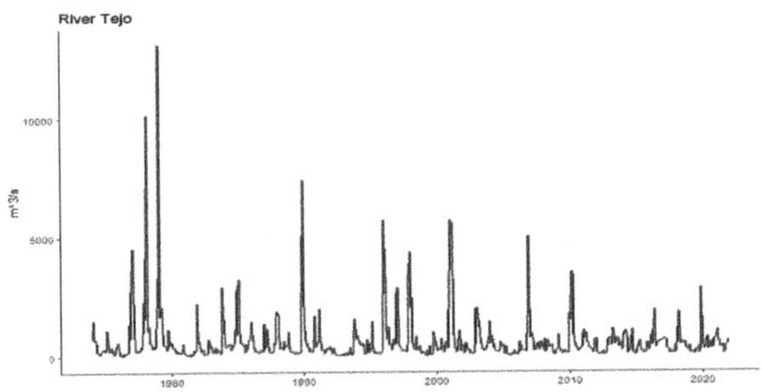

Figure 9.3. *Monthly maximum flow discharge*

The main results of a graphical and descriptive analysis of this data are shown in Figure 9.4. They reveal a tail heavier than that of the normal.

n	min	max	skewness	kurtosis
576	0.99	13102.55	5.7495	47.373

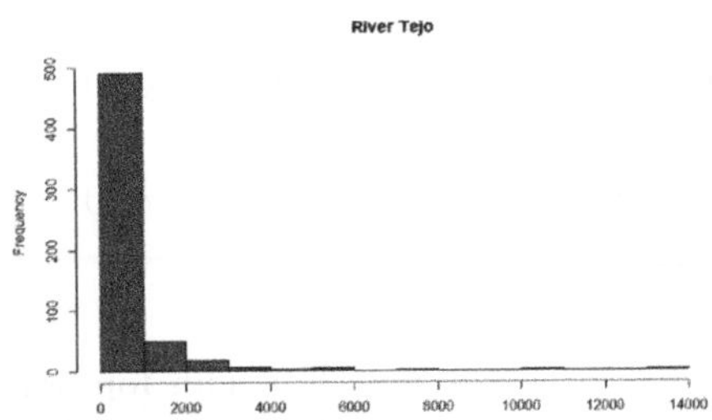

Figure 9.4. *Descriptive statistics measures and histogram for monthly maximum flow discharge*

The various diagnostic plots for assessing the accuracy of the GEV distribution fitted to the monthly maximum flow discharge are shown in Figure 9.5. In probability plot and quantile plot, each set of plotted points is near-linear. The return level curve asymptotes to a finite level, and the curve in density plot provides a satisfactory representation of the empirical estimates. All four diagnostic plots lend support to the fitted GEV distribution.

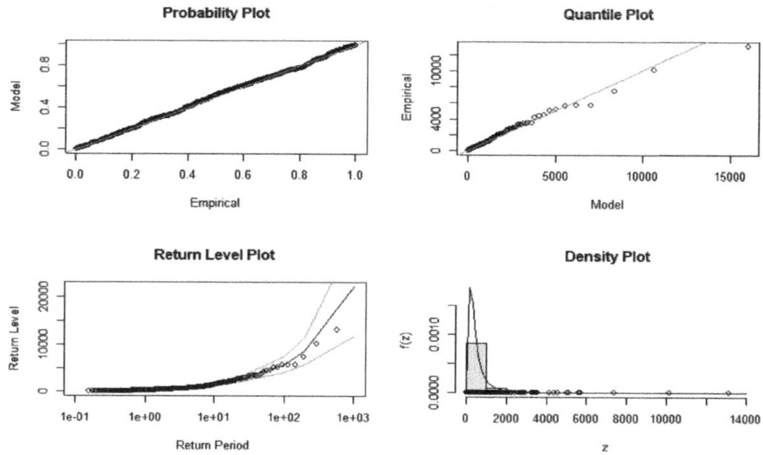

Figure 9.5. *Diagnostic plots for GEV fit to the monthly maximum flow discharge. For a color version of this figure, see www.iste.co.uk/dimotikalis/data4.zip*

Then, we estimate the parameters (δ, ξ, λ) of G_ξ by maximum likelihood and the parameter EI by using the R package `ismev` and `fExtremes`, respectively, where estimators [9.6], [9.7] and [9.9] are implemented.

Table 9.1 summarizes the maximum likelihood estimates (MLE) for GEV distribution parameters and estimates of EI for the monthly maximum flow discharge data. The EI estimates are sensitive to the choice of threshold. By estimating the EI over an expanding range of thresholds (quantiles values between 0.95 and 0.98 with lags 0.0001) and graphing the results, we considered the threshold as a value where the graphs revealed a relative stability. A one-month block length of $r = 22$ days is required for the runs and block length. The extremal index is estimated as $\widehat{\theta}^B = 0.6$ and $\widehat{\theta}^I = 0.72$ suggesting only a weak dependence at extreme values and $\widehat{\theta}^R = 0.35$ suggesting a strong tail dependence.

$\widehat{\delta}$	$\widehat{\xi}$	$\widehat{\lambda}$	$\widehat{\theta}^B$	$\widehat{\theta}^R$	$\widehat{\theta}^I$
228.758	0.585	264.134	0.6	0.35	0.72

Table 9.1. *MLE for GEV parameters (left) and EI estimates (right)*

Regarding the quantile estimation, two approaches are shown in Table 9.2:

– First, the quantile were calculated through the following equation:

$$\widehat{\chi}_{1-q} := \widehat{\lambda} - \frac{\widehat{\delta}}{\widehat{\xi}}\left[1 - \{-\log(1-q)\}^{-\widehat{\xi}}\right]. \qquad [9.12]$$

The results are shown on the left side of Table 9.2 and the 0.99 and 0.999 quantile estimates are equal to $\hat{\chi}_{0.99} = 5640.026$ and $\hat{\chi}_{0.999} = 22110.972$, respectively.

– On the right side of Table 9.2, the EI estimate was considered and the location and scale estimates were upgraded through the relationship [9.10], so we have

$$\widehat{\lambda}_\theta = \widehat{\lambda} - \widehat{\delta}\frac{1-\theta^{\widehat{\xi}}}{\widehat{\xi}}, \quad \widehat{\delta}_\theta = \widehat{\delta}\theta^{\widehat{\xi}} \text{ and } \widehat{\xi}_\theta = \widehat{\xi}.$$

In other words, due to dependence, the 0.99 quantile estimates obtained are now $\hat{\chi}_{0.99,\hat{\theta}} = 4150.331$, 2993.597 and 4631.750 and 0.999 quantile estimates obtained are $\hat{\chi}_{0.999,\hat{\theta}} = 16366.556$, 11906.073 and 18222.958, with blocks, runs and intervals estimates for EI, respectively. This means that if we neglect EI here, then we risk overestimating the quantile.

$1-q$	$\hat{\chi}_{1-q}$	Estimator	$\hat{\theta}$	$\hat{\chi}_{1-q,\hat{\theta}}$
		Blocks	0.6	4150.331
0.99	5640.026	Runs	0.35	2993.597
		Intervals	0.72	4631.750
		Blocks	0.6	16366.556
0.999	22110.972	Runs	0.35	11906.073
		Intervals	0.72	18222.958

Table 9.2. *Parametric quantile estimates*

In the semi-parametric approach and considering the Weissman estimator of quantiles, in [9.11], and with $\xi_n^\bullet$ equal to $\mathrm{H}(k)$, $\mathrm{CH}(k)$ or $\mathrm{L}_p(k)$, for some values of p, the sample paths of the estimates are plotted in Figure 9.6. It shows some stability around $5,000$ for 0.99 quantile and around $15,000$ for 0.999 quantile.

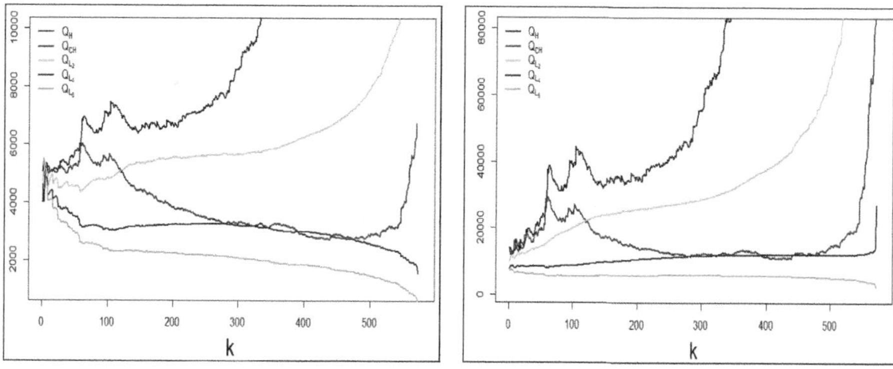

Figure 9.6. 0.99 *quantile estimates (left) and* 0.999 *quantile estimates (right). For a color version of this figure, see www.iste.co.uk/dimotikalis/data4.zip*

9.6. Conclusion and work in progress

The estimation of extreme quantiles is of great importance in several areas of application, as already mentioned above. In this study, some EVI and EI estimators were reviewed to exemplify the need to consider the EI estimation in situations of dependency. Ignoring the EI results in an overestimation of extreme quantiles and a misinterpretation of its meaning. An extensive simulation study is underway to better understand and exemplify the effect of the lack of estimation of that parameter, which arises in the context of dependence, on the estimation of other parameters of interest.

9.7. Acknowledgments

This work was funded by national funds through the FCT – Fundação para a Ciência e a Tecnologia, I.P., under the scope of the projects UIDB/00297/2020 and UIDP/00297/2020 (Center for Mathematics and Applications) and under the project UIDB/00006/2020 (CEAUL).

9.8. References

Beirlant, J., Goegebeur, Y., Segers, J. (2004). *Statistics of Extremes. Theory and Applications*. John Wiley & Sons, Hoboken.

Caeiro, F., Gomes, M.I., Pestana, D. (2005). Direct reduction of bias of the classical hill estimator. *REVSTAT-Statistical Journal*, 3(2), 113–136.

Ferro, C.A.T. and Segers, J. (2003). Inference for clusters of extreme values. *Journal of the Royal Statistical Society: Series B (Statistical Methodology)*, 65(2), 545–556.

Fisher, R.A. and Tippett, L.H.C. (1928). Limiting forms of the frequency distribution of the largest or smallest member of a sample. *Mathematical Proceedings of the Cambridge Philosophical Society*, 24(2), 180–190.

Fraga Alves, M.I., Gomes, M.I., Haan, L. (2003). A new class of semi-parametric estimators of the second order parameter. *Portugaliae Mathematica*, 60(2), 193–214.

Fraga Alves, M.I., Gomes, M.I., de Haan, L., Neves, C. (2007). A note on second order conditions in extreme value theory: Linking general and heavy tails conditions. *Revstat*, 5(3), 285–305.

Fréchet, M. (1927). Sur la loi de probabilité de l' écart maximum. *Annales de la Société Polonaise de Mathématique*, 6, 93–116.

Gnedenko, B. (1943). Sur la distribution limite du terme maximum d'une série aleatoire. *Annals of Mathematics*, 44(3), 423–453.

Gomes, M.I. and Martins, M.J. (2002). "Asymptotically unbiased" estimators of the tail index based on external estimation of the second order parameter. *Extremes*, 5(1), 5–31.

Gumbel, E. (1935). Les valeurs extrêmes des distributions statistiques. *Annales de l'institut Henri Poincaré*, 5(2), 115–158.

Haan, L. (1970). *On Regular Variation and its Application to the Weak Convergence of Sample Extremes*. Mathematisch Centrum, Amsterdam.

Haan, L. and Ferreira, A. (2006). A. *Extreme Value Theory: An Introduction*. Springer, New York.

Hill, B.M. (1975). A simple general approach to inference about the tail of a distribution. *The Annals of Statistics*, 3, 5.

Hsing, T. (1991). Estimating the parameters of rare events. *Stochastic Processes and their Applications*, 37, 117–139.

Hsing, T. (1993). Extremal index estimation for a weakly dependent stationary sequence. *Annals of Statistics*, 21, 2043–2071.

Leadbetter, M.R. (1983). Extremes and local dependence in stationary sequences. *Zeitschrift für Wahrscheinlichkeitstheorie und verwandte Gebiete*, 65(2), 291–306.

Leadbetter, M.R., Lindgren, G., Rootzén, H. (1983). *Extremes and Related Properties of Random Sequences and Processes*. Springer, New York.

O'Brien, G. (1987). Extreme values for stationary and Markov sequences. *Annals of Probability*, 15(1), 281–289.

Penalva, H. (2017). Contributos computacionais e metodológicos na estimação do indíce de valores extremos. PhD Thesis, ISA, Universidade de Lisboa, Lisbon.

Penalva, H., Gomes, M.I., Caeiro, F., Neves, M. (2020). A couple of non reduced bias generalized means in extreme value theory: An asymptotic comparison. *REVSTAT-Statistical Journal*, 18(3), 281-298.

Smith, R. and Weissman, I. (1994). Estimating the extremal index. *Journal of the Royal Statistical Society B*, 56, 515–528.

Von Mises, R. (1936). La distribution de la plus grande de nvaleurs. *Revue mathématique de l'Union interbalkanique*, 1, 141–160.

Weissman, I. (1978). Estimation of parameters and large quantiles based on the k largest observations. *Journal of the American Statistical Association*, 73(364), 812–815.

Weissman, I. and Novak, S. (1998). On blocks and runs estimators of the extremal index. *Journal of Statistical Planning and Inference*, 66, 281–288.

10

Some Properties on Optimal Maintenance Policies for k-out-of-n:G Systems Considering Imperfect Repair with Controllable Repair Levels

Most recent research on condition-based maintenance has assumed that repair can restore the system to an as-new-as-good state. However, repairs are sometimes imperfect, which means the repair restores the system to a state between as-good-as-new and as-bad-as-old. This research investigates optimal maintenance policies for k-out-of-n:G systems considering imperfect repair with controllable repair levels. In such a system, there are total n components. The system functions if and only if k or more of the n components function. The component deteriorates in accordance with a continuous stochastic process, and the deterioration state can only be inspected at some equally spaced time intervals. Based on the inspection results, the decision-maker decides whether to perform preventive maintenance of the whole system/part of components or to operate until the next inspection. This research formulates the optimal decision-making problem over an infinite horizon using a Markov decision process, where the optimal maintenance policy can minimize the total expected discounted operating and maintenance cost. Under certain conditions, we obtained some properties of the optimal maintenance policy that the optimal action changes at some control limits of the deterioration state. Furthermore, a numerical example is presented to illustrate the applicability of the proposed model.

10.1. Introduction

Condition-based maintenance (CBM) plays an important role in maintaining and improving system availability, safety and product quality, especially with the rapid advances in the industry. Over the past few decades, maintenance methods have

Chapter written by Sota IKENOYA and Lu JIN.

evolved from time-based to condition-based maintenance. The CBM approach, based on information monitoring, can help prevent inopportune interventions and reduce maintenance costs.

The first important step in implementing CBM is to model the deterioration process properly. Many stochastic deterioration models have been proposed for this purpose. For example, the Markov chain is a general model of a system with discrete deterioration states. With the fast development of sensor technology in recent decades, the deterioration states can be precisely measured. This research takes advantage of this and considers continuous deterioration states. For such deterioration systems, three commonly used stochastic deterioration models are the Wiener process, the Gamma process and the inverse Gaussian process (IG process) (Ye and Xie 2015).

The Wiener process is typically implemented, when the deterioration path is non-monotonic (Ye and Xie 2015). Gamma and inverse Gaussian processes are used to describe deterioration with monotonic characteristics, and the gamma process is particularly suitable for modeling gradual damage such as wear, fatigue, corrosion, crack growth and erosion (Noortwijk 2009). For example, Wiener processes have been applied to model the deterioration of LED devices (Huang et al. 2015), while inverse Gaussian processes have been applied to GaAs laser deterioration and fatigue crack growth (Hao et al. 2019). Moreover, the gamma processes have been applied to model the deterioration of wind turbine blades (Shafiee et al. 2015).

Most recent research on CBM has focused on single-component systems, i.e. the target system consists of one component (Alaswad and Xiang 2017). Chen et al. (2015) investigated the properties of optimal maintenance policy for single-component systems.

Many multi-component systems employ redundancy, the most common approach to increase system availability and prevent downtime (Moghaddass et al. 2012). One of the most common forms of redundancy is the k-out-of-n:G system, which has a wide range of applications and is one type of multi-component system. In this research, we focused on a k-out-of-n: G system (hereinafter referred to as k-out-of-n), which offers a compromise between the low reliability of series systems and the high cost of parallel systems. In a k-out-of-n system, there are n components, and due to component redundancy, the system can operate if and only if k or more of the n components function; for example, aircraft with multiple engines, air traffic control systems with multiple displays, oil supply systems with multiple pipelines, etc. (Zhang et al. 2023). A failed component is typically replaced immediately, while in a k-out-of-n system, corrective maintenance (CM) can be postponed, making the system more cost-effective due to economic dependence (Keizer et al. 2017). Economic dependence implies that costs can be saved when several components are jointly maintained.

Regarding CBM for k-out-of-n systems, Barbera et al. (1999) investigated the optimal maintenance policy for serial systems, which can be treated as two-out-of-two systems based on numerical results. Keizer et al. (2016) extended the model of Barbera et al. (1999) to k-out-of-n systems and derived similar results. Xu et al. (2021) considered imperfect maintenance, which is represented by a reduction in the deterioration level, and found the optimal maintenance policy when the underlying deterioration of components is represented by a continuous stochastic process. Wang and Zhu (2021) described the underlying deterioration of a component using Wiener and gamma processes. They analytically derived the monotonicity of the expected total cost considering inventory control and obtained some properties of the maintenance policies, based on simulation results. Sun et al. (2018) proved that the optimal maintenance policy follows a two-dimensional control-limit policy for a one-out-of-two system when the underlying deterioration of components is represented by a Wiener process. The properties of the policy when there are more than three components have not been specifically considered. Zhang et al. (2023) analytically derived the properties of optimal maintenance policies for a k-out-of-n system considering failure dependence when the underlying deterioration of components is represented by a pure jump Lévy process. Most of the existing CBM models have been limited to perfect maintenance actions. However, the actual maintenance work is sometimes imperfect, and it is more realistic in real situations that maintenance actions are imperfect, merely restoring a maintained system's condition to somewhere between good-as-new and bad-as-old (Zhang et al. 2015; Alaswad and Xiang 2017).

In this research, we employ the deterioration of each component using a gamma process, which is best suited for monotonic deterioration processes, and investigate the optimal CBM policy that minimizes the total expected discounted cost over an infinite time period for a k-out-of-n system. We derive the properties of optimal maintenance policies for a k-out-of-n system, considering imperfect repair. The properties discuss under both simulation-based and analysis-based results.

10.2. System description

10.2.1. *Deterioration state*

We consider a k-out-of-n system with n identical and independent components. Let $S_i(t), i \in \{1, \ldots, n\}$ denote the underlying deterioration state of component i at time t. Typically, the initial deterioration state for a brand new component is zero, i.e. $S_i(0) = 0, i = 1, \ldots, n$, and the component fails whenever its deterioration state first exceeds a predefined threshold L. Periodic inspections are carried out with every fixed time interval τ.

The deterioration of each component is represented by a gamma process. Thus, $S(t_2) - S(t_1)$ follows a gamma distribution $Ga(\alpha t, \beta)$ with shape parameter $\alpha(> 0)$ and scale parameter $\beta(> 0)$ for any $t_2 > t_1(\geq 0)$.

In this research, the deterioration state of the whole system is evaluated using an n-dimensional information vector $\boldsymbol{s} = (s_1, \ldots, s_n)$. The observed value of the deterioration state at the next time period is $\boldsymbol{s}' = (s'_1, \ldots, s'_n)$. Let $f(s'_i|s_i)$ be the probability that the deterioration state of component i goes from s_i to s'_i at unit time τ as follows:

$$f(s'_i|s_i, \tau) = \frac{(s'_i - s_i)^{\alpha\tau - 1}}{\Gamma(\alpha\tau)\beta^{\alpha\tau}} e^{-\frac{s'_i - s_i}{\beta}} \qquad [10.1]$$

where $\Gamma(a) = \int_0^\infty z^{a-1} e^{-z} dz$ is a gamma function. Let T be the failure time of the k-out-of-n: G system as follows:

$$T = \inf_t \left\{ \sum_{i=1}^{n} 1_{T_i \leq t} \geq n - k + 1 \right\}$$

where $I_A(x)$ is an indicator function and $T_i = \inf_t\{S_i(t) \geq L\},\ i = 1, \cdots, n$ is the failure time of the component i. The failure probability of component i at t when the current deterioration state of component i is s_i is expressed as follows:

$$f_{T_i}(L|s_i, t) = \frac{(L - s_i)^{\alpha t - 1}}{\Gamma(\alpha t)\beta^{\alpha t}} e^{-\frac{L - s_i}{\beta}}. \qquad [10.2]$$

10.2.2. *Maintenance actions*

We assume a system failure is not self-announcing and can only be detected upon inspection. If the system has failed, CM, which means replacing all the components, is performed immediately with cost c_c. Let $s_{(k)}$ be the k-th element, with the deterioration state of each component sorted in decreasing order. When $s_{(k)} = L$, the degradation states of $n-k+1$ components exceed failure threshold L, which indicates that the system is failing; when $s_{(k)} < L$, (1) do nothing until the next inspection (DN); (2) perform imperfect repair (IR); (3) perform preventive replacement (PR) actions is then selected. We treat IR and PR as PM. If the decision-maker decides to perform IR or PR, they must determine which component(s) is/are to receive maintenance. The deterioration state of the component performed PR is restored to 0 afterward, and the deterioration state of the component performed IR is restored to any deterioration state $s'_i(0 < s'_i < s_i)$ between good-as-new and bad-as-old afterward. Setup cost c_s and IR cost $C(s_i, s'_i)$ or PR cost $C(s_i, 0)$ for each component are incurred. We assume that the cost of PM for all n components is less than the cost of CM. That is, $c_c > c_s + nC(s_i, 0)$. We further assume that replacement requires one period.

10.3. Total expected discounted cost

Let $V^{(N)}(\boldsymbol{s})$ be the total expected discounted cost for the remaining n periods if the deterioration state is $\boldsymbol{s}$, and let $V^{(0)}(\boldsymbol{s})$ be 0. The total expected discounted cost can then be expressed as

$$V^{(N)}(\boldsymbol{s})=\begin{cases} c_c + e^{-r\tau}V^{(N-1)}(0,\ldots,0), & s_{(k)} \geq L \\ \min\{C^{(N)}_{(0,0)}(\boldsymbol{s}), C^{(N)}_{(|S_{IR}|,|S_{PR}|)}(\boldsymbol{s})\} & \text{otherwise} \end{cases},$$

where

$$C^{(N)}_a(\boldsymbol{s})=\begin{cases} D_\tau(\boldsymbol{s}) + e^{-r\tau}\displaystyle\int_{s_n}^{\infty}\cdots\int_{s_1}^{\infty} f(s_1'|s_1)\cdots f(s_n'|s_n) & a=(0,0) \\ \quad \times V^{(N-1)}(\boldsymbol{s}')ds_1'\cdots ds_n' & \\ c_s + \displaystyle\sum_{i\in S_{IR}} C(s_i,s_i') + \sum_{j\in S_{PR}} C(s_j,0) & a=(|S_{IR}|,|S_{PR}|) \\ \quad + e^{-r\tau}V^{(N-1)}(\boldsymbol{s}') & \end{cases}$$

Here, S_{IR} is the set of components for which IR is performed and S_{PR} is the set of components for which PR is performed, and $|\cdot|$ is a number of elements in the set. Note that $0 \leq |S_{IR}|+|S_{PR}| \leq n$. r is a discount factor. $C^{(N)}_{(0,0)}(\boldsymbol{s})$ represents the total expected cost over N time periods following a decision to do nothing and then continuing to select actions in accordance with the optimal policy from the next period. $C^{(N)}_{(|S_{IR}|,|S_{PR}|)}(\boldsymbol{s})$ represents the total expected cost over N time periods following a decision to imperfect repair for the $|S_{IR}|$ components and preventive replacement for the $|S_{PR}|$ components selected at the current time. Table 10.1 shows maintenance actions for a k-out-of-three system as an example.

Action $a=(\|S_{IR}\|,\|S_{PR}\|)$	Action description	$\|S_{IR}\|+\|S_{PR}\|$
$a=(0,0)$	Do nothing	0
$a=(1,0)$	IR for one component	1
$a=(0,1)$	PR for one component	1
$a=(2,0)$	IR for two components	2
$a=(1,1)$	IR for one component and PR for one component	2
$a=(0,2)$	PR for two components	2
$a=(3,0)$	IR for three components	3
$a=(2,1)$	IR for two components and PR for one component	3
$a=(1,2)$	IR for one component and PR for two components	3
$a=(0,3)$	PR for three components	3

Table 10.1. *Description of action in the k-out-of-three system*

The downtime cost from the previous inspection epoch to the current inspection epoch is defined as

$$d(T_f) = \int_{T_f}^{\tau} c_d \exp(-ru)du = \frac{c_d[\exp(-rT_f) - \exp(-r\tau)]}{r} \qquad [10.3]$$

where T_f is the elapsed time from the last inspection to the failure, and c_d is the downtime cost per time unit. If no failure occurs between two successive inspections, then $d(T) = 0$. Let $f_T(s,t)$ be the probability that the system fails at t given a deterioration state s. The expected downtime cost during two inspection epochs is defined as

$$D_\tau(s) = E[d(T_f)|S_1 = s_1, \ldots, S_n = s_n] = \int_0^\tau \frac{c_d(e^{-rt} - e^{-r\tau})}{r} f_T(s,t)dt$$

$$= \sum_{j=1}^{\kappa} \int_0^\tau \frac{c_d(e^{-rt} - e^{-r\tau})}{r}$$

$$\left(\int_{ll_1(C_j)}^{ul_1(C_j)} \cdots \int_{ll_n(C_j)}^{ul_n(C_j)} f_{T_1}(s_1'|s_1,t) \cdots f_{T_n}(s_n'|s_n,t) ds_1' \cdots ds_n' \right) dt$$

where $C_1, \ldots, C_\kappa$ denotes the cut set in a k-out-of-n system. As an example, for a two-out-of-three system, $C_1 = \{1,2\}, C_2 = \{1,3\}, C_3 = \{2,3\}, C_4 = \{1,2,3\}$. Furthermore, the lower and upper limits of integration, respectively, are defined as

$$ll_i(C_j) = \begin{cases} L & i \in C_j \\ s_i & i \notin C_j \end{cases}, ul_i(C_j) = \begin{cases} \infty & i \in C_j \\ L & i \notin C_j \end{cases}, \quad i = 1, 2, \ldots, n.$$

When the remaining period N is infinite, the standard argument of the contraction mapping theorem guarantees that $V^{(N)}(s) = V(s)$ (Puterman 2014). The total expected cost over the infinite horizon can then be written as

$$V(s) = \begin{cases} c_c + e^{-r\tau} V(0, \ldots, 0), & s_{(k)} \geq L \\ \min\{C_{(0,0)}(s), C_{(|S_{IR}|, |S_{PR}|)}(s)\} & \text{otherwise} \end{cases},$$

where

$$C_a(s) = \begin{cases} D_\tau(s) + e^{-r\tau} \int_{s_n}^\infty \cdots \int_{s_1}^\infty f(s_1'|s_1) \cdots f(s_n'|s_n) & a = (0,0) \\ \quad \times V(s') ds_1' \cdots ds_n' & \\ c_s + \sum_{i \in S_{IR}} C(s_i, s_i') + \sum_{j \in S_{PR}} C(s_j, 0) & a = (|S_{IR}|, |S_{PR}|) \\ \quad + e^{-r\tau} V(s') & \end{cases}.$$

10.4. Optimization of maintenance policy

Firstly, we introduce the stochastic orders used in this research and then provide the assumption and Lemmas necessary to obtain the monotonicity of the total expected discounted cost. The properties of the optimal maintenance policy are then investigated.

DEFINITION 10.1.– *Stochastic increasing (SI) (Sun et al. 2018): a random variable X is said to be stochastically larger than a random variable Y, written $X \succ_{SI} Y$, if* $\Pr(X > t) \geq \Pr(Y > t)$ *for all t.*

ASSUMPTION.– PM cost $C(s_i, s_i')$ is increasing in s_i and decreasing in s_i'.

This assumption implies that more resources must be committed to improving the deterioration state of the system (Özekici 1995).

LEMMA 10.1.– *The conditional distribution function of the deterioration state $F(s_i'|s_i)$ is non-increasing in s_i for any $i \in \{1, \ldots, n\}$ if the deterioration of each component follows a gamma process. That is,*

$$F(s_i'|s_i^-) \geq F(s_i'|s_i^+) \qquad [10.4]$$

for $s_i^- < s_i^+$ and any $i \in \{1, \ldots, n\}$.

PROOF.– Since the conditional density function for a gamma process is expressed by equation [10.1], the conditional distribution function can be written as follows:

$$\begin{aligned} F(s_i'|s_i) &= \int_{s_i}^{s_i'} \frac{(v_i - s_i)^{\alpha\tau - 1}}{\Gamma(\alpha\tau)\beta^{\alpha\tau}} e^{-\frac{v_i - s_i}{\beta}} dv_i \\ &= \int_0^{s_i' - s_i} \frac{x_i^{\alpha\tau - 1}}{\Gamma(\alpha\tau)\beta^{\alpha\tau}} e^{-\frac{x_i}{\beta}} dx_i \ (x_i = v_i - s_i) \\ &= \frac{\gamma(\alpha\tau, \frac{s_i' - s_i}{\beta})}{\Gamma(c\tau)} \end{aligned} \qquad [10.5]$$

where $\gamma(a, z)(a > 0)$ is an incomplete gamma function as follows:

$$\gamma(a, z) = \int_0^z t^{a-1} e^{-t} dt. \qquad [10.6]$$

Differentiating the incomplete gamma function in equation [10.6] with respect to z yields $z^{a-1}e^{-z}$, and the incomplete gamma function is a non-increasing function in z $(z > 0)$. Therefore, equation [10.5] is a non-increasing function in s_i' for any $i \in \{1, \ldots, n\}$. Thus,

$$\gamma\left(\alpha\tau, \frac{s_i' - s_i^-}{\beta}\right) \geq \gamma\left(\alpha\tau, \frac{s_i' - s_i^+}{\beta}\right) \qquad [10.7]$$

holds for any $s_i^- < s_i^+$, and Lemma 10.1 is thus proved.

LEMMA 10.2 (Sun et al. 2018).– *If $X \succ_{SI} Y$, then, for all increasing functions $f(\cdot)$,* $E[f(X)] \geq E[f(Y)]$.

LEMMA 10.3.– *Assume that the conditional probability distributions for a failure time are* Y_1, Y_2. *If* $s_1^+ \geq s_1^-$, *then* $Y_1(T|S_1(k\tau) = s_1^+, S_2(k\tau) = s_2, \ldots, S_n(k\tau) = s_n) \succ_{SI} Y_2(T|S_1(k\tau) = s_1^-, S_2(k\tau) = s_2, \ldots, S_n(k\tau) = s_n)$ *for any time* $k\tau$.

PROOF.– If component 1 fails, the probability that the system fails at t $(t \geq k\tau)$ can be expressed as

$$\begin{aligned}
&\Pr(T \leq t, S_1(t) \geq L|S_1(k\tau) = s_1^-, S_2(k\tau) = s_2, \ldots, S_n(k\tau) = s_n) \\
&= \Pr(T_1 \leq t|S_1(k\tau) = s_1^-)\times \\
&\left\{\sum_{K=n-k}^{n-1}\left(\prod_{i\in S_K}\Pr(T_i \leq t|S_i(k\tau) = s_i)\prod_{j\notin S_K}(1-\Pr(T_j \leq t|S_j(k\tau) = s_j))\right)\right\} \\
&\leq \Pr(T_1 \leq t|S_1(k\tau) = s_1^+)\times \\
&\left\{\sum_{K=n-k}^{n-1}\left(\prod_{i\in S_K}\Pr(T_i \leq t|S_i(k\tau) = s_i)\prod_{j\notin S_K}(1-\Pr(T_j \leq t|S_j(k\tau) = s_j))\right)\right\} \\
&= \Pr(T \leq t, S_1(t) \geq L|S_1(k\tau) = s_1^+, S_2(k\tau) = s_2, \ldots, S_n(k\tau) = s_n)
\end{aligned} \quad [10.8]$$

where S_K is the set of all possible combinations of K component failures. If component 1 does not fail, the probability of the system failing at t can be expressed as

$$\begin{aligned}
&\Pr(T \leq t, S_1(t) < L|S_1(k\tau) = s_1^-, S_2(k\tau) = s_2, \ldots, S_n(k\tau) = s_n) \\
&= \Pr(T \leq t, S_1(t) < L|S_1(k\tau) = s_1^+, S_2(k\tau) = s_2, \ldots, S_n(k\tau) = s_n).
\end{aligned} \quad [10.9]$$

According to equations [10.8] and [10.9], we can conclude $\Pr(T \leq t|S_1(k\tau) = s_1^-, S_2(k\tau) = s_2, \ldots, S_n(k\tau) = s_n) \leq \Pr(T \leq t|S_1(k\tau) = s_1^+, S_2(k\tau) = s_2, \ldots, S_n(k\tau) = s_n)$. Therefore, Lemma 10.3 is proved.

LEMMA 10.4.– *The total expected downtime cost* $D_\tau(\mathbf{s})$, *where* $\mathbf{s} = (s_1, s_2, \ldots, s_n)$, *is a non-decreasing function in* s_i *for any* $i \in \{1, \ldots, n\}$.

PROOF.– Let $S_2(k\tau) = s_2, \ldots, S_n(k\tau) = s_n$ and $s_1^- < s_1^+$. For $t \geq k\tau$, we have

$$\begin{aligned}
\Pr(S_1(t) \leq s|S_1(k\tau) = s_1^-) &= \Pr(S_1(t) \leq s + s_1^+ - s_1^-|S_1(k\tau) = s_1^+) \\
&> \Pr(S_1(t) \leq s|S_1(k\tau) = s_1^+)
\end{aligned}$$

for all $s \geq s_1^+ > s_1^-$. Hence, $\forall t \geq k\tau, X(S_1(t)|S_1(k\tau) = s_1^-) \prec_{SI} X(S_1(t)|S_1(k\tau) = s_1^+)$, where $X(\cdot)$ is the conditional probability distribution for the deterioration state. Then

$$\begin{aligned}\Pr(T_1 \leq t|S_1(k\tau) = s_1^-) &= \Pr(S_1(t) > L|S_1(k\tau) = s_1^-)\\ &\leq 1 - \Pr(S_1(t) \leq L|S_1(k\tau) = s_1^+)\\ &= \Pr(S_1(t) > L|S_1(k\tau) = s_1^+)\\ &= \Pr(T_1 \leq t|S_1(k\tau) = s_1^+)\end{aligned} \qquad [10.10]$$

which implies $Y(T_1|S_1(k\tau) = s_1^-) \prec_{SI} Y(T_1|S_1(k\tau) = s_1^+)$. Here, $Y(\cdot)$ is the conditional probability distribution for a failure time and $T_i = \inf_t\{S_i(t) \geq L\}$, $i = 1, \cdots, n$ is the failure time of the component i.

Based on Lemma 10.3, we have $Y(T|S_1(k\tau) = s_1^-, S_2(k\tau) = s_2, \ldots, S_n(k\tau) = s_n) \prec_{SI} Y(T|S_1(k\tau) = s_1^+, S_2(k\tau) = s_2, \ldots, S_n(k\tau) = s_n)$. According to Lemma 10.2 and equation [10.3], we can conclude

$$\begin{aligned}D_\tau(s_1^-, s_2, \ldots, s_n) &= E[d(T|S_1(k\tau) = s_1^-, S_2(k\tau) = s_2, \ldots, S_n(k\tau) = s_n]\\ &\leq E[d(T|S_1(k\tau) = s_1^+, S_2(k\tau) = s_2, \ldots, S_n(k\tau) = s_n]\\ &= D_\tau(s_1^+, s_2, \ldots, s_n)\end{aligned} \qquad [10.11]$$

which means that $D_\tau(\boldsymbol{s})$ is non-decreasing in s_1.

Similarly, $D_\tau(\boldsymbol{s})$ is a non-decreasing function in s_i for any $i \in \{2, \ldots, n\}$. Therefore, Lemma 10.4 is proved. Next, we derive a proposition on the total expected discounted cost.

PROPOSITION 10.1.– *The total expected discounted cost $V(\boldsymbol{s})$ is a non-decreasing function in s_i for any $i \in \{1, \ldots, n\}$.*

PROOF.– We prove proposition 10.1 using mathematical induction. Firstly, let $V^{(0)}(\boldsymbol{s}) = 0$ for $N = 0$ holds for any $\boldsymbol{s}$. Thus, $V^{(0)}(\boldsymbol{s})$ is a non-decreasing function in s_i for any $i \in \{1, \ldots, n\}$. Next, we assume that $V^{(l)}(\boldsymbol{s})$ is non-decreasing in s_i for $N = l$. When $N = l + 1$ and $s_{(k)} \geq L$, $V^{(l+1)}(\boldsymbol{s})$ can be expressed as

$$V^{(l+1)}(\boldsymbol{s}) = c_c + e^{-r\tau}V^{(l)}(0, \ldots, 0) \qquad [10.12]$$

where the right-hand side is a constant function in s_i for any $i \in \{1, \ldots, n\}$. When $s_{(k)} < L$, it can be expressed as

$$V^{(l+1)}(\boldsymbol{s}) = \min\left\{C_{(0,0)}(\boldsymbol{s}), C_{(|S_{ir}|,|S_{pr}|)}(\boldsymbol{s})\right\}. \qquad [10.13]$$

From Lemma 10.4, the expected downtime cost $D_\tau(\boldsymbol{s})$ is a non-decreasing function in s_i for any $i \in \{1, \ldots, n\}$, we can replace $C^{(l+1)}_{(0,0)}(\boldsymbol{s}) - D_\tau(\boldsymbol{s})$ by $U^{(l+1)}(\boldsymbol{s})$ as follows:

$$U^{(l+1)}(\boldsymbol{s}) = e^{-r\tau}\mathrm{E}\left[V^{(l)}\left(S^{(l)}_1, \ldots, S^{(l)}_n\right)|S^{(l)}_1 = s_1, \ldots, S^{(l)}_n = s_n\right].$$

From the inductive hypothesis, Lemmas 10.1 and 10.2,

$$\begin{aligned}U^{(l+1)}(\boldsymbol{s}^-) &\equiv e^{-r\tau}\mathrm{E}\left[V^{(l)}\left(S^{(l)}_1, \ldots, S^{(l)}_n\right)|S^{(l)}_1 = s^-_1, \ldots, S^{(l)}_n = s_n\right]\\ &\le e^{-r\tau}\mathrm{E}\left[V^{(l)}\left(S^{(l)}_1, \ldots, S^{(l)}_n\right)|S^{(l)}_1 = s^+_1, \ldots, S^{(l)}_n = s_n\right]\\ &\equiv U^{(l+1)}(\boldsymbol{s}^+)\end{aligned}$$

holds for any $\boldsymbol{s}^- \prec_c \boldsymbol{s}^+$. The preceding argument implies that $C^{(l+1)}_{0,0}(\boldsymbol{s})$ is non-decreasing in s_i for any $i \in \{1, \ldots, n\}$. From the inductive hypothesis, $C^{(l+1)}_a(\boldsymbol{s})$ for $a \neq (0,0)$ is also non-decreasing in s_i for any $i \in \{1, \ldots, n\}$. Thus, all components on the right-hand side of equation [10.13] are non-decreasing in s_i for any $i \in \{1, \ldots, n\}$.

Consequently, the inductive hypothesis holds for all N. We therefore conclude that the total expected discounted cost $V^{(N)}(\boldsymbol{s})$ is a non-decreasing function in s_i for any $i \in \{1, \ldots, n\}$. From the standard argument of contraction mapping theory (Puterman 2014), $V^{(N)}(\boldsymbol{s}) = V(\boldsymbol{s})$ holds. Therefore, proposition 10.1 is proved. Next, we derive a proposition for the properties of policies.

PROPOSITION 10.2.– *The difference between the expected cost $C_{(x,x')}(\boldsymbol{s}))$ of IR for x components and PR for x' components and the expected cost $C_{(0,y)}(\boldsymbol{s})$ $(0 \le (x + x') < y \le n)$ of PR for y components is non-decreasing in $s_{(k)}$ $(n - y < k \le n - (x + x'))$.*

PROOF.– The following equation is shown to be monotonically non-decreasing. Firstly, we consider the case that $(x, x') = (0, 0)$,

$$\begin{aligned}&C_{(0,0)}(\boldsymbol{s}) - C_{(0,y)}(\boldsymbol{s})\\ &= \left(D_\tau(\boldsymbol{s}) + e^{-r\tau}\int_{s_n}^{\infty}\cdots\int_{s_1}^{\infty} f(s'_1|s_1)\cdots f(s'_n|s_n)V^{(N-1)}(\boldsymbol{s}')ds'_1\cdots ds'_n\right)\\ &- \left(c_s + \sum_{j\in S_{pr}}^{y} C(s_j, 0) + e^{-r\tau}V^{(N-1)}(\boldsymbol{s}^-)\right)\end{aligned}$$

holds. From proposition 10.1, $C_{(0,0)}(\boldsymbol{s})$ is a non-decreasing function in s_i for any $i \in \{1, \ldots, n\}$ and $C_{(0,y)}(\boldsymbol{s})$ is constant in $s_{(k)}$ $(n - y < k \leq n - (x + x'))$. Also, we consider the case $(x, x') \neq (0, 0)$,

$$
\begin{aligned}
& C_{(x,x')}(\boldsymbol{s}) - C_{(0,y)}(\boldsymbol{s}) \\
&= \left(c_s + \sum_{i \in S_{ir}}^{x} C(s_i, s_i') + \sum_{j \in S_{pr}}^{x'} C(s_j, 0) + e^{-r\tau} V^{(N-1)}(\boldsymbol{s}^+) \right) \\
&- \left(c_s + \sum_{j \in S_{pr}}^{y} C(s_j, 0) + e^{-r\tau} V^{(N-1)}(\boldsymbol{s}^-) \right)
\end{aligned}
$$

holds. From the relation $0 \leq (x + x') < y \leq n$, the deterioration state of the system when PM$(x + x')$ is performed is $\boldsymbol{s}^+$, and the deterioration state of the system when PM(y) is performed is $\boldsymbol{s}^-$, then $\boldsymbol{s}^- \prec_c \boldsymbol{s}^+$. $e^{-r\tau} V(\boldsymbol{s}^+)$ is non-decreasing in $s_{(k)}$ $(n - y < k \leq n - (x + x'))$ and $e^{-r\tau} V(\boldsymbol{s}^-)$ is constant. Therefore, the difference between the expected cost $C_{(x,x')}$ of IR for x components and PR for x' components and the expected cost $C_{(0,y)}(\boldsymbol{s})$ $(0 \leq (x + x') < y \leq n)$ of PR for y components is non-decreasing in $s_{(k)}$ $(n - y < k \leq n - (x + x'))$. From propositions 10.1 and 10.2, we obtain the following corollary that demonstrates the structural properties of the optimal maintenance policies.

COROLLARY 10.1.– *Consider a k-out-of-n system with identical and independent components. Given the system's initial deterioration state $\boldsymbol{s} = (s_1, s_2, \ldots, s_n)$, define $s_{(1)}, s_{(2)}, \ldots, s_{(n)}$ as the ordered vector of $\boldsymbol{s}$ with $s_{(i)}$ representing the ith largest element in $\boldsymbol{s}$; then the optimal maintenance policy has the following properties:*

1) There exists $s^*_{(1)}$ as the switching point between "DN" and "PR for 1 component". When $s_{(1)} \leq s^*_{(1)}$, "DN" is preferable to "PR for 1 component". Otherwise, "PR for 1 component" is preferable to "DN".

2) For $i = 2, 3, \ldots, n$ there exists $s^*_{(i)}$ as the switching point between "Perform PM for $i - 1$ or less components" and "Perform PR for i components". When $s_{(i)} \leq s^*_{(i)}$, "Perform PM for $i - 1$ or fewer components" is preferable to "Perform PR for i components". Otherwise, the latter action is preferable.

The switching point between optimal actions limits the candidate of optimal policy to a small set. Therefore, this corollary makes the search for optimal policies easier.

10.5. Numerical studies

10.5.1. *Optimal maintenance policies for a two-out-of-three system*

We consider a two-out-of-three system. The deterioration parameters for each component are $\alpha = 1.2$ and $\beta = 1.5$. The system is periodically inspected at intervals of $\tau = 1$, and the deterioration state of component i obtained is classified into 12 levels: $s_i = 0$ if the deterioration amount locates in the interval $[0, 1)$ and $s_i = 1, 2, 3, 4, 5, 6, 7, 8, 9, 10$ and 11 if it is in the intervals $[1, 2), [2, 3), [3, 4), [4, 5), [5, 6), [6, 7), [7, 8), [8, 9), [9, 10), [10, 11)$ and $[11, +\infty)$, respectively. Let the failure threshold L be 11, which means this component is failed if the deterioration amount reaches 11. When PM is performed, setup cost $c_s = 200$ and PR cost $C(s_i, 0) = 200$ are incurred for each component. If we decide to perform IR, we also assume that the deterioration state of component i is restored from the current deterioration state $s_i(s_i > 2)$ to $s_i' = s_i - 2$, and the IR cost is $C(i, i-2) = 60 + 10i(i = 3, \ldots, L)$. When the system fails, the downtime cost per unit time is $c_d = 400$, and the CM cost $c_c = 3000$, and the system is restored to an as-good-as-new state. The incurred cost is discounted by $e^{-0.01}$.

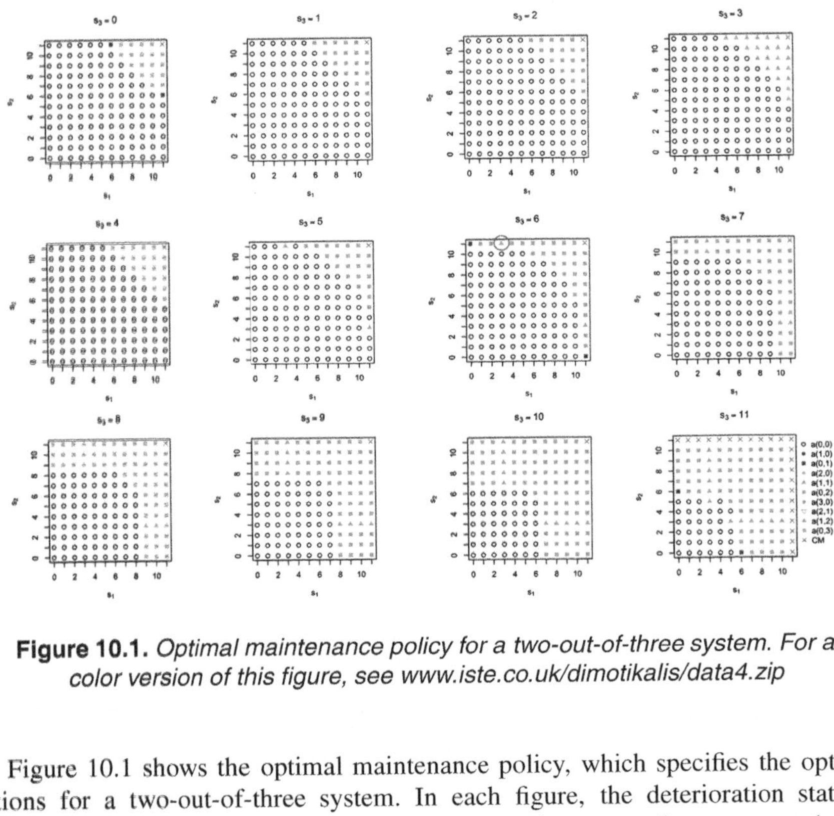

Figure 10.1. *Optimal maintenance policy for a two-out-of-three system. For a color version of this figure, see www.iste.co.uk/dimotikalis/data4.zip*

Figure 10.1 shows the optimal maintenance policy, which specifies the optimal actions for a two-out-of-three system. In each figure, the deterioration state of component 3 is fixed, the x-axis is the deterioration state of component 1, and the y-axis is the deterioration state of component 2. Each mark represents the corresponding optimal actions for that deterioration state. As shown in Figure 10.1, the maintenance area (excluding $a(0, 0)$) tends to increase as the deterioration state of the system increases, and maintenance with a larger scale is preferable to be selected.

On the other hand, some maintenance areas exist where the scale of maintenance decreases as the deterioration state of the system increases. This is because the total expected discounted cost over a long-run period can be reduced by keeping operation until other components deteriorate more and simultaneously replacing multiple components at the next period onward, more than immediately replacing them. There exist cases where maintenance is mostly PR (square markers), but with some IR (circle, triangle and inverted triangle markers) mixed in (e.g. $\boldsymbol{s} = (3, 11, 6)$). Here, a PR was performed for $s_3 = 11$, do nothing was performed for $s_2 = 6$, and IR was performed for $s_1 = 3$. This is because in a two-out-of-three system, the probability of system failure is low if two components are in good states, and IR was performed for deterioration state 3 can restore the system to near-new condition at a low cost.

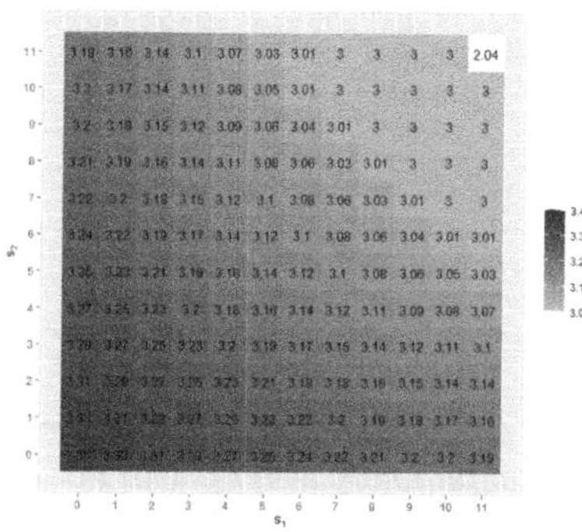

Figure 10.2. *Cost reduction rate for each deterioration state with* $s_3 = 0$

Next, Figure 10.2 shows the total expected discounted cost reduction rate for each deterioration state with and without considering IR. Let $V(\boldsymbol{s})$ be the total expected discounted cost considering IR and $V_{PR}(\boldsymbol{s})$ be the total expected discounted cost without considering IR, then the reduction rate $Rr(\boldsymbol{s})$ can be expressed as follows:

$$\text{Cost reduction rate } Rr(\boldsymbol{s}) = \frac{V_{PR}(\boldsymbol{s}) - V(\boldsymbol{s})}{V_{PR}(\boldsymbol{s})} \times 100\%.$$

Figure 10.2 shows that the total expected discount cost could be reduced by 2–3% by considering IR in any deterioration state. Figure 10.2 shows the case of $s_3 = 0$, and similar results can obtained for $s_3 = 1, \ldots, L$. This is because there are more options to restore the deterioration state at a lower cost than PR.

10.5.2. *Sensitivity analysis*

In this section, we investigate the effects of various factors on optimal maintenance decisions, and several parameters of sensitivity analysis are conducted. Firstly, we investigate the effects of the gamma process parameters, which describe the difference in the deterioration process. The parameters used in the sensitivity analysis are summarized in Table 10.2.

	α	β
base line	1.2	1.5
low deterioration	1.0	1.1
high deterioration	2.0	1.25

Table 10.2. *Gamma process parameters*

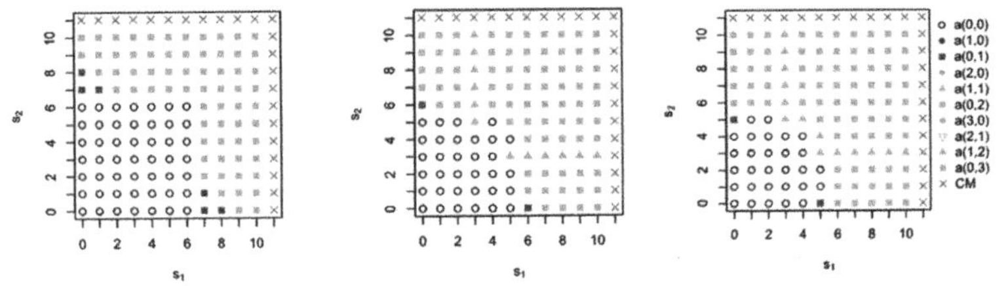

(a) $\alpha = 1.0, \beta = 1.1$ (b) $\alpha = 1.2, \beta = 1.5$ (c) $\alpha = 2.0, \beta = 1.25$

Figure 10.3. *Effects to optimal maintenance policies with respect to gamma process parameters with $s_3 = L$. For a color version of this figure, see www.iste.co.uk/dimotikalis/data4.zip*

As shown in Figure 10.3, the faster the system deteriorates, the greater the maintenance area (excluding $a(0,0)$). IR (circle, triangle and inverted triangle markers) is performed more often when the system deteriorates faster and less often when it deteriorates slower. This is because of the increased probability of system failure. Also, the area for action $a = (0,3)$ becomes smaller as changing from $\alpha = 1.2, \beta = 1.5$ to $\alpha = 2.0, \beta = 1.25$. This is because replacing two components is less expensive in the long term than replacing all, since the system will not fail as long as the two components are working.

Secondly, we investigate the effects of the recovery amount of IR. In this case, the optimal maintenance policies were derived from the current deterioration state s_i for the cases of $s_i' = s_i - 1, s_i' = s_i - 2, s_i' = s_i - 3$, and $s_i' = s_i - 4$.

As shown in Figure 10.4, the greater the recovery amount of IR, the larger the area of IR, and a larger-scale maintenance is selected. This is because IR can reduce the probability of system failure at a lower cost than PR.

Finally, we investigate the effects of the cost function. We focused on setup costs and IR costs. Setup costs were set at $c_s = 100, 200$ and 300.

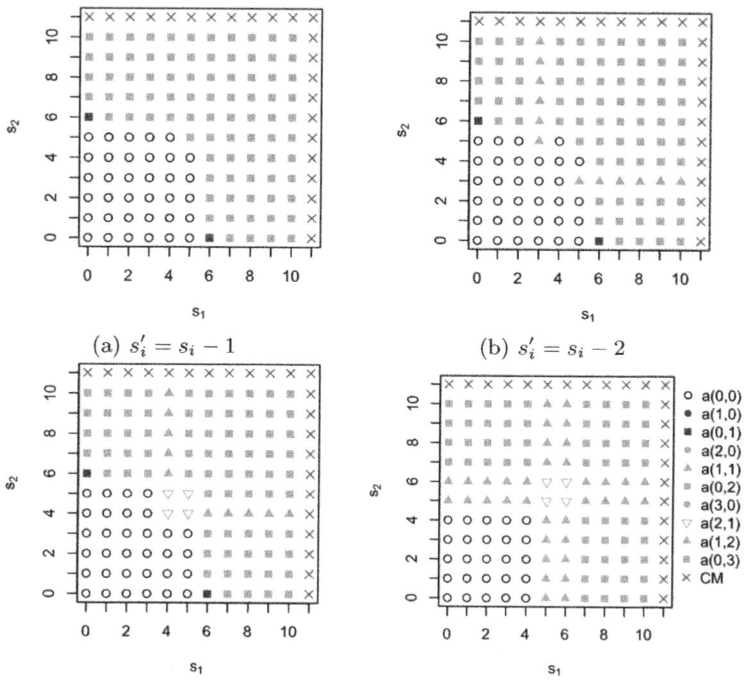

(a) $s_i' = s_i - 1$ (b) $s_i' = s_i - 2$

(c) $s_i' = s_i - 3$ (d) $s_i' = s_i - 4$

Figure 10.4. *Effects to optimal maintenance policies with respect to s_i', the recovery amount of IR, with $s_3 = L$. For a color version of this figure, see www.iste.co.uk/dimotikalis/data4.zip*

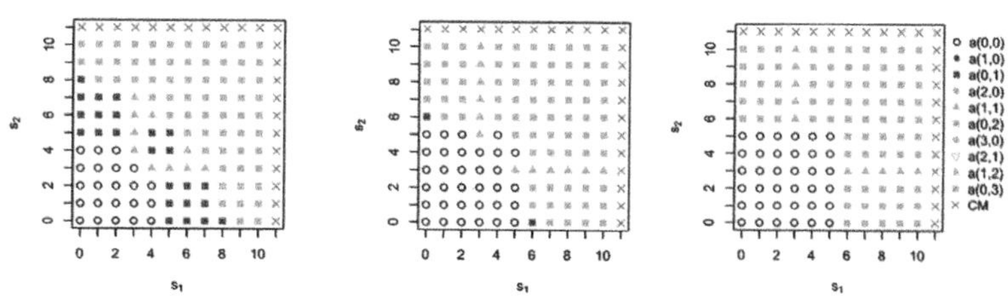

(a) $c_s = 100$ (b) $c_s = 200$ (c) $c_s = 300$

Figure 10.5. *Effects to optimal maintenance policies with respect to setup cost with $s_3 = L$. For a color version of this figure, see www.iste.co.uk/dimotikalis/data4.zip*

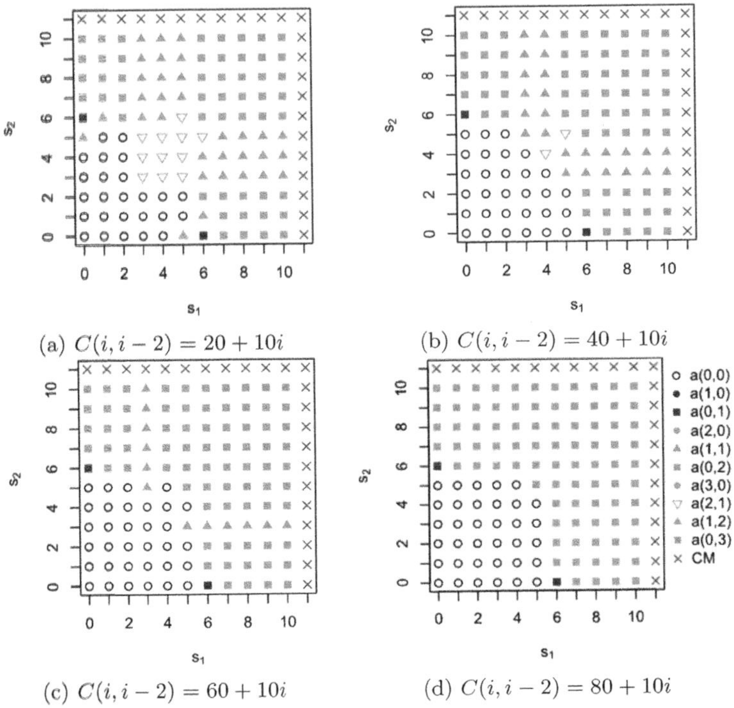

Figure 10.6. *Effects to optimal maintenance policies with respect to IR cost with $s_3 = L$. For a color version of this figure, see www.iste.co.uk/dimotikalis/data4.zip*

As shown in Figure 10.5, the larger the setup cost, the larger the scale maintenance is selected. This is because the larger the setup costs, the impact of economic dependence is greater. Due of this, when setup costs are small, the effect of economic dependence is smaller, and maintenance for only one component increases.

IR costs were set as $C(i, i-2) = 20 + 10i, C(i, i-2) = 40 + 10i, C(i, i-2) = 60 + 10i$ and $C(i, i-2) = 80 + 10i$ $(i = 3, \ldots, L)$.

As shown in Figure 10.6, the lower the cost of IR, the larger the area of IR. This is because IR is more cost-effective than PR. However, PR is always the choice in a deterioration state where the system is close to failure because it is not cost-effective to reduce the probability of failure by IR.

10.6. Conclusion

We deal with a k-out-of-n system of which the deterioration follows a Gamma process. Considering IR, we have formulated the optimal decision-making problem of

CBM over an infinite horizon. Under an assumption related to cost, we demonstrated the monotonicity of the total expected discounted cost for each deterioration state, which indicates the degree of system deterioration. Furthermore, we clarified the structural properties of the optimal maintenance policy.

This research formulated the deterioration of components using a gamma process. However, there are several stochastic processes that represent deterioration. We also assumed independent components. In reality, the failure or deterioration of one component can affect the deterioration of other components. Future work includes using a continuous stochastic process other than a gamma process and considering component-dependent deterioration.

10.7. References

Alaswad, S. and Xiang, Y. (2017). A review on condition-based maintenance optimization models for stochastically deteriorating system. *Reliability Engineering & System Safety*, 157, 54–63.

Barbera, F., Schneider, H., Watson, E. (1999). A condition based maintenance model for a two-unit series system. *European Journal of Operational Research*, 116, 281–290.

Chen, N., Ye, Z., Xiang, Y., Zhang, L. (2015). Condition-based maintenance using the inverse Gaussian degradation model. *European Journal of Operational Research*, 243, 190–199.

Gu, X., Guo, W., Jin, X. (2020). Performance evaluation for manufacturing systems under control-limit maintenance policy. *Journal of Manufacturing Systems*, 55, 221–232.

Hao, S., Yang, J., Berenguer, C. (2019). Degradation analysis based on an extended inverse Gaussian process model with skew-normal random effects and measurement errors. *Reliability Engineering & System Safety*, 189, 261–270.

Huang, J., Golubović, D., Koh, S., Yang, D., Li, X., Fan, X., Zhang, G. (2015). Degradation modeling of mid-power white-light LEDs by using Wiener process. *Optics Express*, 23, A966–A978.

Keizer, M., Teunter, R., Veldman, J. (2016). Clustering condition-based maintenance for systems with redundancy and economic dependencies. *European Journal of Operational Research*, 251, 531–540.

Keizer, M., Flapper, S., Teunter, R. (2017). Condition-based maintenance policies for systems with multiple dependent components: A review. *European Journal of Operational Research*, 261, 405–420.

Liu, B., Wu, S., Xie, M., Kuo, W. (2017). A condition-based maintenance policy for degrading systems with age-and state-dependent operating cost. *European Journal of Operational Research*, 263, 879–887.

Ministry of Land, Infrastructure, Transport and Tourism (2021). Strategic maintenance and management of rivers (in Japanese) [Online]. Available at: http://www.river.or.jp/kougi2021_4.pdf.

Moghaddass, R., Zuo, M., Pandey, M. (2012). Optimal design and maintenance of a repairable multi-state system with standby components. *Journal of Statistical Planning and Inference*, 142, 2409–2420.

Noortwijk, J. (2009). A survey of the application of gamma processes in maintenance. *Reliability Engineering & System Safety*, 94, 2–21.

Özekici, S. (1995). Optimal maintenance policies in random environments. *European Journal of Operational Research*, 82, 283–294.

Puterman, M. (2014). *Markov Decision Processes: Discrete Stochastic Dynamic Programming*. John Wiley & Sons, New York.

Qiao, W. and Lu, D. (2015). A survey on wind turbine condition monitoring and fault diagnosis – Part I: Components and subsystems. *IEEE Transactions on Industrial Electronics*, 62, 6536–6545.

Shafiee, M., Finkelstein, M., Bérenguer, C. (2015). An opportunistic condition-based maintenance policy for offshore wind turbine blades subjected to degradation and environmental shocks. *Reliability Engineering & System Safety*, 142, 463–471.

Sun, Q., Ye, Z., Chen, N. (2018). Optimal inspection and replacement policies for multi-unit systems subject to deterioration. *IEEE Transactions on Reliability*, 67, 401–413.

Wang, J. and Zhu, X. (2021). Joint optimization of condition-based maintenance and inventory control for a k-out-of-n:f system of multi-state degrading components. *European Journal of Operational Research*, 290, 514–529.

Xu, J., Liang, Z., Li, Y., Wang, K. (2021). Generalized condition-based maintenance optimization for multi-component systems considering stochastic dependency and imperfect maintenance. *Reliability Engineering & System Safety*, 211, 107592.

Ye, Z. and Xie, M. (2015). Stochastic modelling and analysis of degradation for highly reliable products. *Applied Stochastic Models in Business and Industry*, 31, 16–32.

Zhang, M., Gaudoin, O., Xie, M. (2015). Deterioration-based maintenance decision using stochastic filtering for systems under imperfect maintenance. *European Journal of Operational Research*, 245, 531–541.

Zhang, N., Fouladirad, M., Barros, A., Zhang, J. (2020). Condition-based maintenance for a K-out-of-N deteriorating system under periodic inspection with failure dependence. *European Journal of Operational Research*, 287, 159–167.

Zhang, N., Tian, S., Cai, K., Zhang, J. (2023). Condition-based maintenance assessment for a deteriorating system considering stochastic failure dependence. *IISE Transactions*, 55, 687–697.

11

Stochastic Orders and Reliability Properties for the Deficit at Ruin and Bounds for the Laplace Transform of a Compound Geometric Distribution

In this chapter, we give stochastic comparison results, in terms of the Laplace transform order, for quantities of interest in the Sparre Andersen model of risk theory. We also discuss how these results may yield bounds for the Laplace transform of a compound geometric distribution.

11.1. Introduction

It is well-known that the Laplace transform (LT) is an effective tool in the analysis of stochastic models in various areas such as economics, engineering and computer science. There are many types of stochastic orders based on LT that have been studied in the literature. Alzaid et al. (1991) have studied the LT order, which compares two random variables via their respective LT. They also provide some interesting interpretations in life insurance, finance and reliability theory. Moreover, Denuit (2001) showed the importance of this stochastic order in actuarial science and utility theory by deriving several results and applications. See Shaked and Shanthikumar (2007) for more details on stochastic orders related to the LT.

Moreover, the theory of stochastic orders is an efficient way to derive useful bounds for quantities of interest in complicated stochastic models. In the actuarial literature, stochastic orders have been widely studied and used in risk theory (see Goovaerts et al. 1990). While comparison between risks is of key interest in actuarial

---

Chapter written by Lazaros KANELLOPOULOS and Konstantinos POLITIS.

science, and numerous papers employ stochastic orders to deal with this issue in recent years, the use of LT orders in an actuarial context is rather rare. An advantage for considering LT orders in collective risk theory is that for various quantities of interest there, their exact distribution is not available but their LT is. A typical example concerns compound distributions, which are encountered most frequently in risk theory or, more generally, distributions that arise by taking the convolution of a compound distribution with another distribution on $[0, \infty)$.

Initially, for a non-negative variable X with d.f. F, the variable $X_t \equiv [X-t|X > t]$ is known as the residual life of X at time t. Also define a random variable X^e with tail $\overline{F}_e(x) = \int_x^\infty \overline{F}(t)dt / \int_0^\infty \overline{F}(t)dt$. The d.f. F_e is known as the equilibrium distribution associated with F. Next, in the following definition, we give the notion of some stochastic orders. For further details and properties of these and other stochastic orders, the reader is referred to the book by Shaked and Shanthikumar (2007).

DEFINITION 11.1.– *Let X, Y be two non-negative random variables (r.v.'s) having distribution function (d.f.) F_X, F_Y, respectively, with support $l_X = sup\{t : F_X(t) < 1\}$ for X and $l_Y = sup\{t : F_Y(t) < 1\}$ for Y. Then, X is said to be smaller than Y in the*

(i) *usual stochastic order (denoted by $X \leq_{st} Y$) if*

$$\overline{F}_X(x) \leq \overline{F}_Y(x) \quad \text{for all} \quad x;$$

(ii) *LT order (denoted by $X \leq_{Lt} Y$) if*

$$\mathcal{L}_X(s) = \int_0^\infty e^{-sx} dF_X(x) \geq \int_0^\infty e^{-sx} dF_Y(x) = \mathcal{L}_Y(s) \quad \text{for all} \quad s \geq 0;$$

(iii) *hazard rate order (denoted by $X \leq_{hr} Y$) if*

$$r_X(t) = \frac{f_X(t)}{\overline{F}_X(t)} \geq \frac{f_Y(t)}{\overline{F}_Y(t)} = r_Y(t) \quad \text{is increasing in} \quad t \geq 0;$$

(iv) *LT order of residual lives (denoted by $X \leq_{Lt-rl} Y$) if $X_t \leq_{Lt} Y_t$ for all $t \in [0, l_X) \cap [0, l_Y)$.*

We also recall the definition of some classes of lifetime distributions arising from reliability theory. In particular, the following classes of distributions are defined via stochastic comparisons of a residual lifetime X_t and the original variable $X = X_0$ (see Belzunce et al. 2001). Let X be a non-negative random variable with distribution F. We say that X (or F) is new better than used (denoted by $X \in NBU$ or $F \in NBU$) if $X_t \leq_{st} X$ for all $t \geq 0$. A r.v. X (or F) is new better than used in the Laplace order (denoted by $X \in NBU_{Lt}$ or $F \in NBU_{Lt}$) if $X_t \leq_{Lt} X$ for all $t \geq 0$.

Note that the NBU class is contained in the NBU_{Lt}. As a result, we obtain, in particular, that the NWU_{Lt} (NBU_{Lt}) class contains the class of distributions with increasing (decreasing) mean residual life (IMRL, respectively, DMRL, see, for example, Willmot and Lin 2001). Furthermore, using an example (as in Franco et al. (2001), see Example 2.7), we can show that the NBU class is strictly smaller than the NBU_{Lt} class.

The rest of the chapter is organized as follows: in section 11.2, we present stochastic comparisons for the deficit at ruin and the maximal aggregate loss in the Sparre Andersen model of risk theory. In section 11.3, we show that stochastic orders can give bounds for the LT of maximal aggregate losses in the classical risk model. Finally, in section 11.4, we illustrate these bounds by giving two examples.

11.2. Model description and results

We consider the Sparre Andersen risk model with a surplus process

$$U(t) = x + ct - \sum_{i=1}^{N(t)} Y_i, \quad t \geq 0, \qquad [11.1]$$

where $x \geq 0$ is the initial surplus, $c > 0$ is the constant premium rate and the positive, independent and identically distributed (i.i.d.) r.v.'s $\{Y_i\}_{i\geq 1}$ with d.f. $P(x) = 1 - \overline{P}(x) = Pr(Y \leq x)$ denote the claim sizes. The arrival of claims is modeled by a renewal counting process $\{N(t) : t \geq 0\}$, so that $N(t) = max\{n \in \mathbb{N} : \Xi_1 + \Xi_2 + \cdots + \Xi_n \leq t\}$, where the interclaim times Ξ_i are assumed to be i.i.d. with d.f. $H(t) = 1 - \overline{H}(t) = Pr(\Xi \leq t)$, independent of the claim sizes. We assume throughout that $cE\Xi > EY$, providing a positive safety loading. More specifically, we assume that $c = (1+\theta)EY/E\Xi$, where $\theta > 0$ is the relative security loading. An important special case of this model is the *classical risk model*, where the arrival process $\{N(t) : t \geq 0\}$ is a Poisson process. See, for example, Willmot and Lin (2001) and Asmussen and Albrecher (2010) for a detailed description and various results on these models.

Let $T = \inf\{t : U(t) < 0\}$ be the time of ruin; then the probability of ruin is defined by

$$\psi(x) = Pr(T < \infty | U(0) = x).$$

The ruin probability satisfies the following defective renewal equation (d.r.e.):

$$\psi(x) = \phi \int_0^x \psi(x-t)dF(t) + \phi\overline{F}(x), \qquad [11.2]$$

whose solution is

$$\psi(x) = \frac{\phi}{1-\phi} \int_{0^-}^x \overline{F}(x-t)dG(t), \qquad [11.3]$$

where $\phi = \psi(0)$, $G(x) = 1 - \psi(x)$ is the probability of non-ruin with initial capital x and $F(x)$ is the d.f. $F(x) = Pr(X_F \leq x)$, of the descending ladder height associated with the surplus process, i.e. the (proper) distribution of the drop in the surplus given that a drop occurs. It is well established that $\psi(x)$ is the tail of the compound geometric distribution associated with a r.v. $L = X_F^{(1)} + X_F^{(2)} + \cdots X_F^{(N)}$, which satisfies

$$\overline{G}(x) = 1 - G(x) = (1-\phi)\sum_{n=1}^{\infty} \phi^n \overline{F^{*n}}(x), \quad x \geq 0, \qquad [11.4]$$

where $\overline{F^{*n}}(x) = Pr(X_F^{(1)} + X_F^{(2)} + \cdots X_F^{(n)} > x)$ is the tail of the n-th fold convolution of F with itself and $0 < \phi < 1$. The variable L here is the maximal aggregate loss in the surplus process. Also, N is a counting random variable, independent of $\{X_F^{(i)} : i \geq 1\}$, with $Pr(N = n) = (1-\phi)\phi^n, n = 0, 1, ...$ Note that $G(x)$ has a mass point at 0, $G(0) = 1 - \phi$.

The deficit at ruin (given that ruin occurs) is of central interest in ruin theory. Gerber et al. (1987) introduced the defective d.f. of the deficit (or the severity) at ruin, given by $G(x,y) = Pr(|U_T| \leq y, T < \infty | U(0) = x), y \geq 0$. If we set $\overline{G}(x,y) = \psi(x) - G(x,y)$ for $x \geq 0$ and $y \geq 0$, then $\overline{G}(x,y)$ satisfies the d.r.e.

$$\overline{G}(x,y) = \phi\overline{F}(x+y) + \phi\int_0^x \overline{G}(x-t,y)dF(t), \qquad [11.5]$$

which generalizes [11.2]. The solution of [11.5] is given by (see Willmot (2002))

$$\overline{G}(x,y) = \frac{\phi}{1-\phi}\int_{0-}^{x} \overline{F}(x+y-t)dG(t). \qquad [11.6]$$

Let now Z_x be a random variable which represents the deficit at ruin, given that ruin occurs with initial surplus x. The distribution of Z_x is denoted by G_x, while the associated tail is

$$\overline{G}_x(y) = 1 - G_x(y) = \frac{\overline{G}(x,y)}{\overline{G}(x)}.$$

Willmot (2002) studied the function $\overline{G}_x$ using results from reliability theory and obtained some inequalities for the tail $\overline{G}_x$ when the corresponding d.f. of ladder height belongs to a reliability class. Psarrakos (2009) gave results about stochastic comparisons for a compound geometric distribution convolved with another distribution, termed a compound geometric convolution, which is an extension of the deficit at ruin. The following proposition extends the results of Psarrakos (2009) as it gives a result for the LT order between the deficit at ruin and the corresponding ladder height.

PROPOSITION 11.1.– *If the d.f. F is $NBU_{Lt}(NWU_{Lt})$, then*

$$Z_x \leq_{Lt} (\geq_{Lt}) X_F.$$

PROOF.– Assume that the d.f. F is NBU$_{\text{Lt}}$. Then, taking LT on both sides of [11.6], we derive that

$$\begin{aligned}\int_0^\infty e^{-sy}\overline{G}(x,y)dy &= \int_0^\infty e^{-sy}\frac{\phi}{1-\phi}\int_0^x \overline{F}(x+y-t)dG(t)dy \\ &\leq \frac{\phi}{1-\phi}\int_0^x\int_0^\infty e^{-sy}\overline{F}(x-t)\overline{F}(y)dydG(t) \\ &= \frac{\phi}{1-\phi}\int_0^x \overline{F}(x-t)dG(t)\int_0^\infty e^{-sy}\overline{F}(y)dy.\end{aligned}$$

By dividing both sides of the last inequality by $\overline{G}(x)$, the result follows. The NWU$_{\text{Lt}}$ case may be proved in a similar manner.

Another type of stochastic order defined in Definition 11.1 is the hazard rate order. It is somewhat surprising that only a few papers in risk theory discuss results for this order. In general, the $\leq_{hr}$ order is not closed under convolution. In the following theorem, we show that the $\leq_{Lt}$ order between ladder heights of two different surplus processes implies, under some conditions, the hazard rate order for the corresponding maximal aggregate losses.

THEOREM 11.1.– *Let two different surplus processes as in* [11.1], *with respective ladder heights denoted generically by X_F, Y_F and with relative security loadings θ_X, θ_Y, respectively, such as $\theta_X \geq \theta_Y$. If $X_F \in NBU_{Lt}$ and $Y_F \in NWU_{Lt}$, then*

$$X_F \leq_{Lt} Y_F \Rightarrow L_X \leq_{hr} L_Y.$$

PROOF.– Willmot (2002) proved that LT of residual lifetime of L is

$$\int_0^\infty e^{-sy}\psi_t(y)dy = \frac{1-E(e^{-s\cdot L})\cdot E(e^{-s\cdot Z_t})}{s}, \qquad [11.7]$$

where $\psi_t(y) = \overline{G}(t+y)/\overline{G}(t)$. Then, by Proposition 11.1, it follows that

$$X_F \in NBU_{Lt} \Rightarrow Z_t^X \leq_{Lt} X_F,$$

$$Y_F \in NBU_{Lt} \Rightarrow Z_t^Y \geq_{Lt} Y_F.$$

Therefore, using the transitivity of the LT order and the assumption in the statement, we get that $Z_t^X \leq X_F \leq_{Lt} Y_F \leq_{Lt} Z_t^Y$, or equivalently, for $s \geq 0$

$$\mathcal{L}_{Z_t^X}(s) \geq \mathcal{L}_{Z_t^Y}(s). \qquad [11.8]$$

It is well-known that the LT order is closed under convolution (see Denuit 2001). Hence, by assumption that $X_F \leq Y_F$ and $\theta_X \geq \theta_Y$, it follows $L_X \leq_{Lt} L_Y$, or equivalently for $s \geq 0$

$$\mathcal{L}_{L_X}(s) \geq \mathcal{L}_{L_Y}(s). \qquad [11.9]$$

By [11.7], [11.8] and [11.9], it follows

$$\int_0^\infty e^{-sy}\psi_t^X(y)dy \leq \int_0^\infty e^{-sy}\psi_t^Y(y)dy, \quad s \geq 0,$$

or $L_X \leq_{Lt-rl} L_Y$. Belzunce et al. (2004) proved that the LT of the residual lives order is equivalent to the hazard order $X \leq_{Lt-rl} Y \Leftrightarrow X \leq_{hr} Y$ and the assertion follows from the last two expressions.

11.3. Bounds for the LT of the maximal aggregate loss

Stochastic order is an effective tool in order to derive bounds. In particular, the usual stochastic order gives bounds for the tail of a distribution and the LT order gives bounds for the LT associated with a r.v. Bounds for the LT of a r.v. have been considered by many authors; see, for example, Hu and Lin (2008) and Zhang (2012). In Goovaerts et al. (1990, pp. 65–66), the authors discuss how a weak type of ordering (stop-loss order) between claim sizes implies ordering of the respective ruin probabilities.

We mentioned in the Introduction that in many cases (e.g. when claim sizes have a heavy tail, such as that of a Pareto or a lognormal distribution), it is impossible to extract an explicit expression of the ruin probability or other quantities associated with it. However, LT of several functions of interest are available analytically. Here, we compare the LT of the maximal aggregate losses L_X, L_Y and L_Z of three compound Poisson models with the same relative security loading in order to derive upper bounds for the LT of the maximal aggregate loss, when the corresponding claim size follows a Pareto distribution.

More specifically, consider the following two surplus processes:

$$U_1(t) = x + ct - S_1(t) \quad t \geq 0, \qquad [11.10]$$

and

$$U_2(t) = x + ct - S_2(t), \quad t \geq 0, \qquad [11.11]$$

where $S_1(t) = \sum_{i=1}^{N_1(t)} X^{(i)}$ and $S_2(t) = \sum_{i=1}^{N_2(t)} Y^{(i)}$ are two compound Poisson processes. We assume that the claim sizes $X^{(1)}, X^{(2)}, \ldots$ are i.i.d. and distributed as

X, while claim sizes $Y^{(1)}, Y^{(2)}, ...$ are i.i.d. and distributed as Y. Moreover, the two Poisson processes $\{N_1(t)\}, \{N_2(t)\}$ have the same rate λ. Now let L_X and L_Y be the maximal aggregate loss associated with the risk processes [11.10] and [11.11], respectively.

In the following corollary, we demonstrate that the $\leq_{Lt}$ order between claim sizes in the classical Poisson risk model implies the same order (with reverse sign) for the maximal aggregate loss.

COROLLARY 11.1.– *Let X and Y be the r.v.'s representing claim sizes of the surplus processes* [11.10] *and* [11.11], *respectively, such as $EX = EY$. Then,*

$$X \geq_{Lt} Y \Rightarrow L_X \leq_{Lt} L_Y.$$

PROOF.– In the classical model, it is well-known that the distribution of the (descending) ladder height is the equilibrium distribution associated with the d.f. of claim sizes. Also, by Denuit (2001, Property 2.4), it follows that

$$X \geq Y \Leftrightarrow X^e \leq_{Lt} Y^e.$$

Now since these two surplus processes have the same λ, c and $EX = EY$, we get $\theta_X = c/(\lambda EX) - 1 = c/(\lambda EY) - 1 = \theta_Y$. Using the closure under compounding of the LT order (see Denuit 2001, Property 2.3), we obtain $L_X \leq_{Lt} L_Y$.

11.4. Examples

To illustrate the Theorem 11.1 and the Corollary 11.1, we give two examples. Firstly, in the classical model case, we show that LT order between two ladder heights in the classical model implies hazard rate order between the corresponding maximal aggregate losses. Next, we derive bounds for the LT of r.v. L when the claim size follows a Pareto distribution and we compare it with two bounds by Hu and Lin (2001, 2008), respectively.

EXAMPLE 11.1.– *Let $X \sim Exp(5/4)$ and Y has the tail $\overline{F}_Y(t) = (1/5)e^{-(1/2)t} + (4/5)e^{-2t}, t \geq 0$ representing claim sizes of* [11.10] *and* [11.11], *such that $EX = EY = 4/5$. It is easy to see that (by MATHEMATICA)*

$$\mathcal{L}_X(s) = \frac{5/4}{5/4+s} \leq \frac{1}{10(1/2+s)} + \frac{8}{5(2+s)} = \mathcal{L}_Y(s), \quad s \geq 0.$$

or equivalently $X \geq_{Lt} Y$. In the classical model case, we have that the ladder height d.f. is the equilibrium distribution and by Denuit (2001, Property 2.4), it follows that $X^e \leq_{Lt} Y^e$. Also, it is well known that a mixture of two exponentials belongs *to NWU$_{LT}$ and an exponential distribution is both NBU$_{LT}$ and NWU$_{LT}$. Finally, by Theorem* 11.1, *it follows that*

$$r_{L_X}(t) = \frac{-\psi'_X(t)}{\psi_X(t)} \geq \frac{-\psi'_Y(t)}{\psi_Y(t)} = r_{L_Y}(t), \quad t \geq 0,$$

where $\frac{-\psi'_X(t)}{\psi_X(t)} = 0.1136$ *and* $\frac{-\psi'_Y(t)}{\psi_Y(t)} = \frac{0.0833e^{-1.2933t}+0.1232e^{-0.0702t}}{0.0644e^{-1.2933t}+1.7537e^{-0.0702t}}$.

From Figure 11.1, we observe that $L_X \leq_{hr} L_Y$ *as we expected.*

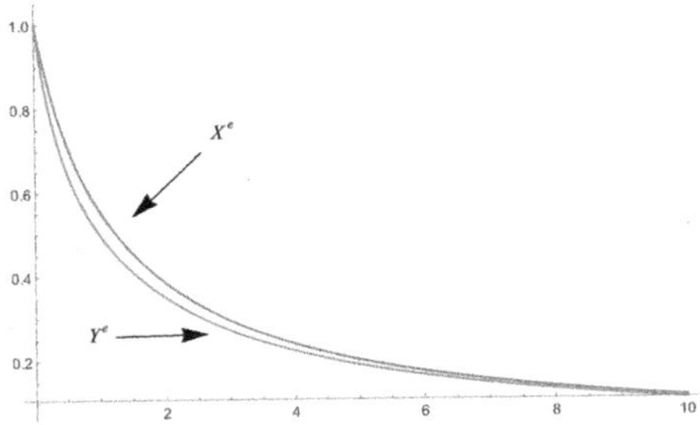

(a) Laplace transforms of densities of X^e and Y^e

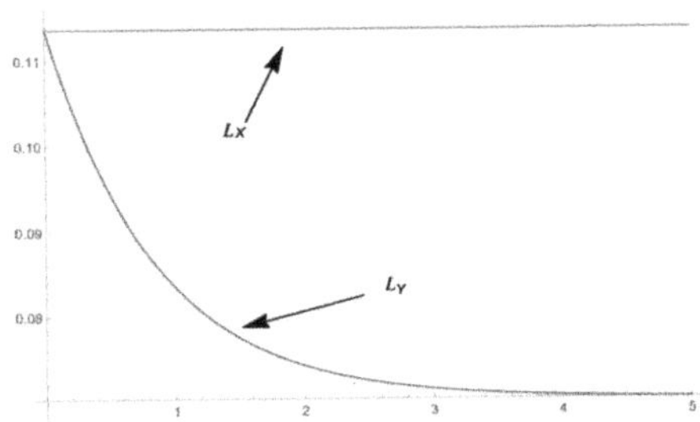

(b) hazard rate functions of L_X, L_Z and UB_{HL}

Figure 11.1. *For a color version of this figure, see www.iste.co.uk/dimotikalis/data4.zip*

EXAMPLE 11.2.– *Let X and Y have the tails* $\overline{F}_X(t) = \frac{1}{3}e^{-2t} + \frac{2}{3}e^{-4t}$ *and* $\overline{F}_Y(t) = 1/(1+t)^4$, *so that* $EX = EY = 1/3$. *Also, let Z follow an exponential distribution with parameter* 3. *Then, it is easy to check that*

$$\mathcal{L}_Z(s) \leq \mathcal{L}_X(s) \leq \mathcal{L}_Y(s), \quad s \geq 0.$$

By Corollary 11.1, *we get* $\mathcal{L}_{L_Z}(s) \geq \mathcal{L}_{L_X}(s) \geq \mathcal{L}_{L_Y}(s)$. *It turns out that the functions* $\mathcal{L}_{L_X}(s)$ *and* $\mathcal{L}_{L_Z}(s)$ *can serve as upper bounds of* $\mathcal{L}_Y(s)$. *Now let a non-negative r.v. W with the finite second moment* $EW^2 < \infty$. *Hu and Lin (2001) derived an upper bound for the LT* L_W *as follows:*

$$UB_{HL1}(s) := 1 - s \cdot \mu_W \cdot exp\{-sEW^2/2\mu_W\}, \quad s \geq 0.$$

Moreover, Hu and Lin (2008) gave another upper bound for the LT of W,

$$UB_{HL2}(s) := 1 - \frac{(EW)^2}{EW^2} + \frac{(EW)^2}{EW^2} \cdot exp\{-sEW^2/\mu_W\}, \quad s \geq 0.$$

In Figure 2(a), we show the LT order of densities for X, Y and Z. Also, in Figure 2(b), we present the LT of the corresponding maximal aggregate losses when the random variables of claim sizes follow a mixture of two exponentials, or an exponential with the same mean. It is clear that they are better upper bounds than UB_{HL1} and UB_{HL2} for $s \in (0.2, \infty)$.

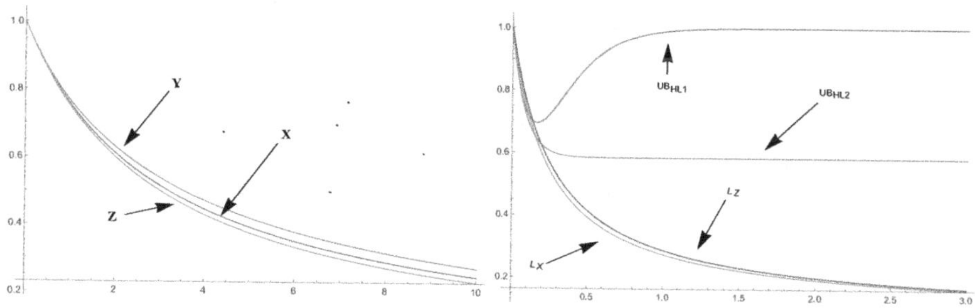

(a) Laplace transforms of densities of X, Y and Z

(b) Laplace transforms of densities for L_X, L_Z and UB_{HL}

Figure 11.2. *For a color version of this figure, see www.iste.co.uk/dimotikalis/data4.zip*

11.5. References

Alzaid, A., Kim, J.S., Proschan, F. (1991). Laplace ordering and its applications. *J. Appl. Probab.*, 28, 116–130.

Asmussen, S. and Albrecher, H. (2010). *Ruin Probabilities*, 2nd edition. World Scientific, Singapore.

Belzunce, F., Ortega, E.M., Ruiz, J.M. (2001). A note on stochastic comparisons of excess lifetimes of renewal processes. *J. Appl. Probab.*, 38(3), 747–753.

Belzunce, F., Gao, X., Hu, F. (2004). Characterizations of the hazard rate order and IFR aging notion. *Stat. Probab. Lett.*, 70, 235–242.

Denuit, M. (2001). Laplace transform ordering of actuarial quantities. *Ins. Math. Econ.*, 29, 83–102.

Franco, M., Ruiz, J.M., Ruiz, M.C. (2001). On closure of the IFR(2) and NBU(2) classes. *J. Appl. Prob.*, 38, 235–241.

Gerber, H.U., Goovaerts, M.J., Kaas, R. (1987). On the probability and severity of ruin. *ASTIN Bulletin*, 39, 151–163.

Goovaerts, M.J., Kaas, R., Van Heerwaarden, A.E., Bauwelinckx, T. (1990). *Effective Actuarial Methods*. North Holland, Amsterdam.

Hu, C.-Y. and Lin, G.D. (2001). On the geometric compounding model with applications. *Probab. Math. Statist.*, 21, 135–147.

Hu, C.-Y. and Lin, G.D. (2008). Some inequalities for Laplace transforms. *J. Math. Anal. Appl.*, 340, 675–686.

Psarrakos, G. (2009). A note on convolutions of compound geometric distributions. *Stat. Probab. Lett.*, 79, 1231–1237.

Shaked, M. and Santhikumar, J.G. (2007). *Stochastic Orders*. Springer, New York.

Willmot, G.E. (2002). Compound geometric residual lifetime distributions and the deficit at ruin. *Ins. Math. Econ.*, 30, 421–438.

Willmot, G.E. and Lin, X.S. (2001). *Lundberg Approximations for Compound Distributions with Insurance Applications*. Springer, New York.

Zhang, Z. (2012). Bounds for characteristic functions and Laplace transforms of probability distributions. *Soc. Indust. Appl. Math.*, 56(2), 350–358.

12

A New Family of Continuous Univariate Distributions with Applications in Actuarial Science

In this work, we introduce a wide family of continuous univariate distributions with support $(0, \infty)$. The new family, denoted by ${D_g}^+(h)$, contains distributions with the cumulative distribution function of the form $F(x; \boldsymbol{\theta}) = g^{-1}(h(x; \boldsymbol{\theta}))$ where g and h satisfy specific conditions. Several properties of ${D_g}^+(h)$ are studied, including unimodality, aging and probability bounds, and a condition is given so that a member of ${D_g}^+(h)$ has heavy tails. The last result as well as the aging properties are of special interest for the actuarial science where distributions with heavy tails are of major significance.

12.1. Introduction

The search for families of distributions that can be exploited as appropriate parametric models for empirical data has a long history in the statistics literature. The premier example in this area, and probably the oldest one, is Pearson's system of differential equations (see Pearson 1895).

Two additional pioneering methods that appeared before 1980 were Johnson's method of transformations (see Johnson 1949) and the method of quantiles suggested in Hastings et al. (1947) and Tukey (1960).

After 1980, there has been a renewed interest in developing more flexible distributions, with special emphasis drawn in generating skewed and heavy tailed distributions. The last properties are essential when fitting empirical

---

Chapter written by Markos V. KOUTRAS and Spiros D. DAFNIS.

economic/financial data, as well as for data arising in the actuarial field (claims/losses of insurance companies).

The majority of methodologies in that period can be described as "methods of combination", since they combine existing distributions into new ones or add parameters to an existing distribution. Lee et al. (2013) have classified the developments under this framework in the following four categories:

– Generation of skew distributions, with driving force the works of Azzalini (1985, 1986). For a detailed review of this approach up to 2005, see Vicari and Kotz (2005).

– Generation of new distributions by adding an extra parameter to an existing cumulative distribution function (cdf) $F(x)$, for example, by considering the so-called Neyman alternatives $F^{\alpha}(x)$ and $1-(1-F(x))^{\alpha}$. See Marshall and Olkin (1997) or Mudholkar and Srivastava (1993) for an alternative approach of this type.

– The class of Beta-generated distributions or more generally, the method of probability integral transformation of a $(0,1)$ random variable. According to this, we start with a random variable over $(0,1)$ (e.g. Beta) and consider the integral of its density from 0 to $F(x)$, where $F(x)$ is the cdf of another random variable. The first work on this class was by Eugene et al. (2002) (see also Jones 2004), and since then, numerous publications exploiting this approach have appeared. Special attention should be given to the $T-X$ family which was introduced by Alzaatreh et al. (2013).

– The composite method which combines two truncated distributions with overlapping supports in a new distribution (see Cooray and Ananda 2005).

For more details on the methods of generating families of univariate continuous distributions, the interested reader is referred to the excellent review article by Lee et al. (2013).

Recently, Koutras et al. (2014) introduced a new distribution by exploiting the well-known property of the logistic distribution that the logit transformation $ln\frac{F(x)}{1-F(x)}$ of its cdf $F(x)$ is a linear function of x. In their approach, the linear function of x was replaced by a polynomial function and for the resulting parametric model, they used the term polynomial logistic distribution.

Motivated by the above approach, we observed that the majority of the classical continuous distributions whose cdf $F(x)$ admits a closed expression, there exists a monotone transformation of $F(x)$ that leads to a simple function of x (usually linear).

This condition is used in section 12.2 of this chapter to define a new general class of distributions that includes as special cases most of the classical parametric families. In the following sections of this chapter, we study the properties of the new family. In section 12.3, we develop a probability bound. In section 12.4, we study aging properties and provide conditions so that the members of the new family are unimodal. In section 12.5, we study the tail behavior of the family. Finally, in section 12.6, we summarize the contents of this chapter and discuss future research directions.

12.2. Definitions and notations

For many classical continuous univariate distributions, there exists a monotone transformation, say $g(\cdot)$, of their cdf $F(x)$, so that

$$g(F(x,\boldsymbol{\theta})) = h(x;\boldsymbol{\theta}), \qquad [12.1]$$

where

- $g(x)$ does not involve any of the distribution parameters;
- $h(x;\boldsymbol{\theta})$ contains the parameters of the distribution.

In this case, we may easily estimate the parameter vector $\boldsymbol{\theta}$, using a sample $X_1, X_2, \ldots, X_n$ as follows: if $x_1, x_2, \ldots, x_n$ are the observed values of $X_1, X_2, \ldots, X_n$, $\hat{F}(x_i)$ is the empirical cdf for the $i-th$ observation and $\hat{y}_i = g(\hat{F}(x_i))$, we may estimate $\boldsymbol{\theta}$ so that $\hat{y}_i \cong h(x_i;\boldsymbol{\theta})$ for $i = 1, 2, \ldots, n$ using, for example, the ordinary least squares (OLS) method or a method of numerical analysis to fit a function $h(x;\boldsymbol{\theta})$ to the points $(x_i, \hat{y}_i)$, $i = 1, 2, \ldots, n$.

As an illustration, let us consider three different cases of the Pareto distribution with cdf

$$F(x;\alpha,\lambda) = 1 - \left(\frac{\lambda}{x+\lambda}\right)^{\alpha}, \; x > 0.$$

In the first case, let us assume that the parameter α is known and, therefore, $\theta = \lambda$. Then, for

$$g(x) = \left(\frac{1}{1-x}\right)^{\frac{1}{\alpha}},$$

it is very easy to verify that $g(F(x;\lambda))$ is a linear function of x, more specifically $g(F(x;\lambda)) = bx + 1$, with $b = \frac{1}{\lambda}$. By setting

$$\hat{y}_i = \ln\left(\frac{1}{1-\hat{F}(x_i)}\right)^{\frac{1}{\alpha}} - 1,$$

we can use OLS to fit a line (without a constant term) to the points $(x_i, \hat{y}_i)$, $i = 1, 2, \ldots, n$, thereby obtaining an estimator $\hat{b}$ of b and then estimating λ as $\hat{\lambda} = \frac{1}{\hat{b}}$.

Next, let us consider the case when the parameter λ is known and, therefore $\theta = \alpha$. Then, introducing the function $g(x) = -\ln(1-x)$, we get

$$g(F(x;\alpha)) = \alpha \ln(\frac{x}{\lambda} + 1) = h(x;\alpha).$$

Using our data, we can compute the points $(x_i', \hat{y_i})$, $i = 1, 2, \ldots, n$ with

$$x_i' = \ln(\frac{x_i}{\lambda} + 1),\ \hat{y_i} = -ln(1 - \hat{F}(x_i))$$

and the estimation of α can be easily achieved by fitting a line (with no constant term) to the points $(x_i', \hat{y_i})$, $i = 1, 2, \ldots, n$.

Finally, let us consider the case when both parameters of the Pareto distribution are unknown and, therefore, $\boldsymbol{\theta} = (\alpha, \lambda)$. If $g(x) = 1/(1-x)$, we may write

$$g(F(x, \boldsymbol{\theta})) = \left(\frac{x}{\lambda} + 1\right)^{\alpha} = h(x; \boldsymbol{\theta}).$$

Then, an estimate of α and λ can be obtained by using classical methods of numerical analysis to fit a curve of the form $y = \left(\frac{x}{\lambda} + 1\right)^{\alpha}$ to the points $(x_i, \hat{y_i})$ with

$$\hat{y_i} = \frac{1}{1 - \hat{F}(x_i)},\ i = 1, 2, \ldots, n.$$

The procedures described above provide a method to fit the Pareto distribution to the observed sample $x_1, x_2, \ldots, x_n$ of size n. It is clear that similar procedures can be described for any distribution for which formula [12.1] can be established.

Returning back to [12.1], we will exploit this expression to introduce a new family of univariate distributions with support $(0, \infty)$. More specifically, we will consider continuous univariate distributions with cdf $F(x)$ of the form

$$F(x; \boldsymbol{\theta}) = g^{-1}(h(x; \boldsymbol{\theta})).$$

In the sequel, we will refer to $g(x)$ by the term "generator" and to $h(x; \boldsymbol{\theta})$ by the term "parametric part". Table 12.1 provides a list of classical univariate distributions and their transformations according to [12.1].

From now on, for typographical convenience, the parameter $\boldsymbol{\theta}$ will be suppressed. Therefore, instead of $F(x; \boldsymbol{\theta}) = g^{-1}(h(x; \boldsymbol{\theta}))$, we will write

$$F(x) = g^{-1}(h(x)). \qquad [12.2]$$

Distribution	$F(x)$	$\boldsymbol{\theta}$	Transformation	$g(x)$	$h(x;\boldsymbol{\theta})$
Exponential	$1-e^{-\lambda x}$	λ	$-\ln(1-F)=\lambda x$	$-\ln(1-x)$	λx
Weibull	$1-e^{-\lambda x^{\alpha}}$	(α,λ)	$-\ln(1-F)=\lambda x^{\alpha}$	$-\ln(1-x)$	λx^{α}
Pareto with known α	$1-(\frac{\lambda}{x+\lambda})^{\alpha}$	λ	$(\frac{1}{1-F})^{\frac{1}{\alpha}}=\frac{x}{\lambda}+1$	$(\frac{1}{1-x})^{\frac{1}{\alpha}}$	$\frac{x}{\lambda}+1$
Pareto with known λ	$1-(\frac{\lambda}{x+\lambda})^{\alpha}$	α	$-\ln(1-F)=a\ln(\frac{x}{\lambda}+1)$	$-\ln(1-x)$	$a\ln(\frac{x}{\lambda}+1)$
Pareto with unknown α and λ	$1-(\frac{\lambda}{x+\lambda})^{\alpha}$	(α,λ)	$\frac{1}{1-F}=(\frac{x}{\lambda}+1)^{\alpha}$	$\frac{1}{1-x}$	$(\frac{x}{\lambda}+1)^{\alpha}$
Gompertz with known α	$1-e^{-\alpha(e^{\lambda x}-1)}$	λ	$\frac{-\ln(1-F)}{\alpha}=e^{\lambda x}-1$	$\frac{-\ln(1-x)}{\alpha}$	$e^{\lambda x}-1$
Gompertz with unknown α	$1-e^{-\alpha(e^{\lambda x}-1)}$	(α,λ)	$-\ln(1-F)=\alpha(e^{\lambda x}-1)$	$-\ln(1-x)$	$\alpha(e^{\lambda x}-1)$
Dagum with known p	$\left(1+(\frac{x}{\lambda})^{-\alpha}\right)^{-p}$	(α,λ)	$(F^{-1/p}-1)^{-1}=(\frac{x}{\lambda})^{\alpha}$	$\frac{1}{-1+x^{-1/p}}$	$(\frac{x}{\lambda})^{\alpha}$
Dagum with unknown p	$\left(1+(\frac{x}{\lambda})^{-\alpha}\right)^{-p}$	(α,p,λ)	$-\ln F=p\ln\left(1+(\frac{x}{\lambda})^{-\alpha}\right)$	$-\ln x$	$p\ln\left(1+(\frac{x}{\lambda})^{-\alpha}\right)$
Exponential-logarithmic with known p	$1-\frac{\ln(1-(1-p)e^{-\lambda x})}{\ln p}$	λ	$-\ln(\frac{1-p^{1-F}}{1-p})=\lambda x$	$-\ln(\frac{1-p^{1-x}}{1-p})$	λx
Exponential-logarithmic with unknown p	$1-\frac{\ln(1-(1-p)e^{-\lambda x})}{\ln p}$	(p,λ)	$-e^{1-F}=((1-p)e^{-\lambda x}-1)^{\ln p}$	$-e^{1-x}$	$((1-p)e^{-\lambda x}-1)^{\ln p}$
Log-logistic with known α	$\frac{x^{\alpha}}{\lambda^{\alpha}+x^{\alpha}}$	λ	$(\frac{F}{1-F})^{\frac{1}{\alpha}}=\frac{x}{\lambda}$	$(\frac{x}{1-x})^{\frac{1}{\alpha}}$	$\frac{x}{\lambda}$
Log-logistic with known λ	$\frac{x^{\alpha}}{\lambda^{\alpha}+x^{\alpha}}$	α	$\ln(\frac{F}{1-F})=\alpha\ln(\frac{x}{\lambda})$	$\ln(\frac{x}{1-x})$	$\alpha\ln(\frac{x}{\lambda})$
Log-logistic with unknown α and λ	$\frac{x^{\alpha}}{\lambda^{\alpha}+x^{\alpha}}$	(α,λ)	$\frac{F}{1-F}=(\frac{x}{\lambda})^{\alpha}$	$\frac{x}{1-x}$	$(\frac{x}{\lambda})^{\alpha}$

Table 12.1. *Generators and parametric parts for classical continuous univariate distributions with support* $(0,\infty)$

In view of the previous discussions, we proceed to the formal introduction of a new family of continuous univariate distributions with support the positive real axis $(0, \infty)$.

DEFINITION 12.1.– *Let $F(x)$ be the cdf of a distribution with support $(0, \infty)$. We will say that F belongs to the family ${D_g}^+(h)$ (notation: $F \in {D_g}^+(h)$) if $F(x) = g^{-1}(h(x))$, where*

– *C1. $g : (0, 1) \rightarrow \mathbb{R}$ is strictly increasing;*

– *C2. $h : (0, \infty) \rightarrow \mathbb{R}$ is increasing;*

– *C3. g, h differentiable;*

– *C4. $lim_{x \to 1^-} g(x) = lim_{x \to \infty} h(x) = \infty$;*

– *C5a. $lim_{x \to 0^+} g(x) = lim_{x \to 0^+} h(x) = l \in \mathbb{R}$ or C5b. $lim_{x \to 0^+} g(x) = lim_{x \to 0^+} h(x) = -\infty$.*

We will first prove that F is a proper cdf for the case C5a (the proof for the case C5b. is similar).

It is straightforward that the domain of F is $(0, \infty)$. Moreover,

– Since g, and consequently g^{-1}, is strictly increasing and h is increasing, we conclude that $F = g^{-1} \circ h$ is also increasing. Moreover, F is continuous, since it is differentiable.

– The conditions $lim_{x \to 0^+} F(x) = lim_{x \to 0^+} g^{-1}(h(x)) = lim_{u \to l} g^{-1}(u) = 0$ hold true, since $h : (0, \infty) \rightarrow (l, \infty)$ and $g^{-1} : (l, \infty) \rightarrow (0, 1)$ are increasing functions.

– The conditions $lim_{x \to \infty} F(x) = lim_{x \to \infty} g^{-1}(h(x)) = lim_{u \to \infty} g^{-1}(u) = 1$ hold true, since $h : (0, \infty) \rightarrow (l, \infty)$ and $g^{-1} : (l, \infty) \rightarrow (0, 1)$ are increasing functions.

Therefore, $F = g^{-1} \circ h$ is a proper cdf.

It is easy to verify that all the classical distributions depicted in Table 12.1 are members of the class ${D_g}^+(h)$ with g and h as shown there.

For illustration purposes, let us consider the exponential distribution (see the first row in Table 12.1). Figure 12.1 provides graphs of the functions $F(x)$, $g(x)$ and $h(x)$ for $\lambda = 2$. It is of special interest to note that, in this case, $h(x)$ is a linear function of x. We will further elaborate the consequences of the linearity of $h(x)$ in sections 12.4 and 12.5.

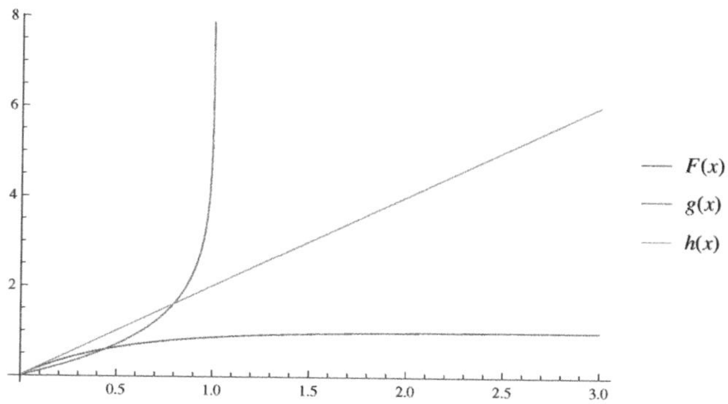

Figure 12.1. *Functions $F(x)$, $g(x)$ and $h(x)$ of exponential distribution for $\lambda = 2$. For a color version of this figure, see www.iste.co.uk/dimotikalis/data4.zip*

12.3. Probability bounds

In this section, we will develop a bound for the probability

$$P(x_1 < X < x_2) = \int_{x_1}^{x_2} f(x)dx.$$

Firstly, note that the probability density function (pdf) $f(x)$ can be written as

$$f(x) = \frac{h'(x)}{g'(F(x))}. \qquad [12.3]$$

This can be easily deduced by first differentiating [12.2] to obtain

$$f(x) = F'(x) = (g^{-1})'(h(x))h'(x)$$

and then making use of the well-known formula

$$(g^{-1})'(x) = \frac{1}{g'(g^{-1}(x))}$$

which leads to

$$f(x) = \frac{h'(x)}{g'(g^{-1}(h(x)))} = \frac{h'(x)}{g'(F(x))}.$$

With this in mind, we next note that, for the functions $g(x)$ shown in Table 12.1, we may easily verify that, in most cases, the derivative of the function $g(x)$ is lower bounded by a positive constant (an illustration is provided in Figure 12.2). Motivated by this observation, we may state the following result.

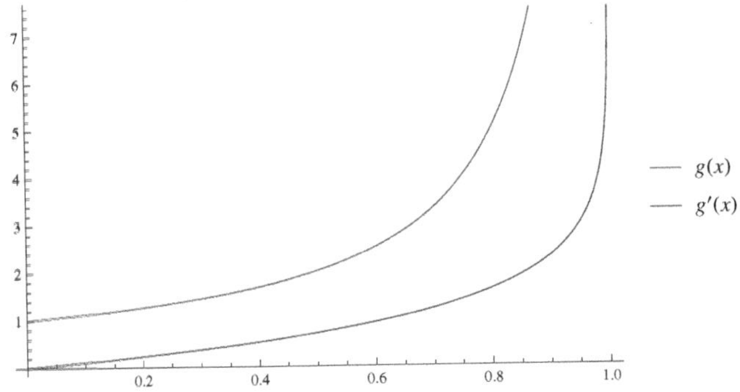

Figure 12.2. *Functions $g(x)$ and $g'(x)$ of the Weibull distribution and Pareto distribution with known λ. For a color version of this figure, see www.iste.co.uk/dimotikalis/data4.zip*

PROPOSITION 12.1.– *If $F \in {D_g}^+(h)$ and LB is a positive lower bound for the function g', i.e.*

$$g'(x) \geq LB, \text{ for all } x \in (0,1), \tag{12.4}$$

then

$$P(x_1 < X < x_2) \leq \frac{h(x_2) - h(x_1)}{LB},$$

for every x_1, x_2 with $0 < x_1 < x_2$.

PROOF.– Making use of [12.4] and [12.3], we may write

$$f(x) \leq \frac{h'(x)}{LB}, \; x > 0$$

and integrating both sides from $x = x_1$ to $x = x_2$, we obtain

$$\int_{x_1}^{x_2} f(x)dx \leq \frac{1}{LB}\int_{x_1}^{x_2} h'(x)dx = \frac{1}{LB}[h(x)]_{x_1}^{x_2} = \frac{h(x_2) - h(x_1)}{LB}.$$

Therefore,

$$P(x_1 < X < x_2) = \int_{x_1}^{x_2} f(x)dx \leq \frac{h(x_2) - h(x_1)}{LB}.$$

As an application, let us draw our attention to the family of continuous distributions ${D_g}^+(h)$ with $g(x) = -\ln(1-x)$. Then

$$g'(x) = \frac{1}{1-x} \geq 1 = LB, \text{ for all } x \in (0,1) \tag{12.5}$$

and Proposition 12.1 yields the following simple upper bound:

$$P(x_1 < X < x_2) \leq h(x_2) - h(x_1). \qquad [12.6]$$

Applying the last inequality for the special case $x_1 = 0$, $x_2 = x > 0$, we deduce the next upper bound for the cdf of all continuous distributions $F \in {D_g}^+(h)$ with $g(x) = -\ln(1-x)$:

$$F(x) \leq h(x) - h(0). \qquad [12.7]$$

Since the lower bound in inequality [12.5] is close to $g'(x)$ for values of x close to 0, the quality of the approximation provided by [12.6] and [12.7] for the respective probabilities shown in the LHS will improve as x_1, x_2, x approach 0.

As an illustration, let us consider the Weibull distribution with

$$F(x) = 1 - e^{-\lambda x^\alpha}.$$

In this case, we have $g(x) = -ln(1-x)$, $h(x) = \lambda x^\alpha$ (see Table 12.1) and therefore [12.7] takes on the form

$$F(x) = 1 - e^{-\lambda x^\alpha} \leq h(x) - h(0) = \lambda x^\alpha. \qquad [12.8]$$

The last inequality can also be justified by appealing to the classical result of elementary calculus $e^{-x} \geq 1 - x$, $x > 0$. Table 12.2 depicts the percentage error for several values of α and x, when the RHS of [12.8] is used as an approximation for the cdf of the Weibull distribution with $\lambda = 1.2$. All the numerical results in the table have been rounded to six decimal points.

α	x	$F(x)$	Upper bound [12.8]	Distance	Percentage error
0.5	0.001	0.037236	0.037947	0.000711	1.9094 %
	0.01	0.113080	0.120000	0.006920	6.1196 %
	0.05	0.235343	0.268328	0.032985	14.0157 %
	0.1	0.315778	0.379473	0.063695	20.1708 %
1.0	0.001	0.001199	0.001200	0.000001	0.0834 % %
	0.01	0.011928	0.012000	0.000072	0.5952 %
	0.05	0.058236	0.060000	0.001764	3.0291 %
	0.1	0.113080	0.120000	0.006920	6.1196 %
1.5	0.001	0.000037	0.000037	0.000000	0%
	0.01	0.001199	0.001200	0.000001	0.0834 %
	0.05	0.013327	0.013416	0.000089	0.6678 %
	0.1	0.037236	0.037947	0.000711	1.9094 %

Table 12.2. *Approximating the cdf of the Weibull distribution*

To conclude this section, we mention that there are quite a few classical distributions that belong to the family ${D_g}^+(h)$ with $g(x) = -ln(1-x)$, for example, the exponential and Weibull distribution, the Pareto distribution with known λ and the Gompertz distribution with unknown α (see Table 12.1). In all these cases, we can use inequalities [12.6] and [12.7] to get simple upper bounds for $P(x_1 < X < x_2)$ and $F(x)$, which provide accurate estimates for them, when x_1, x_2 and x are close to 0.

12.4. Aging properties and unimodality

In the remaining sections of this chapter, we will provide several general results for the family ${D_g}^+(h)$ for the special case when $h(x)$ is a linear function of x, i.e. $h(x) = cx + d$ with $c > 0$. According to Definition 12.1, the conditions needed for $g(x)$ in this case are that $g : (0, 1) \to \mathbb{R}$ is strictly increasing and differentiable with

$$lim_{x \to 0^+} g(x) = d \text{ and } lim_{x \to 1^-} g(x) = \infty.$$

It should be emphasized that, for the development of the results that follow in this section and section 12.5, the function $g(x)$ that leads to the transformation

$$F(x) = g^{-1}(h(x)) = g^{-1}(cx + d) \qquad [12.9]$$

is not necessarily free of parameters. This condition was imposed originally only for describing an easy-to-apply procedure for the estimation of the parameters of $F \in {D_g}^+(h)$. This option offers enhanced flexibility in the task of determining g and h so that $h(x)$ becomes linear.

In the sequel, we will use the notation ${D_g}^+(c, d)$ to refer to the family ${D_g}^+(h)$, with $h(x) = cx+d$. In Table 12.3 we indicate how the classical univariate distributions with support the real axis can be viewed as members of ${D_g}^+(c, d)$.

PROPOSITION 12.2.– *Let $F \in {D_g}^+(c, d)$ and w be the function defined on $\Delta \subseteq (0, 1)$ by the formula*

$$w(x) = \frac{1}{g'(x)}.$$

1) If w' is decreasing on $F(\Delta)$ (w concave), then $F \in {D_g}^+(c, d)$ is (strongly) unimodal and an increasing failure rate (IFR) on Δ.

2) If w' is increasing on $F(\Delta)$ (w convex), then $F \in {D_g}^+(c, d)$ is a decreasing failure rate (DFR) on Δ.

3) If w' is constant on $F(\Delta)$, then $F \in {D_g}^+(c, d)$ has a constant failure rate (CFR) on Δ.

PROOF.– (a) It suffices to prove that the pdf $f(x)$ is logconcave, i.e. $ln(f(x))$ is concave (see Dharmadhikari and Joag 1988, pages 20, 225).

Distribution	$F(x)$	Transformation	$g(x)$	$h(x)$	c	d
Exponential	$1-e^{-\lambda x}$	$-\ln(1-F)=\lambda x$	$-\ln(1-x)$	λx	λ	0
Weibull	$1-e^{-\lambda x^{\alpha}}$	$(-\ln(1-F))^{\frac{1}{\alpha}}=\lambda^{\frac{1}{\alpha}}x$	$(-\ln(1-x))^{\frac{1}{\alpha}}$	$\lambda^{\frac{1}{\alpha}}x$	$\lambda^{\frac{1}{\alpha}}$	0
Pareto	$1-(\frac{\lambda}{x+\lambda})^{\alpha}$	$(\frac{1}{1-F})^{\frac{1}{\alpha}}=\frac{x}{\lambda}+1$	$(\frac{1}{1-x})^{\frac{1}{\alpha}}$	$\frac{x}{\lambda}+1$	$\frac{1}{\lambda}$	1
Gompertz	$1-e^{-\alpha(e^{\lambda x}-1)}$	$\ln(\frac{-\ln(1-F)}{\alpha}+1)=\lambda x$	$\ln(\frac{-\ln(1-x)}{\alpha}+1)$	λx	λ	0
Dagum	$\left(1+(\frac{x}{\lambda})^{-\alpha}\right)^{-p}$	$(F^{-1/p}-1)^{-\frac{1}{\alpha}}=\frac{x}{\lambda}$	$(x^{-1/p}-1)^{-\frac{1}{\alpha}}$	$\frac{x}{\lambda}$	$\frac{1}{\lambda}$	0
Exponential-logarithmic	$1-\frac{\ln(1-(1-p)e^{-\lambda x})}{\ln p}$	$-\ln(\frac{1-p^{1-F}}{1-p})=\lambda x$	$-\ln(\frac{1-p^{1-x}}{1-p})$	λx	λ	0
Log-logistic	$\frac{x^{\alpha}}{\lambda^{\alpha}+x^{\alpha}}$	$(\frac{F}{1-F})^{\frac{1}{\alpha}}=\frac{x}{\lambda}$	$(\frac{x}{1-x})^{\frac{1}{\alpha}}$	$\frac{x}{\lambda}$	$\frac{1}{\lambda}$	0
Logistic	$\frac{1}{1+e^{-\frac{x-\mu}{\sigma}}}$	$ln(\frac{F}{1-F})=\frac{x-\mu}{\sigma}$	$ln(\frac{x}{1-x})$	$\frac{x-\mu}{\sigma}$	$\frac{1}{\sigma}$	$-\frac{\mu}{\sigma}$

Table 12.3. *Transformation of the cdf of classical distributions in the form* $g(F(x))=cx+d$

Since $h(x) = cx + d$, $c > 0$ expression [12.3] yields, for $x \in \Delta$,

$$f(x) = \frac{c}{g'(F(x))} \qquad [12.10]$$

and

$$f'(x) = -\frac{cg''(F(x))f(x)}{(g'(F(x)))^2}.$$

Therefore,

$$(\ln f(x))' = \frac{f'(x)}{f(x)} = \frac{-cg''(F(x))}{(g'(F(x)))^2}.$$

Since $w'(x) = -g''(x)/(g'(x))^2$, the last expression takes on the form

$$(\ln f(x))' = cw'(F(x)),\ x \in \Delta. \qquad [12.11]$$

Since w is concave on $F(\Delta)$ and $c > 0$, the RHS of [12.11] is decreasing and, therefore, $f(x)$ is logconcave.

(b) The proof follows by observing that in this case, the RHS of [12.11] is increasing.

(c) When w' is constant on $F(\Delta)$, the RHS of [12.11] is also constant. In order to provide some illustrative examples, let us first consider the Weibull distribution. As indicated in the second line of Table 12.3, in this case, we have $g(x) = (-\ln(1-x))^{\frac{1}{\alpha}}$ and $h(x) = \lambda^{\frac{1}{\alpha}} x$. Therefore,

$$w(x) = \frac{1}{g'(x)} = \alpha(1-x)(-\ln(1-x))^{1-\frac{1}{\alpha}}$$

and the second derivative of $w(x)$ reads

$$w''(x) = \frac{(\alpha-1)(-\ln(1-x))^{-\frac{1+\alpha}{\alpha}}(\alpha\ln(1-x)-1)}{\alpha(1-x)}.$$

We may easily verify that $w''(x) < 0$ for all $x \in F(\Delta) = (0,1)$ if $\alpha > 1$ (w' decreasing), $w''(x) > 0$ for all $x \in F(\Delta) = (0,1)$ if $\alpha > 1$ (w' increasing) and $w''(x) = 0$ for all $x \in F(\Delta) = (0,1)$ if $\alpha = 1$ (w' constant). A direct application of Proposition 12.2 leads to the conclusion that the Weibull distribution is IFR and unimodal on $\Delta = (0,\infty)$ for $\alpha > 1$, DFR on $\Delta = (0,\infty)$ for $\alpha < 1$ and CFR on $\Delta = (0,\infty)$ for $\alpha = 1$.

Let us next consider the Pareto distribution. We recall (see Table 12.3) that in this case, we have $g(x) = (\frac{1}{1-x})^{\frac{1}{\alpha}}$ and $h(x) = \frac{x}{\lambda} + 1$. Therefore,

$$w(x) = \frac{1}{g'(x)} = \alpha(1-x)^{\frac{1}{\alpha}+1}$$

which is convex on $F(\Delta) = (0,1)$, since

$$w'(x) = \alpha(\frac{1}{\alpha} + 1)(1-x)^{\frac{1}{\alpha}}$$

is increasing on $F(\Delta) = (0,1)$. Therefore, by Proposition 12.2, we deduce that F is DFR on $\Delta = (0,\infty)$.

In the next proposition, we present a result on the aging properties of $F \in {D_g}^+(c,d)$ which requires a condition on the function $Q^*(x) = e^{-x}g'(x)$ (instead of $w(x) = \frac{1}{g'(x)}$).

PROPOSITION 12.3.– *Let $F \in {D_g}^+(c,d)$, $\Delta \subseteq (0,1)$ and $Q^*(x) = e^{-x}g'(x)$. If g' is differentiable on $F(\Delta)$ and Q^* is decreasing on $F(\Delta) \subseteq (0,1)$, then $F \in {D_g}^+(c,d)$ is IFR on Δ.*

PROOF.– The failure rate $r(x)$ is expressed as (see, for example, Barlow and Proschan 1965)

$$r(x) = \frac{f(x)}{1-F(x)}, \quad x > 0.$$

If $F \in {D_g}^+(c,d)$, making use of [12.10], we obtain

$$r(x) = \frac{c}{g'(F(x))(1-F(x))},$$

or equivalently, on setting $Q(x) = g'(x)(1-x)$, $0 < x < 1$,

$$r(x) = \frac{c}{Q(F(x))}, \quad x > 0. \tag{12.12}$$

Since Q^* is decreasing and g' is differentiable, we may conclude that

$$(Q^*(x))' = e^{-x}(g''(x) - g'(x)) \leq 0 \Rightarrow g''(x) - g'(x) \leq 0, \text{ for all } x \in F(\Delta)$$

which implies that

$$\begin{aligned} Q'(x) &= g''(x)(1-x) - g'(x) \\ &= (g''(x) - g'(x))(1-x) - g'(x)x < 0, \text{ for all } x \in F(\Delta) \end{aligned}$$

and therefore Q is decreasing on $F(\Delta)$. Therefore, the failure rate [12.12] is increasing on $F(\Delta)$, which leads to the conclusion that F is IFR on Δ.

12.5. Tail behavior of ${D_g}^{+}(h)$

In this section, we will present a result pertaining to the behavior of the right tail of ${D_g}^{+}(c, d)$.

PROPOSITION 12.4.– *Let* $Q(x) = g'(x)(1-x)$ *and assume that*

$$\lim_{x \to 1^-} Q(x) = \infty.$$

Then, $F \in {D_g}^{+}(c, d)$ *is heavy-tailed.*

PROOF.– As already indicated in the proof of Proposition 12.3, for $F \in {D_g}^{+}(c, d)$, the failure rate function takes on the form shown in [12.12] and therefore,

$$\lim_{x \to \infty} r(x) = \lim_{x \to \infty} \frac{c}{Q(F(x))},$$

or, alternatively

$$\lim_{x \to \infty} r(x) = \lim_{x \to 1^-} \frac{c}{Q(x)}.$$

Since $c > 0$ and $\lim_{x \to 1^-} Q(x) = \infty$, we conclude that

$$\lim_{x \to \infty} r(x) = 0,$$

which implies that $F \in {D_g}^{+}(c, d)$ is heavy-tailed (see, for example, Foss et al. 2011). Let us provide an illustration of how Proposition 12.4 can be applied to classical heavy-tailed distributions. Considering the Weibull distribution, we will have $g(x) = (-\ln(1-x))^{\frac{1}{\alpha}}$ and $h(x) = \lambda^{\frac{1}{\alpha}} x$ (see Table 12.3). Then

$$\lim_{x \to 1^-} Q(x) = \lim_{x \to 1} g'(x)(1-x) = \lim_{x \to 1^-} \frac{1}{\alpha}(-\ln(1-x))^{\frac{1-\alpha}{\alpha}} = \begin{cases} \infty, & \text{if } \alpha < 1, \\ 1, & \text{if } \alpha = 1, \\ 0, & \text{if } \alpha > 1. \end{cases}$$

Therefore, the Weibull distribution is heavy-tailed for $\alpha < 1$.

In the case of the Pareto distribution, we have $g(x) = (\frac{1}{1-x})^{\frac{1}{\alpha}}$ and $h(x) = \frac{x}{\lambda} + 1$ (see Table 12.3). Therefore,

$$\lim_{x \to 1} Q(x) = \lim_{x \to 1} g'(x)(1-x) = \lim_{x \to 1} \frac{1}{\alpha}(\frac{1}{1-x})^{\frac{1}{\alpha}} = \infty,$$

which implies that the Pareto distribution is heavy-tailed for all $\alpha > 0$.

12.6. Conclusion

In the present chapter, we introduced a class of continuous distributions defined on the positive real axis that includes as special cases the majority of classical continuous distributions. In addition, new distributions can be obtained by appropriate choices of the generator of the class.

The new class, under certain conditions on the generator, may encompass desirable aging properties and tail behavior, a fact that turns it into a useful tool for the analysis of data arising in the insurance and actuarial science.

The results pertaining to aging properties and tail behavior have been developed in the case where, applying the generator on the cdf of the new distribution, leads to a linear function. Nevertheless, we believe that this restriction could be relaxed and more general results might be established under the assumption that, the application of the generator on the cdf produces a function with specific properties, for example, convexity or concavity. Such a generalization, which we will be chasing in our future research on this topic, will enhance the flexibility of our family and will provide a powerful tool for producing new classes of continuous distributions.

12.7. Acknowledgment

This research was financially supported by the MSc program in Actuarial Science and Risk Management of the University of Piraeus through the grant "C.908: Development of new methodologies in insurance and risk management".

12.8. References

Alzaatreh, A., Lee, C., Famoye, F. (2013). A new method for generating families of continuous distributions. *Metron*, 71, 63–79.

Azzalini, A. (1985). A class of distributions which includes the normal ones. *Scandinavian Journal of of Statistics*, 12, 171–178.

Azzalini, A. (1986). Further results on a class of distributions which includes the normal ones. *Statistica*, 46, 199–208.

Barlow, R.E. and Proschan, F. (1965). *Mathematical Theory of Reliability*. John Wiley and Sons, New York.

Cooray, K. and Ananda, M.M.A. (2005). Modeling actuarial data with a composite lognormal-Pareto model. *Scandinavian Actuarial Journal*, 5, 321–334.

Dharmadhikari, S. and Joag, K.-D. (1988). *Unimodality, Convexity, and Applications*. Elsevier, Amsterdam.

Eugene, N., Lee, C., Famoye, F. (2002). The beta-normal distribution and its applications. *Communications in Statistics Theory and Methods*, 31, 497–512.

Foss, S., Korshunov, D., Zachary, S. (2011). *An Introduction to Heavy-Tailed and Subexponential Distributions*. Springer, New York.

Hastings, J.C., Mosteller, F., Tukey, J.W., Windsor, C. (1947). Low moments for small samples: A comparative study of order statistics. *Annals of Statistics*, 18, 413–426.

Johnson, N.L. (1949). Systems of frequency curves generated by methods of translation. *Biometrika*, 36, 49–176.

Jones, M.C. (2004). Families of distributions arising from distributions of order statistics. *Test*, 13, 1–43.

Koutras, V.M., Drakos, K., Koutras, M.V. (2014). A polynomial logistic distribution and its applications in finance. *Communications in Statistics Theory and Methods*, 43, 2045–2065.

Lee, C., Famoye, F., Alzaatreh, A.Y. (2013). Methods for generating families of univariate continuous distributions in the recent decades. *Computational Statistics*. doi: 10.1002/wics.1255.

Marshall, A.W. and Olkin, I. (1997). A new method for adding a parameter to a family of distributions with application to the exponential and Weibull families. *Biometrika*, 84, 641–652.

Mudholkar, G.S. and Srivastava, D.K. (1993). Exponentiated Weibull family for analyzing bathtub failure-rate data. *IEEE Transactions on Reliability*, 42, 299–302.

Pearson, K. (1895). Contributions to the mathematical theory of evolution. II. Skew variation in homogeneous material. *Philosophical Transactions of the Royal Society A*, 186, 343–414.

Tukey, J.W. (1960). The practical relationship between the common transformations of percentages of counts and amounts. Technical Report 36, Statistical Techniques Research Group, Princeton University, Princeton.

Vicari, S.K.D. and Kotz, S. (2005). Survey of developments in the theory of continuous skewed distributions. *Metron*, 63, 225–261.

13

Simple Form of Probability Density Functions via Sampling

A critical point in statistical analysis is the determination of the probability density function (p.d.f.) of the random variables entered by the problem under study. The effort needed for the determination is often extremely time-consuming if we insist on using classic methods. Sampling can contribute to the study of the distribution of a random variable with very good results in terms of accuracy and especially speed. Therefore, the data used here is sampling data. In the last two decades, the coefficient of variation (Cv) has been used for the above determination, which has already heavily reduced the time needed to determine the p.d.f. in multiple instances. In this chapter, we study the case where the graph of the p.d.f. does not pass through the origin of the X and Y axes: i.e. it is f(0)=m>0. Here, X is the random variable values and Y is the frequencies of those values. Throughout this chapter, we deal with continuous random variables and illustrating examples are given.

13.1. Introduction

The analytical definition of the distribution of a random variable X is an important process for the study of the random variable X. Usually, analytically defining the distribution of a random variable is a time-consuming process, and for many important random variables this process can take years or decades. The methods used to analytically define the distribution of a random variable differ according to object of the random variable. Since the beginning of the year 2000, the idea of the coefficient of variation (Cv) has been used to approximate the definition (estimation) of the p.d.f. (Farmakis 2003, 2010, 2015; Papatsouma 2018). The p.d.f. (symbol f(x)) presented in the previous chapters are polynomials of $\nu>-1$ degree, and usually, specific p.d.f. refers to continuous random variables X. An increasing form

Chapter written by Maria LEDAKI and Myrto PAPAGEORGIOU.

of p.d.f. is studied in this chapter (Farmakis 2010; Papatsouma 2018), with the property f(x)=m>0. With these methods, the Cv, particularly the square of its inverse (i.e. the parameter $q = ICv^2 = Cv^{-2}$), is deployed, where $Cv=\sigma/\mu$, μ=mean and σ= standard deviation of random variable X. In these implementations, the estimations of parameters q, μ, σ and Cv are used. Furthermore, the basic form of p.d.f. is reached via a two-step process. After the presentation of the method with its theoretical calculations, some illustrated examples are given.

13.2. The sense and the method

For the analytical presentation of the distribution of a random variable X, the most manageable form of p.d.f. is obviously a polynomial formula (Farmakis 2010, 2015; Papatsouma 2018). There are many kinds of p.d.f. in terms of the scheme of the graph, such as symmetric (Farmakis 2003), increasing (Farmakis 2010), decreasing (Papatsouma 2018), etc. All of the above can be imagined as passing through the origin of the axial coordinates. This means that it is f(0)=0.

NOTE.– The idea and scope of this chapter is to study and analyze another kind of random variable with p.d.f., which the graph does not pass through the origin O(0,0) of the axial coordinates, i.e. f(x)=m>0. We deal especially with random variables having increasing p.d.f. (see Figure 13.1).

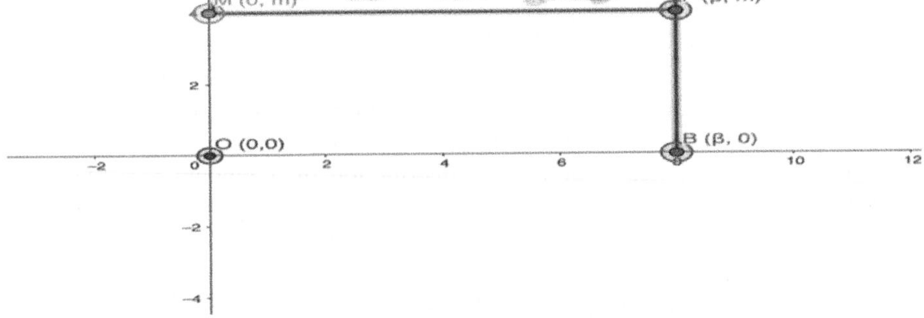

Figure 13.1. *For a color version of this figure, see www.iste.co.uk/dimotikalis/data4.zip*

The analytical form of the p.d.f. of the random variable X is:

$$f(x)=\begin{cases}\frac{1}{(1+m\beta)}\left(m+\frac{h}{1-m\beta}\left(\frac{x}{\beta}\right)^{\nu}\right) & x\in[0,\beta] \\ 0 \quad , & x\notin[0,\beta]\end{cases}, \nu\neq-1,\text{m},\text{h}>0 \qquad [13.1]$$

Of course, it is

$$\int_{0}^{\beta} f(x)\,dx=1 \qquad [13.2]$$

and in the next section, we reach [13.1] in two steps by looking at Figure 13.1. First, we note that the measure of area OBAM is (OBAM)=1, given by [13.2].

13.2.1. *The first step*

By a theoretical point of view using the p.d.f. in equation [1.1] we can calculate the mean of X, the EX, the variance and standard deviation of X, the VarX and SDX, and finally the coefficient of variation of X

$$CvX=\frac{SDX}{EX} \qquad [13.3]$$

In order to solve [13.3] against the exponent $\nu=\varphi(Cv)$ and also to find the value of the coefficient $h=\omega(\nu)=\omega(\nu(q))$, where $q=Cv^{-2}$. Since the suitable calculations are very complicated, we will try some kind of transformation; after this, we will work with a simple p.d.f. g(x), which passes through the origin of a suitable axial system of coordinates (i.e. g(0)=0) (see also Farmakis 2010; Papatsouma 2018). This is reached by adopting the MΓA area instead of the OBAM one. Therefore, we have to adopt some more transformations in order to take the measure of the MΓA surface as 1 and afterwards work with a new p.d.f., as is shown in the next section.

13.2.2. *The second step*

The measure of the AMΓ area is (AMΓ)=1-mβ=(OBAM)-(OBΓM). If we substitute the axis of X's by the line MΓ, then a very well-operating model for the p.d.f. will be the one

$$g(x)=\begin{cases} \frac{h}{1-m\beta}\left(\frac{x}{\beta}\right)^{\nu} & , x\in[0,\beta] \\ 0 & , x \notin[0,\beta] \end{cases}, \nu\neq -1. \qquad [13.4]$$

In order to prove it, we only need to see that

$$\int_0^\beta g(x)dx=1. \qquad [13.5]$$

Obviously, since it is

$$h=\frac{(1-m\beta)\cdot(\nu+1)}{\beta}, \qquad [13.6]$$

the

$$\int_0^\beta g(x)dx=\frac{h\beta}{1-m\beta}\int_0^\beta\left(\frac{x}{\beta}\right)^{\nu}d\left(\frac{x}{\beta}\right)=...=1$$ is obtained.

After this, we use [13.4] to calculate the mean, the variance, the standard deviation and the coefficient of variation for the random variable X. Therefore, we have:

Mean value

$$EX=\int_0^\beta x\cdot g(x)dx=\frac{h}{(1-m\beta)\cdot\beta^{\nu}}\int_0^\beta x^{\nu+1}dx=...=\frac{\nu+1}{\nu+2}\beta \qquad [13.7]$$

Mean of squares

$$EX^2=\int_0^\beta x^2\cdot g(x)dx=\frac{h}{(1-m\beta)\cdot\beta^{\nu}}\int_0^\beta x^{\nu+2}dx=...=\frac{\nu+1}{\nu+3}\beta^2 \qquad [13.8]$$

Variance

$$VarX=EX^2-(EX)^2=\frac{\nu+1}{\nu+3}\beta^2-\left(\frac{\nu+1}{\nu+2}\beta\right)^2=...=\frac{(\nu+1)\cdot\beta^2}{(\nu+3)\cdot(\nu+2)^2} \qquad [13.9]$$

Coefficient of variation

$$Cv = \frac{\sqrt{VarX}}{EX}, \quad q = Cv^{-2} = (\nu+1)\cdot(\nu+3) \qquad [13.10]$$

And the relation $\nu = -2 + \sqrt{1+q}$ is finally obtained. [13.11]

13.3. Using sampling data

In the real world of applications, we use sampling data with sample of size n, and after checking x_{min} and x_{max}, we find the range of the distribution $R \cong x_{max} - x_{min}$. This range a little bit more than the difference x_{max}-x_{min} by taking $X_{max} \geq x_{max}$, $X_{min} \leq x_{min}$, where the capital symbols are the values from the real world. If x_{min} is near zero, we adopt the zero value for X_{min} and so it is x_{max}=β and the definition field for the p.d.f. is [0, β]. We divide the space [0, β] in κ subspaces of the same size w=β/κ. The subspaces are [0, w), [w, 2w), [2w, 3w),…[(κ-1)w, β]. We see on the sample data, and we distribute to the suitable subspace each one of them. We count and note the frequency n_i of observations in the subspace [(i-1)w, iw), i=1,2,3,…,κ. So, a table is prepared with the classes (=subspaces), their centers and the suitable data frequencies are presented. We use this table to calculate the parameters of the random variable X, as we will see in the following illustrating examples (see also Farmakis 2001).

EXAMPLE 1.– We asked n=310 students about the time in minutes they spend browsing the internet. The random variable is time spent browsing the Internet, and was found to be x_{max}=69 minutes and x_{min}=3 minutes. The distribution of the observations or the frequencies is shown in the 3rd column of Table 13.1. In this table, we see seven classes of length w=10 minutes and the range is β=70minutes, (β: from the Greek word βεληνεκές = range). We chose as temporary average mean value the r=35, the center of the 4th class (the middle class). The sixth column is the one of the transformed values of centers, i.e. $x_i'=(x_i-r)/w$, i=1,2,…,7(=κ). Since for the distributions of the Table 13.1, we have n_1=22>0, we have not the condition f(x)=0 and we have to subtract from any class frequency the quantity u=22=n_1 or a frequency near n_i, for example, 20. Therefore, in the fifth column, we see the stump frequencies n_i-u=n_i-20. The quantity u is connected with the parameter m in [13.1]. It is $m = \frac{n_1}{n \cdot w} = 0.0071$. This is useful to obtain a p.d.f. passing from the origin of the axial system of coordinates. It can also be useful to have the value 1-mβ=0.503. Now, we can work to find the increasing p.d.f. g(x), with g(0)=0.

Class	Center x_i	n_i	N_i	n_i'	x_i'	$n_i'*x_i'$	$n_i'*x_i'^2$	Pi	θi	X^2
[0,10)	5	22	22	2	-3	-6	18	0,06184	19,171	25,246
[10,20)	15	33	55	13	-2	-26	52	0,08955	27,760	39,229
[20,30)	25	38	93	18	-1	-18	18	0,11663	36,154	39,940
[30,40)	*35*	45	138	25	0	0	0	0,14338	44,446	45,561
[40,50)	45	50	188	30	1	30	30	0,16990	52,669	47,467
[50,60)	55	58	246	38	2	76	152	0,19625	60,837	55,295
[60,70]	65	64	310	44	3	132	396	0,22246	68,963	59,395
		310		**170**		**188**	**666**	**1,00000**	**310**	**2,132**

Table 13.1. *For a color version of this table, see www.iste.co.uk/dimotikalis/data4.zip*

Now we are ready for the calculations. The sums of columns 7th and 8th are T_1 and T_2, respectively. So, working with the frequencies of the 5th column, we obtain:

$$\overline{x} = r + \frac{w \cdot T_1}{n} = 35 + \frac{10 \cdot 188}{170} = 46.06 \text{ Mean value}$$

$$s^2 = \frac{w^2}{n'-1} \cdot \left(\mathrm{T}_2 - \frac{\mathrm{T}_1^2}{n'} \right) = \frac{100}{169} \cdot \left(666 - \frac{188^2}{170} \right) = 271.0616 \text{ and s=16.46.}$$

So, it is also $Cv = \frac{s}{\overline{x}} = \frac{16.46}{46.06} = 0.3574$ q=Cv^{-2}=7.8287.

Finally, the exponent is v=-2+$(1+q)^{0.5}$=0.9713 and the coefficient

$$h = \frac{(1 - m\beta) \cdot (v + 1)}{\beta} = \frac{0.503 \cdot 1.9713}{70} = 0.014165.$$

The quantity 1+mβ=1.497 will be also useful to obtain the implemented form of equation [13.1]

$$f(x) = \begin{cases} 1.497 \left(0.0071 + \frac{0.014165}{0.503} \left(\frac{x}{70} \right)^{0.9713} \right), & x \in [0,70] \\ 0 \qquad , & x \notin [0,70] \end{cases} \qquad \text{[Ex1.1]}$$

or

$$f(x)=\begin{cases} 0.010629+0.04216\cdot\left(\dfrac{x}{70}\right)^{0.9713} & , x\in[0,70] \\ 0 \quad , & x\notin[0,70] \end{cases} \quad \text{[Ex1.2]}$$

From the above [Ex1.2] by integration for every class, we have the κ=7 theoretic frequencies in the 10th column of Table 13.1:

$$\theta_i = n\cdot\int_{w_{i-1}}^{w_i} f(x)dx = n\cdot\int_{10(i-1)}^{10i} f(x)dx, i=1,2,...,7=\kappa \quad \text{[Ex1.3]}$$

A test X^2 between the frequencies of the columns 3rd and 10th gives a "good fit" of that frequencies at a significance level α=0.05, since X^2= 2.132 at the bottom of 11th column.

EXAMPLE 2.– We asked n=315 students to answer, after a short internet search, the question "when was the Parthenon built?"

We counted the time taken to make this search for every student in seconds.

The random variable is time spends for browsing the Internet, and it was found x_{max}=277 seconds and x_{min}=10 minutes. The distribution of the observations or the frequencies is shown in the 3rd column of Table 13.2. In this table, we see seven classes of length w=40 minutes and the range is β=280 seconds (we chose as the temporary average mean value the r=140 seconds the center of the 4th class (the middle class)). The sixth column is the one of transformed values of centers, i.e. $x_i'=(x_i-r)/w$, i=1,2,…,7(=κ). Since for the distributions of Table 13.2, we have n_1=22>0, the condition f(x)=0 is not valid and so we have to subtract from any class frequency the quantity u=22=n_1 or a frequency near n_1, for example, 21. This is useful to obtain a p.d.f. passing from the origin of the axial system of coordinates. We see in the 5th column the stump frequencies n_i-u=n_i-21. The quantity $u\cong n_1$ is connected with the parameter m in [13.1] . It is $m=\dfrac{n_1}{n\cdot w}=0.00175$. It also be useful to have the value 1-mβ=0.511. Now, we can work to find the increasing p.d.f. g(x), with g(0)=0.

Classes	Center x_i	n_i	N_i	n_i'	x_i'	$n_i'{*}x_i'$	$n_i'{*}x_i'^2$	P_i	θ_i	X^2
[0,40)	20	22	22	1	-3	-3	9	0,05863	18,469	26,2060
[40,80)	60	33	55	12	-2	-24	48	0,08476	26,701	40,7855
[80,120)	100	38	93	17	-1	-17	17	0,11258	35,461	40,7205
[120,160)	***140***	46	139	25	0	0	0	0,14133	44,520	47,5291
[160,200)	180	50	189	29	1	29	29	0,17077	53,794	46,4739
[200,240)	220	60	249	39	2	78	156	0,20075	63,236	56,9293
[240,280]	260	66	315	45	3	135	405	0,23117	72,819	59,8196
		315		**168**		**198**	**664**	**1,00000**	**315**	**3,464**

Table 13.2. *For a color version of this table, see www.iste.co.uk/dimotikalis/data4.zip*

Next we look at some calculations.

The sums of columns 7th and 8th are the T_1 and T_2 respectively. Therefore, by working with the frequencies of the fifth column, we have:

$$\overline{x} = r + \frac{w \cdot T_1}{n} = 140 + \frac{40 \cdot 198}{168} = 187.14 \text{ Mean value}$$

$$s^2 = \frac{w^2}{n'-1} \cdot \left(T_2 - \frac{T_1^2}{n'} \right) = \frac{1600}{167} \cdot \left(664 - \frac{198^2}{168} \right) = 4125.9196 \text{ and } s=64.23.$$

Therefore, it is also $Cv = \frac{s}{\overline{x}} = \frac{64.23}{187.14} = 0.3432$ $q=Cv^{-2}=8.4899$

Finally, the exponent is $v=-2+(1+q)^{0.5}=1.0806$ and the coefficient

$$h = \frac{(1-m\beta)\cdot(v+1)}{\beta} = \frac{0.511 \cdot 2.0806}{280} = 0.003797 .$$

The quantity $1+m\beta=1.49$ will be also useful to obtain the implemented form of [13.1]

$$f(x) = \begin{cases} 1.49\left(0.00175 + \frac{0.003797}{0.511}\left(\frac{x}{70}\right)^{1.0806}\right), & x \in [0,280] \\ 0 \qquad , & x \notin [0,280] \end{cases} \qquad \text{[Ex2.1]}$$

or

$$f(x)=\begin{cases}0.0026075+0.01107\left(\dfrac{x}{280}\right)^{1.0806} & ,x\in[0,280]\\ 0 \qquad , & x\notin[0,280]\end{cases} \qquad \text{[Ex2.2]}$$

From the above [Ex1.2] by integration for every class, we have the κ=7 theoretic frequencies in the 10th column of Table 13.2:

$$\theta_i = n\cdot\int_{w_{i-1}}^{w_i} f(x)dx = n\cdot\int_{10(i-1)}^{10i} f(x)dx, i=1,2,...,7=\kappa \qquad \text{[Ex2.3]}$$

A test X^2 between the frequencies of the columns 3rd and 10th gives a "good fit" of that frequencies at a significance level α=0.05, since X^2= 3.464 at the bottom of 11th column.

13.4. Results and discussion

In this chapter, we have studied the p.d.f. for a random variable X, the f(x) with f(0)=m>0 and we try determine f(x) with the help of p.d.f. g(x), g(0)=0, well known already (Farmakis 2010). This is achieved by substitution of the axis of X by the line f(x)=m getting g(x)=f(x)-m, for which g(0)=f(0)-m=m-m=0.

The remaining area "under" the f(x) curve is now equal to $1-m\beta=\int_0^b g(x)dx$.

Thus, the calculations take into account this area and the parameters, exponent ν and coefficient h, are calculated suitably, i.e. finally the format of the p.d.f. has in the denominator the quantity 1-mβ and so it is $\int_0^\beta (p.d.f.)dx=1$. Next step is to add to the final format of p.d.f. the subtracted quantity m, getting as the x-axis the previous one. The area "under" the new resulting φ(x)=p.d.f.+m is now equal to 1+mβ. In order to have again a kind of p.d.f., we have the task of dividing the resulting function φ(x) by 1-mβ and the requested function is obtained: the function f(x) in [13.1] is checked by [13.2].

The function f(x) gives theoretic frequencies θ_i, i=1,2,3…,κ for all the κ classes with a good fitting to the observed frequencies n_i, i=1,2,3,…,κ, as shown in examples using the X^2 test.

13.5. References

Farmakis, N. (2001). *STATISTICS, Brief Theory, Exercises*. Christodoulidi, S.O., Kallipos, Thessaloniki (in Greek).

Farmakis, N. (2003). Estimation of coefficient of variation: Scaling of symmetric continuous distributions. *Statistics in Transition*, 6(1), 83–96.

Farmakis, N. (2010). Coefficient of variation: Connecting sampling with some increasing distribution models. In *Proceedings of Stochastic Modeling Techniques & Data Analysis International Conference (SMTDA-2010)*, 8–11 June, Chania, Crete.

Farmakis, N. (2015). *Sampling and Applications*. Greek Academic Depository, Athens (in Greek).

Farmakis, N. (2016). *Introduction to Sampling*. Kyriakidis Bros, S.A., Thessaloniki (in Greek).

Moysiadis, P. (2000). *Advanced Mathematics*. Christodoulidi, S.O., Thessaloniki (in Greek).

Papatsouma, I. (2018). Contribution to the sampling highlight of model distributions using the coefficient of variation. PhD Dissertation, Aristotle University of Thessaloniki, Thessaloniki (in Greek).

14

Optimizing Financial Trading Strategies Using Dynamic Bayesian Networks

Devising a financial trading strategy that allows for long-term gains is a very common problem in finance. This chapter aims to formulate a mathematically rigorous framework for the problem and compare and contrast the results obtained. The main approach considered is based on dynamic Bayesian networks (DBNs). Within the DBN setting, a long-term as well as a short-term trading strategy are considered and applied on different sets of equities. It was concluded that both the long-term and the short-term strategies proposed in this chapter outperform the benchmark buy-and-hold (B&H) trading strategy. Despite the clear advantages of the former trading strategies, the limitations of this model are discussed along with the number of possible improvements which can be implemented.

14.1. Introduction

In this chapter, dynamic Bayesian networks (DBNs) are used to study the problem of obtaining and testing a financial strategy whose return is higher than the buy and hold strategy for a given equity. A Bayesian network (BN) is a graphical and compact representation of a joint probability density function (PDF) that makes use of conditional independence and can be used to model a system under one time instance. DBNs extend the BN to more than one time period, which is to say that DBNs are a temporally driven extension to BNs.

Some benefits of using DBNs over other models, such as basic time series models, are the following. Firstly, DBNs have the capacity of incorporating what are known as hidden (or latent) variables, which either govern, or are thought to govern, the observations of the observable random variable. These hidden variables are random variables whose true value cannot be measured directly, sometimes due

Chapter written by Karl LEWIS, Mark Anthony CARUANA and David Paul SUDA.

to instrumental inadequacies; other times, simply because the existence of these variables is hypothesized. Examples of such hidden variables are the intelligence of an individual (which cannot be measured precisely using any instrument) or the state (bull or bear) of a financial market (whose existence itself is hypothetical). Secondly, since they are an offshoot of BNs, DBNs allow for compact representations of an otherwise possibly cumbersome joint distribution. Russell and Norvig (1995) argue that due to conditional independence, representing a joint distribution as a DBN may eliminate any redundant terms which, in turn, also makes parameter estimation simpler. Murphy (2002) states that another benefit of DBNs is the ease with which variations to the model at hand can be introduced. DBNs can be used to alternatively represent both basic Hidden Markov Models (HMMs), and HMMs with variations, such as HMMs with a mixture-of-Gaussian outputs, auto-regressive HMMs, input–output HMMs and hierarchical HMMs. DBNs can also be used to represent Kalman filter models where, contrary to HMMs, the hidden state is continuous rather than discrete. Lastly, DBNs also have the capacity of answering questions about different types of reasoning or inference, such as *diagnostic* inference (from effects to causes), *causal* inference (from causes to effects), *intercausal* inference (between causes of the same effect) and mixed inference (a mixture of any two of the above types of inference).

Historically, Paul Dagum is thought to have kick-started the development of DBNs in the early 1990s, namely in Dagum et al. (1992, 1995). Since then, DBNs have been used in various areas, particularly in finance and economics. However, other areas include (and are not limited to) speech recognition (Zweig and Russell 1998; Murphy 2002; Nefian et al. 2002), (Murphy and Mian 1996; Raval et al. 2002; Yao et al. 2008), robotics (Patel et al. 2010; Prembida et al. 2016), image processing (Delage et al. 2006; de Paz et al. 2011) and fault detection (Cozar et al. 2017). Parameter estimation techniques of DBNs were discussed in Benhamou et al. (2018); whereas, Murphy (2001) worked on the theoretical foundations of DBNs.

The rest of this chapter is structured as follows. Section 14.2 introduces the theoretical underpinnings of DBNs. In section 14.3, DBNs are applied to a financial data set and present the results obtained. Finally, in the concluding section, the key points and results obtained are highlighted.

14.2. Theoretical framework

This chapter is based on the work of Wang (2016), which proposes a model which exploits two behavioral finance phenomena – *behavioral volatility* and *mean reversion*. Behavioral volatility refers to the phenomenon whereby market-related events such as irrational trades executed by inexperienced traders cause the trading price of a stock to deviate away from its "true" value. Events like these continually affect market price either until the effects caused cancel each other out, or until rational investors balance these effects out with their rational trades. This phenomenon is known as *mean reversion*. The theory of mean reversion is applicable not only to the price of a stock, but to any price-related metric, such as the Price to Earnings (PE) ratio (share price divided by the earnings per share). As a result, we can decide to buy (or sell) a stock only when some metric that follows the mean reversion theory is far away from the mean, knowing that the "true" value of the metric will be returned to at some point in the future.

A *Directed Graphical Model* (DGM) is a representation of a probabilistic model that uses conditional independence assumptions through a directed graph where the vertices[1] of the graph represent random variables and the arcs represent conditional dependence between pairs of random variables. An arc from vertex A to vertex B represents the statement "A causes B" (Murphy 2002). DGMs are convenient due to their compactness in exhibiting some joint probability distribution – for N binary random variables, the general closed form of the joint probability distribution of these random variables may need $O(2^N)$ parameters; whereas, the graphical model may give the same information using less parameters due to the omission of terms via conditional independence statements.

A *Bayesian Network* is a DGM that represents a set of random variables $X_1, ..., X_n$ and their conditional dependencies through a directed *acyclic* graph (DAG), denoted by $G = (\mathcal{V}, \mathcal{E})$. Each vertex in $\mathcal{V}$ represents a random variable X_i, and each directed edge in $\mathcal{E}$ represents the conditional dependence a random variable has on another. A conditional probability distribution is associated with each node X_i and the joint probability distribution on the vertex set $\mathcal{V}$ is given by $\mathbb{P}[\mathcal{V}] = \prod_{i=1}^{n} \mathbb{P}[X_i \mid parents(X_i)]$. The generalization of a BN to multiple time slices gives rise to the definition of a DBN. A *Dynamic Bayesian Network* is defined to be a pair $(B_0, B_{\rightarrow})$, where B_0 is the BN representing the *prior probability* (or the initial state probability), i.e. the probability distribution of the random variables at time 0, and $B_{\rightarrow}$ is a two-slice temporal BN which describes *transition probabilities* from time $t-1$ to time t for any node X in the vertex set $\mathcal{V}$ of the DAG $G = (\mathcal{V}, \mathcal{E})$, denoted by $\mathbb{P}[X_t | X_{t-1}]$. The joint probability distribution of the vertex set $\mathcal{V}$ over all time slices is given by:

$$\mathbb{P}[\mathcal{V}] = \mathbb{P}[\mathcal{V}_0]\,\mathbb{P}[\mathcal{V}_{1:T}] = \prod_{X_i \in \mathcal{V}} \mathbb{P}[X_{i_0} \mid parents(X_{i_0})] \prod_{t=1}^{T} \prod_{X_i \in \mathcal{V}} \mathbb{P}[X_{i_t} \mid parents(X_{i_t})],$$

where $\mathcal{V}_{t_1:t_2}$ refers to the set of all vertices indexed from time t_1 up to time t_2. A DBN can be parameterized by its transition matrix $\mathbb{A}_t = \mathbb{P}[X_t = j \mid X_{t-1} = i]$, and its prior distribution $\pi(i) = \mathbb{P}[X_1 = i]$. If the transition probabilities are assumed to be constant for all time slices ($\mathbb{A}_t = \mathbb{A}$), then they are said to be *homogeneous* and have a

1 Note that the terms "state", "random variable", "node" and "vertex" may be used interchangeably.

much more compact joint distribution function. When representing a DBN pictorially, two or three time slices are typically shown – the initial time slice and the subsequent one or two – since its structure is assumed to replicate throughout time.

An important property of DAGs is that "nodes can be ordered such that parents come before children. This is called a *topological ordering*, and it can be constructed from any DAG" (Murphy 2012). Given such an ordering, the *Ordered Markov property* (or *Local Markov property*) is defined to be the "assumption that a node only depends on its parents, not on all its predecessors in the ordering" (Murphy 2012; Wang 2016). This assumption is in fact a generalization of the Markov property for Markov chains.

14.2.1. *Inference for DBNs*

The objective in inference is to infer the value of the latent states, given the observations of the observable states; i.e. inferring the marginals $\mathbb{P}[X_t = i \mid y_{1:\tau}]$. If $\tau = t$, the process is known as *filtering* (or *"now-casting"*); if $\tau > t$, then this is *smoothing*; and if $\tau < t$, then we would perform *prediction* (or *forecasting*). A commonly used inference algorithm for DBNs is the *forward–backward algorithm*. In this algorithm, dynamic programming is implemented through two steps, known as *passes*, that run in a counter-directional manner – one runs forward in time while the other runs backward. Note that it is assumed that the transition probability matrix, emission probability matrix and prior probabilities are all known. In the *forward pass*, the value of $\alpha_t(i) := \mathbb{P}[X_t = i \mid y_{1:t}]$ is found in a recursive manner. In the *backward pass*, the value of $\beta_t(i) := \mathbb{P}[y_{t+1:T} \mid X_t = i]$ is also found recursively, but moving in counter chronological order (from time T to time 2). After the forward and backward passes are complete, the value for $\gamma_t(i) := \mathbb{P}[X_t = i \mid y_{1:T}]$ can be finally obtained:

$$\gamma_t(i) = \mathbb{P}[X_t = i \mid y_{1:T}] = \frac{\mathbb{P}[y_{t+1:T} \mid X_t = i]\,\mathbb{P}[X_t = i \mid y_{1:t}]}{\mathbb{P}[y_{1:T}]}$$

where $\mathbb{P}[y_{1:T}] = \prod_{t=1}^{T} c_t$.

14.2.2. *Learning DBNs*

In this context, learning refers to the parameter estimation process. In parameter estimation, learning can be tackled either through a Maximum Likelihood (ML) approach or through the Maximum A Posteriori (MAP) approach. If using ML, then the data is used to obtain parameter estimates via the solution of the optimization problem: $\theta^*_{ML} = \arg\max_\theta \left\{\mathbb{P}[Y \mid \theta]\right\} = \arg\max_\theta \left\{\log \mathbb{P}[Y \mid \theta]\right\}$, where θ is the set of parameters to be estimated. Typically, θ contains the transition matrix and parameters pertaining to the probability distribution used in the emission matrix.

On the other hand, if using the MAP method, the optimization problem above is adjusted slightly to become $\theta^*_{MAP} = \arg\max_\theta \Big\{ \log \mathbb{P}[Y \mid \theta] + \log \mathbb{P}[\theta] \Big\}$, where $\mathbb{P}[\theta]$ is the parameter prior distribution. The approach to solving the optimization problems above is through an adaptation of the Expectation-Maximization (EM) algorithm known as the *Baum–Welch* algorithm, proven to give a local optimum to the optimization problems above (Baum et al. 1970; Dempster et al. 1977). It uses the forward–backward algorithm as a subroutine. Hence, in cases where the model parameters are unknown, the Baum–Welch algorithm is first used to estimate (or learn) the model parameters. Then, the forward–backward algorithm is used to infer the posterior marginals.

14.2.3. *Application of theory*

The main hypothesis of the model proposed by Wang (2016) is that the stock price of a firm is not always equal to the firm's "true" intrinsic value. Using the phenomena of behavioral volatility and mean reversion, temporary effects that cause stock metrics to deviate from their "true" value are classified into two: short-term effects (length of a few days) and medium-term effects (length of several weeks).

It is hypothesized that the fundamental value of a company i at time t, denoted by $P^*_{i,t}$, is directly proportional to its annual earnings at time t, denoted by $E_{i,t}$, with the *fundamental PE ratio*, denoted by $PE^*_{i,t}$, acting as the constant of proportionality:

$$P^*_{i,t} = (PE^*_{i,t})(E_{i,t}).$$

On the other hand, the *observed PE ratio* (openly available on the public domain), denoted by $PE_{i,t}$ is given by $PE_{i,t} = \frac{P_{i,t}}{E_{i,t}}$ where $P_{i,t}$ denotes the actual trading price of a company i at time t.

Note that from this point onward, the index i is dropped as the analysis on stocks is done univariately. The model equation that results from the above is given by:

$$\begin{aligned} P_t = P^*_t(1+Z_t)(1+\varepsilon_t) \quad &\implies \quad y_t = \ln\Big[PE^*(1+Z_t)\Big] + \ln\Big[1+\varepsilon_t\Big] \\ &\implies \quad y_t = \ln\Big[PE^*(1+Z_t)\Big] + \varepsilon_t \qquad [14.1] \end{aligned}$$

where $y_t = \ln\left[\frac{P_t}{E_t}\right]$, $\{Z_t\}_{t\in\mathbb{N}}$ is a discrete-time Markov chain modeling the medium-term noise effects, and $\varepsilon_t \sim \mathcal{N}(0, \sigma^2)$ is a random variable modeling the short-term noise effects. Due to the above model equation, the model used is only applicable for firms that have positive earnings throughout the period under study. Furthermore, we must note that y_t is an observable quantity (since both P_t and E_t are); however, PE^* and Z_t are not. It is assumed that both Z_t and PE^* are discrete-valued;

hence, $Z_t \in \{a_1, \ldots, a_M\}$ and $PE^* \in \{b_1, \ldots, b_N\}$ where M and N represent the number of possible latent states of Z_t and PE^*, respectively.

The conditional independence assumptions used in this model are presented next:

$$\forall\, t \geq 1, \forall\, i, j \geq 1,$$

$$Z_t \perp PE^* \mid \emptyset. \qquad [14.2]$$

$$Z_i \perp Z_j \mid Z_k \qquad \exists\, k \in \{i+1, \ldots, j-1\} \qquad [14.3]$$

$$y_i \perp Z_j \mid Z_k, PE^* \quad \exists\, k \in \{i, \ldots, j-1\} \text{ or } k \in \{j+1, \ldots, i\}. \qquad [14.4]$$

$$y_i \perp y_j \mid Z_k, PE^* \quad \exists\, k \in \{i, \ldots, j\}. \qquad [14.5]$$

For $t \geq 2$ and $r, s \in \{1, \ldots, M\}$, the matrix $\mathbb{W} := [w_{rs}]_{M \times M}$ is defined to be the *transition probability matrix*, where

$$w_{rs} := \mathbb{P}[Z_t = a_s | Z_{t-1} = a_r].$$

Note that $w_{rs} \in [0, 1]$ and $\sum_{s=1}^{M} w_{rs} = 1$. For $t \geq 1$, $m \in \{1, \ldots, M\}$ and $n \in \{1, \ldots, N\}$, the matrix $\mathbb{D}_t := [d_{mn}(y_t)]_{M \times N}$ is defined to be the *emission probability matrix* at time t, where

$$d_{mn}(y_t) := \mathbb{P}[y_t \mid Z_t = a_m, PE^* = b_n].$$

where $d_{mn}(y_t) \sim \mathcal{N}(\ln[b_n(1 + a_m)], \sigma^2)$. For $m \in \{1, \ldots, M\}$ and $n \in \{1, \ldots, N\}$, the vectors $\boldsymbol{u} := (u_m)_{m \in \mathbb{N}}$ and $\boldsymbol{v} := (v_n)_{n \in \mathbb{N}}$ are defined to be the *initial probability vectors* that contain the initial probability distributions, where

$$u_m := \mathbb{P}[Z_1 = a_m]; \qquad v_n := \mathbb{P}[PE^* = b_n].$$

Note that $u_m, v_n \in [0, 1]$, $\sum_{m=1}^{M} u_m = 1$ and $\sum_{n=1}^{N} v_n = 1$. These prior distributions serve to incorporate any expert knowledge that the researcher may have available.

Having laid out the principles needed for inference, the aim of the analysis now makes itself clearer – that of inferring the value of PE^* so as to estimate the fundamental price of a stock and formulate a trading strategy based on this knowledge. Furthermore, inferring the value of Z_t is also useful as it can be used to test an alternative trading strategy. In this context, the data used will be split into a training and test set. The set of model parameters is given by $\theta = \{\mathbb{W}, \boldsymbol{u}, \boldsymbol{v}, \sigma^2\}$. The space of possible parameters is given by the set:

$$\Theta = \left\{ \theta : u_m, v_n, w_{rs} \in [0, 1], \sum_{m=1}^{M} u_m = 1, \sum_{n=1}^{N} v_n = 1, \sum_{s=1}^{M} w_{rs} = 1, \sigma^2 > 0 \right\}. \qquad [14.6]$$

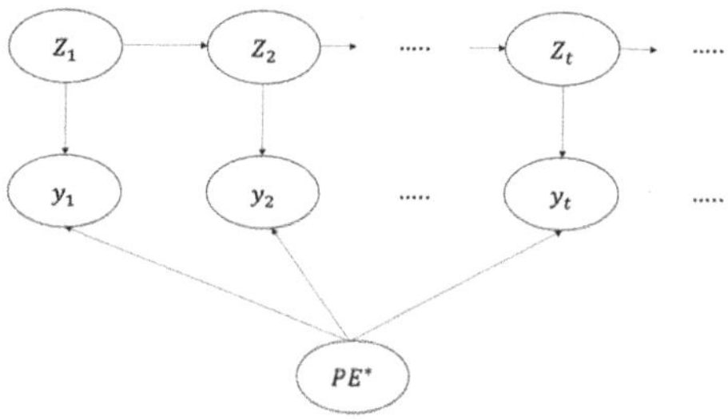

Figure 14.1. *Representation of the model described above using a DBN, where y_t is observable and PE^* and Z_t are latent, discrete variables*

Learning and inference then follow. Since the parameters in θ are unknown, they will first need to be estimated (learning procedure). As mentioned, the algorithm used to obtain the MAP estimates is the Baum–Welch algorithm. After the unknown model parameters are estimated, the forward–backward algorithm is used on the parameter estimates to infer the constant value of PE^* for the training set and test set, and to infer the value of Z_t through smoothing for the training set, and through filtering for the test set:

– filtering probabilities: $\mathbb{P}[Z_T, PE^* \mid y_{1:T}, \theta]$;

– smoothing probabilities: $\mathbb{P}[Z_t, PE^* \mid y_{1:T}, \theta]$, where $t \in \{1, \ldots, T-1\}$.

14.2.4. *Inference with known parameters*

According to the forward pass of the forward–backward algorithm, the following definitions are made and equations derived for the filtering probabilities:

$$\forall\, t \in \{1, \ldots, T\}, m \in \{1, \ldots, M\}, n \in \{1, \ldots, N\},$$

$$\alpha_{tmn} := \mathbb{P}\left[Z_t = a_m, PE^* = b_n \mid y_{1:t}, \theta\right] \;;$$

$$\alpha_{1mn} = \frac{d_{mn}(y_1)\, u_m v_n}{\sum_{m'=1}^{M} \sum_{n'=1}^{N} d_{m'n'}(y_1)\, u_{m'} v_{n'}} \;;$$

$$\alpha_{tmn} = \frac{d_{mn}(y_t) \sum_{i=1}^{M} \mathbb{P}\left[Z_{t-1} = a_i, PE^* = b_n \mid y_{1:t-1}\right] w_{mi}}{c_t} \;;$$

$$c_t := \sum_{m=1}^{M} \sum_{n=1}^{N} d_{mn}(y_t) \sum_{i=1}^{M} \mathbb{P}\left[Z_{t-1} = a_i, PE^* = b_n \mid y_{1:t-1}\right] w_{mi}.$$

After defining the filtering probabilities, the smoothing probabilities are given through the estimate denoted by γ_{tmn}:

$$\forall\, t \in \{1, \ldots, T-1\}, m \in \{1, \ldots, M\}, n \in \{1, \ldots, N\},$$

$$\gamma_{tmn} := \mathbb{P}\left[Z_t = a_m, PE^* = b_n \mid y_{1:T}\right].$$

Next, according to the backward pass of the forward–backward algorithm, the definition of β_{tmn} is to be given, so as to be able to obtain the values for γ_{tmn}:

$$\beta_{tmn} := \frac{\mathbb{P}\left[y_{t+1:T} \,|\, Z_t = a_m, PE^* = b_n\right]}{\mathbb{P}\left[y_{t+1:T} \mid y_{1:t}\right]} = \frac{\mathbb{P}\left[y_{t+1:T} \mid Z_t = a_m, PE^* = b_n\right]}{\prod_{t'=t+1}^{T} c_{t'}}$$

Therefore, according to the forward–backward algorithm, we have:

$$\gamma_{tmn} = \alpha_{tmn}\beta_{tmn}.$$

What remains to be derived are the expressions for β_{tmn} $\forall\, t \in \{1, \ldots, T-1\}$:

$$\beta_{(T-1)mn} = \frac{\beta'_{(T-1)mn}}{c_T} = \frac{\sum_{i=1}^{M} d_{in}\left(y_T\right) w_{im}}{\sum_{m=1}^{M}\sum_{n=1}^{N} c_T}.$$

For β_{tmn} $\forall\, t \in \{1, \ldots, T-2\}, m \in \{1, \ldots, M\}, n \in \{1, \ldots, N\}$:

$$\beta'_{tmn} = \sum_{i=1}^{M} \beta'_{(t+1)in} d_{in}\left(y_{t+1}\right) w_{im}\,; \qquad \beta_{tmn} = \frac{\sum_{i=1}^{M} \beta_{(t+1)in} d_{in}\left(y_{t+1}\right) w_{im}}{c_{t+1}}.$$

With expressions found for both the smoothing and filtering probabilities, the most probable values of the latent variables PE^* and Z_t are found through marginalization:

$$\widehat{PE^*} = \arg\max_{b_n}\left\{\sum_{m=1}^{M} \mathbb{P}\left[Z_t = a_m, PE^* = b_n \mid y_{1:T}\right]\right\} = \arg\max_{b_n}\left\{\sum_{m=1}^{M} \gamma_{tmn}\right\}$$

To find the estimate $\widehat{Z_t}$ for the latent state Z_t, smoothing is used on the training set while filtering is applied on the test set:

$$\widehat{Z_t} = \arg\max_{a_m}\left\{\sum_{n=1}^{N} \gamma_{tmn}\right\} \quad \forall\, t \in \{t : y_t \in \mathbb{X}_{train}\};$$

$$\widehat{Z_t} = \arg\max_{a_m}\left\{\sum_{n=1}^{N} \alpha_{tmn}\right\} \quad \forall\, t \in \{t : y_t \in \mathbb{X}_{test}\}.$$

where $\mathbb{X}_{train}$ and $\mathbb{X}_{test}$ denote the training set and test set, respectively.

14.2.5. *Learning unknown parameters*

The optimization problem in learning is given by $\widehat{\theta_{MAP}} = \arg\max_{\theta\in\Theta}\left\{\mathbb{P}\left[\theta \mid y_1^T\right]\right\}$ and is solved using the Baum–Welch Algorithm[2]:

1. Set $j = 1$.
2. Set $\theta^{(1)} - \theta^{(0)} > \delta$.
3. *While* $\theta^{(j)} - \theta^{(j-1)} > \delta$ *do*

   (i) Calculate probabilities $\mathbb{P}\left[Z_t = a_m, PE^* = b_n \mid y_{1:T}, \theta^{(j)}\right] \;\; \forall\, t, m, n.$

   (ii) Solve the constrained maximization problem

$$\widehat{\theta^{(j+1)}} = \arg\max_{\theta\in\Theta}\left\{Q\left(\theta;\theta^{(j)}\right) + \ln\mathbb{P}[\theta]\right]\}$$

   where $Q\left(\theta;\theta^{(j)}\right) = \mathbb{E}_{Z_{1:T},PE^*|y_{1:T},\theta^{(j)}}\left[\ln\mathbb{P}\left[y_{1:T}, Z_{1:T}, PE^* \mid \theta\right]\right].$

   (iii) Increment j.

An expression in closed form can be obtained for $Q\left(\theta;\theta^{(j)}\right)$ by using the smoothing probabilities:

$$\begin{aligned}Q\left(\theta;\theta^{(j)}\right) =& \sum_{t=1}^{T-1}\sum_{m=1}^{M}\sum_{n=1}^{N}\alpha_{tmn}^{(j-1)}\beta_{tmn}^{(j-1)}\ln[d_{mn}(y_t)] + \sum_{m=1}^{M}\sum_{n=1}^{N}\alpha_{Tmn}^{(j-1)}\ln[d_{mn}(y_T)]\\&+\sum_{t'=2}^{T-1}\sum_{i,m=1}^{M}\sum_{n=1}^{N}\beta_{tmn}^{(j-1)}\left(\frac{d_{mn}^{(j-1)}(y_t)}{c_t^{(j-1)}}\right)w_{mi}^{(j-1)}\alpha_{(t-1)in}^{(j-1)}\ln[w_{mi}]\\&+\sum_{i,m=1}^{M}\sum_{n=1}^{N}\left(\frac{d_{mn}^{(j-1)}(y_T)}{c_T^{(j-1)}}\right)w_{mi}^{(j-1)}\alpha_{T-1,in}^{(j-1)}\ln[w_{mi}]\\&+\sum_{m=1}^{M}\sum_{n=1}^{N}\alpha_{1mn}^{(j-1)}\beta_{1mn}^{(j-1)}(\ln[u_m]+\ln[v_n]).\end{aligned}$$

In the argument of the maximization problem above, $\ln\mathbb{P}[\theta]$ is the logarithm of the prior distribution $\mathbb{P}[\theta]$, where $\mathbb{P}[\theta] = \mathbb{P}[\boldsymbol{u}]\mathbb{P}[\boldsymbol{v}]\mathbb{P}[\mathbb{W}]\mathbb{P}[\sigma^2]$ since independence of priors is assumed. Within this prior distribution, two types of expert knowledge can be included – prior knowledge on the ballpark value of PE^* and prior knowledge on the persistence of the medium-term noise effects, which are encoded through the prior $\mathbb{P}[\boldsymbol{v}]$ and the prior $\mathbb{P}[\mathbb{W}]$, respectively.

2 Note that in the forthcoming expressions, θ should technically be written with a hat superscript (ˆ) since it is a set of parameter estimates.

The prior for the vector $\boldsymbol{v}$ is represented by the Dirichlet distribution:

$$f(\boldsymbol{v}) = \frac{\Gamma(k_1 + k_2 + \ldots + k_N)}{\Gamma(k_1)\Gamma(k_2)\ldots\Gamma(k_N)} \prod_{n=1}^{N} v_n^{k_n - 1}. \quad [14.7]$$

The values k_n for $n \in \{1, \ldots, N\}$ intuitively correspond to the degree of belief an expert has on the event that b_n is the "true" value for PE^*. For this analysis, $k_n = 1 \ \forall n$. The prior for the matrix $\mathbb{W}$ is also derived from the Dirichlet distribution $f(\mathbb{W}) = \prod_{m=1}^{M} f(\boldsymbol{w}_m)$, where $\boldsymbol{w}_m = (w_{im})_{i=1,\ldots,M}$ and

$$f(\boldsymbol{w}_m) = \frac{\Gamma(k_{1m} + k_{2m} + \ldots + k_{Mm})}{\Gamma(k_{1m})\Gamma(k_{2m})\ldots\Gamma(k_{Mn})} \prod_{m=1}^{M} w_{im}^{k_{im}-1}.$$

Since $\mathbb{W}$ is the transition matrix for the hidden Markov chain $\{Z_t\}_{t\in\mathbb{N}}$, the diagonal entries of $\mathbb{W}$ represent the probability that a particular state will persist (remain as it is at the next time point). The greater the value of Z_t (or, correspondingly, a_m), the greater the stat's persistence. In this analysis, the off-diagonal entries[3] are set to 0.

Taking all the above into account, the logarithm of the prior $\mathbb{P}[\theta]$ becomes

$$\ln \mathbb{P}[\theta] = \ln \mathbb{P}[\mathbb{W}] + \ln \mathbb{P}[\boldsymbol{v}] = \sum_{m=1}^{M}\sum_{i=1}^{M} (k_{im} - 1)\ln[w_{im}] + \sum_{n=1}^{N} (k_n - 1)\ln[v_n] + s_1,$$

where $s_1 = \ln\left[\frac{\Gamma(k_1+k_2+\ldots+k_N)}{\Gamma(k_1)\Gamma(k_2)\ldots\Gamma(k_N)}\right] + \ln\left[\frac{\Gamma(k_{1m}+k_{2m}+\ldots+k_{Mm})}{\Gamma(k_{1m})\Gamma(k_{2m})\ldots\Gamma(k_{Mn})}\right]$. The constant s_1 is only included for completeness' sake – it is rendered irrelevant when maximizing in the Baum–Welch algorithm.

With the priors set, the constrained optimization problem is now fully defined. Note that only the equality constraints in [14.6] will be considered as the inequality constraints will end up still being satisfied. Therefore, the method of Lagrange multipliers can be used to solve this optimization problem. The expressions for the estimators of the four variables in question are given below:

$$\widehat{u_m^{(j)}} = \sum_{n=1}^{N} \alpha_{1mn}^{(j-1)} \beta_{1mn}^{(j-1)}; \quad [14.8]$$

$$\widehat{v_n^{(j)}} = \frac{\sum_{m=1}^{M} q_{1mn}^{(j)}(Z_1, PE^*) + (k_n - 1)}{1 + \sum_{n'=1}^{N}(k_{n'} - 1)} = \frac{\sum_{m=1}^{M} \alpha_{1mn}^{(j-1)} \beta_{1mn}^{(j-1)} + (k_n - 1)}{1 + \sum_{n'=1}^{N}(k_{n'} - 1)}; \quad [14.9]$$

3 The reader is suggested to refer to Wang (2016) for more information on the values of the off-diagonals.

$$\widehat{w_{mi}^{(j)}} = \frac{\sum_{t'=2}^{T}\sum_{n=1}^{N} q_{t',m,i,n}^{(j)}\left(Z_{t'}, Z_{t'-1}, PE^*\right) + (k_{mi}-1)}{\sum_{t'=2}^{T}\sum_{m=1}^{M}\sum_{n=1}^{N} q_{t',m,i,n}^{(j)}\left(Z_{t'}, Z_{t'-1}, PE^*\right) + \sum_{m'=1}^{M}(k_{m'i}-1)}$$
$$= \frac{\omega_{t\prime,m,i,n}^{(j)}}{\sum_{m'=1}^{M}\omega_{t\prime,m,i,n}^{(j)}}, \quad [14.10]$$

where

$$\omega_{t\prime,m,i,n}^{(j)} = \sum_{t'=2}^{T-1}\sum_{n=1}^{N}\beta_{t'mn}^{(j-1)}\left(\frac{d_{mn}^{(j-1)}(y_{t'})}{c_{t'}^{(j-1)}}\right)w_{mi}^{(j-1)}\alpha_{t'-1,i,n}^{(j-1)} + \sum_{n=1}^{N}\left(\frac{d_{mn}^{(j-1)}(y_T)}{c_T^{(j-1)}}\right)w_{mi}^{(j-1)}\alpha_{(T-1)in}^{(j-1)} + (k_{mi}-1)$$

$$\widehat{\sigma^{2(j-1)}} = \frac{\sum_{t=1}^{T-1}\sum_{m=1}^{M}\sum_{n=1}^{N}\alpha_{tmn}^{(j-1)}\beta_{tmn}^{(j-1)}\left(y_t - \ln\left[b_n\left(1+a_m\right)\right]\right)^2}{\sum_{t=1}^{T-1}\sum_{m=1}^{M}\sum_{n=1}^{N}\alpha_{tmn}^{(j-1)}\beta_{tmn}^{(j-1)} + \sum_{m=1}^{M}\sum_{n=1}^{N}\alpha_{Tmn}^{(j-1)}}$$
$$+ \frac{\sum_{m=1}^{M}\sum_{n=1}^{N}\alpha_{Tmn}^{(j-1)}\left(y_T - \ln\left[b_n\left(1+a_m\right)\right]\right)^2}{\sum_{t=1}^{T-1}\sum_{m=1}^{M}\sum_{n=1}^{N}\alpha_{tmn}^{(j-1)}\beta_{tmn}^{(j-1)} + \sum_{m=1}^{M}\sum_{n=1}^{N}\alpha_{Tmn}^{(j-1)}}. \quad [14.11]$$

14.3. Methodology of analysis and results

Twelve equities were chosen to be analyzed in this chapter (see Table 14.1) – nine from a developed market (US) and three from emerging markets (Brazil and China). The training set contains data from January 1, 2011 to December 31, 2019 while the test set contains data from January 1, 2020 to September 30, 2020. Two datasets were collected for each stock for the above-mentioned period: daily price data and quarterly earnings per share data.

After the preliminary data cleaning and preparation phase, the initial values of vectors $\boldsymbol{a} = (a_m)$ and $\boldsymbol{b} = (b_n)$ are set next. Priors of the vector $\boldsymbol{v}$ and matrix $\mathbb{W}$ are set as discussed earlier; the prior for $\boldsymbol{u}$ is set to be the discrete uniform distribution and the initial value of σ^2 is set to 5. Parameter learning is then performed before inference of the latent states $\widehat{PE^*}$ and $\widehat{Z_t}$. Simulation of the trading strategies follows.

Stock	Thresholds for the LT strategy				Thresholds for the MT strategy				Profit from
	0.05	0.10	0.15	0.20	0.03	0.05	0.07	0.10	B&H
AAPL (US)	55.30%	55.30%	55.30%	55.30%	69.51%	57.82%	48.06%	76.02%	55.30%
ADBE (US)	25.46%	37.86%	44.45%	0%	46.65%	46.65%	46.65%	46.65%	46.65%
BLK (US)	12.98%	12.98%	12.98%	12.98%	33.92%	34.66%	20.85%	20.85%	12.98%
COST (US)	22.59%	22.59%	22.59%	22.59%	50.12%	42.85%	28.21%	0%	22.59%
HD (US)	28.71%	28.71%	28.71%	28.71%	57.76%	51.31%	37.99%	47.35%	28.71%
ITUB (BZ)	-39.86%	-29.36%	-29.36%	-27.57%	9.10%	7.07%	7.07%	-9.59%	-55.85%
MA (US)	27.17%	29.34%	61.09%	60.41%	47.70%	32.57%	24.66%	34.39%	11.93%
MCD (US)	11.38%	11.38%	11.38%	11.38%	18.94%	18.94%	30.63%	30.63%	11.38%
NTES (CHN)	47.89%	50.84%	57.35%	39.54%	39.54%	39.54%	39.54%	39.54%	39.54%
NVDA (US)	125.90%	125.90%	125.90%	125.90%	149.00%	156.79%	125.90%	125.90%	125.90%
SAN (BZ)	-2.08%	-14.35%	-17.78%	-17.78%	-57.17%	-57.17%	-57.17%	-57.17%	-57.17%
UNH (US)	7.95%	7.95%	15.90%	19.88%	72.41%	21.83%	38.58%	2.87%	7.95%
Average	26.12%	25.07%	32.38%	27.61%	44.79%	37.74%	32.60%	29.79%	20.83%
W/D/L	4/7/1	4/7/1	5/6/1	4/7/1	9/3/0	9/3/0	7/4/1	6/4/2	
Totals	17/27/4				31/14/3				

Table 14.1. *Table of results, showing the return on investment as a percentage of the sum invested*

The trading strategies proposed by Wang (2016) and used in this chapter will be compared to the benchmark B&H strategy. For both the proposed trading strategies, let I_t denote the amount of cash available at time t; let N_t denote the units of a security held at time t; let T_{train} represent the size of the training set; and let T represent the size of the dataset (sum of sizes of training and test sets). Both the long-term and the medium-term trading strategies can be described by three possible courses of action (labeled (i), (ii) and (iii) below) at time t; i.e. courses of action (i) through (ii) are common to both trading strategies:

(i) If $PE_t \leq A_t(1 - Tr)$ and $I_t > 0$, then buy the security using all the available cash I_t. Hence, $N_{t+1} = \frac{I_t}{P_T}$ and $I_{t+1} = 0$.

(ii) If $PE_t \geq A_t(1 + Tr)$ and $I_t = 0$, then sell all the units held N_t. Hence, $N_{t+1} = 0$ and $I_{t+1} = P_t N_t$.

(iii) If neither (i) nor (ii) are satisfied, do not execute any trades. Hence, $N_{t+1} = N_t$ and $I_{t+1} = I_t$.

Note that A_t is considered to be a baseline and depends on the trading strategy. The threshold value $Tr \in (0, 1)$ acts as a sensitivity gauge defining how much the investor wants to allow $PE_t = \frac{P_t}{E_t}$ to deviate from the baseline A_t before triggering a particular course of action in the trading strategies. This is clear from how the courses of action are defined. The total profit at the end of the trading period is given by $I_T + P_T N_T - I_{T_{train}+1}$.

The first trading strategy proposed by Wang (2016) is the so-called "long-term strategy", where trading is done with respect to the constant value of $\widehat{PE^*}$, so $A_t = \widehat{PE^*}$. The alternative strategy is the "medium-term strategy", where trading is done with respect to the dynamic values of $\widehat{PE^*}(1 + \widehat{Z_t})$, where each $\widehat{Z_t}$ is dynamically estimated through filtering. Therefore, for the medium-term strategy, $A_t = \widehat{PE^*}(1 + \widehat{Z_t})$.

The results on the BLK stock are presented in this chapter. Firstly, the long-term strategy on the BLK stock data suggests that the investor buys the stock at time point $2265 = T_{train} + 1$ and holds the stock for the rest of the period. Clearly, this strategy coincides with the B&H strategy and, as a result, profit from the long-term-strategy would be equal to profit from the B&H strategy, which is equal to \$1298.04, equaling a 12.98% return on the initial investment of \$10000. On the other hand, the medium-term strategy suggests that the investor buys the stock at time points 2265, 2301 and 2437, sells it at time points 2289 and 2431, and holds it for the rest of the time points. This would yield a profit of \$3391.85; equaling a 33.92% return on the initial investment of \$10000 in the nine-month period that the testing set covers. This means that the medium-term strategy beats the B&H strategy by 20.94%. Figure 14.2 illustrates the long-term strategy and medium-term strategy.

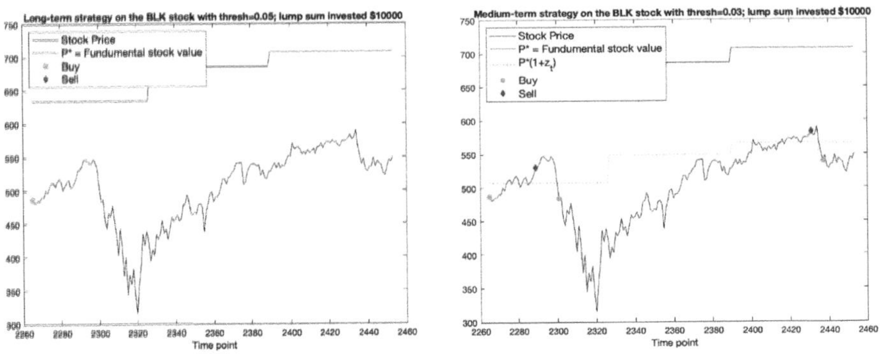

(a) Long-term strategy (b) Medium-term strategy

Figure 14.2. *Simulated strategies for the BLK stock. For a color version of this figure, see http://www.iste.co.uk/dimotikalis/data4.zip*

14.4. Conclusion

Through the use of DBNs, a model for stock movement was built as proposed by Wang (2016). This model includes two latent states – one modeling the medium-term noise effects and the other modeling the true fundamental PE ratio of a firm, the latter assumed to be constant throughout the period under study. The forward–backward algorithm and the Baum–Welch algorithm (variant of the EM algorithm) are used to perform parameter learning and inference. Based on this fitted model, the trading strategies (also proposed by Wang) were applied to the 12 stocks studied here, with nine of these stocks trading on a developed market and the rest on an emerging one. Overall, both the long-term and medium-term strategies outperform the benchmark B&H trading strategy, 17 and 31 times, respectively, out of a total of 48 experiment runs for each strategy (four for each of the 12 stocks). The strategies proposed by Wang only lose out to the B&H four and three times, respectively. Furthermore, the outperformance of these trading strategies is substantial. Whereas the average profit over all stocks when using the B&H is 20.83%, the average profit over all stocks and over all thresholds for the long-term strategy is 27.78%, and that for the medium-term strategy is 36.23%. Lastly, it results that these trading strategies provide the investor with trading suggestions that, in certain cases, can even turn a loss under the B&H strategy into a profit, as was shown to be the case for the ITUB stock. This stock was on a downfall, but the medium-term strategy still yielded a profit on the sum invested. All these results are as displayed in Table 14.1.

As with any statistical model, the model implemented in this work has its own flaws and potential improvements. The first and most significant limitation is the fact that only stocks that had a positive EPS during the period under study can be modeled by the model. This is due to the left-hand side of the model equation, i.e. equation [14.1]. In certain times such as during pandemics or during recessions, it may be considerably difficult to find a firm who has not registered a loss in at least one quarter for the period under study.

A second limitation is the lack of use of expert knowledge. In real-world investing, expertise in the field is considered highly valuable, and only seasoned investors are generally advised to trade actively. Since the model in this chapter allows for the incorporation of expert knowledge, it is indeed a limitation that such knowledge is not made use of.

Another limitation related to expert knowledge is that no trading fees or commissions are taken into account in this analysis. Although Wang (2016) allows for commissions to be considered in her trading strategies, no knowledge on the actual values of fees or commissions charged was available at the time of writing, and hence, such expenses could not be taken into account. It is well-known that certain trading fees can sometimes tally up when executing numerous trades, in such a way that a profit can turn into a loss when these fees are brought to the fore.

Improvements on the above-mentioned limitations can add value to the model and should be considered in future works. In addition, another improvement that makes the model here more applicable in real-life scenarios is the incorporation of some variable that measures the liquidity of a stock. This is because the suggestions provided by the trading strategies on when to buy and sell a stock are rendered useless if the stock itself is not liquid. Prices may change by the time the stock becomes liquid enough for an actual trading opportunity to arise, and if the price changes significantly, that obviously renders the suggestion itself useless.

Finally, another improvement that can be implemented in future studies is further and deeper experimentation and testing. To begin with, experimentation on a portfolio level (as considered by Wang 2016) can be implemented with the stocks studied here to understand how the profits change when a group of stocks are considered together. For instance, samples of nine stocks from the 12 studied here can be taken to form portfolios and the "optimal" portfolio can be identified. Apart from this, more time can be spent on cross-validation in future studies to further improve on the suggestions provided by the trading strategies in this work. Furthermore, properties of all the estimators used could be derived in future works, to better understand their behavior.

14.5. References

Baum, L.E., Petries, T., Soules, G., Weiss, N. (1970). A maximization technique occurring in the statistical analysis of probabilistic functions of Markov chains. *The Annals of Mathematical Statistics*, 41(1), 167–171.

Benhamou, E., Atif, J., Laraki, R. (2018). A new approach to learning in dynamic Bayesian networks (DBNs). *SSRN Electronic Journal*, arXiv:1812.09027v2.

Cozar, J., Puerta J., Gamez, J.A. (2017). An application of dynamic Bayesian networks to condition monitoring and fault prediction in a sensored system: A case study. *International Journal of Computational Intelligence Systems*, 10(1), 176.

Dagum, P., Galper, A., Horvitz, E. (1992). Dynamic network models for forecasting. *Proceedings of the Eighth Conference on Uncertainty in Artificial Intelligence*, 41–48.

Dagum, P., Galper, A., Horvitz, E. (1995). Uncertain reasoning and forecasting. *International Journal of Forecasting*, 11(1), 73–87.

Delage, E., Lee, H., Ng, A.Y. (2006). A dynamic Bayesian network model for autonomous 3D reconstruction from a single indoor image. *2006 IEEE Computer Society Conference on Computer Vision and Pattern Recognition (CVPR'06)*, 2, 2418–2428. doi: 10.1109/CVPR.2006.23.

Dempster, A.P., Laird, N.M., Rubin, D.B. (1977). Maximum likelihood from incomplete data via the EM algorithm. *Journal of the Royal Statistical Society: Series B (Methodological)*, 39(1), 1–22.

Murphy, K. (2001). An introduction to graphical models. Technical Report [Online]. Available at: https://www.cs.ubc.ca/murphyk/Bayes/bnintro.html.

Murphy, K. (2002). Dynamic Bayesian networks: Representation, inference and learning. PhD Dissertation, University of California, Berkeley.

Murphy, K. (2012). *Machine Learning: A Probabilistic Perspective*. MIT Press, Cambridge, MA.

Murphy, K. and Mian, S. (1996). Modelling gene expression data using dynamic Bayesian networks. Technical Report [Online]. Available at: https://www.cs.ubc.ca/murphyk/Papers/ismb99.pdf.

Nefian, A., Liang, L., Pi, X., Liu, X., Murphy, K. (2002). Dynamic Bayesian networks for audio-visual speech recognition. *EURASIP Journal on Advances in Signal Processing*, 11.

Patel, M., Miro, J.V., Dissanayake, G. (2010). Dynamic Bayesian networks for learning interactions between assistive robotic walker and human users. *KI 2010: Advances in Artificial Intelligence*, 333–340 [Online]. Available at: https://opus.lib.uts.edu.au/bitstream/10453/16294/1/2010000382.pdf.

de Paz, R.C., Flores, M.J., Marin-Gomez, J. (2011). Dynamic Bayesian networks for gesture recognition [Online]. Available at: https://www.jmartinez-gomez.com/uploads/5/2/8/0/52807/waf11.pdf.

Prembida, C., Souza, F.A.A., Faria, D.R. (2016). Dynamic Bayesian network for semantic place classification in mobile robotics. *Autonomous Robots*, 5(41), 1161–1172.

Raval, A., Ghahramani, Z., Wild, D.L. (2002). A Bayesian network model for protein fold and remote homologue recognition. *Bioinformatics*, 6(18), 788–801.

Russell, S. and Norvig, P. (1995). *Artificial Intelligence: A Modern Approach*, 2nd edition. Prentice Hall, Upper Saddle River, NJ.

Wang, H. (2016). Bayesian probabilistic inference on firm-level stock price dynamics. PhD Dissertation, Suranaree University of Technology.

Yao, X.Q., Zhu, H., She, Z. (2008). A dynamic Bayesian network approach to protein secondary structure prediction. *BMC Bioinformatics*, 1, 9.

Zweig, G. and Russell, S. (1998). Speech recognition with dynamic Bayesian networks. *Proceedings of the fifteenth national/tenth conference on Artificial intelligence/Innovative applications of artificial intelligence (AAAI '98/IAAI '98). American Association for Artificial Intelligence, USA*, 173–180 [Online]. Available at: http://www.cse.msu.edu/cse841/papers/zweig.pdf.

15

Quantitative Methods for Analysing the Risk and Timing of Bankruptcy of Small and Medium Enterprises

Statistical modeling has many applications in business and finance, for example, in credit scoring and predicting business failures. Nowadays, the preferred methods are logistic regression, when only the occurrence of the event is of interest, and survival analysis if the timing of the event also needs to be examined. Another approach to these analyses is to use machine learning techniques. The problem presented by imbalanced data due to a low relative frequency of the event is discussed. The survival analysis methodology that is applied most often is Cox's semi-parametric proportional hazards regression, and the important extension of this to competing risk is presented and illustrated by application to data on the failure of Small Business Enterprises in Italy. The two main approaches to hazard modeling with competing risks – cause-specific hazards and subdistribution hazards – are discussed.

15.1. Introduction

Finance is essentially a quantitative field. Consequently, developments in quantitative methodology – drawn originally from statistical science and, more recently, also from the field of machine learning – have been introduced over the years in order to improve the analysis and modeling of financial phenomena. The general aim is to provide an objective basis for decisions such as providing credit, where the lending institution seeks to minimize the costly error of extending credit to a firm or individual that will default. In the case of firms' failures through bankruptcy or other causes, investors wish to use the quantitative information provided in balance sheets in order to detect financial distress and predict the failure. In both of these applications of risk assessment, the basic structure of the problem is to construct a

Chapter written by Francesca PIERRI and Chrys CARONI.

rule for assigning a unit (an applicant for credit or a firm) to the "good" or "bad" group on the basis of measured covariates. This is done by fitting a model to a training set of historical data which contains both good and bad units (this procedure is known as supervised learning). The progressive development of statistical approaches to such problems was reviewed by Balcaen and Ooghe (2006). In parallel with a trend that occurred generally throughout applied statistics, the method of discriminant analysis which was employed in the first applications following Altman (1968), subsequently gave way to logistic regression analysis (introduced into this area by Ohlson (1981)), which has now become the standard statistical methodology for these applications. Other, non-statistical approaches are being employed increasingly often, such as the use of neural networks (see, for example, Yang et al. 1999; Atiya 2001).

Another major statistical innovation was to extend the modeling of the event of failure so as to examine its timing, instead of simply determining whether or not it happened within a fixed interval of time. This required the introduction of the methods of lifetime data analysis generally known as survival analysis. Thus, Shumway (2001), following earlier work such as Kiefer (1988) and Banasik et al. (1999), used hazard models for forecasting bankruptcy. His model had the best performance in the comparative study of Wu et al. (2010). The most widely used technique for modeling lifetimes in relation to covariates using hazard functions is Cox's semi-parametric proportional hazards regression model (Cox 1972). This and its various extensions have now been applied many times in banking, finance and economics. A more detailed review was carried out by Bisogno et al. (2018).

15.2. Approaches to statistical modeling

Breiman (2001) drew attention to the existence of two cultures in statistical modeling. What might be called the traditional statistical approach (including both sides of the frequentist–Bayesian divide) generally proceeds from the assumption of a probability model. This is often in the form of "signal plus noise", as in linear regression. On the contrary, a great deal of data analysis nowadays is carried out using an algorithmic approach, with examples such as neural networks and other techniques from the area of machine learning. In both approaches, the objective is to use a set of data on a response variable y and a vector of explanatory variables or predictors x to derive individual predictions $\hat{y} = f(x)$ for each unit that is close to the corresponding observed values of y according to some criterion (e.g. least squares). In regression-type models, the predictor may simply be $\beta' x$, where the parameters β are estimated to optimize fit to the data. By examining the values of the estimates of the elements of β, and possibly using tests of statistical significance and other variable selection techniques, a model can be obtained that is interpretable, in the sense that it shows which predictors affect the response y and how much. In contrast, interpretability is not a target of the algorithmic approach, which concentrates almost exclusively on the quality of prediction (although some techniques may produce an indication of variable importance). The details of the link between x and y are hidden inside a black box. Another difference is that the algorithmic approach is much more oriented and adapted to big data. A more recent overview of the two cultures is presented by Efron (2020) and the contributed discussion that follows it.

This division relates directly to credit scoring, bankruptcy prediction and other applications in the financial field. In many cases – particularly credit scoring – it is likely that achieving good prediction from the available data on the credit applicants is the only objective. Nothing is gained by reducing the number of predictors that form the input to the procedure or from determining which predictors are the most important. Consequently, the statistical modeling approaches such as logistic regression cease to be relevant and can be replaced by machine learning methods, if these perform better. The classic objective of statistical modeling of obtaining a parsimonious model that has been reduced to the few essential predictors applies chiefly to cases such as medical data analyses, where collecting the data on a predictor may require an expensive test and establishing which predictors influence the response y probably has substantial scientific interest. Bankruptcy prediction may have both objectives. The pure prediction aspect may be important in itself, but the identification of which of the financial indexes that have been employed as predictors are the best indicators of future failure, may be what the financial analyst really wants to know.

15.3. Imbalanced data

A major practical problem that may arise in predicting failure is imbalance between the two groups in the data, in the sense that the "good" group is much bigger than the "bad" group, because the event under study occurs relatively rarely. For example, Shumway's data included only 118 filings for bankruptcy among 1,822 firms (6.5%) (Shumway 2001). In our study of the closing down of Small Business Enterprises in Italy (Pierri and Caroni 2017), the closure rate was about 3% each year. Other examples can be far more extreme than these: Baesens et al. (2021) indicate that investigations into fraud in transactions encounter rates typically below 0.5%. There is now a large literature on the problems posed by imbalanced data and how they can be handled. Essentially, there are two problems, which align with the two approaches to modeling discussed above. One is the effect on the quality of estimation of the parameters of a statistical model. We mainly consider the case of logistic regression, which has been well studied and is the method most often applied to the area that we are considering here. The other problem is the effect of data imbalance on the quality of prediction, which is discussed very extensively in the machine learning literature (see, for example, Haixiang et al. 2017).

15.3.1. *Estimating the logistic regression model with imbalanced data*

Logistic regression is usually estimated by maximum likelihood. Although the method's asymptotic properties are excellent, it is well known that small sample estimates of regression coefficients may be biased and this can be severe with imbalanced data. This was discussed and analyzed in detail by King and Zeng (2001). Solutions have been developed in modern statistical analysis and are applied in logistic regression and Cox regression. In particular, Firth's penalized estimation method (Puhr et al. 2017; Kosmidis and Firth 2021) can be applied using the R package "brglm" (Kosmidis 2021).

In fact, the absolute number of events, not only the proportion, seems to be a crucial factor for the quality of estimation. A result is often cited from simulation studies that indicated that for successful logistic regression and proportional hazards regression, there should be ten times as many events as there are predictor variables in the analysis. This would mean that a study that investigated, say, 20 potential predictors would require a data set containing at least 200 events. Also, if the data were split at random into training and test sets, using an 80%:20% split as is often done, the total number of events required in order for the training set to contain the recommended number would increase to 250. Of course, any simulation study can only examine a limited number of factors and range of circumstances, and Vittinghoff and McCulloch (2007) subsequently suggested that this 10-times criterion may be too severe as a general rule.

Generally, having few events and many variables tends to lead to overfitting: the fitted model is closely adapted to chance associations in the data set, which are unlikely to be reproduced in further data. Therefore, the model's out-of-sample performance may be poor. One aspect of this is poor calibration, meaning that the fitted probabilities of an event are not close to the true probabilities. This can be detected by a test proposed by Cox (1958), 60 years ago. Let the estimated logistic regression coefficients (including the constant term) from the training set be $\hat{\boldsymbol{\beta}}$. Applied to the test set, this gives for unit i which has covariate vector $\mathbf{x}_i$ the linear predictor (risk score) $r_i = \hat{\boldsymbol{\beta}}'\mathbf{x}_i$. If the model is well calibrated, these risk scores should be close to optimal for the test set as well. In other words, although obtained from the training set, they nearly give the correct right-hand side for a logistic regression in the test set. Hence, logistic regression carried out in the test set, with this risk score as the only predictor (and no intercept), should give a regression slope close to one. In practice, it is expected to be less than one. If it is much less, this shows poor calibration in the sense of overestimating the probability of the event for high-risk units and underestimating it for lower-risk units.

The problem of overfitting can be greatly reduced by using appropriate procedures for selecting variables and shrinking the estimates of the coefficients (Pavlou et al.

2016). The following artificial example illustrates how this produces an improvement. From our original data set of Small Business Enterprises (described below), we drew randomly for this illustration 4,900 firms that survived and 100 firms that closed down in a five-year period. From this illustrative data set, a training set of 4,000 firms was drawn by simple random sampling, with the remaining 1,000 firms constituting a test set. A logistic regression was fitted to the training set, using nine potential predictors and backwards elimination of non-significant predictors. As described above, risk scores in the test set were constructed and logistic regression gave a slope of 0.925. This is not particularly small, since the number of events just meets the ten-per-variable suggestion. However, repeating this procedure after applying the lasso method of variable selection in the training set improved the slope to 0.961, a value which shows that the calibration is excellent and the issue of overfitting has been eliminated by using the lasso.

15.3.2. *Separate sampling of good and bad units*

As noted above, the parameter estimation problem induced by rare events is attributable to their low absolute frequency in the data rather than to the existence of imbalance between good and bad units. However, many studies have avoided this imbalance by separate sampling of good and bad units. If there is a marginal cost involved in sampling each unit and recording its data, this avoids wasting resources on the unnecessary inclusion of a very large number of good units. This strategy is discussed in detail by King and Zeng (2001). The most familiar example of separate sampling is the case–control study design in epidemiology (choice-based sampling in econometrics). Anderson (1972) showed that the estimators of the logistic regression coefficients of the covariates are the same under separate sampling as for sampling from the population mixture of good and bad units (see also Prentice and Pyke 1979; Kagan 2001). Only the constant term is affected, and this can be adjusted to refer to any desired mixture. Further details are given by Pierri et al. (2016).

A case–control study can also be executed with matching. In this situation, every failed unit is matched on the basis of selected characteristics with one or possibly several of the units that have not failed. The characteristics might include, for example, the firm's sector of economic activity, the location, year of foundation and number of employees. Appropriate techniques of statistical analysis must be used. While matching usually implies a gain in sensitivity of the analysis, there are various drawbacks, such as the impossibility of assessing the effect of the matching characteristics on the event of interest. This approach was used by Beaver (1966) in a pioneering study of the probabilistic prediction of bankruptcy and by many others since.

15.3.3. *Modifying the sample to deal with imbalanced data*

The problem of imbalanced data in prediction is usually illustrated by taking an example such as a 98%–2% split between the majority and minority classes. Then, simply predicting that all units belong to the majority class has only a 2% error rate. However, the errors all concern the minority class, which is usually the class of interest that needs to be detected. A solution that may be implemented and is discussed extensively in the machine learning literature is to remove the imbalance by modifying the data. This could be done simply by either undersampling (units are deleted at random from the majority class in order to reduce its size) or oversampling (randomly selected units from the minority class are duplicated in order to increase its size), although various, more elaborate methods are available and improve performance. Review papers, including those focused on bankruptcy and business failure (e.g. Marques et al. 2013; Veganzones and Severin 2018), tend to support oversampling as the preferred method. A prominent method in this category is SMOTE introduced by Chawla et al. (2002), in which new cases representing the minority class are generated by interpolation within clusters of existing minority cases, instead of just duplicating existing cases. Many developments of this have appeared (see, for example, Santos et al. 2018). In R, the SMOTE technique and varieties of it can be found in the package "smotefamily" (Siriseriwan 2016). Several other recently developed oversampling techniques are available in "imbalance" (Cordn 2017).

15.4. Competing risks

The discussion so far has been in the context of there being two classes in the data, corresponding to whether or not an event of interest – such as a firm's "failure" – occurred. However, there are often multiple mutually exclusive types of event to be considered. For example, our study of the closure of small businesses in Italy included three different types of failure: voluntary winding-up, dissolution or liquidation; bankruptcy; and closure without action by creditors or the courts (Caroni and Pierri 2020). In the terminology of survival analysis, different causes of failure are "competing risks". The occurrence of any one of them terminates the "lifetime" of the unit under study. If, instead of survival analysis, multiple outcomes are analyzed on the basis of their occurrence or otherwise in a fixed time frame, then an appropriate statistical analysis is to use the extension of logistic regression to the multinomial logistic model. In the context of the prediction problem, the extension of methods for the two-class problem to the multiclass case currently appears not to be very soundly established. Methods that have been proposed seem to concentrate on changing the multiclass problem to a set of two-class problems (Fernandez et al. 2013). In one approach, all the possible pairs of classes are analyzed (one-versus-one, OVO). Alternatively, each class is compared to all the rest put together (one-versus-all, OVA). The latter has the disadvantage of probably worsening class imbalance, which is likely to be present anyway when there are several classes.

The competing risks problem has been extensively analyzed in survival analysis. This makes it possible to examine the occurrence of each cause and the covariates that are involved, which may not be the same for each one. Two approaches to this are described briefly below. The first of these, cause-specific hazards analysis, predominates in competing risks analyses in economics and finance. The second, using sub-distribution hazards, is less familiar in this area.

Under competing risks, it is necessary to distinguish between the rate at which an event is occurring and the risk that it has of occurring by a certain time. The former is given by the hazard function $h(t)$, such that the conditional probability of occurring in the next interval $[t, t+\delta t)$ among the units that have survived as far as time t is $h(t)\delta t$. The risk or cumulative incidence of occurring by t is $F(t) = P(T \leq t) = 1 - S(t)$, where $S(t)$ is the survival function. Modeling takes place most often on the hazard function. In particular, Cox's proportional hazards model assumes that the covariates have a multiplicative effect on an unspecified baseline hazard rate $h_0(t)$

$$h(t|\mathbf{x}) = h_0(t) \exp\{\boldsymbol{\beta}'\mathbf{x}\}, \qquad [15.1]$$

which gives the survival function

$$S(t|\mathbf{x}) = S_0(t)^{e^{\boldsymbol{\beta}'\mathbf{x}}} \qquad [15.2]$$

where the baseline survival function $S_0(t)$ corresponds to the baseline hazard. Therefore, in the absence of competing risks, there is an equivalence between the effects of covariates on both the rate of occurrence of the failure event and the risk of its occurrence. Although one is affected multiplicatively and the other is raised to a power, the same coefficient is involved, and the one effect can be derived from the other. However, this equivalence does not hold when there are competing risks. Then, it is necessary to concentrate on either the rate or the risk, which is why different approaches exist.

The cause-specific hazard for the kth of K causes is defined as

$$h_k(t) = \lim_{\delta t \to 0} \frac{P[t < T \leq t + \delta t \bigcap D = k | T > t]}{\delta t} \qquad [15.3]$$

where D denotes the cause of failure. This is a simple extension of the usual definition of the hazard function: $h_k(t)\delta t$ is the probability of failure from cause k in the interval $[t, t + \delta t)$, given that the firm has survived until time t. This is a straightforward definition of a meaningful quantity. Unfortunately, however, it does not lead to the cumulative incidence (risk) of failure from this cause, along the lines of equation [15.2], because surviving to time t means that the firm must so far have avoided not only this cause of failure but also all the other causes of failure. Therefore, all the hazard functions must be taken into account. The causes cannot be considered separately from each other.

The alternative, which leads to correct estimation of the risk of failure from cause k, is the subdistribution hazard function (Fine and Gray 1999)

$$h_k^s(t) = \lim_{\delta t \to 0} \frac{P[t < T \leq t + \delta t \bigcap D = k | T > t \bigcup (T \leq t \cap D \neq k)]}{\delta t}, \qquad [15.4]$$

which is the instantaneous rate of failure at time t among firms that have not yet experienced an event of type k. However, what is the risk set here? It includes not only the actually surviving firms but also those that have already failed from a cause other than cause k. Due to this, the subdistribution hazard is not interpretable as a real-world quantity, since it refers to the hypothetical possibility of failure of firms at this time point that in fact have already failed at an earlier time. This makes it unattractive to some analysts, for example, Andersen and Keiding (2012). Its usefulness lies in giving the cumulative incidence of failure from cause k by means of the relation

$$h_k^s(t) = -\frac{d}{dt} \ln(1 - F_k(t)), \qquad [15.5]$$

where the subdistribution function of cause k,

$$F_k(t) = P(T \leq t \cap D = k)$$

gives as required the risk of failure from cause k up to time t. The sum of these separate cumulative incidences of the various causes at any time equals the overall cumulative incidence of failure from any cause, as desired.

The multiplicative effects of covariates can be introduced into both versions of the hazard function in the same way as in the proportional hazards model defined by equation [15.1]. We note that there is no connection between the regression coefficients of the same covariate in these two different models. Although, in most cases, the same factors might be expected to influence both the risk and the rate of a particular cause, this is not necessarily true. Furthermore, estimates of the coefficient cannot be compared numerically between the two models, because of the lack of interpretability of the subdistribution hazard.

The cause-specific hazard model is the simpler one to work with. Its definition shows that any program for fitting the basic Cox model can be employed for estimation. For each cause in turn, the standard Cox model is fitted to a modified data set in which only the failures from the cause of interest are treated as failure events. A failure from any other cause is treated as censored at its failure time, and it is removed from the risk set for all subsequent times. However, fitting the subdistribution hazards model, in which a firm that has failed from another cause remains in the risk sets, is more difficult in general. In many applications, there is random right censoring, and then it is necessary to estimate the distribution of censoring times in order to estimate how long the firm would hypothetically have been under observation (and therefore in the risk set) if there had not been failure from another cause. This can be done by using the estimated survival function of time to censoring to weight contributions to the risk set for cause k from the firms that have failed earlier from competing causes. This method is implemented in specialized software such as the R package "cmprsk" (Gray 2022). In a simpler special case, which applies to the present application, all censoring is "administrative" or "complete" (Fine and Gray 1999), i.e. censoring takes place only at a pre-determined time (usually the end of the study). This means that the potential observation time is known exactly, so the standard Cox model can be applied to estimate the subdistribution hazard of failure from one cause k simply by constructing a modified data set in which firms that failed from other causes are right-censored at the end of their potential observation periods.

	Total	Inactive		Closure	Winding-up	Bankruptcy
	n	n	%	%*	%*	%*
Total firms	15184	3049	20.1	33.0	59.3	7.7
Cooperative	1003	256	25.5	21.9	75.4	2.7
Limited liability	13776	2713	19.7	33.1	58.7	8.3
Publicly traded	405	80	19.8	65.0	28.8	6.3

*Among failures

Table 15.1. *Distribution of causes of failure by legal form of the firm, Umbria, 2008–2013*

The above methods were applied to the analysis of the failure of firms in our database. The distribution of the numbers of failures from each of the three causes is shown in Table 15.1, broken down by the legal form of the firm. Results for this covariate are given for illustration, extracted from a model which used all the financial indexes as in our earlier study (Pierri and Caroni 2017), although the lagged variables and time-varying covariates employed in that study were not used here. Estimated hazard ratios – the exponentiated regression coefficients $\exp(\beta_i)$ – from both the cause-specific and subdistribution hazard models are shown in Table 15.2. Results from a simple Cox regression where the event is failure from any cause are also shown for comparison. The 95% confidence intervals for the hazard ratios in the any-cause analysis include the value one, suggesting that the type of firm does not affect failure rates and risks. However, the competing risks analyses show a different picture. While both cooperatives and limited-liability companies have increased hazards for winding-up compared to publicly traded companies, they both have much smaller hazards for closure compared to publicly traded companies. The result for the any-cause analysis concealed these large differences by averaging them out.

The bulk of the discussion and development of survival data analysis takes place in the medical statistics literature, which contains several articles presenting these alternative approaches to the analysis of competing risks, for example, Bakoyannnis and Touloumi (2012) and Austin and Fine (2017). These papers also give some information on available software. Although the two hazard models are different, and despite the fact that a proportional hazards model for the covariates based on the Cox model in equation [15.1] cannot be correct for both of them simultaneously, there is some support in the literature for applying them both in a study, in order to obtain a complete picture (see, for example, Latouche et al. 2013). If only one model is going to be used, the choice depends on which aspect of the problem, risk or rate, is more important. In applications such as credit scoring, subdistribution hazard modeling seems to be the more useful, because estimating the risk of failure is the basic objective.

	Cooperative		Limited Liability	
	HR	95% CI	HR	95%CI
Any cause	1.05	0.81-1.36	0.84	0.67-1.06
Cause-specific				
Winding-up	2.44	1.55-3.78	1.57	1.04-2.39
Closure	0.48	0.33-0.70	0.50	0.38-0.67
Bankruptcy	0.55	0.17-1.80	1.41	0.58-3.43
Subdistribution				
Winding-up	2.61	1.57-4.04	1.67	1.11-2.52
Closure	0.45	0.31-0.66	0.48	0.36-0.65
Bankruptcy	0.56	0.17-1.83	1.30	0.53-3.24

Table 15.2. *Estimated regression coefficients for types of firm in competing risks survival analyses. Reference category: Publicly traded. HR=hazard ratio, CI=confidence interval*

15.5. Conclusion

Logistic regression and Cox's proportional hazards regression model are among the most widely used statistical models. The latter, in particular, has achieved a position of dominance in survival analysis that is probably unmatched by any other statistical model in any field. This can be accounted for by its great simplicity and easy interpretation (with many similarities to logistic regression), along with the freedom from assumptions owing to its semi-parametric nature. However, Cox himself did not make much claim for his model beyond empirical convenience (Cox 1972). There are other models that should be considered more often, such as the accelerated failure time model that is widely used in reliability modeling by engineers, or models such as first hitting time regression that are based on a representation of the underlying process that leads to failure (Lee and Whitmore 2006; Caroni 2017). One major advantage of the Cox model, however, is the fact that it has been very extensively studied and has been extended in every conceivable way. The extension to competing risks that has been presented in this chapter is a particularly important extra tool in the analysis of time-to-event data in order to estimate the risk of default, bankruptcy or other forms of failures. Another important extension allows time-varying covariates, as used by Pierri and Caroni (2017).

In many areas of data analysis, methods characterized as belonging to machine learning have emerged and in some cases have taken over from more traditional statistical models. This was discussed above for logistic regression in particular, but it is a trend that can be seen elsewhere, including survival analysis. In fact, Andersen's recent review of the Cox model on the occasion of its 50th anniversary (Andersen 2022) suggests that, as far as prediction is concerned, machine learning techniques tend to outperform Cox regression.

15.6. References

Altman, E.I. (1968). Financial ratios, discriminant analysis and the prediction of corporate bankruptcy. *Journal of Finance*, 23, 589–609.

Andersen, P.K. (2022). Fifty years with the Cox proportional hazards regression model. *Journal of the Indian Institute of Science*, 102, 1135–1144.

Andersen, P.K. and Keiding, N. (2012). Interpretability and importance of functionals in competing risks and multistate models. *Statistics in Medicine*, 31, 1078–1088.

Anderson, J.A. (1972). Separate sample logistic discrimination. *Biometrika*, 59, 19–35.

Atiya, A.F. (2001). Bankruptcy prediction for credit risk using neural networks: A survey and new results. *IEEE Transactions on Neural Networks*, 12, 929–935.

Austin, P.C. and Fine, J.P. (2017). Practical recommendations for reporting Fine-Gray model analyses for competing risks data. *Statistics in Medicine*, 36, 4391–4400.

Baesens, B., Hoppner, S., Ortner, I., Verdonck, T. (2021). robROSE: A robust approach for dealing with imbalanced data in fraud detection. *Statistical Methods and Applications*, 30, 841–861.

Bakoyannnis, G. and Touloumi, G. (2012). Practical methods for competing risks data: A review. *Statistical Methods in Medical Research*, 21, 257–272.

Balcaen, S. and Ooghe, H. (2006). 35 years of studies on business failure: An overview of the classic statistical methodologies and their related problems. *British Accounting Review*, 38, 63–93.

Banasik, J., Crook, J.N., Thomas, L.C. (1999). Not if but when will borrowers default. *Journal of the Operational Research Society*, 50, 1185–1190.

Beaver, W.H. (1966). Financial ratios as predictors of failure. *Journal of Accounting Research*, 4, 71–111.

Bisogno, M., Restaino, M., Di Carlo, A. (2018). Forecasting and preventing bankruptcy: A conceptual review. *African Journal of Business Management*, 12, 231–262.

Breiman, L. (2001). Statistical modeling: The two cultures. *Statistical Science*, 16, 199–231.

Caroni, C. (2017). *First Hitting Time Regression Models: Lifetime Data Analysis Based on Underlying Stochastic Models*. ISTE Ltd, London, and John Wiley & Sons, New York.

Caroni, C. and Pierri, F. (2020). Different causes of closure of small business enterprises: Alternative models for competing risks survival analysis. *Electronic Journal of Applied Statistical Analysis*, 13, 211–228.

Chawla, N.V., Bowyer, K.W., Hall, L.O., Kegelmeyer, W.P. (2002). SMOTE: Synthetic minority over-sampling technique. *Journal of Artificial Intelligence Research*, 16, 321–357.

Cordn, I. (2017). imbalance: Preprocessing algorithms for imbalanced datasets. R package version 1.0.2.1 [Online]. Available at: https://cran.r-project.org/web/packages/imbalance.

Cox, D.R. (1958). Two further applications of a model for binary regression. *Biometrika*, 45, 562–565.

Cox, D.R. (1972). Regression models and life-tables. *Journal of the Royal Statistical Society Series B*, 34, 187–202.

Efron, B. (2020). Prediction, estimation, and attribution. *International Statistical Review*, 88, S28–S59.

Fernandez, A., Lopez, V., Galar, M., del Jesus, M.J., Herrera, F. (2013). Analysing the classification of imbalanced data-sets with multiple classes: Binarization techniques and ad-hoc approaches. *Knowledge-Based Systems*, 42, 97–110.

Fine, J.P. and Gray, R.P. (1999). A proportional hazards model for the subdistribution of a competing risk. *Journal of the American Statistical Association*, 94, 496–509.

Gray, R. (2022). cmprsk: Subdistribution analysis of competing risks. R package version 2.2-11 [Online]. Available at: https://CRAN.R-project.org/package=cmprsk.

Haixiang, G., Yijing, L., Shang, J., Mingyun, G., Yuanyue, H., Bing, G. (2017). Learning from class-imbalanced data: Review of methods and applications. *Expert Systems with Applications*, 73, 220–239.

Kagan, A. (2001). A note on the logistic link function. *Biometrika*, 88, 599–601.

Kiefer, N.M. (1988). Economic duration and hazard functions. *Journal of Economic Literature*, 26, 646–679.

King, G. and Zeng, L. (2001). Logistic regression in rare events data. *Political Analysis*, 9, 137–163.

Kosmidis, I. (2021). brglm: Bias reduction in binary-response generalized linear models. Rpackage version 0.7.2 [Online]. Available at: https://cran.r-project.org/package=brglm.

Kosmidis, I. and Firth, D. (2021). Jeffreys-prior penalty, finiteness and shrinkage in binomial-response generalized linear models. *Biometrika*, 108, 71–82.

Latouche, A., Allignol, A., Bayersmann, J., Labopin, M., Fine, J.P. (2013). A competing risks analysis should report results on all cause-specific hazards and cumulative incidence functions. *Journal of Clinical Epidemiology*, 66, 648–653.

Lee, M.-L.T. and Whitmore, G.A. (2006). Threshold regression for survival analysis: Modeling event times by a stochastic process reaching a boundary. *Statistical Science*, 21, 501–513.

Marques, A.I., Garcia, V., Sanchez, J.S. (2013). On the suitability of resampling techniques for the class imbalance problem in credit scoring. *Journal of the Operational Research Society*, 64, 1060–1070.

Ohlson, J.A. (1981). Financial ratios and the probabilistic prediction of bankruptcy. *Journal of Accounting Research*, 18, 109–131.

Pavlou, M., Ambler, G., Seaman, S.R., Di Iorio, M., Omar, R.Z. (2016). Review and evaluation of penalised regression methods for risk prediction model in low-dimensional data with few events. *Statistics in Medicine*, 35, 1159–1177.

Pierri, F. and Caroni, C. (2017). Bankruptcy prediction by survival models based on current and lagged values of time-varying financial data. *Communications in Statistics: Case Studies, Data Analysis and Applications*, 3, 62–70.

Pierri, F., Stanghellini, E., Bistoni, N. (2016). Risk analysis and retrospective unbalanced data. *Revstat – Statistical Journal*, 14, 157–169.

Prentice, R.L. and Pyke, R. (1979). Logistic disease incidence models and case-control studies. *Biometrika*, 66, 403–411.

Puhr, R., Heinze, G., Nold, M., Lusa, L., Geroldinger, A. (2017). Firth's logistic regression with rare events: Accurate effect estimates and predictions? *Statistics in Medicine*, 36, 2302–2317.

Santos, M.S., Soares, J.P., Abreu, P.H., Araujo, H., Santos, J. (2018). Cross-validation for imbalanced datasets: Avoiding overoptimistic and overfitting approaches. *IEEE Computational Intelligence Magazine*, 13, 59–76.

Shumway, T. (2001). Forecasting bankruptcy more accurately: A simple hazard model. *The Journal of Business*, 74, 101–124.

Siriseriwan, W. (2016). smotefamily: A collection of oversampling techniques for class imbalance problem based on SMOTE. R package version 1.3.1 [Online]. Available at: https://cran.r-project.org/web/packages/smotefamily.

Veganzones, D. and Severin, E. (2018). An investigation of bankruptcy prediction in imbalanced datasets. *Decision Support Systems*, 112, 111–124.

Vittinghoff, E. and McCulloch, C.E. (2007). Relaxing the rule of ten events per variable in logistic and Cox regression. *American Journal of Epidemiology*, 165, 710–718.

Wu, Y., Gaunt, C., Gray, S. (2010). A comparison of alternative bankruptcy prediction models. *Journal of Contemporary Accounting & Economics*, 6, 34–45.

Yang, Z.R., Platt, M.B., Platt, H.D. (1999). Probabilistic neural networks in bankruptcy prediction. *Journal of Business Research*, 44, 67–74.

16

Network of Adaptive Frequency Oscillators in a Ballistic, Non-Gaussian, Noisy Environment

Based on the well-known Kuramoto model, a collection of coupled phase oscillators with adapting frequencies is considered. The global network dynamics is set in a fluctuating environment with a noise source emanating from non-Gaussian, superdiffusive (i.e. ballistic component), stochastic processes. For arbitrary network topologies, we can analytically calculate (for the linearized system) the probability densities for the phases and frequencies of the resulting stochastic process and explicitly observe the influence of the non-Gaussian noise source on the mean vector for the state variables. The network connectivity influences the covariance matrix of the phases but not the covariance matrix of the frequencies. Numerical experiments on the nonlinear system confirm the analytical results obtained for the linear dynamical system impacted by a ballistic noise source.

16.1. Introduction

Frequency adaptation (i.e. the "plasticity" of oscillators to adapt their own frequency) has been broadly studied in the realm of deterministic dynamics, whether in biology (Ermentrout 1991), in robotics (Gams et al. 2009; Petrič 2011; Righetti et al. 2006, 2021), in adaptive control and human–robot interactions (Ronsse et al. 2011; Gams et al. 2016; Petrič 2020), or in the field of human rehabilitation and locomotion assistance with the use of exoskeletons (Yan et al. 2017; Laloyaux et al. 2023), and thus for time delayed interactions or time-dependent random switching networks (Rodriguez 2013).

Chapter written by Julio RODRIGUEZ.

However, random perturbations can strongly impact their capability to adapt – hence the interest to investigate this phenomenon of adaptation in noisy environments specifically. To the best of the author's knowledge, networks of adapting frequency oscillators in the presence of external ballistic, non-Gaussian noise sources have not been studied. Closely related to this note is the contribution (Taylor et al. 2010), where the All-to-All network of phase oscillators with slow frequency adaptation is investigated with adaptive mechanisms subjected to Gaussian noise and containing a "confining potential" in order to constrain the values of natural frequencies in a certain range. The aim of this work is to analytically calculate the resulting probability densities of the state variables in the long run (i.e. neglecting transient effects) and this for arbitrary network topology (not only All-to-All).

This contribution is organized as follows: first, the dynamical system and noise source are presented in section 16.2. In section 16.3, the resulting dynamics is analytically discussed, continuing with numerical simulations in section 16.4, with discussions and perspectives in section 16.5.

16.2. Dynamics of the network

The dynamical system of interest in this contribution is

$$\begin{aligned} \dot{\phi}_k &= \omega_k - \mathsf{c}\sum_{j=1}^{n} a_{k,j}\sin(\phi_k - \phi_j) + \epsilon\zeta_k(t) \\ \dot{\omega}_k &= -\mathsf{s}\sum_{j=1}^{n} a_{k,j}\sin(\phi_k - \phi_j) \end{aligned} \qquad k = 1,\ldots,n \qquad [16.1]$$

Equation [16.1] represents n local systems, each consisting of a phase oscillator with individual instantaneous frequencies ω_k. These local systems are coupled (i.e. interact with one another) through a connected, undirected network whose entries of the adjacency matrix A are $a_{k,j} \in \{0, 1\}$, and since the network is undirected, then $a_{k,j} = a_{j,k}$. The strength of the diffusive coupling is given by a coupling constant $0 < \mathsf{c}$. In this coupled system, an additional degree of freedom is provided to each phase oscillator so that it may adapt its own frequency ω_k: the ω_k are time-dependent and not constant. This type of unsupervised learning (i.e. adaptation) is governed by the phase interactions via the same network (i.e. the same entries of the adjacency matrix). The rate of adaptation is controlled by a susceptibility constant $0 < \mathsf{s}$. Finally, the dynamics of each phase is perturbed by an external noise source $\zeta_k(t)$ with intensity ϵ.

In this contribution the noise sources $\zeta_k(t)$ in equation [16.1] are formal derivatives $\zeta_k(t) := \frac{dZ_k}{dt}(t)$ of nonlinear diffusion processes $Z_k(t)$ with the Langevin equation

$$\frac{dZ_k}{dt}(t) = \beta\tanh(\beta Z_k(t)) + \xi_k(t) \quad \text{and} \quad Z_k(0) = 0 \qquad [16.2]$$

for $k = 1, \ldots, n$, $\beta > 0$ and where the $\xi_k(t)$ are independent white Gaussian noise processes verifying

$$\mathrm{E}[\xi_k(t)] = 0 \quad \text{and} \quad \mathrm{E}[\xi_k(t)\xi_j(s)] = \delta_{k,j}\, \delta(t-s)$$

with Kronecker delta $\delta_{k,j}$ and Dirac delta $\delta(t)$. To investigate the resulting dynamics given by equation [16.1], some features of the noise source given by equation [16.2] are presented here. For this purpose, the subscript k is omitted.

I) The transition probability density $f(z,t)$ associated with the nonlinear diffusion process from equations [16.2] reads as (Hongler 1979; Hongler et al. 2006)

$$\begin{aligned} f(z,t \mid 0,0) &= \cosh(\beta z)\tfrac{1}{\sqrt{2\pi t}} \exp(-\tfrac{\beta^2 t^2 - z^2}{2t}) \\ &= \tfrac{1}{2} f_+(z,t) + \tfrac{1}{2} f_-(z,t)\,, \end{aligned} \qquad [16.3]$$

with $f_\pm(z,t) = \frac{1}{\sqrt{2\pi t}} \exp(-\frac{(z \pm \beta t)^2}{2t})$. This transition probability density is the sum of two Gaussian densities and therefore the non-Gaussian character of noise source $\zeta(t)$.

II) For the first two moments and the covariance, we have

$$\mathrm{E}[Z(t)] = 0\,, \quad \mathrm{E}[Z(t)^2] = t + \beta^2 t^2 \quad \text{and} \quad \mathrm{E}[Z(t)Z(s)] = \min(t,s) + \beta^2 ts$$

and hence the superdiffusive behavior of the noise since the variance is of order two.

III) Rogers and Pitman (1981, see example 2, page 581) remarked that $Z(t)$ can be represented as the random Gaussian mixture (see also equation [16.3]):

$$Z(t) = B\beta t + W(t) \quad Z(0) = 0 \qquad [16.4]$$

where $W(t)$ is the standard Wiener process and $B \in \{-1, +1\}$ is a symmetric Bernoulli variable independent of $W(t)$. As nicely phrased in Hongler (2013), each stochastic process given by equations [16.2] can be seen as follows: "at initial time operate the Bernoulli choice of the drift and then evolve according to the resulting $\pm\beta$-drifted (Wiener process)".

It is important to state that in the limiting case when $\beta = 0$, we have the usual white Gaussian noise source (respectively, the usual non-drifted Wiener process) and therefore we have at disposal the parameter β to investigate the influence of the nonlinear superdiffusive behavior of the noisy environment.

This superdiffusive noise source has been investigated in physics (Hongler et al. 2006), in optimal control problems (Filliger and Hongler 2007), in finance (Hongler 2013) and recently in economics (Arcand 2020).

Having briefly discussed the noise source and some of its properties, we can now study its influence on the network dynamics.

16.3. Analyzing the dynamics

Equations [16.1] form a system of stochastic differential equations that can be explicitly written as (omitting the time argument t)

$$\begin{aligned} d\phi_k &= \big(\omega_k - \mathsf{c}\sum_{j=1}^{n} a_{k,j}\sin(\phi_k - \phi_j)\big)dt + \epsilon dZ_k \\ d\omega_k &= \big(-\mathsf{s}\sum_{j=1}^{n} a_{k,j}\sin(\phi_k - \phi_j)\big)dt \qquad\qquad k = 1,\ldots,n \qquad [16.5] \\ dZ_k &= \beta\tanh(\beta Z_k)dt + dW_k \end{aligned}$$

It is important to remark that, independently of the type of the noise source, equations [16.1] possess a constant of motion, namely:

$$\sum_{k=1}^{n}\dot{\omega}_k = -\mathsf{s}\underbrace{\sum_{k=1}^{n}\left(\sum_{j=1}^{n} a_{k,j}\sin(\phi_k - \phi_j)\right)}_{=0} \quad\Rightarrow\quad \sum_{k=1}^{n}\omega_k(t) = \sum_{k=1}^{n}\omega_k(0) \text{ for all } t$$

and hence (see Rodriguez 2013 for details), in the deterministic case when $\epsilon = 0$, if the global dynamical system reaches a consensual oscillatory state in the sense that

$$\lim_{t\to\infty} \|\big(\phi_k(t), \omega_k(t)\big) - \big(\omega_c t, \omega_c\big)\| = 0 \quad \forall k \qquad [16.6]$$

then the value of ω_c is given as

$$\omega_c = \frac{1}{n}\sum_{k=1}^{n}\omega_k(0)$$

Details of the deterministic case (i.e. $\epsilon = 0$), especially concerning the proof of convergence with Lyapunov functions and results on convergence rate are found in Rodriguez (2013).

Since the $Z_k(t)$ realizations coincide with those from $\pm\beta$-drifted Wiener process (i.e. $Z_k(t) = B_k\beta t + W_k(t)$ (see equation [16.4]), and therefore we formally have infinitesimal increments as $dZ_k(t) = B_k\beta dt + dW_k(t)$), the stochastic process of interest in this contribution is given by

$$\begin{aligned} d\phi_k &= \big(\omega_k + B_k\epsilon\beta - \mathsf{c}\sum_{j=1}^{n} a_{k,j}\sin(\phi_k - \phi_j)\big)dt + \epsilon dW_k(t) \qquad k=1,\ldots,n \\ d\omega_k &= \big(-\mathsf{s}\sum_{j=1}^{n} a_{k,j}\sin(\phi_k - \phi_j)\big)dt \end{aligned}$$

[16.7]

For analytical tractability, the linearized system given by equations [16.7] is considered and can be rewritten in a compact form as

$$\begin{pmatrix} d\phi \\ d\omega \end{pmatrix} = \left(\begin{pmatrix} -\mathrm{c}L & I \\ -\mathrm{s}L & \mathbf{0} \end{pmatrix} \begin{pmatrix} \phi \\ \omega \end{pmatrix} + \epsilon\beta \begin{pmatrix} B \\ \vec{0} \end{pmatrix} \right) dt + \epsilon \begin{pmatrix} dW_t \\ \vec{0} \end{pmatrix}$$
$$\iff \begin{pmatrix} \dot{\phi} \\ \dot{\omega} \end{pmatrix} = \begin{pmatrix} -\mathrm{c}L & I \\ -\mathrm{s}L & \mathbf{0} \end{pmatrix} \begin{pmatrix} \phi \\ \omega \end{pmatrix} + \epsilon\beta \begin{pmatrix} B \\ \vec{0} \end{pmatrix} + \epsilon \begin{pmatrix} \xi_t \\ \vec{0} \end{pmatrix} \qquad [16.8]$$

where $L := D^A - A$ is the Laplacian matrix associated with the adjacency matrix A of the given undirected network (and D^A is the diagonal matrix with the degree of each vertex on its diagonal, i.e. $d_{k,k} := \sum_{j=1}^{n} a_{k,j}$), I is the $n \times n$ identity matrix, $\mathbf{0}$ is the $n \times n$ matrix with 0 as entries, $d\phi = (d\phi_1, \ldots, d\phi_n)^\top$, $d\omega = (d\omega_1, \ldots, d\omega_n)^\top$, $B = (B_1, \ldots, B_n)^\top$ are mutually independent symmetric Bernoulli variables each with values in $\{-1, +1\}$ and also independent of the n-dimensional independent Wiener processes $W_t = (W_1(t), \ldots, W_n(t))^\top$ (respectively n independent white Gaussian noise processes $\xi_t = (\xi_1(t), \ldots, \xi_n(t))^\top$) and $\vec{0} = (0, \ldots, 0)^\top$ an n-dimensional vector with 0 as entries.

Since the random vector B is independent of W_t (i.e. the outcome of B does not influence the outcome of W_t), we can proceed to the analysis of the dynamics by considering an outcome of B and afterwards analyze the random effects of B on the resulting dynamics. Therefore, at this stage, let $\vec{b} = (b_1, \ldots, b_n)$ be a realization of the random vector B, so that for each j, $b_j = 1$ or $b_j = -1$. Changing the variables with the help of a 2×2 bloc matrix with each bloc of size $n \times n$ and with $O^\top$ on its bloc diagonal (i.e. $(X(t), Y(t)) := (O^\top \phi(t), O^\top \omega(t))$), we have

$$\begin{pmatrix} \dot{X} \\ \dot{Y} \end{pmatrix} = \begin{pmatrix} -\mathrm{c}D^\lambda & I \\ -\mathrm{s}D^\lambda & \mathbf{0} \end{pmatrix} \begin{pmatrix} X \\ Y \end{pmatrix} + \epsilon\beta \begin{pmatrix} O^\top \vec{b} \\ \vec{0} \end{pmatrix} + \epsilon \begin{pmatrix} \check{\xi}_t \\ \vec{0} \end{pmatrix} \qquad [16.9]$$

with D^λ a diagonal matrix with the eigenvalues of L as diagonal entries $(0, \lambda_2, \ldots, \lambda_n)$. Since the network is connected, it has only one eigenvalue that is zero (i.e. $\lambda_1 = 0$) with eigenvector $\frac{1}{\sqrt{n}}(1, \ldots, 1)^\top$ and all other eigenvalues are strictly positive (i.e. $\lambda_k > 0$ for $k = 2, \ldots, n$). Without loss of generality, the eigenvector $\frac{1}{\sqrt{n}}(1, \ldots, 1)^\top$ is the first row of matrix $O^\top$. The vector $O^\top \vec{b} =: (\check{b}_1, \ldots, \check{b}_n)$ is the image of the realization $\vec{b}$ through $O^\top$. Finally, vector $\check{\xi}_t := O^\top \xi_t$ consists of n independent white Gaussian noise processes since it is the image of an orthogonal transformation of ξ_t. This change of variables leads to n 2×2 systems given as

$$\begin{pmatrix} \dot{X}_k \\ \dot{Y}_k \end{pmatrix} = \begin{pmatrix} -\mathrm{c}\lambda_k & 1 \\ -\mathrm{s}\lambda_k & 0 \end{pmatrix} \begin{pmatrix} X_k \\ Y_k \end{pmatrix} + \begin{pmatrix} \epsilon\beta\check{b}_k \\ 0 \end{pmatrix} + \begin{pmatrix} \epsilon\check{\xi}_k(t) \\ 0 \end{pmatrix} \qquad k = 1, \ldots, n \qquad [16.10]$$

For $k = 1$, then $\lambda_1 = 0$, and therefore we have the following stochastic differential equation written in its differential form and equivalently as a stochastic integral equation:

$$\begin{aligned} dX_1(t) &= \big(Y_1(t) + \epsilon\beta\check{b}_1\big)dt + \epsilon d\check{W}_1(t) \\ dY_1(t) &= 0 \end{aligned}$$

$$\Longleftrightarrow \qquad \begin{aligned} X_1(t) &= X_1(0) + \int_0^t Y_1(t) + \epsilon\beta\check{b}_1\, dt + \epsilon \int_0^t d\check{W}_1(t) \\ Y_1(t) &= Y(0) \end{aligned} \qquad [16.11]$$

with increments $d\check{W}_1(t) = \check{\xi}_1(t)dt$ and with solution

$$X_1(t) = X_1(0) + (Y_1(0) + \epsilon\beta\check{b}_1)t + \epsilon\check{W}_1(t) \quad \text{and} \quad Y_1(t) = Y_1(0)$$

with $X_1(0) = \frac{1}{\sqrt{n}}\sum_{j=1}^{n} \phi_j(0)$, $Y_1(0) = \frac{1}{\sqrt{n}}\sum_{j=1}^{n} \omega_j(0)$ and $\check{b}_1 = \frac{1}{\sqrt{n}}\sum_{j=1}^{n} b_j$.

For $k = 2, \ldots, n$, then $\lambda_k > 0$ and we have $n - 1$ stochastic differential equations of the form

$$\begin{aligned} dX_k(t) &= \big(Y_k(t) - \mathsf{c}\lambda_k X_k(t) + \epsilon\beta\check{b}_k\big)dt + \epsilon d\check{W}_k(t) \\ dY_k(t) &= -\mathsf{s}\lambda_k X_k(t)dt \end{aligned} \qquad k = 2, \ldots, n \qquad [16.12]$$

The solution for each k in equation [16.12] is a Gaussian process (see Appendix 16.6.1 for details) and for large t, we can approximate the expected value and covariance matrix as (see end remark in Appendix 16.6.1 – note that here $-\mathsf{c}\lambda_k < 0$ and $-\mathsf{s}\lambda_k < 0$ for $k = 2, \ldots, n$)

$$\begin{pmatrix} \mathrm{E}[X_k(t)] \\ \hat{A}\ \mathrm{E}[Y_k(t)] \end{pmatrix} = \begin{pmatrix} 0 \\ -\epsilon\beta\check{b}_k \end{pmatrix} \quad \text{and} \quad \mathrm{K}[X_k(t), Y_k(t)] = \begin{pmatrix} \frac{\epsilon^2}{2\mathsf{c}\lambda_k} & 0 \\ 0 & \frac{\epsilon^2 \mathsf{s}}{2\mathsf{c}} \end{pmatrix}$$

This means that the network dynamics, described in the variables $(X(t), Y(t)) = (X_1(t), \ldots, X_n(t), Y_1(t), \ldots, Y_n(t))$ and for one realization of B, tends (i.e. for large t) towards a Gaussian process with

$$\mathrm{E}[X(t)] = \begin{pmatrix} X_1(0) + (Y_1(0) + \epsilon\beta\check{b}_1)t \\ 0 \\ \vdots \\ 0 \end{pmatrix} \qquad \mathrm{E}[Y(t)] = \begin{pmatrix} Y_1(0) \\ -\epsilon\beta\check{b}_2 \\ \vdots \\ -\epsilon\beta\check{b}_n \end{pmatrix}$$

$$\mathrm{K}[X(t)] = \begin{pmatrix} \epsilon^2 t & 0 & \ldots & 0 \\ 0 & \frac{\epsilon^2}{2\mathsf{c}\lambda_2} & \ldots & 0 \\ \vdots & & \ddots & \vdots \\ 0 & \ldots & & \frac{\epsilon^2}{2\mathsf{c}\lambda_n} \end{pmatrix} \quad \text{and} \quad \mathrm{K}[Y(t)] = \begin{pmatrix} 0 & 0 & \ldots & 0 \\ 0 & \frac{\epsilon^2 \mathsf{s}}{2\mathsf{c}} & \ldots & 0 \\ \vdots & & \ddots & \vdots \\ 0 & \ldots & & \frac{\epsilon^2 \mathsf{s}}{2\mathsf{c}} \end{pmatrix}$$

Under these assumptions, changing the variables back with the help of the 2×2 bloc matrix with each bloc of size $n \times n$ and with O on its bloc diagonal (i.e. $(\phi(t), \omega(t)) = (OX(t), OY(t))$), we have a Gaussian process with expected values and covariance matrices (see Appendix 16.6.2 for details)

$$\mathrm{E}[\phi(t)] = ((\bar{\omega} + \epsilon\beta\bar{b})t + \bar{\phi})\vec{1} \qquad \mathrm{E}[\omega(t)] = \bar{\omega}\vec{1} - \tfrac{\epsilon\beta}{n} L^{\mathfrak{a}}\vec{b}$$

$$\mathrm{K}[\phi(t)] = \frac{\epsilon^2}{n}(t\mathbb{1} + \frac{1}{2cn}(I - \frac{1}{n}L^{\mathfrak{c}})^{-1}L^{\mathfrak{a}}) \qquad \mathrm{K}[\omega(t)] = \frac{\epsilon^2 \mathsf{s}}{2nc}L^{\mathfrak{a}}$$

with $\bar{\omega} := \frac{1}{n}\sum_{j=1}^{n} \omega_j(0)$, $\bar{b} := \frac{1}{n}\sum_{j=1}^{n} b_j$, $\bar{\phi} := \frac{1}{n}\sum_{j=1}^{n} \phi_j(0)$, $\vec{1}$ being the vector with 1 for all entries, $L^{\mathfrak{a}}$ being the Laplacian matrix associated with the "All-to-All" network, and $L^{\mathfrak{c}}$ being the (Laplacian) complement matrix of L, i.e. $L^{\mathfrak{c}} := L^{\mathfrak{a}} - L$. Note that β influences the expected vectors $\mathrm{E}[\phi(t)]$ and $\mathrm{E}[\omega(t)]$ but not the covariance matrices.

16.3.1. *The effect of the random vector* B

So far, the analysis has been carried out with one realization of the random vector B and therefore, to account for all of the randomness in the system, we need to include the distributions of

(I) the scalar random variable $\bar{B} := \frac{1}{n}\sum_{j=1}^{n} B_j$;

(II) the random vector $L^{\mathfrak{a}}B$;

(III) each component of the random vector $L^{\mathfrak{a}}B$.

These are explicitly determined as (see Appendix 16.6.3 for details)

For (I)

$$\mathrm{P}(\bar{B} = \frac{-n + 2k}{n}) = \binom{n}{k}(\frac{1}{2})^n \quad k = 0, 1, \ldots, n$$

For (II)

$$\mathrm{P}(L^{\mathfrak{a}}B = \vec{0}) = \frac{2}{2^n} \quad \text{and} \quad \mathrm{P}(L^{\mathfrak{a}}B = \vec{v}_j) = \frac{1}{2^n}$$

for $j \in \{1, 2, \ldots, 2^n - 1\}$ and where $\vec{v}_j$ is the image of $L^{\mathfrak{a}}b_j$, with b_j being a realization of B which is neither $\vec{1}$ nor $-\vec{1}$. The v_j are distinct and hence the uniform distribution.

For (III)

for $j = 1, 2, \ldots, n$

$$\mathrm{P}(R_j = -2(n-1) + 2k) = \frac{1}{2}\binom{n-1}{k}(\frac{1}{2})^{n-1} \qquad k = 0, \ldots, n-2$$

$$\mathrm{P}(R_j = 0) = (\frac{1}{2})^{n-1}$$

$$\mathrm{P}(R_j = 2(n-1) - 2k) = \frac{1}{2}\binom{n-1}{k}(\frac{1}{2})^{n-1} \qquad k = 0, \ldots, n-2$$

where R_j is the jth component of $L^a B$. Note that all R_j have identical distribution but are not independent.

16.3.2. *Main results*

Given the independence between the random variables B and W_t, we can directly compute the probability densities for $\phi = (\phi_1, \ldots, \phi_n)$ and $\omega = (\omega_1, \ldots, \omega_n)$ (for large t) which are

$$f_\phi(x,t) = \sum_{k=0}^{n} \binom{n}{k}(\frac{1}{2})^n \frac{\exp\left((x - \mu_\phi(t,k))^\top \mathrm{K}[\phi(t)]^{-1}(x - \mu_\phi(t,k))\right)}{\sqrt{(2\pi)^n \mid \mathrm{K}[\phi(t)] \mid}}$$

with $\mu_\phi(t,k) = ((\bar{\omega} + \epsilon\beta(\frac{-2k-n}{n}))t + \bar{\phi})\vec{1}$ and

$$f_\omega(y) = \frac{2}{2^n} \frac{\exp\left((x - \bar{\omega}\vec{1})^\top \mathrm{K}[\omega]^{-1}(x - \bar{\omega}\vec{1})\right)}{\sqrt{(2\pi)^n \mid \mathrm{K}[\omega] \mid}}$$
$$+ \sum_{k=1}^{2^n-2} (\frac{1}{2})^n \frac{\exp\left((x - \mu_\omega(k))^\top \mathrm{K}[\omega]^{-1}(x - \mu_\omega(k))\right)}{\sqrt{(2\pi)^n \mid \mathrm{K}[\omega] \mid}}$$

with $\mu_\omega(k) = \bar{\omega}\vec{1} - \frac{\epsilon\beta}{n} L^a \vec{b}_k$ and $\vec{b}_k$ being a realization of B.

With the notation for a Gaussian "bell curve"

$$N(x, \mu, \sigma^2) = \frac{1}{\sqrt{2\pi\sigma^2}} \exp(-\frac{1}{2}\frac{(x-\mu)^2}{\sigma^2})$$

the marginal distributions for each ϕ_j and ω_j are

$$f_{\phi_j}(x,t) = \sum_{k=0}^{n} \binom{n}{k}(\frac{1}{2})^n N(x, (\bar{\omega} + \epsilon\beta\bar{b}_k)t + \bar{\phi}, \sigma^2_{\phi_j}(t))$$

with $\sigma^2_{\phi_j}(t) := \mathrm{K}[\phi(t)]_{j,j}$ and $\bar{b}_k := \frac{-n+2k}{n}$ for $k = 0, 1, \ldots, n$, and

$$f_{\omega_j}(y) = \frac{1}{2}\sum_{k=0}^{n-2}\binom{n-1}{k}(\frac{1}{2})^{n-1}N(y, \bar{\omega} - \frac{\epsilon\beta}{n}r_k^-, \sigma^2_{\omega_j}) + (\frac{1}{2})^{n-1}N(y, \bar{\omega}, \sigma^2_{\omega_j})$$

$$+\frac{1}{2}\sum_{k=0}^{n-2}\binom{n-1}{k}(\frac{1}{2})^{n-1}N(y, \bar{\omega} - \frac{\epsilon\beta}{n}r_k^+, \sigma^2_{\omega_j})$$

with $\sigma^2_{\omega_j} := \mathrm{K}[\omega(t)]_{j,j} = \frac{\epsilon^2 \mathsf{s}(n-1)}{2n\mathsf{c}}$ and $r_k^- := -2(n-1)+2k$, $r_k^+ := 2(n-1)-2k$ for $k = 0, \ldots, n-2$. We can clearly appreciate that these marginal distributions are sums of Gaussian "bell curves" with "binomial weights". This is observed in numerical simulation as shown in Figure 16.1. Note that for both cases (either for ϕ_j of for ω_j), only the mean value of Gaussian "bell curves" depends on the outcome of the random vector B. That is, each Gaussian "bell curve" in the marginal distributions have mean values depending on the outcome of B but not on the variances. Also, the topology influences the variances of each Gaussian "bell curve" for each ϕ_j but it does not influence the marginal distributions of the ω_j.

Parameter values:

- $\mathsf{c} = 0.5$, $\mathsf{s} = 0.025$
- $\epsilon = 0.1$, $\beta = 2$

Initial conditions:

- $\phi_k(0) = 0$
- $\omega_k(0) = 0.95 + \frac{k-1}{60}$ $k = 1, 2, \ldots, 7$

(evenly spaced between 0.95 and 1.05)

- $Z_k(0) = 0$

for $k = 1, 2, \ldots, n$

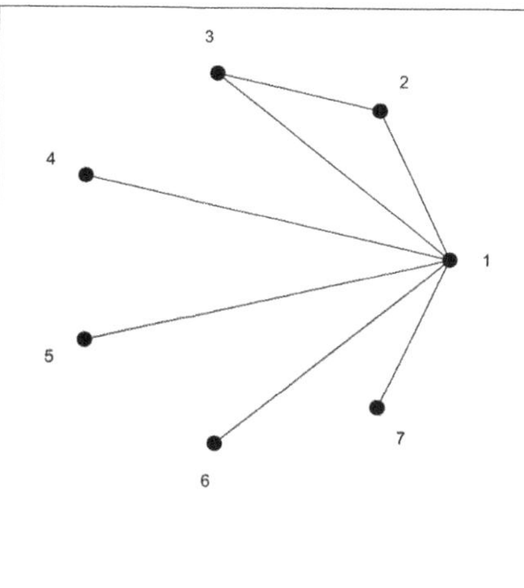

Table 16.1. *Values of the parameters, initial conditions and topology of the network*

16.4. Numerical simulations

We can numerically integrate the nonlinear stochastic differential equation given by equations [16.5] numerous times and empirically study the distributions of ϕ_j and ω_j. This was done 10,000 times (i.e. the number of samples) where each realization (i.e. each numerical integration) consisted of a connected network with $n = 7$ adaptive frequency oscillators on each vertex and with topology given in Table 16.1. The integration was done with Euler's method with step size $h = 0.01$ and the time of integration was $T = 100$. The values of the parameters of the dynamical system as well as the initial conditions are given in Table 16.1. Note that these values are chosen such that the linear approximation holds. Figure 16.1 shows the histogram as well as the theoretical marginal distributions for ϕ_7 and ω_5.

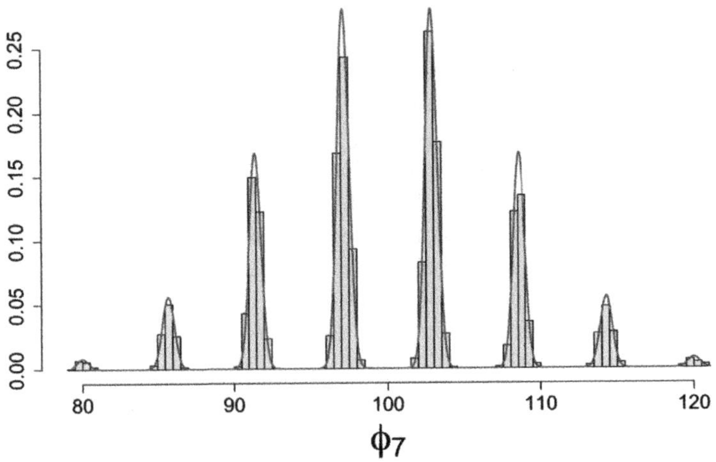

(a)

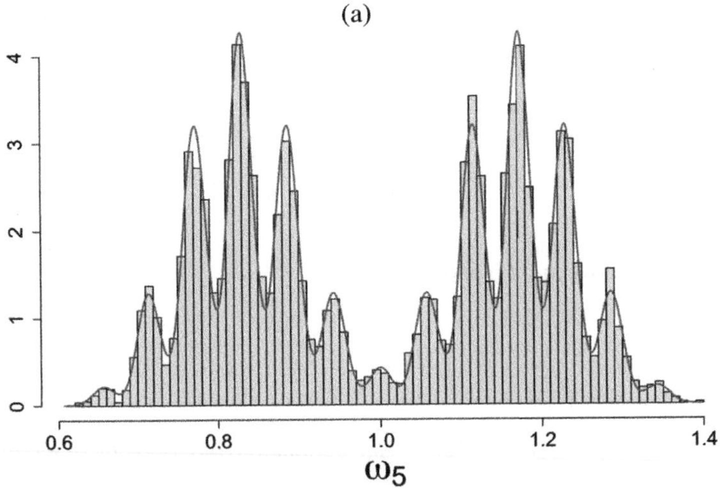

(b)

Figure 16.1. *(a) The histogram with the theoretical marginal distribution (red curve) for ϕ_7. (b) The histogram with the theoretical marginal distribution (red curve) for ω_7. For both (a) and (b), the histograms contain a sample of 10,000 realizations. For a color version of this figure, see www.iste.co.uk/dimotikalis/data4.zip.*

16.5. Discussion and perspectives

This work discusses a system of coupled stochastic differential equations where the deterministic part is linear, but where the noise source emanates from nonlinear diffusion processes exhibiting superdiffusive behavior. For this system and for large t (i.e. transient effects can be neglected), we can analytically calculate the probability densities for ϕ and ω and this for arbitrary network topology. Put simply, the probability density for ϕ is a sum of "binomially" weighted Gaussian "bell curves", for which the covariance matrices depend on the topology, and the probability density for ω is a sum of "equiprobability" weighted Gaussian "bell curves", with here, covariance matrices independent of the network connections. For both cases, the "ballisticity" of the noise source (controlled by parameter β) influences the respective expected vectors (but not the respective covariance matrices). For $\beta = 0$, we recover the model with classical Gaussian noisy perturbations. From a didactical point of view, this ballistic, non-Gaussian, noise source is a nice example to leave the Gaussian world... without too many difficulties!

Considering the real world, these types of models can, for example, be used to investigate the influence of stochastic environments on the network frequency of electrical grids, where the ballistic input corresponds to random run-of-rivers and the equations can be generalized to incorporate the typical class of "generator" and "load" models. These are typically (see, for example, Dörfler 2013; and Berner et al. 2021) of the form

Generators $j = 1, \ldots, n_g$

$$\mathsf{I}_j \ddot{\phi}_j + \mathsf{d}_j \dot{\phi}_j = \omega_j - \mathsf{c} \sum_{k=1}^{n} a_{j,k} \sin(\phi_j - \phi_k) + \epsilon \zeta_j(t)$$

$$\dot{\omega}_j = -\mathsf{s} \sum_{j=1}^{n} a_{j,k} \sin(\phi_j - \phi_k)$$

Loads $l = n_g + 1, \ldots, n$

$$\mathsf{d}_l \dot{\phi}_l = \omega_l - \mathsf{c} \sum_{k=1}^{n} a_{l,k} \sin(\phi_l - \phi_k) + \epsilon \zeta_l(t)$$

$$\dot{\omega}_l = -\mathsf{s} \sum_{j=1}^{n} a_{l,k} \sin(\phi_l - \phi_k)$$

As in Munyayev et al. (2022), the presence of inertia I_j, may cause other types of dynamical behavior, which open new questions and perspectives. Further investigations include (1) the analysis of the resulting stochastic process of the order parameter (i.e. $\frac{1}{n}\sum_{j=1}^{n} \exp(i\phi_j)$), (2) the study of the dynamical system with multiplicative noise (i.e. non-Gaussian noise source multiplying the coupling terms), (3) considering the stochastic process with heterogeneous (i.e. node dependent) "ballisticity" β_k and (4) inspecting the quality of the winding number of the oscillators with and without the possibility to adapt the frequencies.

16.6. Appendices

16.6.1. *Appendix 1: Solution of the linear stochastic differential equation*

Consider the following differential equation:

$$\begin{pmatrix} \dot{x} \\ \dot{y} \end{pmatrix} = \begin{pmatrix} p & 1 \\ q & 0 \end{pmatrix} \begin{pmatrix} x \\ y \end{pmatrix} + \begin{pmatrix} b_x \\ b_y \end{pmatrix}$$

The eigenvectors for the matrix

$$M := \begin{pmatrix} p & 1 \\ q & 0 \end{pmatrix} \quad \text{are} \quad \begin{pmatrix} \gamma_1 \\ q \end{pmatrix} \quad \text{and} \quad \begin{pmatrix} \gamma_2 \\ q \end{pmatrix}$$

with eigenvalues

$$\gamma_1 = \frac{p + \sqrt{p^2 + 4q}}{2} \text{ and } \gamma_2 = \frac{p - \sqrt{p^2 + 4q}}{2}$$

since

$$\begin{vmatrix} p - \gamma & 1 \\ q & -\gamma \end{vmatrix} \stackrel{!}{=} 0 \iff 0 = \gamma^2 - p\gamma - q$$

and

$$\begin{pmatrix} p - \gamma_j & 1 \\ q & -\gamma_j \end{pmatrix} \begin{pmatrix} p - \gamma_j \\ q \end{pmatrix} = \begin{pmatrix} \gamma_j p + q \\ \gamma_j q \end{pmatrix} = \begin{pmatrix} \gamma_j^2 \\ \gamma_j q \end{pmatrix} = \gamma_j \begin{pmatrix} \gamma_j \\ q \end{pmatrix}$$

for $j = 1, 2$. A fundamental matrix is

$$\begin{aligned} \Phi(t) &:= \begin{pmatrix} \exp(\gamma_1 t)\gamma_1 & \exp(\gamma_2 t)\gamma_2 \\ \exp(\gamma_1 t)q & \exp(\gamma_2 t)q \end{pmatrix} \\ &= \begin{pmatrix} \gamma_1 & \gamma_2 \\ q & q \end{pmatrix} \begin{pmatrix} \exp(\gamma_1 t) & 0 \\ 0 & \exp(\gamma_2 t) \end{pmatrix} \\ &= \Phi(0) D^{e^{\gamma t}} \end{aligned}$$

with

$$\Phi(0) = \begin{pmatrix} \gamma_1 & \gamma_2 \\ q & q \end{pmatrix} \qquad D^{e^{\gamma t}} := \begin{pmatrix} \exp(\gamma_1 t) & 0 \\ 0 & \exp(\gamma_2 t) \end{pmatrix}$$

$$\text{and} \quad \Phi(0)^{-1} = \tfrac{1}{q(\gamma_1 - \gamma_2)} \begin{pmatrix} q & -\gamma_2 \\ -q & \gamma_1 \end{pmatrix}$$

and therefore the solution is

$$\begin{pmatrix} x(t) \\ y(t) \end{pmatrix} = \Phi(t)\Phi(0)^{-1} \begin{pmatrix} x_0 \\ y_0 \end{pmatrix}$$

with

$$\Phi(t)\Phi(0)^{-1} = \frac{1}{q(\gamma_1-\gamma_2)}\begin{pmatrix} e^{\gamma_1 t}\gamma_1 q - e^{\gamma_2 t}\gamma_2 q & e^{\gamma_2 t}\gamma_2\gamma_1 - e^{\gamma_1 t}\gamma_1\gamma_2 \\ e^{\gamma_1 t}q^2 - e^{\gamma_2 t}q^2 & e^{\gamma_2 t}q\gamma_1 - e^{\gamma_1 t}q\gamma_2 \end{pmatrix}$$

$$= \frac{1}{\sqrt{p^2+4q}}\begin{pmatrix} \gamma_1 e^{\gamma_1 t} - \gamma_2 e^{\gamma_2 t} & e^{\gamma_1 t} - e^{\gamma_2 t} \\ q(e^{\gamma_1 t} - e^{\gamma_2 t}) & \gamma_1 e^{\gamma_2 t} - \gamma_2 e^{\gamma_1 t} \end{pmatrix}$$

since $\gamma_1 - \gamma_2 = \sqrt{p^2+4q}$ and $\gamma_1\gamma_2 = -q$. We denote $R(t) := \Phi(t)\Phi(0)^{-1}$ as the fundamental matrix of the homogeneous linear differential equation

$$\dot{R}(t) = MR(t) \quad R(0) = I$$

Therefore, the solution to the stochastic differential equation

$$\begin{pmatrix} dX_t \\ dY_t \end{pmatrix} = \begin{pmatrix} p & 1 \\ q & 0 \end{pmatrix}\begin{pmatrix} X_t \\ Y_t \end{pmatrix} dt + \begin{pmatrix} b_x \\ b_y \end{pmatrix} dt + \epsilon \begin{pmatrix} dW_t \\ 0 \end{pmatrix} \qquad [16.13]$$

is (see, for example, Chapter 8 of Arnold (1974))

$$\begin{aligned} \begin{pmatrix} X_t \\ Y_t \end{pmatrix} &= R(t)\Big(\begin{pmatrix} X_0 \\ Y_0 \end{pmatrix} + \int_0^t R(s)^{-1}\Big(\begin{pmatrix} b_x \\ b_y \end{pmatrix} ds + \epsilon \begin{pmatrix} dW_s \\ 0 \end{pmatrix}\Big)\Big) \\ &\overset{*}{=} R(t)\begin{pmatrix} X_0 \\ Y_0 \end{pmatrix} + \int_0^t R(t-s)\Big(\begin{pmatrix} b_x \\ b_y \end{pmatrix} ds + \epsilon \begin{pmatrix} dW_s \\ 0 \end{pmatrix}\Big) \qquad [16.14] \\ \vec{X}_t &\overset{**}{=} R(t)\vec{X}_0 + M^{-1}(R(t)-I)\vec{b} + \epsilon \int_0^t R(t-s)\, d\vec{W}_s \end{aligned}$$

with

$$\vec{X}_t = \begin{pmatrix} X_t \\ Y_t \end{pmatrix} \quad \vec{X}_0 = \begin{pmatrix} X_0 \\ Y_0 \end{pmatrix} \quad \vec{b} = \begin{pmatrix} b_x \\ b_y \end{pmatrix} \quad d\vec{W}_s = \begin{pmatrix} dW_s \\ 0 \end{pmatrix}$$

and because:

* we can compute the product of $R(t)R(s)^{-1}$ as

$$\begin{aligned} R(t)R(s)^{-1} &= \Phi(t)\Phi(0)^{-1}(\Phi(s)\Phi(0)^{-1})^{-1} = \Phi(t)\Phi(0)^{-1}(\Phi(0)\Phi(s)^{-1}) \\ &= \Phi(t)\Phi(s)^{-1} = \Phi(0)D^{e^{\gamma t}}(D^{e^{\gamma s}})^{-1}\Phi(0)^{-1} \\ &= \Phi(0)D^{e^{\gamma(t-s)}}\Phi(0)^{-1} = \Phi(t-s)\Phi(0)^{-1} = R(t-s) \end{aligned}$$

** since $\vec{b}$ is not time-dependent, then $\int_0^t R(t-s)\vec{b}\,ds = (\int_0^t R(t-s)\,ds)\vec{b}$, and we can integrate the matrix $\int_0^t R(t-s)\,ds$ as

$$\begin{aligned}\int_0^t R(t-s)\,ds &= \int_0^t \Phi(0)D^{e^{\gamma(t-s)}}\Phi(0)^{-1}\,ds = \Phi(0)\left(\int_0^t D^{e^{\gamma(t-s)}}\,ds\right)\Phi(0)^{-1}\\ &= \Phi(0)\left[-(D^{\gamma})^{-1}D^{e^{\gamma(t-s)}}\right]_0^t\Phi(0)^{-1}\\ &= \Phi(0)(D^{\gamma})^{-1}\left(D^{e^{\gamma t}}-I\right)\Phi(0)^{-1}\\ &= \Phi(0)(D^{\gamma})^{-1}\Phi(0)^{-1}\cdot\Phi(0)D^{e^{\gamma t}}\Phi(0)^{-1}-\Phi(0)(D^{\gamma})^{-1}\Phi(0)^{-1}\\ &= M^{-1}R(t)-M^{-1}=M^{-1}(R(t)-I)\end{aligned}$$

or simply using the fact that $R'(x) = MR(x)$ for all $x \in \mathbb{R}$, we have $R'(t-s) = MR(t-s)$. Therefore, by integrating with respect to s, we have

$$\begin{aligned}\int_0^t R'(t-s)\,ds &= \int_0^t MR(t-s)\,ds\\ [-R(t-s)]_0^t &= M\int_0^t R(t-s)\,ds\\ -(R(0)-R(t)) &= M\int_0^t R(t-s)\,ds\\ \int_0^t R(t-s)\,ds &= M^{-1}(R(t)-I)\end{aligned}$$

The solution [16.14] is a Gaussian process that is determined by its expected value and covariance matrix which is now calculated. The integral in solution [16.14] has expected value zero, hence

$$\mu_{\vec{X}_t} := \mathrm{E}[\vec{X}_t] = R(t)\vec{X}_0 + M^{-1}(R(t)-I)\vec{b} =: \begin{pmatrix}\mu_{X_t}\\ \hat{A}\,\mu_{Y_t}\end{pmatrix}$$

The covariance matrix is

$$\mathrm{K}[X_t,Y_t] = \mathrm{E}[(\vec{X}_t-\mu_{\vec{X}_t})(\vec{X}_t-\mu_{\vec{X}_t})^{\top}] = \begin{pmatrix}\mathrm{Var}[X_t] & \mathrm{Cov}[X_t,Y_t]\\ \mathrm{Cov}[X_t,Y_t] & \mathrm{Var}[Y_t]\end{pmatrix}$$

with variances

$$\mathrm{Var}[X_t] = \mathrm{E}[X_t^2]-\mu_{X_t}^2 \qquad \mathrm{Var}[Y_t] = \mathrm{E}[Y_t^2]-\mu_{Y_t}^2$$

and covariance

$$\mathrm{Cov}[X_t,Y_t] = \mathrm{E}[(X_t-\mu_{X_t})(Y_t-\mu_{Y_t})] = \mathrm{E}[X_tY_t]-\mu_{X_t}\mu_{Y_t}$$

determined through the following calculations:

$$\begin{aligned}
\mathrm{E}[X_t^2] &= \mathrm{E}[(\mu_{X_t} + \epsilon \int_0^t r_{1,1}(t-s)\, dW_s)^2] \\
&= \mathrm{E}[\mu_{X_t}^2] + \underbrace{\mathrm{E}[2\mu_{X_t}\epsilon \int_0^t r_{1,1}(t-s)\, dW_s]}_{=0} + \mathrm{E}[(\epsilon \int_0^t d_{1,1}(t-s)\, dW_s)^2] \\
&= \mu_{X_t}^2 + \epsilon^2 \mathrm{E}[\int_0^t r_{1,1}(t-s)^2\, ds] \\
&= \mu_{X_t}^2 + \frac{\epsilon^2}{p^2+4q} \int_0^t (\gamma_1 e^{\gamma_1(t-s)} - \gamma_2 e^{\gamma_2(t-s)})^2\, ds \\
&= \mu_{X_t}^2 + \frac{\epsilon^2}{p^2+4q} \int_0^t \gamma_1^2 e^{2\gamma_1(t-s)} - 2\underbrace{\gamma_1\gamma_2}_{=-q} \exp((\underbrace{\gamma_1+\gamma_2}_{p})(t-s)) + \gamma_2^2 e^{2\gamma_2(t-s)}\, ds \\
&= \mu_{X_t}^2 + \frac{\epsilon^2}{p^2+4q} \left[\frac{\gamma_1^2 e^{2\gamma_1(t-s)}}{-2\gamma_1} + \frac{2qe^{p(t-s)}}{-p} + \frac{\gamma_2^2 e^{2\gamma_2(t-s)}}{-2\gamma_2} \right]_0^t \\
&= \mu_{X_t}^2 + \frac{\epsilon^2}{p^2+4q}(-1)\left(\frac{\gamma_1}{2} + \frac{2q}{p} + \frac{\gamma_2}{2} - \frac{\gamma_1 e^{2\gamma_1 t}}{2} - \frac{2qe^{pt}}{p} - \frac{\gamma_2 e^{2\gamma_2 t}}{2} \right) \\
&= \mu_{X_t}^2 + \frac{\epsilon^2}{p^2+4q}\left(\frac{2qe^{pt}}{p} + \frac{1}{2}(\gamma_1 e^{2\gamma_1 t} + \gamma_2 e^{2\gamma_2 t}) - \frac{p^2+4q}{2p} \right) \\
&= \mu_{X_t}^2 - \frac{\epsilon^2}{2p} + \underbrace{\frac{\epsilon^2}{p^2+4q}\left(\frac{2qe^{pt}}{p} + \frac{1}{2}(\gamma_1 e^{2\gamma_1 t} + \gamma_2 e^{2\gamma_2 t}) \right)}_{=:h_X(t)}
\end{aligned}$$

and therefore $\mathrm{Var}[X_t] = -\frac{\epsilon^2}{2p} + h_X(t)$, then

$$\begin{aligned}
\mathrm{E}[Y_t^2] &= \mathrm{E}[(\mu_{Y_t} + \epsilon \int_0^t r_{2,1}(t-s)\, dW_s)^2] \\
&= \mathrm{E}[\mu_{Y_t}^2] + \underbrace{\mathrm{E}[2\mu_{Y_t}\epsilon \int_0^t r_{2,1}(t-s)\, dW_s]}_{=0} + \mathrm{E}[(\epsilon \int_0^t r_{2,1}(t-s)\, dW_s)^2]
\end{aligned}$$

$$= \mu_{Y_t}^2 + \epsilon^2 \mathrm{E}[\int_0^t r_{2,1}(t-s)^2\, ds]$$

$$= \mu_{Y_t}^2 + \frac{\epsilon^2 q^2}{p^2+4q} \int_0^t (e^{\gamma_1(t-s)} - e^{\gamma_2(t-s)})^2\, ds$$

$$= \mu_{Y_t}^2 + \frac{\epsilon^2 q^2}{p^2+4q} \int_0^t e^{2\gamma_1(t-s)} - 2\exp((\underbrace{\gamma_1+\gamma_2}_{p})(t-s)) + e^{2\gamma_2(t-s)}\, ds$$

$$= \mu_{Y_t}^2 + \frac{\epsilon^2 q^2}{p^2+4q} \left[\frac{e^{2\gamma_1(t-s)}}{-2\gamma_1} + \frac{2e^{p(t-s)}}{p} + \frac{e^{2\gamma_2(t-s)}}{-2\gamma_2} \right]_0^t$$

$$= \mu_{Y_t}^2 + \frac{\epsilon^2 q^2}{p^2+4q} \left(\frac{2}{p} - \frac{1}{2\gamma_1} - \frac{1}{2\gamma_2} + \frac{e^{2\gamma_1 t}}{2\gamma_1} - \frac{2e^{pt}}{p} + \frac{e^{2\gamma_2 t}}{2\gamma_2} \right)$$

$$= \mu_{Y_t}^2 + \frac{\epsilon^2 q^2}{p^2+4q} \left(\frac{2}{p} - \frac{\gamma_2}{2\gamma_1\gamma_2} - \frac{\gamma_1}{2\gamma_1\gamma_2} + \frac{\gamma_2 e^{2\gamma_1 t}}{2\gamma_1\gamma_2} + \frac{\gamma_1 e^{2\gamma_2 t}}{2\gamma_1\gamma_2} - \frac{2e^{pt}}{p} \right)$$

$$= \mu_{Y_t}^2 + \frac{\epsilon^2 q^2}{p^2+4q} \left(\frac{2}{p} + \frac{p}{2q} - \frac{\gamma_2 e^{2\gamma_1 t} + \gamma_1 e^{2\gamma_2 t}}{2q} - \frac{2e^{pt}}{p} \right)$$

$$= \mu_{Y_t}^2 + \frac{\epsilon^2 q^2}{p^2+4q} \left(\frac{p^2+4q}{2pq} - \frac{\gamma_2 e^{2\gamma_1 t} + \gamma_1 e^{2\gamma_2 t}}{2q} - \frac{2e^{pt}}{p} \right)$$

$$= \mu_{Y_t}^2 + \frac{\epsilon^2 q}{2p} - \underbrace{\frac{\epsilon^2 q^2}{p^2+4q} \left(\frac{\gamma_2 e^{2\gamma_1 t} + \gamma_1 e^{2\gamma_2 t}}{2q} + \frac{2e^{pt}}{p} \right)}_{=:h_Y(t)}$$

and therefore $\mathrm{Var}[Y_t] = \frac{\epsilon^2 q}{2p} - h_Y(t)$ and finally

$$\mathrm{E}[X_t Y_t] = \mathrm{E}[(\mu_{X_t} + \epsilon \int_0^t r_{1,1}(t-s)\, dW_s)(\mu_{Y_t} + \epsilon \int_0^t r_{2,1}(t-s)\, dW_s)]$$

$$= \mathrm{E}[\mu_{X_t}\mu_{Y_t}] + \underbrace{\mathrm{E}[\mu_{X_t}\epsilon \int_0^t r_{2,1}(t-s)\, dW_s]}_{=0} + \underbrace{\mathrm{E}[\mu_{Y_t}\epsilon \int_0^t r_{1,1}(t-s)\, dW_s]}_{=0}$$

$$+ \mathrm{E}[(\epsilon \int_0^t r_{1,1}(t-s)\, dW_s)(\epsilon \int_0^t r_{2,1}(t-s)\, dW_s)]$$

$$= \mu_{X_t}\mu_{Y_t} + \epsilon^2 \mathrm{E}[\int_0^t r_{1,1}(t-s) r_{2,1}(t-s)\, ds]$$

$$= \mu_{X_t}\mu_{Y_t} + \frac{\epsilon^2 q^2}{p^2+4q} \int_0^t (\gamma_1 e^{\gamma_1 (t-s)} - \gamma_2 e^{\gamma_2 (t-s)})(e^{\gamma_1 (t-s)} - e^{\gamma_2 (t-s)})\, ds$$

$$= \mu_{X_t}\mu_{Y_t} + \frac{\epsilon^2 q^2}{p^2+4q} \left[-\frac{1}{2} \left(e^{\gamma_1 (t-s)} - e^{\gamma_2 (t-s)} \right)^2 \right]_0^t$$

$$= \mu_{X_t}\mu_{Y_t} + \frac{\epsilon^2 q^2}{p^2+4q} (-\frac{1}{2}) \left(0 - (e^{\gamma_1 t} - e^{\gamma_2 t})^2 \right)$$

$$= \mu_{X_t}\mu_{Y_t} + \frac{\epsilon^2 q^2}{2(p^2+4q)} \left(e^{\gamma_1 t} - e^{\gamma_2 t} \right)^2$$

and therefore $\mathrm{Cov}[X_t, Y_t] = \frac{\epsilon^2 q^2}{2(p^2+4q)} \left(e^{\gamma_1 t} - e^{\gamma_2 t} \right)^2$. Therefore, the covariance matrix is

$$\mathrm{K}[X_t, Y_t] = \begin{pmatrix} -\frac{\epsilon^2}{2p} + h_X(t) & \frac{\epsilon^2 q^2}{2(p^2+4q)} \left(e^{\gamma_1 t} - e^{\gamma_2 t} \right)^2 \\ \frac{\epsilon^2 q^2}{2(p^2+4q)} \left(e^{\gamma_1 t} - e^{\gamma_2 t} \right)^2 & \frac{\epsilon^2 q}{2p} - h_Y(t) \end{pmatrix}$$

Behavior of the dynamics for large t: if t is large (i.e. $1 << t$ so that we neglect the transient effects) and if $\mathrm{Re}(\gamma_1) < 0$ and $\mathrm{Re}(\gamma_2) < 0$, then the following approximation holds:

$$\mu_{\vec{X}_t} \approx -M^{-1}\vec{b} = (-1)(\frac{-1}{q}) \begin{pmatrix} 0 & -1 \\ -q & p \end{pmatrix} \begin{pmatrix} b_x \\ b_y \end{pmatrix} = \frac{1}{q} \begin{pmatrix} -b_y \\ -q b_x + p b_y \end{pmatrix}$$

$$\text{and} \quad \mathrm{K}[X_t, Y_t] \approx \begin{pmatrix} -\frac{\epsilon^2}{2p} & 0 \\ 0 & \frac{\epsilon^2 q}{2p} \end{pmatrix}$$

since the entries of the matrix $R(t)$ converge to 0 as $t \to +\infty$, just as well as the functions $h_X(t)$, $h_Y(t)$ and $t \mapsto \frac{\epsilon^2 q^2}{2(p^2+4q)} \left(e^{\gamma_1 t} - e^{\gamma_2 t} \right)^2$.

16.6.2. *Appendix 2: Calculations for changing back the variables, expected values and covariance matrices*

From a distribution point of view, the global stochastic process resulting from equations [16.8] is (for large t and for one realization of B)

$$\begin{array}{ll} X_1(t) \sim \mathcal{N}((Y_1(0)+\epsilon\beta\check{b}_1)t + X_1(0), \epsilon^2 t) & Y_1(t) = Y(0) \\ X_2(t) \sim \mathcal{N}(0, \frac{\epsilon^2}{2\mathfrak{c}\lambda_2}) & Y_2(t) \sim \mathcal{N}(-\epsilon\beta\check{b}_2, \frac{\epsilon^2 \mathfrak{s}}{2\mathfrak{c}}) \\ \vdots & \vdots \\ X_n(t) \sim \mathcal{N}(0, \frac{\epsilon^2}{2\mathfrak{c}\lambda_n}) & Y_n(t) \sim \mathcal{N}(-\epsilon\beta\check{b}_n, \frac{\epsilon^2 \mathfrak{s}}{2\mathfrak{c}}) \end{array}$$

which can be rewritten as

$$\begin{pmatrix} X_1(t) \\ X_2(t) \\ \vdots \\ X_n(t) \end{pmatrix} = \begin{pmatrix} (Y_1(0)+\epsilon\beta\check{b}_1)t + X_1(0) \\ 0 \\ \vdots \\ 0 \end{pmatrix} + \epsilon \underbrace{\begin{pmatrix} \sqrt{t} & 0 & \dots & 0 \\ 0 & \frac{1}{\sqrt{2\mathfrak{c}\lambda_2}} & & 0 \\ \vdots & & \ddots & \vdots \\ 0 & \dots & & \frac{1}{\sqrt{2\mathfrak{c}\lambda_n}} \end{pmatrix}}_{=:\sqrt{D\frac{t}{2\mathfrak{c}\lambda}}} \underbrace{\begin{pmatrix} N_{x_1} \\ N_{x_2} \\ \vdots \\ N_{x_n} \end{pmatrix}}_{=:N_x}$$

$$\begin{pmatrix} Y_1(t) \\ Y_2(t) \\ \vdots \\ Y_n(t) \end{pmatrix} = \begin{pmatrix} Y_1(0) \\ -\epsilon\beta\check{b}_2 \\ \vdots \\ -\epsilon\beta\check{b}_n \end{pmatrix} + \epsilon\sqrt{\frac{\mathfrak{s}}{2\mathfrak{c}}} \underbrace{\begin{pmatrix} 0 \\ N_{y_2} \\ \vdots \\ N_{y_n} \end{pmatrix}}_{=:N_y}$$

with $N_{x_j} \sim \mathcal{N}(0,1)$, $N_{y_j} \sim \mathcal{N}(0,1)$ and mutual independence: $N_{x_j} \perp\!\!\!\perp N_{x_k}$, $N_{x_j} \perp\!\!\!\perp N_{y_k}$ and $N_{y_j} \perp\!\!\!\perp N_{y_k}$ for all $j = 1, \dots, n$ and $k = 2, \dots, n$ (and with the notation "$X \sim \mathcal{N}(\mu, \sigma^2)$" meaning: random variable X with normal distribution and expected value μ and variance σ^2). Changing the variables back with the help of the 2×2 bloc matrix with each bloc of size $n \times n$ and with O on its bloc diagonal (i.e. $(\phi(t), \omega(t)) = (OX(t), OY(t))$), we have a Gaussian process with

$$\phi(t) = OX(t) = ((\bar{\omega} + \epsilon\beta\bar{b})t + \bar{\phi})\vec{1} + \epsilon O\sqrt{D\tfrac{t}{2\mathfrak{c}\lambda}}N_x$$

$$\omega(t) = OY(t) = \bar{\omega}\vec{1} - \frac{\epsilon\beta}{n}L^{\mathfrak{a}}\vec{b} + \epsilon\sqrt{\frac{\mathfrak{s}}{2\mathfrak{c}}}ON_y$$

with $\bar{\omega} := \frac{1}{n}\sum_{j=1}^{n}\omega_j(0)$, $\bar{b} := \frac{1}{n}\sum_{j=1}^{n} b_j$, $\bar{\phi} := \frac{1}{n}\sum_{j=1}^{n}\phi_j(0)$, $\vec{1}$ being the vector with 1 for all entries, and $L^{\mathfrak{a}}$ being the Laplacian matrix associated with the "All-to-All" network. This results from the following calculations:

For $\phi(t)$

Since the first column of matrix O is $\frac{1}{\sqrt{n}}(1,\ldots,1)^\top$, then

$$\phi(t) = OX(t) = \begin{pmatrix} \frac{1}{\sqrt{n}}(Y_1(0)+\epsilon\beta\check{b}_1)t + \frac{1}{\sqrt{n}}X_1(0) \\ \frac{1}{\sqrt{n}}(Y_1(0)+\epsilon\beta\check{b}_1)t + \frac{1}{\sqrt{n}}X_1(0) \\ \vdots \\ \frac{1}{\sqrt{n}}(Y_1(0)+\epsilon\beta\check{b}_1)t + \frac{1}{\sqrt{n}}X_1(0) \end{pmatrix} + \epsilon O\sqrt{D^{\frac{t}{2c\lambda}}}N_x$$

$$= \left((\bar{\omega}+\epsilon\beta\bar{b})t+\bar{\phi}\right)\vec{1} + \epsilon O\sqrt{D^{\frac{t}{2c\lambda}}}N_x$$

because $\frac{1}{\sqrt{n}}Y_1(0) = \frac{1}{n}\sum_{j=1}^{n}\omega_j(0) = \bar{\omega}$, $\quad \frac{1}{\sqrt{n}}\check{b}_1 = \frac{1}{n}\sum_{j=1}^{n}b_j = \bar{b}$ and $\frac{1}{\sqrt{n}}X_1(0) = \frac{1}{n}\sum_{j=1}^{n}\phi_j(0) = \bar{\phi}$.

For $\omega(t)$

Again, since the first column of matrix O is $\frac{1}{\sqrt{n}}(1,\ldots,1)^\top$, then

$$\omega(t) = OY(t) = \begin{pmatrix} \frac{1}{\sqrt{n}}Y_1(0) \\ \vdots \\ \frac{1}{\sqrt{n}}Y_1(0) \end{pmatrix} + O\begin{pmatrix} 0 \\ -\epsilon\beta\check{b}_2 \\ \vdots \\ -\epsilon\beta\check{b}_n \end{pmatrix} + \epsilon\sqrt{\frac{\mathsf{s}}{2\mathsf{c}}}ON_y$$

$$= \bar{\omega}\vec{1} - \epsilon\beta\sum_{j=2}^{n}\check{b}_j\vec{o}_j + \epsilon\sqrt{\frac{\mathsf{s}}{2\mathsf{c}}}ON_y$$

$$= \bar{\omega}\vec{1} - \frac{\epsilon\beta}{n}L^{\mathfrak{a}}\vec{b} + \epsilon\sqrt{\frac{\mathsf{s}}{2\mathsf{c}}}ON_y$$

because $\frac{1}{\sqrt{n}}Y_1(0) = \frac{1}{n}\sum_{j=1}^{n}\omega_j(0) = \bar{\omega}$ and since $\check{b}_j = \left\langle \vec{o}_j \mid \vec{b}\right\rangle$ with $\vec{o}_j$ the jth column vector of matrix O, then by direct calculations

$$\frac{1}{n}L^{\mathfrak{a}}\vec{b} = \frac{1}{n}L^{\mathfrak{a}}OO^\top\vec{b} = \frac{1}{n}\left(\vec{0},\, n\vec{o}_2,\, \ldots,\, n\vec{o}_n\right)\begin{pmatrix} \left\langle \vec{o}_1 \mid \vec{b}\right\rangle \\ \left\langle \vec{o}_2 \mid \vec{b}\right\rangle \\ \vdots \\ \left\langle \vec{o}_n \mid \vec{b}\right\rangle \end{pmatrix} = \sum_{j=2}^{n}\underbrace{\left\langle \vec{o}_j \mid \vec{b}\right\rangle}_{=\check{b}_j}\vec{o}_j$$

because the matrix $L^{\mathfrak{a}}$ has eigenvalue 0 for eigenvector $\frac{1}{\sqrt{n}}(1,\ldots,1)^\top$ (i.e. the first column in matrix O) and all other eigenvalues are n (see Appendix 16.6.4).

The expected values and covariance matrices of $\phi(t)$ and $\omega(t)$ are:

For $\mathrm{E}[\phi(t)]$

The expected value of $\phi(t)$ is

$$\mathrm{E}[\phi(t)] = ((\bar{\omega} + \epsilon\beta\bar{b})t + \bar{\phi})\vec{1}$$

because $\sqrt{D^{\frac{t}{2c\lambda}}}N_x$ consists of n-independent normally distributed random variables, all with mean 0 and so the n sums corresponding to the n components of $O\sqrt{D^{\frac{t}{2c\lambda}}}N_x$ are all normally distributed with mean 0.

For $\mathrm{K}[\phi(t)]$

The covariance matrix of $\phi(t)$ is

$$\mathrm{K}[\phi(t)] = \mathrm{K}[OX(t)] = O\mathrm{K}[X(t)]O^\top = \epsilon^2 O \begin{pmatrix} t & 0 & \ldots & 0 \\ 0 & \frac{1}{2c\lambda_2} & \ldots & 0 \\ \vdots & & \ddots & \vdots \\ 0 & \ldots & & \frac{1}{2c\lambda_n} \end{pmatrix} O^\top$$

$$= \epsilon^2 O(\begin{pmatrix} t & 0 & \ldots & 0 \\ 0 & 0 & \ldots & 0 \\ \vdots & & \ddots & \vdots \\ 0 & \ldots & & 0 \end{pmatrix} + \begin{pmatrix} 0 & 0 & \ldots & 0 \\ 0 & \frac{1}{2c\lambda_2} & \ldots & 0 \\ \vdots & & \ddots & \vdots \\ 0 & \ldots & & \frac{1}{2c\lambda_n} \end{pmatrix})O^\top$$

$$= \epsilon^2 (\frac{t}{n}\mathbf{1} + \frac{1}{2cn^2}(I - \frac{1}{n}L^{\mathfrak{c}})^{-1}L^{\mathfrak{a}}) = \frac{\epsilon^2}{n}(t\mathbf{1} + \frac{1}{2cn}(I - \frac{1}{n}L^{\mathfrak{c}})^{-1}L^{\mathfrak{a}})$$

since be direct calculations (i.e. due to the fact that the first column (respectively the first row) of O is $\frac{1}{\sqrt{n}}(1,\ldots,1)^\top$ (respectively of $O^\top$))

$$O \begin{pmatrix} t & 0 & \ldots & 0 \\ 0 & 0 & \ldots & 0 \\ \vdots & & \ddots & \vdots \\ 0 & \ldots & & 0 \end{pmatrix} O^\top = \begin{pmatrix} \frac{t}{\sqrt{n}} & 0 & \ldots & 0 \\ \frac{t}{\sqrt{n}} & 0 & \ldots & 0 \\ \vdots & & \ddots & \vdots \\ \frac{t}{\sqrt{n}} & \ldots & & 0 \end{pmatrix} O^\top = \frac{t}{n}\mathbf{1}$$

with $\mathbf{1}$ the $n \times n$ matrix with 1 as entries and the result for $\frac{1}{2cn^2}(I - \frac{1}{n}L^{\mathfrak{c}})^{-1}L^{\mathfrak{a}}$ follows from the following calculations.

Denote by $L^{\mathfrak{c}}$ the (Laplacian) complement matrix of L, i.e. $L^{\mathfrak{c}} := L^{\mathfrak{a}} - L$. In other words, in $L^{\mathfrak{c}}$, all entries of L outside the diagonal with value -1 are 0 (i.e. removing edges), all entries of L outside the diagonal with value 0 are -1 (i.e. inserting edges) and the diagonal entries of $L^{\mathtt{c}}$ are $L^{\mathtt{c}}_{j,j} = (n-1) - L_{j,j}$. The matrix $L^{\mathtt{c}}$ is the Laplacian matrix associated with the adjacency matrix $A^{\mathtt{c}}$ of the undirected network (not necessarily connected) that is the "complement" network associated with the adjacency matrix A in the sense that the edges in A are removed and vertices that are not directly connected in A are connected in $A^{\mathtt{c}}$.

Since L, $L^{\mathtt{c}}$ and $L^{\mathfrak{a}}$ mutuality commute (i.e. $LL^{\mathtt{c}} = L^{\mathtt{c}}L$, $LL^{\mathfrak{a}} = L^{\mathfrak{a}}L$ and $L^{\mathtt{c}}L^{\mathfrak{a}} = L^{\mathfrak{a}}L^{\mathtt{c}}$) (see Rodriguez (2014) for details), then there exists O such that

$$O^\top L O = \begin{pmatrix} 0 & 0 & \cdots & 0 \\ 0 & \lambda_2 & \cdots & 0 \\ \vdots & & \ddots & \vdots \\ 0 & 0 & \cdots & \lambda_n \end{pmatrix} \quad O^\top L^{\mathtt{c}} O = \begin{pmatrix} 0 & 0 & \cdots & 0 \\ 0 & \lambda^{\mathtt{c}}_2 & \cdots & 0 \\ \vdots & & \ddots & \vdots \\ 0 & 0 & \cdots & \lambda^{\mathtt{c}}_n \end{pmatrix} \quad O^\top L^{\mathfrak{a}} O = \begin{pmatrix} 0 & 0 & \cdots & 0 \\ 0 & n & \cdots & 0 \\ \vdots & & \ddots & \vdots \\ 0 & 0 & \cdots & n \end{pmatrix}$$

with $\lambda^{\mathtt{c}}_1 = 0$ and $\lambda^{\mathtt{c}}_j$ $(j = 2, \ldots, n)$ being the eigenvalues of $L^{\mathtt{c}}$, and, without loss of generality, the eigenvector $\frac{1}{\sqrt{n}}(1, \ldots, 1)^\top$ is the first column of matrix O. Since

$$L^{\mathfrak{a}} = L + L^{\mathtt{c}} \iff O^\top L^{\mathfrak{a}} O = O^\top L O + O^\top L^{\mathtt{c}} O$$

it follows that for $j = 2, \ldots, n$:

$$n = \lambda_j + \lambda^{\mathtt{c}}_j \iff n - \lambda^{\mathtt{c}}_j = \lambda_j \iff \frac{n}{\lambda_j} - \frac{\lambda^{\mathtt{c}}_j}{\lambda_j} = 1$$

and therefore

$$\begin{pmatrix} 0 & 0 & \cdots & 0 \\ 0 & \frac{n}{\lambda_2} & \cdots & 0 \\ \vdots & & \ddots & \vdots \\ 0 & 0 & \cdots & \frac{n}{\lambda_n} \end{pmatrix} - \begin{pmatrix} 0 & 0 & \cdots & 0 \\ 0 & \frac{\lambda^{\mathtt{c}}_2}{\lambda_2} & \cdots & 0 \\ \vdots & & \ddots & \vdots \\ 0 & 0 & \cdots & \frac{\lambda^{\mathtt{c}}_2}{\lambda_n} \end{pmatrix} = \begin{pmatrix} 0 & 0 & \cdots & 0 \\ 0 & 1 & \cdots & 0 \\ \vdots & & \ddots & \vdots \\ 0 & 0 & \cdots & 1 \end{pmatrix}$$

$$\begin{pmatrix} 0 & 0 & \cdots & 0 \\ 0 & \frac{1}{\lambda_2} & \cdots & 0 \\ \vdots & & \ddots & \vdots \\ 0 & 0 & \cdots & \frac{1}{\lambda_n} \end{pmatrix} - \frac{1}{n} \begin{pmatrix} 0 & 0 & \cdots & 0 \\ 0 & \lambda^{\mathtt{c}}_2 & \cdots & 0 \\ \vdots & & \ddots & \vdots \\ 0 & 0 & \cdots & \lambda^{\mathtt{c}}_2 \end{pmatrix} \begin{pmatrix} 0 & 0 & \cdots & 0 \\ 0 & \frac{1}{\lambda_2} & \cdots & 0 \\ \vdots & & \ddots & \vdots \\ 0 & 0 & \cdots & \frac{1}{\lambda_n} \end{pmatrix} = \frac{1}{n^2} \begin{pmatrix} 0 & 0 & \cdots & 0 \\ 0 & n & \cdots & 0 \\ \vdots & & \ddots & \vdots \\ 0 & 0 & \cdots & n \end{pmatrix}$$

and therefore with the notation

$$D^{\frac{1}{\lambda}} = \begin{pmatrix} 0 & 0 & \cdots & 0 \\ 0 & \frac{1}{\lambda_2} & \cdots & 0 \\ \vdots & & \ddots & \vdots \\ 0 & 0 & \cdots & \frac{1}{\lambda_n} \end{pmatrix}$$

we have

$$D^{\frac{1}{\lambda}} - \frac{1}{n} O^\top L^{\mathtt{c}} O D^{\frac{1}{\lambda}} = \frac{1}{n^2} O^\top L^{\mathtt{a}} O$$

$$O D^{\frac{1}{\lambda}} O^\top - \frac{1}{n} L^{\mathtt{c}} O D^{\frac{1}{\lambda}} O^\top = \frac{1}{n^2} L^{\mathtt{a}}$$

$$(I - \frac{1}{n} L^{\mathtt{c}}) O D^{\frac{1}{\lambda}} O^\top = \frac{1}{n^2} L^{\mathtt{a}}$$

$$O D^{\frac{1}{\lambda}} O^\top = \frac{1}{n^2} (I - \frac{1}{n} L^{\mathtt{c}})^{-1} L^{\mathtt{a}}$$

$$O(\frac{1}{2\mathtt{c}} D^{\frac{1}{\lambda}}) O^\top = \frac{1}{2\mathtt{c} n^2} (I - \frac{1}{n} L^{\mathtt{c}})^{-1} L^{\mathtt{a}}$$

since $I - \frac{1}{n} L^{\mathtt{c}}$ is invertible because it can be diagonalized with O

$$O(I - \frac{1}{n} L^{\mathtt{c}}) O^\top = I - \frac{1}{n} O L^{\mathtt{c}} O^\top$$

which has the diagonal entries: $1, 1 - \frac{\lambda_j^{\mathtt{c}}}{n}$ and $0 < \lambda_j^{\mathtt{c}} < n$ for $j = 2, \ldots, n$.

For $\mathrm{E}[\omega(t)]$

The expected value of $\omega(t)$ is

$$\mathrm{E}[\omega(t)] = \bar{\omega}\vec{1} - \frac{\epsilon\beta}{n} L^{\mathtt{a}} \vec{b}$$

because each component of ON_y consists of a sum of $n-1$ independent normally distributed random variables all with mean 0.

For $\mathrm{K}[\omega(t)]$

The covariance matrix of $\omega(t)$ is

$$\mathrm{K}[\omega(t)] = \mathrm{K}[OY(t)] = O\mathrm{K}[Y(t)]O^\top = \frac{\epsilon^2 \mathtt{s}}{2n\mathtt{c}} L^{\mathtt{a}}$$

because

$$O\mathrm{K}[Y(t)]O^\top = O \begin{pmatrix} 0 & 0 & \ldots & 0 \\ 0 & \frac{\epsilon^2 \mathtt{s}}{2\mathtt{c}} & \ldots & 0 \\ \vdots & & \ddots & \vdots \\ 0 & \ldots & & \frac{\epsilon^2 \mathtt{s}}{2\mathtt{c}} \end{pmatrix} O^\top$$

$$= \frac{\epsilon^2 \mathtt{s}}{2\mathtt{c}} O(\begin{pmatrix} 0 & 0 & \ldots & 0 \\ 0 & 1 & \ldots & 0 \\ \vdots & & \ddots & \vdots \\ 0 & \ldots & & 1 \end{pmatrix} + \begin{pmatrix} 1 & 0 & \ldots & 0 \\ 0 & 0 & \ldots & 0 \\ \vdots & & \ddots & \vdots \\ 0 & \ldots & & 0 \end{pmatrix} - \begin{pmatrix} 1 & 0 & \ldots & 0 \\ 0 & 0 & \ldots & 0 \\ \vdots & & \ddots & \vdots \\ 0 & \ldots & & 0 \end{pmatrix}) O^\top$$

$$= \frac{\epsilon^2 \mathsf{s}}{2\mathsf{c}}(OIO^\top - O \begin{pmatrix} 1 & 0 & \dots & 0 \\ 0 & 0 & \dots & 0 \\ \vdots & & \ddots & \vdots \\ 0 & \dots & & 0 \end{pmatrix} O^\top) = \frac{\epsilon^2 \mathsf{s}}{2\mathsf{c}}(I - \frac{1}{n}\mathbf{1}) = \frac{\epsilon^2 \mathsf{s}}{2\mathsf{c}}(\frac{1}{n}L^{\mathfrak{a}})$$

$$= \frac{\epsilon^2 \mathsf{s}}{2n\mathsf{c}} L^{\mathfrak{a}}$$

with I being the $n \times n$ identity matrix.

16.6.3. *Appendix 3: Distributions concerning the random vector* B

For (I)

The random variable $\bar{B} := \frac{1}{n}\sum_{j=1}^{n} B_j$ has a binomial distribution in the following sense ($l \in \{1, 2, \dots\}$):

$$\begin{array}{ll} \text{if } n = 2l & \bar{B} \in \{-1, \frac{-n-2}{n}, \dots, \frac{-2}{n}, 0, \frac{2}{n}, \dots, \frac{n-2}{n}, 1\} \\ \text{if } n = 2l + 1 & \bar{B} \in \{-1, \frac{-n-2}{n}, \dots, \frac{-3}{n}, \frac{-1}{n}, \frac{1}{n}, \frac{3}{n}, \dots, \frac{n-2}{n}, 1\} \end{array}$$

$$\text{with probability:} \quad \mathrm{P}(\bar{B} = \frac{-n + 2k}{n}) = \binom{n}{k}(\frac{1}{2})^n \quad k = 0, 1, \dots, n$$

since a random variable following a standard binomial distribution has support $\{0, 1, \dots, n\}$, and here, the support of $\sum_{j=1}^{n} B_j$ is the set of elements in $\{0, 1, \dots, n\}$ multiplied by 2 and subtracted by n. A further multiplication with $\frac{1}{n}$ (i.e. dividing by n) gives the values of $\bar{B}$.

For (II)

The aim is to determine the distribution of $L^{\mathfrak{a}} B$ with

$$B = \begin{pmatrix} B_1 \\ \vdots \\ B_n \end{pmatrix} \quad \text{and} \quad \mathrm{P}(B_j = 1) = \mathrm{P}(B_j = -1) = \frac{1}{2}, \quad B_j \perp\!\!\!\perp B_k \ \forall\, j, k$$

Denote by $\mathbb{H} := \{x \in \mathbb{R}^n \mid x_j \in \{-1,1\}, j = 1,\dots,n\}$ and so set $\mathbb{H}$ has $|\mathbb{H}| = 2^n$ elements. Let $\vec{b} \in \mathbb{H}$, then $\vec{b} = \sum_{j=1}^{n} \left\langle \vec{o}_j \mid \vec{b} \right\rangle \vec{o}_j$ since

$$\vec{b} = \vec{b} \iff \vec{b} = OO^\top \vec{b} \iff \vec{b} = O \begin{pmatrix} \left\langle \vec{o}_1 \mid \vec{b} \right\rangle \\ \left\langle \vec{o}_2 \mid \vec{b} \right\rangle \\ \vdots \\ \left\langle \vec{o}_n \mid \vec{b} \right\rangle \end{pmatrix} = \sum_{j=1}^{n} \left\langle \vec{o}_j \mid \vec{b} \right\rangle \vec{o}_j$$

Therefore, $L^{\mathfrak{a}}\vec{b} = n \sum_{j=2}^{n} \left\langle \vec{o}_j \mid \vec{b} \right\rangle \vec{o}_j$ and so $L^{\mathfrak{a}}\vec{b} = n(\vec{b} - \left\langle \vec{o}_1 \mid \vec{b} \right\rangle \vec{o}_1)$ since

$$\vec{b} = \left\langle \vec{o}_1 \mid \vec{b} \right\rangle \vec{o}_1 + \sum_{j=2}^{n} \left\langle \vec{o}_j \mid \vec{b} \right\rangle \vec{o}_j \iff n(\vec{b} - \left\langle \vec{o}_1 \mid \vec{b} \right\rangle \vec{o}_1) = n \sum_{j=2}^{n} \left\langle \vec{o}_j \mid \vec{b} \right\rangle \vec{o}_j$$

We have to determine the number of different $L^{\mathfrak{a}}\vec{b}_j$ for $\vec{b}_j \in \mathbb{H}$ and $j = 1,\dots,n$. This is answered by the following lemma:

LEMMA 16.1.– *If* $\vec{b}_1, \vec{b}_2 \in \mathbb{H} \setminus \{-\vec{1}, \vec{1}\}$ *and* $\vec{b}_1 \neq \vec{b}_2 \Rightarrow L^{\mathfrak{a}}\vec{b}_1 \neq L^{\mathfrak{a}}\vec{b}_2$

PROOF.– The proof is done by contradiction. Assume that there exists $\vec{b}_1, \vec{b}_2 \in \mathbb{H} \setminus \{-\vec{1}, \vec{1}\}$ and $\vec{b}_1 \neq \vec{b}_2$ such that $L^{\mathfrak{a}}\vec{b}_1 = L^{\mathfrak{a}}\vec{b}_2$. Then

$$L^{\mathfrak{a}}\vec{b}_1 = L^{\mathfrak{a}}\vec{b}_2 \iff L^{\mathfrak{a}}(\vec{b}_2 - \vec{b}_1) = \vec{0} \iff \vec{b}_2 - \vec{b}_1 \in \mathbb{K}(L^{\mathfrak{a}}) \iff \vec{b}_2 - \vec{b}_1 = \alpha\vec{1}$$

Since $\vec{b}_1 \neq \vec{b}_2$, there exists $j \in \{1,\dots,n\}$ such that $b_{1,j} \neq b_{2,j}$ (with notation: $\vec{b}_1^\top = (b_{1,1},\dots,b_{1,n})^\top$ and $\vec{b}_2^\top = (b_{2,1},\dots,b_{2,n})^\top$). We directly see that $\alpha \neq 0$, since then $\vec{b}_2 - \vec{b}_1 = \vec{0}$ and so $\vec{b}_2 = \vec{b}_1$, which is a contradiction. Since

$$b_{1,j} = \begin{cases} 1 \\ -1 \end{cases} \quad \text{and} \quad b_{2,j} = \begin{cases} 1 \\ -1 \end{cases} \quad \text{then} \quad b_{2,j} - b_{1,j} = \begin{cases} 2 \\ -2 \end{cases} \Rightarrow \alpha = \begin{cases} 2 \\ -2 \end{cases}$$

Assume that there exists $k \in \{1,\dots,n\}$ and $k \neq j$ such that $b_{1,k} = b_{2,k}$, then $b_{2,k} - b_{1,k} = 0$, but then $\alpha = 0$, which is a contradiction. Therefore, all components are different: $\forall\, l \in \{1,\dots,n\}$, then $b_{1,l} \neq b_{2,l}$ which implies that $\vec{v}_2 = -\vec{v}_1$, but then

$$L^{\mathfrak{a}}\vec{b}_1 = \vec{v}_1 \quad \text{and} \quad L^{\mathfrak{a}}\vec{b}_2 = L^{\mathfrak{a}}(-\vec{b}_1) = -\vec{v}_1 \Rightarrow L^{\mathfrak{a}}\vec{b}_1 \neq L^{\mathfrak{a}}\vec{b}_2$$

Therefore, we have

$$L^{\mathfrak{a}}B = \begin{cases} \vec{0} & \text{if } B = b_0 \text{ or } B = b_{2^n-1} \\ n(\vec{b}_j - \left\langle \vec{o}_1 \mid \vec{b}_j \right\rangle) & \text{if } B = b_j \text{ for } j \in \{1,2,\dots,2^n-1\} \end{cases}$$

with $\vec{b}_0^\top = (-\vec{1})^\top, \vec{b}_{2^n-1}^\top = \vec{1}^\top$ and $\vec{b}_j \in \mathbb{H} \setminus \{-\vec{1}, \vec{1}\}$. Hence, the distribution of $L^{\mathfrak{a}}B$ is

$$\mathrm{P}(L^{\mathfrak{a}}B = \vec{0}) = \frac{2}{2^n} \quad \text{and} \quad \mathrm{P}(L^{\mathfrak{a}}B = \vec{v}) = \frac{1}{2^n}$$

with $\vec{v} = n(\vec{b} - \langle \vec{o}_1 \mid \vec{b} \rangle)$ for a realization $B = \vec{b}$ and neither $\vec{b} = \vec{1}$ nor $\vec{b} = -\vec{1}$.

For (III)

The distribution of the jth component of $L^{\mathfrak{a}}B$ is calculated as follows. Define the random variable

$$R_j := (n-1)B_j - \sum_{k \neq j}^{n} B_k =: (n-1)B_j - S_{n-1}$$

The distribution of $(n-1)B_j$ is $\mathrm{P}\big((n-1)B_j = \pm(n-1)\big) = \frac{1}{2}$ and the distribution of S_{n-1} is

if $n = 2l$ $\quad S_{n-1} \in \{-(n-1), -(n-3), \ldots, -3, -1, 1, 3, \ldots, n-3, n-1\}$
if $n = 2l+1$ $\quad S_{n-1} \in \{-(n-1), -(n-3), \ldots, -2, 0, 2, \ldots, n-3, n-1\}$

with probability: $\mathrm{P}(S_{n-1} = -(n-1) + 2k) = \binom{n-1}{k} (\frac{1}{2})^{n-1} \quad k = 0, 1, \ldots, n-1$

If $n = 2l$, the values for $R_j = (n-1)B_j - S_{n-1}$ when $B_j = 1$ are

$(n-1)B_j$:	$n-1$	$n-1$	$\ldots$	$n-1$	$n-1$	$n-1$	$n-1$	$\ldots$	$n-1$	$n-1$
$-S_{n-1}$:	$(n-1)$	$(n-3)$	$\ldots$	3	1	-1	-3	$\ldots$	$-(n-3)$	$-(n-1)$
R_j :	$2(n-1)$	$2(n-2)$	$\ldots$	$n+2$	n	$n-2$	$n-4$	$\ldots$	2	0

and the values for $R_j = (n-1)B_j - S_{n-1}$ when $B_j = -1$ are

$(n-1)B_j$:	$-(n-1)$	$-(n-1)$	$\ldots$	$-(n-1)$	$-(n-1)$	$-(n-1)$	$-(n-1)$	$\ldots$	$-(n-1)$	$-(n-1)$
$-S_{n-1}$:	$(n-1)$	$(n-3)$	$\ldots$	3	1	-1	-3	$\ldots$	$-(n-3)$	$-(n-1)$
R_j :	0	-2	$\ldots$	$-n+4$	$-n+2$	$-n$	$-n-2$	$\ldots$	$-2(n-2)$	$-2(n-1)$

If $n = 2l+1$, the values for $R_j = (n-1)B_j - S_{n-1}$ when $B_j = 1$ are

$(n-1)B_j$:	$n-1$	$n-1$	$\ldots$	$n-1$	$n-1$	$n-1$	$\ldots$	$n-1$	$n-1$
$-S_{n-1}$:	$(n-1)$	$(n-3)$	$\ldots$	2	0	-2	$\ldots$	$-(n-3)$	$-(n-1)$
R_j :	$2(n-1)$	$2(n-2)$	$\ldots$	$n+1$	$n-1$	$n-3$	$\ldots$	2	0

and the values for $R_j = (n-1)B_j - S_{n-1}$ when $B_j = -1$ are

$(n-1)B_j$:	$-(n-1)$	$-(n-1)$	$\ldots$	$-(n-1)$	$-(n-1)$	$-(n-1)$	$\ldots$	$-(n-1)$	$-(n-1)$
$-S_{n-1}$:	$(n-1)$	$(n-3)$	$\ldots$	2	0	-2	$\ldots$	$-(n-3)$	$-(n-1)$
R_j :	0	-2	$\ldots$	$-n+3$	$-n+1$	$-n-1$	$\ldots$	$-2(n-2)$	$-2(n-1)$

The random variable R_j takes $2(n-1)+1=2n-1$ distinct values in

$$\{-2(n-1),-2(n-2),\ldots,-2,0,2,\ldots,2(n-2),2(n-1)\}$$

with the following probability distribution:

$$\mathrm{P}(R_j=-2(n-1)+2k)=\frac{1}{2}\binom{n-1}{k}(\frac{1}{2})^{n-1} \qquad k=0,\ldots,n-2$$

$$\mathrm{P}(R_j=0)=(\frac{1}{2})^{n-1}$$

$$\mathrm{P}(R_j=2(n-1)-2k)=\frac{1}{2}\binom{n-1}{k}(\frac{1}{2})^{n-1} \qquad k=0,\ldots,n-2$$

We can easily check that the sum of the probabilities adds up to one, since $\sum_{j=0}^{n-2}\binom{n-1}{j}+1=2^{n-1}$ and therefore

$$\sum_{j=0}^{n-2}(\mathrm{P}(R_j=-2(n-1)+2j)+\mathrm{P}(R_j=2(n-1)-2j))+\mathrm{P}(R_j=0)$$

$$=\sum_{j=0}^{n-2}\binom{n-1}{j}(\frac{1}{2})^{n-1}+(\frac{1}{2})^{n-1}=(\frac{1}{2})^{n-1}(\underbrace{\sum_{j=0}^{n-2}\binom{n-1}{j}+1}_{=2^{n-1}})=1$$

Note that the random variables $R_1,R_2,\ldots,R_n$ are not independent.

16.6.4. *Appendix 4: Eigenvalues of the Laplacian matrix of the "All-to-All" network*

LEMMA 16.2.– *Every nonzero vector orthogonal to $\vec{1}$ (i.e. the vector with 1 for all entries) is an eigenvector of L^{a} with eigenvalue n.*

PROOF.– Let v be a vector orthogonal to $\vec{1}$ (i.e. $\sum_{j=1}^{n}v_j=0 \iff v_k=-\sum_{j\neq k}^{n}v_j$). The kth line of the product L^a is

$$\sum_{j=1}^{n}l_{k,j}v_j=\underbrace{l_{k,1}}_{=-1}v_1+\underbrace{l_{k,2}}_{=-1}v_2+\cdots+\underbrace{l_{k,k}}_{=(n-1)}v_k+\cdots+\underbrace{l_{k,n}}_{=-1}v_n$$

$$=-\sum_{j\neq k}^{n}v_j+(n-1)v_k$$

$$=nv_k$$

since, if $v_k \neq 0$, then $-\sum_{j\neq k}^{n} v_j + (n-1)v_k = v_k + nv_k - v_k = nv_k$ and if $v_k = 0$, then $-\sum_{j\neq k} v_j + (n-1)v_k = -\sum_{j\neq k}^{n} v_j = v_k = 0 = nv_k$. Therefore, $L^a v = nv$.

16.7. References

Arcand, J.-L., Hongler, M.-O., Rinaldo, D. (2020). Increasing risk: Dynamic mean-preserving spreads. *Journal of Mathematical Economics*, 86, 69–82.

Arnold, L. (1974). *Stochastic Differential Equations: Theory and Applications*. John Wiley & Sons, New York.

Berner, R., Yanchuk, S., Schöll, E. (2021). What adaptive neuronal networks teach us about power grids. *Physical Review E*, 103, 042315.

Dörfler, F., Chertkov, M., Bullo, F. (2013). Synchronization in complex oscillator networks and smart grids. *Proceedings of the National Academy of Sciences*, 110, 2005–2010.

Ermentrout, B. (1991). An adaptive model for synchrony in the firefly *Pteroptyx malaccae*. *Journal of Mathematical Biology*, 29, 571–585.

Filliger, R. and Hongler, M.-O. (2007). Explicit Gittins indices for a class of superdiffusive processes. *Journal of Applied Probability*, 44, 554–559.

Gams, A., Ijspeert, A.J., Schaal, S., Lenarčič, J. (2009). On-line learning and modulation of periodic movements with nonlinear dynamical systems. *Autonomous Robots*, 27, 3–23.

Gams, A., Petrič, T., Do, M., Nemeca, B., Morimoto, J., Asfour, T., Ude, A. (2016). Adaptation and coaching of periodic motion primitives through physical and visual interaction. *Robotics and Autonomous Systems*, 75, 340–351.

Hongler, M.-O. (1979). Exact solutions of a class of non-linear Fokker-Planck equations. *Physics Letters A*, 75, 3–4.

Hongler, M.-O. (2013). Super-diffusive noise source in asset dynamics. *Journal of Mathematical Finance*, 3, 53–58.

Hongler, M.-O., Filliger, R., Blanchard, P. (2006). Soluble models for dynamics driven by a super-diffusive noise. *Physica A*, 370, 301–315.

Laloyaux, H., Livolsi, C., Pergolini, A., Crea, S., Vitiello, N., Ronsse, R. (2023). Simplified motor primitives for gait symmetrization: Pilot study with an active hip orthosis. *IEEE International Conference on Robotics and Automation*, London, 10436–10442.

Munyayev, V.O., Bolotov, M.I., Smirnov, L.A., Osipov, G.V., Belykh, I.V. (2022). Stability of rotatory solitary states in Kuramoto networks with inertia. *Physical Review E*, 105, 024203.

Petrič, T. (2020). Phase-synchronized learning of periodic compliant movement primitives (P-CMPs). *Frontiers in Neurorobotics*, 14, 599889.

Petrič, T., Gams, A., Ijspeert, A.J., Žlajpah, L. (2011). On-line frequency adaptation and movement imitation for rhythmic robotic tasks. *The International Journal of Robotics Research*, 30(14), 1775–1788.

Righetti, L., Buchli, J., Ijspeert, A.J. (2006). Dynamic Hebbian learning in adaptive frequency oscillators. *Physica D*, 216, 269–281.

Righetti, L., Buchli, J., Ijspeert, A.J. (2021). Slow-fast dynamics of strongly coupled adaptive frequency oscillators. *SIAM Journal on Applied Dynamical Systems*, 20, 1985–2012.

Rodriguez, J. (2013). Noise and delays in adaptive interacting oscillatory systems. PhD Thesis, Universität Bielefeld, Bielefeld.

Rodriguez, J. (2014). Random parametric resonance in time-dependent networks of adaptive frequency oscillators. *Discontinuity, Nonlinearity, and Complexity*, 3(3), 347–365.

Rogers, L. and Pitman, J. (1981). Markov functions. *The Annals of Probability*, 9, 573–582.

Ronsse, R., Lenzi, T., Vitiello, N., Koopman, B., van Asseldonk, E., De Rossi, S.M.M., van den Kieboom, J., van der Kooij, H., Carrozza, M.C., Ijspeert, A.J. (2011). Oscillator-based assistance of cyclical movements: Model-based and model-free approaches. *Medical & Biological Engineering & Computing*, 49, 1173–1185.

Taylor, D., Ott, E., Restrepo, J.G. (2010). Spontanous synchronization of coupled oscillator systems with frequency adaptation. *Physical Review E*, 81, 046214.

Yan, T., Parri, A., Ruiz Garate, V., Cempini, M., Ronsse, R., Vitiello, N. (2017). An oscillator-based smooth real-time estimate of gait phase for wearable robotics. *Autonomous Robots*, 41, 759–774.

17

Penalised Regression Adaptations of the Longstaff–Schwartz Algorithm for Pricing American Options

One of the most popular techniques for evaluating the American put option is the Longstaff–Schwartz algorithm, a Monte Carlo type algorithm where orthogonal polynomials are typically used to estimate the expected future payoff, given the current value of the American option from simulated paths of the process. An optimal exercise strategy then ensues for each of these paths, where the average payoff over all paths becomes equivalent to the fair price of the American option. Convergence results have been proven which show that, under certain regularity conditions, and using a least squares estimation approach, this average payoff converges to the true price as the sample size of the paths and the order of the orthogonal polynomial go simultaneously to infinity. Various alternative modeling and estimation approaches have been attempted to make the Longstaff–Schwartz algorithm more accurate and computationally efficient. However, studies on the use of penalized regression approaches are scarce. Under different sample path and polynomial order settings, in this chapter, an empirical assessment is conducted of the benchmark least squares method in comparison with the Ridge, LASSO and elastic net estimation; this is to see which of these methods is the best in terms of accuracy and computational efficiency. This comparison is made on three staple processes in finance, namely geometric Brownian motion, the Heston stochastic volatility and a model based on the Meixner jump processes, while convergence properties for the standard Longstaff–Schwarz approach is used to determine a benchmark for accuracy. Across most settings in the simulation design, LASSO resulted in the best precision across the four algorithm variations, followed closely by elastic net. Ridge regression often produced results that were less accurate than LASSO and elastic net; however, these were also often more precise than the least squares approach. Therefore, a discussion on the computational aspect is made, determining for each process which methods achieve the best compromise between precision and execution time.

Chapter written by David Paul SUDA, Monique BORG INGUANEZ and Lara CILIA.

17.1. Introduction

An option is defined as a contract between two parties: a buyer and a seller, which gives the holder the right but not the obligation to buy some asset at some predetermined price (known as the strike price). These instruments can be found in all major financial markets and can be used to trade various types of assets including equity, commodities, currencies and interest, with these assets being referred to as the underlying asset of the option. Options are split into two main types – put and call options. For put options, the seller has the right but not the obligation to sell an asset at a specified strike price. For call options, the buyer has the right but not the obligation to buy an asset at a specified strike price. Thus, if the strike price has not been reached, the holder can opt to not exercise the option. If, instead, the strike price has been reached, it is stated that the option is in-the-money, since there is an opportunity for a profit for the holder of the option if it is exercised. There are various types of options, with the variations mostly dependent on the possible times at which an option can be exercised. The most basic type of option is the European option, where the only possible exercise time is at the end of the contract. Let this time be denoted by T. Another form of commonly traded option is the American option, which allows an option to be exercised at any point from the start of a contract up to a terminal time T. For an American call option which is not interest-bearing, it is never optimal to exercise the option prior to the end of the contract. This makes the American call option equivalent to the European call option, and thus only, the put option will be considered in this study. The mathematical derivation to support this statement can be found in Elliot and Kopp (2004), section 1.6. On the contrary, a discretized version of the American option is the Bermuda option, which may be exercised at multiple discrete points during the contract period, with these exercise dates being pre-determined within the option contract. The Longstaff–Schwartz (LS) algorithm introduced in the following section approximates the American option by a Bermuda option.

The LS algorithm by Longstaff and Schwartz (2001) is a popular method for evaluating American options, where a number of sample paths are obtained via Monte Carlo simulation, and working backward, the expected future payoff (a conditional expectation) is estimated via ordinary least squares (OLS) estimation by using the prices at the particular time t as variables in an orthogonal polynomial regression model. In this study, modifications to the LS algorithm are proposed, wherein the OLS approach will be substituted with one of three penalized regression approaches, namely Ridge, LASSO and elastic net (EN). In the literature, there are many studies on alternatives to OLS estimation within the LS algorithm. Examples of these are smoothing spline estimates by Kohler (2008), modifications on the least squares algorithm by Areal (2008) and artificial neural networks by Kohler et al. (2010) and Lapeyre and Lelong (2021), who looked into least squares neural network estimates to obtain approximations for the expected future payoff at each point in time. In the context of regularized regression, Tompaidis and Yang (2014) focus on the Ridge regression, matching projection pursuit and modified matching projection pursuit. In addition, they also consider regression trees. The main novelty in this study is the use of LASSO and elastic net. The aim is to produce estimates of the fair price which are closer to the true price of the American option than those obtained using the original LS algorithm with a smaller number of paths, and a simulation design will be devised for this purpose. While the OLS approach has been shown theoretically to converge to the true price of the American option under certain regularity conditions, this convergence is achieved only by simultaneously increasing the number of basis functions and the number of sample paths. Moreover, it has been shown empirically by Tompaidis and Yang (2014) that OLS estimation is prone to overfitting and tends to produce inaccurate estimates for a small number of paths. A main advantage of penalized regression methods is that these work by decreasing the variance in the estimated results. However, in these methods, the variance is decreased at the cost of introducing some bias in the model. Thus, it is aimed to ensure that the bias introduced through these methods is limited as much as possible. In the next section, the LS algorithm and its most fundamental assumptions are discussed.

17.2. The Longstaff–Schwartz algorithm and proposed extensions

The LS algorithm is a simulation based method used to estimate the optimal price and exercise strategy of the American option. It involves a regression step using an orthogonal polynomial, since regular polynomials face issues with multicollinearity. Orthogonal polynomials are polynomials of the type $f(x) = \sum_{j=0}^{M} \beta_j \phi_j(x)$, where the $\phi_j(x)$ are orthonormal basis functions. Types of orthogonal polynomials include Laguerre, Legendre, Hermite and Chebyshev polynomials (see, for example, Moreno and Navas (2003) for further detail on their formulation). For reasons explained later, in this chapter, the Laguerre and the Legendre polynomials are implemented in the analysis. When it comes to Laguerre polynomials, the basis functions are given by $\phi_j(x) = e^{-x/2} \frac{e^x}{j!} \frac{d^j}{dx^j}(x^j e^{-x})$, while for the Legendre polynomials, the first two terms are given by $\phi_0(x) = 1$ and $\phi_1(x) = x$, while the general term is given by $(j + 1)\phi_{j+1}(x) = (2j + 1)x\phi_j(x) - l\phi_{j-1}(x)$. An overview of the LS algorithm is the following:

1) Discretize a continuous time interval $[0, T]$ into $m + 1$ equally spaced points such that $t_i = i\Delta$ and $T = t_m = m\Delta$ and simulate N independent paths $\left\{S_{\Delta}^{(j)}, \ldots, S_{m\Delta}^{(j)}\right\}$ for $j = 1, \ldots, N$.

2) Let the payoff function at time t_i be given by $h_i(x) = e^{-rt_i} max\{0, K - x\}$. Let $V_m(x) = h_m(x)$ and $V_i(x) = max\{h_i(x), C_i(x)\}$ for $i = 1, \ldots, m$, where $C_i(x) = E\left[V_{i+1}\left(S_{(i+1)\Delta}\right) | S_{i\Delta} = x\right]$ is referred to as the continuation value of the American put option. Starting with time t_{m-1}, and working recursively backwards at each time t_i until time t_0, $V_{i+1}\left(S_{(i+1)\Delta}\right)$ is regressed with the current value of the American option $S_{i\Delta}$ for pairs $\left(S_{i\Delta}^{(j)}, V_{i+1}\left(S_{(i+1)\Delta}^{(j)}\right)\right)$. For paths which

are in-the-money, i.e. $h_i\left(S_{i\Delta}^{(j)}\right) > 0$, this expectation is estimated through OLS orthogonal polynomial regression given M basis functions.

3) For in-the-money paths, if $h_i\left(S_{i\Delta}^{(j)}\right)$ is greater or equal to the estimated expectation of $C_i\left(S_{i\Delta}^{(j)}\right)$, then let $V_i\left(S_{i\Delta}^{(j)}\right) = h_i\left(S_{i\Delta}^{(j)}\right)$, else let $V_i\left(S_{(i)\Delta}^{(j)}\right) = V_{i+1}\left(S_{(i+1)\Delta}^{(j)}\right)$. For out-of-the-money paths, on the contrary, also let $V_i\left(S_{(i)\Delta}^{(j)}\right) = V_{i+1}\left(S_{(i+1)\Delta}^{(j)}\right)$.

4) The estimated fair price of $V_0\left(S_0\right)$ – denoted by $V_0^{(N,M)}$ – is estimated by averaging the $V_1\left(S_1^{(j)}\right)$s.

A number of convergence results have been derived for $V_0^{(N,M)}$, but the most useful ones in the context of this study are the ones proven in Stentoft (2004). The authors first start by making a number of assumptions, including the independence of the simulated paths, the assumption that the optimal stopping time will never be correctly identified except at the limit, that the support of the observation process is a Cartesian product of compact connected intervals on which it has a probability density function bounded below by some $\epsilon > 0$, and that the conditional expectation function is smooth. Under these assumptions, they show (in two separate theorems) that if $M = M(N)$ is increasing in N such that $M \rightarrow \infty$ and $\frac{M^3}{N} \rightarrow 0$, then $V_0^{(N,M)}$ converges in probability to V_0 and is also mean square convergent. The full theorem and complementary assumptions are given in the supplementary material in Suda (2023). The general applicability of these assumptions allows us to apply these theorems not only to basic models such as geometric Brownian motion but also to models with stochastic volatility, stochastic dividends and stochastic interest rates (see Stentoft 2004).

In this study, the aim is to tweak the LS algorithm by substituting the OLS approach with a penalized regression approach for a linear model of the type $= E\left[Y|X_1 = x_1, \ldots, X_p = x_p\right] + \epsilon$, where Y is the dependent variable, $X_1, \ldots, X_p$ are the independent variables and $\beta_1, \ldots, \beta_p$ are the regression coefficients of the model such that $E\left[Y|X_1 = x_1, \ldots, X_p = x_p\right] = \beta_0 + \sum_{j=1}^{p} \beta_j X_j$. Consider an observation set of size N, where the ith observation constitutes the vector $(Y_i, X_{1i}, \ldots, X_{pi})$. Furthermore, let $\boldsymbol{\beta} = (\beta_1, \ldots, \beta_p)$ be the coefficient vector for the model in regression equation excluding the intercept. The general penalized regression estimator is given by:

$$\hat{\boldsymbol{\beta}}_{PR} = \arg\min_{(\beta_0, \boldsymbol{\beta}')'} \left\{ \sum_{i=1}^{n} \left[Y_i - \left(\beta_0 + \sum_{j=1}^{p} \beta_j X_{ij} \right) \right]^2 + \psi\left(\boldsymbol{\beta}\right) \right\} \qquad [17.1]$$

where the penalty term $\psi(\boldsymbol{\beta})$ in equation [17.1] is either of the form $\psi(\boldsymbol{\beta}) = \lambda||\boldsymbol{\beta}||_q$ (for LASSO estimation $q = 1$ and for Ridge estimation $q = 2$), or else for EN estimation, $\psi(\boldsymbol{\beta}) = \lambda(\alpha||\boldsymbol{\beta}||_1 + (1-\alpha)||\boldsymbol{\beta}||_2)$. It must be noted that Ridge estimation has an explicit solution and, furthermore, the coefficients may go close to 0 but are not allowed to be 0; however, LASSO and EN, on the contrary, while having no explicit solution, can truncate some predictors altogether from the equation by setting their coefficients to zero. Of course, the main issue with all penalized regression approaches is that of finding the ideal shrinkage parameter λ. This is typically done using cross-validation with a goodness-of-fit criterion. In this chapter, an 80/20 cross-validation approach is used in the simulation analysis and the mean squared error of prediction (MSEP) as goodness-of-fit criterion. Orthogonal polynomial regression can, of course, be viewed as a special form of regression, whereby the predictors X_j are substituted with the basis functions $\phi_j(X)$. Section 17.3 introduces the underlying asset price models we shall consider in this chapter, their risk-neutrality conditions and also, since one of the models we introduce in this chapter is a Lévy process, convergence results relate to this specific process since the aforementioned convergence results do not apply.

17.3. Stochastic processes in finance and relevant theoretical considerations

In this chapter, the simulation study for American option pricing will be implemented on three stochastic processes: geometric Brownian motion, the Heston stochastic volatility model and a Meixner process-based stock price model. In order for an option to be economically viable and marketable, we must exclude all scenarios of riskless profit (also called arbitrage opportunity). Also, by the fundamental theorem of arbitrage pricing (see Pliska 1997), it is known that the presence of a risk neutral probability measure is sufficient to guarantee that no arbitrage opportunities exist. Let $\mathbb{Q}$ be a risk neutral probability measure – under this measure, given a stock price process $(S_t)_{t\geq 0}$ is a martingale when discounted. If, as will be assumed throughout this study, the riskless interest rate is r and constant in time, then $e^{-rt}S_t$ must be a martingale. The aforementioned stochastic processes will now be reviewed, including their parameterization under the risk neutrality assumption, and also any other convergence considerations under the OLS setup of the LS algorithm, given that these may not be satisfied for all of the three processes.

Geometric Brownian motion has been chosen due to the fact that it is one of the most standard and classical model in finance – indeed, it is the model on which the well-known Black–Scholes model for European option pricing is based. This is given by the stochastic differential equation (SDE):

$$dS_t = \mu S_t dt + \sigma S_t dW_t \qquad [17.2]$$

where μ and σ are the drift and volatility parameter, respectively, and $(W_t)_{t\geq 0}$ is a standard Brownian motion. It is a well-known result that, under the risk neutral measure, the drift parameter of geometric Brownian motion in equation [17.2] is equal to r. However, geometric Brownian motion makes a number of assumptions which are known to be unsuitable for current stock price dynamics. For this reason, a stochastic volatility model is also considered (which caters for the volatility clustering phenomenon) and a Lévy process which allows for jump behavior.

The stochastic volatility considered is the Heston model. Generally, this model is given by the following bivariate SDE:

$$\begin{aligned} dS_t &= \mu S_t dt + \sqrt{V_t} S_t dW_t^{(1)} \\ dV_t &= \gamma\left(\theta - V_t\right) dt + \sigma\sqrt{V_t} dW_t^{(2)} \end{aligned} \qquad [17.3]$$

where μ is the drift of the stock price SDE, $(V_t)_{t\geq 0}$ is an unobserved variance process, θ refers to the long-term variance of the stock price process, γ is the mean reversion speed, σ is the volatility of the variance process and controls the kurtosis of the stock price return distribution, and $\left(W_t^{(1)}\right)_{t\geq 0}$ and $\left(W_t^{(2)}\right)_{t\geq 0}$ are two correlated Weiner processes such that $dW_t^{(1)} dW_t^{(2)} = \rho dt$. The risk neutral parameterization of the Heston stochastic volatility model (see Heston 2008) is obtained by substituting the drift term in the stock price equation of the Heston equation in [17.3] by the riskless rate r, and γ and θ in the volatility equation by $\gamma + \phi$ and $\frac{\gamma\theta}{\gamma+\phi}$, respectively, for some constant ϕ. ϕ is not unique, which may be an issue as different ϕs may yield different option prices. However, Heston (2008) suggests estimating this by using average returns on option positions that are hedged against the risk of changes in the stock price. This aspect of the Heston model will not be delved into in this study.

Finally, a stock price model $S_t = S_0 e^{M_t}$ is considered where (M_t) is an infinite variation Lévy type process called the Meixner process, which is a stochastic process with $M_0 = 0$, where the increments are stationary and independent, and where $M_t \sim Meixner(a, b, mt, dt)$. According to the Lévy–Itô decomposition, Lévy processes may consist of a drift part, a Brownian part and a jump part. The Meixner process does not contain the Brownian part, but instead, it contains a jump portion determined by the Lévy measure $\nu(dx)$ given by $\nu(dx) = \frac{de^{\frac{bx}{a}}}{x \sinh\frac{\pi x}{a}} dx$ such that $\int_{-1}^{1} |x| \nu(dx) = \infty$, hence of infinite variation (see, for example, Mazzola and Muliere 2011). To ensure risk neutrality of the Meixner-based process, we require that $S_t = S_0 \frac{e^{rt} e^{M_t}}{E[e^{M_t}]}$ where the parameter m is replaced by $r - 2d \log\left(\frac{\cos\frac{b}{2}}{\cos\frac{a+b}{2}}\right)$ (see Schoutens 2002).

To conclude, it is important to discuss the convergence properties of the LS algorithm related to these processes. As mentioned in section 17.2, the theorems in

Stentoft (2004) apply not only to geometric Brownian motion but also to models with stochastic volatility. However, for a Lévy process, it is more complex to show the applicability of the convergence theorems due to the discontinuities inherent in the process. Gerhold (2011) studies this problem in detail, looking into Lévy processes, and in particular Meixner processes, and their convergence properties in the context of the LS algorithm. The author proves that the convergence of the true price is still satisfied, provided the risk neutral dynamics of the underlying asset are $S_t = S_0 e^{M_t}$, where M_t is a Meixner process with $M_0 = 0$ such that the support of M_t is the whole real line, mild integrability conditions on S_t, at most linearly growing payoff functions, shifted Legendre polynomials as basis functions, independence of the simulated paths, the assumption that the optimal stopping time will never be correctly identified except at the limit and the assumption that the continuation values are in the L^2-span of the regressors. The full theorem and complementary assumptions are given in the supplementary material in Suda (2023). Section 17.4 gives an overview of the simulation design prior to presenting the results for the simulation study.

17.4. Simulation design

In this section, the simulation design compares the penalized regression methods in their accuracy in estimating the fair price within the context of an LS-type algorithm, with comparison to OLS. The comparison of the estimates obtained is made possible by the convergence properties of the LS algorithm discussed earlier, where given certain regularity conditions, as the number of basis functions M and the number of sampled paths N increases towards infinity, the estimate of the fair price obtained by the LS algorithm using OLS estimation approaches the true price. This allows us to obtain high precision estimates of the true price using OLS estimation given sufficiently large values for M and N which can be used as benchmarks for comparison (we use 1 million paths and 10 basis functions). Three different well-known processes are considered for modeling the prices of the underlying assets of the American option – geometric Brownian motion, the Heston stochastic volatility model and the Meixner process. Most studies in this field tend to focus on orthogonal polynomials using three basis functions, but the number of basis functions in this study will be allowed to range between 3 and 10. The number of paths for each of the runs of the algorithm will vary between 2,000 and 100,000, at intervals of 1,000. This allows us to examine any improvement in accuracy of the price estimates across the four estimation methods as the number of basis functions and the number of paths are increased. Thus, the simulation design will study a combination of four different regression estimators, eight polynomials of different orders and nine variations on the number of paths (288 combinations in total). Furthermore, each combination will be subjected to 20 runs, so that the price estimate is based on a mean of the runs. The simulations are run using *Matlab* software, whereby tailor-made modifications to a code called *LongstaffSchwartzAmericanOptionPricer* available on *Mathworks* (see Sansom 2024) are affected. The input parameters for the original

LongstaffSchwartzAmericanOptionPricer are the following: the strike price of the option, the initial price of the option, the interest rate, the number of days for the option to mature, the daily drift and volatility rates for the geometric Brownian motion process, the mean reversion rate for the geometric Brownian motion process, the number of paths to be simulated, the seed used for random number generation and the polynomial order. Furthermore, there are also two Boolean flags – one that determines whether it is a put or call option (which will always be set to put option) and one that determines whether discrete or continuous discounting is used (which will always be set to discrete in line with the original LS algorithm). To extend the analysis to other regression methods, an additional parameter will be added to this function with options for regular OLS, Ridge, LASSO and EN. In addition, due to the requirement of catering for various forms of the underlying price process, the geometric Brownian motion specific parameters for drift, volatility and mean reversion will be made redundant and an input will be included, which will receive the simulated paths. Hence, it was decided that the altered *Matlab* function will receive an $N \times m$ matrix of the simulated paths as input parameter. Externally from the function, simulation of geometric Brownian motion and the Heston stochastic volatility model could be easily performed using the Euler method (see, for example, Kloeden and Platen 1992). On the contrary, to simulate from the Meixner process, it is necessary to simulate the Meixner distributed increments. For this, R is used, as no *Matlab* functions were found for this purpose. This was done using the *udmeixner* function within the package *Runuran*. The matrix of simulated paths for the Meixner process was then exported to a CSV file and fed to the required American option pricer function. Finally, two versions of the function were created – one that uses Laguerre polynomials (as in the original *LongstaffSchwartzAmericanOptionPricer* function) and another one that uses Legendre polynomials, due to the fact that for the Meixner process, convergence results are specific to Legendre polynomials.

All penalized regression methods considered require a value for the shrinkage parameter λ as input, where the returned estimated regression coefficients correspond to this value. If the value of the λ parameter is not provided for this *Matlab* function, this returns the estimated regression coefficients for 100 different values of λ, identically distributed between 0 and 1. However, this would clearly require an extensive amount of computational time for the penalized regression methods, especially in comparison to OLS; therefore, it was decided to use an array of six values as λ input parameters to the *Matlab* function, ranging between 0.001 and 0.3 – in particular, 0.001, 0.01, 0.1, 0.15, 0.2 and 0.3. It must be noted that larger values for λ were not included to keep the bias small in the regression coefficient estimates obtained. The next step in the implementation was to determine which of the six sets of regression coefficient estimates obtained provided the best fit. When the number of observations permit, an 80/20 cross validation approach is used to select the value of λ, which is then applied on the entire data set. However, there will also be iterations at which very few paths are in-the-money and even instances where no such paths exist, especially close to the initial time t_0, where no path will have yet reached the strike price and thus none of the paths will result in a positive payoff, in which case, regular OLS will be applied. For EN estimation, the value for the α parameter is set to be 0.5. Prior to selecting this value, test runs were carried out using values for α of 0.25, 0.5 and 0.75. However, the results for all three values were similar, and thus it was decided to use the value of 0.5.

Finally, the parameters assigned to each process are given. All three processes are considered in their risk neutral form over a period of 365 days, a riskless annual interest rate of 6% and a simulation discretization of 0.01. For geometric Brownian motion, the strike price is taken to be $K = 20$, the spot price taken to be 24, and the volatility parameter is taken to be $\sigma = 0.02$. For the Heston model, the strike price is taken to be $K = 23$, the spot price is taken to be 24, and the parameters are taken to be $\theta = 0.01$, $\gamma = 2$, and $\lambda = -0.09$. Finally, for the Meixner-type model, the strike price is taken to be $K = 20$, the spot price to be 24, $a = 0.298$, $b = 0.1271$, and $d = 0.0573$.

17.5. Results

In this section, the results pertaining to the simulation design described in section 17.4 will be presented. Figure 17.1 shows the precision of each regression approach (absolute difference from the mean in 20 runs) for the different chosen processes, only when dealing with three basis functions.

When comparing equivalent number of paths, in the case of geometric Brownian motion, regularized methods (Ridge, LASSO and EN) offer a marginally better precision than OLS for the same number of paths. In the case of the Heston model, LASSO and EN offer significantly superior precision to Ridge, which in turn is also significantly superior in terms of precision to OLS. Finally, in the case of the Meixner-based model, LASSO and EN offer significantly superior precision to Ridge and OLS which, in this case, perform similarly.

In Table 17.1, the best method by process, number of basis functions and number of paths is presented. When considering all combinations of number of basis functions and number of paths, the following is deduced:

– For GBM, regularized methods were generally superior to OLS, which only resulted as the superior method in five combinations of sample size and number of basis functions. Ridge regression, on the contrary, proved superior in 26 combinations, LASSO regression in 27 combinations and EN in 14 combinations.

– For the Heston model and Meixner-based model, LASSO and EN are always superior to both OLS and Ridge. For the Heston model, EN is superior in 18 combinations, while LASSO is superior in 54 combinations. For the Meixner-based model, EN is superior in 24 combinations and LASSO in 48 combinations.

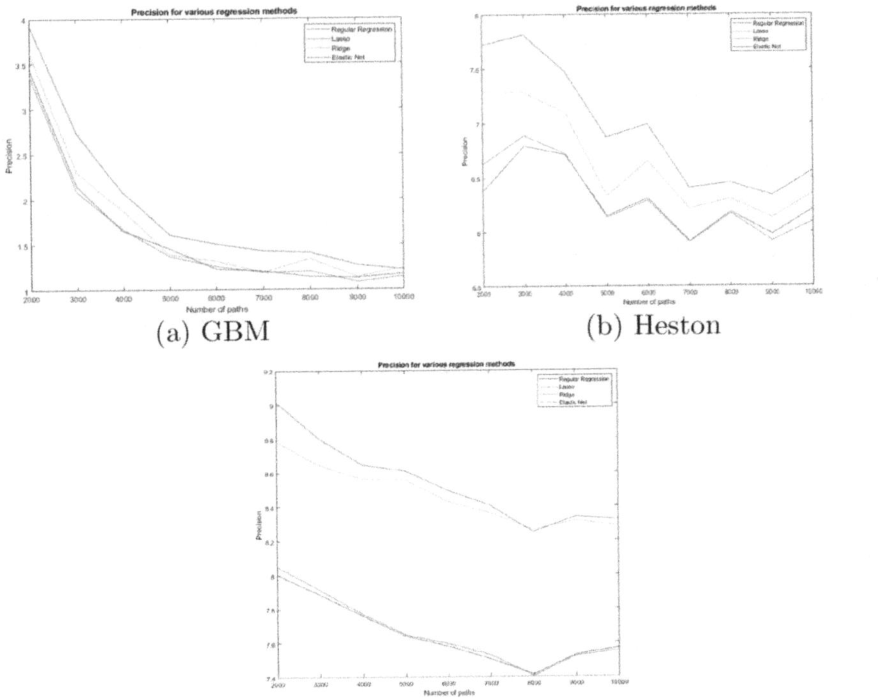

(a) GBM (b) Heston

(c) Meixner

Figure 17.1. *Precision for different number of sample paths for (a) GBM, (b) Heston and (c) Meixner when using polynomials with three basis functions. For a color version of this figure, see www.iste.co.uk/dimotikalis/data4.zip*

Table 17.2 provides the precision for all sample size/number of basis functions combinations for each process considered. A green color gradient is used based on the absolute difference in precision from the best method (ADPBM) for that particular combination, where darker shades indicate higher ADPBM than lighter ones. It can be noted that LASSO is generally the better method, especially for the Heston model and the Meixner-based model, while OLS is frequently the worst method, although there are some exceptions for GBM where it is the best. There is generally no trend in the precision depending on the number of basis functions used. This issue is of particular importance as increasing the number of basis functions used also increases the computational expense. Furthermore, it is also necessary to address whether the more computationally intensive LASSO and EN approaches are worthwhile when it comes to improved precision, as these can be significantly more computationally intensive than OLS and Ridge. It is therefore important to further explore the relationship between execution time and precision for the different methods.

GBM - No. of paths (in thousands)									
No. of b.f.s	2	3	4	5	6	7	8	9	10
3	R	R	R	R	R	R	R	EN	EN
4	R	L	L	L	L	L	OLS	L	R
5	L	L	L	L	EN	EN	L	OLS	OLS
6	OLS	R	R	EN	EN	OLS	R	L	R
7	L	R	R	R	R	R	R	R	R
8	L	R	EN	EN	EN	L	EN	L	EN
9	L	L	L	L	L	R	R	R	R
10	L	EN	L	EN	L	L	EN	L	L

Heston - No. of paths (in thousands)									
No. of b.f.s	2	3	4	5	6	7	8	9	10
3	EN	EN	EN	L	L	L	L	L	L
4	L	EN	L	L	L	L	L	L	L
5	EN	L	L	L	L	L	L	L	L
6	L	EN	L	EN	L	EN	L	L	L
7	L	L	L	L	L	L	L	L	L
8	L	L	EN	EN	EN	EN	L	L	L
9	L	L	EN	EN	EN	L	L	EN	L
10	EN	L	L	L	L	L	EN	L	L

Meixner - No. of paths (in thousands)									
No. of b.f.s	2	3	4	5	6	7	8	9	10
3	EN	EN	EN	EN	EN	EN	L	L	L
4	EN	EN	EN	EN	EN	EN	EN	EN	EN
5	L	EN	L	EN	EN	L	L	EN	L
6	L	EN	L	EN	L	L	EN	L	L
7	L	L	L	L	L	L	L	L	L
8	L	EN	L	L	L	L	L	L	EN
9	L	L	L	L	L	L	L	L	L
10	L	L	L	L	L	L	L	L	L

Table 17.1. *Best method by process, number of basis functions and number of paths*

Figure 17.2 shows smoothed execution time versus precision values for the different simulation design combinations, which has been achieved via nonlinear regression estimation of the power function. In Figure 17.2, only results for 3 and 10 basis functions are shown, with results for the other basis functions given in Suda (2023). We must keep in mind that the computational intensity computed is dependent on the computational efficiency of the simulators used and the regression routines available on *Matlab*.

When analyzing execution time against precision for GBM, we can see that Ridge regression and OLS regression offer better precision for the same execution time, which indicates that they are the better choice for this process. Ridge regression is marginally better than OLS regression for a small number of basis functions, but the discrepancy between the two becomes negligible as the number of basis functions increases. For the Heston model, LASSO regression is the most computationally efficient when considering a lower number of basis functions. For a higher number of basis functions, Ridge regression is the most computationally efficient if a higher precision is required. Finally, for the Meixner-based model, Ridge regression and OLS regression offer low precision with small number of basis functions. EN regression and LASSO regression offer high precision and a higher computational cost; however, superior precision is achieved for similar execution time. If we increase the number of basis functions, LASSO regression, Ridge regression and OLS regression offer similar execution time versus precision benefits. EN regression is more computationally costly in such instances.

(a) GBM

Number of basis functions	2	3	4	5	6	7	8	9	10
					Number of paths (in thousands)				
OLS									
3	3.67%	3.08%	2.81%	2.05%	2.04%	2.11%	1.98%	1.61%	1.62%
4	3.95%	2.58%	2.35%	1.97%	1.45%	1.22%	1.32%	1.35%	1.41%
5	2.51%	2.14%	1.66%	1.55%	1.34%	1.26%	1.36%	1.25%	1.29%
6	3.02%	2.46%	2.06%	1.86%	1.50%	1.33%	1.54%	1.50%	1.51%
7	4.33%	3.21%	2.94%	2.14%	2.03%	1.80%	1.79%	1.76%	1.79%
8	4.72%	3.92%	2.44%	1.77%	1.70%	1.82%	1.63%	1.40%	1.20%
9	5.74%	4.30%	3.76%	2.98%	2.69%	2.60%	2.31%	2.36%	2.14%
10	6.11%	4.48%	3.67%	3.14%	2.80%	2.55%	2.24%	2.14%	1.82%
LASSO									
3	3.97%	3.13%	2.68%	2.29%	1.95%	2.00%	1.84%	1.45%	1.51%
4	3.40%	2.47%	1.96%	1.83%	1.43%	1.21%	1.34%	1.32%	1.17%
5	2.61%	2.14%	1.66%	1.55%	1.34%	1.26%	1.36%	1.25%	1.29%
6	3.43%	2.32%	2.08%	1.70%	1.59%	1.57%	1.44%	1.16%	1.15%
7	3.24%	2.70%	2.18%	1.94%	1.63%	1.71%	1.63%	1.72%	1.71%
8	3.21%	2.96%	1.86%	1.43%	1.61%	1.41%	1.39%	1.23%	1.16%
9	4.27%	3.17%	2.91%	2.37%	2.29%	2.09%	1.93%	1.99%	1.70%
10	4.49%	3.30%	2.89%	2.42%	1.83%	1.69%	1.70%	1.52%	1.41%
Ridge									
3	3.32%	2.13%	2.03%	1.71%	1.84%	1.75%	1.53%	1.56%	1.53%
4	3.34%	3.12%	2.04%	2.56%	2.09%	1.95%	1.51%	1.32%	1.15%
5	3.41%	2.77%	2.31%	1.76%	2.00%	1.50%	1.51%	1.24%	1.21%
6	3.70%	2.09%	2.05%	2.01%	1.56%	1.44%	1.24%	1.21%	0.96%
7	3.65%	2.48%	1.96%	1.72%	1.37%	1.33%	1.16%	1.36%	1.31%
8	4.15%	2.89%	2.62%	2.28%	2.29%	2.13%	2.06%	1.81%	1.73%
9	4.33%	3.70%	3.20%	2.54%	2.34%	1.96%	1.72%	1.62%	1.58%
10	5.01%	3.60%	3.02%	2.46%	2.15%	1.98%	1.77%	1.87%	1.74%
Elastic Net									
3	3.79%	3.00%	2.76%	2.26%	1.99%	2.12%	1.78%	1.44%	1.49%
4	3.40%	2.47%	1.96%	1.83%	1.43%	1.21%	1.34%	1.32%	1.17%
5	2.53%	2.22%	1.69%	1.62%	1.27%	1.17%	1.43%	1.32%	1.16%
6	3.25%	2.17%	2.18%	1.69%	1.44%	1.61%	1.31%	1.25%	1.20%
7	3.46%	2.62%	2.00%	1.92%	1.79%	1.83%	1.63%	1.63%	1.63%
8	3.34%	3.02%	1.83%	1.28%	1.41%	1.48%	1.35%	1.24%	1.05%
9	4.34%	3.25%	3.06%	2.43%	2.34%	2.13%	1.95%	2.01%	1.75%
10	4.50%	3.20%	3.09%	2.37%	2.05%	1.81%	1.66%	1.55%	1.55%

(b) Heston

Number of basis functions	2	3	4	5	6	7	8	9	10
					Number of paths (in thousands)				
OLS									
3	7.73%	7.82%	7.48%	6.87%	6.99%	6.41%	6.45%	6.33%	6.57%
4	9.82%	9.15%	8.41%	7.69%	7.28%	6.79%	6.51%	5.99%	6.04%
5	8.54%	7.69%	6.49%	7.86%	7.45%	7.08%	6.73%	6.35%	6.22%
6	8.78%	8.59%	7.52%	7.21%	7.08%	7.00%	6.80%	6.87%	6.77%
7	10.86%	9.47%	8.59%	8.53%	8.13%	7.77%	7.55%	7.17%	7.13%
8	8.98%	8.16%	8.29%	7.55%	7.36%	7.23%	7.20%	7.10%	6.94%
9	8.92%	8.93%	8.52%	8.21%	8.29%	8.16%	7.80%	7.66%	7.46%
10	9.18%	8.21%	8.16%	7.44%	7.47%	7.40%	7.10%	7.20%	7.08%
LASSO									
3	6.63%	6.89%	6.73%	6.13%	6.29%	5.91%	6.17%	5.92%	6.10%
4	9.06%	8.11%	7.42%	7.13%	6.61%	6.50%	6.16%	5.83%	5.52%
5	6.97%	5.78%	5.14%	6.60%	6.31%	5.98%	5.72%	5.57%	5.57%
6	7.89%	7.00%	5.96%	5.78%	5.84%	5.96%	5.76%	5.77%	5.69%
7	9.07%	7.88%	7.48%	7.09%	6.84%	6.71%	6.43%	6.61%	6.44%
8	6.88%	6.47%	6.97%	6.57%	6.42%	6.23%	6.25%	6.06%	6.20%
9	7.26%	7.43%	7.34%	7.03%	7.07%	7.13%	6.86%	6.91%	6.69%
10	7.54%	6.97%	6.99%	6.71%	6.58%	6.47%	6.86%	6.84%	6.74%
Ridge									
3	7.30%	7.29%	7.10%	6.33%	6.65%	6.21%	6.30%	6.13%	6.35%
4	9.15%	8.52%	7.62%	7.31%	7.04%	6.55%	6.31%	5.95%	5.76%
5	7.68%	6.61%	5.91%	6.97%	6.72%	6.51%	6.37%	5.83%	6.02%
6	9.84%	8.13%	7.65%	6.43%	6.46%	6.44%	6.51%	6.24%	6.35%
7	9.60%	8.55%	8.26%	7.65%	7.40%	7.24%	7.14%	6.96%	6.91%
8	7.35%	6.87%	7.13%	6.71%	6.80%	6.42%	6.48%	6.37%	6.40%
9	7.57%	7.56%	7.63%	7.56%	7.28%	7.32%	7.12%	7.22%	7.06%
10	7.77%	7.46%	7.66%	7.33%	7.22%	6.97%	7.28%	7.33%	7.27%
Elastic Net									
3	6.38%	6.80%	6.72%	6.15%	6.31%	5.91%	6.18%	5.98%	6.21%
4	9.10%	8.08%	7.52%	7.07%	6.69%	6.47%	6.20%	5.82%	5.53%
5	7.17%	6.10%	5.15%	6.51%	6.35%	6.01%	5.73%	5.58%	5.65%
6	7.92%	7.12%	6.22%	6.08%	5.96%	6.07%	5.84%	5.95%	5.78%
7	9.19%	8.26%	7.59%	7.19%	6.96%	6.88%	6.60%	6.77%	6.69%
8	7.13%	6.54%	6.92%	6.55%	6.40%	6.21%	6.33%	6.25%	6.30%
9	7.26%	7.47%	7.21%	7.00%	7.03%	7.15%	6.91%	6.85%	6.71%
10	7.52%	7.08%	7.07%	6.84%	6.71%	6.71%	6.84%	6.95%	6.76%

(c) Meixner

Number of basis functions	2	3	4	5	6	7	8	9	10
					Number of paths (in thousands)				
OLS									
3	9.02%	8.80%	8.65%	8.61%	8.49%	8.41%	8.25%	8.34%	8.32%
4	9.34%	9.14%	8.99%	8.95%	8.78%	8.65%	8.58%	8.58%	8.62%
5	9.53%	9.35%	9.11%	9.01%	8.82%	8.71%	8.62%	8.67%	8.66%
6	9.74%	9.56%	9.24%	9.15%	8.95%	8.79%	8.71%	8.79%	8.80%
7	10.01%	9.65%	9.43%	9.29%	9.05%	8.94%	8.87%	8.89%	8.86%
8	10.15%	9.74%	9.42%	9.29%	9.11%	8.95%	8.90%	8.90%	8.88%
9	10.26%	9.87%	9.50%	9.29%	9.11%	8.98%	8.96%	8.95%	8.94%
10	10.25%	9.86%	9.59%	9.39%	9.16%	9.04%	8.95%	8.95%	8.98%
LASSO									
3	8.05%	7.91%	7.77%	7.65%	7.59%	7.53%	7.40%	7.52%	7.55%
4	8.44%	8.44%	8.22%	8.16%	8.07%	8.03%	7.94%	8.01%	8.08%
5	8.67%	8.65%	8.47%	8.46%	8.33%	8.25%	8.17%	8.24%	8.27%
6	8.80%	8.79%	8.59%	8.57%	8.48%	8.40%	8.34%	8.35%	8.38%
7	8.92%	8.92%	8.68%	8.66%	8.52%	8.48%	8.38%	8.42%	8.47%
8	8.99%	9.03%	8.72%	8.64%	8.55%	8.46%	8.40%	8.43%	8.50%
9	9.13%	9.01%	8.83%	8.73%	8.67%	8.51%	8.45%	8.45%	8.47%
10	9.21%	9.15%	8.88%	8.82%	8.70%	8.57%	8.51%	8.52%	8.57%
Ridge									
3	8.78%	8.65%	8.56%	8.56%	8.43%	8.36%	8.26%	8.32%	8.28%
4	8.96%	8.86%	8.68%	8.70%	8.56%	8.43%	8.37%	8.39%	8.45%
5	8.99%	8.99%	8.76%	8.79%	8.71%	8.53%	8.48%	8.50%	8.53%
6	9.07%	9.09%	8.93%	8.81%	8.69%	8.57%	8.49%	8.58%	8.56%
7	9.35%	9.18%	8.91%	8.89%	8.73%	8.63%	8.56%	8.60%	8.58%
8	9.41%	9.24%	9.02%	9.00%	8.76%	8.65%	8.56%	8.68%	8.61%
9	9.45%	9.35%	9.14%	8.99%	8.87%	8.75%	8.70%	8.70%	8.69%
10	9.67%	9.32%	9.18%	9.15%	8.97%	8.79%	8.72%	8.79%	8.77%
Elastic Net									
3	8.00%	7.89%	7.76%	7.64%	7.58%	7.50%	7.41%	7.53%	7.57%
4	8.34%	8.36%	8.12%	8.05%	7.98%	7.89%	7.81%	7.93%	7.98%
5	8.73%	8.58%	8.50%	8.46%	8.32%	8.27%	8.18%	8.23%	8.28%
6	8.94%	8.76%	8.64%	8.57%	8.51%	8.42%	8.32%	8.38%	8.43%
7	9.13%	8.98%	8.73%	8.69%	8.55%	8.49%	8.42%	8.47%	8.48%
8	9.06%	9.00%	8.76%	8.73%	8.58%	8.50%	8.43%	8.49%	8.49%
9	9.31%	9.09%	8.90%	8.79%	8.70%	8.61%	8.49%	8.51%	8.56%
10	9.38%	9.20%	8.99%	8.86%	8.72%	8.64%	8.57%	8.60%	8.60%

Table 17.2. *Precisions obtained for (a) GBM, (b) Heston model and (c) Meixner-based process, with green color gradients used to illustrate the ADPBM between the estimation methods for same sample size/number of basis function combination. For a color version of this table, see www.iste.co.uk/dimotikalis/data4.zip*

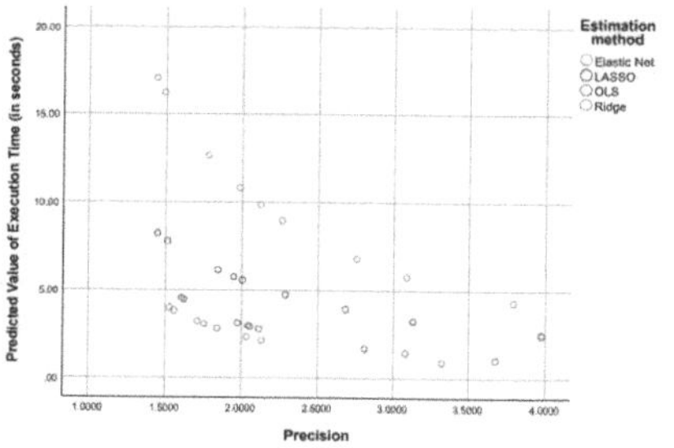

(a) GBM - 3 b.f.s

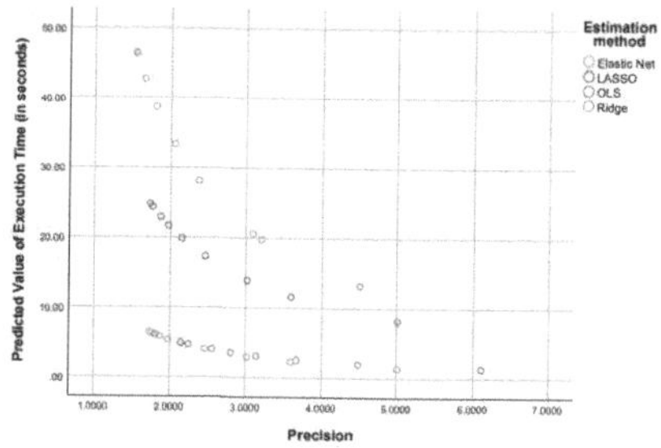

(b) GBM - 10 b.f.s

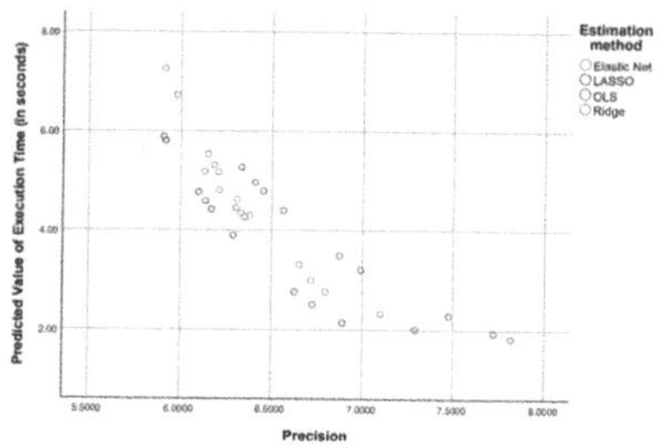

(c) Heston - 3 b.f.s

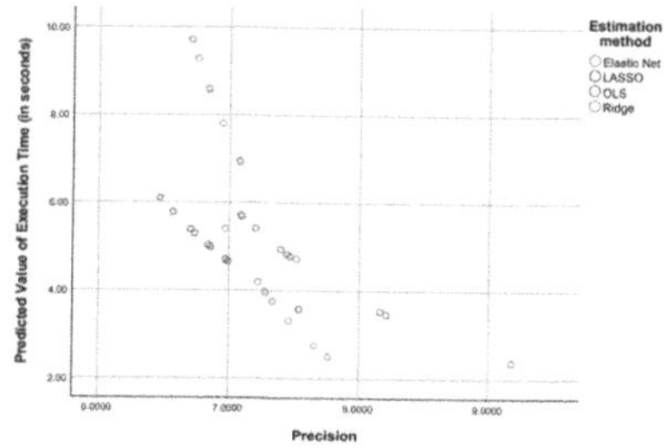

(d) Heston - 10 b.f.s

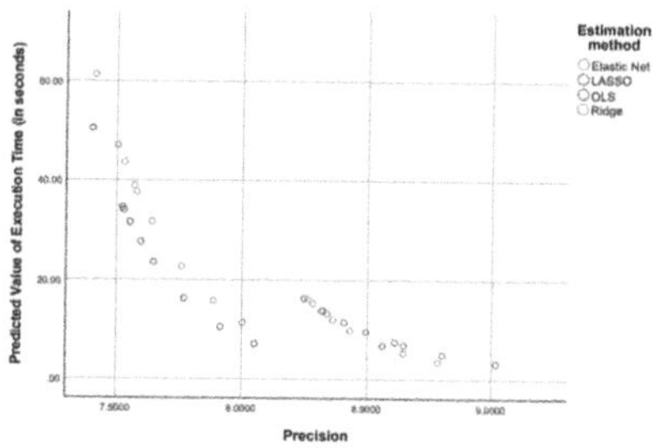

(e) Meixner - 3 b.f.s

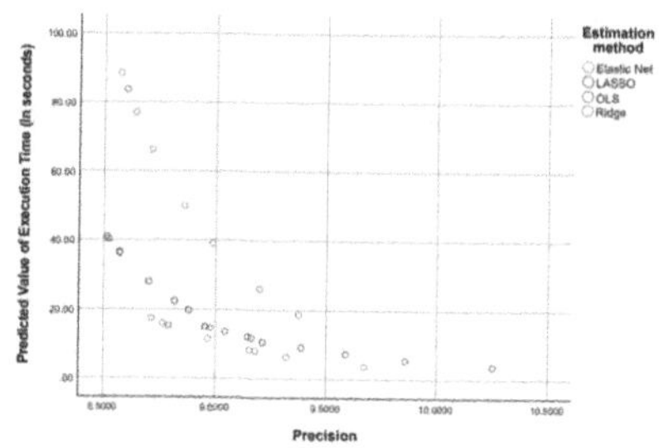

(f) Meixner - 10 b.f.s

Figure 17.2. *Execution times versus precision for polynomials with 3 and 10 basis functions for the different methods (see legend) and the different processes. For a color version of this figure, see www.iste.co.uk/dimotikalis/data4.zip*

17.6. Conclusion

This chapter presents a simulation design on three processes – GBM, the Heston model a Meixner based model – to analyze the percentage precision of the achieved American price option. The simulation design consisted of different combinations of number of sample paths and number of basis functions. The execution time was also calculated for each of these combinations. It has been concluded that a LASSO-type regression within the LS framework can be a desirable adaptation for the LS algorithm as it can often yield the best precision for comparable execution time, particularly with more complex models, such as the Heston and the Meixner-based one. EN, on the contrary, can offer similar precision to LASSO for the same sample size/number of basis functions but at higher computational expense. It has thus indicated not to provide any purposeful benefits. OLS and Ridge adaptations are less computationally intensive, but generally inferior for more complex processes than GBM. This study, however, does indicate that Ridge regression outperforms OLS in terms of precision, while having a similar computational expense. This conclusion is corroborated in Tompaidis and Yang (2014). It has also been shown that increasing the number of basis functions increases the computational time but does not provide any added benefit in terms of precision.

Further work in this field could include the use of other regularization approaches that have not yet been attempted, and a more in-depth investigation of execution time versus precision benefits could be tackled. Furthermore, the performance of such methods using other important models in finance such as the double Heston model in Christoffersen et al. (2009) could also be investigated.

17.7. References

Areal, N., Rodrigues, A., Armada, M.R. (2008). On improving the least squares Monte Carlo option valuation method. *Review of Derivatives Research*, 11(1), 119–151.

Christoffersen, P., Heston, S., Jacobs, K. (2009). The shape and term structure of the index option smirk: Why multifactor stochastic volatility models work so well. *Management Science*, 55(12), 1914–1932.

Elliot, R. and Kopp, P. (2004). *Mathematics of Financial Markets*, 2nd edition. Springer, New York.

Gerhold, S. (2011). The Longstaff-Schwartz algorithm for Lévy models: Results on fast and slow convergence. *The Annals of Applied Probability*, 22(2), 589–608.

Heston, S.L. (2008). A closed-form solution for options with stochastic volatility with applications to bond and currency options. *The Review of Financial Studies*, 6(2), 327–343.

Kloeden, P.E. and Platen, E. (1992). *Numerical Solutions of Stochastic Differential Equations*. Springer, Berlin, Heidelberg.

Kohler, M. (2008). A regression-based smoothing spline Monte Carlo algorithm for pricing American options. *AStA Advances in Statistical Analysis*, 92(2), 553–178.

Kohler, M., Krzyzak, M., Todorovic, N. (2010). Pricing of high-dimensional American options by neural networks. *Mathematical Finance: An International Journal of Mathematics, Statistics and Financial Economics*, 20(3), 383–410.

Lapeyre, B. and Lelong, J. (2021). Neural network regression for Bermudan option pricing. *Monte Carlo Methods and Applications*, 27(3), 227–247.

Longstaff, F.A. and Schwartz, E.S. (2001). Valuing American options by simulation: A simple least squares approach. *Review of Financial Studies*, 14(1), 113–147.

Mazzola, E. and Muliere, P. (2011). Reviewing alternative characterizations of Meixner process. *Probability Surveys*, 8, 127–154.

Moreno, M. and Navas, J.F. (2003). On the robustness of least-squares Monte Carlo (LSM) for pricing of American derivatives. *Review of Derivatives Research*, 6, 107–128.

Pliska, S. (1997). *Introduction to Mathematical Finance*. Blackwell Publishers, Oxford.

Sansom, A. (2024). Longstaff Schwartz American option price analysis. Matlab Central File Exchange [Online]. Available at: https://www.mathworks.com/matlabcentral/fileexchange/64716-longstaff-schwartz-american-option-price-analysis.

Schoutens, W. (2002). The Meixner process: Theory and applications in finance. *Finance. Mini-proceedings: 2nd MaPhySto Conference on Levy Processes – Theory and Applications*, Aarhus.

Stentoft, L. (2004). Convergence of the least squares Monte Carlo approach to American option valuation. *Management Science*, 50(9), 1193–1203.

Suda, D., Borg Inguanez, M., Cilia, L. (2023). Supplementary material – penalised regression adaptations of the longstaff-schwartz algorithm for pricing American options. Github [Online]. Available at: https://github.com/davidsuda80/sudaborginguanezcilia.

Tompaidis, S. and Yang, C. (2014). Pricing American-style options by Monte Carlo simulation: Alternatives to ordinary least squares. *Journal of Computational Finance*, 18(1), 121–143.

18

International Auditing Standards and Their Contribution to the Limitation of Accounting Fraud

The globalization of the economy and the constantly evolving financial environment have led to the rise of falsification of financial statements. This phenomenon of accounting fraud has been highlighted by the international literature, from real cases such as the example of Enron. The effects of this phenomenon can be catastrophic. The reasons for the appearance of this form of accounting fraud are due to many different factors and motivations, which auditors try to discover in order to limit this form of fraud. The role of International Auditing Standards is significant, in terms of preventive measures and solutions similar incidents. Therefore, this research aims to highlight the most important factors and motivations of financial statement falsification and the most important treatment of financial statement falsification from both the auditors' and the large audited companies' point of view, as well as the positive contribution of the current institutional framework to limit fraud. For these research purposes, two different questionnaires were sent – to auditors and to audited companies – in order to compare their opinions. The results of the research highlighted the "*lack of an effective control system*" as the most important factor in the falsification of financial statements, as well as the "*maximization of profits*" as the most important motivation that leads to the phenomena of fraud and "*the positive contribution of the institutional framework to the limitation of fraud*". Finally, the "*mandatory and faithful implementation of accounting and auditing standards*" is, according to the results, the best treatment in this phenomenon.

18.1. Introduction

Nowadays, one of the most important topics that accounting and auditing science deals with is the internationally and widely accepted International Auditing Standards. The globalization of the economy and the abolition of financial borders

Chapter written by Efthalia TABOURATZI and Leonidas FANOURAKIS.

created new data in the modern way of operation of auditing companies, gradually changing their way of acting in relation to their compliance with International Auditing Standards, with the ultimate goal of prevention to avoid fraud phenomena and above all to ensure a better quality audit. The need, therefore, for a more reliable and objective audit led to the gradual revision of these standards, where, over time, more and more countries began to respond and adopt these standards in the implementation of audits.

As competition increases, companies increasingly intensify their desire to maximize their profits and gain a more advantageous position in the market, engaging in fraudulent actions of falsification-alteration of financial statements, bringing about significant negative financial consequences. The concept of accounting fraud mainly refers to the "beautification" of financial statements in order to provide fictitious information that creates a platonic environment for the company, leading it closer to its goals as well as misinforming the concerned users.

In an economy, therefore, where over time accounting frauds and scandals increase rapidly, there is an urgent need to ensure the reliability of the companies' financial statements, through audit procedures. The establishment of the audit came as a result of the emergence of huge accounting frauds with the involvement of world-renowned audit firms, both in the USA and in Europe, which led to the subsequent establishment of a new legislative framework and audit mechanisms, mainly aiming at better reliability of financial statements, through stricter audits.

The contribution of International Auditing Standards to the limitation of accounting fraud has proven to be particularly effective by ensuring the reliability of the financial data of companies. The International Standards on Auditing essentially illustrate the guidelines that auditors should follow in order to provide a more credible audit (Simunic et al. 2016)[1].

The topic presented in this chapter is the presentation and analysis of the International Auditing Standards, the assurance of the quality of the audit, as well as the effective treatment of fraud and irregularities in the financial statements of economic entities. More specifically, the primary objective is to understand the way in which the modern audit process works, within the framework of the International Auditing Standards adopted by countries, in order to ensure a better quality, and more correct and safer audit methods that will reduce fraud phenomena to a minimum through the financial statements of the companies, as well as the subsequent potential challenges of huge scandals. Also, one of the main purposes of

1 Simunic, D.A., Ye, M., Zhang, P. (2016). The joint effects of multiple legal system characteristics on auditing standards and auditor behavior. *Contemporary Accounting Research*, 34(1), 7–38.

this work is to answer essential questions regarding the contribution of International Auditing Standards to the limitation of accounting fraud. Essentially, through the international bibliography, an effort will be made to perceive and understand the observance of the International Auditing Standards, the reasons and causes of the appearance of accounting frauds in the financial statements of the companies, the subsequent consequences, as well as the ways of dealing with them.

18.2. Literature review

18.2.1. *International Auditing Standards*

The International Standards of Auditing (ISA) are professional standards for conducting financial audits of financial statements. These standards are issued by IFAC, through the International Accounting and Assurance Standards Board (IAASB), which operates under the supervision of the International Federation of Accountants. The ultimate goal of the Federation is the creation of high-quality audit standards, which will facilitate auditors in their audit procedures as well as strengthening cooperation with other international organizations (Ghafran and O'Sullivan 2017)[2].

In their research, Simunic et al. (2016)[3] emphasized that the need to create International Auditing Standards came as a result of the alarming increase in continuous fraud in the financial statements of mainly colossal companies, which resulted in the subsequent explosion of huge scandals. The gradual development and evolution of these standards aimed to ensure the provision of more reliable and truthful financial statement information to interested users, and it is also worth noting that over time, more and more countries began to adopt the standards in their audit procedures in order to ensure a better quality and creditable control.

Audit quality has become a vital part of the financial market as it promotes a sense of trust and credibility. According to the research of Perera and Wijerathna (2020)[4], there are five indicators of audit quality corresponding to five indicators. Firstly, individual auditor activity refers to how the activity of the independent auditor could be reflected in audit quality. Secondly, the auditor's mood or influence accounts for how the auditor's mood or outcome could be reflected in audit quality.

---

2 Ghafran, C. and O'Sullivan, N. (2017). The impact of audit committee expertise on audit quality: Evidence from UK audit fees. *The British Accounting Review*, 49(6), 578–593.

3 Simunic, D.A., Ye, M., Zhang, P. (2016). The joint effects of multiple legal system characteristics on auditing standards and auditor behavior. *Contemporary Accounting Research*.

4 Perera, P. and Wijerathna, H.S. (2020). Audit quality: Perception of audit practitioners in Sri Lanka. *17th International Conference on Business Management (ICBM 2020)*.

Thirdly, the size of the audit firm can be measured using the number of partners in the audit profession. Also, the business, accounting and auditing environment is the fourth indicator which refers to the way in which the business, accounting and auditing environment could reflect the quality of the audit. Finally, legal requirements indicate that an audit must be conducted in accordance with relevant legal and regulatory requirements.

The main purpose of the International Standards on Auditing, therefore, is to provide auditors with an authoritative guideline on modern auditing practice that should contribute to safeguarding not only the interests of interested users of financial statements but also of the auditor themselves. To achieve this goal, auditing standards must reflect modern legislation. It is quite important for auditors to keep themselves fully informed of all legal responsibilities that may apply to them (Gantz 2014)[5].

18.2.2. *Accounting fraud – falsification of financial statements*

The concept of accounting fraud is broad and refers mainly to the intentional manipulation of financial statements, which aims to create an illusion, regarding the wealth of a company in order to either claim a more favorable financing or to avoid debt obligations. Accounting fraud is mainly rooted in the unethical behavior of a person who does not have sufficient ethical training, while it has a significant negative impact on the reputation and financial position of the company (Tutino and Berlo 2019)[6].

Wuerges and Borba (2010)[7] state that "accounting fraud is defined as the deliberate inaccuracy of financial reports, in violation of generally accepted accounting principles, with the aim of forcing certain individuals to act against their interests".

The term "*Accounting Fraud*" refers to illegal actions on the accounting books of an economic entity in order to mislead the concerned users regarding the true picture of the audited economic entity (Tommasetti et al. 2021)[8]. As stated in the research

5 Gantz, S.D. (ed.) (2014). Audit-related organizations, standards, and certifications. In *The Basics of IT Audit Purposes, Processes, and Practical Information*. Syngress, Waltham, MA, 197–219.

6 Tutino, M. and Berlo, M. (2019). Accounting fraud: A literature review. *Risk Governance and Control: Financial Markets & Institutions*, 9(1), 8–25.

7 Wuerges, A.F.E. and Borba, J.A. (2010). Accounting fraud detection: Is it possible to quantify undiscovered cases?. *SSRN Electronic Journal*.

8 Tommasetti, R., Leite, R.O., Maia, V.M., Macedo, M.A.D.S. (2021). Revisiting the accounting fraud components: A bottom-up approach using the twitter platform. *SAGE Open*, 11(4), 1–12.

by Amina (2021)[9], the International Standards on Auditing (ISA) define fraud as follows: "Fraud is an intentional act committed by one or more persons among the members of management or of third parties, which includes the use of misleading information to obtain an unjustified or illegal advantage". In a constantly changing environment, due to new international requirements and rapid changes, the problem of accounting fraud detection has become more important. More specifically, the falsification of financial statements aims to mislead interested users regarding the performance of the respective economic entity, in order to conceal any improprieties and to present an improved and false image of the business in terms of its profits and efficiency. This act, as literature has shown, in most cases brings temporary "positive" results by satisfying the people who falsify, but in the medium term, these frauds are revealed, bringing dramatic consequences to the future operation and viability of the business (Pazarskis et al. 2017)[10].

International Standard on Auditing 240, defines fraud as "an intentional act committed by one or more persons in the management group who are responsible to the entity's government, employees or third parties, which involves the use of deception to obtain unfair or illegal advantage". Based on this standard, the errors are considered to be mainly due to fraudulent financial data leading in turn to the misleading image of the financial statements of the audited company using various techniques such as, for example, the manipulation or falsification of accounting records or even the incorrect implementation of generally accepted accounting principles (Josiah et al. 2020)[11].

In addition, one of the most frequent forms of falsification of financial statements is deliberate omissions and disclosures or even the presentation of insufficient disclosures regarding accounting standards, principles and practices as well as the use of unfair accounting tricks and practices regarding the management of profits of the company, thus presenting an altered image of the company in terms of its sustainability (Rezaee 2005)[12]. Also, senior executives may often commit

9 Amina, Z. (2021). Financial fraud detection and the importance of internal control. *International Journal of Accounting and Financial Reporting*, 11(4), 28.

10 Pazarskis, M., Drogalas, G., Baltzi, K. (2017). Detecting false financial statements: Evidence from Greece in the period of economic crisis. *Investment Management and Financial Innovations*, 14(3), 102–112.

11 Josiah, M., Ekundayo, G., Adeboye, Moses, O. (2020). Audit-quality-and-auditors-independence. *AE-Funai Journal of Accounting, Business and Finance (FJABAF)*, 6(1), 107–118.

12 Rezaee, Z. (2005). Causes, consequences, and deterence of financial statement fraud. *Critical Perspectives on Accounting*, 16(3), 277–298. doi: 10.1016/s1045-2354(03)00072-8.

12 C.R.I.M.E.: Cooking, Recipes, Incentives, Monitoring, End Results.

falsification of financial statements to defraud investors and lenders or to inflate profits to earn higher salaries and bonuses (Spathis et al. 2002)[13].

18.2.3. *The Fraud Triangle*

The Fraud Triangle theory is an idea that examines the cause of fraud. This concept was first coined by Donald R. Cressey in 1953, who called it the "*Fraud Triangle*". The Fraud Triangle is a model for explaining the factors that cause someone to commit professional fraud. It consists of three elements, which collectively lead to potentially fraudulent behavior. More specifically, this aforementioned model is based on the premise that fraud is likely to result from a combination of three factors, which are *motivation/pressure*, *opportunity* and *rationalization/behavior*.

The first element of the Fraud Triangle's tripartite that of *motivation/pressure*, regarding the manifestation of fraud through the preparation of altered financial statements, is evident in cases where this pressure primarily leads business executives to take substantial risks in order to succeed their goals. Key motivations that drive executives and management to commit fraud are the obsession for systematic success, expensive lifestyle habits, high debts and, in general, pressure from management regarding pay or promotion. The usual reason for this element according to the international literature is the pressure to achieve the desired financial results and by extension the maximization of profits.

As for the second element, that of *opportunity*, this appears when internal audit is non-existent or when the rules and limits set are not fully clarified. Fraud in this case can be carried out mainly when people of "trust" hold important positions and know exactly the weaknesses that exist in the inner workings of each company, and by taking advantage of their position and the weaknesses of the company they can easily carry out fraudulent phenomena for their own benefit their (Gaganis and Zopounidis 2009)[14].

Finally, the third element, which refers to *rationalization/behavior*, means that the employee has found ways to justify the involved fraud in their conscience. Essentially, in this case, the workers are led to methods of deception and illegal acts in cases such as when they feel wronged in terms of their wages from the company,

---

13 Spathis, C., Doumpos, M., Zopounidis, C. (2002). Detecting falsified financial statements: A comparative study using multicriteria analysis and multivariate statistical techniques. *The European Accounting Review*, 11(3), 509–535.

14 Gaganis, Ch. and Zopounidis, K. (2009). *Recognition of Falsified Accounting Statements*. Kleidaritmos, Athens.

compared to the hours worked. Such actions are often carried out by honest people due to the possible pressure they may be under as mentioned above (Loumiotis and Tzifas 2017)[15].

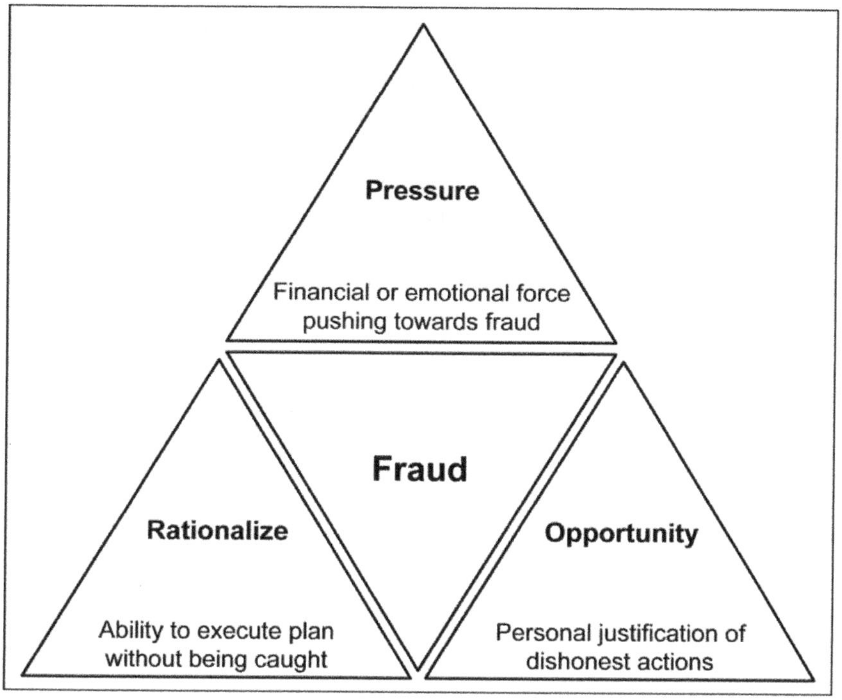

Figure 18.1. *Fraud Triangle (source: Sanchez et al. 2018)*[16]

The triptych described by the Fraud Triangle has over time helped auditors quite a bit in identifying and preventing accounting fraud phenomena, becoming one of the most important accounting fraud detection tools. The lack of moral value and skepticism, safe internal barriers and the pressure that individuals are under in many cases are the main reasons why the Fraud Triangle is helping auditors to understand the drivers of accounting fraud.

15 Loumiotis, V. and Tzifas, V. (2017). *Basic Guidelines for the Implementation of International Auditing Standards*. SOL, Athens.

16 Sanchez, M., Torres, J., Zambrano, P., Flores, P. (2018). FraudFind: Financial fraud detection by analyzing human behavior. *2018 IEEE 8th Annual Computing and Communication Workshop and Conference (CCWC)*.

18.2.4. *Fraud Diamond*

Over time, the well-known Fraud Diamond was created by Wolfe and Hermanson in 2004, which added another factor, that of the fraudster's *capability* to avoid detection. In general, it can be concluded that pressure is the motivation to commit fraud by giving the perpetrator the opportunity to commit fraud, while rationalization is the justification for manipulation to be done and is supported by the perpetrator's ability.

The *capability* is the advantageous position and the ability of the employees to penetrate the internal audits of the company, to exploit this advantageous position and to obtain more and more benefits, misappropriating elements of the business and thereby falsifying the financial statements in the course of management and auditors (Umar et al. 2020)[17].

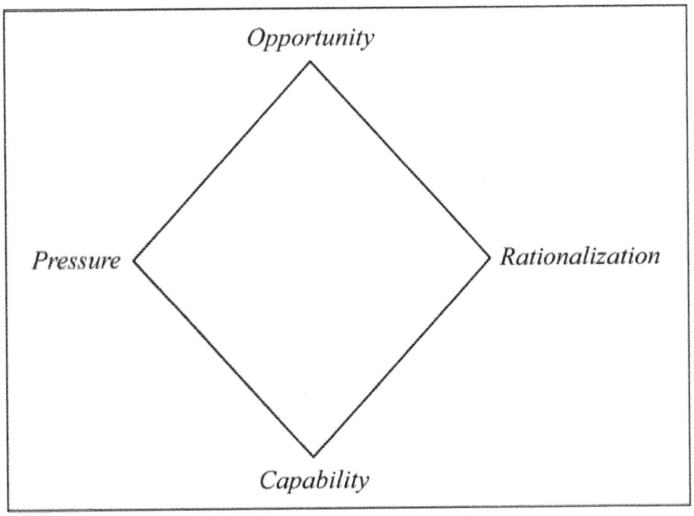

Figure 18.2. *Fraud Diamond (source: Umar et al. 2020)*

Essentially, the fourth element added with the Fraud Diamond was the *ability* of the individual to commit illegal activities by exploiting the weaknesses of the internal audit system, taking advantage of any opportunity to commit fraud either for their own benefit or for the benefit of the business. Therefore, the fraud can come

17 Umar, H., Partahi, D., Purba, R. (2020). Fraud Diamond analysis in detecting fraudulent financial report. *April 2020 International Journal of Scientific & Technology Research*, 9(3), 6638–6646.

from the right person who has the right position in the company, exploits the gaps in the internal security barriers and has the ability to do so, turning the opportunity into reality (Wolfe and Hermanson 2004)[18].

18.2.5. *Detection and prevention of accounting fraud*

Detecting and preventing accounting fraud is one of the most important objectives of auditors, as it demonstrates their effective contribution and work. Essentially, it is a challenge for them as they are called upon to discover and identify falsification phenomena and any irregularities, while protecting both the audited company itself and the domestic financial situation in general.

As Mangala and Kumari (2017)[19] state, detecting accounting fraud is not always easy, while appropriate procedures and control mechanisms are needed to combat it. An economic entity must develop a four-point anti-fraud framework consisting of *knowledge, prevention, detection* and *action*, as shown in Figure 18.3.

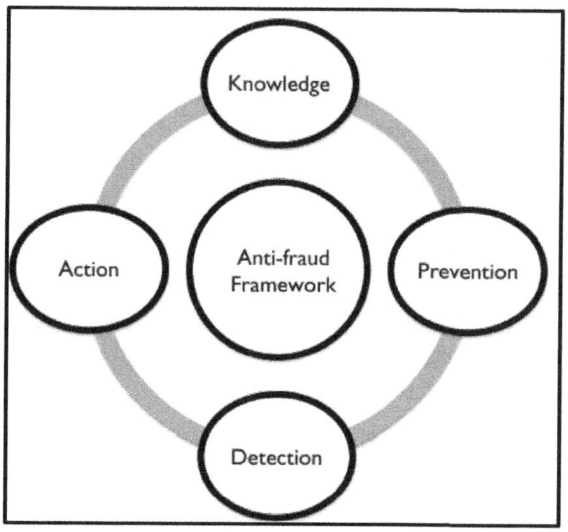

Figure 18.3. *Anti-fraud framework (source: Albrecht et al. 2012)*[20]

18 Wolfe, D.T. and Hermanson, D.R. (2004). The Fraud Diamond: Considering the four elements of fraud. *CPA Journal*, 74(12), 38–42.

19 Mangala, D. and Kumari, P. (2014). Auditors' perceptions of the effectiveness of fraud prevention and detection method. *Indian Journal of Corporate Governance*, 10(2), 118–142.

20 Albrecht, W.S., Albrecht, C.O., Albrecht, C.C., Zimbelman, M.F. (2012). *Fraud Examination*, 4th edition. Cengage Learning, Mason.

Knowledge and *prevention* are proactive measures to combat fraud, while *detection* and *action* are subsequent measures. The basis for combating fraud is knowledge about the concept and nature of fraud, the reasons and causes for which it exists as well as the subsequent consequences. Once the roots of the fraud are understood, prevention and follow-up measures must be taken to ensure that it does not occur again (Bolton and Hand 2002)[21].

The detection of accounting fraud can come with the help of various methods such as statutory audit, effective corporate governance and internal audit. The appearance of fraud or a material error creates the subsequent need to take strict measures, such as dismissal from the company, demotion, the use of criminal actions, as well as even reporting to the judicial authorities in order for the law to proceed and bring the parties involved into compliance. This creates a sense of fear of committing future fraud as it effectively "warns" involved members of the consequences of fraud.

One of the most important fraud prevention methods is internal audit, according to Rezaee (2005)[22]. Internal auditors are well aware of the organizational environment and structure of the audited company. In addition, they are responsible for internal oversight and ensure compliance with laws and regulations. Therefore, the effectiveness of internal audit as a means of combating fraud is becoming more and more evident. Also, the external audit is also an important fraud prevention method as according to the law and the ISA, 450 auditors are required to report fraud or material misstatements to either management or the audit committee and the government (Alleyne and Howard 2005[23]; Loumiotis and Tzifas 2017)[24].

The PwC research report (2011) found that 14% of fraud cases could be detected by risk assessment. In addition, PwC (2016) highlighted real-life examples that underlie accounting fraud phenomena such as lavish lifestyles, fake accounts, as well as incomplete documents (Salleh and Othman 2016)[25].

---

21 Bolton, R.J. and Hand, D.J. (2002). Statistical fraud detection: A review. *Statistical Science*, 17(3), 235–249.

22 Rezaee, Z. (2005). Causes, consequences, and deterrence of financial statement fraud. *Critical Perspectives on Accounting*.

23 Alleyne, P. and Howard, M. (2005). An exploratory study of auditors' responsibility for fraud detection in Barbados. *Managerial Auditing Journal*, 20(3), 284–303.

24 Loumiotis, V. and Tzifas, V. (2017). *Basic Guidelines for the Implementation of International Auditing Standards*. SOL, Athens.

25 Salleh, S.M. and Othman, R. (2016). Board of director's attributes as deterrence to corporate fraud. *Procedia Economics and Finance*, 35, 82–91.

It is worth emphasizing that employees are a key part of every company and act as an important tool for fraud audit. Therefore, employees should be properly trained in order to be aware not only of the concept of fraud, but also to recognize any suspicious movement that leads to fraud. Therefore, it is important that businesses make deliberate efforts to educate employees about their role in creating a healthy company, with no incentive for fraud and wrongdoing (Mangala and Kumari 2017)[26].

In addition, the auditor analyzes the financial statements for material inaccuracies, according to the ISA 240. According to Baesens et al. (2015)[27], the fight against fraud is based on two very important elements, the detection and prevention of fraud. Fraud detection refers to the ability to identify or discover fraudulent activities, while fraud prevention refers to measures that can be taken to avoid or minimize fraud. These two elements can complement each other, in order to fulfill their goal, i.e. to eliminate the phenomena of accounting fraud that exist and those that lurk. The fraud life cycle as highlighted by Baesen et al. (2015)[28] depicts four main activities – fraud detection, amplification, confirmation and prevention.

18.3. Empirical analysis

18.3.1. *Introduction*

This research aims, through the implementation of two written anonymous questionnaires, to examine the opinion of both auditors and audited companies regarding the phenomena of accounting fraud. More specifically, the first questionnaire was addressed exclusively to external, internal and trainee auditors, in order to make an anonymous record of their opinions on how to manage, deal with and prevent accounting fraud phenomena. The second questionnaire was addressed to large audited companies[29] – listed and unlisted – operating throughout the

26 Mangala, D. and Kumari, P. (2014). Auditors' perceptions of the effectiveness of fraud prevention and detection method. *Indian Journal of Corporate Governance*, 10(2), 118–142.

27 Baesens, B., Van Vlasselaer, V., Verbeke, W. (2015). *Fraud Analytics Using Descriptive, Predictive, and Social Network Techniques: A Guide to Data Science for Fraud Detection.* John Wiley & Sons Inc, Hoboken.

28 Baesens, B., Van Vlasselaer, V., Verbeke, W. (2015). *Fraud Analytics Using Descriptive, Predictive, and Social Network Techniques: A Guide to Data Science for Fraud Detection.* John Wiley & Sons Inc, Hoboken.

29 Large companies: according to Law 4308/2014 (G.A.S.), entities are classified on the basis of their size as large, if at least two of the three following limits apply in the year of closing their balance sheet: 1. Total Balance Sheet (Assets) >€20,000,000, 2.Net Turnover >€40,000,000, and 3. Average Number of Staff in Use >250.

territory of Greece, with the ultimate goal of also recording their opinions regarding the falsification of financial statements, the motivations, the factors as well as the relationship – cooperation they have with the auditors. Essentially, the primary purpose of this chapter is to present the opinions of both parties – auditors and audited companies – regarding the falsification of financial statements, and mainly a comparative picture of the way in which the contracting parties perceive this falsification, both in terms of the motivations and benefits they believe they can derive and in terms of the factors, management and countermeasures of this fraud. The main research questions concern the factors, motivations, the appropriateness of the institutional framework as well as the prevention of phenomena of falsification of financial statements by the contracting parties of both questionnaires, in order to arrive at a comparative analysis of their opinions and their skepticism.

18.3.2. *Sample*

The sample for this research consists of a different audience for each questionnaire. More specifically:

1) For the questionnaire addressed exclusively to auditors, the sample consists of auditors who practice the profession (internal, external and trainee auditors) throughout Greece.

2) For the questionnaire that was addressed exclusively to large audited companies, the sample consists of executives of listed and un-listed large companies throughout the territory of Greece, who hold board positions, chef of accounting, accounting assistants, as well as office employees.

Both questionnaires of the present survey were sent via the Internet, while they were designed using the survey management software Google Forms. The sending of both questionnaires started in October 2022 and was completed after one month with 55 responses for the auditors and 102 responses for the audited companies. The response rate for both questionnaires was quite satisfactory for the number of questionnaires sent and the time taken.

18.3.3. *Methodology*

The achievement of the above objective was achieved by using closed-type questions through the Likert scale for both questionnaires, in order to measure the opinion of the parties involved – auditors and large audited companies – regarding their attitude to the phenomena of falsification of financial statements. The use of the Likert scale, according to Cohen et al. (2008)[30], gives the possibility of providing multiple answers for a compared question, being a widespread and accepted tool used in modern researches. All questions were aimed at obtaining more and more useful information in order to conduct the following results on the views and perceptions of the stakeholders. The final gathering and processing of the responses was carried out with the help of the Microsoft Excel spreadsheet program and the SPSS statistical software. The diagrams' representation used is in the form of a bar, as they were drawn from the Excel program[31].

18.3.4. *Simple linear regression*

In the first stage, we calculated the simple linear regression through the SPSS statistical software in order to identify if there is a positive correlation between the dependent variable "Job Position" and the independent variables "Factor", "Motivation", "Treatment" and "Institutional Framework". The following are the model assumptions for both questionnaires:

Research cases: auditors

H1: Positive correlation between the job position – auditors and the factors of falsification of financial statements.

H2: Positive correlation between job position – auditors and motivations to falsify financial statements.

H3: Positive correlation between the job position – auditors and the treatment of falsification.

H4: Positive correlation between the job position – auditors and the institutional framework.

Research cases: audited companies

H1: Positive correlation between job position and financial statement falsification factors.

H2: Positive correlation between job position and motivations to falsify financial statements.

H3: Positive correlation between job position and treatment of falsification.

---

30 Cohen, L., Manion, L., Morrison, K. (2008). *Research Methods in Education*, 5th edition. METAIHMIO, Athens.

31 With reference to the percentages below, rounding has been done to the first decimal place.

H4: Positive correlation between the job position and the institutional framework.

Coefficients: Auditors[a]

Model		Unstandardized Coefficients B	Std. Error	Standardized Coefficients Beta	t	Sig.
1	(Constant)	1,519	,347		4,377	,161
	Institutional Framework	,059	,095	,094	,627	,534
	Factor	,129	,108	,181	1,193	,239
	Motivation	,007	,072	,014	,102	,919
	Treatment	,056	,073	,106	,768	,446

a. Dependent Variable: Job Position

Table 18.1.

Coefficients :Companies[a]

Model		Unstandardized Coefficients B	Std. Error	Standardized Coefficients Beta	t	Sig.
1	(Constant)	1,379	,331		4,165	,068
	Factor	,024	,050	,051	,486	,628
	Motivation	,050	,109	,047	,461	,646
	Institutional Framework	,074	,121	,063	,611	,543
	Treatment	,023	,037	,064	,630	,530

a. Dependent Variable: Job Position

Table 18.2.

– Auditors: Job Position = 1.519 + 0.059*Institutional Framework + 0.129*Factor + 0.007*Motivation + 0.056*Treatment.

– Audited companies: Job Position= 1.379 + 0.074*Institutional Framework + 0.024*Factor + 0.050*Motivation + 0.023*Treatment.

As we can see from the regression, there is a positive correlation between the independent variable and the dependent variables in both questionnaires. This shows that the answers to the questionnaires are valid. The results for auditors and companies are presented in more detail below, as well as their comparison.

18.3.5. *Analysis of auditors' questionnaire data*

The results of the auditors as presented in Table 18.3 refer to responses of 55 respondents.

No.	Questions	Answer	
		Frequency	Percent
1.	**Gender**		
	Man	39	71%
	Woman	16	29%
	Total	55	100%
2.	**Age**		
	24-30	11	20%
	30-40	20	36%
	40-50	16	29%
	>50	8	15%
	Total	55	100%
3.	**Education**		
	Ph.D	3	5%
	Professional Certifications (A.C.C.A., C.I.A., C.F.E, A.C.A. C.P.A. e.t.c..)	34	62%
	Master Degree	12	22%
	Higher Education (Bachelor)	6	11%
	Total	55	100%
4.	**Work Experience**		
	1 - 5 έτη	12	22%
	10 - 15 έτη	15	27%
	15 - 20 έτη	7	13%
	5 - 10 έτη	7	13%
	> 20 έτη	14	25%
	Total	55	100%
5.	**Job Position**		
	Trainee Auditor	6	11%
	External Auditor	38	69%
	Internal Auditor	11	20%
	Total	55	100%

Table 18.3.

In more detail, as shown in Table 18.3, a total of 55 auditors responded to the research, with the majority of participants being men (39 responses) and 16 women with a percentage of 71% and 29%, respectively. The work experience results show that most have been working as auditors for 10–15 years with a percentage of 27% (15 responses), as well as more than 20 years with a percentage of 23% (14 responses); this highlights how representative, suitable and experienced the sample is to answer the following questions, collecting reliable responses. Then, follow with a percentage of 22% for the people working in the field for 1–5 years (12 people) and finally the auditors with a previous service of 5–10 years and 15–20 years with a percentage of 7% each.

Regarding the educational level of the respondents, we note that most of the respondents hold some professional certification (C.P.A., A.C.C.A., C.I.A., C.F.E, A.C.A.) with a percentage of 62%; a percentage of the order of 22% hold a master's degree, 11% are graduates of higher education, while only 5% hold a PhD. Therefore, we note that most participants hold some professional certification, which according to ELTE, is pre-requisite for obtaining the license of auditors. Also, for the job position held by the respondents, 69% (38 responses) work as external auditors, 20% (11 responses) as internal auditors, while only 11% (6 responses) are trainee auditors in audit firms.

The results regarding the factors of falsification of financial statements are also quite interesting. In more detail, participants were asked to answer who they consider to be the "most important factor" in falsifying financial statements, in a wide range of responses, as listed in Table 18.4.

Factors of Falsifying Financial Statements										
									Total	
Question	None		A little		Plenty		Enough			
	Frequency	Percentage	Frequency	Percentage	Frequency	Percentage	Frequency	Percentage	Frequency	Percentage
Conceal Obligations and Expenses	6	11%	13	24%	21	38%	15	27%	55	100%
Lack of effective control system	2	4%	17	31%	28	51%	8	14%	55	100%
Unusual transactions at the end of the year that affect the company's profits	1	2%	18	33%	22	40%	14	25%	55	100%
Virtual Income	5	9%	18	33%	16	29%	16	29%	55	100%
Significant deficits in assets	4	7%	15	27%	26	47%	10	19%	55	100%
Insufficient staff in the company	3	6%	18	33%	20	36%	14	25%	55	100%
Data distortion	3	6%	20	36%	17	31%	15	27%	55	100%

Table 18.4.

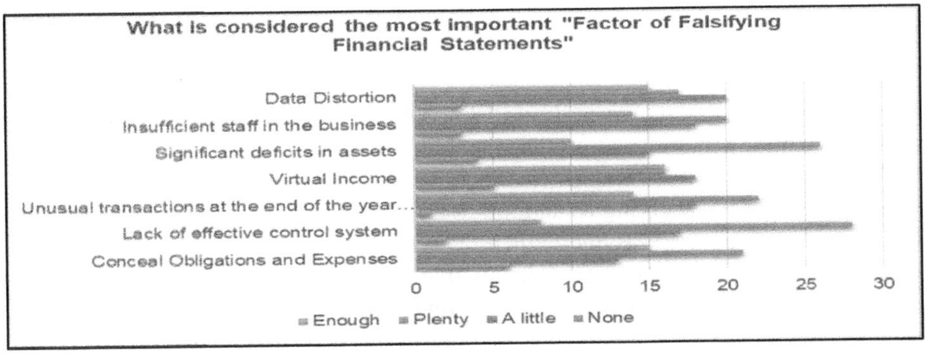

Figure 18.4. *For a color version of this figure, see www.iste.co.uk/dimotikalis/data4.zip*

Regarding the factors of falsification of financial statements, we can conclude that the most important factor of falsification of financial statements, according to the answers of the respondents, is, with a percentage of 51%, the lack of an effective control system in the company, while virtual revenues with 29% is another important factor. Also, 36% chose the distortion of data as a slightly important factor in the falsification of financial statements, while finally the largest percentage in the "none important factor" category, 11%, considers the concealment of obligations and expenses as none important factor in falsification.

Then, the next question refers to the motives for falsifying the financial statements. Similar to the previous question, participants were asked to select on a scale, none to quite a lot, regarding the most common motives for falsifying financial statements and which they consider most important.

Motivations to Falsify Financial Statements												
Question	None		A little		Medium		Plenty		Enough		Total	
	Frequency	Percentage	Frequency	Percentage	Frequency	Percentage	Frequency	Percentage	Frequency	Percentage	Frequency	Percentage
Frequency of audit in the company	5	9%	13	24%	15	27%	15	27%	7	13%	55	100%
Excessive trust in employees serving in key positions	2	4%	11	20%	11	20%	20	36%	11	20%	55	100%
Maximizing business profits	1	2%	5	9%	10	19%	21	38%	18	33%	55	100%
Tax evasion	0	0%	4	7%	15	27%	18	33%	18	33%	55	100%
Unrealistic repayment of loans on the predetermined repayment dates	2	4%	10	19%	17	31%	14	25%	12	21%	55	100%
Financial difficulties	3	6%	8	14%	19	35%	13	24%	12	21%	55	100%
Remuneration of the accountant/auditor	15	27%	11	20%	11	20%	11	20%	7	13%	55	100%

Table 18.5.

Therefore, we conclude that the most important motives for falsifying financial statements, according to the auditors, are tax evasion with a percentage of 33% and maximization of company profits with a percentage of 38%, followed by excessive trust in employees serving in key positions with a percentage of 36%. On the contrary, we observe that the remuneration of the accountant-auditor is not at all a significant motivation to falsify the financial statements according to the rate of 27% of the auditors.

Then, the questions refer to the treatments with and measures to prevent accounting fraud phenomena.

Treatment												
Question	None		A little		Medium		Plenty		Enough		Total	
	Frequency	Percentage	Frequency	Percentage	Frequency	Percentage	Frequency	Percentage	Frequency	Percentage	Frequency	Percentage
Mandatory implementation and strict adherence to International Auditing Standards	1	2%	3	5%	6	11%	26	47%	19	35%	55	100%
Regular audit of vulnerable companies	1	2%	1	2%	13	24%	26	47%	14	25%	55	100%
Frequent and continuous staff training	0	0%	1	2%	10	18%	22	40%	22	40%	55	100%
Use of criminal actions	0	0%	2	4%	13	24%	23	42%	17	30%	55	100%
Compliance with statutory and regulatory requirements	0	0%	0	0%	10	18%	22	40%	23	42%	55	100%
Detailed Procedures	0	0%	1	2%	13	24%	17	30%	24	44%	55	100%

Table 18.6.

Therefore, we observe that in general, all the treatments are declared by the auditors to be effective and significant based on the results. The ways of dealing with the most positive results on the "enough" scale seem to be compliance with statutory and regulatory requirements, frequent and continuous staff training and detailed procedures.

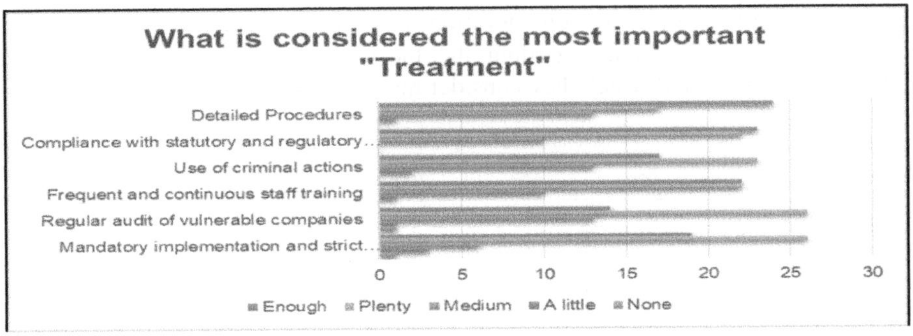

Figure 18.5. *For a color version of this figure, see www.iste.co.uk/dimotikalis/data4.zip*

18.3.6. *Analysis of questionnaire data of large companies*

The analysis of the results for the second questionnaire is performed in a similar way to the auditors' questionnaire. It is important to emphasize that the specific questionnaire was addressed exclusively to large companies that are audited by external auditors and/or have a distinct internal audit department. The main purpose is to compare the results with those of the auditors in terms of how the contracting parties perceive the factors and motivations for falsifying financial statements.

As shown in Table 18.7, a total of executives from 102 companies answered, of which 44% come from listed companies and 56% from un-listed companies, as well as the largest percentage having its headquarters in the Regional Unit of Attica with a percentage of 31%, followed by the region of Crete with a percentage of 23% and the region of Central Macedonia with a percentage of 22%. The 8% comes from businesses in the Aegean region, while 12% is shared equally by 4% in the regions of Western Macedonia, Central Greece and Epirus, as well as just 2% coming from the region of Western Greece.

No.	Questions	Answers	
		Frequency	Percentage
1.	**Company**		
	Listed	45	44%
	Unlisted	57	56%
	Total	102	100%
2.	**Region**		
	Region of Eastern Macedonia and Thrace	3	3%
	Region of Central Macedonia	22	22%
	Region of Western Macedonia	4	4%
	Region of Attica	31	31%
	Region of Central Greece	4	4%
	Epirus Region	4	4%
	Region of Crete	23	23%
	Thessaly Region	1	1%
	Aegean Region	8	8%
	Region of Ionian Islands	0	0%
	Region of Western Greece	2	2%
	Total	102	100%
3.	**Line of Business**		
	Agriculture - Fishing	3	3%
	Clothing & Footwear	10	10%
	Energy	2	2%
	Construction Sector	8	8%
	Transportation & Logistics	12	12%
	Information Technology - Technologies	8	8%
	Tourism industry	18	17%
	Banking - Financial Sector	2	2%
	Food - Drink	25	24%
	Pharmaceutical - Medical Sector	14	14%
	Total	102	100%
4.	**Job Position**		
	Assistant accountant	31	30%
	Chief accountant	21	21%
	Executive (CEO, Chairman of the Board)	14	14%
	Office employee	36	35%
	Total	102	100%
5.	**Education**		
	Ph.D.	5	5%
	Professional Certifications (C.P.A., A.C.C.A., C.I.A., C.F.E, A.C.A. κ.ο.κ.)	3	3%
	Master Degree	51	50%
	Bachelor Degree	43	42%
	Total	102	100%

Table 18.7.

Regarding the *line of business*, we observe that most companies are active in the food and beverage sector with a percentage of 24%, in the tourism sector with a percentage of 17%, followed by the pharmaceutical–medical sector with a percentage of 14%, the transport-logistics sector at 12%, the construction sector with 8%, agriculture – fishing with 3%, and finally the banking sector and the energy sector with 2%. Therefore, we observe that according to the participation, most businesses are active in the food-beverage and tourism sectors.

The largest percentage of participants hold a position as an office employee with a percentage of 36%, followed by assistant accountants with a percentage of 30%, chef accountants with a percentage of 21%, while only 14% of the participants are executives (Board of Directors, President, etc.). Also, regarding the educational background of the participants, 50% hold a master's degree (51 answers), 42% (43 answers) hold a bachelor's degree, 5% hold a PhD (five people), while finally only 3% (three answers) are holders of professional certification.

The next question refers to the most important motive for falsifying financial statements. The aggregated responses are shown in Table 18.8.

Most Important Motivation to Falsify Financial Statements												
Question	None		A little		Medium		Plenty		Enough		Total	
	Frequency	Percentage	Frequency	Percentage	Frequency	Percentage	Frequency	Percentage	Frequency	Percentage		
Frequency of control in the enterprise	24	24%	12	12%	19	18%	24	24%	23	22%	102	100%
Excessive trust in employees serving in key positions	7	7%	12	12%	23	22%	30	30%	30	30%	102	100%
Maximizing business profits	4	4%	4	4%	19	18%	45	44%	30	30%	102	100%
Tax evasion	8	8%	7	7%	19	18%	39	38%	29	29%	102	100%
Unrealistic repayment of loans on the predetermined	11	11%	11	11%	23	22%	36	35%	21	21%	102	100%
Work/financial difficulties	9	9%	18	18%	21	21%	28	27%	26	25%	102	100%
Remuneration of the accountant/auditor	34	33%	17	17%	13	13%	22	21%	16	16%	102	100%

Table 18.8.

Comparing the results, we observe that the participants consider profit maximization, tax evasion, as well as unrealistic repayment of loans on the predetermined repayment dates as the most important motivation for falsifying financial statements. On the contrary, we note that the remuneration of the accountant-auditor is not a sufficiently important motivation as the largest percentage who chose "none" concentrated on this motivation.

As seen in Table 18.9, the largest percentage believes that the most important factor in the falsification of the financial statements is the unusual transactions at the end of the year that affect the company's profits with a percentage of 22.3%, followed by the distortion of data at 20.4% and the lack of an effective quality audit system with a percentage of 16.5%. In a less advantageous position is the concealment of liabilities and expenses with a percentage of 14.6%, virtual income with 12.6%, insufficient staff in the company with 11.7%, while only 1% regarded significant deficits in assets.

Factor of Falsification of Financial Statements

			Factor								
				1. Concealment of liabilities and expenses	2. Non-existence of an effective quality control system	3. Unusual transactions at the end of the year that affect the company's profits	4.Virtual income	5. Significant deficits in assets	6. Insufficient staff in the business	7.Data distortion	Total
Job Position		% within Job Position	100.0%								100.0%
		% within Factor_Fraud	100.0%								1.0%
		% of Total	1.0%								1.0%
	Assistant Accountant	% within Job Position		19.4%	12.9%	25.8%	12.9%	3.2%	6.5%	19.4%	100.0%
		% within Factor_Fraud		40.0%	23.5%	34.8%	30.8%	100.0%	16.7%	28.6%	30.1%
		% of Total		5.8%	3.9%	7.8%	3.9%	1.0%	1.9%	5.8%	30.1%
	Chief Accountant	% within Job Position		9.5%	19.0%	28.6%	14.3%		9.5%	19.0%	100.0%
		% within Factor_Fraud		13.3%	23.5%	26.1%	23.1%		16.7%	19.0%	20.4%
		% of Total		1.9%	3.9%	5.8%	2.9%		1.9%	3.9%	20.4%
	Executive (CEO, Chairman of the Board)	% within Job Position		7.1%	42.9%	7.1%	7.1%		14.3%	21.4%	100.0%
		% within Factor_Fraud		6.7%	35.3%	4.3%	7.7%		16.7%	14.3%	13.6%
		% of Total		1.0%	5.8%	1.0%	1.0%		1.9%	2.9%	13.6%
	Office employee	% within Job Position		16.7%	8.3%	22.2%	13.9%		16.7%	22.2%	100.0%
		% within Factor_Fraud		40.0%	17.6%	34.8%	38.5%		50.0%	38.1%	35.0%
		% of Total		5.8%	2.9%	7.8%	4.9%		5.8%	7.8%	35.0%
Total		% within Job Position	1.0%	14.6%	16.5%	22.3%	12.6%	1.0%	11.7%	20.4%	100.0%
		% within Factor_Fraud	100.0%	100.0%	100.0%	100.0%	100.0%	100.0%	100.0%	100.0%	100.0%
		% of Total	1.0%	14.6%	16.5%	22.3%	12.6%	1.0%	11.7%	20.4%	100.0%

Table 18.9.

The answers given by the companies regarding the following research question on the limitation and prevention of accounting fraud, the largest percentage answered that the faithful implementation of accounting and auditing standards is the best way with 27%, 21% answered that the existence and implementation of appropriate legislation was the best solution, as well as the best cooperation of the company with the auditors throughout the year with a corresponding percentage of 21%. The 16% answered as an option the company's compliance with the auditors' advice, while finally 15% the existence of stricter criminal sanctions.

Company * To limit and prevent accounting fraud it is necessary (Crosstabulation)

			To limit and prevent accounting fraud it is necessary						
				The best cooperation of the company with the auditors throughout the entire period of use	The faithful impementation of accounting and auditing standards	The company's compliance with the auditors' advice	The existence of stricter criminal penalties	The existence and implementation of appropriate legislation	Total
Company		% within Company	100.0%						100.0%
		% within To limit and prevent accounting fraud it is necessary	100.0%						1.0%
		% of Total	1.0%						1.0%
	Listed	% within Company		20.0%	22.2%	11.1%	20.0%	26.7%	100.0%
		% within To limit and prevent accounting fraud it is necessary		40.9%	35.7%	31.3%	60.0%	57.1%	43.7%
		% of Total		8.7%	9.7%	4.9%	8.7%	11.7%	43.7%
	Unlisted	% within Company		22.8%	31.6%	19.3%	10.5%	15.8%	100.0%
		% within To limit and prevent accounting fraud it is necessary		59.1%	64.3%	68.8%	40.0%	42.9%	55.3%
		% of Total		12.6%	17.5%	10.7%	5.8%	8.7%	55.3%
Total		% within Company	1.0%	21.4%	27.2%	15.5%	14.6%	20.4%	100.0%
		% within To limit and prevent accounting fraud it is necessary	100.0%	100.0%	100.0%	100.0%	100.0%	100.0%	100.0%
		% of Total	1.0%	21.4%	27.2%	15.5%	14.6%	20.4%	100.0%

Table 18.10.

18.3.7. Comparative analysis of auditors' and companies' results

According to the above-mentioned analysis of the results, the largest percentage of auditors (51%) answered that they consider the most important factor in the falsification of financial statements to be "Lack of an effective audit system", as a "very" important factor (Figure 18.6).

Similar results were reached by the responses of the company participants. More specifically, as seen in Table 18.11, most of the responses regarding who the participants consider to be the most important factor were concentrated in the factor "unusual transactions at the end of the year regarding the company's profits", with a percentage of 22.3% (=22%), as well as the "Lack of an effective quality control system" percentage of 16.5% (=17%) (Figure 18.7).

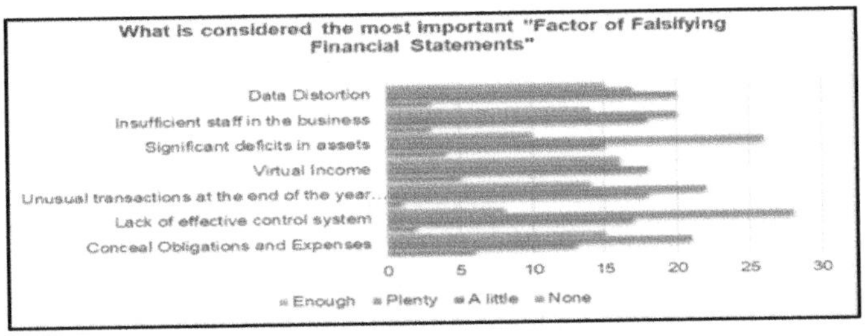

Figure 18.6. *Auditors. For a color version of this figure, see www.iste.co.uk/dimotikalis/data4.zip*

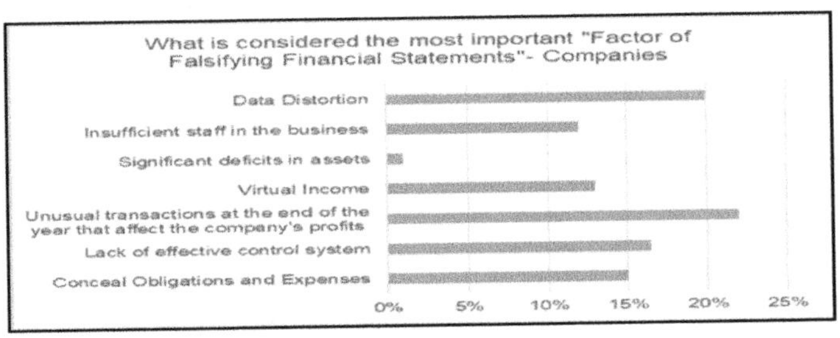

Figure 18.7. *Companies. For a color version of this figure, see www.iste.co.uk/dimotikalis/data4.zip*

These answers regarding the "lack of an effective quality control system", as one of the most important factors in the falsification of financial statements, completely agree with the research of Perera and Wijerathna (2020), as mentioned in the literature review, as they state that the quality of audit has become a vital part of the financial market as it fosters a sense of trust and credibility by citing five important indicators of audit quality.

Regarding the motivations for falsifying financial statements, the results showed that auditors consider the most important motivation to be "maximizing the company's profits" with a percentage of 38%, where 3.6% were answered by practicing auditors, 25.5% by external auditors and 9.1% from internal auditors (Figure 18.8).

It is worth noting that the answers to the second questionnaire of the companies had the same result, with a percentage of 44% (=43.7%), as shown in Figure 18.9.

The maximization of profits as the most important motivation for falsifying financial statements by the participants of both research works is fully consistent with the aforementioned literature of Spathis et al. (2002) and Rezaee (2005).

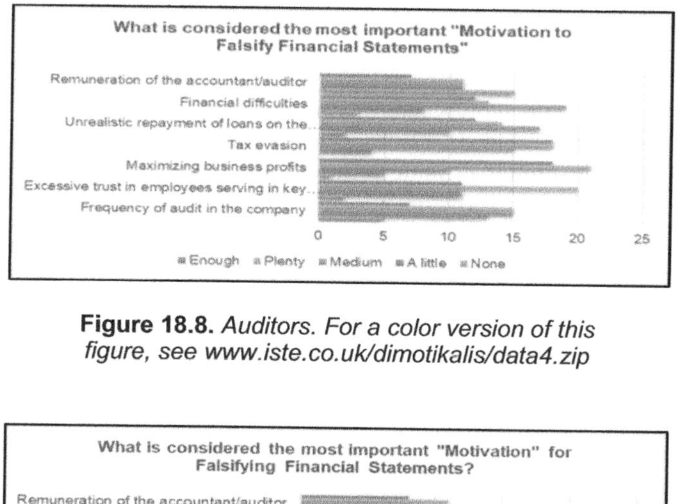

Figure 18.8. *Auditors. For a color version of this figure, see www.iste.co.uk/dimotikalis/data4.zip*

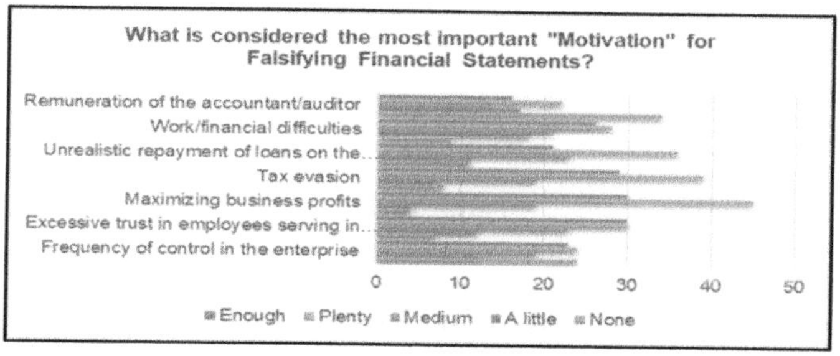

Figure 18.9. *Companies. For a color version of this figure, see www.iste.co.uk/dimotikalis/data4.zip*

The contribution of the institutional framework regarding the limitation of accounting fraud seems to have helped enough to eliminate similar phenomena, as the responses of the participants to both questionnaires were positive. More specifically, in Table 18.11, the answers of the auditors are listed where 5.5% of the trainee auditors answered that they have contributed enough, as well as the percentage of 34.5% and 9.1% of the external and internal auditors, respectively. The largest percentage considers that it contributes positively.

Job Position * Is the current institutional framework considered to have contributed to reducing fraud? (Crosstabulation)

			Is the current institutional framework considered to have contributed to reducing fraud?					
			Enough	None	A little	Plenty	Significant	Total
Job Position	Trainee Auditor	% within Job Position	50.0%	16.7%	33.3%			100.0%
		%within Is the current institutional framework considered to have contributed to reducing fraud?	11.1%	50.0%	14.3%			10.9%
		% of Total	5.6%	1.8%	3.6%			10.9%
	External Auditor	% within Job Position	50.0%	2.6%	28.9%	10.5%	7.9%	100.0%
		%within Is the current institutional framework considered to have contributed to reducing fraud?	70.4%	50.0%	78.6%	57.1%	60.0%	69.1%
		% of Total	34.5%	1.8%	20.0%	7.3%	5.5%	69.1%
	Internal Auditor	% within Job Position	45.5%		9.1%	27.3%	18.2%	100.0%
		%within Is the current institutional framework considered to have contributed to reducing fraud?	18.5%		7.1%	42.9%	40.0%	20.0%
		% of Total	9.1%		1.8%	5.5%	3.6%	20.0%
Total		% within Job Position	49.1%	3.6%	25.5%	12.7%	9.1%	100.0%
		%within Is the current institutional framework considered to have contributed to reducing fraud?	100.0%	100.0%	100.0%	100.0%	100.0%	100.0%
		% of Total	49.1%	3.6%	25.5%	12.7%	9.1%	100.0%

Table 18.11.

The responses of the representatives of the companies, listed and not, were similar, as shown in Table 18.12, as most responses agree with the positive contribution of the institutional framework to limiting fraud phenomena, with these responses agreeing with the above-mentioned research of Gantz (2014).

Job_Position * Is the current institutional framework considered to have contributed to the reduction of fraud? Crosstabulation

				Is the current institutional framework considered to have contributed to the reduction of fraud?		
				Yes	No	Total
Job Position		% within Job Position	100,0%			100,0%
		% within Is the current institutional framework considered to have contributed to the reduction of fraud?	100.0%			1.0%
		% of Total	1,0%			1,0%
	Assistant Accountant	% within Job Position		77.4%	22.6%	100.0%
		% within Is the current institutional framework considered to have contributed to the reduction of fraud?		33.8%	22.6%	30.1%
		% of Total		23.3%	6.8%	30,1%
	Chef Accountant	% within Job Position		81.0%	19.0%	100.0%
		% within Is the current institutional framework considered to have contributed to the reduction of fraud?		23.9%	12.9%	20.4%
		% of Total		16.5%	3.9%	20.4%
	Executive (CEO, Board of Director)	% within Job Position		85.7%	14.3%	100,0%
		% within Is the current institutional framework considered to have contributed to the reduction of fraud?		16.9%	6.5%	13.6%
		% of Total		11.7%	1.9%	13,6%
	Office employee	% within Job Position		50.0%	50.0%	100.0%
		% within Is the current institutional framework considered to have contributed to the reduction of fraud?		25.4%	58.1%	35.0%
		% of Total		17.5%	17.5%	35.0%
Total		% within Job Position	1.0%	68.9%	30.1%	100.0%
		% within Is the current institutional framework considered to have contributed to the reduction of fraud?	100.0%	100.0%	100.0%	100.0%
		% of Total	1.0%	68.9%	30.1%	100,0%

Table 18.12.

In addition, regarding the ways to deal with accounting fraud, most responses focused on the mandatory implementation and strict adherence to International Auditing Standards (47%) as a very important way, where about 7% answered trainee auditors, about 35% came from external auditors and 5.5% from internal auditors. Also, the same percentage of responses were collected for the regular audit of vulnerable businesses, of which approximately 5.5% came from trainee auditors, 30.9% from external auditors and 10.9% from internal auditors.

Job_Position * Mandatory application and strict adherence to International Auditing Standards (Crosstabulation)

			Mandatory application and strict adherence to International Auditing Standards					
			Enough	None	A little	Medium	Plenty	Total
Job Position	Trainee Auditor	% within Job Position	33.3%				66.7%	100.0%
		% within Mandatory application and strict adherence to International Auditing Standards	10.5%				15.4%	10.9%
		% of Total	3.6%				7.3%	10.9%
	External Auditor	% within Job Position	28.9%	2.6%	5.3%	13.2%	50.0%	100.0%
		% within Mandatory application and strict adherence to International Auditing Standards	57.9%	100.0%	66.7%	83.3%	73.1%	69.1%
		% of Total	20.0%	1.8%	3.6%	9.1%	34.5%	69.1%
	Internal Auditor	% within Job Position	54.5%		9.1%	9.1%	27.3%	100.0%
		% within Mandatory application and strict adherence to International Auditing Standards	31.6%		33.3%	16.7%	11.5%	20.0%
		% of Total	10.9%		1.8%	1.8%	5.5%	20.0%
Total		% within Job Position	34.5%	1.8%	5.5%	10.9%	47.3%	100.0%
		% within Mandatory application and strict adherence to International Auditing Standards	100.0%	100.0%	100.0%	100.0%	100.0%	100.0%
		% of Total	34.5%	1.8%	5.5%	10.9%	47.3%	100.0%

Table 18.13.

Job_Position * Regular check on vulnerable businesses (Crosstabulation)

			Regular check on vulnerable businesses					
			Enough	None	A little	Medium	Plenty	Total
Job Position	Trainee Auditor	% within Job Position	16.7%			33.3%	50.0%	100.0%
		% within Regular check on vulnerable businesses	7.1%			15.4%	11.5%	10.9%
		% of Total	1.8%			3.6%	5.5%	10.9%
	External Auditor	% within Job Position	28.9%	2.6%	2.6%	21.1%	44.7%	100.0%
		% within Regular check on vulnerable businesses	78.6%	100.0%	100.0%	61.5%	65.4%	69.1%
		% of Total	20.0%	1.8%	1.8%	14.5%	30.9%	69.1%
	Internal Auditor	% within Job Position	18.2%			27.3%	54.5%	100.0%
		% within Regular check on vulnerable businesses	14.3%			23.1%	23.1%	20.0%
		% of Total	3.6%			5.5%	10.9%	20.0%
Total		% within Job Position	25.5%	1.8%	1.8%	23.6%	47.3%	100.0%
		% within Regular check on vulnerable businesses	100.0%	100.0%	100.0%	100.0%	100.0%	100.0%
		% of Total	25.5%	1.8%	1.8%	23.6%	47.3%	100.0%

Table 18.14.

Similar results were given by the answers of the companies as most of the answers regarding the prevention of accounting fraud phenomena were concentrated on the faithful implementation of the accounting and auditing standards, with a percentage of 27% (=27.2%), where 9.7% came from listed companies and 17.5% from un-listed companies.

Company * To limit and prevent accounting fraud is necessary

				To limit and prevent accounting fraud is necessary					
				The best cooperation of the company with the auditors througnout the entire period of use	The faithful application of accounting and auditing standards	The company's compliance with the auditors' advice	The existence of stricter criminal penalties	The existence and implementation of appropriate legislation	Total
Company		% within Company	100.0%						100.0%
		% within To limit and prevent accounting fraud is necessary	100.0%						1.0%
		% of Total	1.0%						1.0%
	Listed	% within Company		20.0%	22.2%	11.1%	20.0%	26.7%	100.0%
		% within To limit and prevent accounting fraud is necessary		40.9%	35.7%	31.3%	60.0%	57.1%	43.7%
		% of Total		8.7%	9.7%	4.9%	8.7%	11.7%	43.7%
	Unlisted	% within Company		22.8%	31.6%	19.3%	10.5%	15.8%	100.0%
		% within To limit and prevent accounting fraud is necessary		59.1%	64.3%	68.8%	40.0%	42.9%	55.3%
		% of Total		12.6%	17.5%	10.7%	5.8%	8.7%	55.3%
Total		% within Company	1.0%	21.4%	27.2%	15.5%	14.6%	20.4%	100.0%
		% within To limit and prevent accounting fraud is necessary	100.0%	100.0%	100.0%	100.0%	100.0%	100.0%	100.0%
		% of Total	1.0%	21.4%	27.2%	15.5%	14.6%	20.4%	100.0%

Table 18.15.

18.4. Conclusion

In conclusion, the abolition of financial borders and the subsequent globalization of the economy has intensified the phenomena of falsification of financial statements, maintaining them as important perennial problems, where from their embryonic form until today, they have taken on significant dimensions as over time, more and more factors have contributed to the growing trend of counterfeiting and deception.

According to all the above, an attempt was made, through thorough research, to draw conclusions regarding the way in which auditors and audited companies perceive the falsification of financial statements. More specifically, two different questionnaires were distributed – one to auditors and one to large companies – where, through a wide range of questions, an attempt was made to draw conclusions about the reasons, the factors, the motivations as well as the solutions of the phenomena of falsification of financial statements

Comparing the responses of the two questionnaires, we observe that there is a positive course of responses regarding who the participants consider as the most important factor in falsifying financial statements. More specifically, as it turned out, "Lack of an effective control system" is a very important factor for auditors with a percentage of 51% (Table 18.4), and also for companies with a percentage of 17% (Table 18.9). The results regarding the motivations for falsifying the financial statements also came to a similar conclusion, as well as the auditors and the companies considering the "maximization of the company's profits" as the most important motivation, with percentages of 38% (Table 18.5) and 44% (Table 18.8), respectively. The contribution of the institutional framework regarding the limitation of accounting fraud seems to have helped enough to eliminate similar phenomena as the responses of the participants of the two questionnaires are in complete agreement, with the auditors agreeing quite a lot with a percentage of 49% (Table 18.11), and the companies with about 70% (Table 18.12). Finally, regarding the treatment, the answers of the respondents also agree as most believe that the most effective solution is the mandatory implementation and strict adherence to International Auditing Standards, with percentages of around 47% (Table 18.13) and 27% (Table 18.15), for auditors and companies, respectively.

18.5. References

Albrecht, W.S., Albrecht, C.O., Albrecht, C.C., Zimbelman, M.F. (2012). *Fraud Examination*, 4th edition. Cengage Learning, Mason.

Alleyne, P. and Howard, M. (2005). An exploratory study of auditors' responsibility for fraud detection in Barbados. *Managerial Auditing Journal*, 20(3), 284–303.

Amina, Z. (2021). Financial fraud detection and the importance of internal control. *International Journal of Accounting and Financial Reporting*, 11(4), 28.

Baesens, B., Van Vlasselaer, V., Verbeke, W. (2015). *Fraud Analytics Using Descriptive, Predictive, and Social Network Techniques: A Guide to Data Science for Fraud Detection*. John Wiley & Sons Inc, Hoboken.

Bolton, R.J. and Hand, D.J. (2002). Statistical fraud detection: A review. *Statistical Science*, 17(3), 235–249.

Cohen, L., Manion, L., Morrison, K. (2008). *Research Methods in Education*, 5th edition. METAIHMIO, Athens.

Gaganis, Ch. and Zopounidis, K. (2009). *Recognition of Falsified Accounting Statements*. Kleidaritmos, Athens.

Gantz, S.D. (ed.) (2014). Audit-related organizations, standards, and certifications. In *The Basics of IT Audit Purposes, Processes, and Practical Information*. Syngress, Waltham, MA, 197–219.

Ghafran, C. and O'Sullivan, N. (2017). The impact of audit committee expertise on audit quality: Evidence from UK audit fees. *The British Accounting Review*, 49(6), 578–593.

Josiah, M., Ekundayo, G., Adeboye, Moses, O. (2020). Audit-quality-and-auditors-independence. *AE-Funai Journal of Accounting, Business and Finance (FJABAF)*, 6(1).

Loumiotis, V. and Tzifas, V. (2017). *Basic Guidelines for the Implementation of International Auditing Standards*. SOL, Athens.

Mangala, D. and Kumari, P. (2014). Auditors' perceptions of the effectiveness of fraud prevention and detection method. *Indian Journal of Corporate Governance*, 10(2), 118–142.

Pazarskis, M., Drogalas, G., Baltzi, K. (2017). Detecting false financial statements: evidence from Greece in the period of economic crisis. *Investment Management and Financial Innovations*, 14(3), 102–112

Perera, P. and Wijerathna, H.S. (2020). Audit quality: Perception of audit practitioners in Sri Lanka. *17th International Conference on Business Management (ICBM 2020)*.

Rezaee, Z. (2005). Causes, consequences, and deterence of financial statement fraud. *Critical Perspectives on Accounting*, 16(3), 277–298. doi: 10.1016/s1045-2354(03)00072-8.

Salleh, S.M. and Othman, R. (2016). Board of director's attributes as deterrence to corporate fraud. *Procedia Economics and Finance*, 35, 82–91

Sanchez, M., Torres, J., Zambrano, P., Flores, P. (2018). FraudFind: Financial fraud detection by analyzing human behavior. *2018 IEEE 8th Annual Computing and Communication Workshop and Conference (CCWC)*.

Simunic, D.A., Ye, M., Zhang, P. (2016). The joint effects of multiple legal system characteristics on auditing standards and auditor behavior. *Contemporary Accounting Research*.

Spathis, C., Doumpos, M., Zopounidis, C. (2002). Detecting falsified financial statements: A comparative study using multicriteria analysis and multivariate statistical techniques. *The European Accounting Review*, 11(3), 509–535.

Tommasetti, R., de Oliveira Leite, R., Maia, V.M., Da Silva Macedo, M.A. (2021). Revisiting the accounting fraud components: A bottom-up approach using the twitter platform. *SAGE Open*, 11(4), 1–12.

Tutino, M. and Berlo, M. (2019). Accounting fraud: A literature review. *Risk Governance and Control: Financial Markets & Institutions*, 9, 1.

Umar, H., Partahi, D., Purba, R. (2020). Fraud Diamond analysis in detecting fraudulent financial report. *April 2020 International Journal of Scientific & Technology Research*, 9(3), 6638–6646.

Wolfe, D.T. and Hermanson, D.R. (2004). The Fraud Diamond: Considering the four elements of fraud. *CPA Journal*, 74(12), 38–42.

Wuerges, A.F.E. and Borba, J.A. (2010). Accounting fraud detection: Is it possible to quantify undiscovered cases? *SSRN Electronic Journal*.

19

Equivariant Robust Estimators for Moment Condition Models

We present a large class of robust estimators for semi-parametric moment condition models. These estimators are defined by minimizing empirical versions of divergences in dual form, using truncated orthogonality functions instead of the original orthogonality functions of the model. When the moment condition model is invariant with respect to a transformations group, these robust estimators are also equivariant.

19.1. Introduction

A moment condition model is a family $\mathcal{M}^{(1)}$ of probability measures (p.m.), all defined on the same measurable space $(\mathbb{R}^m, \mathcal{B}(\mathbb{R}^m))$, such that (s.t.)

$$\int_{\mathbb{R}^m} f(x,\theta)\, dQ(x) = 0 \quad \text{for all} \quad Q \in \mathcal{M}^{(1)},$$

$\mathcal{B}(\mathbb{R}^m)$ being the Borel σ-field. The parameter of interest θ belongs to a compact set $\Theta \subset \mathbb{R}^d$ and the function $f := (f_1, \ldots, f_\ell)^\top$, with $\ell \geq d$, is defined on $\mathbb{R}^m \times \Theta$, each f_i being real-valued function. The functions $f_1, \ldots, f_l$ and $\mathbf{1}_{\mathbb{R}^m}$ are assumed to be linearly independent. Denote by $M^{(1)}$ the set of all p.m. on $(\mathbb{R}^m, \mathcal{B}(\mathbb{R}^m))$ and for each $\theta \in \Theta$ define

$$\mathcal{M}_\theta^{(1)} := \left\{ Q \in M^{(1)} \text{ s.t. } \int_{\mathbb{R}^m} f(x,\theta)\, dQ(x) = 0 \right\},$$

so that

$$\mathcal{M}^{(1)} = \bigcup_{\theta \in \Theta} \mathcal{M}_\theta^{(1)}. \qquad [19.1]$$

Chapter written by Aida TOMA, Amor KEZIOU, Luiza BĂDIN and Silvia DEDU.

Let $X_1, \ldots, X_n$ be an i.i.d. sample on the random vector X with unknown probability distribution P_0. We consider the problem of estimation of the parameter θ_0 for which

$$\int f(x, \theta_0) dP_0(x) = 0. \quad [19.2]$$

We assume that θ_0 is the unique solution of equation [19.2]. Thus, we assume that information about θ_0 and P_0 is available in the form of $l \geq d$ functionally independent unbiased estimating functions, and we use this information to estimate θ_0.

Among the most known estimation methods for moment condition models, we mention the generalized method of moments (Hansen 1982), the empirical likelihood estimator (Qin and Lawless 1994; Imbens 1997), the continuous updating estimator (Hansen et al. 1996), the exponential tilting estimator (Kitamura and Stutzer 1997) and the generalized empirical likelihood estimators (Newey and Smith 2004). The so-called information and entropy econometric techniques have been proposed to improve the finite sample performance of the general method of moments estimators and tests (see, for example, Imbens (1997); Kitamura and Stutzer (1997)).

Some recent approaches for estimation and testing in moment condition models are based on using divergences. Divergence measures are widely used in statistics and data science, as well as in other areas such as machine learning or pattern recognition. Statistical methods based on divergence minimization extend the likelihood paradigm and often have the advantage to provide a trade-off between efficiency and robustness (see, for example, Pardo (2006); Basu et al. (2011); Pardo and Martin (2021); and Karagrigoriou and Makrides (2023)). A general methodology for estimation and testing in moment condition models was developed by Broniatowski and Keziou (2012). This approach is based on minimizing divergences in their dual form and allows the asymptotic study of the estimators, called minimum empirical divergence estimators, and of the associated test statistics, both under the model and under misspecification of the model. The approach based on minimizing dual forms of divergences was initially used in the case of parametric models (see, for example, Broniatowski and Keziou (2009); Toma and Leoni-Aubin (2010); Toma and Broniatowski (2011); and Toma (2014)). The large class of minimum empirical divergence estimators contains, in particular, the empirical likelihood estimator, the continuous updating estimator, as well as the empirical tilting estimator. All of the minimum empirical divergence estimators have the same efficiency of first order, and moreover, the empirical likelihood estimator, which belong to this class, is superior in higher order efficiency. On the other hand, these minimum empirical divergence estimators are not robust, because the corresponding influence functions are generally not bounded (Toma 2013).

Some robust estimation methods for moment condition models have been proposed in the literature, for example, in Ronchetti and Trojani (2001),

Lô and Ronchetti (2012), Felipe et al. (2018), Keziou and Toma (2021a, 2021b) and Toma (2023). In this chapter, we present a large class of robust estimators for semi-parametric moment condition models. These estimators are defined by minimizing empirical versions of divergences in dual form, using truncated orthogonality functions instead of the original orthogonality functions of the model. When the moment condition model is invariant with respect to a transformations group, these robust estimators are also equivariant.

19.2. Robust estimators for moment condition models

19.2.1. *Statistical divergences*

Let φ be a convex function defined on $\mathbb{R}$ and $[0, +\infty]$ valued, satisfying $\varphi(1) = 0$, and P be some p.m. on the measurable space $(\mathbb{R}^m, \mathcal{B}(\mathbb{R}^m))$. For any signed finite measure Q, on the measurable space $(\mathbb{R}^m, \mathcal{B}(\mathbb{R}^m))$, absolutely continuous with respect to P, the φ-divergence between Q and P is defined by

$$D_\varphi(Q, P) := \int_{\mathbb{R}^m} \varphi\left(\frac{dQ}{dP}(x)\right) dP(x), \tag{19.3}$$

where $\frac{dQ}{dP}$ is the Radon–Nikodym derivative. When Q is not absolutely continuous with respect to P, we set $D_\varphi(Q, P) = +\infty$. This definition extends the one given in Rüschendorf (1984) for divergences between p.m.

A known class of divergences between p.m. is the Cressie–Read class, introduced in Cressie and Read (1984) and defined by the convex functions

$$\varphi_\gamma : x \in \mathbb{R}_+ \mapsto \varphi_\gamma(x) := \frac{x^\gamma - \gamma x + \gamma - 1}{\gamma(\gamma - 1)}, \tag{19.4}$$

for $\gamma \in \mathbb{R} \setminus \{0, 1\}$, $\varphi_0(x) := -\log x + x - 1$ and $\varphi_1(x) := x \log x - x + 1$.

For any $\gamma \in \mathbb{R}$, if $\varphi_\gamma(0)$ is not defined, we set $\varphi_\gamma(0) := \lim_{x \to 0^+} \varphi_\gamma(x)$ which may be finite or infinite. When φ_γ is not defined on $(-\infty, 0)$ or when φ_γ is defined but not convex on whole $\mathbb{R}$, the definition of the corresponding power divergence function $Q \in M^{(1)} \mapsto D_{\varphi_\gamma}(Q, P)$ can be extended on the whole set of signed finite measures by taking the following extension of φ_γ

$$\varphi_\gamma : x \in \mathbb{R} \mapsto \varphi_\gamma(x)\mathbf{1}_{[0,+\infty[}(x) + (+\infty)\mathbf{1}_{]-\infty,0[}(x). \tag{19.5}$$

Some well-known divergences belong to the Cressie–Read class. The Kullback–Leibler divergence is associated with φ_1, the modified Kullback–Leibler to φ_0, the χ^2 divergence to φ_2, the modified χ^2 divergence to φ_{-1} and the Hellinger distance to $\varphi_{1/2}$.

The φ-divergence between some set Ω of signed finite measures and a p.m. P is defined by

$$D_\varphi(\Omega, P) := \inf_{Q \in \Omega} D_\varphi(Q, P). \tag{19.6}$$

19.2.2. *Definition of the estimators*

Consider a reference identifiable model $\{P_\theta; \theta \in \Theta\}$ of p.m. such that, for each $\theta \in \Theta$, $P_\theta \in \mathcal{M}_\theta$, which means that $\int f(x,\theta)\, dP_\theta(x) = 0$ and assume that θ is the unique solution of the equation. $\{P_\theta;\ \theta \in \Theta\}$ is not necessarily a parametric moment condition model. The index θ of P_θ only shows that P_θ belongs to $\mathcal{M}_\theta$. Assume that the p.m. P_0 of the data, here denoted as P_{θ_0}, corresponding to the unknown parameter θ_0 to be estimated, belongs to the reference model. The reference model will be associated with the truncated orthogonality function that will be used to define the robust estimators of θ_0.

Similarly as in Ronchetti and Trojani (2001), using the reference model $\{P_\theta;\ \theta \in \Theta\}$, we define the function $f^c : \mathbb{R}^m \times \Theta \to \mathbb{R}^\ell$,

$$f^c(x,\theta) := H_c\left(A(\theta, P_\theta)\,[f(x,\theta) - \tau(\theta, P_\theta)]\right), \tag{19.7}$$

where $H_c : \mathbb{R}^\ell \to \mathbb{R}^\ell$ is the multidimensional Huber function (see, for example, Hampel et al. (1986); and Ronchetti and Huber (2009))

$$H_c(y) := \begin{cases} y \cdot \min\left(1, \frac{c}{\|y\|}\right) & \text{if } y \neq 0, \\ 0 \text{ if } y = 0, \end{cases} \tag{19.8}$$

and the $\ell \times \ell$ matrix $A(\theta, P_\theta)$ and the ℓ-vector $\tau(\theta, P_\theta)$ are defined by the solutions of the system

$$\begin{cases} \int f^c(x,\theta)\, dP_\theta(x) = 0 \\ \int f^c(x,\theta)\, f^c(x,\theta)^\top\, dP_\theta(x) = I_\ell \end{cases} \tag{19.9}$$

where I_ℓ is the $\ell \times \ell$ identity matrix and c is a given positive constant.

We also use the auxiliary function

$$h^c(x,\theta,A,\tau) := H_c(A\,[f(x,\theta) - \tau]), \tag{19.10}$$

when we need to work with the dependence on the matrix A and on the vector τ. Then

$$h^c(x,\theta,A(\theta,P_\theta),\tau(\theta,P_\theta)) = f^c(x,\theta). \tag{19.11}$$

For given P_θ from the reference model, the triplet $(\theta, A(\theta, P_\theta), \tau(\theta, P_\theta))$ is the unique solution of the system

$$\begin{cases} \int f(x,\theta)\, dP_\theta(x) = 0, \\ \int f^c(x,\theta)\, dP_\theta(x) = 0, \\ \int f^c(x,\theta)\, f^c(x,\theta)^\top\, dP_\theta(x) = I_\ell \end{cases} \qquad [19.12]$$

(see Ronchetti and Trojani 2001, p.48).

Consider the estimation problem of the triplet $(\theta_0, A(\theta_0, P_{\theta_0}), \tau(\theta_0, P_{\theta_0}))$ on the basis of a sample $X_1, \dots, X_n \sim P_{\theta_0}$, $P_{\theta_0} \in \mathcal{M}_{\theta_0}$.

For each $\theta \in \Theta$, using the p.m. P_θ from the reference model, we define $A_n(\theta)$ and $\tau_n(\theta)$ solutions of the system

$$\begin{cases} \int h^c(x,\theta, A_n(\theta), \tau_n(\theta))\, dP_\theta(x) = 0, \\ \int h^c(x,\theta, A_n(\theta), \tau_n(\theta)) h^c(x,\theta, A_n(\theta), \tau_n(\theta))^\top\, dP_n(x) = I_\ell, \end{cases} \qquad [19.13]$$

where $P_n(\cdot)$ is the empirical measure associated with the sample,

$$P_n(\cdot) := \frac{1}{n}\sum_{i=1}^{n} \delta_{X_i}(\cdot),$$

$\delta_x(\cdot)$ being the Dirac measure at the point x, for any x. Then, we define

$$f_n^c(x,\theta) := h^c(x,\theta, A_n(\theta), \tau_n(\theta)) = H_c(A_n(\theta)\,[f(x,\theta) - \tau_n(\theta)]). \qquad [19.14]$$

Note that $f_n^c(x,\theta)$ depends on both the data and the reference probability P_θ.

Consider the moment condition model associated with the truncated function $f_n^c(x,\theta)$, namely

$$\mathcal{M}^{c,n} := \bigcup_{\theta \in \Theta} \mathcal{M}_\theta^{c,n} \qquad [19.15]$$

with

$$\mathcal{M}_\theta^{c,n} := \left\{ Q \in M \text{ s.t. } \int f_n^c(x,\theta)\, dQ(x) = 0 \right\},\ \forall \theta \in \Theta \qquad [19.16]$$

where M is the set of all signed finite measures defined on the measurable space $(\mathbb{R}^m, \mathcal{B}(\mathbb{R}^m))$. Note that the reference model belongs to the extended model $\mathcal{M}^{c,n}$ and particularly, $P_{\theta_0} \in \mathcal{M}_{\theta_0}^{c,n}$.

For a given φ-divergence, $\theta \in \Theta$ and P a p.m., we define the set

$$\Lambda_\theta^{c,n}(P) := \left\{ t := (t_0, t_1, \dots, t_\ell)^\top \in \mathbb{R}^{1+\ell} \text{ s.t. } \int \left|\psi\left(t^\top \overline{f}_n^c(x,\theta)\right)\right| dP(x) < \infty \right\}, \qquad [19.17]$$

where $\overline{f}_n^c := (\mathbf{1}_{\mathbb{R}^m}, f_n^{c\top})^\top$ and $\psi(\cdot)$ is the convex conjugate of $\varphi(\cdot)$ given by

$$\psi(u) = u\varphi'^{-1}(u) - \varphi(\varphi'^{-1}(u)), \; \forall u \in \text{Im}\varphi',$$

with $\text{Im}\varphi' := \{\varphi'(x) \text{ s.t. } x \in \text{dom}\varphi\}$. We denote $\Lambda_\theta^{c,n} := \Lambda_\theta^{c,n}(P_{\theta_0})$ and $\Lambda_\theta^{c,n,n} := \Lambda_\theta^{c,n}(P_n)$.

Since $f_n^c(x, \theta)$ is bounded with respect to x, if we assume that $D_\varphi(\mathcal{M}_\theta^{c,n}, P_{\theta_0})$ is finite, then on the basis of Corollary 1.2 from Broniatowski et al. (2006), the following dual representation holds:

$$D_\varphi(\mathcal{M}_\theta^{c,n}, P_{\theta_0}) = \sup_{t \in \Lambda_\theta^{c,n}} \int m_n^c(x, \theta, t)\, dP_{\theta_0}(x) \qquad [19.18]$$

where $m_n^c(x, \theta, t) := t_0 - \psi(t^\top \overline{f}_n^c(x, \theta))$. Note that $m_n^c(x, \theta, t)$ depends on the reference p.m. P_θ, since $f_n^c(x, \theta)$ depends on P_θ.

The supremum in [19.18] is reached in $t_\theta^{c,n} = t_\theta^{c,n}(P_{\theta_0})$,

$$t_\theta^{c,n} := \arg \sup_{t \in \Lambda_\theta^{c,n}} \int m_n^c(x, \theta, t)\, dP_{\theta_0}(x). \qquad [19.19]$$

According to Proposition 4.2. from Broniatowski and Keziou (2012), for each $\theta \in \Theta$, the condition

$$P_{\theta_0}\left(\{x \in \mathbb{R}^m \text{ s.t. } t^\top \overline{f}_n^c(x, \theta) \neq 0\}\right) > 0, \quad \text{for all } t \in \mathbb{R}^{1+\ell} \backslash \{0\}, \qquad [19.20]$$

assures that $t_\theta^{c,n}$ defined as solution of optimization problem [19.19] is unique. Note that the linear independence of the functions $\mathbf{1}_{\mathbb{R}^m}, f_{n,1}^c(\cdot, \theta), \ldots, f_{n,\ell}^c(\cdot, \theta)$ implies condition [19.20], whenever P_{θ_0} is not degenerate.

A natural estimator of $t_\theta^{c,n}$ is defined by

$$\widehat{t_\theta^c} := \arg \sup_{t \in \Lambda_\theta^{c,n,n}} \int m_n^c(x, \theta, t)\, dP_n(x). \qquad [19.21]$$

Then, a plug-in estimator of $D_\varphi(\mathcal{M}_\theta^{c,n}, P_{\theta_0})$ is

$$\widehat{D}_\varphi(\mathcal{M}_\theta^{c,n}, P_{\theta_0}) := \sup_{t \in \Lambda_\theta^{c,n,n}} \int m_n^c(x, \theta, t)\, dP_n(x). \qquad [19.22]$$

Finally, an estimator of θ_0 is defined by

$$\widehat{\theta_\varphi^c} := \arg \inf_{\theta \in \Theta} \sup_{t \in \Lambda_\theta^{c,n,n}} \int m_n^c(x, \theta, t)\, dP_n(x). \qquad [19.23]$$

Formula [19.23] defines a class of estimators, indexed by the φ-function corresponding to the used φ-divergence. These minimum empirical divergence estimators are robust, since their influence functions are bounded. The influence function of such an estimator, below denoted $\text{IF}(x; T_\varphi^c, P_{\theta_0})$, is proportional to the truncated orthogonality function $f^c(x, \theta_0)$ and consequently is bounded with respect to x

$$\text{IF}(x; T_\varphi^c, P_{\theta_0}) = \left\{ \left[\int \frac{\partial}{\partial \theta} f^c(y, \theta_0) dP_{\theta_0}(y) \right]^\top \int \frac{\partial}{\partial \theta} f^c(y, \theta_0) dP_{\theta_0}(y) \right\}^{-1} \cdot \left[\int \frac{\partial}{\partial \theta} f^c(y, \theta_0)\, dP_{\theta_0}(y) \right]^\top f^c(x, \theta_0). \quad [19.24]$$

19.3. Equivariance of robust minimum empirical divergence estimators

When the moment condition model is invariant with respect to a transformations group, the robust minimum empirical divergence estimators [19.23] are equivariant. We use the notions of group of transformations on a random vector space, the invariance of the model to a group of transformations and equivariant estimators.

19.3.1. *Groups of transformations, invariant models and equivariant estimators*

Let $\mathcal{G}$ be a group of one-to-one transformations from the vector space $\mathbb{R}^m$ to $\mathbb{R}^m$, in the sense that

$$\forall\, g_1, g_2 \in \mathcal{G},\ g_1 \circ g_2 \in \mathcal{G} \text{ and } \forall\, g \in \mathcal{G},\ g^{-1} \in \mathcal{G}. \quad [19.25]$$

Two types of transformations groups are usually considered on the observation space:

– *additive transformations groups*

$$\mathcal{G} := \{x \in \mathbb{R}^m \mapsto x + a \in \mathbb{R}^m, a \in S\} \quad [19.26]$$

where $S \subset \mathbb{R}^m$, respectively

– *multiplicative transformations groups*

$$\mathcal{G} := \{x \in \mathbb{R}^m \mapsto \text{diag}(\lambda_1, \ldots, \lambda_m)x \in \mathbb{R}^m,\ \lambda \in \mathbb{R}^{*m}\} \quad [19.27]$$

where $\text{diag}(\lambda_1, \ldots, \lambda_m)$ is the diagonal matrix with entries $\lambda_1, \ldots, \lambda_m$.

We consider that the moment condition model $\mathcal{M}$ is invariant with respect to the group of transformations $\mathcal{G}$, in the sense that

$$\text{for any random vector } X, \text{if } P_X \in \mathcal{M}, \text{ then } P_{g(X)} \in \mathcal{M}, \forall g \in \mathcal{G} \qquad [19.28]$$

where P_X denotes the probability distribution associated with the random vector X.

If a moment condition model $\mathcal{M}$ is invariant with respect to a group of transformations $\mathcal{G}$, then the group $\mathcal{G}$ induces on the parameter space Θ a group $\overline{\mathcal{G}}$ defined as follows. Let $\mathcal{G}$ be the group of transformations on the observation space, $g \in \mathcal{G}$ and X a random vector such that $P_X \in \mathcal{M}$. By the identifiability assumption, there exists a unique $\theta \in \Theta$ such that $P_X \in \mathcal{M}_\theta$. On the basis of the invariance of the model $\mathcal{M}$ with respect to the group $\mathcal{G}$, it holds $P_{g(X)} \in \mathcal{M}$. Again, there exists a unique $\overline{\theta} \in \Theta$ such that $P_{g(X)} \in \mathcal{M}_{\overline{\theta}}$. Denoting by $\overline{g}$ the bijection induced by g on the parameter space Θ, namely

$$\overline{g} : \theta \in \Theta \mapsto \overline{g}(\theta) := \overline{\theta} \in \Theta, \qquad [19.29]$$

the group induced on the parameter space is defined by

$$\overline{\mathcal{G}} := \{\overline{g}; g \in \mathcal{G}\}. \qquad [19.30]$$

For each $\theta \in \Theta$, the orbit $\Theta(\theta)$ is defined by

$$\Theta(\theta) := \{\overline{g}(\theta); \overline{g} \in \overline{\mathcal{G}}\}. \qquad [19.31]$$

We assume that there exists only one orbit on Θ, in the sense that $\Theta(\theta) = \Theta$, $\forall \theta \in \Theta$. This means that $\overline{\mathcal{G}}$ is reach enough allowing to go from any point from Θ in any other point in Θ. In such a case, the group $\overline{\mathcal{G}}$ is called transitive over Θ.

EXAMPLE 19.1.– *Let $X_1, \ldots, X_n$ be an i.i.d. sample of a random variable X with mean $\mathbb{E}(X) = \theta$ and assume that $\mathbb{E}(X^2) = h(\theta)$, where $h(\cdot)$ is a known function. Our aim is to estimate θ. The information about the probability distribution P_0 of X can be expressed in the form of the model [19.1] by taking*

$$f(x, \theta) := (f_1(x, \theta), f_2(x, \theta)) = \left(x - \theta, x^2 - h(\theta)\right)^\top \qquad [19.32]$$

(see, for example, Qin and Lawless 1994).

For $\Theta = \mathbb{R}$, the model $\mathcal{M}^{(1)}$ associated with the function $f(x, \theta)$ defined in [19.32] is invariant to the additive group

$$\mathcal{G} := \{g : x \in \mathbb{R} \mapsto g(x) := x + a;\ a \in \mathbb{R}\} \qquad [19.33]$$

if $h(\theta) := \theta^2 + b$*, for some* $b \geq 0$*, and is also invariant to the multiplicative group*

$$\mathcal{G} := \{g : x \in \mathbb{R} \mapsto g(x) := \lambda x;\ \lambda \in \mathbb{R}_+^*\} \quad [19.34]$$

if $h(\theta) := b\theta^2$*, for some* $b > 0$.

The groups induced on the parameter space $\Theta := \mathbb{R}$ *are*

$$\overline{\mathcal{G}} := \{\overline{g} : \theta \in \mathbb{R} \mapsto \overline{g}(\theta) := \theta + a;\ a \in \mathbb{R}\}$$

$$\overline{\mathcal{G}} := \{\overline{g} : \theta \in \mathbb{R} \mapsto \overline{g}(\theta) := \lambda\theta;\ \lambda \in \mathbb{R}_+^*\}$$

respectively.

Let $\mathcal{M}$ be a moment condition model invariant with respect to the transformations group $\mathcal{G}$, and let $\overline{\mathcal{G}}$ be the group induced on the parameter space Θ. An estimator $\widehat{\theta}_n = \widehat{\theta}_n(X_1, \ldots, X_n)$ of the parameter $\theta_0 \in \Theta$ is called equivariant if

$$\widehat{\theta}_n(g(X_1), \ldots, g(X_n)) = \overline{g}(\widehat{\theta}_n(X_1, \ldots, X_n)),\ \ \forall g \in \mathcal{G}. \quad [19.35]$$

19.3.2. *Equivariance of robust minimum empirical divergence estimators*

Assume that the model $\mathcal{M}$ and the group of transformations $\mathcal{G}$ are such that

$$f(g(x), \overline{g}(\theta)) = f(x, \theta),\ \forall x \in \mathbb{R}^m,\ \forall \theta \in \Theta,\ \forall g \in \mathcal{G}. \quad [19.36]$$

Assume also that there exists only one orbit on Θ generated by the group $\overline{\mathcal{G}}$ induced on the parameter space, so $\overline{\mathcal{G}}$ is transitive over Θ.

Let $X_1, \ldots, X_n$ be a sample on X with the probability distribution $P_X = P_{\theta_0} \in \mathcal{M}_{\theta_0}$, $g \in \mathcal{G}$ and the sample $g(X_1), \ldots, g(X_n)$ on $g(X)$ with the law $P_{g(X)} \in \mathcal{M}_{\overline{g}(\theta_0)}$. By imposing condition [19.36], we show that the robust minimum empirical divergence estimators $\widehat{\theta}_\varphi^c$ defined in [19.23] are equivariant

$$\widehat{\theta}_\varphi^c(g(X_1), \ldots, g(X_n)) = \overline{g}(\widehat{\theta}_\varphi^c(X_1, \ldots, X_n)),\ \ \forall g \in \mathcal{G}. \quad [19.37]$$

First note that, the property of the function f given in condition [19.36] also holds for the truncated orthogonality function $f_n^c(x, \theta)$, namely

$$f_n^c(g(x), \overline{g}(\theta)) = f_n^c(x, \theta),\ \forall x \in \mathbb{R}^m,\ \forall \theta \in \Theta,\ \forall g \in \mathcal{G}. \quad [19.38]$$

Here, $f_n^c(g(x), \overline{g}(\theta))$ is based on the sample $g(X_1), \ldots, g(X_n)$ on $P_{\overline{g}(\theta_0)}$, while $f_n^c(x, \theta)$ is based on the sample $X_1, \ldots, X_n$ on P_{θ_0}.

Indeed, using condition [19.36] for the orthogonality function f, we get

$$f_n^c(g(x),\overline{g}(\theta)) = H_c\left(A_n(\overline{g}(\theta))[f(g(x),\overline{g}(\theta)) - \tau_n(\overline{g}(\theta))]\right) \quad [19.39]$$

$$= H_c\left(A_n(\overline{g}(\theta))[f(x,\theta) - \tau_n(\overline{g}(\theta))]\right). \quad [19.40]$$

The elements $A_n(\overline{g}(\theta))$ and $\tau_n(\overline{g}(\theta))$, based on the sample $g(X_1),\ldots,g(X_n)$, are solutions of the system of equations

$$\begin{cases} \int H_c(A[f(y,\overline{g}(\theta)) - \tau])\,dP_{\overline{g}(\theta)}(y) = 0, \\ \frac{1}{n}\sum_{i=1}^n H_c(A[f(g(X_i),\overline{g}(\theta)) - \tau])H_c(A[f(g(X_i),\overline{g}(\theta)) - \tau])^\top = 0 \end{cases} \quad [19.41]$$

which can be rewritten as

$$\begin{cases} \int H_c(A[f(g^{-1}(y),\theta) - \tau])\,dP_{\overline{g}(\theta)}(y) = 0, \\ \frac{1}{n}\sum_{i=1}^n H_c(A[f(X_i,\theta) - \tau])H_c(A[f(X_i,\theta) - \tau])^\top = 0 \end{cases}. \quad [19.42]$$

Since $Y = g(X)$, the system can also be written as

$$\begin{cases} \mathbb{E}[H_c(A[f(X,\theta) - \tau])] = 0, \; X \sim P_\theta \\ \frac{1}{n}\sum_{i=1}^n H_c(A[f(X_i,\theta) - \tau])H_c(A[f(X_i,\theta) - \tau])^\top = 0 \end{cases}. \quad [19.43]$$

The solution of the system [19.43] is given by $A_n(\theta)$ and $\tau_n(\theta)$ based on the sample $X_1,\ldots,X_n$. Whenever the solution of the system is unique, we obtain the equalities

$$A_n(\overline{g}(\theta))(g(X_1),\ldots,g(X_n)) = A_n(\theta)(X_1,\ldots,X_n)$$

$$\tau_n(\overline{g}(\theta))(g(X_1),\ldots,g(X_n)) = \tau_n(\theta)(X_1,\ldots,X_n).$$

Consequently, [19.40] becomes

$$f_n^c(g(x),\overline{g}(\theta)) = H_c\left(A_n(\theta)[f(x,\theta) - \tau_n(\theta)]\right) = f_n^c(x,\theta). \quad [19.44]$$

By the definition [19.23] of a minimum empirical divergence estimator $\hat{\theta}_\varphi^c$, we obtain

$$\hat{\theta}_\varphi^c(g(X_1),\ldots,g(X_n)) = \arg\inf_{\theta\in\Theta}\sup_{t\in\mathbb{R}^{\ell+1}}\left\{t_0 - \frac{1}{n}\sum_{i=1}^n \psi\left(t^\top \overline{f}_n^c(g(X_i),\theta)\right)\right\} \quad [19.45]$$

$$= \arg\inf_{\theta\in\Theta}\sup_{t\in\mathbb{R}^{\ell+1}}\left\{t_0 - \frac{1}{n}\sum_{i=1}^n \psi\left(t^\top \overline{f}_n^c(g(X_i),\overline{g}(\overline{g}^{-1}(\theta)))\right)\right\} \quad [19.46]$$

$$= \arg\inf_{\theta\in\Theta}\sup_{t\in\mathbb{R}^{\ell+1}}\left\{t_0 - \frac{1}{n}\sum_{i=1}^n \psi\left(t^\top \overline{f}_n^c(X_i,\overline{g}^{-1}(\theta))\right)\right\} \quad [19.47]$$

$$= \arg\inf_{\theta\in\Theta} \left\{ \widehat{t_0^c}(\overline{g}^{-1}(\theta)) \right.$$

$$\left. - \frac{1}{n}\sum_{i=1}^{n} \psi\left(\widehat{t^c}(\overline{g}^{-1}(\theta))\overline{f}_n^c(X_i, \overline{g}^{-1}(\theta))\right) \right\}. \quad [19.48]$$

Denote $\widetilde{\theta} := \overline{g}^{-1}(\theta)$. By its very definition, $\widehat{\theta_\varphi^c}(X_1, \ldots, X_n)$ realizes the infimum over Θ of the criterion

$$\widetilde{U}(\widetilde{\theta}) := \left\{ \widehat{t_0^c}(\widetilde{\theta}) - \frac{1}{n}\sum_{i=1}^{n} \psi\left(\widehat{t^c}(\widetilde{\theta})\overline{f}_n^c(X_i, \widetilde{\theta})\right) \right\}$$

which means that

$$\widetilde{U}(\widehat{\theta_\varphi^c}(X_1, \ldots, X_n)) \leq \widetilde{U}(\widetilde{\theta}), \quad \forall\widetilde{\theta} \in \Theta. \quad [19.49]$$

Denoting $U(\theta) := \widetilde{U}(\overline{g}^{-1}(\theta)) = \widetilde{U}(\widetilde{\theta})$, relation [19.49] becomes

$$U(\overline{g}(\hat{\theta}_\varphi^c(X_1, \ldots, X_n))) \leq U(\theta), \ \forall\theta \in \Theta, \quad [19.50]$$

on the basis of the fact that the group $\overline{\mathcal{G}}$ is transitive over Θ. Since the criterion optimized in [19.48] is even $U(\theta)$, using [19.50], we deduce that $\overline{g}(\widehat{\theta_\varphi^c}(X_1, \ldots, X_n))$ realizes the infimum in [19.48], hence

$$\widehat{\theta_\varphi^c}(g(X_1), \ldots, g(X_n)) = \overline{g}(\widehat{\theta_\varphi^c}(X_1, \ldots, X_n)). \quad [19.51]$$

The fact that all of the estimators of the presented class are robust and equivariant brings the perspective of considering the robust minimum risk equivariant estimator corresponding to this class. The problem of characterization and approximation for the robust minimum risk equivariant estimator pertaining of this class will be the theme of a future research study.

19.4. Acknowledgments

This work was supported by a grant of the Ministry of Research, Innovation and Digitization, CNCS CCCDI – UEFISCDI, project number PN-III-P4-ID-PCE-2020-1112, within PNCDI III.

19.5. References

Basu, A., Shioya, H., Park, C. (2011). *Statistical Inference: The Minimum Distance Approach.* Chapman & Hall, London.

Broniatowski, M. and Keziou, A. (2006). Minimization of ϕ-divergences on sets of signed measures. *Studia Sci. Math. Hungar.*, 43, 403–442.

Broniatowski, M. and Keziou, A. (2009). Parametric estimation and tests through divergences and the duality technique. *J. Multivariate Anal.*, 100, 16–36.

Broniatowski, M. and Keziou, A. (2012). Divergences and duality for estimation and test under moment condition models. *J. Statist. Plann. Inference*, 142, 2554–2573.

Cressie, N. and Read, T.R.C. (1984). Multinomial goodness-of-fit tests. *J. Roy. Statist. Soc. Ser. B*, 46, 440–464.

Felipe, A., Martín, N., Miranda, P., Pardo, L. (2018). Testing with exponentially tilted empirical likelihood. *Methodol. Comput. Appl. Probab.*, 20, 1319–1358.

Hampel, F.R., Ronchetti, E., Rousseeuw, P.J., Stahel, W. (1986). *Robust Statistics: The Approach Based on Influence Functions*. John Wiley & Sons, New York.

Hansen, L.P. (1982). Large sample properties of generalized method of moments estimators. *Econometrica*, 50, 1029–1054.

Hansen, L.P., Heaton, J., Yaron, A. (1996). Finite-sample properties of some alternative GMM estimators. *Journal of Business and Economic Statistics*, 14, 462–2800.

Imbens, G.W. (1997). One-step estimators for over-identified generalized method of moments models. *Rev. Econom. Stud.*, 64, 359–383.

Karagrigoriou, A. and Makrides, A. (2023). Information and divergence measures. *Entropy*, 25(4), 683.

Keziou, A. and Toma, A. (2021a). A robust version of the empirical likelihood estimator. *Mathematics*, 9, 829.

Keziou, A. and Toma, A. (2021b). Robust empirical likelihood. In *International Conference on Geometric Science of Information*. Springer International Publishing, Paris, 841–848.

Kitamura, Y. and Stutzer, M. (1997). An information-theoretic alternative to generalized method of moments estimation. *Econometrica*, 65, 861–874.

Lô, S.N. and Ronchetti, E. (2012). Robust small sample accurate inference in moment condition models. *Comput. Statist. Data Anal.*, 56, 3182–3197.

Newey, W.K. and Smith, R.J. (2004). Higher order properties of GMM and generalized empirical likelihood estimators. *Econometrica*, 72, 219–255.

Pardo, L. (2006). *Statistical Inference based on Divergence Measures*. Chapmann & Hall, London.

Pardo, L. and Martin, N. (2021). Robust procedures for estimating and testing in the framework of divergence measures. *Entropy*, 23, 430.

Qin, J. and Lawless, J. (1994). Empirical likelihood and general estimating equations. *Ann. Statist.*, 22, 300–325.

Ronchetti, E.M. and Huber, P.J. (2009). *Robust Statistics*. John Wiley & Sons, New York.

Ronchetti, E. and Trojani, F. (2001). Robust inference with GMM estimators. *J. Econometrics*, 101, 37–69.

Rüschendorf, L. (1984). On the minimum discrimination information theorem. *Statist. Decisions*, (suppl. 1), 263–283.

Toma, A. (2013). Robustness of dual divergence estimators for models satisfying linear constraints. *C. R. Math. Acad. Sci. Paris*, 351, 311–316.

Toma, A. (2014). Model selection criteria using divergences. *Entropy*, 16, 2686–2698.

Toma, A. (2023). Robust Z-estimators for semiparametric moment condition models. *Entropy*, 25(7), 1013.

Toma, A. and Broniatowski, M. (2011). Dual divergence estimators and tests: Robustness results. *J. Multivariate Anal.*, 102, 20–36.

Toma, A. and Leoni-Aubin, S. (2010). Robust tests based on dual divergence estimators and saddlepoint approximations. *J. Multivariate Anal.*, 101, 1143–1155.

20

Continuous Increasing Probability Density Functions: An Approach Through Sampling

A critical goal in statistical analysis is the determination of the probability density function (p.d.f.) of the random variables entered by any problem under study. The effort needed for the determination is often extremely time-consuming. For a time-saving process, we need the help of sampling techniques and the use of the idea of coefficient of variation (Cv) for a random variable X. Sampling can contribute to the study of the distribution of a random variable with very good results in terms of accuracy and more especially of speed. Therefore, the data used in this chapter is sampling data. Since the early 2000s, the coefficient of variation (Cv) has been used for the above determination, which has already heavily reduced the time needed to determine the p.d.f. in multiple instances. There have been a lot of publications since 2003, basically for continuous random variables. In this chapter, we study the case where the graph of an increasing p.d.f. passes through the origin of the axial system of the coordinates X and Y, i.e. in the case of f(0)=0. Here, X is the random variable values and Y=f(x) is the frequencies of those values. Throughout this chapter, we deal with continuous random variables and illustrating examples are given.

20.1. Introduction

For any case of statistical analysis, the idea of random variable X dominates. In some studies, there are hundreds of random variables. The researcher's basic duty is to find or determine the probability density function (p.d.f.) for every random variable involved in the study. The effort for the determination is sometimes an extremely time-consuming process. In the present chapter, we deal with continuous random variables taking their values in the interval $[0, \beta]$. Their p.d.f. values are

---

Chapter written by Maria TSIFOUTIDOU and Nikolaos FARMAKIS.

increasing and passing from the origin of the axial system of X and Y: X for the random variable and Y=f(x) for the suitable p.d.f. of X. It is of course f(0)=0.

In this chapter, our basic duty and the new idea are to use sampling data and the concept of the coefficient of variation (Cv) in order to achieve the determination of the p.d.f. of a continuous random variable X. The p.d.f. here is taken as an increasing one. The approach is made in minimal time, much quicker than the time required by an already-known method. This method gives the form of the p.d.f. at the best level of accuracy.

The theoretical approach of the p.d.f. f(x) will be on the basis of a polynomial function of degree v and all efforts are to find this degree expressed in terms of the Cv concept. After this, an expression of the appropriate coefficient(s) in terms of Cv and v completes the whole effort. For the convenience of the researcher, the squared inverse coefficient of variation $q=Cv^{-2}=ICv^2$, instead of Cv, will be used.

20.2. Theoretical approach

Suppose we have a continuous random variable X with distribution expressed by an increasing p.d.f. f(x). The random variable X takes its values in the range [0, β]. Such a p.d.f. can be found in Farmakis (2010). Here, we will introduce a new one similar with slightly better behavior. This is the next one:

$$f(x)=\begin{cases}\left(\dfrac{ax}{\beta}\right)^{v}, x\in[0,\beta] \\ 0 \quad , \quad x\notin[0,\beta]\end{cases}, v\neq-1, a>0 \tag{20.1}$$

First of all, we demand

$$\int_0^{\beta} f(x)\,dx=1 \tag{20.2}$$

which leads to

$$\int_0^{\beta}\left(\frac{ax}{\beta}\right)^{v}dx=\frac{a^{v}}{\beta^{v}\cdot(v+1)}\cdot x^{v+1}\Big|_0^{\beta}=\frac{a^{v}\cdot\beta}{v+1}=1\Rightarrow a^{v}=\frac{v+1}{\beta}, a=\left(\frac{v+1}{\beta}\right)^{\frac{1}{v}}. \tag{20.3}$$

In order to calculate the parameters Cv and its squared inverse q, we need the three basic parameters of the random variable: (a) mean value EX, (b) variance VarX and (c) standard deviation SDX. So it is:

$$EX = \int_0^{\beta} x \cdot f(x)\,dx = \frac{a^{\nu}}{\beta^{\nu}} \int_0^{\beta} x^{\nu+1} dx = \ldots = \frac{a^{\nu} \cdot \beta^2}{\nu+2} = \frac{\nu+1}{\nu+2} \cdot \beta \qquad [20.4]$$

$$EX^2 = \int_0^{\beta} x^2 \cdot f(x)\,dx = \frac{a^{\nu}}{\beta^{\nu}} \int_0^{\beta} x^{\nu+2} dx = \ldots = \frac{a^{\nu} \cdot \beta^3}{\nu+3} = \frac{\nu+1}{\nu+3} \cdot \beta^2 \qquad [20.5]$$

$$VarX = EX^2 - (EX)^2 = \ldots = \frac{(\nu+1) \cdot \beta^2}{(\nu+3) \cdot (\nu+2)^2}, \quad SDX = \frac{\beta}{\nu+2} \cdot \sqrt{\frac{(\nu+1)}{(\nu+3)}} \qquad [20.6]$$

and of course

$$Cv = \sqrt{\frac{1}{(\nu+1) \cdot (\nu+3)}} = \sqrt{\frac{1}{q}} \text{ or}$$

$$Cv^{-2} = q = (\nu+1) \cdot (\nu+3) \Rightarrow \nu = -2 + \sqrt{1+q}\,. \qquad [20.7]$$

So instead of [20.1] we finally take the new form of f(x) as

$$f(x) = \begin{cases} \dfrac{\nu+1}{\beta^{\nu+1}} \cdot x^{\nu}, & x \in [0, \beta] \\ 0, & x \notin [0, \beta] \end{cases}, \nu \neq -1 \qquad [20.1a]$$

and it remains to devise an algorithm that with the help of [20.1a] leads from sample data to the appropriate p.d.f. The steps of this algorithm are according to Farmakis (2001):

Step 1: Put the sample data in order of increasing size.

Step 2: Divide the range $R = X_{max} - X_{min}$ by the number of classes κ=4,5,6,…,20 estimated to be required (usually used κ=4,5,6,..,11). It is good to take range of classes w=[R/κ]+1 at least, with [x]=integer part of the real x. So the random variable X has field of values [0, β], β=κw.

Step 3: In each class $\left[w\cdot(i-1),w\cdot i\right]$, i=1,2,…,κ assign the frequency n_i of occurrence of values of the random variable X in this class and the class center $x_i=\left(w\cdot(i-1)+w\cdot i\right)/2$. The center represents the value of X in the class.

Step 4: Put all of the above in a table and calculate the parameters of X: Mean=EX, VarX, SDX, Cv, q, ν, α or α^{ν}.

Step 5: Write the p.d.f. of X in the form of [20.1a] and calculate the theoretical frequencies θ_i, i=1,2,…,κ by integrating (1a) over all the κ classes and multiplying the probabilities by the size n of the sample.

Step 6: Make the good fitting X^2 test between the observed frequencies n_i and the theoretic ones θ_i. Degrees of freedom k-3 and significance level a=0.05 or 0.01. END of the algorithm.

Some illustrative examples in the next paragraph will give a clearer icon of the method.

20.3. Examples for illustration

In the examples below, it is undertaken that we have a continuous random variable (r.v.) X with distribution expressed by an increasing p.d.f. f(x), like this in [20.1]. The r.v. X takes its values in the range [0, β].

EXAMPLE 20.1.– A sample of n=340 students is drawn from all the high schools of a region. The members of the sample face the question:

"*Who was the architect of the Parthenon?*"

They have to search for an answer on the Internet, and a searching machine counts and records the time in minutes consumed until an answer is given. We observed the values X_{max}=48 min and X_{min}=2 min. So we adopt a range R=49 minutes divided into κ=7 classes with the same width w=7 minutes, as shown in Table 20.1. We note by X the random variable "time consumed", and we distribute the frequencies of its values into the third column of Table 20.1. In the fourth column of Table 20.1 is the cumulative frequency of the values of X. The center value of the fourth class is taken as temporary average value noted by m=24.5. The values hosted by the fifth column are $x_i'=\left(x_i-m\right)/w=\left(x_i-24.5\right)/7$. After this, we calculate the values of the parameters of X: mean, variance, standard deviation, coefficient of variation (Cv), inverse squared coefficient of variation (ICv^{-2}=q) and the exponent ν (Farmakis 2001, 2003). The calculations follow:

Classes	xi	ni	Ni	xi′	ni*xi ′	ni*xi ′^2	Pi	θi	X^2
[0, 7)	3.5	5	5	-3	-15	45	0.017	5.8	4.32
[7, 14)	10.5	19	24	-2	-38	76	0.056	18.9	19.10
[14, 21)	17.5	35	59	-1	-35	35	0.097	33.0	37.11
[21, 28)	***24.5***	50	109	0	0	0	0.140	47.7	52.45
[28, 35)	31.5	66	175	1	66	66	0.185	62.7	69.43
[35, 42)	38.5	77	252	2	154	308	0.230	78.1	75.89
[42, 49]	45.5	88	340	3	264	792	0.276	93.8	82.58
		340			**T_1= 396**	**T_2=1,322**	**1**	**340.0**	**340.9**

Table 20.1.

Mean value $\overline{x} = m + \frac{w \cdot T_1}{n} = 24.5 + \frac{7 \cdot 396}{340} = 32.65$

Variance $s^2 = \frac{w^2}{n-1}\left(T_2 - \frac{T_1^2}{n}\right) = \frac{7^2}{339}\left(1322 - \frac{396^2}{340}\right) = 124.4190$

Standard deviation $s = \sqrt{124.4190} = 11.15$

Coefficient of variation $Cv = \frac{s}{\overline{x}} = 0.3415$ and $q = ICv^2 = Cv^{-2} = 8.5747$

Exponent $v = -2 + \sqrt{1+q} = 1.0943$ and according to (1a), we get the p.d.f. of X:

$$f(x) = \begin{cases} \frac{2.0943}{49^{2.0943}} \cdot x^{v} = 0.000604 \cdot x^{v}, x \in [0,49] \\ 0 \qquad , \qquad x \notin [0,49] \end{cases} . \qquad [20.8]$$

Thanks to the p.d.f., we calculate the theoretic frequencies θ_i, i=1,2,…,7 for the values of the random variable X into the 7 classes. They are already located in the ninth column of Table 20.1. An X^2 test was performed to check the goodness of fit of observed to theoretical frequencies. A good fit is established and certified. So [20.8] is the p.d.f. describing the distribution of the time consumed for research.

EXAMPLE 2.– A sample of n=320 members is drawn from college students. The members of the sample face the question:

"*How much time do you spent per day online on average in minutes?*"

All responses are recorded and ranked in ascending order. We observed the values X_{max}=139 min and X_{min}=3 min. So we adopt a range R=140 minutes divided into κ=7 classes with the same width w=20 minutes, as shown in Table 20.2. We note by X the random variable "time spent", and we distribute the frequencies of its values in the third column of Table 20.2. In the fourth column of Table 20.2 is the cumulative frequency of the values of X. The center value of the 4th class is taken as temporary average value noted by m=70. The values hosted by the fifth column are $x_i' = (x_i - m)/w = (x_i - 70)/7$. After this, we calculate the values of the parameters of X: mean, variance, standard deviation, coefficient of variation (Cv), inverse squared coefficient of variation (ICv^{-2}=q) and the exponent v (Farmakis 2001, 2003). The calculations follow:

Classes	xi	ni	Ni	xi′	ni*xi ′	ni*xi ′^2	Pi	θi	X^2
[0, 20)	10	3	3	-3	-9	27	0.014	4.6	1.96
[20, 40)	30	17	20	-2	-34	68	0.051	16.2	17.83
[40, 60)	50	32	52	-1	-32	32	0.092	29.6	34.62
[60, 80)	*70*	47	99	0	0	0	0.137	44.0	50.21
[80, 100)	90	60	159	1	60	60	0.185	59.2	60.81
[100, 120)	110	73	232	2	146	292	0.234	75.0	71.02
[120, 140]	130	88	320	3	264	792	0.286	91.4	84.72
		320			**395**	**1,271**	**1**	**320.0**	**321.2**

Table 20.2.

Mean value $\bar{x} = m + \frac{w \cdot T_1}{n} = 70 + \frac{20 \cdot 395}{320} = 94.69$

Variance $s^2 = \frac{w^2}{n-1}\left(T_2 - \frac{T_1^2}{n}\right) = \frac{20^2}{319}\left(1271 - \frac{395^2}{320}\right) = 982.3472$

Standard deviation $s = \sqrt{982.3472} = 31.34$

Coefficient of variation $Cv = \frac{s}{\overline{x}} = 0.3310$ and $q = ICv^2 = Cv^{-2} = 9.1273$

Exponent $\nu = -2 + \sqrt{1+q} = 1.1823$ and according the (1a) we get the p.d.f. of X:

$$f(x) = \begin{cases} \frac{2.1823}{140^{2.1823}} \cdot x^{\nu} = 0.0000452 \cdot x^{\nu}, & x \in [0,140] \\ 0, & x \notin [0,140] \end{cases} . \qquad [20.9]$$

Thanks to the p.d.f., we can calculate the theoretic frequencies θ_i, i=1,2,...,7 for the values of the random variable X into seven classes. They are already located in the ninth column of Table 20.2. An X^2 test was performed to check the goodness of fit of observed to theoretical frequencies. A good fit is established and certified. So [20.9] is the p.d.f. describing the distribution of the time consumed for research.

20.4. Results and discussion

The above two examples very clearly showed that:

The model [20.1] can be a very successful kind of p.d.f., for the suitable random variable X. In the present case, the distribution of the random variable is an increasing function. The value of the X^2 index coming out from the sampling data is very small (vanishing) in relation to the degrees of freedom, (d.f.=7-1-2=4) and the significance level α=0.05. We face X^2=0.88 for the case of Example 1 and X^2=1.18 for the case of Example 2 against the critical value X^2=9.88 (Farmakis 2001).

The biggest advantage of this method, with the coefficient of variation, is the speed with which we reach the result. It is hundreds or even thousands of times shorter than the time required to have the p.d.f. from the corresponding time that another method would need, without using the coefficient of variation (Cv).

For future applications, it would be very interesting to face the analogous problem in decreasing distribution with some model like the one in [20.1] of the present chapter.

20.5. References

Farmakis, N. (2001). *STATISTICS, Brief Theory, Exercises*. Christodoulidi, S.O., Kallipos, Thessaloniki (in Greek).

Farmakis, N. (2003). Estimation of coefficient of variation: Scaling of symmetric continuous distributions. *Statistics in Transition*, 6(1), 83–96.

Farmakis, N. (2010). Coefficient of variation: Connecting sampling with some increasing distribution models. In *Proceedings of Stochastic Modeling Techniques & Data Analysis International Conference (SMTDA-2010)*, 8–11 June, Chania, Crete.

Farmakis, N. (2015). *Sampling and Applications*. Greek Academic Depository, Athens (in Greek).

Farmakis, N. (2016). *Introduction to Sampling*. Kyriakidis Bros, S.A., Thessaloniki (in Greek).

Papatsouma, I. (2018). Contribution to the sampling highlight of model distributions using the coefficient of variation. PhD Dissertation, Aristotle University of Thessaloniki, Thessaloniki, (in Greek).

21

The Importance of the Initial Selection of Suppliers in the Food Service Divisions of Hotels, the Current Situation in the Supply Chain of Greece

Strategic supply chain management has become more important with the impact of globalization. The main idea of supply chain management is to establish good relationships between the members of the chain to serve customers accurately. The success of the supply chain depends largely on strong cooperation among the chain members, where the selection of supplier is a strategic decision-making process that affects all supply chain performance. In this chapter, the current situation of the Greek hotel industry in terms of supply chains is analyzed mainly from the perspective of initial supplier selection. At some stages, correlation of factors and influence of environmental variables on supply chain management are analyzed with a degree of importance. The sample concerns 653 Greek hotel companies and was conducted in the first quarter of 2019. The findings of the study highlight the importance of the function in the initial selection of suppliers, the problems and the process of initial selection of suppliers.

21.1. Introduction

The synchronization of business processes is the main objective of supply chain management (SCM) (Min 2015). In addition, it enables the rational flow of information, goods and services, with the aim of increasing speed, flexibility, availability and quality of goods while reducing costs. Firms gain competitive advantages by implementing a supply chain where the end user receives supplies of quality products at competitive prices.

Chapter written by Konstantinos VASILAKAKIS, Efthalia TABOURATZI and Despoina SDRALI.

The utility of rational real-time information flow throughout the supply chain enables immediate customer service and reduces inventories in warehouses. Today, to be competitive, enterprises need partnerships and synergies between effective supply chain management. The use of real-time information and communication technology (ICT) is essential to search for products, ensure timely and secure delivery, ensure the requirement of little inventory and, in essence, use just-in-time (JIT) concepts.

In addition, the use of ICT helps hotels with SCM functions such as customer relationship management (CRM), market research, demand forecasting, event planning, decision-making, inventory management, etc.

SCM is defined, according to Cousins et al. (2019), as a management philosophy that includes a set of activities that directly and indirectly affect the supply chain member organizations and supply chain performance. SCM is the effective management of all processes from the design of a product or service to its sale and distribution by the end consumer. The supply chain assessment capability includes all activities related to the flow of goods from raw material supply to final condition, as well as the associated information flows. Looking at the definitions for SCM, most of them emphasize the performance of the supply chain as a whole and introduce the ultimate goal of SCM. Therefore, it is clear that the purpose of measuring the effective management of a supply chain is to determine the overall objectives. SCM is an integrated process that transforms raw materials into finished products, which are offered to customers through distribution or retailing.

Implementing good supply chain management has many benefits for both the supplier and the hotel. The relationship between the supplier and the hotel becomes stronger with the development of appropriate buying and selling policies. The implemented policies regarding procurement result in the emergence of reliable suppliers, with greater efficiency. In addition, appropriate policies lead to cost reduction and improvement in the purchasing process.

The analysis of the results of this research, adopted the logic of Milovanovic, Paunović and Avramovski (2021) from their research in hotels in the Republic of Serbia, where it included descriptive statistics, t-test and ANOVA, using SPSS v25.0.

This chapter emphasizes the importance of initial supplier selection and the testing of the regularity of these initial selection stages. In addition, it is done on the correlation of factors and the influence of environmental variables on supply chain management in hotel catering divisions in Greek hotel enterprises.

This work is considered to be original because nothing similar has been studied regarding the initial supplier selection for the food service divisions of Greek hotels. In addition, its originality is defined in that so far studies have investigated supplier selection as a whole and not the important concept of initial supplier selection.

21.2. Literature review

Ayers (2006) defined supply chain as "life cycle processes that include physical, information, financial and knowledge flows whose purpose is to understand consumer demands with products and services from multiple connected suppliers". Grant et al. (2017) defined another dimension of SCM as "a function of linking important business functions and processes across firms in a high-performance business model". Through the supply chain, users become strategic partners and the relationships between them change from simple transactions to sophisticated partnerships (Wallner et al. 2015).

Moreover, according to Gonzalez-Torres et al. (2021), collaborations between users of the tourism supply chain is the most important parameter for it to work efficiently and benefit all participating firms. Timely information about any operation of the chain is a prerequisite so that there are no blockages in their work schedules. The responsibility of the supply chain manager is to evaluate the business decisions in the whole chain and not only in specific users (Ilić and Tešić 2016). The strategic importance of supply chain management is that companies without partnerships can no longer be competitive.

According to Schlegel (1999), the benefits of a good supply chain management can be improved customer service and value-added, more rational use of assets and increased sales and profitability. The competitive advantage of such firms can be achieved either by a low-cost strategy or by a diversification strategy. The low-cost strategy expects lower prices to attract uneconomic customers. The diversification strategy is oriented towards the needs of customers in order to offer high-quality products. SCM creates the conditions for firms to use both strategies at the same time and to avoid the traditional strategies. As a result, SCM makes it easier for its users to reduce delivery time, increase the availability of products/services, reduce costs and improve their quality.

Vasilakakis and Sdrali (2022) reported that, adopting a quality system can support compliance, profitability and the development of a quality-driven culture. Quality management requires a systematic approach that uses strategy, data and effective communications to integrate the quality discipline into the culture and activities of the organization.

Tellioglu (2021) stated that in the modern hotel enterprises, cost and quality of services are of paramount importance. Selecting supply chain partners and conducting an effective SCM provides quality services and results in repeat and satisfied guests in hotels. All supply chain users must have access to real-time information and incorporate learning and business process improvement. Knowledge management is another prerequisite for a reliable supply chain, along with information gathering among its members (Lopes de Sousa Jabbour et al. 2020).

Abdelsalam and Elbelehy (2020) defined the members of the tourism supply chain (TSC) as producers, distributors and suppliers of food and other products, hoteliers, as well as transport companies, tour operators, and restaurants, attractions and shops. Each tourism supply chain (TSC) includes participants, attractions and a specific destination. According to Zhang et al. (2009, p. 345), tourism supply chain management (TSC) is referred to as "a set of approaches used to effectively manage operations within a specific tourist destination to meet the needs of tourists from selected markets and achieve the business objectives of different firms within the chain".

Tour operators link supply and demand by combining products and services from different suppliers into a homogeneous package, which is made available to tourists or by travel agencies. They therefore play an important role in TSC (Tigu and Calaretu 2013).

Vasilakakis and Sdrali (2022) said that suppliers must pay constant attention to maintaining the quality of the products they offer, along with the quality of food systems and the stable economic policy. Thus, the adoption of quality assurance procedures may assist. The tourism supply has a variety of products and services; therefore, effective and adequate coordination of all of these suppliers is of great importance.

This chapter focuses on the selection of suppliers and the initial selection of suppliers in Greek hotel enterprises.

21.3. Benefits of supply chain management

Suppliers and hotels benefit from an established supply chain management system. The relationship between the supplier and the hotel is made stronger by professional management in the form of developing appropriate purchasing policies. This could also lead to concentration on a few reliable suppliers, rather than a large and inefficient supplier base. Newer and more efficient suppliers could be identified, which would lead to increased efficiency. This leads to a significant reduction in costs and also helps to continuously evaluate and improve the purchasing process. It could increase the product range or perhaps even reduce it, due to the intensive market research that is carried out.

The supplier base is huge in the hotel industry, which has its positives. Conscious steps should be taken to identify committed suppliers who are willing to follow the goals of the hotel enterprise, participate and appreciate and support changes in organizational requirements. In addition, supplier evaluation is a critical process, and the ability of suppliers to deliver the right goods at the right time with the right specifications must be reviewed. Contracts are awarded after careful negotiations with the supplier.

Once suppliers have fulfilled their obligation by delivering the required goods as per specification, it is the responsibility of the purchasing division to ensure that suppliers' accounts are paid promptly, and occasionally good suppliers are lost due to late payments. Therefore, it is very important to maintain a strong relationship with the supplier; thus, supplier management needs to be strengthened. Finally, it is a very critical step in supply chain management. Careful consideration of this process will contribute to efficiency and cost savings.

21.4. Research methodology

The aim of the research was to examine the stages and factors that influence the initial selection of suppliers in the food service divisions in the Greek hotel industry, from the perspective of purchasing managers.

The survey was conducted with a structured closed-ended questionnaire in 2019. The sampling was based on the hotel industry in Greece (2019). The questionnaire was answered only by hotels with a fully operational food service division located in Greece (4 and 5 stars, about 2,274 hotels). The sample was more than 10% of all hotels in Greece.

The final sample collected was 653 valid questionnaires, with a response rate of 29% out of the total of 2,274 hotels in the Greek territory.

21.4.1. *The questionnaire*

From studying the literature (Saunders 1994; Biljanoska and Martinoska 2010; Ho et al. 2010; Onder and Kabadayi 2015; Ninemeier 2018; Taherdoost and Brard 2019), a closed-ended questionnaire was structured based on the research question. The questionnaire was divided into three sections. In the first section, there were general questions about supplier evaluation and selection. The second section included questions about the most important factors in supplier selection and reasons for discontinuing them. Finally, in the third section, there were questions about the profile of the sample participants.

To capture the stages, factors influencing the initial selection of suppliers, participants were asked to rate on a five-point Likert scale, how important are the following 11 initial stages: problem identification/buying need, description of raw material specifications, determining necessary quantities of raw materials, identifying potential suppliers, gathering alternative bidding options, evaluating potential suppliers, selecting suppliers, signing a supply contract, determining raw material orders, receiving, and controlling supplies and continuous evaluation of supplies.

21.5. Data analysis

Responses were processed and analyzed using descriptive and factorial statistics. After the completion of the 653 questionnaires from Greek hotel companies, the coding of the variables followed and the data were entered into the statistical package SPSS v25.0. In order to record the results of the field survey in terms of their supplier evaluation and selection criteria, the results of descriptive statistics were analyzed and then examined whether there are correlations between selected variables that attribute particular characteristics of the survey. The data obtained from the questionnaires provided a significant range of information on the characteristics of the respondents.

21.5.1. *Reliability analysis*

Reliability is usually checked using the widely used *Cronbach's Alpha reliability coefficient.* This should be close to 0.7 (although there is also a view in the literature that the threshold should be less than 0.6) (Cohen et al. 2008).

Reliability analysis was implemented using the Reliability *Analysis* command of SPSS software[1]. Therefore, the result is as follows (see Table 21.1):

– *0.851*: found high relative to the theoretical threshold of *0.7*.

Cronbach's alpha	N of items
.851	11

Table 21.1. *Reliability analysis of Question 5 (Composite variable)*

1 SPSS: Analyze^Scale^Reliability analysis^Statistics^Scale if item deleted.

21.5.2. *Results*

The profile of the sample

The accommodation category that received a high percentage of about 48% were four and five star hotels, three star hotels a percentage of about 30%, and two star hotels 15%. The majority of respondents who answered the survey were hotel managers and owners (72% of respondents).

Importance of initial supplier selection stages

Table 21.2 presents the mean and variance of the 11 initial stages, and initial supplier selection factor responses. For the importance of the stages in the initial selection of suppliers, 83.5% reported "very important" and "very important", the first stage, that of "identifying the problem". Also, almost 92% defined "description of raw material specifications" as very and very important.

	Q51 Problem identification	Q52 Identification of raw Materials	Q53 Essential quantities of raw materials	Q54 Potential suppliers	Q55 Alternative tender options
Average Standard Deviation	4.04 .766	4.35 .687	4.18 .735	4.14 .761	4.27 .755
	Q56 Rating of potential suppliers	Q57 Selection of suppliers	Q58 Sub-agreement purchasing	Q59 Specification of orders for pr. materials	Q510 Receipt, control of supplies
Average Standard Deviation	4.08 .824	4.43 .718	3.28 1.264	4.10 .778	4.55 .638
			Q511 Continuous evaluation of supplies		
Average Standard Deviation			4.22 .895		

Table 21.2. *Average and divergence of initial supplier selection stages*

Furthermore, 6.5% defined the "determining quantities" stage as "very important" and "very important". "Finding potential suppliers" as a stage scored 84% ("very important" and "very important") and "gathering alternative bidding options", 87%.

A further 81% said it was highly important at the "evaluating potential suppliers" stage and a disproportionate 15% said it was "moderately important". The "supplier selection" stage was set at a high importance ("very important" and "very important"), 93%.

At the "supplier contract signing" stage, a high percentage of 29% indicated the "fragile" relationship (stating "moderately important") that exists between hotels and suppliers. A signed contract as shown is not as important a stage when initially selecting suppliers, but specifications and quantities of raw materials are high on the list.

At other stages, "determining raw material orders" and "continuous evaluation of supplies" reach high importance at over 83%. The highest percentage is given to "receipt, control of supplies" which 95% indicated importance at the level of "very important" and "very important".

It is therefore observed that hotel companies place greater emphasis on raw materials (specifications and quantities), as well as on the receipt and control of these supplies.

From the initial stages of supplier selection studied, "problem recognition", i.e. the need for proper selection of personnel, was considered by a large percentage (57.9%) to be very important in the initial selection of suppliers. In addition, stocks and availability of suppliers has a high weight in terms of initial supplier selection with the stage "necessary quantities of raw materials" reaching a percentage of importance of (52.4%). The definition of "potential suppliers" as an initial stage also has a high importance (50.7%), as well as the evaluation of them (48.5%).

A stage that indirectly reflects its great importance in the initial selection is the "determination of raw material orders" after the selection of the supplier that has been answered in a very significant percentage of 53.1% that they want companies to define in advance specific quantities of order and receipt (61.4% importance rate). This shows the great mass production and distribution of products in the hotel industry and gives greater importance to the evaluation and selection of suppliers in this sector.

Factor analysis of initial supplier selection stages

Regarding the factor of initial supplier selection stages (ISS), the measures of central tendency & variance of $\mathbf{F_{ISS}}$ are shown in Table 21.3 and graph, where it is shown to have a relatively high value (4.19/max=5.0).

Valid	653
N	
Missing	4
Mean	**4.1498**
Median	4.1800
Fashion	4.00
std. deviation	**.51854**
Variance	.269
Range	4.00
Minimum	1.00

Table 21.3. *GDP Stages Factor Analysis* (F_{ISS})

It is observed that the factor does not follow the normal distribution, it has extreme values.

Regularity check of initial supplier selection stages

In order to check for possible correlations between the factors (of F_{ISS} with other factors) of the present chapter, a first normality test (Gaussian curve) was carried out, with the results shown in Table 21.4[2].

– All variables and the factor F_{ISS} in the next table do not have a normal distribution since in both *K-S* & *S-W* tests, the significance is less than 0.05 (Sig.<0.05) (Chen and Zhu 2001; Field 2009; Munro 2001), and in the corresponding Box & Whisker plots, the median is not approximately in the middle and neither of the two extremes are equally spaced from the rectangle, and there is evidence of outliers at some end(s) (Chen and Zhu 2001; Field 2009; Munro 2001).

2 Analyze ^ Descriptive Statistics ^ Explore ^ Dependent List ^ Plots ^ Histogram ^ Normality plots with tests [SPSS]

	Kolmogorov–Smirnov[a]			Shapiro–Wilk		
	Statistic	df	**Sig.**	Statistic	df	**Sig.**
Q1 EVALUATION PROCEDURES	.527	533	**.000**	.362	533	**.000**
Q4 SUPPLIER EVALUATION	.284	533	**.000**	.791	533	**.000**
Q6 PERFORMANCE TEST	.353	533	**.000**	.636	533	**.000**
Q11 CHANGE IN SUPPLY NO.	.386	533	**.000**	.663	533	**.000**
Q13 SUPPLIER REEVALUATION PROCEDURES	.457	533	**.000**	.556	533	**.000**
Q16 TYPE OF ACCOMMODATION	.451	533	**.000**	.546	533	**.000**
Q17 CATEGORY OF ACCOMMODATION	.194	533	**.000**	.893	533	**.000**
INITIAL SELECTION OF SUPPLIER (F_{ISS})	.075	533	**.000**	.931	533	**.000**

Table 21.4. *Normality test for Par - variables*

In addition, the other survey factors also have a non-normal distribution (Table 21.5).

	Kolmogorov–Smirnov[a]			Shapiro–Wilk		
	Statistic	df	**Sig.**	Statistic	df	**Sig.**
CRITERIA RAW MATERIALS	.302	653	**.000**	.636	653	**.000**
SUPPLIER CRITERIA	.272	653	**.000**	.700	653	**.000**
CRITERIA ENVIRONMENT	.162	653	**.000**	.916	653	**.000**
REASONS FOR INTERRUPTION OF COOPERATION. SUPPLIER	.072	653	**.000**	.946	653	**.000**

Table 21.5. *Normality check of other survey factors*

Correlation of factors

Therefore, the correlation between all factors and variables, *Spearman's* correlation coefficient (due to non-normality) was used, where it showed the following[3,4] (Table 21.6).

		INITIAL CHOICE OF SUPPLIER
INITIAL CHOICE OF	correlation coefficient	1.000
SUPPLIER	Sig. (2-tailed)	.
	N	653
CRITERIA RAW	correlation coefficient	**.550****
MATERIALS	Sig. (2-tailed)	.000
SPEARMAN'S RHO	N	653
SUPPLIER CRITERIA	correlation coefficient Sig. (2-tailed)	**.453**** .000
	N	653
REASONS FOR	correlation	
INTERRUPTION OF	coefficient	**.382****
COOPERATION.	Sig. (2-tailed)	.000
SUPPLIER	N	653
	correlation	**.260****
CRITERIA	coefficient	
ENVIRONMENT	Sig. (2-tailed)	.000
	N	653

Table 21.6. *Correlation table of factors*

According to the Spearman coefficient value framework (Brosius 2002, p. 501):

3 Use a Spearman correlation coefficient because at least one of the factors has a non-normal distribution, and use a Pearson coefficient when both factors have a normal distribution.

4 Analyze ^ Correlate ^ Bivariate ^ Spearman [SPSS]

– 0	No correlation
– 0–0.2	Very weak correlation
– 0.2–0.4	Weak correlation
– 0.4–0.6	Moderate correlation
– 0.6–0.8	Strong correlation
– 0.8–1.0	Very strong correlation
– 1.0	Perfect correlation

Findings

– A high statistical significance is found between the factor F_{ISS} and the factor ORIGINAL MATERIALS (<0.01), with a moderate positive correlation (0.550) (when one factor increases, the other increases accordingly), i.e. the initial supplier selection stages are moderately influenced by the supplier evaluation criteria.

– A high statistical significance is found between the factor F_{ISS} and the factor SUPPLIER (<0.01), with a moderate positive correlation (0.453) (when one factor increases, the other increases accordingly), i.e. the initial supplier selection stages are moderately influenced by the supplier criteria.

– A high statistical significance is found between the factor F_{ISS} and the factor REASONS FOR STOPPING COOPERATION WITH SUPPLIERS (<0.01), with a weak positive correlation (0.382) (when one factor increases, the other increases accordingly), i.e. the initial supplier selection stages are affected to a small extent by the reasons for stopping cooperation with suppliers.

– A high statistical significance is found between the factor F_{ISS} and the factor PRIMARY MATERIALS (<0.01), with a weak positive correlation (0.260) (when one factor increases, the other increases accordingly), i.e. the initial supplier selection stages are influenced to a small extent by environmental criteria.

Effect of environmental variables

Thus, since the factor F_{ISS} and the variables have a *non-normal distribution*, nonparametric statistical tests are chosen to test their effect. More specifically:

– the nonparametric test, *Kruskal–Wallis test*, which is the equivalent of the parametric *one-way ANOVA test* and involves more than two independent samples;

– or the nonparametric test, *Mann–Whitney U Test*, instead of the T-test, and involves two independent samples.

Therefore, the following were found:

– *Evaluation procedures* (Question 1). It was found that the factor F_{ISS} is influenced by the evaluation process with high statistical significance (Sig.: 0.000) (Table 21.7).

Null Hypothesis	Test	Sig.	Decision
The distribution of INITIAL SUPPLIER SELECTION is the same across categories of Q1 EVALUATION PROCEDURES.	Independent Samples Mann–Whitney U Test	.000	Reject the null hypothesis

Asymptotic significances are displayed. The significance level is .05,

Table 21.7. *Impact Check F_{ISS} – Question 1 (Q1) Hypothesis Test Summary*

By analyzing the trend of the means (medians), we find that F_{ISS} changes (incrementally), from the YES option to the NO option, i.e. the factor increases when there are supplier-procurement evaluation procedures, as shown in Tables 21.7a and 21.7b.

Valid	500
N	
Missing	0
Mean	**4.2280**
Median	**4.2700**
Fashion	4.00
std. deviation	.45550
Variance	.207
Range	3.82
Minimum	1.18

Table 21.7a. *Analysis of F_{ISS} – variable Question 1 (option: YES)*

– *Frequency of evaluation* (Question 1). It was found that the factor F_{ISS} is influenced by supplier-supply evaluation frequency with statistical significance (Sig.: 0.026) (Table 21.8).

Valid	152
N	
Missing	0
Mean	**3.8941**
Median	**3.9100**
Fashion	4.09
std. deviation	.62365
Variance	.389
Range	4.00
Minimum	1.00

Table 21.7b. *Analysis of F_{ISS} – variable Question 1 (option: NO)*

Null Hypothesis	Test	Sig.	Decision
The distribution of INITIAL SUPPLIER SELECTION is the same across categories of Q4 SUPPLIER EVALUATION	Independent- Samples Kruskal–Wallis Test	.026	Reject the null hypothesis

Asymptotic significances are displayed. The significance level is .05,

Table 21.8. *Impact Check F_{ISS} – Question 4 (Q4) Hypothesis Test Summary*

– *Accommodation category* (question 17). The factor F_{ISS} was found to be influenced by accommodation categories with high statistical significance (Sig.: 0.000) (Table 21.9).

Null Hypothesis	Test	Sig.	Decision
The distribution of INITIAL SUPPLIER SELECTION is the same across categories of Q17 ACCOMMODATION CATEGORY	Independent- Samples Kruskal–Wallis Test	.000	Reject the null hypothesis

Asymptotic significances are displayed. The significance level is .05,

Table 21.9. *Impact Check F_{ISS} – Question 17 (Q17) Hypothesis Test Summary*

Analyzing the trend of the averages (medians), we see that the F_{ISS} (fluctuation) changes by accommodation category, as shown in Table 21.10.

Select	Median
Other	4.18
1*	3.91
2*	4.0
3*	4.09
4*	4.31
5*	4.27

Table 21.10. *Analysis of F_{ISS} – variable Question 17 (all options)*

21.6. Discussion

Highlighting that there are not many relevant empirical studies that study supplier evaluation and initial selection criteria, procedures, stages, etc. in tourism (hotel) enterprises, but mainly the opinions of scientists make our work more important and interesting.

İkinci and Tipi (2021) pointed out that selecting the right supplier for firms is very important and is needed for them to be able to achieve high-quality products at relatively low cost, increasing profitability and customer satisfaction. Through proper evaluation and selection of suppliers and targeted criteria, firms improve their competitiveness.

The purpose of this study was to investigate the factors that influence initial supplier selection in the Greek food and beverage segments of the hotel industry, as well as the factors that are taken into account for initial supplier selection. This study can be considered as a first review in this field, conducted in Greece.

In addition, many authors have defined that it is necessary in supply chain management to improve social, economic and environmental practices of supplier selection (Amindoust et al. 2012; Grimm et al. 2014; Shen et al. 2016). It would be reasonable to repeat the survey at a reasonable time to observe how much these factors have changed following specific events and circumstances, such as the Covid-19 pandemic.

Professional supply chain management ensures that each supplier is committed to leading standards of product and service quality. Effective supply chain management helps to significantly reduce costs by developing and implementing contracts and agreements with suppliers of hospitality products and services, ensuring hotels are competitively priced, whether for food and beverage, rooms or property operations.

The study leads to a better understanding of the factors that contribute to the correct initial selection of suppliers in the food segments of the hotel industry in Greece. Understanding the main factors related to initial selection is an important step for a company to establish a supplier selection process and continuous evaluation of the selected suppliers, thus providing a supplier network that meets the company's objectives. Finally, major pressures on the environment have resulted in a greater focus on supply chain management as businesses incorporate environmental attributes and considerations into their supplier selection and evaluation. Integrating environmental considerations is a necessary condition for long-term competitiveness of firms and their supplier selection (Grimm et al. 2014).

Vasilakakis and Sdrali (2022) reported that one of our most basic needs is food and therefore many countries invest in the food industry. However, due to climate change, population growth, urbanization, natural disasters and the changing competitive conditions, firms must control their production, marketing and supply chain process.

21.7. Conclusion

This study fills the gap in the literature, as it is the first to examine the initial supplier selection criteria in Greece in the food and beverages divisions in the Greek hotel industry. In summary, the results showed that the primary objectives of initial supplier selection in the food service divisions of hotels are related to initial identification of the problem and finding potential suppliers, as well as in evaluating them and the reliability of supply delivery confirm previous research. Therefore, a sample involving more tourism business disciplines is suggested for future research. Furthermore, this research was conducted in 2019; therefore, an updated survey for the post-Covid-19 era would be of interest to explore whether the results may have varied.

21.8. References

Abdelsalam, A. and Elbelehy, C. (2020). The early impact of COVID-19 on tourism industry: Assessment of Egyptian tourism supply chain. In *10th International Conference on Operations and Supply Chain Management*. Victoria University of Wellington & Institut Teknologi Sepuluh Nopember (ITS), Indonesia, 1–12.

Amindoust, A., Ahmed, S., Saghafinia, A., Bahreininejad, A. (2012). Sustainable supplier selection: A ranking model based on fuzzy inference system. *Applied Soft Computing*, 12(6), 1668–1677. doi: 10.1016/j.asoc.2012.01.023.

Ayers, J.B. (2006). *Handbook of Supply Chain Management*. CRC Press, Boca Raton.

BDO Canada. (2021). Procurement and supply chain strategies for COVID-19 [Online]. Available at: https://www.bdo.ca/insights/procurement-and-supply-chain-strategies-during-covid-19.

Biljanoska, J. and Martinoska, S. (2010). Supplier selection criteria as a critical point in the menu quality. In *Tourism & Hospitality Management 2010, Conference Proceedings*, 266–272 [Online]. Available at: https://eprints.uklo.edu.mk/648/1/203%20Biljanoska%20145.pdf [Accessed 10 December 2022].

Brosius, F. (2002). *SPSS 11*. MITP Verlag, Bonn.

Chadee, D., Ren, S., Tang, G. (2021). Is digital technology the magic bullet for performing work at home? Lessons learned for post COVID-19 recovery in hospitality management. *International Journal of Hospitality Management*, 92, 1–8. doi: 10.1016/j.ijhm.2020.102718.

Chen, A. and Zhu, W. (2001). Revisiting the assumptions for inferential statistical analyses: A conceptual guide. *Quest*, 53, 418–439.

Christopher, M. and Peck, H. (2004). Building the resilient supply chain. *The International Journal of Logistics Management*, 15(2), 1–14. doi: 10.1108/09574090410700275.

Clark, J. (2020) The impact of COVID-19 on your hospitality supply chain [Online]. Available at: https://www.ukhospitality.org.uk/blogpost/1721400/357732/The-Impact-of-COVID-19-on-your-Hospitality-Supply-Chain [Accessed 14 December 2021].

Cohen L., Manion, L., Morrison, K. (2018). *Research Methods in Education*, 8th edition. Routledge Falmer, London.

Cousins, P.D., Lawson, B., Petersen, K.J., Fugate, B.S. (2019). Investigating green supply chain management practices and performance. *International Journal of Operations & Production Management*. doi: 10.1108/IJOPM-11-2018-0676.

Field, A. (2009). *Discovering Statistics Using SPSS*, 3rd edition. Sage Publications Ltd., London.

González-Torres, T., Rodríguéz-Sánchez, J.L., Pelechano-Barahona, E. (2021). Managing relationships in the tourism supply chain to overcome epidemic outbreaks: The case of COVID-19 and the hospitality industry in Spain. *International Journal of Hospitality Management*, 92. doi: 10.1016/j.ijhm.2020.102733.

Grant, B.D., Trautrims, A., Wong, Y.C. (2017). *Sustainable Logistics and Supply Chain Management. Principles and Practices for Sustainable Operations and Management*, 2nd edition. Kogan Page Ltd, New York.

Grimm, J.H., Hofstetter, J.S., Sarkis, J. (2014). Critical factors for sub-supplier management: A sustainable food supply chains perspective. *International Journal of Production Economics*, 152, 159–173. doi: 10.1016/j.ijpe.2013.12.011.

Ho, W., Xu, X., Dey, P.K. (2010). Multi criteria decision making approaches for supplier evaluation and selection: A literature review. *European Journal of Operational Research,* 202(1), 16–24. doi: 10.1016/j.ejor.2009.05.009.

İkinci, M. and Tipi, T. (2021). Food supplier selection in the catering industry using the analytic hierarc hyprocess. *Food Science and Technology*, v42, e48420. doi: 10.1590/fst. 48420.

Ilić, D. and Tešić, A. (2016). The relationship between supply chain management strategy, marketing, logistics and company performance for breweries in Serbia. *Ekonomika poljoprivrede*, 63, 1157–1168.

Kim, S.S., Kim, J., Badu-Baiden, F., Giroux, M., Choi, Y. (2021). Preference for robot service or human service in hotels? Impacts of the COVID-19 pandemic. *International Journal of Hospitality Management*, 93, 1–12. doi: 10.1016/j.ijhm.2020.102795.

Lopes de Sousa, Jabbour, A.B., Chiappetta Jabbour, C.J., Hingley, M., Vilalta-Perdomo, E.L. Ramsden, G., Twigg, D. (2020). Sustainability of supply chains in the wake of the coronavirus (COVID-19/SARS-CoV-2) pandemic: Lessons and trends. *Modern Supply Chain Research and Applications*, 2(3), 117–122. doi: 10.1108/MSCRA-05-2020-0011.

Loukaidis, K.A. (2011). *Statistical Data Processing using IBM SPSS STATISTICS 19: A Guide to Entering, Managing, Analysing, Interpreting and Presenting Statistical Data in the Social Sciences*. Epifanios Publications, Nicosia.

Milovanovic, V. (2021). The COVID-19 pandemic effects on the hotel industry. In *The Sixth International Scientific Conference – TOURISM CHALLENGES AMID COVID-19*. Thematic Proceedings, Vrnjačka Banja, 570–587. doi: 10.52370/TISC21570VM.

Milovanovic, V., Paunović, M., Avramovski, S. (2021). The impact of COVID-19 on the hotel supply chain management. *Hotel and Tourism Management*, 9(2), 63–78. doi: 10.5937/menhottur2102063M.

Min, H. (2015). *The Essentials of Supply Chain Management – New Business Concepts and Applications*. Pearson FT Press, New York.

Munro, B.H. (2001). *Statistical Methods for Health Care Research*, 4th edition. Lippincott, Philadelphia, PA.

Ninemeier, J.D. (2018). *Planning and Control for Food and Beverage Operations*, 9th edition. American Hotel & Lodging Educational Institute, Orlando.

Nova-Kaltsouni, X. (2006). *Methodology of Empirical Research in Social Sciences*. Gutenberg Publications, Athens.

OECD (2020). Food supply chains and COVID-19: Impacts and policy lessons [Online]. Available at: https://www.oecd.org/coronavirus/policy-responses/food-supply-chains-and-covid-19-impacts-and-policy-lessons-71b57aea/ [Accessed 14 November 2022].

Onder, E. and Kabadayi, N. (2015). Supplier selection in hospitality industry using ANP. *International Journal of Academic Research in Business and Social Sciences*, 5(1), 166–186. doi: 10.6007/IJARBSS/v5-i1/1417.

Saunders, A. (1994). Supplier audits as part of a supplier partnership. *The TQM Magazine*, 6(2), 41–42. doi: 10.1108/09544789410054028.

Schlegel, G.L. (1999). Supply chain optimization: A practitioner's perspective. *Supply Chain Management Review*, 11(4), 50–57.

Shen, H., Deng, Q., Lao, R., Wu, S. (2016). A case study of inventory management in a manufacturing company in China. *Nang Yan Business Journal*, 5, 20–40. doi: 10.1515/nybj-2017-0003.

Taherdoost, H. and Brard, A. (2019). Analyzing the process of supplier selection criteria and methods. *Business Procedia Manufacturing*, 32, 1024–1034. doi: 10.1016/J.PROMFG. 2019.02.317.

Tasnim, Z. (2020). Disruption in global food supply chain (FSCs) due to Covid-19 pandemic and impact of digitalization through block chain technology in FSCs management. *European Journal of Business and Management*, 12(17), 73–84.

Tellioglu, S. (2021). The impact of COVID-19 on supply chains of all-inclusive hotels. *GeoJournal of Tourism and Geosites*, 35(2), 464–470. doi: 10.30892/gtg.35226-673.

Tigu, G. and Calaretu, B. (2013). Supply chain management performance in tourism Continental hotels chain case. *Amfiteatru Economic*, 15(33), 103–115.

Vasilakakis, K. and Sdrali, D. (2022). Supplier selection criteria in the Greek hotel food and beverage divisions. *Journal of Hospitality and Tourism Insights*. doi: 10.1108/JHTI-07-2021-0169.

Wallner, M., Brunner, U., Zsifkovits, H. (2015). Modelling complex planning processes in supply chains. In *Operational Excellence in Logistics and Supply Chains*, Blecker, T., Kersten, W., Ringle, C.M. (eds). Hamburg University of Technology, Hamburg.

Welch, C. (2021). Global supply chain disruption: How the COVID-19 pandemic impacted the hospitality industry. EIS [Online]. Available at: https://www.elkayinteriorsystems.com/en/covid-19-response/innovation-through-%20design/global-supply-chain-disruption.html [Accessed 30 November 2022].

Zhang, X., Song, H., Huang, G.Q. (2009). Tourism supply chain management: A new research agenda. *Tourism Management*, 30(3), 345–358. doi: 10.1016/j.tourman.2008.12.010.

22

Compliance with IUU Fisheries of Manila Clams in the Tagus Estuary

The high exploitation of the Manila clam in the Tagus estuary is carried out in an IUU (Illegal, Unreported and Unregulated fishing) fishing scenario. The livelihood of several families depends on this resource, which represents great economic importance for all players involved in the process, from harvesters to the final consumer. Since 2011, the fishing community has been transferring its harvesting effort to this clam and the number of harvesters has increased significantly, including immigrants, people with professions not related to fisheries, unemployed, without recreational or professional license. All these factors cause uncertainty evaluation of the stock of this species, as it does not pass through legal channels, and leads to uncertain information that does not reflect the reality or the extent of the problem.

This study has the following research objectives: 1: Characterization of IUU fishing of the Manila clam in the Tagus estuary based on literature review, analysis of a questionnaire carried out to shellfish harvesters in the Tagus estuary and analysis of the bivalves auction landings in the jurisdiction of the captaincies of Setúbal and Lisbon. 2: Analysis of the factors that influence compliance with the allowed daily quotas for harvesting the Manila clam in the Tagus estuary. 3: Analysis of the factors that influence compliance with the fishing gear allowed for harvesting the Manila clam in the Tagus estuary.

For the last two objectives, the present study applied an OP and probit (binary) deterrence model to analyze the determinants of non-compliance with regulations that included socio-economic, deterrence and normative variables. The obtained results indicated that the fishing gear influences the probability of violation; individuals who use illegal gear are more likely to fail daily quotas. One of the suggested measures to combat non-compliance is to increase monitoring, control and surveillance efforts and effectiveness and resort to sufficiently dissuasive penalties.

The identification of the causes of each IUU activity allows the competent authorities to design policies that are more incisive and adequate to each of the problems, promote sustainable management and increase the fight against illegality and the existence of parallel markets.

Chapter written by Margarida XAVIER, Ana LORGA DA SILVA and Paula CHAINHO.

22.1. Introduction

Unreported and unregulated illegal fishing began to gain expression globally in 1950 with the sharp decline in stocks of marine species (Le Gallic and Cox 2006). This issue has cast a shadow over the sustainable development of marine species (Shen and Huang 2021). By definition, anything that violates the law is illegal, so that IUU fishing covers a wide range of behaviors (Coelho et al. 2013). This term "IUU fishing" refers to fishing activities that do not comply with national, international or regional fisheries conservation and management legislation or measures (Newman 2015). IUU fishing is a worldwide problem that impacts ecosystems and causes socio-economic imbalances. This problem is more pronounced in countries where fisheries regulation and inspection are still weak, but it can also be relevant in developed countries, when the competent authorities and regulations are not yet adapted to manage a new fishery.

Several studies have been conducted to study compliance with fisheries' regulations. The approaches of these studies differ in the type of deterrence models used, which can have static approaches or dynamic approaches (Sanaa 2015). Static deterrence models follow Becker's approach (Becker 1968) and assume that the violator faces a single decision problem for a period of time to make the decision to maximize the expected utility of illegal fishing, i.e. whether they choose to follow the regulations ("compliance") or whether they choose to infringe it. In this context, the main determinants that lead the fisherman to choose to infringe are the profit that the fisherman obtains, resulting from the practice of an illegal activity and the low probability of detection combined with a "small" fine (enforcement) (Sanaa 2015).

Many authors follow Becker's static approach (with only one period) (e.g. Furlong 1991; Kuperan and Sutinen 1998; Hatcher and Gordon 2005). However, some authors carried out an extension of the model, in which they began to consider the effects of avoidance behavior (Charles et al. 1999). The results of the study show that fishermen react to enforcement by focusing more on avoiding it than on reducing the violation rate (Charles et al. 1999). Some studies indicate that the determinants that lead the fisherman to infringe are not enough to explain their decisions. Based on this argument, they decided to incorporate normative factors in the static model, such as moral, social and legitimacy determinants. These factors measure the fisherman's behavior, their beliefs regarding their peer group and how the peer group's opinion influences their values. It also measures the fisherman's perception of violation and the legitimacy of regulations (Hatcher et al. 2000)).

The influence of normative factors has also been analyzed in the existing literature, both in theoretical and empirical applications, and has shown different results. These factors were considered positive when the fisherman considered violating behavior as "bad behavior" and negative when the fisherman considered violating behavior as "normal" (Abusin and Hassan 2015). Although some authors consider deterrence factors to be of greater importance (Hatcher and Gordon 2005), most authors consider normative factors and deterrence factors to be of equal importance (Abusin and Hassan 2015).

Normative variables have been measured in several ways, such as (Abusin and Hassan 2015):

– the fisherman's perception of the number of violators (peer pressure and peer behavior);

– how fishermen view the legitimacy of the imposed regulations (whether they consider the regulations adequate);

– moral and social position of the fisherman in society.

Some flaws are pointed out to the statistical model, such as the assumption that two different agents understand the same restrictions and the only factor that differentiates them is their affinity for taking risks. A limitation pointed out to the model is that it does not take into account the effect of discounting future benefits, i.e. discount rates (which proved to be significant among poor fishermen). By nature, the static model cannot measure the optimal breach rate over time (Sanaa 2015).

Dynamic models consider that the fisherman maximizes their profits with time until they are caught, because the crime is committed repeatedly. The dynamic model includes the effect of the discount rate and modifies the detection probability, which in the static model is subjective and in the dynamic model becomes conditional, explaining that the profit from the violation is conditioned to the survival of the offender (Sanaa 2015).

The arguments used to resort to this model in the study of illegal activities are based on the repetitive nature of the crime (the violation occurs several times), the change in the danger of being caught over time and the differences in preferences regarding the future (discount rates). Extensions to this model were made, such as replacing "intensity" with "frequency" to measure the breach rate and/or compliance. This rate has been measured in different ways in different countries. Studies that classify fishermen by their violation rate believe that the classification will help formulate policies adapted to the needs of each group. Breach frequency as a measure of breach rate has also been measured in a variety of ways. Frequency substitution was due to four factors: the intensity of the violation, which may work for developed countries, but does not "work" in the case of developing countries because quota rights are not well defined and the probability of evading detection is quite high; seasonality; the use of frequency help to classify fishermen into different categories of violators, thus the typology can help formulate policies tailored to each group; illegal catches are not sold in formal markets but sold outside monitoring and formal markets (Abusin and Hassan 2015).

IUU fishing constitutes a threat to the sustainable management of fishing resources and to the conservation of biodiversity in aquatic systems, as is the case in the Tagus estuary where IUU fishing for Manila clams (*Ruditapes philippinarum*), combined with the invasive nature of the species, has contributed to a sharp decrease in the population of the native species, the grooved carpet shell (*Ruditapes decussatus*) (Chainho et al. 2015; Ramajal et al. 2016; Mamede et al. 2020).

The occurrence of a great abundance of Manila clams in the Tagus estuary and its extensive distribution substantially altered the reality of bivalve fisheries in this system. There was an exponential increase in harvesters dedicated to the Manila clam and using new fishing gear (Coelho et al. 2020).

The removal of a species on a large scale (illegally, unregulated and unregulated) causes an imbalance in ecosystems and disturbs their stability and productivity (Ma 2020).

Manila clams can be caught using various fishing gears, and four predominant groups of catchers (i.e. manual gathering, clam rake, Scuba diving and clam dredge) were identified in the Tagus estuary (Figure 22.1) (Picard and Ramajal 2015).

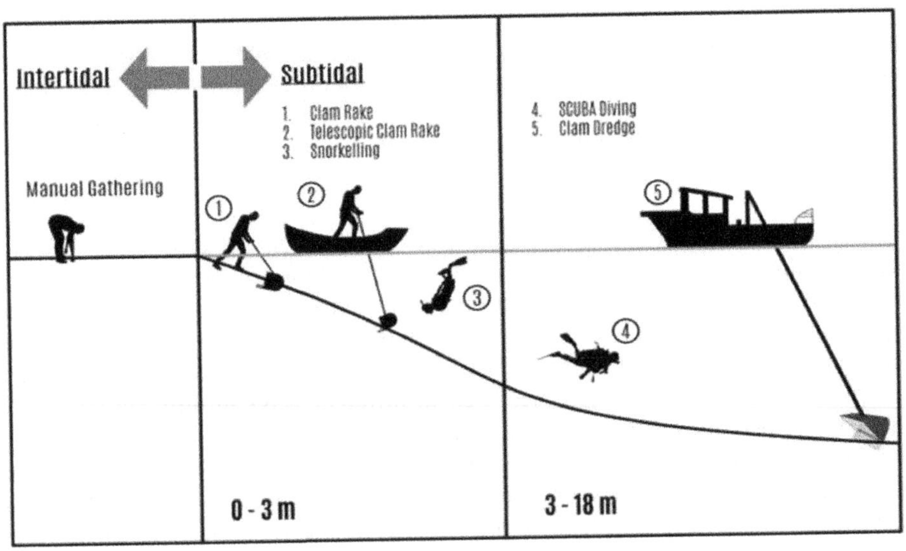

Figure 22.1. *Manila clam harvesting techniques used in the Tagus estuary (adapted from Ramajal et al. (2016)). For a color version of this figure, see www.iste.co.uk/dimotikalis/data4.zip*

Most shellfish harvesters do not have a license, and they practice this activity using illegal fishing gear, with a high negative impact on the ecosystem (Carvalho 2017). The most significant volume of catches recorded in the Tagus estuary comes from illegal fishing gear such as the clam dredge (Ramajal et al. 2016; Carvalho 2017; Coelho et al. 2020). In environmental terms, the clam dredge is harmful because it destroys the benthic species habitat and it affects productivity (Cunha 2012). The clam dredge towed by vessel is more harmful because it intervenes in the sediment at greater depth (due to the greater length of the teeth) (Ramajal et al. 2016; Coelho et al. 2020).

The importance of two factors that contributed to the disproportionate increase in new harvesters should be noted (Coelho et al. 2020):

– easy access to harvesting areas;

– high monetary return of the exploitation of the Manila clam, given its high productivity.

Several problems arise from this exploitation scenario in the Tagus estuary, associated to IUU fishing activities of the Manila clam (Carvalho 2017; Mamede et al. 2020), such as use of illegal fishing gear, public health risk, risk of overfishing, decrease in the price of the resource, high social cost that cannot be internalized, lack of harvesting licenses, and damage to the ecosystem (e.g. reduction of native species in the estuary).

That said, and as this species is a significant economic resource with a social and ecological impact associated with problems of illegal exploitation, it becomes necessary to find an effective solution for harvesting this clam, to promote sustainable management, increase the fight against illegality and the existence of parallel markets. Due to these assumptions, this study has the following research objectives:

1) Analysis of the factors that influence compliance with the daily quotas for harvesting Manila clams in the Tagus estuary.

2) Analysis of the factors that influence compliance with the fishing gear allowed for capturing Manila clams in the Tagus estuary.

22.2. Research methodology

The methodological approach of this study included i) the selection of indicators and the respective variables that represent them; ii) the analyses of compliance with fishing regulations; and iii) the design of the model used to identify factors that influence compliance.

As already mentioned, this study was carried out in the Tagus estuary, and the database was obtained through the questionnaire of the PROMAR Manila clam project (Costa et al. 2015). This questionnaire was carried out in situ by the MARE (Marine and Environmental Research Centre) research team, belonging to the Faculty of Sciences of the University of Lisbon (FCUL) during the period from June 2015 to September 2015, with a view to obtaining the first information on the Manila clam fishing in the Tagus estuary and to characterize the fishing community that operates in this area.

The object of study is the Manila clam, which, since 2011, has become a commercially exploited resource due to its commercial value, productivity and resilience to a broad range of environmental conditions, when compared to native species (Ramajal et al. 2016).

The choice of variables aims to characterize and, when possible, quantify IUU fishing activities in the estuary. The most common IUU fishing activities are (Coelho et al. 2013): fishing without a license, harvesting the native protected species (grooved carpet shell), offenses related to fishing gear, disrespect for quotas, not declaring catches, misreporting and deliberately and erroneously declaring harvest.

A statistical analysis of the variables considered relevant to characterize and quantify the main IUU fishing activities in the Tagus estuary was made based on the data collected through the responses to the questionnaire conducted on the fishing community that operates in this area (see Carvalho (2017) for the detailed answers to the questionnaire). This analysis was also subsequently used for variables considered relevant to the Deterrence model (explained below). For data analysis, descriptive statistics (measures of central tendency and dispersion) and estimation of models, the software used was Stata Statistical Software: Release 17, which focused on the following variables: age of the harvesters (age), price of Manila clams practiced at the level of the harvester (price/kg), years of practice of the activity (experience), gender of the harvesters (gender), fishing gear used for harvesting Manila clams (fishing gear), quantity of Manila clams (kg) caught by type of fishing gear (kg/day), number of respondents who fish above and below the allowed daily quota, whether they practice the activity of harvesting clams alone, accompanied or in both ways (they practice the activity alone, accompanied or both), whether they have professional fishing license or not (license), whether in the harvester's opinion the regulations for the Tagus estuary are respected or not by other harvesters (respected regulations), whether they are aware of the legislation in force for the Tagus estuary (do you know the legislation), if fishing in the Tagus estuary is their main activity or is it a complementary activity (main or complementary activity), and if they consider the management and inspection in the Tagus estuary adequate (adequate management and inspection).

In order to quantify IUU fishing activity "deliberately and erroneously declaring harvests", the official auction landings were used as an indicator of catches in the Tagus estuary. Landings from the Tagus estuary and Sado estuary for the period referring to the questionnaire (2015) were analyzed. This analysis of the auction landings from the Sado estuary was done because a large part of the Manila clam catches from the Tagus estuary is declared to have been caught in the Sado estuary due to the false declarations, motivated by the absence of regulation of the Manila clam harvesting in the Sado estuary (with no daily quotas established) and by the frequent classification of the Tagus estuary as zone C (microbiological and metal contamination); this constrains the possible destinations of the harvested bivalves (see Ma (2020) for further details).

One of the objectives of this study was to characterize and quantify IUU fishing activities and to understand the determinants that catalyze each IUU activity present in the Tagus estuary, in order to identify what is failing and its causes.

A static ordered probit (OP) model was used to understand the factors that influence the probability of violating the daily kg quota; additionally, marginal effects were calculated to understand the flexibility of each individual's choice. The probit model (binary) was used to understand the factors that influence the probability of violating the fishing gear allowed for catching Manila clams, following Abusin and Hassan (2015).

22.3. Analysis and interpretation of results

The results of the questionnaire showed that 35.1% of the catchers use illegal gear and that the associated determinant is economic, since these gears allow access to locations with higher abundance of this species; therefore, more catches equal a higher income. The responses to the questionnaire also indicated that 91.5% of the harvesters do not have a license, the associated determinant being low levels of enforcement (such as low levels of MCV and fines that are not sufficiently deterrent) and low levels of compliance on the part of fishermen. It was estimated that 15.96% of the harvesters capture the species above the allowed daily quota. The reasons associated to these infringements are of an economic nature such as profit. It was determined that there is the capture of the native protected species (grooved carpet shell); however, it was not possible to quantify this activity because the catches are not declared, the inherent reason being the bycatch because the arts are not selective and profit (the grooved carpet shell has a higher monetary value). According to data estimated by Costa et al. (2015), the annual catch of the Manila clam in 2015 was 6,000–17,000 tons, while the records of auction landings in the captaincy of Setúbal only declared 4,000 tons of the Manila clam coming from the Tagus estuary; the designated causes for not declaring catches were lack of professional license, tax evasion and profit. With the analysis of the discharges in batch of the captaincy of Setúbal and the surrounding scenario of the Tagus estuary and the Sado estuary, it was determined that the catches were declared wrongly and deliberately. This happens because the Tagus estuary is assigned the zone classification C and the Sado estuary is classified as zone B[1]. Identifying the causes of each IUU activity will allow the competent authorities to design policies that are more incisive and adequate to each of the problems (Coelho et al. 2021). Regarding the fishing community that captures Manila clams in the Tagus estuary, the analysis of the descriptive statistics of our sample allowed us to verify that the average age of the harvesters is 43 years old, 95.7% of which are male, and the most representative fishing technique is manual harvesting (43.6%), although the fishing gear that presents a higher average of kg captured per day is the trawl ≈107 kg/harvester.

The OP model, the results of which are presented below, was estimated with the variables described, and as mentioned earlier, the dependent variable is an ordinal variable that classifies catchers into three categories: non-violators (NV), moderate violators (MV), chronic violators (CV).

Within the explanatory socio-economic variables whose coefficients are statistically significant, it is possible to measure:

The explanatory variable gender has a coefficient with a negative sign, i.e. being a woman negatively influences the probability of choosing to violate the daily kg quota, while being a man positively influences the probability of choosing to violate the daily kg quota per day.

This result was expected since the vast majority of harvesters in our sample are male and the catch of larger numbers is associated with the use of fishing gears that require greater physical robustness, namely scuba diving and using a clam rake; therefore, the probabilities of violation also show greater expression for males.

Regarding the explanatory variable practices, the activity accompanied, alone or both, the estimated coefficient associated with this variable has a positive sign, i.e. when the fisherman practices the activity accompanied, the probability of deciding to violate the daily quota (kg) is lower and when they practice activity alone, the

1 The European Union (EU) has developed a classification system for estuarine-lagoon zones for the production of bivalves. This classification is based on the levels of microbiological contamination of water according to the analysis of the bacteriological content (*Escherichia coli*) and metal contamination levels. The estuarine-lagoon zones can be classified into A, B, C, Probiden. Class A–Bivalves may be caught and marketed for direct human consumption. Class B–Bivalves can be caught and destined for purification, transposition or transformation into an industrial unit. Class C–Bivalves may be caught and intended for prolonged transposition or transformation into an industrial unit.

probability of deciding to violate the daily quota (kg) is greater. Having more crew on the same boat (or practicing the activity accompanied) seems to discourage the violation, which could be associated to the relatively higher risk of being caught and fined with a large crew.

Variables	Coefficient	Standard deviation
Socio-economic variables		
Years of experience	0.317*	0.162
Main or complementary activity	0.763	0.945
Gender	-5.007***	1.157
Age	0.0195	0.021
Price/kg	0.627	1.029
Practice the activity alone, accompanied or both	2.431*	1.402
Dissuasion variables		
License	-0.971	0.864
Fishing gear used	-2.608***	0.937
Ethics variables		
Considers the regulations respected by other fishermen	-4.484***	0.963
Legitimacy variables		
Considers adequate management and supervision	4.098***	0.961
Know the legislation	-0.448	0.477
* $p < 0.10$, ** $p < 0.05$, *** $p < 0.01$		
P>chi$^{2=}$ 0.0000; maximum likelihood= -21.06 Number of observations=93; pseudo R^2=0.548		

Table 22.1. *Results estimated by the OP model on the probability of violation related to the allowed daily kg quotas*

Regarding the explanatory variable years of experience, the estimated coefficient associated with this variable has a positive sign, so the more years of activity the catcher has, the greater the probability of choosing to violate the daily quota (kg). This sign was already expected because the majority of Manila clam harvesters who use fishing gear that collect higher abundances, are harvesters who already harvested other species in the estuary and abandoned the activity to start collecting the Manila clam in 2011, while the "new" harvesters are mostly manual harvesters.

Within the explanatory variables of deterrence that are associated with statistically significant coefficients, it is possible to measure:

Alluding to the explanatory variable fishing gear used, the estimated coefficient associated with this variable has a negative sign, which means that manual harvesters are less likely to violate the daily quota (kg); however, trawl catchers are more likely to violate the permissible daily quota. This signal was already expected, since harvesters who use the clam dredge mostly violate the allowed daily quota, since they use a gear that covers a large fishing area, in addition to not depending on tides. On the contrary, the manual harvesters are limited by the accessibility to the collection sites, which are predominantly conditioned by tides, so this limitation does not allow violating of the daily capture limit.

Within the explanatory variables of ethics that are associated with statistically significant coefficients, it is possible to measure:

The variable considering the regulations respected by the other harvesters displays an estimated coefficient with a negative sign, i.e. the harvesters who do not consider the regulations respected by the other harvesters have a greater probability of violating the daily quota. This variable exposes the conception of the opinion of the harvesters in relation to the other catchers. The existing literature shows that the tendency to violate increases if the peer group also violates (Eggert and Lokina 2010).

Within the legitimacy variables that are associated with statistically significant coefficients, it is possible to measure:

Regarding the variable "considers the management and supervision adequate", the estimated coefficient has a positive sign; therefore, harvesters who consider the management and supervision adequate are more likely to choose to violate the daily quota. Kuperan and Sutinen (1998) emphasize that the "willingness to comply" with the regulations is strongly dependent on the fisherman's perception of the legitimacy of the authorities and their respective authorities.

The estimated coefficients associated with the remaining explanatory variables are not significant in influencing the probability of violating the allowed daily quotas.

Half of the explanatory variables whose estimated coefficients are statistically significant are found in socio-economic variables.

Regarding the following table and in order to measure the effects of the factors that influence the probability of belonging to any of the categories of fishermen

(NV; MV; CV), it is understood that a negative sign represents the willingness of a harvester to leave the group, i.e. discouraging factors. The opposite is the positive sign, which means the incentive to stay in the same group or increase the association with the current position.

From Tables 22.2 and 22.3, it is apparent that the variables' age, price/kg and main or complementary activity are all statistically unimportant. Similar to our model, Hatcher and Gordon (2005) in their OP model of marginal effects also did not find any statistical relevance in the age variable.

Among socio-economic variables, more years of experience seem to encourage non-violators to leave the group and move to higher violation categories (MV and CV), i.e. it encourages violation; whereas, more years of experience seem to encourage chronic violators to stay in the group or even increase group membership. Gender influences the NV to remain, i.e. it discourages the violation while in the CV, the gender tends to encourage the change to lower violation categories (MV and NV). This indicates that among the socio-economic factors, the indicators that seem to discourage violation (within the NV and CV) are years of experience and gender.

Regarding deterrence variables, the fishing gear used encourages the probability of NV to remain in the group and chronic violators to leave the group for lower violation categories (MV; NV). The suggested interpretation is that illegal fishing gear is more common among chronic violators, so the probability of suffering a penalty (fine) is higher for using a prohibited gear, while non-violators do not interact with this danger, so their willingness to stay in the group remains. Therefore, the fishing gear used seems to discourage violation.

The ethical factor namely believing that the regulations are respected by the other catchers discourages the violation. With this belief, the NV tend to remain in the group; whereas, with this belief the VC are encouraged to leave the group. Eggert and Lokina (2010) obtained the same result with this variable which they named Precomp, concluding that the higher the perceived percentage of violators, the lower the probability of the fisherman remaining a non-violator. Abusin and Hassan (2015) and Akpalu (2008) also reach this conclusion. This variable checks the importance of normative factors in the decision-making of the catchers between violating and cooperating with fishing regulations.

Finally, the legitimacy factor, namely considering adequate management and supervision, seems to unexpectedly encourage the NV to leave the group and the VC to remain in the group; therefore, this factor encourages violation. We found no logical explanation for this result. Unlike our model (Eggert and Lokina 2010) for this variable, which they named Adequate, they measured a positive sign suggesting that if fishermen consider the inspection adequate, the probability of not being violators increases. Abusin and Hassan (2015) also obtain for this variable the opposite signs to those estimated in our model and conclude that the belief that law enforcement is adequate represents an incentive for the strategy of being an occasional violator, rather than a chronic violator.

	Non Violators		Moderate Violators		Chronic Violators	
Variables	dy/dx	t stat	dy/dx	t stat	dy/dx	t stat
Socioeconomic Variables						
Years of experience	-0.0261**	-2.20	0.00799	1.44	0.0182**	2.23
Main or complementary activity	-0.0629	-0.79	0.0192	0.67	0.0437	0.83
Gender	0.413***	2.92	-0.126	-1.50	-0.287***	-3.38
Age	-0.00160	-0.96	0.000490	0.86	0.00111	0.96
Price/kg	-0.0517	-0.64	0.0158	0.60	0.0359	0.64
Practice the activity alone, accompanied or both	-0.200*	-1.71	0.0612	1.44	0.139	1.59
Dissuasion Variables						
License	0.0801	1.17	-0.0245	-0.93	-0.0556	-1.23
Fishing gear used	0.215***	3.56	-0.0657*	-1.71	-0.149***	-3.55
Ethics Variables						
Considers the regulations respected by other fishermen	0.370***	6.02	-0.113**	-1.96	-0.257***	-4.92
Legitimacy Variables						
Considers adequate management and supervision	-0.338***	-3.18	0.103*	1.71	0.235***	3.06
Know the legislation	0.0369	0.90	-0.0113	-0.81	-0.0256	-0.90
N=93; * $p < 0.10$, ** $p < 0.05$, *** $p < 0.01$						

Table 22.2. *Marginal effects on the determinants of the decision to violate ordered probit*

The conclusions of Akpalu's model (Akpalu 2008) also refer to a positive influence on the compliance of this variable. The probit model specified in Table 22.3 was estimated with the variables described above. As mentioned, the dependent variable is a dummy variable that classifies catchers into two categories: Illegal and Legal. The model only presents two variables with statistically significant estimated coefficients, and both belong to the category of socio-economic variables. Regarding the explanatory variable main or complementary activity, this has an estimated coefficient with a negative sign, so the catchers who capture Manila clams as their main activity are more likely to use illegal fishing gear, while fishermen who capture Manila clams as a complementary activity have a higher (binary) probability of using legal fishing gear. A possible interpretation is that fishermen who are more dependent on income from fishing (main activity) prefer illegal gear because it allows them to capture more kg and therefore obtain more income. Catchers who are less dependent on fishing income (fishing is a complementary activity) do not need to make as much profit from catches; therefore, legal gear serves the purpose.

Variables	dy/dx	*t* stat
Socioeconomic Variables		
Years of experience	0.00157	0.11
Main or complementary activity	-0.306***	-2.98
Gender	0.106	0.58
Age	0.00250	0.68
Price/kg	0.0631	0.75
Practice the activity alone, accompanied or both	-0.393***	-4.87
Dissuasion Variables		
License	-0.141	-1.03
Ethics Variables		
Considers the regulations respected by other fishermen	-0.161	-1.22
Legitimacy Variables		
Know the legislation	-0.0492	-0.62
*$p < 0.10$, **$p < 0.05$, ***$p < 0.01$		
P>Chi²=0.0101; Maximum Likelihood = -40.27 Number of observations =93; pseudo R^2=0.3405		

Table 22.3. *Marginal effects on the determinants of the decision to violate: probit*

Alluding to the variable who practices the activity alone, accompanied or both, this has an estimated coefficient with a negative sign. This means that the catchers who practice the activity alone are more likely to choose illegal fishing gear, while the catchers who practice the activity accompanied are more likely to choose legal fishing gear.

The other variables do not present statistically significant estimated coefficients.

22.4. Conclusion

IUU fishing has cast a shadow over the sustainable management of marine resources. In Portugal, this scenario has been present since 2010 with the IUU fishing of Manila clams in the Tagus estuary.

For the last two objectives, the present study applied a deterrence model to analyze the determinants of the problem of non-compliance with regulations. The studied determinants would include socio-economic variables, deterrence variables and normative variables (legitimacy variables and ethical variables). The models used in the analysis were the OP and BP models; they had three purposes, namely to examine the determinants that affect the probability of choosing between violating and cooperating with daily kg quotas allowed, to examine the determinants that influence the probability of choosing between violating and cooperating with daily kg quotas based on three categories (NV, VM, VC) and to analyze the determinants that influence the probability of using legal fishing gear or illegal fishing gear.

Regarding the determinants that influence the probability of violating the daily kg quotas and within the deterrence category, it was determined that the fishing gear influences the probability of violation, namely individuals who use illegal gear are more likely not to respect the daily quotas, and the license variable did not show any relevance in the decision-making probability of the harvesters. This may happen due to low levels of enforcement by the competent authorities. One of the suggested measures to combat non-compliance would be to increase efforts to combat the effectiveness of monitoring, control and surveillance and sufficiently dissuasive penalties.

Normative factors also proved to be important showing significant coefficients, recommending that they are equally important as dissuasion factors in explaining compliance with regulations. The results suggest that the harvester is more likely to comply if they perceive that the other catchers comply and/or if the other fishermen censure cases of violation of norms/regulations. The results suggest: having fewer years of experience, practice the activity accompanied, and consider that regulations are respected are incentives to cooperate with regulations. Having said that, a suggested measure is the implementation of a co-management mechanism, as indicated in the literature that argues that the fishing communities that have this regime and tolerate certain “illegal” actions (e.g. poaching), are capable of establishing boundaries between actions that violate fisheries regulations by differentiating between acceptable and unacceptable. Informing harvesters about the impact fishing gear has on the ecosystem and how it affects juveniles and other species are some low-cost management options (Xavier 2021). These solutions combined with dissuasion measures can contribute to the development of sustainable exploitation of this resource.

Regarding the determinants that influence the probability of choosing a legal or illegal fishing gear, it was determined that the variable of activity has the main or complementary influence on the probability of choosing gear, namely individuals whose main activity is fishing are more likely to violate. Offering alternative income or employment opportunities outside of fishing would be important to encourage the use of legal fishing gear.

Ultimately, the objectives of this study were to provide support on what measures should be taken to encourage compliance and combat violations with the goal of promoting sustainable fishing of this resource, which has proven to be so important for the surrounding communities of the Tagus estuary.

22.5. Acknowledgments

This work had the funding support granted to MARE (UIDB/04292/2020) by Fundação para a Ciência (FCT) e Tecnologia and project NIPOGES (MAR01.03.02-FEAMP-0013). P. Chainho was funded by a senior researcher scholarship (2020.01797.CEECIND) granted by FCT.

22.6. References

Abusin, S. and Hassan, R. (2015). Legitimacy and ethics or deterrence factors : Which are more important for compliance with regulations among the artisanal fishers of Sudan? *African Journal of Agricultural and Resource Economics*, 9(3), 239–252.

Akpalu, W. (2008). Individual discount rate and regulatory compliance in a developing country fishery. *Environment and Development Economics*, 13, 591–606.

Becker, G.S. (1968). Crime and punishment: An economic approach. *The Journal of Political Economy*, 76(2), 169–217.

Carvalho. F.B. (2017). Estado atual da população de amêijoa-japonesa (*Ruditapes philippinarum*) do estuário do Tejo e impactes da sua introdução. Master's Dissertation, Faculdade de Ciências da Universidade de Lisboa.

Chainho, P., Fernandes, A., Amorim, A., Ávila, S.P., Canning-Clode, J., Castro, J.J., Costa, A.C., Costa, J.L., Cruz, T., Gollasch, S. et al. (2015). Nonindigenous species in Portuguese coastal areas, coastal lagoons, estuaries and islands. *Estuarine, Coastal and Shelf Science*, 167, 199–211.

Charles, T.A., Mazany, L., Cross, L.M. (1999). The economics of illegal fishing: A behavioral model. *Marine Resource Economics*, 14, 95–11.

Coelho, P. (2020). Análise de cenários de governança na gestão da apanha da amêijoajaponesa (*Ruditapes philippinarum*) em Portugal. Master's Dissertation, Faculdade de Ciências da Universidade de Lisboa.

Coelho, M., Filipe, J.A., Ferreira, M.A.M., Utl, I. (2013). Modelling enforcement and compliance in fisheries: A survey. *International Journal of Latest Trends in Finance & Economic Sciences*, 3(2), 464–469.

Coelho, P., Carvalho, F., Goulding, T., Chainho, P., Guerreiro, J. (2021). Management models of the Manila clam (*Ruditapes philippinarum*) fisheries in invaded European coastal systems. *Frontiers in Marine Science*, 8.

Costa, J.L., Chainho, P., Carvalho, F.B. (2015). Determinação da distribuição espacial de *Ruditapes philippinarum* no estuário do Tejo e condições ambientais favoráveis; Estimativa do número de apanhadores, artes de pesca utilizadas e zonas de pesca. Relatório final do projeto Amêijoa-japonesa. (PROMAR 31-03-01-FEP161), Centro de Ciências do Mar e do Ambiente.

Cunha, V. (2012). Redução do teor de contaminantes químicos provenientes do Estuário do Tejo. Master's Dissertation, Instituto Supeior de Agronomia da Universidade Técnica de Lisboa.

Eggert, H. and Lokina, R.B. (2010). Regulatory compliance in lake Victoria fisheries. *Environment and Development Economics*, 15(2), 197–217.

Furlong, W.J. (1991). The deterrent effect of regulatory enforcement in the fishery. *Land Economics*, 67, 116–129.

Hatcher, A. and Gordon, D. (2005). Further investigations into the factors affecting compliance with U.K. fishing quotas. *Land Economics*, 81(1), 71–86.

Hatcher, A., Jaffry, S., Thebaud, O., Bennett, E. (2000). Normative and social influences affecting compliance with fishery regulations. *Land Economics*, 76(3), 448–461.

Kuperan, K. and Sutinen, J.G. (1998). Blue water crime: Deterrence, legitimacy, and compliance in fisheries. *Law & Society Review*, 32(2), 309–338.

Kuperan, K., Abdullah, N., Susilowati, I., Cynthia Ticao, I.M.S (1997). Enforcement and compliance with fisheries regulations in Malaysia, Indonesia and the Philippines. *Proceedings of the International Workshop on Fisheries Co-management.*

Le Gallic, B. and Cox, A. (2006). An economic analysis of illegal, unreported and unregulated (IUU) fishing: Key drivers and possible solutions. *Marine Policy*, 30(6), 689–695.

Ma, X. (2020). An economic and legal analysis of trade measures against illegal, unreported and unregulated fishing. *Marine Policy*, 117(April), 103980.

Mamede, R., Ricardo, F., Santos, A., Díaz, S., Santos, S.A.O., Bispo, R., Domingues, M.R.M. Calado, R. (2020). Revealing the illegal harvesting of Manila clams (*Ruditapes philippinarum*) using fatty acid profiles of the adductor muscle. *Food Control*, 118(February), 107368.

Newman, S. (2015). A case study on illegal fishing and the role of rights-based fisheries management in improving compliance. *Case Study Compiled as Part of the EFFACE Project*, Institute for European Environmental Policy, London, 4(1).

Picard, D. and Ramajal, J. (2015). Caracterização da pesca e comercialização da amêijoajaponesa – cadeia de valor da apanha e potencial de mercado em Portugal, no âmbito do projecto amêijoa-japonesa (PROMAR).

Ramajal, J., Picard, D., Costa, J.L., Carvalho, F., Gaspar, M., Chainho, P. (2016). Amêijoajaponesa, uma nova realidade no estuário do rio tejo: pesca e pressão social e impacto socio-económico. *BRASPOR*.

Sanaa, A. (2015). Approaches and methods used in analyzing compliance with fishery regulations. *African Journal of Agricultural Research*, 10(19), 2104–2112.

Shen, H. and Huang, S. (2021). China's policies and practice on combatting IUU in distant water fisheries. *Aquaculture and Fisheries*, 6(1), 27–34.

Xavier, M. (2021). Pesca Ilegal, não regulada e não regulamentada da Ameijoa Japonesa no Estuário do Tejo e os fatores que afetam o compliance com os regulamentos de pesca. Master Thesis, Lusófona University.

23

The Expectation of a Mixed Moving Average Process Subject to Ambiguous Lévy Basis

A mixed moving average process (MMA process) is a superposition of infinitely many affine stochastic differential equations. It is a tractable mathematical model of jump-driven processes having a sub-exponential memory. The probability measure for the superposition is often ambiguous due to the data limitation in applications, motivating us to operate the model and accounting for the ambiguity. We present a suitable optimization framework for bounding nominal statistics based on the Tsallis divergence, which is a proper risk measure for dealing with the sub-exponential memory structure. This is an application example of the proposed framework to the streamflow time series data that have qualitatively different memory structures.

23.1. Introduction

The long memory, or a sub-exponentially decaying autocorrelation function, is ubiquitous in a variety of engineering problems (Dissanayake et al. 2018, Beaulieu et al. 2020; Alkathery and Chaudhuri 2022). Widely used classical stochastic process models such as first-order autoregressive models and Ornstein–Uhlenbeck (OU) models are inappropriate for dealing with such problems due to having the exponential memory decaying too fast.

The superposition as an integration of (infinitely) many OU processes with mutually different reversion speeds (i.e. multiple timescales) has been studied (Barndorff-Nielsen 2001). This process has been called the supOU process. Its advantage is that the analytical tractability of the OU process is not critically lost

Chapter written by Hidekazu YOSHIOKA and Yumi YOSHIOKA.

while realizing the model generating a long memory. The latter is due to the coexistence of OU processes, thereby realizing multi-scale time series.

The superposition is defined through the Lévy Basis, often called the independently scattered random measure as an ideal mathematical model of infinite-dimensional white noise processes (Pedersen 2003). The probability measure governing the distribution of the reversion speed, here called the reversion measure, is the key element as it directly determines the decaying speed of the autocorrelation function as well as the fundamental statistics, such as mean and variance. However, its identification would not always be free from errors in applications due to the data limitation; this issue has not been studied well so far, motivating us to study statistical evaluation of supOU processes.

The objective of this chapter is to propose and apply an optimization framework that can bound the variance of a stationary supOU process, both from below and above. The approach of this work for the variance is also applicable to the other statistical moments as they share the common functional form for the supOU and further to some advanced processes (Yoshioka et al. 2023). The evaluation of an inverse moment of the distributed reversion speed plays an indispensable role. Conventionally, the Kullback–Leibler divergence has been used for the statistical evaluation of model distortion, which is the distortion of the reversion measure in this work (Hansen and Sargent 2011). However, it turns out that the Kullback–Leibler divergence becomes indefinite in the sense that the integral to define it blows up. We avoid this issue by using the Tsallis divergence, which is a generalization of the Kullback–Leibler divergence (Tsallis 2019). The optimization framework is novel and is also analytically tractable as closed-form solutions are available. Nevertheless, it needs some care from the standpoint of the optimization in reflexive Banach spaces (Zeidler 1995). Its applicability and limitation will be discussed through the theoretical analysis. The proposed framework is finally applied to the available hourly data of streamflow discharge in Japan.

23.2. supOU process

We briefly review the jump-driven supOU process following the literature (Barndorff-Nielsen 2001; Yoshioka et al. 2023). The supOU process X is a continuous-time and continuous-state stochastic process defined at each time $t \in \mathbb{R}$ as

$$X_t = \int_0^{+\infty} \int_0^{+\infty} \int_{-\infty}^{t} \exp\left(-r(t-s)\right) \mu(\mathrm{d}s, \mathrm{d}z, \mathrm{d}r), \qquad [23.1]$$

where μ is the Poisson random measure of bounded variation jumps with the compensated measure $\mathrm{d}s \times v(\mathrm{d}z) \times \pi(\mathrm{d}r)$ extended over the whole real time line

$t \in \mathbb{R}$, v is the Lévy measure of a subordinator satisfying the integrability conditions

$$M_1 = \int_0^{+\infty} z v(\mathrm{d}z) < +\infty,\ M_2 = \int_0^{+\infty} z^2 v(\mathrm{d}z) < +\infty, \quad [23.2]$$

and π is the probability measure, called the reversion measure, which satisfies $\int_0^{+\infty} \pi(\mathrm{d}r) = 1$. The parameter $r > 0$ is the reversion speed distributed according to π, and jump size z and its frequency are determined by the measure v. Each sample path of the supOU process contains a series of jumps followed by gradual recessions, as typically found in the time series data of streamflow discharge (Yoshioka et al. 2023). We assume the existence of the inverse moment

$$R = \int_0^{+\infty} \frac{1}{r} \pi(\mathrm{d}r). \quad [23.3]$$

More specifically, we assume the Gamma reversion measure (Yoshioka et al. 2023), given by

$$\pi(\mathrm{d}r) = \frac{1}{\Gamma(\alpha)\beta^{\alpha}} r^{\alpha-1} e^{-\frac{r}{\beta}} \mathrm{d}r,\ r > 0 \quad [23.4]$$

with $\alpha > 1$ and $\beta > 0$ so that we have $R = \{\alpha(\beta - 1)\}^{-1} > 0$.

Under [23.2] and [23.3], the supOU process exists globally in time as a weakly stationary process with the mean

$$\mathbb{E}[X_t] = R \int_0^{+\infty} z v(\mathrm{d}z) = R M_1, \quad [23.5]$$

variance

$$\mathbb{E}\left[(X_t - \mathbb{E}[X_t])^2\right] = \frac{R}{2} \int_0^{+\infty} z^2 v(\mathrm{d}z) = \frac{R}{2} M_2, \quad [23.6]$$

and the autocorrelation function (ACF) for time lag $\tau \geq 0$:

$$\mathrm{ACF}(\tau) = \frac{1}{R} \int_0^{+\infty} \frac{\exp(-r\tau)}{r} \pi(\mathrm{d}r) = \left(\frac{1}{1 + \beta\tau}\right)^{\alpha-1}. \quad [23.7]$$

Higher-order statistical moments are also available under additional conditions (Yoshioka 2021). The ACF [23.7] clearly has an algebraically decaying memory corresponding to a slower decay than exponential ACFs. In particular, the ACF is not integrable over $(0,+\infty)$ if $1<\alpha\le 2$, which is the truly long-memory case focused on in our application study.

The closed-form formulas [23.5]–[23.7] show that reasonably identifying the inverse moment R and hence the reversion measure π is of great importance for the modeling and analysis of the supOU process.

23.3. Optimization problems

23.3.1. *Problem description*

The optimization problems considered in this work are intended to bound the variance [23.6], considering the ambiguity of the reversion measure π. The ambiguity is represented by using a Radon–Nikodým derivative as a measurable mapping $\phi:(0,+\infty)\to(0,+\infty)$ such that

$$\int_0^{+\infty}\phi(r)\pi(\mathrm{d}r)=1, \tag{23.8}$$

so that the distorted reversion measure $\phi(r)\pi(\mathrm{d}r)$ becomes a probability measure equivalent to $\pi(\mathrm{d}r)$.

Now, we formulate a pair of optimization problems, which are **Problem D** and **Problem U**. For that purpose, set the Tsallis divergence defined for Radon–Nikodým derivatives and the shape parameter $q>0$ (the special case $q=1$, the Kullback–Leibler case, is understood through the classical l'Hôpital rule):

$$I_q(\phi)=\frac{1}{1-q}\int_0^{+\infty}\left(1-q+q\phi(r)-\{\phi(r)\}^q\right)\pi(\mathrm{d}r). \tag{23.9}$$

Problem D

Find a minimizing ϕ of

$$J_+(\phi)=\frac{M_2}{2}\int_0^{+\infty}\frac{1}{r}\{\phi(r)\}^q\,\pi(\mathrm{d}r)+\psi I_q(\phi) \tag{23.10}$$

and the minimized J_+.

Problem U

Find a maximizing ϕ of

$$J_{-}(\phi)=\frac{M_2}{2}\int_0^{+\infty}\frac{1}{r}\{\phi(r)\}^q\,\pi(\mathrm{d}r)-\psi I_q(\phi) \qquad [23.11]$$

and the maximized J_{-}.

Here, $\psi>0$ is the ambiguity aversion parameter. The first term in [23.11] is the distorted variance defined through the Radon–Nikodým derivative ϕ in the sense of Tsallis. The second term in [23.10] represents the penalization of the ambiguity where the penalization is stronger with larger ψ. From the viewpoint of statistical decision-making, choosing a larger ψ allows for attaining a smaller divergence $I_q(\phi)$, hence representing a stronger confidence about the benchmark (i.e. non-distorted) reversion measure π.

Problem D is a minimization problem of the distorted variance subject to a penalization about the model ambiguity measured by the Tsallis divergence. Similarly, **Problem U** is a maximization problem of the distorted variance subject to a penalization about the model ambiguity measured by the Tsallis divergence. Each problem will be separately studied in the following sections, showing that their well-posedness needs asymmetrical settings with each other and further, the classical Kullback–Leibler divergence fails.

23.3.2. *Problem D: Underestimation problem*

Problem D is an infinite-dimensional minimization problem, and hence choosing a proper admissible set, hereafter denoted as $\mathfrak{C}$, of ϕ is a key issue. Under [23.8], **Problem D** can be stated equivalently as follows.

Problem D (reformulated)

Find a minimizing ϕ of

$$J_{+}(\phi)=\int_0^{+\infty}\left(\frac{M_2}{2}\frac{1}{r}+\frac{\psi}{q-1}\right)\{\phi(r)\}^q\,\pi(\mathrm{d}r)+\frac{\psi}{1-q} \qquad [23.12]$$

and the minimized J_{+}.

The second term of [23.12] is independent of ϕ. We consider the problem in a reflexive Banach space (Zeidler (1995), Chapter 2.9) that is a common approach toward infinite-dimensional optimization problems. Namely, we want to well-pose **Problem D** in the context of the unique existence of the minimizer. Then, we need some boundedness of ϕ so that the integral in [23.12] exists, as well as strict convexity and sequentially lower semi-continuity of J_+.

We found that the following definition of $\mathfrak{C}$ is suitable for **Problem D**.

DEFINITION 23.1.– The admissible set $\mathfrak{C}$ for **Problem D** for $q>1$ is a collection of all measurable mapping $\phi:(0,+\infty)\to(0,+\infty)$ such that the condition [23.8] and

$$\int_0^{+\infty}\{\phi(r)\}^q\left(\frac{1}{r}+1\right)\pi(\mathrm{d}r)<+\infty \text{ and } 0<\phi(r)<C\left(1+r^{\frac{1}{q-1}}\right) \text{ for } r>0 \quad [23.13]$$

are satisfied. Here, $C>0$ is a constant depending on q but not on ϕ.

The restriction $q>1$ is imposed not only to make the objective strictly convex with respect to $\phi\in\mathfrak{C}$ but also to identify the set $\mathfrak{C}$ as a convex and closed sub-sect of the reflexive Banach space equipped with the weighted norm

$$\|\phi\|_q=\left(\int_0^{+\infty}\{\phi(r)\}^q\left(\frac{1}{r}+1\right)\pi(\mathrm{d}r)\right)^{\frac{1}{q}}<+\infty. \quad [23.14]$$

The convexity of $\mathfrak{C}$ is clear considering the constraint [23.8], and the closedness can be checked as well. The case $q=1$, i.e. the Kullback–Leibler case, is naturally excluded from the consideration, since the Banach space equipped with the norm $\|\phi\|_1$ is clearly not reflexive and the weak convergence of bounded sequences (Zeidler (1995), Proposition 6 of Chapter 2.8) is not necessarily guaranteed.

With **Definition 23.1** in mind, we obtain the following proposition on the unique solvability of **Problem D**. Before stating the result, we define the q-exponential function for brevity:

$$\exp_q(x)=\begin{cases}(1+(1-q)x)^{\frac{1}{1-q}} & (q\neq 1)\\ \exp(x) & (q=1)\end{cases} \text{ for } 1+(1-q)x>0. \quad [23.15]$$

Proposition 23.1

Assume $q > 1$ and sufficiently large C. ***Problem D*** *with the admissible set* $\mathfrak{C}$ *in the sense of* ***Definition 23.1*** *is uniquely solved by* $\phi = \phi_* \in \mathfrak{C}$ *given by*

$$\phi_*(r) = \left[\int_0^{+\infty} \exp_q\left(-\frac{M_2}{2}\frac{1}{\psi r}\right)\pi(\mathrm{d}r)\right]^{-1} \exp_q\left(-\frac{M_2}{2}\frac{1}{\psi r}\right),\ r > 0. \quad [23.16]$$

The proof of **Proposition 23.1** is omitted here because it is based on the direct variational differentiation of [23.12] with respect to ϕ (Zeidler (1995), Theorem 2.E(1) in Chapter 2.9). The strict convexity and the continuity are clear because the first term of J_+ is equivalent to $\|\cdot\|_q^q$. The sequentially lower semi-continuity follows from this norm equivalence as well as the convexity and closedness of $\mathfrak{C}$.

We are also interested in the extreme case $\psi \to +0$ corresponding to the largest ambiguity penalizable by the Tsallis divergence. From [23.15] and [23.16], we have the following proposition based on an elementary calculation.

Proposition 23.2

Under **Proposition 23.1**, the minimizer $\phi = \phi_* \in \mathfrak{C}$ converges locally uniformly to

$$\underline{\phi}(r) = \left(\int_0^{+\infty} r^{\frac{1}{q-1}}\pi(\mathrm{d}r)\right)^{-1} r^{\frac{1}{q-1}},\ r > 0. \quad [23.17]$$

This $\underline{\phi}$ *still belongs to* $\mathfrak{C}$.

Indeed, we have

$$\phi_*(r) = \left[\int_0^{+\infty}\left(\psi + (q-1)\frac{M_2}{2}\frac{1}{r}\right)^{-\frac{1}{q-1}}\pi(\mathrm{d}r)\right]^{-1}\left(\psi + (q-1)\frac{M_2}{2}\frac{1}{r}\right)^{-\frac{1}{q-1}}. \quad [23.18]$$

The integrand is integrable for all $\psi > 0$ as well as $\psi = 0$, and hence we can pass to the limit $\psi \to 0$. Consequently, **Problem D** was solved completely.

23.3.3. *Problem U: Overestimation problem*

As for **Problem D**, we reformulate **Problem U** under the condition [23.8]. Note that we have rewritten the maximization problem to a minimization problem without any loss of generality.

Problem U (reformulated)

Find a minimizing ϕ of

$$-J_{-}(\phi)=-\int_0^{+\infty}\left(\frac{M_2}{2}\frac{1}{r}+\frac{\psi}{1-q}\right)\{\phi(r)\}^q\,\pi(\mathrm{d}r)+\frac{\psi}{1-q} \qquad [23.19]$$

and the minimized $-J_{-}$.

Choosing a proper admissible set $\mathfrak{C}$ of ϕ is also a key issue for **Problem U**. Unfortunately, **Problem U** is more difficult than **Problem D** because the direct method based on reflexive Banach spaces seems not to work, although at least we can find a candidate of minimizers. First of all, formally the convexity of the functional $-J_{-}$ requires $0<q<1$, again excluding the Kullback–Leibler case. The candidate of minimizer is found though a naïve variational differentiation as

$$\phi^*(r)=\left[\int_0^{+\infty}\exp_q\left(\frac{M_2}{2}\frac{1}{\psi r}\right)\pi(\mathrm{d}r)\right]^{-1}\exp_q\left(\frac{M_2}{2}\frac{1}{\psi r}\right),\ r>0. \qquad [23.20]$$

The integral term of $-J_{-}$ with $\phi=\phi^*$ is bounded only if

$$0<q<1-\alpha^{-1}. \qquad [23.21]$$

Namely, we need to choose the shape parameter q considering the parameter α of the Gamma reversion measure [23.4]. In the other word, the possible range of q is more restricted for the longer memory structures according to the ACF [23.7]. To make the matters worse, we can use the norm [23.14] only for $q\geq 1$. Therefore, the approach based on reflexive Banach spaces, which served well for **Problem D**, is not applicable to **Problem U**.

Fortunately, we can directly apply the recent theoretical result concerning nonlinear expectations by Ma (2021). More specifically, Theorem 4.1 of Ma (2021) directly applies to our problem by setting "$X=1/r$" in this literature. We then obtain the following optimality result.

Proposition 23.3

Assume [23.21]. *Then,* $\phi = \phi^*$ *of* [23.20] *is a minimizer of* $-J_-$ *among all measurable* $\phi:(0,+\infty)\to(0,+\infty)$ *complying with* [23.8] *and the lower boundedness of* $-J_-$.

Then, as in **Proposition 23.2**, we can consider the extreme case with the largest ambiguity penalizable by the Tsallis divergence.

Proposition 23.4

Under **Proposition 23.3**, the maximizer ϕ^* converges locally uniformly to

$$\bar{\phi}(r) = \left(\int_0^{+\infty} r^{-\frac{1}{1-q}} \pi(\mathrm{d}r)\right)^{-1} r^{-\frac{1}{1-q}} = \underline{\phi}(r),\ r > 0. \qquad [23.22]$$

Interestingly, we have $\bar{\phi} = \underline{\phi}$, while they are defined for mutually different ranges of q with each other.

23.4. Application

23.4.1. *Study sites*

We apply the proposed optimization framework to streamflow discharge data at two study sites of different first-class river systems in Japan with each other. The dimension of the variable X here is m^3/s.

The first study site is Kamishima (Station K) in Hii River, Shimane Prefecture, Japan (132°49’49″E, 35°20’23″N). The downstream reach of Station K has a huge diversion channel for the flood mitigation of city areas extending around the river course, called Hii River Diversion Channel (Figure 23.1, left) (Yoshioka and Yoshioka 2022). Statistical evaluation of the streamflow discharge at Station K is therefore important for the flood risk analysis around Hii River.

The second study site is Tsurugi (Station T) in Tedori River, Ishikawa Prefecture, Japan (136°37’13″E, 36°26’57″N). Station T is located near the apex of the Tedori River alluvial fan over which agricultural areas such as paddy fields extend (Yoshioka et al. 2016). In addition to the agricultural water resources management around Tedori River, flood mitigation of the downstream area of Station T is also a concern because the alluvial fan is a lowland area. Tengu Bridge serves as a landmark of Station T (Figure 23.1, right), at which we will able to observe both downstream and upstream river reaches of Tedori River and the surrounding lowland areas.

Figure 23.1. *Hii River Diversion Channel (left) and Tengu Bridge (right) seen from the upstream. Photographs have been taken by Hidekazu Yoshioka. For a color version of this figure, see www.iste.co.uk/dimotikalis/data4.zip*

23.4.2. *Parameter estimation*

For the parameter estimation of the supOU process at each study site, we use the public data available at the Water Information System (http://www1.river.go.jp/) by Ministry of Land, Infrastructure, Transport and Tourism of Japan. The data periods are from 01:00:00 January 1, 2016 to 24:00:00 December 31, 2020 for Station K and 01:00:00 January 1, 2018 to 24:00:00 December 31, 2021 for Station T (Figure 23.2).

We employ the model identification method based on the ACF and statistical moments that has already been applied to different study sites (Yoshioka 2021; Yoshioka et al. 2023). Identified parameter values of α (-) and β (1/hour) are $(\alpha,\beta)=(2.09,0.047)$ at Station K and $(\alpha,\beta)=(1.74,0.037)$ at Station T, showing that the latter is of the long memory type, while the former is not.

By assuming a tempered stable-type v, the empirical and modeled variances at Station K are 3,547 (m^6/s^2) and 3,557 (m^6/s^2), respectively. Similarly, the empirical and modeled variances at Station T are 5,849 (m^6/s^2) and 5,837 (m^6/s^2), respectively. The mean, skewness and kurtosis have been fitted with the relative errors smaller than 3% at Station T and smaller than 10% at Station T. The theoretical values of M_2 (m^6/s^2/hour) appearing in the variance formula [23.6] is 5,182 at Station K and 25,568 at Station T.

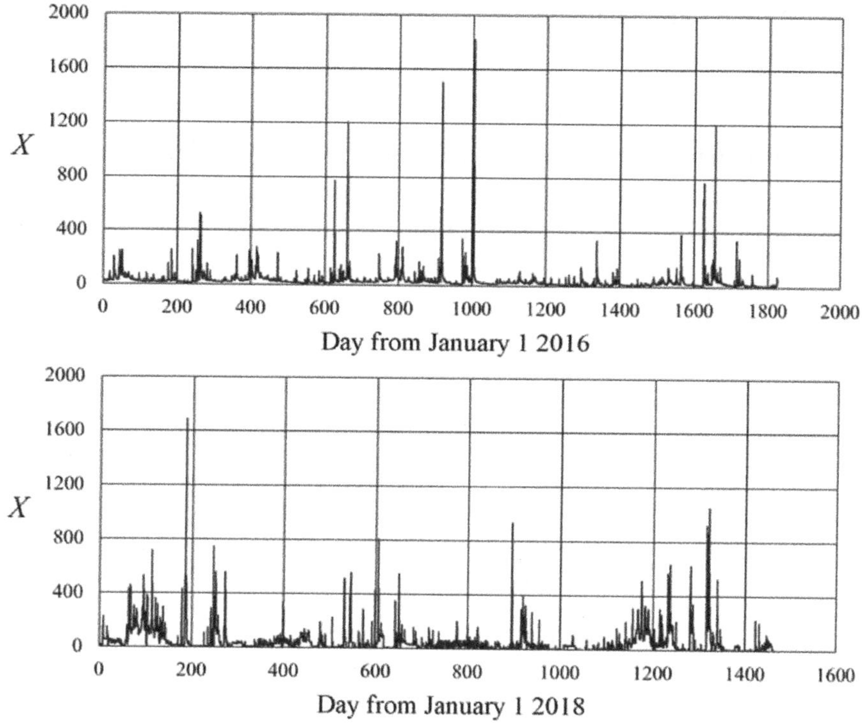

Figure 23.2. *The discharge time series data at Station K (top) and at Station T (bottom). For a color version of this figure, see www.iste.co.uk/dimotikalis/data4.zip*

23.4.3. *Results and discussion*

We compute **Problems D** and **U** at each station to compute their optimizers (denoted for simplicity as ϕ) as well as the corresponding distorted variance (V, the first term of [23.10] or [23.11]) and the Tsallis divergence (here denoted for simplicity as I) for different values of the ambiguity aversion parameter ψ. In this way, we can obtain Pareto frontier of V and I parameterized by ψ.

Figure 23.3 shows the Pareto frontiers of **Problem D** at Station K (left) and Station T (right) with $q = 1.33$. Similarly, Figure 23.4 shows the Pareto frontiers of **Problem U** at Station K (left) and Station T (right) with $q = 0.33$. Increasing the Tsallis divergence I decreases (resp., increases) the distorted variance V for

Problem D (resp., **Problem U**) with the lower-bound (resp., upper-bound) of V is finite, which corresponds to the case $\psi = 0$ of **Propositions 23.2** and **23.4**.

Figures 23.5 and 23.6 show the optimal Radon–Nikodým derivatives ϕ obtained by solving **Problems D** and **U** at Station T, respectively. The ambiguity ϕ becomes more distorted as the ambiguity aversion parameter ψ decreases, and eventually becomes the worst-case ones obtained in **Propositions 23.2** and **23.4**.

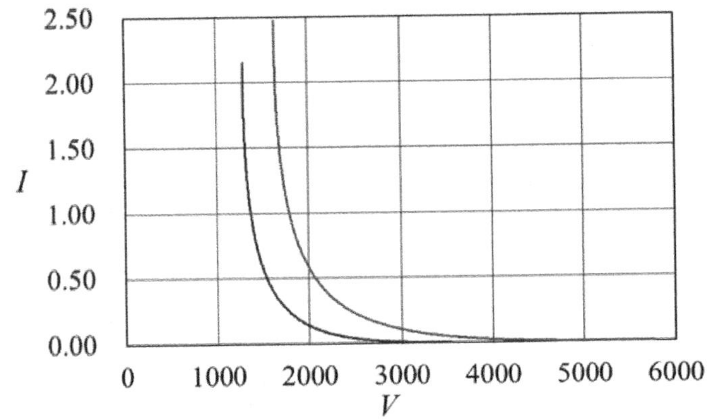

Figure 23.3. *Pareto frontiers of* ***Problem D*** *at Station K (blue) and Station T (red). For a color version of this figure, see www.iste.co.uk/dimotikalis/data4.zip*

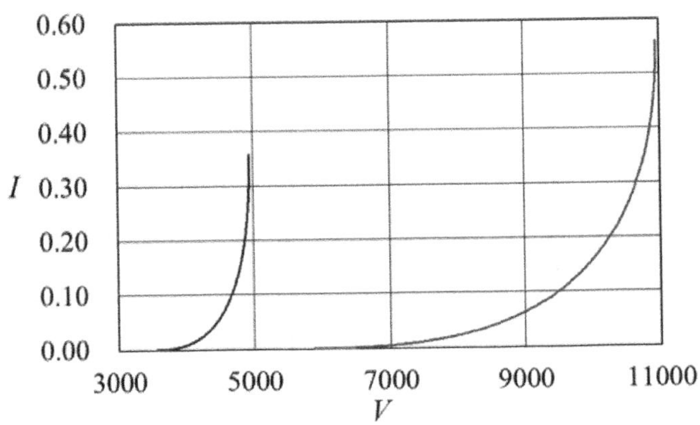

Figure 23.4. *Pareto frontiers of* ***Problem U*** *at Station K (blue) and Station T (red). For a color version of this figure, see www.iste.co.uk/dimotikalis/data4.zip*

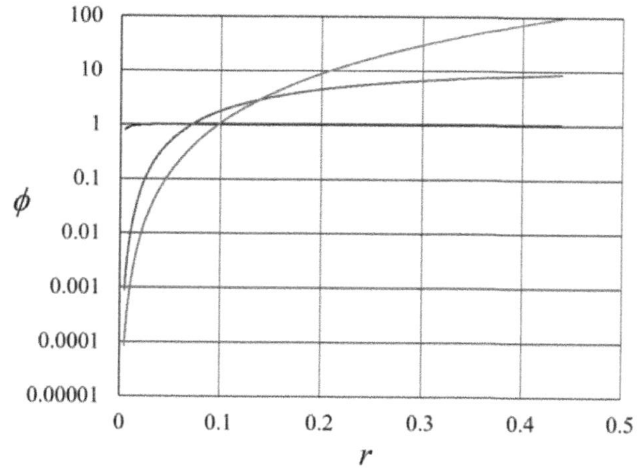

Figure 23.5. *The optimal Radon–Nikodým derivatives* **Problem D** *at Station T; the values of I are 0.0028 (blue), 0.79 (red) and 2.5 (green). For a color version of this figure, see www.iste.co.uk/dimotikalis/data4.zip*

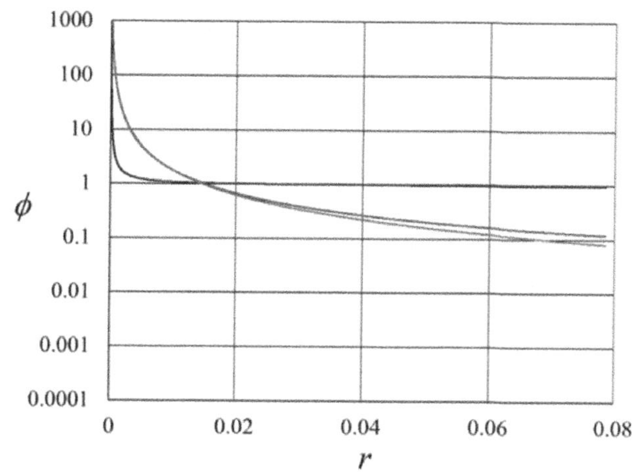

Figure 23.6. *The optimal Radon–Nikodým derivatives* **Problem U** *at Station T: the values of I are 0.0035 (blue), 0.49 (red) and 0.56 (green). For a color version of this figure, see www.iste.co.uk/dimotikalis/data4.zip*

23.5. Conclusion

The optimization framework based on the Tsallis divergence served well for the evaluation of the variance of the supOU process, subject to the ambiguity. The shape parameter of the Tsallis divergence had to be chosen properly to well define the optimization problems. Nevertheless, they cover the cases that the classical Kullback–Leibler divergence completely failed. The brief application study demonstrated the effectivity of the proposed mathematical approach in dealing with real time series data. An important future topic will be an extension of the optimization problems so that non-stationary long memory processes can be dealt with. Case studies of time series data other than the streamflow discharge would also be interesting.

23.6. Acknowledgments

This work was supported by Japan Society for the Promotion of Science (22K14441, 22H02456) and Environmental Research Projects from the Sumitomo Foundation (203160).

23.7. References

Alkathery, M.A. and Chaudhuri, K. (2022). Implications of clean energy, oil and emissions pricing for the GCC energy sector stock. *Energy Economics*, 112, 106119.

Barndorff-Nielsen, O.E. (2001). Superposition of ornstein–uhlenbeck type processes. *Theory of Probability & Its Applications*, 45(2), 175–194.

Beaulieu, C., Killick, R., Ireland, D., Norwood, B. (2020). Considering long-memory when testing for changepoints in surface temperature: A classification approach based on the time-varying spectrum. *Environmetrics*, 31(1), e2568.

Dissanayake, G.S., Peiris, M.S., Proietti, T. (2018). Fractionally differenced Gegenbauer processes with long memory: A review. *Statistical Science*, 33(3), 413–426.

Hansen, L.P. and Sargent, T.J. (2011). *Robustness*. Princeton University Press, Princeton.

Ma, H. (2021). Generalized entropic risk measures and related BSDEs. *Statistics & Probability Letters*, 174, 109110.

Pedersen, J. (2003). The Lévy-Ito decomposition of an independently scattered random measure. Research Report, MaPhySto, Department of Mathematical Sciences, University of Aarhus.

Tsallis, C. (2019). *Introduction to Nonextensive Statistical Mechanics: Approaching a Complex World*, Springer, New York.

Yoshioka, H. (2021). Fitting a superposition of Ornstein–Uhlenbeck process to time series of discharge in a perennial river environment. *ANZIAM Journal*, 63, C84–C96.

Yoshioka, H. and Yoshioka, Y. (2022). Dynamic optimization with tempered stable subordinators for modeling river hydraulics. In *Data Analysis and Related Applications 2, Multivariate, Health and Demographic Data Analysis*, Zafeiris K.N. et al. (eds). ISTE Ltd, London, and John Wiley & Sons, New York, 105–117.

Yoshioka, Y., Nakamura, K., Horino, H., Kawashima, S. (2016). Numerical assessments of the impacts of climate change on regional groundwater systems in a paddy-dominated alluvial fan. *Paddy and Water Environment*, 14(1), 93–103.

Yoshioka, H., Tanaka, T., Yoshioka, Y., Hashiguchi, A. (2023). Stochastic optimization of a mixed moving average process for controlling non-Markovian streamflow environments. *Applied Mathematical Modelling*, 116, 490–509.

Zeidler, E. (1995). *Applied Functional Analysis: Main Principles and Their Applications*. Springer, New York.

List of Authors

Mario ABUNDO
Department of Mathematics
Università di Roma "Tor Vergata"
Italy

Roberto ASCARI
Department of Economics
Management and Statistics
University of Milano-Bicocca
Italy

Achref BACHOUCH
Division of Mathematics and Physics
Mälardalen University
Västerås
Sweden

Luiza BĂDIN
Department of Applied Mathematics
Bucharest University of Economic Studies
and
Institute of Mathematical Statistics and Applied Mathematics
Romanian Academy
Romania

Yana BELOPOLSKAYA
Sirius University of Science and Technology
St Petersburg
Russia

Abigail BERTA
Department of Mathematics and Mathematical Statistics
Umeå University
Sweden

Monique BORG INGUANEZ
Department of Statistics and Operations Research
University of Malta
Msida
Malta

Frederico CAEIRO
Department of Mathematics
NOVA University
Lisbon
Portugal

Chrys CARONI
Department of Mathematics
National Technical University of Athens
Zografou
Greece

Mark Anthony CARUANA
Department of Statistics and Operations Research
University of Malta
Msida
Malta

Michaela ČERVEŇANSKÁ
Department of Hydraulic Engineering
Slovak University of Technology in Bratislava
Slovakia

Paula CHAINHO
Department of Animal Biology
University of Lisbon
Portugal

Andrey CHUBATOV
Sirius University of Science and Technology
St Petersburg
Russia

Lara CILIA
University of Malta
Valletta
Malta

Spiros D. DAFNIS
Department of Statistics and Insurance Science
University of Piraeus
Greece

Silvia DEDU
Department of Applied Mathematics
Bucharest University of Economic Studies
Romania

Marko DIMITROV
Division of Mathematics and Physics
Mälardalen University
Västerås
Sweden

Yiannis DIMOTIKALIS
Department of Management Science and Technology
Hellenic Mediterranean University
Heraklion
Crete
Greece

Christian EWALD
Department of Mathematics and Mathematical Statistics
Umeå University
Sweden

Leonidas FANOURAKIS
Department of Accounting and Finance
Hellenic Mediterranean University
Heraklion
Crete
Greece

Nikolaos FARMAKIS
Aristotle University of Thessaloniki
Greece

Kentaro FUJIOKA
Department of Informatics
University of Electro-Communications
Tokyo
Japan

Gloria GHENO
Ronin Institute
Montclair
USA

Alice GIAMPINO
Department of Economics
Management and Statistics
University of Milano-Bicocca
Italy

Dora Prata GOMES
Department of Mathematics
NOVA University
Lisbon
Portugal

Sota IKENOYA
University of Electro-Communications
Tokyo
Japan

Lu JIN
Department of Informatics
University of Electro-Communications
Tokyo
Japan

Jana KALICKÁ
Institute of Computer Science and Mathematics
Slovak University of Technology in Bratislava
Slovakia

Lazaros KANELLOPOULOS
Department of Statistics and Insurance Science
University of Piraeus
Greece

Amor KEZIOU
Université de Reims Champagne-Ardenne
France

Markos V. KOUTRAS
Department of Statistics and Insurance Science
University of Piraeus
Greece

Maria LEDAKI
Aristotle University of Thessaloniki
Greece

Karl LEWIS
Department of Statistics and Operations Research
University of Malta
Msida
Malta

Ana LORGA DA SILVA
Lusófona University
Lisbon
Portugal

Ayana MATEUS
Department of Mathematics
NOVA University
Lisbon
Portugal

Sonia MIGLIORATI
Department of Economics
Management and Statistics
University of Milano-Bicocca
Italy

M. Manuela NEVES
Instituto Superior de Agronomia
Universidade de Lisboa
Lisbon
Portugal

Ying NI
Division of Mathematics and Physics
Mälardalen University
Västerås
Sweden

Myrto PAPAGEORGIOU
Aristotle University of Thessaloniki
Greece

Francesca PIERRI
Department of Economics
University of Perugia
Italy

Konstantinos POLITIS
Department of Statistics and
Insurance Science
University of Piraeus
Greece

Julio RODRIGUEZ
School of Engineering and Computer
Science
Bern University of Applied Sciences
Biel
Switzerland

Despoina SDRALI
Department of Economics and
Sustainable Development
Harokopio University
Kallithea
Greece

Christos H. SKIADAS
Technical University of Crete
Chania
and
ISAST
Athens
Greece

Dominika SÓNAK BALLOVÁ
Department of Mathematics and
Descriptive Geometry
Slovak University of Technology in
Bratislava
Slovakia

David Paul SUDA
Department of Statistics and
Operations Research
University of Malta
Msida
Malta

Efthalia TABOURATZI
Department of Accounting and
Finance
Laboratory of Accounting and
Financial Management (LAFIM)
Hellenic Mediterranean University
Heraklion
Crete
Greece

Aida TOMA
Department of Applied Mathematics
Bucharest University of Economic Studies
and
Institute of Mathematical Statistics and Applied Mathematics
Romanian Academy
Romania

Maria TSIFOUTIDOU
Aristotle University of Thessaloniki
Greece

Konstantinos VASILAKAKIS
Department of Economics and Sustainable Development
Laboratory of Accounting and Financial Management (LAFIM)
Hellenic Mediterranean University
Heraklion
Crete
Greece

Margarida XAVIER
Auchan Retail Portugal
Portugal

Hidekazu YOSHIOKA
Japan Advanced Institute of Science and Technology
Nomi
Japan

Yumi YOSHIOKA
Shimane University
Matsue
Japan

Index

G, H

I, J

K, L

M, O

P, R

S, T, V

Other titles from

iSTE

in

Innovation, Entrepreneurship and Management

2024

AÏT-EL-HADJ Smaïl
Environmental Transition and Technological Change
(Smart Innovation – Volume 43)

ALBERT-CROMARIAS Anne, ALBERTINI Thérèse, TERRAMORSI Patrice
Collective Dynamics and Territories: 9 Issues for Competitive, Innovative and Sustainable Territories
(Territorial Entrepreneurship and Innovation – Volume 3)

BRASSEUR Martine, BARTOLI Annie, CHABAUD Didier, GROUIEZ Pascal, ROUET Gilles
Inclusive Territories 2: Role of Institutions and Local Actors
(Territorial Entrepreneurship and Innovation Set – Volume 2)

COURIE-LEMEUR Aline
Innovation, Collective Intelligence and Resiliency in Healthcare Organizations
(Health and Innovation Set – Volume 4)

DELÉCOLLE Thierry, JACOB Florence, PRIM-ALLAZ Isabelle
New Frontiers of Customer Strategy: Managing Sustainable, Environmental and Ethical Transitions

DIMOTIKALIS Yannis, SKIADIS Christos H.
Data Analysis and Related Applications 3: Theory and Practice – New Approaches
(Big Data, Artificial Intelligence and Data Analysis Set – Volume 11)

FLORA Luigi, GRENIER Corinne, PONISGNON Frédéric
Experience in Healthcare Innovation: Fad or New Paradigm?
(Health and Innovation – Volume 5)

PARMENTIER Guy
Organizational Creative Capabilities: Management Factors, Processes and Devices
(Organizational Creativity Set – Volume 1)

RUIZ Émilie
The Creative Capabilities of Open Organizations
(Organizational Creativity Set – Volume 2)

VERNIER Marie-France
Eco-Design and Ecological Transition: Questioning the Economic Model
(Smart Innovation Set – Volume 42)

2023

BOLLINGER Sophie
Management Control and Creativity: Challenges of Managing Innovation Processes
(Smart Innovation Set – Volume 41)

BOUVIER-PATRON Paul
Frugal Innovation and Innovative Creation
(Smart Innovation Set – Volume 40)

BRASSEUR Martine, BARTOLI Annie, CHABAUD Didier, GROUIEZ Pascal, ROUET Gilles
Inclusive Territories 1: Role of Enterprises and Organizations
(Territorial Entrepreneurship and Innovation Set – Volume 1)

CASADELLA Vanessa, UZUNIDIS Dimitri
Agri-Innovations and Development Challenges: Engineering, Value Chains and Socio-economic Models
(Innovation in Engineering and Technology Set – Volume 8)

DARTIGUEPEYROU Carine, SALOFF-COSTE Michel
Futures: The Great Turn
(Innovation and Technology Set – Volume 18)

PEYROUX Élisabeth, RAIMOND Christine, VIEL Vincent, LAVIE Émilie
Development and Territorial Restructuring in an Era of Global Change: Theories, Approaches and Future Research Perspectives

SAULAIS Pierre
Knowledge and Ideation: Inventive Knowledge Analysis for Ideation Stimulation
(Innovation and Technology Set – Volume 17)

2022

AOUINAÏT Camille
Open Innovation Strategies
(Smart Innovation Set – Volume 39)

BOUCHÉ Geneviève
Productive Economy, Contributory Economy: Governance Tools for the Third Millennium
(Innovation and Technology Set – Volume 15)

BRUYÈRE Christelle
Caring Management in Health Organizations: A Lever for Crisis Management
(Health and Innovation Set – Volume 3)

ENJOLRAS Manon
Innovation and Export: The Joint Challenge of the Small Company
(Smart Innovation Set – Volume 37)

FLEURY Sylvain, RICHIR Simon
Immersive Technologies to Accelerate Innovation: How Virtual and Augmented Reality Enables the Co-Creation of Concepts
(Smart Innovation Set – Volume 38)

HELLER David
Valuation of the Liability Structure by Real Options
(Modern Finance, Management Innovation and Economic Growth Set – Volume 5)

MATHIEU Valérie
A Customer-oriented Manager for B2B Services: Principles and Implementation

MORALES Lucía, DZEVER Sam, TAYLOR Robert
Asia-Europe Industrial Connectivity in Times of Crisis
(Innovation and Technology Set – Volume 16)

NOËL Florent, SCHMIDT Géraldine
Employability and Industrial Mutations: Between Individual Trajectories and Organizational Strategic Planning
(Technological Changes and Human Resources Set – Volume 4)

DE SAINT JULIEN Odile
The Innovation Ecosystem as a Source of Value Creation: A Value Creation Lever for Open Innovation
(Diverse and Global Perspectives on Value Creation Set – Volume 4)

SALOFF-COSTE Michel
Innovation Ecosystems: The Future of Civilizations and the Civilization of the Future
(Innovation and Technology Set – Volume 14)

SOULÉ Bastien, HALLÉ Julie, VIGNAL Bénédicte, BOUTROY Éric, NIER Olivier
Innovation in Sport: Innovation Trajectories and Process Optimization
(Smart Innovation Set – Volume 35)

VALLIER Estelle
Innovation in Clusters: Science–Industry Relationships in the Face of Forced Advancement
(Smart Innovation Set – Volume 36)

VAYRE Emilie
Digitalization of Work: New Spaces and New Working Times
(Technological Changes and Human Resources Set – Volume 5)

ZAFEIRIS Konstantinos N, SKIADIS Christos H, DIMOTIKALIS Yannis, KARAGRIGORIOU Alex, KARAGRIGORIOU-VONTA Christina
Data Analysis and Related Applications 1: Computational, Algorithmic and Applied Economic Data Analysis
(Big Data, Artificial Intelligence and Data Analysis Set – Volume 9)
Data Analysis and Related Applications 2: Multivariate, Health and Demographic Data Analysis
(Big Data, Artificial Intelligence and Data Analysis Set – Volume 10)

2021

ACH Yves-Alain, RMADI-SAÏD Sandra
Financial Information and Brand Value: Reflections, Challenges and Limitations

ARCADE Jacques
Strategic Engineering
(Innovation and Technology Set – Volume 11)

BÉRANGER Jérôme, RIZOULIÈRES Roland
The Digital Revolution in Health
(Health and Innovation Set – Volume 2)

BOBILLIER CHAUMON Marc-Eric
Digital Transformations in the Challenge of Activity and Work: Understanding and Supporting Technological Changes
(Technological Changes and Human Resources Set – Volume 3)

BUCLET Nicolas
Territorial Ecology and Socio-ecological Transition
(Smart Innovation Set – Volume 34)

DIMOTIKALIS Yannis, KARAGRIGORIOU Alex, PARPOULA Christina, SKIADIS Christos H
Applied Modeling Techniques and Data Analysis 1: Computational Data Analysis Methods and Tools
(Big Data, Artificial Intelligence and Data Analysis Set - Volume 7)
Applied Modeling Techniques and Data Analysis 2: Financial, Demographic, Stochastic and Statistical Models and Methods
(Big Data, Artificial Intelligence and Data Analysis Set – Volume 8)

DISPAS Christophe, KAYANAKIS Georges, SERVEL Nicolas, STRIUKOVA Ludmila
Innovation and Financial Markets
(Innovation between Risk and Reward Set – Volume 7)

GAUDIN Thierry, MAUREL Marie-Christine, POMEROL Jean-Charles
Chance, Calculation and Life

GASMI Nacer
Corporate Innovation Strategies: Corporate Social Responsibility and Shared Value Creation
(Smart Innovation Set – Volume 33)

GIORGINI Pierre
The Contributory Revolution
(Innovation and Technology Set – Volume 13)

GOGLIN Christian
Emotions and Values in Equity Crowdfunding Investment Choices 1: Transdisciplinary Theoretical Approach
Emotions and Values in Equity Crowdfunding Investment Choices 2: Modeling and Empirical Study

GRENIER Corinne, OIRY Ewan
Altering Frontiers: Organizational Innovations in Healthcare (Health and Innovation Set – Volume 1)

GUERRIER Claudine
Security and Its Challenges in the 21st Century (Innovation and Technology Set – Volume 12)

HELLER David
Performance of Valuation Methods in Financial Transactions (Modern Finance, Management Innovation and Economic Growth Set – Volume 4)

LEHMANN Paul-Jacques
Liberalism and Capitalism Today

LIMA Marcos
Entrepreneurship and Innovation Education: Frameworks and Tools (Smart Innovation Set – Volume 32)

MACHADO Carolina, DAVIM J. Paulo
Sustainable Management for Managers and Engineers

MEUNIER François-Xavier
Dual Innovation Systems: Concepts, Tools and Methods (Smart Innovation Set – Volume 31)

UZUNIDIS Dimitri, KASMI Fedoua, ADATTO Laurent
Innovation Economics, Engineering and Management Handbook 1: Main Themes
Innovation Economics, Engineering and Management Handbook 2: Special Themes

2020

ANDREOSSO-O'CALLAGHAN Bernadette, DZEVER Sam, JAUSSAUD Jacques, TAYLOR Robert
Sustainable Development and Energy Transition in Europe and Asia (Innovation and Technology Set – Volume 9)

BEN SLIMANE Sonia, M'HENNI Hatem
Entrepreneurship and Development: Realities and Future Prospects (Smart Innovation Set – Volume 30)

CHOUTEAU Marianne, FOREST Joëlle, NGUYEN Céline
Innovation for Society: The P.S.I. Approach (Smart Innovation Set – Volume 28)

CORON Clotilde
Quantifying Human Resources: Uses and Analysis (Technological Changes and Human Resources Set – Volume 2)

CORON Clotilde, GILBERT Patrick
Technological Change (Technological Changes and Human Resources Set – Volume 1)

CERDIN Jean-Luc, PERETTI Jean-Marie
The Success of Apprenticeships: Views of Stakeholders on Training and Learning (Human Resources Management Set – Volume 3)

DELCHET-COCHET Karen
Circular Economy: From Waste Reduction to Value Creation (Economic Growth Set – Volume 2)

DIDAY Edwin, GUAN Rong, SAPORTA Gilbert, WANG Huiwen
Advances in Data Science (Big Data, Artificial Intelligence and Data Analysis Set – Volume 4)

DOS SANTOS PAULINO Victor
Innovation Trends in the Space Industry (Smart Innovation Set – Volume 25)

GUILHON Bernard
Venture Capital and the Financing of Innovation
(Innovation Between Risk and Reward Set – Volume 6)

JURCZENKO Emmanuel
Machine Learning for Asset Management: New Developments and Financial Applications

LATOUCHE Pascal
Open Innovation: Human Set-up
(Innovation and Technology Set – Volume 10)

MAKRIDES Andreas, KARAGRIGORIOU Alex, SKIADAS Christos H.
Data Analysis and Applications 3: Computational, Classification, Financial, Statistical and Stochastic Methods
(Big Data, Artificial Intelligence and Data Analysis Set – Volume 5)
Data Analysis and Applications 4: Financial Data Analysis and Methods
(Big Data, Artificial Intelligence and Data Analysis Set – Volume 6)

MASSOTTE Pierre, CORSI Patrick
Complex Decision-Making in Economy and Finance

MICHAUD Thomas
Science Fiction and Innovation Design
(Innovation in Engineering and Technology Set – Volume 6)

MONINO Jean-Louis
Data Control: Major Challenge for the Digital Society
(Smart Innovation Set – Volume 29)

MORLAT Clément
Sustainable Productive System: Eco-development versus Sustainable Development (Smart Innovation Set – Volume 26)

SAULAIS Pierre, ERMINE Jean-Louis
Knowledge Management in Innovative Companies 2: Understanding and Deploying a KM Plan within a Learning Organization
(Smart Innovation Set – Volume 27)

UZUNIDIS Dimitri
Systemic Innovation: Entrepreneurial Strategies and Market Dynamics

2019

AMENDOLA Mario, GAFFARD Jean-Luc
Disorder and Public Concern Around Globalization

BARBAROUX Pierre
Disruptive Technology and Defence Innovation Ecosystems
(Innovation in Engineering and Technology Set – Volume 5)

DOU Henri, JUILLET Alain, CLERC Philippe
Strategic Intelligence for the Future 1: A New Strategic and Operational Approach
Strategic Intelligence for the Future 2: A New Information Function Approach

FRIKHA Azza
Measurement in Marketing: Operationalization of Latent Constructs

FRIMOUSSE Soufyane
Innovation and Agility in the Digital Age
(Human Resources Management Set – Volume 2)

GAY Claudine, SZOSTAK Bérangère L.
Innovation and Creativity in SMEs: Challenges, Evolutions and Prospects
(Smart Innovation Set – Volume 21)

GORIA Stéphane, HUMBERT Pierre, ROUSSEL Benoît
Information, Knowledge and Agile Creativity
(Smart Innovation Set – Volume 22)

HELLER David
Investment Decision-making Using Optional Models
(Economic Growth Set – Volume 2)

HELLER David, DE CHADIRAC Sylvain, HALAOUI Lana, JOUVET Camille
The Emergence of Start-ups
(Economic Growth Set – Volume 1)

HÉRAUD Jean-Alain, KERR Fiona, BURGER-HELMCHEN Thierry
Creative Management of Complex Systems
(Smart Innovation Set – Volume 19)

LATOUCHE Pascal
Open Innovation: Corporate Incubator
(Innovation and Technology Set – Volume 7)

LEHMANN Paul-Jacques
The Future of the Euro Currency

LEIGNEL Jean-Louis, MÉNAGER Emmanuel, YABLONSKY Serge
Sustainable Enterprise Performance: A Comprehensive Evaluation Method

LIÈVRE Pascal, AUBRY Monique, GAREL Gilles
Management of Extreme Situations: From Polar Expeditions to Exploration-Oriented Organizations

MILLOT Michel
Embarrassment of Product Choices 2: Towards a Society of Well-being

N'GOALA Gilles, PEZ-PÉRARD Virginie, PRIM-ALLAZ Isabelle
Augmented Customer Strategy: CRM in the Digital Age

NIKOLOVA Blagovesta
The RRI Challenge: Responsibilization in a State of Tension with Market Regulation
(Innovation and Responsibility Set – Volume 3)

PELLEGRIN-BOUCHER Estelle, ROY Pierre
Innovation in the Cultural and Creative Industries
(Innovation and Technology Set – Volume 8)

PRIOLON Joël
Financial Markets for Commodities

QUINIOU Matthieu
Blockchain: The Advent of Disintermediation

RAVIX Joël-Thomas, DESCHAMPS Marc
Innovation and Industrial Policies
(Innovation between Risk and Reward Set – Volume 5)

ROGER Alain, VINOT Didier
Skills Management: New Applications, New Questions
(Human Resources Management Set – Volume 1)

SAULAIS Pierre, ERMINE Jean-Louis
Knowledge Management in Innovative Companies 1: Understanding and Deploying a KM Plan within a Learning Organization
(Smart Innovation Set – Volume 23)

SERVAJEAN-HILST Romaric
Co-innovation Dynamics: The Management of Client-Supplier Interactions for Open Innovation
(Smart Innovation Set – Volume 20)

SKIADAS Christos H., BOZEMAN James R.
Data Analysis and Applications 1: Clustering and Regression, Modeling-estimating, Forecasting and Data Mining
(Big Data, Artificial Intelligence and Data Analysis Set – Volume 2)
Data Analysis and Applications 2: Utilization of Results in Europe and Other Topics
(Big Data, Artificial Intelligence and Data Analysis Set – Volume 3)

VIGEZZI Michel
World Industrialization: Shared Inventions, Competitive Innovations and Social Dynamics
(Smart Innovation Set – Volume 24)

2018

BURKHARDT Kirsten
Private Equity Firms: Their Role in the Formation of Strategic Alliances

CALLENS Stéphane
Creative Globalization
(Smart Innovation Set – Volume 16)

CASADELLA Vanessa
Innovation Systems in Emerging Economies: MINT – Mexico, Indonesia, Nigeria, Turkey
(Smart Innovation Set – Volume 18)

CHOUTEAU Marianne, FOREST Joëlle, NGUYEN Céline
Science, Technology and Innovation Culture
(Innovation in Engineering and Technology Set – Volume 3)

CORLOSQUET-HABART Marine, JANSSEN Jacques
Big Data for Insurance Companies
(Big Data, Artificial Intelligence and Data Analysis Set – Volume 1)

CROS Françoise
Innovation and Society
(Smart Innovation Set – Volume 15)

DEBREF Romain
Environmental Innovation and Ecodesign: Certainties and Controversies
(Smart Innovation Set – Volume 17)

DOMINGUEZ Noémie
SME Internationalization Strategies: Innovation to Conquer New Markets

ERMINE Jean-Louis
Knowledge Management: The Creative Loop
(Innovation and Technology Set – Volume 5)

GAUDIN Thierry, LACROIX Dominique, MAUREL Marie-Christine, POMEROL, Jean-Charles
Life Sciences, Information Sciences

GILBERT Patrick, BOBADILLA Natalia, GASTALDI Lise, LE BOULAIRE Martine, LELEBINA Olga
Innovation, Research and Development Management

VAN HOOREBEKE Delphine
The Management of Living Beings or Emo-management

IBRAHIMI Mohammed
Mergers & Acquisitions: Theory, Strategy, Finance

LEMAÎTRE Denis
Training Engineers for Innovation

LÉVY Aldo, BEN BOUHENI Faten, AMMI Chantal
Financial Management: USGAAP and IFRS Standards
(Innovation and Technology Set – Volume 6)

LOISY Catherine, COULET Jean-Claude
Competence and Program-based Approach in Training: Tools for Developing Responsible Activities
Innovation and Responsibility Set – Volume 1)

MILLOT Michel
Embarrassment of Product Choices 1: How to Consume Differently

PANSERA Mario, OWEN Richard
Innovation and Development: The Politics at the Bottom of the Pyramid
(Innovation and Responsibility Set – Volume 2)

RICHEZ Yves
Corporate Talent Detection and Development

SACHETTI Philippe, ZUPPINGER Thibaud
New Technologies and Branding
(Innovation and Technology Set – Volume 4)

SAMIER Henri
Intuition, Creativity, Innovation

TEMPLE Ludovic, COMPAORÉ SAWADOGO Eveline M.F.W.
Innovation Processes in Agro-Ecological Transitions in Developing Countries
(Innovation in Engineering and Technology Set – Volume 2)

UZUNIDIS Dimitri
Collective Innovation Processes: Principles and Practices
(Innovation in Engineering and Technology Set – Volume 4)

2017

AÏT-EL-HADJ Smaïl
The Ongoing Technological System
(Smart Innovation Set – Volume 11)

D'ANDRIA Aude, GABARRET Inés
Building 21st Century Entrepreneurship
(Innovation and Technology Set – Volume 2)

BAUDRY Marc, DUMONT Béatrice
Patents: Prompting or Restricting Innovation?
(Smart Innovation Set – Volume 12)

BÉRARD Céline, TEYSSIER Christine
Risk Management: Lever for SME Development and Stakeholder Value Creation

CHALENÇON Ludivine
Location Strategies and Value Creation of International Mergers and Acquisitions

CHAUVEL Danièle, BORZILLO Stefano
The Innovative Company: An Ill-defined Object
(Innovation between Risk and Reward Set – Volume 1)

CORSI Patrick
Going Past Limits To Growth

DAIDJ Nabyla
Cooperation, Coopetition and Innovation
(Innovation and Technology Set – Volume 3)

FERNEZ-WALCH Sandrine
The Multiple Facets of Innovation Project Management
(Innovation between Risk and Reward Set – Volume 4)

FOREST Joëlle
Creative Rationality and Innovation
(Smart Innovation Set – Volume 14)

GUILHON Bernard
Innovation and Production Ecosystems
(Innovation between Risk and Reward Set – Volume 2)

HAMMOUDI Abdelhakim, DAIDJ Nabyla
Game Theory Approach to Managerial Strategies and Value Creation
(Diverse and Global Perspectives on Value Creation Set – Volume 3)

LALLEMENT Rémi
Intellectual Property and Innovation Protection: New Practices and New Policy Issues
(Innovation between Risk and Reward Set – Volume 3)

LAPERCHE Blandine
Enterprise Knowledge Capital
(Smart Innovation Set – Volume 13)

LEBERT Didier, EL YOUNSI Hafida
International Specialization Dynamics
(Smart Innovation Set – Volume 9)

MAESSCHALCK Marc
Reflexive Governance for Research and Innovative Knowledge
(Responsible Research and Innovation Set – Volume 6)

MASSOTTE Pierre
Ethics in Social Networking and Business 1: Theory, Practice and Current Recommendations
Ethics in Social Networking and Business 2: The Future and Changing Paradigms

MASSOTTE Pierre, CORSI Patrick
Smart Decisions in Complex Systems

MEDINA Mercedes, HERRERO Mónica, URGELLÉS Alicia
Current and Emerging Issues in the Audiovisual Industry
(Diverse and Global Perspectives on Value Creation Set – Volume 1)

MICHAUD Thomas
Innovation, Between Science and Science Fiction
(Smart Innovation Set – Volume 10)

PELLÉ Sophie
Business, Innovation and Responsibility
(Responsible Research and Innovation Set – Volume 7)

SAVIGNAC Emmanuelle
The Gamification of Work: The Use of Games in the Workplace

SUGAHARA Satoshi, DAIDJ Nabyla, USHIO Sumitaka
Value Creation in Management Accounting and Strategic Management: An Integrated Approach
(Diverse and Global Perspectives on Value Creation Set –Volume 2)

UZUNIDIS Dimitri, SAULAIS Pierre
Innovation Engines: Entrepreneurs and Enterprises in a Turbulent World
(Innovation in Engineering and Technology Set – Volume 1)

2016

BARBAROUX Pierre, ATTOUR Amel, SCHENK Eric
Knowledge Management and Innovation
(Smart Innovation Set – Volume 6)

BEN BOUHENI Faten, AMMI Chantal, LEVY Aldo
Banking Governance, Performance And Risk-Taking: Conventional Banks Vs Islamic Banks

BOUTILLIER Sophie, CARRÉ Denis, LEVRATTO Nadine
Entrepreneurial Ecosystems
(Smart Innovation Set – Volume 2)

BOUTILLIER Sophie, UZUNIDIS Dimitri
The Entrepreneur
(Smart Innovation Set – Volume 8)

BOUVARD Patricia, SUZANNE Hervé
Collective Intelligence Development in Business

GALLAUD Delphine, LAPERCHE Blandine
Circular Economy, Industrial Ecology and Short Supply Chains
(Smart Innovation Set – Volume 4)

GUERRIER Claudine
Security and Privacy in the Digital Era
(Innovation and Technology Set – Volume 1)

MEGHOUAR Hicham
Corporate Takeover Targets

MONINO Jean-Louis, SEDKAOUI Soraya
Big Data, Open Data and Data Development
(Smart Innovation Set – Volume 3)

MOREL Laure, LE ROUX Serge
Fab Labs: Innovative User
(Smart Innovation Set – Volume 5)

PICARD Fabienne, TANGUY Corinne
Innovations and Techno-ecological Transition
(Smart Innovation Set – Volume 7)

2015

CASADELLA Vanessa, LIU Zeting, DIMITRI Uzunidis
Innovation Capabilities and Economic Development in Open Economies
(Smart Innovation Set – Volume 1)

CORLOSQUET-HABART Marine, GEHIN William, JANSSEN Jaques, MANCA Raimondo
Asset and Liabilities Management for Banks and Insurance Companies

CORSI Patrick, MORIN Dominique
Sequencing Apple's DNA

CORSI Patrick, NEAU Erwan
Innovation Capability Maturity Model

FAIVRE-TAVIGNOT Bénédicte
Social Business and Base of the Pyramid

GODÉ Cécile
Team Coordination in Extreme Environments

MAILLARD Pierre
Competitive Quality and Innovation

MASSOTTE Pierre, CORSI Patrick
Operationalizing Sustainability

MASSOTTE Pierre, CORSI Patrick
Sustainability Calling

2014

DUBÉ Jean, LEGROS Diègo
Spatial Econometrics Using Microdata

LESCA Humbert, LESCA Nicolas
Strategic Decisions and Weak Signals

2013

HABART-CORLOSQUET Marine, JANSSEN Jacques, MANCA Raimondo
VaR Methodology for Non-Gaussian Finance

2012

POMEROL Jean-Charles
Decision-Making and Action

SZYLAR Christian
UCITS Handbook

2011

LESCA Nicolas
Environmental Scanning and Sustainable Development

LESCA Nicolas, LESCA Humbert
Weak Signals for Strategic Intelligence: Anticipation Tool for Managers

MERCIER-LAURENT Eunika
Innovation Ecosystems

2010

SZYLAR Christian
Risk Management under UCITS III/IV

2009

COHEN Corine
Business Intelligence

ZANINETTI Jean-Marc
Sustainable Development in the USA

2008

CORSI Patrick, DULIEU Mike
The Marketing of Technology Intensive Products and Services

DZEVER Sam, JAUSSAUD Jacques, ANDREOSSO Bernadette
Evolving Corporate Structures and Cultures in Asia: Impact of Globalization

2007

AMMI Chantal
Global Consumer Behavior

2006

BOUGHZALA Imed, ERMINE Jean-Louis
Trends in Enterprise Knowledge Management

CORSI Patrick, CHRISTOFOL Hervé, RICHIR Simon, SAMIER Henri
Innovation Engineering: the power of intangible networks

Printed and bound by CPI Group (UK) Ltd, Croydon, CR0 4YY
13/09/2026
14961049-0008